D0015871

TED MORGAN

SIMON & SCHUSTER
New York • London • Toronto
Sydney • Tokyo • Singapore

A SHOVEL
OF STARS

The Making of the American West

1800 to the Present

SIMON & SCHUSTER
Rockefeller Center
1230 Avenue of the Americas
New York, New York 10020

Copyright © 1995 by Ted Morgan
All rights reserved
including the right of reproduction
in whole or in part in any form.
SIMON & SCHUSTER *and colophon are*
registered trademarks of Simon & Schuster Inc.
Designed by Edith Fowler
Manufactured in the United States of America

10 9 8 7 6 5 4 3 2 1

Library of Congress Cataloging-in-Publication Data

Morgan, Ted.
   A shovel of stars : the making of the American
West, 1800 to the present / Ted Morgan.
      p.   cm.
   Includes bibliographical references and index.
   1. West (U.S.)—History.   2. Frontier and
pioneer life—West (U.S.)   I. Title.
F591.M865   1995
978—dc20   94-43838   CIP
ISBN: 0-671-79439-6

TITLE PAGE: Many a Wyoming town was born with the cutting and grading of the first railroad bed. Some of these sprawling terminal camps became ghost towns when the crews moved on, but Green River City survived. Here it is shown in 1869, a year after its section of the Union Pacific was completed. Against the backdrop of dramatic sandstone cliffs, with Castle Rock at the left, two trains are passing through the tidy town, one heading east and one heading west. *Print collection, The New York Public Library.*

This book is for Mary Tyler Simpson Donald Nagel,
Kentucky-born and Pennsylvania-wed.

In the darkness with a great bundle of grief
the people march.
In the night, and overhead a shovel of stars for keeps,
the people march:
"Where to? What next?"

CARL SANDBURG

CONTENTS

INTRODUCTION

The character of a country is the sum total of the character of the little punks.

FRANK CAPRA

Huck Finn, at the end of Twain's great novel, says, "I reckon I got to light out for the Territory ahead of the rest, because Aunt Sally she's going to adopt me and sivilize me, and I can't stand it." Since it lay outside the United States, the territory signified freedom. It beckoned to the imagination as a place unregulated and uncivilized, whose inhabitants lived beyond the reach of law and the constraints of polite behavior.

Even today, that phantasmal region lingers in the American psyche as a shimmering mirage of the American dream, far from judges, revenuers, and other pests. The territories were ephemeral, doomed to eventual promotion to statehood. But the dream of unsettled land as a haven from the nuisance of government and as a proper arena for unfettered self-realization continues to reverberate in our minds. Like Huck Finn, some of us may wish we could "light out for the territory"—America as it should have been, and was, for one exalted but fugitive measure of time.

After the thirteen original states had won their independence from England, the young nation kept doubling in size from conquest and purchase until it stretched from ocean to ocean. The story of America has to do with the occupation of newly acquired land, coming in faster than it could be settled. In the process of westward expansion, thirty-seven more states were made, and all but six—Vermont, Kentucky, Maine, Texas, California, and West Virginia—went through the territorial interlude.

They remained territories for periods that ranged from two years for Alabama to sixty-two years for New Mexico. A child born in New Mexico Territory at its formation in 1850 was in his sixties when statehood arrived in 1912. Some interlude!

This book aims to tell the story of how the last thirty-four states were made. I described the creation of the first sixteen in my first volume, *Wilderness at Dawn*. My method is to take each new territory through its formative years until it becomes a state. I am not writing about theories of government. I am trying to duplicate the actual experience of settlement through the people who were there, a mass of ordinary men and women actually on the land.

As in my previous book, I am also trying to include all those whom previous histories of "the American people" left out—women, Indians, Chinese coolies, freed slaves—all of those who make up that large American class of the overlooked. This rich cast of characters both personifies some aspect of settlement and advances the story in time. If one individual drama unfolds in 1845, the next one plays itself out in 1850, and so on. In writing "from the ground up," in using the settlers' own language, and in keeping my focus on the territories rather than on Washington, I hope I have offered a new way of looking at the making of the United States.

The territorial arrangement was neocolonial in principle, but laissez-faire in practice. Since the territories existed far from the center of power, the system accommodated the free play of local influences, allowing the greatest degree of personal freedom that any modern nation-state had ever seen. But the territory was a temporary frontier unit, which in time had to trade some of that freedom for the benefits of statehood.

The territorial years, from the creation of the Northwest Territory in 1787 to the statehood of Alaska and Hawaii in 1959, were chaotic, combative, and colorful. This was America's heroic period. It came to an end not when the census declared the frontier closed in 1890, but when there were no more states to be made.

For some, it came when men no longer carried firearms on the western plains, when with the arrival of the sewing-machine agent the gunman gave up in sheer disgust. The frontiersman was plucked from the saddle and in poured what he saw as the evils of the east—women's suffrage, prohibition, antigun laws, hunting licenses, sheep, and inspectors galore. Gone were the days.

PART ONE
THE LOUISIANA PURCHASE
AND THE GULF STATES

BRITISH

Claimed
by U.S.
and
Britain

Columbia R.

OREGON
COUNTRY

Claimed by U.S.,
Britain, Spain,
and Russia

Missouri R.

Yellowstone R.

Missouri R.

LOUISIANA
TERRITORY
(1805)

Pacific Ocean

Colorado R.

VICEROYALTY OF NEW

Original 13 States

Other States and Territories

Louisiana Purchase
Boundary (1803)

Route of Lewis and Clark
(1804-1806)

Spanish   British

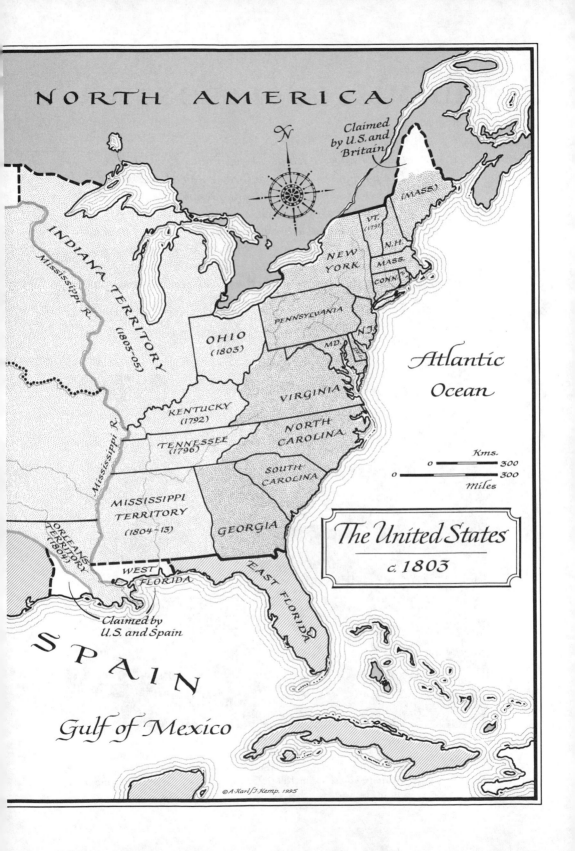

NORTH AMERICA

N

Claimed
by U.S. and
Britain

(MASS.)

INDIANA TERRITORY (1803-05)

Mississippi R.

VT. (1791)

NEW YORK

N.H.

MASS.

CONN.

Mississippi R.

OHIO (1803)

PENNSYLVANIA

N.J.

MD.

KENTUCKY (1792)

VIRGINIA

TENNESSEE (1796)

NORTH CAROLINA

SOUTH CAROLINA

MISSISSIPPI TERRITORY (1804-13)

GEORGIA

ORLEANS TERRITORY (1804)

WEST FLORIDA

EAST FLORIDA

Claimed by
U.S. and Spain

SPAIN

Gulf of Mexico

Atlantic Ocean

Kms.
0 ———— 300
0 ———— 300
Miles

The United States
c. 1803

© A. Karl / J. Kemp. 1995

CHAPTER ONE

THE MISSOURI FRONTIER

I do not know much about gods; but I think that the river
Is a strong brown god — sullen, untamed and intractable,
Patient to some degree, at first recognized as a frontier;
Useful, untrustworthy as a conveyor of commerce;
Then only a problem confronting the builder of bridges.
The problem once solved, the brown god is almost forgotten
By the dwellers in the cities — ever, however, implacable,
Keeping his seasons and rages, destroyer, reminder
Of what men choose to forget.

T. S. ELIOT

Art Resources
This Mandan village on the Missouri, near today's Stanton, North
Dakota, was painted in 1838 by George Catlin. Lewis and Clark
wintered close by in 1804–05, 1,800 miles from their starting point
in St. Louis.

Captain Amos Stoddard, an artillery officer in the United States Army, arrived in St. Louis in February 1804 in the midst of a peculiar situation. An embryonic town fronting the Mississippi River on a two-mile-long limestone bluff, St. Louis was then a part of Louisiana Territory, so extensive a region that three of its four boundaries were natural—the Gulf of Mexico to the south, the Rocky Mountains to the west, and the Mississippi River to the east. The vast area had changed hands so many times that it was hard to keep up with who owned it.

Louis XIV had ceded it to Spain in 1762, as a gratuity for having been its ally in the war against England. In a secret treaty in 1800, however, Spain returned the Louisiana Territory to France, then governed by Napoleon Bonaparte, who promised in return to place an unemployed nephew of the Spanish king on the throne of Tuscany. Three years later, absorbed in his European strategy of war with England, Napoleon sold the Louisiana Territory to the United States. That transaction is what brought Captain Amos Stoddard to St. Louis.

Stoddard's counterpart, Colonel Charles Dehault Delassus, had come to St. Louis in 1799 as Spain's lieutenant governor. Delassus found the usual problems: horse stealing was endemic, and the Osages were murdering settlers. In March 1800, a nine-year-old boy was found with his head cut off, his face smeared with blood, and a small piece of maple sugar in his mouth. Aside from the Indians, Delassus also had to arbitrate quarrels over unpaid debts between rival trading companies.

Colonel Delassus learned in November 1803 that since the province had been turned over to France he was out of a job. But it was only French for a split second before being sold to the Americans. As the man in charge, it was up to Colonel Delassus to handle the formalities. Upon his arrival in Cahokia, on the American side of the river, Captain Stoddard wrote the colonel "to demand and receive in the name of the United States the quiet and peacable possession of Upper Louisiana." Delassus answered that he was ready to comply "on the day and hour you may name."

On Friday, March 9, 1804, Captain Stoddard crossed the river accompanied by his troops and an infantry officer, Captain Meriwether Lewis, who had traveled to the area to prepare for an expedition. In a brief ceremony at the fort, the Spanish standard came down and the French flag was run up just long enough to mark French ownership. Then the Americans hoisted their Stars and Stripes and took possession of the outpost.

Captain Stoddard remained in charge for seven months. His instructions from President Jefferson were to conduct business as usual so as not to alarm the inhabitants, who were averse to the cession out of fear that they would lose their slaves. Stoddard simply continued the Spanish regime, using the same officials and the same archives, the only difference being that English was spoken.

Most urgent among the difficulties Captain Stoddard inherited was the climate of corruption that the Spanish administration had fostered. William C. Carr, one of the first American lawyers to set up practice in St. Louis, wrote Attorney General John Breckenridge that the Spanish "thirst for money has not been less than the most mercenary despot of Tripoli or Morocco." In court cases, the one who paid the largest bribe carried the day.

In September 1804, civil authority, in the form of William Henry Harrison, relieved Captain Stoddard of his duties. Harrison was governor of Indiana Territory, to which St. Louis was briefly attached before becoming a part of Louisiana Territory.

Embracing the future states of Indiana, Illinois, Michigan, and Wisconsin, Indiana Territory had once been part of the Northwest Territory won from England during the Revolutionary War. In May 1800, Northwest Territory was divided in half, the western side making up Indiana Territory, and the area in the east soon to become the state of Ohio.

The population of Indiana Territory in 1800 was 4,875, while the total population of the sixteen United States was 5,305,366. Besides the original thirteen states, Vermont, Kentucky, and Tennessee had been added to the expanding nation in the 1790s.

As for Captain Stoddard, he was mortally wounded during the War of 1812, in the action at Fort Meigs, Ohio, in May 1813. He had his moment in the opening up of the west, and gave his life for his country.

Initially, President Jefferson's interest in the Louisiana Territory had to do with the issue of freedom of navigation on the Mississippi. The Spanish blockaded the river at New Orleans, preventing Americans from getting their farm products and livestock to the Gulf of Mexico. The western outcry at the closure policy created a crisis for Jefferson, and made him all the more conscious of New Orleans's importance. As Secretary of State James Madison protested to the Spanish, the Mississippi was America's vital artery, "the Hudson, the Delaware, the Potomac, and all the navigable rivers of the Atlantic states, formed into one stream."

By this time, Jefferson had sent an envoy to France. Robert R. Livingston, a Hudson Valley landowner and former chancellor of New York, arrived in Paris in December 1801. When Jefferson learned about the secret treaty ceding Louisiana back to France, he wrote Livingston to express his concern that once the French controlled New Orleans they would bar American goods and people. He authorized Livingston to offer to buy New Orleans, which was east of the Mississippi. No one at this point had thought of acquiring land on the western side of the river.

Livingston spent all of 1802 trying to negotiate the purchase of New Orleans, but got nowhere. In 1803, however, Napoleon's thoughts turned to impending war with England. When hostilities broke out, he realized, the British would immediately attack vulnerable Louisiana. Better to sell it to the Americans before the British seized it. Instead of losing it by force, he could finance the war with its sale.

As Napoleon was scheming, James Madison disembarked in France on April 8, 1803, with a firm offer of $10 million for New Orleans. The American envoys were stunned when Napoleon offered to sell not only New Orleans but the entire Louisiana Territory. After weeks of haggling, a deal was struck for about $15 million.

The treaty was signed on May 2. Monroe and Livingston had gone far beyond Jefferson's instructions, but consultations with Washington would have meant a three-month delay. When the news reached the president in July 3, he quickly apprehended that this new acquisition was larger than the existing United States. And he was finally rid of the French on the continent of North America to boot.

Not everyone saw the purchase as a matchless achievement. Writing in the *Boston Columbian Centennial* on July 13, a columnist who called himself "Fabricus" complained: "We are to give money of which we have too little for land of which we have too much." With the Senate's approval of the purchase on October 20, 1803, however, the United States became a continental power, thanks to a French chief of state's strategic goals and financial needs.

For about 4 cents an acre, the United States acquired 828,000 square miles, more than doubling the country's size and bringing its western border within reach of the Pacific. From this huge hunk of land would be carved the present states of Louisiana, Arkansas, Missouri, Iowa, Oklahoma, Kansas, Nebraska, the Dakotas, and parts of Minnesota, New Mexico, Colorado, Wyoming, and Montana. The problem in 1803 was how to explore the new territory, and how to settle it.

Originally, Thomas Jefferson's plan to dispatch an expedition into the land beyond the Mississippi had nothing to do with the Louisiana Purchase. Jefferson had wanted to send explorers west since the days of the Continental Congress, when he asked George Rogers Clark to go to California—but the War of Independence intervened. Now that he was president, Jefferson's adventurous impulse expressed itself in the context of the administration's Indian policy.

The act establishing government trading-houses with the Indians was about to expire at the end of 1802. Jefferson thought that he might get congressional sanction for a westward foray if he asked for it in a rider to a new trading-house act. In a confidential message to Congress on January 18, 1803, he proposed, as one of a series of changes in the act, sending an exploring party to the headwaters of the Missouri "and even to the western ocean."

Jefferson was concerned that by establishing more government trading-houses east of the Mississippi, private traders would be driven away. In compensation, some opportunities might be found for them on the Missouri, where the Spanish presence was practically nil. The time was right for taking action to learn about the lay of the land, the disposition of the tribes, and the presence of foreign traders. Jefferson knew by then that

Spain had ceded Louisiana to France, even though the Spanish retained physical possession of the territory. Spain therefore was in no position to oppose the president's plan.

When Congress appropriated $2,500 for the expedition, it specified that the money was "for the purpose of extending the external commerce of the United States." Of course, the Louisiana Purchase "increased infinitely the interest we felt in the Expedition," Jefferson wrote. On July 3, 1803, he learned that his envoys to France had succeeded. That was two days before the departure from Washington of the expedition's leader, Captain Meriwether Lewis, who had been Jefferson's private secretary since his inauguration in 1801.

As a boy growing up in Charlottesville, Lewis had shown what might be called a "wilderness vocation," slipping out at night with his dogs at the age of eight to hunt raccoons. As an army officer, he served with distinction and won promotion to captain. Jefferson had been grooming him for the expedition, sending the young man to Philadelphia so that he might study botany, zoology, and celestial navigation.

Lewis's enthusiasm for the mission verged on obsession. Jefferson's attorney general, Levi Lincoln, commented that "from my ideas of Captain Lewis, he will be much more likely, in case of difficulty, to push too far, than to recede too soon." Lewis was not quite thirty when he left Washington on July 5, 1803, in such a hurry to get going that he forgot his wallet, which Jefferson forwarded to him in Pittsburgh.

Lewis recruited William Clark as his second-in-command. Four years older than Lewis, the redheaded Clark was the younger brother of the Revolutionary War hero George Rogers Clark. He had served in several Indian campaigns under General Anthony Wayne, and had retired from the army as a captain on account of ill health.

In order to be allowed to take part in the expedition, Clark was recommissioned in March 1804, at the lower rank of second lieutenant. As he later wrote the historian Nicholas Biddle, "I did not think myself very well treated . . . [but] I was not disposed to make any noise about the business." Wanting to be a part of this important mission, Clark swallowed his pride.

Once Lewis and Clark got under way, on May 14, 1804, it was as equal partners, shorn of uniforms and insignia. Off the "Corps of Discovery" went, carrying their ink powder and astronomical instruments, up the Missouri in a twenty-two-oar keelboat with a square sail. When they got to the river's headwaters in Montana at today's Three Forks, they named them the Gallatin, the Madison, and the Jefferson. They took the Jefferson to the approach of the Rockies, crossed over the mountain range, and then shot into the westward-moving river system of the Salmon, the Snake, and the Columbia, finally reaching the Pacific. They returned safely to St. Louis on September 26, 1806, having lost only one man, a young sergeant who died of a burst appendix.

But illness had plagued the two-year-and-four-month voyage. Lewis wrestled with occasional bouts of dysentery, which he treated by drinking a bitter potion of boiled chokeberry twigs. Clark had a painful rheumatism in his neck, to which he applied a hot stone wrapped in flannel. Sergeant Nathaniel Pryor dislocated his shoulder while taking down the mast of one of the boats, and was in later years listed as disabled.

The men suffered from a wide assortment of afflictions, including boils and abscesses, colds and pleurisy. Bad water brought on diarrhea, for which they took essence of peppermint and laudanum. In the North Dakota winter, when it got as cold as 72 below zero, members of the party returned from hunting buffalo in the snow with frostbitten feet. In the wet second winter on the northwest Pacific coast, the explorers came down with pneumonia.

Venereal disease became a problem in the time they spent among the Arikaras and Mandans, whose women were all too willing. On March 29, 1805, Clark worrisomely noted that "venereal is common with Indians and have been communicated to many of our party . . . those favors being easily acquired."

Then there were the dangers of the trip. The men were chased by bears, fought off Indians, slipped to the edge of precipices, nearly drowned in capsized canoes as they watched their baggage float down the current, and struggled against wind-whipped sand that stung their eyes and got into their watches. All the calamities of wilderness travel befell them. Worst was the accidental shooting of Meriwether Lewis in the thigh, when the expedition's one-eyed hunter Pierre Cruzatte mistook Jefferson's emissary for an elk.

But there were wonderful moments too, for example when they reached the Missouri's headwaters and continued up the Jefferson. They had followed the great river 2,500 miles to the point where it narrowed into a trickle, and were climbing to the Great Divide at Lemhi Pass. To mark the occasion, Private Hugh McNeal straddled the narrow stream, with one foot on each bank, declaring; "I thank my God that I have lived to bestride the mighty and heretofore-deemed-endless Missouri." They had reversed the scale of nature, where man was dwarfed by the immense and interminable river, and were now giants bestriding it.

On April 26, 1805, in that unknown sanctuary where all the great western rivers were born, they came to the fork of the Missouri and the Yellowstone. That night, in a modest celebration, the weary travelers called for a "gill" of brandy—the official army ration of four fluid ounces—and Pierre Cruzatte broke out his fiddle and played French tunes. This may have been the journey's finest moment, before it got caught in the twists and turns of politics and conquest. For on this particular evening, the men sang under the stars, and a sense of limitless possibility filled their hearts.

The expedition was a success in many ways. Lewis and Clark reached their destination. They drew maps and collected a vast body of information. They sent back botanical specimens. They planted the flag on virgin land. But in one important respect, they had mixed results, and this was in their dealings with the Indians.

One of their instructions had immediate and disastrous consequences. "If a few of their influential chiefs, within practicable distance, wish to visit us," Jefferson wrote, "arrange such a visit with them, and furnish them with authority to call on our officers on their entering the United States, to have them conveyed to this place [Washington] at the public expense."

A first group of fourteen Osage Indians were escorted to Washington just as the explorers were getting under way, arriving in the capital on July 11, 1804. The next day, they were taken to see President Jefferson, who declared: "In the name of the 17 nations, I take you by the hand."

On July 16, the president delivered his official talk concerning the new state of affairs: "By late arrangement with France and Spain, we now take their place as your neighbors, friends, and father; and we hope you will have no cause to regret the change." Jefferson added that he had sent "a beloved man, one of my own household," up the river to arrange the terms of a mutually beneficial trade.

The standard guided tour given to this and subsequent Indian delegations included seeing Congress in session. When the Osage delegation that summer observed a meeting of the House of Representatives, a European visitor, Charles William Janson, was present, and noted that their presence in the chamber was announced by the jingle of little bells fastened to their clothes. The Osages listened politely to the debate, though they did not understand a word. Then, at a signal from one of their chiefs, they all got up in unison and left.

Janson also attended a performance of Indian dances at a theater on Pennsylvania Avenue, announced by handbills. The Osages were given half the proceeds and a ration of rum, of which they made such liberal use that they screamed in horrid discord, frightening some of the audience away. More spectators left after the scalping scene, acted with such adroitness that the deception of a wig was not perceived. The next day, the principal dancer was found dead in his bed, a victim of overexertion and overdrinking.

The delegation was back in St. Louis on October 3. James Bruff, the military commandant of the territory, described them as "puffed up with ideas of their great superiority over other nations—on account of the distinction paid them by our government."

The importance of Lewis and Clark's mission to the tribes had been underlined in the breakdown of how the $2,500 congressional appropriation was to be spent. Among the various expenses, such as $217 for "mathematical instruments" and $81 for "arms and accoutrements," the largest item by far was $696 for Indian presents. Such gifts were the key to good relations. As the Indians put it, they "brightened the chain of friendship." Presents were a toll for traveling on populated rivers, payment for Indian food and hospitality, and an incentive to further trade.

So that even though the Corps of Discovery left their camp on the Wood River with fourteen bales and one box of Indian presents, Clark worried that it was not enough for the multitudes of Indians they would encounter. Chosen with care to appeal to tribal tastes, the gifts included richly laced coats, knives and tomahawks, pewter looking glasses and calico shirts, 4,600 sewing needles, 2,800 fishhooks, and two corn grinders, personally chosen by Jefferson.

As ambassadors to the native population, the explorers devised a series of riverside meetings that came to be known as "the Lewis and Clark medicine show." They would arrive at a village, send invitations to the chiefs, convert the keelboat's main sail into an awning for shade, open a bale, and unpack the presents. Before the program, however, came the commercial, in the form of a windy speech full of father-child imagery that concluded with an invitation to visit Washington.

Usually, the chiefs professed to be delighted with the new regime and asked the white emissaries to act as mediators in quarrels with neighboring tribes. As Lewis and Clark soon learned, these river tribes were always at war, over as slight a matter as a stolen horse or an insult to a squaw.

The "distribution of presents" scene, with three different grades of medals, and a "spoonful of milk" (whiskey), was repeated often as the expedition proceeded upriver, from Missouri to Nebraska to South Dakota. In the first two months, the Indians were amicable, displaying not the slightest hostile intent. But as Lewis and Clark navigated the Missouri's pretzel-shaped Big Bend in the middle of South Dakota, they approached those notorious river pirates the Teton Sioux, who preyed on the Arikaras to the north and on the Omahas to the south.

On September 25, they camped at the juncture of the Missouri and Bad rivers, two miles from a large Teton band. This time the "medicine show" turned into a fracas as the hostile Tetons erupted in a threatening manner, backing off when the swivel gun was aimed at them.

The embassy to the Tetons proved futile. Since they were outlaws who despoiled their neighbors, they had no intention of joining a trade network, and no interest in visiting the Great White Father in Washington. They were determined to maintain the status quo, based on a policy of plunder. Lewis's description of the Teton Sioux, read before Congress in February 1806, called them "the vilest miscreants of the savage race."

By October 7, 1804, the Corps of Discovery had reached the mouth of the Grand, near today's Mobridge, South Dakota, where they found an Arikara village three miles long. The Arikaras were the first of the northern Plains villagers, sedentary farmers who lived in circular earth lodges with a fire pit. The "squaw drudges" planted corn and beans and squash, while the men hunted buffalo and other game. Wedged between the Sioux and the Mandans, the Arikaras made war with both but also traded with both.

Warfare and smallpox had reduced the number of their villages from eighteen to three.

Unlike the Teton Sioux, the Arikaras were friendly and welcoming, and did not touch alcohol. When Lewis and Clark offered whiskey, they said they were surprised that their father would give them something that would turn them into fools. The explorers did not understand the cultural differences between the tribes. They appeared on the scene with their all-American homogenizing instincts, ignoring the evidence before them.

They were, for instance, under the impression that the Arikaras were victimized by the Teton Sioux. As Clark put it, "the Sioux exchange some merchandise of small value . . . for corn, etc. and have great influence over this people, treat them roughly and keep them in continual dread." But Clark did not perceive the multiple facets of the relationship. In fact, the Sioux needed Arikara produce, which they traded for guns and other European goods. The Arikaras also had a surplus of horses, which they obtained from the Cheyenne and traded to the Sioux. In trying to wean the Arikaras from the Sioux, Lewis and Clark failed to see a well-established and mutually advantageous trading system that worked reasonably well.

Nor did they understand the offering of women, the Indian form of "distribution of presents." As Clark noted on October 12: "A curious custom with the Sioux as well as the Arikaras is to give handsome squaws to those whom they wish to show some acknowledgement to. . . . The Arikaras sent two handsome squaws to follow us, they came up this evening and persisted in their civilities" (whether their persistence was rewarded is left unsaid).

But women were not, as Clark imagined, merely a way to return a favor. The real benefit was a perceived transfer of power. With their boats and cannon and compasses, these white men had potent magic. Some of that magic could be passed to the tribe via the squaws. The Indians regarded sex as a conduit for the passage of spiritual capabilities, a way of gaining access to the white man's skills, in much the same way that by eating the heart of a brave enemy you could gain his courage.

On October 12, Lewis and Clark visited all three Arikara villages. They were pleased to find that the chiefs wanted to end the war with their neighbors to the north, the Mandans. One of the chiefs, Eagle's Feather, agreed to accompany Lewis and Clark upriver to confer with the Mandans. "I must go," he said; "I also wish to go, perhaps I may when I return make my people glad."

On October 26, they reached the two remaining Mandan villages (the tribe was much reduced by smallpox) at the juncture of the Missouri and the Knife, near today's Stanton, North Dakota. The Mandans were farmers, but since they occupied the hub of a major trade route, they also acted as middlemen between the Arikaras and Sioux to the south, and the Hidatsas and Assiniboins to the north.

The Hidatsas, whose three villages were just a few miles up the Knife

River, coexisted peacefully as friendly neighbors. The Assiniboins, however, were liquor-loving bandits who traded with the British at their forts in southern Saskatchewan. Lewis and Clark hoped to detach the Mandans from the influence of British traders and bring them into a peaceful confederation of American-controlled river tribes, an alliance of sedentary farmers against plains nomads.

The linchpin of the river-tribe system was the partnership between the Arikaras and the Mandans, which is why Lewis and Clark had brought an Arikara chief to smoke the peace pipe. This happy event took place on October 29, when the explorers once again performed their flag-and-sail act.

What they did not know was that on this seemingly congenial occasion one of the Mandan chiefs, Big Man, had privately harangued Eagle's Feather, saying that his nation was made up of bad men and liars, who had broken the peace several times already.

But there were both hawks and doves among the Mandans, and the peace party prevailed. On October 31, Lewis and Clark met the principal Mandan chief, Black Cat, who threw a decorated buffalo robe over Clark's shoulders and told him that his tribe had agreed to make peace with the Arikaras.

Peace could be seen as more beneficial than war, which interrupted a tribe's normal activities. But in a society where the women did the farming while the men did the hunting and fighting, a case could be made for a permanent state of war. For one thing, halting raids on enemies would leave the death of relatives unavenged, which was very bad medicine. Also, chiefs were chosen from among the bravest in battle, and "if they were in a state of peace with their neighbors," Clark wrote, "what would the nation do for chiefs . . . who were now old and must shortly die, and the nation could not exist without chiefs." Even in their peacekeeping efforts, the explorers were disrupting the social organization of the tribes.

Having (as they thought) sealed the peace among the tribes, Lewis and Clark decided to winter among the Mandans, and built a triangular stockade in a cottonwood grove south of today's Stanton. By mid-November, they were filling in the chinks between the logs with clay, and were about ready to move in.

In one of the Hidatsa villages, they found a French-Canadian trader named Toussaint Charbonneau, who had two young wives proficient in the Snake language. One of the wives was six months pregnant, but Clark nonetheless hired the entire family because of their linguistic skills. Sacagawea, the pregnant wife, was a Shoshone from the Idaho-Montana border who had been taken prisoner as a child by a Hidatsa raiding party. Later romanticized accounts portrayed her as a sort of heroine, though all she really did was mend moccasins.

Lewis and Clark spent five months among the Mandans. Living with Indians, as they learned, was very different from passing through and waving the flag. They got entangled in quarrels over women, and drawn into competition with British traders, who made "unfavorable and ill-founded assertions" to undermine the Corps of Discovery.

More seriously, the peace process began to unravel in November, when a half-Sioux and half-Arikara war party attacked a hunting party of five Mandans. Chief Big Man took Clark to task, saying, "We did listen to your good talk, for when you told us that the other nations were inclined to peace with us, we went out carelessly in small parties." And now one of their hunters had been killed and two wounded. "I knew the Arikaras were liars," Big Man concluded.

Clark tried to explain that, though a few Arikaras might be bad apples, it did not mean that the tribe as a whole was breaking the peace. It might have been the old political problem of extremists trying to sabotage the peace process. "You say the Arikaras were with the Sioux," he said. "Some bad men may have been with the Sioux, you know there are bad men in all nations, do not get mad at the Arikaras until we know if those bad men are countenanced by their nation. . . ."

Another result of the corps's long stay was their chance to witness an important ceremony that took place only once a year. On January 5, 1805, Clark sent an observer to attend the Buffalo Dance, a rite meant to give young hunters the necessary magic to kill buffalo.

Based on a belief in the sexual passage of power, the dance went on for three nights. It began when the old, experienced hunters sat cross-legged on buffalo skins around a fire in the middle of the lodge, each with a female doll in front of him. The young hunters arrived with their wives behind them, naked under a robe. Each young man chose one of the elders as a sort of Doppelgänger, presenting him with a pipe that they smoked together. Then the young man asked the older man to take his wife and sleep with her. The old man, often stooped and arthritic and hardly able to walk, was led by the girl to what Clark called "a convenient place for the business." If the old man refused, Clark wrote, the young husband "throws a nice robe over the old man and begs him not despise him and his wife."

In this manner, the old hunters' experience and skill were transmitted to the young men for the upcoming buffalo hunt. According to Clark, the observer he had charged with watching the proceedings was invited to participate, and "they gave him four girls."

On February 11, 1805, Sacagawea gave birth to a fine son, named Jean-Baptiste and nicknamed Pompy. To induce labor, she swallowed the ground-up rattle from a rattlesnake with some water. Pompy became the youngest member of the Corps of Discovery, and later a mountain man and fur trader.

On February 28, the explorers learned that the Teton Sioux were preparing to attack the Mandans, and declaring that if they ever saw Lewis and Clark again they would kill them. Evidently, not all the tribes wanted to become a part of the American grand design. But the explorers could not do much about it, since in March the ice on the river started to break and they had to prepare for departure.

On Sunday, April 7, 1805, the Corps of Discovery split into two sections. A group of thirty-two, in two dugouts and six canoes, traveled upriver toward the Missouri headwaters. At the same time, seven Americans and four Frenchmen headed downriver toward St. Louis in the keelboat, which was too big for the narrowing river and had to turn back.

On the way to St. Louis, the keelboat picked up forty-five chiefs from various tribes who wanted to visit Washington. Among them was the Arikara chief, Eagle's Feather. From May to October the chiefs stayed in St. Louis, since travel during the summer months was considered dangerous. Some of them caught colds or had bouts of dysentery, and nineteen of the forty-five were sent home, too sick to make the long trip east.

On October 22, the remaining twenty-six chiefs from eleven nations left St. Louis under the care of Captain Amos Stoddard, the officer who had taken possession of the Louisiana Territory from the Spanish the previous year. The wisdom of removing Indians from their natural habitat to take them on long and tiring trips was questionable, for illness plagued the delegation en route, and one chief died in Kentucky.

In early January 1806, the weary entourage finally arrived in Washington, but visiting Indians were no longer a novelty, and Secretary of War Henry Dearborn, who was responsible for the chiefs, complained that he was so overwhelmed with delegations that in the future they should come only when Congress was not in session.

As for Eagle's Feather, the trip, the excitement, and the change of diet proved too much for him. He died on April 7, four days before the group's scheduled departure. In his farewell speech, Jefferson expressed sorrow that several chiefs had died, adding, "Man must die, at home or abroad."

Jefferson gave the interpreter Joseph Gravelines, who was taking the delegation home, some presents and a letter of condolence for the Arikaras, which said: "On his return [from a side trip to Philadelphia], Eagle's Feather was taken sick . . . it pleased the Great Spirit to take him from among us. We shed many tears over his grave." The presents, including powder and lead, were to help "wipe away the tears." Henry Dearborn noted on April 9 that "what is more especially to be regretted is the death of the very respectable and amiable Ricara chief, which happened on the 7th instant." It was regrettable for a number of reasons, as we shall see.

As Joseph Gravelines headed for St. Louis with his traveling Indians, the Corps of Discovery crossed the Assiniboin country to the fork of the Missouri and the Yellowstone, then headed past the Milk and the Musselshell to the Great Falls, a sheet of water 300 feet wide and 80 feet high that hurled clouds of spray against the rock ledge.

The only way around the falls was an eighteen-mile portage, during which a bruising hailstorm broke over them and prickly pear pierced their moccasins. On July 25, 1805, they came to the Three Forks, taking the Jefferson and the Beaverhead to the Lemhi Pass at 8,000 feet, where they crossed the Continental Divide, leaving the territory of the Louisiana Purchase and heading into the truly unknown.

While reconnoitering on foot on August 13, Lewis came upon a party of Rocky Mountain Indians, the Shoshones. Having never seen a white man, they jumped from their horses to rub cheeks with the captain and clap him on the back. Four days later, Clark's group arrived with Sacagawea, who discovered that the Shoshone chief Cameawhait was the brother she had not seen since childhood.

Other Indians were less benign. When a canoe capsized on the Snake River on October 8, the explorers had to place sentinels over the goods spread out to dry, since the Indians, "though kind and disposed to give us every aid during our distress, could not resist the temptation of pilfering some of the small articles."

As the expedition headed down the Columbia River to the Pacific, they found as many Indians as they had seen on the Missouri, for the river had an abundance of salmon and other fish. In November, as they approached salt water, they realized that the more the tribes had been in contact with seafaring white traders, the more larcenous and disagreeable they tended to be. On November 4, some Indians wearing sailors' jackets arrived on the pretext of a visit, plucked a pipe out of a crewman's mouth, and relieved another of his greatcoat.

On November 7, seeing the ocean and hearing the roar of the breakers, Clark gave way to a rare emotional outburst and wrote, "Ocean in view! O! The joy!" Then it was winter quarters again, and four months billeted at the mouth of the Columbia among the Clatsop Indians—four months of nonstop rain, and of living like muskrats in their holes, with nothing to do but shoot elk, make salt, and dicker with the natives, who started out asking three times the value of what they were selling and little by little dropped their demands. The Indians were so used to trading with white men that they had picked up some English words, such as "musket," "powder," and "damned rascal."

On March 22, 1806, the Corps of Discovery started back up the Columbia on the long voyage home. This time they had far more trouble than on the trip out. One reason was that "the whole stock of goods on which we are to depend for the purchase either of horses or of goods during the long tour of 4000 miles is so much diminished that it might all be tied in two handkerchiefs."

Unable to trade, Lewis and Clark let their morals lapse and stole a canoe from the Clatsops, "as a reprisal for some elk which some of them had stolen from us in the winter." It seemed that the wilderness imposed its own set of rules. On April 21, while negotiating a tricky portage near a Skilloot village, Lewis saw an Indian pilfer a boat's iron oar socket in broad daylight. He lost his temper, already frayed by two years of slogging, and struck the Indian "several severe blows . . . I now informed the

Indians that I would shoot the first of them that attempted to steal an article from us."

When the next day an Indian stole a buffalo robe that had fallen from an explorer's horse, Lewis threatened to burn their village to the ground. The patience and goodwill the explorers had started out with was worn down to the nub.

In July, the Corps was back on the Missouri, moving smoothly with the current. Leaving the Great Falls on July 17, they came upon shortgrass plains as flat as "a well-shaved bowling green." Captain Lewis took three men on a side trip to explore the Marias River, which runs into the Missouri at today's Loma, Montana. Ten miles from the Rockies, they set up their camp, christening it Camp Disappointment.

On July 26, they ran into a hunting party of eight Piegan Blackfeet, nomadic buffalo hunters so named because their moccasins were darkened by the ash of prairie fires. The Blackfeet wanted to smoke, which Lewis took as a good sign. He proposed that they camp together that night, so that he could give them his "American alliance" lecture.

Other tribes had already joined, he said, not realizing that some of the tribes he mentioned, such as the Shoshones and the Nez Percés, were the Blackfeet's traditional enemies. Thus, his entire purpose was spoiled, for by telling the Blackfeet that their enemies were now obtaining weapons and goods from American trading posts, he was driving them further into the embrace of the British at Saskatchewan. Thanks to British arms, the Blackfeet were the power on the plains, but now saw their dominance threatened by the American alliance that Lewis wanted them to be part of. Once again, Lewis had failed to grasp the dynamics among the tribes.

The white men and the Indians camped together that evening near today's Shelby, Montana. The Blackfeet hunters, who outnumbered the explorers two to one, resolved to steal their guns. At sunrise on July 27, they crowded around the fire near Joseph Fields, who, although on guard duty, had left his rifle near his sleeping brother, Reuben. As one of the Blackfeet took the Fieldses' guns, the brothers chased him, and in the ensuing scuffle, Reuben Fields stabbed him through the heart. The Black-foot ran fifteen steps and fell to the ground. As Reuben put it, "He drew but one breath and the wind of his breath followed the knife and he fell dead."

Meanwhile, several other Blackfeet grabbed the rifles of Captain Lewis and Georges Drouillard. The Frenchman wrestled with the Indian who had his weapon, shouting, "Damn you, let go of my gun," which awakened Lewis from a sound sleep. Reaching out and finding his rifle gone, the captain drew his pistol from his belt, ran after the Indian who had his gun, and ordered him to lay it down. The Blackfoot dropped the rifle and walked slowly away. Minutes later, Lewis saw the same man driving horses off with a second Blackfoot. When he pursued them, they ducked into a crev-ice in the bluff on the riverbank with the horses. Seeing Lewis give chase, one of them jumped behind some mushroom-shaped rocks, while the other stopped, thirty steps away. Lewis raised his gun and shot him in the gut. The Blackfoot sank to his knees, leaning on his right elbow, and fired, but the shot was high. Bareheaded, Lewis felt the whoosh of the bullet through his hair as it flew by. Since he didn't have his shotpouch and couldn't reload, he went back to camp.

Lewis had a peace medal placed around the neck of the Blackfoot that Reuben Fields had killed, so that "they might be informed who we were," a gesture that smacked somehow of those defilements that Indians committed on the bodies of their victims. As an added insult, he cut the amulets off the Indian shields. Begun with decorous negotiations, the expedition ended with a shoot-out, in a situation where diplomacy, presents, and the prestige of a young nation had no effect whatever.

On September 3, the Corps passed the Vermillion River, at the border of Nebraska and South Dakota, and sixty miles farther, they came upon the trader James Aird, who was heading upriver to visit the Sioux. Having heard nothing of events in the United States since their departure in May 1804, the explorers were starved for news, and spent much of the night asking Aird what had happened in their absence. Aird tried to fill them in. General James Wilkinson was now governor of Louisiana. Two British men-of-war had fired on an American ship in the port of New York. Aaron Burr and Alexander Hamilton had fought a duel and Hamilton had been killed.

On September 12, Lewis and Clark were on the broad Missouri between Kansas City and St. Louis when they met a trading party heading upriver with Joseph Gravelines, who was on his way to the Arikara village with $300 worth of presents and a letter from the president. Gravelines was not looking forward to having to tell the Arikaras that their chief, Eagle's Feather, was dead, and may have hoped that they would not blame the messenger for the message.

On September 22, 1806, the men of the Corps reached St. Louis and received a hearty welcome. Theirs was an amazing exploit, a triumph in every respect but one. Their Indian diplomacy had failed. You couldn't just come in and tell the Indians, "This is what the Great Father wants." You couldn't just hand out medals and flags and turn them into docile American subjects. Longtime inhabitants of the land, the Indians had their own diplomacy and their own balance of power, and it was presumptuous to think otherwise.

The return of Lewis and Clark to St. Louis was like the return of Ulysses to Ithaca. No one expected to see them, since they had been gone for more than two years. Now they were back bearing wondrous tales of unknown lands accessible by the river route, and telling of places where the buffalo blackened the plain, where the tiniest rivulet had its beaver dam.

To the queries of inquisitive traders, they provided encouraging answers. What was the reception from the Indians on the upper Missouri?

On the whole good, with the exception of the Teton Sioux. What sort of boats could carry trade goods and navigate the river? Keelboats with plank sides and flat bottoms could usually clear the shallows and be pulled over sandbars. What about the winter? Well, in the winter the river froze and they had to hibernate until spring.

A grateful Congress named Lewis governor of Louisiana Territory and Clark superintendent of Indian Affairs, presenting each with 1,600 acres of land. In the meantime, the vision of untapped riches along the upper Missouri had ignited the imagination of the St. Louis trader Manuel Lisa. A Spaniard born in New Orleans in 1772, Lisa arrived in St. Louis in 1798, intending to get a piece of the Indian trade.

Under the Spanish system, based on favoritism and bribery, Lisa had been able to win the Osage concession for five years. Then came the news of the American takeover, signifying the end of the preferential system and the opening up of the territory to free enterprise.

Lewis and Clark's return was the turning point in Lisa's life, for he had the prescience to see that the two explorers had opened up a vast area to trade. The merchant followed on the heels of the explorer. By April 1807, less than seven months after the return of Lewis and Clark, Lisa was ready to embark on the first commercial venture into the upper Missouri and the Rockies. Quick to strike, he was ahead of the long-established Chouteau firm and all his other rivals. On April 19, his two keelboats, laden with goods, started up the river, carrying crews that were mainly French *engagés* (hired hands) or veterans of the Lewis and Clark trip.

The Missouri, Lisa soon saw, had a personality all its own, described by settlers as "too thin to plow and too thick to drink." The current was too strong for the keelboats, which had to hug the shore in shallow water. Each boat had a mast with a square-rigged sail that was hoisted on those rare occasions when the wind and the boats were moving in the same direction. Most of the time, the methods of propulsion consisted of poling and cordelling.

Poling resembled the technique employed by Venetian gondoliers, except that the keelboats required twenty gondoliers. Cleats were nailed for surer footing on each side of the deck. The men lined up ten on a side, facing the stern, and walked their way back, all the while throwing their shoulders against the padded ends of their poles in unison. They then dashed sixty feet to the bow and started over.

If the water was too deep to pole, they used the cordelle, a towline attached to the mast. The men scampered on shore and dragged the cordelle through mud and nettles and brush as chiggers bit their ankles and mosquitoes buzzed around their heads. It was backbreaking work, tedious and primitive, but no other way existed. In this manner, they advanced perhaps five or ten miles a day. In addition, the river was like a minefield, dense with sunken trees known as sawyers, clotted with great tangles of vines and roots called *embarras*.

Poling and cordelling across South Dakota, Lisa's boats appeared at the Arikara village near today's Mobridge in early August 1807. This was the village whose chief, Eagle's Feather, had died in Washington. Only months before, Joseph Gravelines had brought presents and a letter from President Jefferson to tell them the sad news. The Arikaras had been so angry at the death of their chief that Gravelines barely escaped with his life.

When Lisa approached the village, he did not know that the Arikaras were mourning their lost chief and blaming the white men for his death. But warriors lining the banks fired on his boats and told them to land. Lisa ordered the swivel guns aimed at the Indians, who drew back, but soon came forward again holding peace pipes. After smoking with the chiefs and distributing presents, Lisa and his party left the village without further hostilities.

In the meantime, Meriwether Lewis, now governor of Louisiana, was in St. Louis arranging for the return of another chief, Big White, to his Mandan village. He ordered Sergeant Nathaniel Pryor of the Corps of Discovery to take the chief upriver with a fourteen-soldier escort. Attached to this military mission was a trading party of twenty-three led by Pierre Chouteau, Jr. Aware that Lisa had a head start on the upper Missouri, the Chouteaus were eager to establish a trading post with the Mandans.

Nathaniel Pryor left with Big White on May 18, 1807, having been promoted to ensign for the occasion. Moving slowly upriver, they reached the Arikara village on September 9, about a month after Lisa had passed through. Seeing armed warriors lining the bank, Pryor directed Big White to secure himself in the keelboat cabin by piling trunks and boxes against the door.

Pryor held a council with one of the hostile chiefs, to whom he gave a medal, and made ready to embark when he saw that some warriors had seized the cable of Chouteau's barge. The Arikara chief threw the medal on the ground and demanded that Pryor bring Big White on shore. Suddenly, some warriors concealed behind a clump of willows sixty yards away opened fire, killing four white men and wounding three more.

Pryor ordered a retreat, not wanting to risk Big White's capture or death. The two boats floated back to St. Louis on the current. Pryor estimated that it would take four hundred men to break through the Arikara bottleneck and get Big White home. He blamed the ambush on Manuel Lisa, for he had been told by a Mandan woman captive of the Arikaras that Lisa had given them guns and powder and ball. Pryor reasoned that Lisa had been "obliged to divert the storm which threatened his own boat, by diverting the attention of the Arikaras to ours."

Lisa himself had reached the fork of the Missouri and the Yellowstone at the border of North Dakota and Montana. He traveled up the Yellowstone another two hundred miles until early November, when he arrived at its juncture with the Bighorn, east of present-day Billings.

Having built winter quarters on a wooded point between the two rivers, he sent his men out to trap beaver, even though it was late in the season. In May 1808, he went back to St. Louis with a boatload of furs, leaving most of his men behind to continue trapping in the beaver-rich streams of the northern Rockies.

Lisa and his two partners made a handsome profit from this initial trip. They sold the furs for $9,000, and Lisa received a $1,000 bonus for leading the expedition. They were now established on the upper Missouri, with the only trading post at the foot of the Rockies, and a crew of forty men engaged in trapping there.

Since Lisa had the inside track, his rivals the Chouteaus grew amenable to a merger. Lisa agreed, in order to obtain more capital and spread the risk, and on March 3, 1809, the two parties formed the St. Louis Missouri Fur Company.

In St. Louis, Meriwether Lewis was still grappling with the problem of getting Big White back to his tribe. Jefferson had written him on August 24, 1808, emphasizing that the chief's return was an urgent matter involving American credibility. "That is an object which presses on our honor," the president said. But by the time Jefferson left office in March 1809, to be replaced by James Madison, Big White was still moldering in Fort Bellefontaine above St. Louis, where he had resided for two years.

The formation of the St. Louis Missouri Fur Company, on the verge of sending an expedition upriver, gave Lewis the chance he was looking for. He signed a contract with the company, stipulating that they would take the chief home and receive a payment of $7,000. This sum would cover the cost of hiring 160 militiamen, including 40 expert riflemen, to force the Arikara barrier.

This was by far the largest corps ever to go up the Missouri, a total of 350 men, divided into two detachments, and carried in thirteen keelboats and barges. The first group of 160 militiamen left St. Louis on May 17, 1809, under the command of Pierre Chouteau, Jr., followed a month later by Manuel Lisa and his 190-man trading party.

Lisa's men included Canadian engagés and Americans, and between the two groups there was some animosity. The Americans felt that Lisa worked them too hard and that the engagés got preferential treatment. The engagés saw the Americans as a bunch of lazy complainers who wanted two men to an oar. When one of the Americans went to get his share of food from the provision boat, the engagé in charge offered him a bear's head, saying it was good enough for "you fellows," to indicate the low esteem in which the Americans were held.

When they reached the juncture with the Osage River, the Americans began to jump ship, until thirty-two men had deserted, representing both a loss of manpower and a financial debacle in terms of sums advanced and debts incurred.

On September 12, 1809, the militiamen disembarked at the Arikara village, hauling their cannon and marching in formation toward the palisaded dwellings. When they saw this large armed corps drawing near, the Arikaras made loud protestations of friendship. A council was held, and

Pierre Chouteau told them: "You permitted yourselves to fire upon the colors of your father and to attack his men. I have orders to destroy your nation."

An apologetic Arikara chief clasped Big White's hand and said, "If we fired upon you the first time it was because the death of our chief in the United States was a cause of great dissatisfaction in our nation." All was forgiven when the Arikaras promised to mend their ways.

Big White finally went home. On September 22, 1803, the detachment reached the Mandan village near today's Bismarck, North Dakota. The Mandans were at first frantic with joy to have their old chief back. But the joy turned to disappointment when, instead of distributing the presents he had received on his trip to Washington, he kept everything for himself.

In St. Louis, Meriwether Lewis was in hot water over his contract with the St. Louis Missouri Fur Company. With Madison replacing Jefferson, and William Eustis taking over from Henry Dearborn as secretary of war, Lewis had lost his friends in high places. Questions now arose about the propriety of giving an official mission to a trading company in which Lewis's brother Reuben, as well as his friend William Clark, served as partners.

The government audited Lewis's accounts. The $7,000 for the cost of the expedition was allowed, but Eustis bridled at two additional bills, $500 for presents to the Indians and $440 for an assaying furnace. On July 15, 1809, Eustis wrote Lewis a letter of reprimand. Why had an expedition financed by the government combined military and commercial objectives? And why these other bills—neither of which, Eustis informed Lewis, would be honored.

In another letter on August 7, Eustis berated Lewis over his estimates for Indian affairs expenditures. "It does not seem necessary," he wrote, "that the expenses attending our relations with the Indians in the territory of Louisiana should be four times as much as the whole expense of supporting its civil government." Bent on economy, as newly installed cabinet members tend to be, Eustis wanted to prune the War Department payroll of Indian interpreters.

Lewis replied on August 18 that "the feelings it [Eustis's letter] excites are truly painful." "I have never received a penny of public money," he protested. Then he drifted into the paranoid vein by saying; "I have been informed representations have been made against me." And he magnified what was basically an example of bureaucratic hairsplitting by imagining that he was being accused of treason. "Be assured," he wrote, "that my country can never make a 'Burr' out of me [Aaron Burr had been tried for treason in 1807]. . . . She may reduce me to poverty; but she can never sever my attachments from her."

Because his bills had been refused, Lewis's credit rating fell and his creditors called in $4,000 in debts. He had to put up his property as collateral. On top of that, the government was questioning his integrity. It was intolerable . . . he must go to Washington to explain himself.

That the personality of Meriwether Lewis had a pathological side was something President Jefferson had observed years before in his secretary. He later'wrote in a memoir that "while he lived with me in Washington I observed at times sensible depressions of mind," which Jefferson thought he had inherited from his father. In St. Louis, Jefferson went on, "these depressions returned to him with redoubled vigor and began seriously to alarm his friends."

It may be that Lewis was a manic-depressive, or that Jefferson used the word "depression" as a euphemism for alcoholism, since Lewis had a serious drinking problem. But at the same time, these "depressions" did not prevent Jefferson, an astute judge of men, from choosing Lewis for a difficult mission. His bravery and intelligence were not in doubt, and he proved to be an able leader. Lewis and Clark performed one of the epic feats in the nation's history, while enduring hardships of every description.

Perhaps the nerve-wracking riddle of navigating the unknown and the daily threat of Indian harassment had left their mark on Lewis, creating a kind of "wilderness fatigue." With his nerves permanently frayed, he might have resorted to liquor as a painkiller. Yet he could deal with the expedition's practical difficulties far better than with written attacks accusing him of dishonesty. He must have felt a terrible injustice in having his Washington bosses treat him like a malefactor when he had repeatedly risked his life in his country's service, without the slightest thought of gain.

In any case, the thirty-five-year-old Lewis snapped. What actually happened has only become known in the last fifteen years, through the publication of Donald Jackson's two volumes of Lewis and Clark papers.

Lewis left St. Louis to make his case in Washington at the end of August 1809. Taking a boat down the Mississippi, he reached Fort Pickering on September 15, at the site of today's Memphis, then known as Chickasaw Bluffs.

Captain Gilbert Christian Russell of the 5th Infantry, who commanded the fort, welcomed him. Lewis was, Russell later wrote Jefferson, already in a state of mental derangement when he arrived. The riverboat crew reported that he had made two suicide attempts on the boat, one of which had nearly succeeded.

Captain Russell kept Lewis at the fort for two weeks to dry him out and bring him back to health. "The free use he made of liquor," wrote the captain, ". . . he acknowledged very candidly to me after his recovery and expressed a firm determination never to drink any more spirits or use snuff again, both of which I deprived him of for several days and confined him to claret and a little white wine. But after leaving this place by some means or other his resolution left him."

Lewis and his two servants left Fort Pickering on September 29, heading east across Tennessee, in Chickasaw country. James Neeley, the federal agent to the Chickasaws, happened to be at the fort, and offered to go with him. Lewis packed his voluminous papers on a horse, and they set out together. But as Neeley later observed, "I discovered that he appeared at times deranged in mind."

They rode due east about a hundred miles and came to the Tennessee River. Fording it, they lost two horses. Neeley stayed behind to look for them, while Lewis went ahead, saying he would stop at the first cabin he saw. This turned out to be a "stand," or bed-and-breakfast place, belonging to Mr. and Mrs. Grinder, about seventy miles southwest of Nashville. Grinder was away, and when Lewis arrived at sunset on October 10, he brought in his saddle and asked Mrs. Grinder if he could stay the night. His servants arrived soon after.

Mrs. Grinder prepared his bed in the main cabin, but he insisted on sleeping on the floor, telling his servants to bring his bearskins and buffalo robe. Mrs. Grinder went off to sleep in the kitchen while the servants stayed in the barn two hundred yards away. She could hear Lewis pacing and talking to himself "like a lawyer."

At three o'clock on the morning of October 11, Mrs. Grinder heard the crack of a pistol and the words "O Lord!" Then another shot rang out, followed by the words "O Madam! Give me some water, and heal my wounds." Through the unplastered cracks in the kitchen's log wall, she could see Lewis stumble into the yard, stagger, and fall. He crawled to the kitchen door and scraped the water bucket with a gourd . . . but she was too terrified to move.

When day broke, she sent two of her children for the servants, who entered the cabin and saw Lewis lying on the bed. He turned to show them where one of the bullets had entered—a piece of his forehead was blown off, exposing his brains. Begging for his rifle to finish the job, he kept repeating, "I am no coward, but I am so strong, so hard to die." He expired two hours later, as the sun rose over the trees. "He lay down and died," said Captain Russell's statement, "with the declaration to the boy [the servant] that he had killed himself to deprive his enemies of the pleasure of doing it."

At this point, James Neeley arrived, attended to the burial, and removed Lewis's papers. On October 18, Neeley wrote Jefferson from Nashville about Lewis's death, "and I am sorry to say, by suicide." Jefferson himself, in a letter dated August 18, 1813, wrote that Lewis "did the deed which plunged his friends into affliction."

Mrs. Grinder's fearful inability to help—as well as a reluctance to believe that an American hero could take his own life—has led to speculation that the Grinders murdered Lewis. But since there is not a shred of evidence to support this notion, the verdict of suicide should stand. As it turned out, Lewis's contested bills were posthumously allowed in part, and on March 4, 1812, the Accountant's Office determined that the Treasury owed Lewis $636.25. The money was paid to his estate.

•   •

After dropping off Big White at the Mandan village on September 22, 1809, Lisa and his people continued about ten miles up the Missouri, where they built a trading post that could also serve as a base for trapping sorties. The sore feelings between Lisa and the American boatmen persisted. One of the boatmen, Thomas James, said: "Lisa we thoroughly detested and despised, both for his acts and his reputation. . . . Rascality sat on every feature of his dark complexioned, Mexican face—gleamed from his black, Spanish eyes, and seemed enthroned in a forehead 'villainous low.' "

But James had a particular gripe against Lisa, for when the sailor got back to St. Louis in mid-July 1810, expecting a large sum in back pay, he was told instead that he owed the company $200. He had been duped by the old company-store routine. Whiskey that cost Lisa $2 a gallon in St. Louis was sold at the Mandan post for $12. Since the trappers had no cash, the company took payment in beaver skins at $1.50 each, and then sold them in St. Louis for $6, so that the trappers got swindled twice. James vowed never to go trapping again.

But in 1810, conditions changed for the company. A competitor, John Jacob Astor, had formed the Pacific Fur Company and was planning a chain of fur-trading posts extending all the way to the western ocean. Astor sent one of his best men to St. Louis, twenty-eight-year-old Wilson Price Hunt. Both mild of temperament and firm of purpose, Hunt arrived in St. Louis in September 1810 and began to prepare for an expedition in the spring of 1811. The rivalry with Lisa blossomed when Hunt hired away some of his men.

The spring trip upriver took on the aspect of a race. Hunt left on March 12 with four keelboats and sixty men. He also agreed to take a hitchhiker, the Englishman John Bradbury, the first trained botanist to go west of the Mississippi. Lisa, although he had only one boat and twenty men, did not get started until April 2, giving Hunt a twenty-one-day head start. Lisa also had a special passenger on board, a twenty-five-year-old law student from Pittsburgh, Henry Brackenridge, who was tagging along to study the fur trade, "the theater of American enterprise," as he put it.

One of the reasons for Lisa's delay, Brackenridge observed, was the difficulty of getting the men out of the taverns and into the boat. The barkeeps let them run up tabs, knowing that the company would settle. On the river, Lisa had "unruly hands to manage, who think themselves perfectly at liberty when out of reach of law," Brackenridge wrote.

Bent on catching up with Hunt, Lisa now manned the helm, now wrestled with the grappling iron, now maneuvered the pole, and inquired of everyone he saw along the banks as to when his rival had come through. But the wind and the current worked against them, and the going was slow.

Hunt by then was at the site of today's Leavenworth, where John Bradbury marveled at finding eleven species of snakes under rocks. First came the explorer, then the merchant, and now the botanist, whose only interest was in removing plant specimens from the wilderness. Although disparaged by the crewmen as a trivial and somewhat ridiculous activity, collecting plants was no simple matter. Each specimen had to be pressed in paper and kept free of damp. Descriptions of the plant and its habitat had to be written up. Then the specimens were packed and carried over long distances through numerous hazards, like boats overturning and pack animals losing their footing.

The French *engagés* called Bradbury *le fou* (the madman) and laughed at his efforts, saying, "*Il est après ramasser des racines* [He is gathering roots]." Whatever was happening, whether Indians were about to attack or the boat was caught in an eddy, Bradbury with peculiar single-mindedness examined his flora, oblivious to his surroundings. He asked to land twenty times a day, while Hunt wanted to keep moving. He was never around when the crew stood ready to embark. He jumped into the icy river in March to chase a single clump of grass. In the midst of a tornado, as the boat was about to go under, he sat in the cabin taking notes.

At Council Bluffs, he was collecting specimens when an old Indian galloped up, shook hands, and pointed at his shrubs, asking, "*Bon pour manger?* [Good to eat?]." To which he replied, "*Pas bon.*" The Indian then asked, "*Bon pour médecine?* [Good for medicine?] and Bradbury answered in the affirmative.

On June 1, in the Great Bend of the Missouri, Hunt and his men met a war party of one hundred Arikaras and Mandans, who said they could not go home without proof of having seen the white man. This meant they wanted presents. The next day, Hunt gave them some powder and ball and three dozen knives. At this point, an Indian ran up to announce that a boat was in sight. It was Manuel Lisa, who had finally caught up by ruthlessly pushing his men. He joined Hunt's flotilla, and all five boats proceeded upstream together.

On June 12, they reached the Arikara village. Here Hunt decided to continue overland on horseback. His goal was to find the Columbia River and take it all the way to the Pacific. He sold Lisa his four boats and bought horses from the Arikaras, who also wanted to market their wives, sisters, and daughters. A group of squaws clustered around Bradbury and the trader Donald McKenzie, whose long green coat enthralled the Indian women. Having never seen the color green in clothing, several offered their favors in exchange for a swatch, outlining a small rectangle with their fingers. "Watch out," said Bradbury, "lest your coat become a spencer [a waist-length coat]." While the trade in women was going on, Bradbury climbed up to the bluff, where fourteen buffalo skulls were placed in a row. The cavities of their eyes and nostrils had been filled with sagebrush to appease the spirits.

Eager to bring his several thousand specimens back to St. Louis, Bradbury stayed with Lisa, who continued upriver to the Mandan trading post. On the first of July, the botanist was picking shrubs three miles from the post when an Indian with a gun on his shoulder approached him and made the gesture for trade—crossing two forefingers one over the other. He had a squaw behind him, and it soon became clear that he wished to exchange the squaw for Bradbury's shirt. When Bradbury declined the offer, the Indian called him a *sale crapaud*—a dirty toad. When the Indian took his gun off his shoulder, Bradbury raised his own, and they slowly backed away from each other.

On July 17, Lisa sent two fur-laden boats downriver with Bradbury and Brackenridge. They moved along the current at a brisk nine miles an hour. Lisa had assured the botanist that the boats would stop to allow him to search for more specimens, but the promise was not kept, and Bradbury felt "greatly mortified and chagrined" when they passed a number of plants that would for the moment escape nomenclature. Returning to St. Louis on July 29, after an incredibly swift descent, Bradbury mailed his specimens to his sponsor, the Liverpool Botanical Society. The frontier, he reflected, was a classless society with no privileged orders. "That species of hauteur which one class of society in some countries show in their intercourse with the other, is here utterly unknown."

The partners in St. Louis were especially glad to see the two boats bursting with furs, for the price of beaver had gone up. But the return on their investments did not meet their expectations, and when Lisa got back in October 1811, they dissolved the company. Lisa formed still another company, and made his fourth and final expedition in the spring of 1812, consisting of two boats and $11,000 worth of goods. They left on May 8, and less than a month later the War of 1812 was declared.

The war dramatically changed river politics. When Lisa reached the Arikara village on August 7, he found the Indians sullen and unfriendly. The alliance of river tribes envisioned by Lewis and Clark had broken down completely. Now, as Lisa learned, the Arikaras and Mandans were united against the Americans. There was nothing for this gifted entrepreneur to do but return to St. Louis, dissolve the new company, and sit out the war.

Six years later, in August 1820, Manuel Lisa died of an undiagnosed illness. He was a major figure in the opening up of the American west, for he realized his vision of an upper Missouri fur empire extending to the Rockies, and based on friendly relations with the tribes. He became the recognized leader of the river trade, for he had the stomach to go on the expeditions, while his partners sat in their countinghouses making up the balance sheets.

Being a good trader was no simple matter. You had to know that one tribe wanted a three-point blanket of solid red while another tribe preferred a blue stripe. There were many styles of knives, mirrors, and tomahawks, each with its clientele. The more tribes you traded with, the greater the variety of goods you had to carry. You didn't want to be over- or understocked. You didn't want to return with unsalable goods or run out of a popular item.

The good trader needed Job-like patience and a courtier's tact. Presents to the chief had to be offered in a designated sequence. If the chief was miffed, the trade was ruined. The good trader priced fairly and kept a strict control over his liquor supply, because he wanted the Indians cheerful but not drunk.

Lisa had a good reputation on all counts, except for the way he treated his men. The Missouri River became his home, for between 1807 and 1815 he spent much of his time navigating it. He knew which channel to pick, and how to use favorable winds. He learned to respect the river because each trip took its toll, and his achievement was tempered by fathoms as much as it was measured in miles. "I go a great distance," he said, "while some are considering whether they will start today or tomorrow."

THE MISSISSIPPI FRONTIER

*"If General Jackson hadn't run the Creeks up the creek,
Simon Finch would never have paddled up the Alabama,
where would we be if he hadn't?"*

HARPER LEE

Purchased by the United States in April 1803, the 828,000 square miles the French called Louisiana were divided into two territories: To the south lay Orleans Territory, almost identical with the pres-

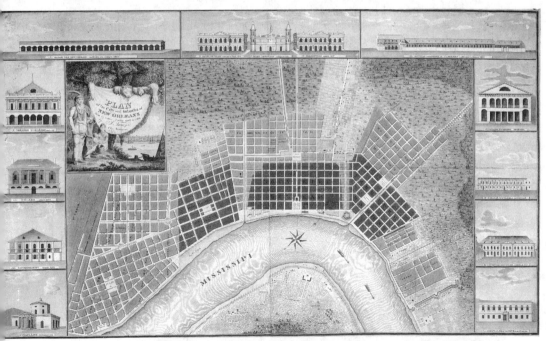

The New York Public Library
This plan of New Orleans, published in 1817, shows the city's crescent shape on a bend of the Mississippi, and the neat grid plan of the different neighborhoods, or *faubourgs*. Closeups of major buildings in the border inset include a firehouse (lower left-hand corner), a meat market (upper left-hand corner), and a military hospital (upper right-hand corner).

ent state of Louisiana, except for the wedge east of the Mississippi and north of Lake Pontchartrain that was still a part of Spanish West Florida. To the north stretched Louisiana Territory, governed first by James Wilkinson and then by Meriwether Lewis, a huge and sprawling area that covered a dozen future states.

Though comparatively small, Orleans Territory was like a densely populated foreign country, inhabited by a predominantly French population and managed by a Spanish administration. New Orleans, for instance, was run by a *cabildo*, or council of twelve notables. The governor, Manuel Salcedo, had a reputation for selling offices and judgeships to the highest bidder. Schools did not exist, and half the population was illiterate.

These people knew nothing about American laws and institutions. They had developed a stratified, class-conscious society, characterized by an odd mix of despotic laws and haphazard enforcement, a tropical chaos that found its brightest example in the cosmopolitan city of New Orleans.

The man President Jefferson chose in 1803 for the serious assignment of governing Orleans Territory was twenty-eight-year-old William Charles Coles Claiborne, a textbook example of how a precocious youth with a good education and a strong sense of party loyalty could climb the political ladder in the early days of the republic.

Born in Virginia in 1775, Claiborne got a job at the age of fifteen with the clerk of Congress, then sitting in New York. Bright and energetic, he attracted the attention of Jefferson, who urged him to go back to Virginia and study law. This he promptly did, and then headed with his Blackstone under his arm for Tennessee, where he established a thriving criminal practice.

In 1796, at the age of twenty-one, Claiborne served at the convention that framed the Tennessee constitution. A year later he was elected as Tennessee's only member of the House of Representatives, even though he was under the constitutional age of twenty-five. When Jefferson ran for president, Claiborne campaigned so strenuously that he brought Tennessee into the Democratic camp. This good deed led to his appointment as governor of Mississippi Territory in 1801.

Two years later Jefferson needed someone to take possession of Louisiana from the French and to govern Orleans Territory. He believed that ruling this Catholic Franco-Spanish population was the second-most-important office in the administration, and wanted someone with maturity and authority.

But his first and second choices, Lafayette (who had been given American citizenship) and James Monroe, were unavailable, for both were in France. So he fell back on William Claiborne, while at the same time realizing his limitations. For one thing, Claiborne could not speak French or Spanish. For another, grown men thought of him as a mere boy. For a third, people described him as "awkward," "slovenly," and "below his place." But the fact of his availability outweighed these drawbacks.

And so it was that on December 20, 1803, William Claiborne arrived in New Orleans under military escort, and the Stars and Stripes were unfurled and the territory amicably surrendered by the French prefect Pierre Laussat. In the face of many tribulations, Claiborne remained in office for more than eight years, until Orleans Territory became the state of Louisiana in 1812.

Governing Orleans Territory turned out to be life-threatening employment, though the newly arrived Claiborne saw his mission simply as bringing the people of Louisiana into the American fold. Among Americans, New Orleans had an unsavory reputation. As the New York merchant John Pintard wrote Secretary of the Treasury Albert Gallatin on September 14, 1803, "The government of a city exposed to the riots of untractable sailors, drunken Indians, and Kentucky boatmen, and more vicious and savage than either, must be considerably energetic." As for the customs officers, "none of the present can be trusted—they are all hacknied in the practices of bribery and cheating the revenue."

Though Claiborne was impressed by New Orleans, whose spacious streets and fine houses reminded him of Baltimore, he tended to agree that the previous government "had scarcely a nerve not wounded by corruption." His task was to gradually replace the Spanish system with the American, but it proved slow work, for the Spaniards were in no hurry to turn over their archives and public buildings.

For the moment, American and Spanish troops bunked together in the New Orleans barracks. The people had existed in a state of passive obedience and were unprepared for the demands of a representative government. Jury trials were a sore point, since not one person in fifty spoke English. Some of the hundred inmates in the New Orleans prison had languished there for ten or a dozen years without ever coming to trial. A humane man, Claiborne began to release them, not wanting, as he put it, to be "disgraced by the rattle of a single chain."

In this transition period, some form of government had to be chosen. The law in Orleans Territory derived from Spanish codes, while French was the language of the courts. The territory's economy rested on the brutal slavery of the sugarcane plantations. Jefferson decided on a system based on the Northwest Ordinance, appointing a governor, a secretary, and judges. In addition, a twenty-four-man council was named to represent the local population.

Claiborne found the people of New Orleans to be in a state of "mental darkness." On January 16, 1804, he wrote Jefferson that the population was "uninformed, indolent, luxurious—in a word, ill-fitted to be useful citizens for a Republic." The French were a particularly sharp thorn in his side. The prefect Laussat, who had been quite helpful at first, now occupied himself with shanghaiing French sailors to complete the crew on the brig charged with taking him back to France.

Rowdy French soldiers filled the streets, trumpeting their love of Napoleon and ready to defend his honor on the flimsiest pretext. It was the presence of all these troops, Claiborne reflected, that led to disorders.

Finally, in March 1804 the French and Spanish troops began to leave, and Congress passed the act that created Orleans Territory. But the local citizens complained that the new territory was too far from the seat of power. "Favoritism is like fire," they said. "Only when you are near it do you feel its warmth."

Claiborne felt that he was not so much governing as managing one crisis after another—riots, robberies, arson, runaway slaves hiding in the bayous, unlicensed traders called *gabateurs* who went upriver in canoes and bartered the runaways' stolen goods for rum and coffee.

When the new governor visited some outlying parishes in May, it seemed that everyone had a grievance. Merchants clamored for courts that would help them recover their debts. Bonaventure Babin accused his neighbor of cutting down his cypress swamp. In the Attakapas District, two priests competed for the same church, and each had his following, which caused a near riot.

In June, the lady abbess of the Ursuline Convent sent Claiborne an embroidered fan "as an offensive and defensive weapon against our common enemy the mosquito." It was not, however, a very effective weapon, for during the summer months, the yellow fever raged, and Claiborne's wife and little daughter succumbed. His secretary also died, and Claiborne fell seriously ill, cursing the climate, for the real culprit was as yet unknown.

He hung on, and slowly made progress. By December, the council was in place and a judge had arrived. It took time, but the people began to change, and Claiborne wrote Jefferson on December 16, 1804, that "they begin to view their connexion with the United States as permanent and to experience the benefits thereof." He kept to himself his opinion that the population still did not entirely trust the federal government, considering themselves "a distinct and acquired branch of the American family," stepchildren rather than natural offspring.

In March 1805, an act of Congress elevated Orleans Territory to the second stage prior to statehood. This meant the establishment of a legislative assembly, and the promise of statehood when the population reached 60,000 white male inhabitants—in effect postponing statehood until after the 1810 census. The second stage also imposed a ban on the importation of slaves—though allowing the slaves already there—and the voiding of Spanish land grants drawn up after October 1800.

A twenty-five-member assembly was elected and the territory divided into twelve counties, each with its own court. But beneath the surface, Orleans remained a boiling cauldron of cultural conflict. The ban on the slave trade was viewed as tyrannical, and a group of malcontents asked for redress in a petition to Congress, which a Democratic rhymester interpreted as follows:

> *Receive us to your arms as Brothers*
> *And grant us to make slaves of others.*

On July 16, Claiborne wrote Secretary of State Madison, "Scarcely a week passes by, but something occurs to create anxiety and to occasion me trouble."

Claiborne made another swing through the upland parishes in the summer of 1806, and it pleased him to see the inhabitants beginning to understand and abide by American law. In one trial, a judge sentenced his own son-in-law to a month in prison and fined him $500 for assault and battery—which seemed to show that favoritism was on the wane, except that the object of the assault was the defendant's wife. In another case, when a Spaniard was tried for murder, his lawyer asked for a jury of his peers—that is, other Spaniards—which the judge denied.

The French, however, grumbled about the introduction of English common law, and were disgusted by the swarms of lawyers, whom they called speculators in distress, and whose only aim, they said, was to encourage litigation. Sugar planters were irate because they could no longer pay their debts with their crop. When a local sheriff told Claiborne that a sugar planter, protected by a troop of his slaves, refused to accept a subpoena from Superior Court, Claiborne advised him to go back with a detachment of armed men and arrest the planter.

In August, while visiting Opelousas, Claiborne was approached by a French lady who said; "You Americans will all take another bottle." Apparently, the new county commissioner was overfond of drink. "Already an opinion prevails here," Claiborne wrote Gallatin, "that the Americans are for the most part drunkards."

On July 4, 1807, an incident occurred that led to cries of military despotism. The officers and men aboard one of the gunboats anchored on the Mississippi heard a woman's cries coming from the shore. Approaching, they saw a plantation overseer whipping a female slave. Acting on their humane feelings, several officers took a dinghy to shore and ordered the slave released. When the news got out, a great outcry arose among the planters, who said it was the kind of interference that would lead to general insubordination. A serious problem already existed of runaways finding sanctuary in Spanish Texas, they told Claiborne.

So far, Claiborne had escaped the Indian trouble that plagued the other territories. But it erupted in 1809, when several tribes of Alabama Indians migrated to Louisiana, and squatters tried to force them off their land. When four young warriors killed several squatters, a court convicted them of murder under the territorial statutes.

In October, Claiborne pardoned two of the Indians, who were not directly implicated. He felt that leniency was in order, and recalled the words of a chief: "The time will come, and it is not far distant, when in this whole tract of country, there will not be left one solitary Indian for a white man's dog to bark at."

Eighteen hundred and nine brought personal tragedy to Claiborne, who had married again. His second wife, Clarissa Duralde, died of the yellow fever that summer "in the bloom of life." This misfortune, he said, "has nearly undone me."

Claiborne continued to feel unsure that the mongrel population was ready for statehood, when so many could not speak English. The statehood movement, however, advanced relentlessly. In March 1810, the territorial legislature made its application, though the magic number of 60,000 adult white males had not been reached. Yellow fever, which killed off hundreds, didn't help.

In November 1811, a convention assembled to draft a constitution. In May 1812, a month before the outbreak of the war with England, the bill to admit Louisiana passed both houses of Congress. Louisiana became the eighteenth state and, needless to say, a slave state (Ohio was the seventeenth, in 1803).

William Claiborne served as a benign Jeffersonian proconsul, with no precedents to guide him, and repeatedly showed an inclination to help the disadvantaged—the Indians, the slaves, and the convicts. Having survived heart-wrenching personal loss, a near fatal duel, and his own heroic efforts to Americanize the young nation's most intractable population, he won election to the United States Senate in 1817. But, debilitated by his bouts with yellow fever, he died before he could take office, at the age of forty-three.

When forty-four-year-old Andrew Ellicott left Philadelphia for Natchez on September 16, 1796, embarking on the most important mission of his life, he already had quite a career behind him. Born in Bucks County, Pennsylvania, of Quaker parents, he did not have a great deal of schooling. But he had a mechanical turn of mind, and at fifteen he helped his father make an intricate musical clock that was considered a masterpiece. It played the tunes of the day, such as "The Lass with the Delicate Air" and "The Hounds Are All Out."

Sent to Philadelphia to study mathematics with a tutor, Andrew started making transits, surveying instruments that measure vertical and horizontal angles. Then came the War of Independence; overcoming his Quaker pacifism, Andrew served as a major under George Washington. Back in Philadelphia in 1782, this man of many talents composed and published an almanac, which combined editorials on the decline of England with recipes for pickling hams.

Surveying, however, claimed him. In 1784, he served by appointment on a team that had been commissioned to continue the work of two British astronomers—Mason and Dixon—on the Pennsylvania-Maryland frontier. In 1791, he surveyed the ten-mile square that Maryland and Virginia had ceded for a "seat of government." This kept him busy for two years. In 1794, he laid out the town of Erie, Pennsylvania, and plotted a road between Erie and Reading.

It's easy to see that, given his nomadic surveyor's life, Ellicott wasn't home much, though he did get back often enough to help his wife Sally have nine children. He made up for his absences with tender letters in which he called her "my dearest of all earthly beings."

In 1796, President Washington chose Ellicott for a job that required both a diplomat's talent and a surveyor's skill. Spain, which kept Louisiana until 1803, continued also to hold on to West Florida, a territory that included the southernmost portions of present-day Alabama and Mississippi. But in 1795, Spain expected a war with England and wished to be on good terms with the United States. Relations between the two countries were strained due to the closing of the Mississippi, which had caused widespread resentment in the American west. In a sudden conciliatory mood, Spain signed the Treaty of San Lorenzo on October 27, 1795.

Pinckney's Treaty, as it became known, signaled the beginning of the end of Spain's colonial empire in North America. Among its major provisions was the acceptance by Spain of the United States' southern boundary claims, from the Mississippi to the Atlantic. In practical terms, this meant that most of Mississippi and Alabama were now American territory, while the Spanish retained the coastal strips south of the 31st parallel, forty miles south of Natchez. Accordingly, the Spanish agreed to evacuate their forts on the eastern bank of the Mississippi, from Memphis to Natchez.

The treaty stipulated that within six months of signing, American and Spanish surveyors should meet at Natchez to lay down the new boundary. In May 1796, Andrew Ellicott was picked to head the American team. He rounded up a thirty-man crew and a military escort of twenty more and left Philadelphia on horseback on September 16, the baggage and surveying instruments following by wagon.

Through forests and stretches of cleared land, they rode over axle-breaking roads to Pittsburgh, at that time a center for western migration boasting two hundred houses, fifty of them brick. There Ellicott procured four boats for his men and equipment, and took the water route to Marietta, Cincinnati, and Louisville, following the Ohio into the Mississippi, which was still a Spanish river.

Ellicott expected that after a prompt turnover of the forts, he could set out for the wilderness with his compass and chains. But the Spaniards had no intention of complying with the treaty, for they were busy conspiring with American agents to bring about the secession of the western states from the Union. Once the United States were dismembered, their thinking went, Pinckney's Treaty would be null and void. The military commandant in Natchez, Manuel Gayoso de Lemos, received instructions to use every conceivable delaying tactic to prevent the American surveying party from getting under way.

Reaching New Madrid, the northernmost Spanish post on the Mississippi, on February 1, 1797, Ellicott's little flotilla was fired upon by the fort's artillery. The fort commandant explained that he was under orders from Governor Carondelet in New Orleans not to let the surveyors pass until the posts were evacuated.

Seemingly embarrassed by his own orders, however, the Spaniard allowed them through, but the hostile welcome generated in Ellicott a certain amount of anxiety. If the commandants of the forts further down-river had similar orders, they might not be so obliging, and he would be detained for months in a Spanish maze.

A week later, when the team reached the next Spanish post at Chicka-saw Bluffs (Memphis), events confirmed Ellicott's suspicions. The com-mandant seemed embarrassed to see them, and gave no sign that he was preparing to decamp. In fact, he claimed that he had never heard of Pinck-ney's Treaty. But the Americans were allowed to proceed, and they contin-ued down the Mississippi until they reached Walnut Hill (Vicksburg) on February 19. Here again a cannon shot jarred them, and they encountered another officer who had never heard of the treaty. Ellicott was incredulous. How could the Spaniards at Walnut Hill, so close to Natchez, not have known that he was coming? He was on an official mission stipulated by treaty, yet he was being stopped and questioned like a smuggler.

On February 24, Ellicott presented his credentials to Governor Gay-oso at Natchez, asking when he could begin running the boundary line. Gayoso gave him March 19 as a starting date, but things turned out differ-ently. For more than a year, Ellicott was stuck in Natchez, as the Spanish kept finding new reasons to keep him there.

On February 29, having set up his camp a quarter mile from the fort, Ellicott hoisted the Stars and Stripes. Two hours later a message arrived from Gayoso asking him to take it down. Ellicott refused, even though he was told that parties were forming to remove the flag by force. But nothing happened, and Ellicott wrote in his journal that "the flag wore out upon the staff." Natchez was, after all, full of Americans who wanted to live under their country's colors.

Gayoso, however, had other hands to play. He charged that the officer in command of Ellicott's military escort had arrested some of Natchez's American residents as deserters from the United States Army. These citi-zens, he said, enjoyed Spanish protection. Ellicott responded with a com-plaint of his own. Instead of preparing for evacuation, Gayoso had remounted the cannon at the fort.

And so it went. As letters flew back and forth, March 19 came and went. The months dragged on, the Spanish inventing one ingenious argu-ment after another, all of which had to be transmitted to both Washington and Madrid. Gayoso claimed he could not leave Spain's faithful subjects unprotected and vulnerable to Indian revenge. He then insisted that the king must be consulted as to the conditions of surrender. Should the forts be given up intact or dismantled?

To this quibbling over the forts, Secretary of State Timothy Pickering replied: "It is probably the first time that to 'withdraw' or retire from a place has been imagined to intend its destruction. If, at the formation of the treaty, the demolition of the posts had been intended, it would as-suredly have been expressed."

Then the Spanish argued that they could not leave their forts because they expected an attack from a British force in Canada. Equally absurd, answered Pickering, since the United States was not about to let the British through to invade remaining Spanish territory. If Walnut Hill and Natchez were the only forts capable of stopping the British, Spain would need them forever.

In July of 1797, Gayoso left for New Orleans to replace Carondelet as governor, but the Spanish still made no move to hand over Natchez. Not until January 1798 did Gayoso order the evacuation, and even then he took his time about it, postponing the departure up to March 30. On that day, Ellicott rose at 4 A.M. Walking over to the fort, he found the gate open and went in. From the parapet, he had the pleasure of seeing, as the first light of dawn illuminated them, the Spanish troops embark in their boats and sail down the river until they were out of sight.

Eight days later, Congress passed an act that created Mississippi Territory, with Natchez as its capital, encompassing the present states of Mississippi and Alabama. The legislation permitted slavery, following Ellicott's recommendation that if it was made illegal, American squatters would move to Spanish territory.

In August 1798, the first territorial governor arrived. He was Winthrop Sargent, an original settler of Marietta, Ohio, who had ten years of experience under his belt as secretary of the Northwest Territory. Like Ellicott, Sargent worried about the rebellious character of the American population. His main goal, he wrote Pickering, was to "fix their attachment to the United States."

Mississippi Territory would last for nineteen years. From the outset, it possessed the mentality of a slave state. In Adams County, on June 6, 1799, one of the earliest grand jury presentments stated: "We present as a very great grievance the want of a white man as an Indian interpreter, which has hitherto been effected by a negro slave, to the great shame of a free and independent people."

Among other grievances were the lack of cotton-gin inspectors, the number of disorderly persons who disturbed the Sabbath in the town of Natchez, the problem of hogs running at large, and the Negro slaves hanging about the outlot fences on the Sabbath playing cards and chuck-penny.

The members of the grand jury said they wanted to be good Americans, and they had good American names like Cato West, James Truly, Robert Throckmorton, and Parker Caradine. But at the same time, they chafed under federal regulation. Governor Sargent wrote President John Adams on June 20, 1800, that to these malcontents "a federal governor was a most obnoxious character." When Thomas Jefferson assumed the presidency in 1801, he appointed William Claiborne to succeed the Federalist Winthrop Sargent.

When the Spaniards finally evacuated the Natchez fort, Andrew Ellicott and his surveying team started down the Mississippi to the point where it crossed the 31st parallel. There they met up with the two Spanish surveyors appointed to accompany their party. With them was Governor Gayoso, who wanted to wish Ellicott a successful trip, as if to say, "No hard feelings."

"We met and saluted in the Spanish manner by kissing!" Ellicott wrote his wife. It was a scratchy kiss, for "I had not been shaved for two days." And, to the austere Quaker, a decidedly unmanly way of greeting—"Men's kissing I think a most abominable custom"—yet another indignity to be suffered in the service of his country.

Surveying in May and June through thirty-five-foot-high canebrake matted with vines proved slow going. They were lucky if they made a quarter of a mile a day. It was so swampy that the only way to carry the line was to light fires and send smoke signals at intervals from high points. It took them until November 1798 to reach the Pearl River, which was about 120 miles on a straight line from the Mississippi along the 31st parallel.

It was dangerous work as well, for malaria-bearing mosquitoes killed off one-fourth of Ellicott's men. On some days, the intrepid Quaker felt so sick he had to be lifted into his chair and carried to the site. All the while the Indians stole the surveyors' horses and everything else they could get their hands on. To make matters worse, the one remaining Spanish surveyor dismissed his military escort, making Ellicott feel as vulnerable as a passed pawn in a game of chess. Marauding Indians rustled horses from within two hundred yards of their camp, and when Ellicott built a pen, they broke down the fence and raided it.

But the brave little band pressed on. After running the line between Georgia and Florida, they reached the mouth of St. Marys River on January 16, 1800, and put up the last mound, marking the boundary limit at the Atlantic Ocean. Their job done, the weary surveyors camped in a forest of live oak, where men were cutting timber for American ships. Soon they sailed to Savannah and boarded a ship bound for New York; on May 18, Ellicott was reunited with his wife.

The rest of his life was sedentary. In 1813, West Point made him professor of mathematics, and he remained there until his death in 1820, at the age of sixty-six. In the face of Spanish obstacles, he had established the southern boundary of the United States as it existed in 1800, before the Louisiana Purchase. Like one of the links in his surveyor's chain, he was a link in the chain of American expansion.

Once formed in 1798, Mississippi Territory attracted settlers from slave states like Virginia, Georgia, and the Carolinas. But it was pioneer life with a twist—the settlers brought their slaves with them, movable property at once put to work clearing land and planting cotton. Hastily built log cabins served as the homes of both owners and slaves, who shared the hard times of early settlement, though reaping none of the rewards.

Knowing the land had once belonged to the Indians, the slaves said they could hear sounds at night,—"de goses of dem Injuns mounin' fur dey homes." Terrified of snakes, the slaves said, "Dey is jes as sly as Injuns; dat time yo ain studin' bout um dey pop yo shore." Although they left no diaries or memoirs recounting their experiences (the previous quotes are from the accounts of their owners), the slaves in Mississippi Territory were authentic pioneers.

The settlers were often restless men, migrating from one place to the next, and taking their slaves with them. Hezekiah Lincemum lived in Georgia and Alabama before settling in Mississippi. In the words of his son Gideon: "My father was a powerful man, six feet high and in the prime of life 200 pounds. I saw him when I was a little boy lift a forge hammer at Byrd's Iron Works that weighed 596 pounds and hold it on his arms until a six-inch rule was set under it."

Soon after Gideon's birth in 1793, the family settled on the Oconee River near today's Milledgeville, Georgia, and raised a little cotton. Picking the seeds out with a hand-roller gin, they stuffed the cotton in a meal sack and hauled it to market and sold it for 50 cents a pound.

One day Hezekiah heard about a Yankee schoolmaster by the name of Whitney. People said he had invented an iron gin with two cylinders revolving in opposite directions, one studded with short wire hooks and the other with bristles. Nobody believed it could clean 1,000 pounds of cotton a day, but Hezekiah took Gideon along to take a look at the newfangled contraption. After that they brought their cotton to the gin.

"Father was moving and shackling about," Gideon later recalled, but in time they settled in a place on a creek a mile from today's Eatonton, north of Milledgeville. "When I was 14," Gideon told a collector of oral histories, "I was one of the chain carriers who surveyed the town lots."

Gideon left home after he and his father had a falling out, found a job with an Eatonton merchant for $500 a year, and joined the army during the War of 1812. The war ended and he got married, but "my wife's family was affluent and they were casting slurs at my poverty." Gideon eventually rejoined his father, who now dwelled along the Ocmulgee River near today's Macon, a dividing line between the Georgia settlers and the Creek Indians.

One day Gideon heard that a schoolmaster had been so badly abused by his pupils that he had quit. He volunteered for the job and was offered $10 in cash per head at the expiration of the nine-and-a-half-month term. Of the forty pupils, fifteen were grown men and five were grown women, "all raised among the cows and drunken cowdrivers of the outer borders, the coarsest specimens of the human family I'd ever seen."

"Play time" was the bane of Gideon's day. The students shouted and quarreled, making trouble and throwing blame. When Gideon called them back to their books after an hour of recreation, one of the more unruly pupils cried, "You give but short play time, mister."

To keep order, Gideon set up a court complete with bylaws. When he proposed to read them, an adult pupil asked, "What's up now, hoss?" Gideon explained that the court would be a sort of government, with a judge, a clerk, and a sheriff. The students approved, saying, "Yes, go it, hoss, it's a good thing." After formally voting and signing the bylaws, one of the men, Scatterwhite, declared; "We never had such sort of doings afore in these diggins."

The first miscreant to face the court, Stephen Heard, had thrown a little girl's bonnet up into the branches of a tree. He was found guilty and sentenced to three lashes well laid out with hickory. Gideon, who had cut and trimmed a number of switches, laid them on himself, cutting the back of Heard's homespun waistcoat into three ribands. Heard burst out crying and said he knew some things that he would tell if he had a mind. "Tell it to the court," Gideon said.

The next case involved Elijah Scatterwhite, who had knocked down a little boy. Since "Lige" Scatterwhite also served on the jury, Gideon replaced him with the just-punished Stephen Heard, who presumably was in a vengeful mood. Gideon could hear the jury deliberating on the other side of the room, one juror finally asking, "Well, Steve, what's your verdict?"

"Well, boys," Steve said, "if we all go for thrashing for every little offense, we'll soon get up the spirit of spite. In this case the boy was not hurt but made very angry and his clothes a little soiled. Mind you, I am not in favor of clearing Lige, but fine him." The jury brought in a verdict of "guilty, but not willfully," and the judge sentenced Scatterwhite to pay three dozen good goose quills.

The year proved to be such a success that Gideon was offered another term at the higher rate of $1,000. He declined, for his father had bought a place on the Alabama side of the Tombigbee River, west of Tuscaloosa. "He loved a border life," Gideon explained, "and I had been reared to frequent change. There were now eight children and six Negros plus my wife and two children of mine."

The family set out for Alabama in March 1818, six weeks on the road to cover five hundred miles of wilderness. "It was the most delightful time I ever spent in my life," Gideon recalled, "flanking the wagons and killing deer and turkeys, and at night fishing with pine torches, until we reached Tuscaloosa, a small log cabin village."

Gideon built a little clapboard house in the part of town that hadn't been surveyed. When his money ran out, he rode to town looking for a job. He ran into John Weeks, a man he'd known in Georgia, and asked, "Where are you going with all your whipsaws?"

"I'm in partnership with a man from Tennessee, but he's such a drunk I had to quit him," Weeks said.

"What would you think of me as a partner?" Gideon asked.

"My friend," Weeks replied, "you have never been accustomed to work, and the whipsaw and summer heat will soon upset you."

Gideon insisted that he had to find work to support his family. "All right," Weeks said, "if you will go in with me I must go in with you. Planks are worth four dollars a hundred and we can get cash for all we make. But it is heavy work I can tell you."

The next day the two men hewed out a thousand feet of one-inch planks for a Yankee trader who needed a floor and a counter. He paid them $20, which they split. They were averaging $8 a day when a misfired gun burned Gideon's hands, and that was the end of the whipsaw operation.

Then Hezekiah turned up, saying he'd found some good land in Mississippi, again on the Tombigbee. Gideon packed up his things and they were twelve days en route, blazing their way through the unhacked forest, digging down the banks of streams in order to cross them. Finally, they reached Hezekiah's new spread, three miles above where the city of Columbus now stands, just over the Alabama border.

"It was a beautiful spot," Gideon recalled, "a low bluff with canebrake, and a flat rock projecting six feet into the river, and on top of the rock a big sycamore with its roots fastened in the bluff, and under the roots gushed a spring of pure clean water."

The next morning he shot a twenty-nine-pound turkey, and used the turkey's liver as bait to catch a twenty-five-pound blue catfish. That night he hunted with his brother Garland, tying a frying pan to a stick, packing it with rich cut pine, and setting it on fire, producing enough light to see the eyes of a deer at a hundred yards. "We are surrounded by this wild forest but we have nothing to fear," Gideon's wife said. Aunt Polly, their Negro mammy, chimed in, "No, dat we ha'nt."

Gideon burned off the canebrake and planted corn with a sharp stick. Though bears and raccoons ate a good deal of the harvest, he managed to save 150 bushels. Then he began trading sugar, coffee, and whiskey with the Choctaws, who camped two miles away. Gideon was never sure whether he lived in Alabama or Mississippi—when they ran the state line, it turned out he was fifteen miles from the border on the Mississippi side.

Eventually, Gideon Lincecum moved to Texas and became a collector of natural history specimens. He sent forty-eight specimens of Texas ants to Charles Darwin, six hundred specimens of Texas flora to the Jardin des Plantes in Paris, and an assortment of Texas butterflies to the New York College of Sciences. He died in 1873 at the age of eighty.

Until 1813, the Spanish held West Florida, which included pieces of Alabama and Mississippi, from the 31st parallel to the Gulf of Mexico. The War of 1812, however, had the effect of ousting Spain from those strips, making Baton Rouge, Pensacola, and Mobile American ports.

As of December 16, Mississippi Territory, with its newly acquired southern strip, had a population of 75,512, of whom 45,085 were free and white, 30,061 were slaves, and 366 were free Negroes. To make one state from this large territory seemed impractical, for wilderness claimed much of it. Natchez, the capital, sat on the western border, too far from the people on the eastern edge.

The House Committee on Territories recommended two states divided by a north-south line. A convention met in Natchez in July 1817 to draft a constitution, and on December 10, 1817, Mississippi was admitted to the Union as the twentieth state. The constitution provided that each county should have a Court of Probate "for the trial of slaves." For petty crimes, the punishment was "stripes," with the injunction that they be "well laid on."

As for Alabama, it was not a natural entity, but simply what was left over from Mississippi Territory after Mississippi's statehood. Alabama had four straight sides, except for a squiggle etched by the Chattahoochee River along part of its eastern border, and a fifty-mile-long coastline wedged between Florida and Mississippi, which provided access to the Gulf and to Mobile's fine harbor.

As long as the Spanish held Mobile and choked off trade, charging 12 percent duty on all goods passing through, the economic outlook for Alabama was dim. In 1803, a government trading house was established at St. Stephens, about thirty miles up from Fort Stoddert, which the Americans had built north of Mobile to keep frontiersmen from trying to capture Spanish Mobile.

St. Stephens consisted of an old Spanish fort manned by two companies of infantry, and included a house for the factor, Joseph Chambers, and his assistant, George Strother Gaines.

When the Choctaws arrived bringing furs to trade, Chambers served the chiefs dinner in the officers' mess. Afterward, hosts and guests enjoyed dances and games of hide-the-bullet. On one occasion, a War Department auditor reprimanded the factor for having treated the Indians to anchovies and assorted condiments.

Gaines spent much of his time buying land from the Indians between Natchez and Tombigbee. Settlers trooped in daily to file their claims at the St. Stephens land office, claims that originated in Spanish warrants, donations by act of Congress, and preemptions. Witnessing rich and poor acquire land, Gaines reflected on the rise of the self-made man.

The changes that led to statehood for Alabama came about as the result of the Louisiana Purchase of 1803. The settlements on the Tombigbee at Fort Stoddert and St. Stephens evolved into halfway points on the wilderness route from Georgia to Louisiana. In 1811, a horse path across Alabama was widened into a wagon road, and settlers poured in.

The United States finally pried Mobile loose from Spain in 1813. Now Alabama had its saltwater port. A year later Andrew Jackson slaughtered the Creeks at the battle of Horseshoe Bend on the Tallapoosa, near today's Montgomery, forever destroying their power in the area. Under the terms of the Treaty of Fort Jackson on August 9, 1814, the Creeks ceded twenty million acres in Alabama and Georgia to the United States.

But Indian problems persisted. The Creeks manned the ferries from the Chattahoochee to the Alabama, and customers complained about negligence, absenteeism, and capricious rates. Finally, the Creeks agreed to make the ferries United States property, and began to post rates.

As for the factory system, it broke down because of competition from private traders and feuds between the Indian agent and the factor. Major Daniel Hughes, the factor at Fort Hawkins on the Chattahoochee, in the heart of Creek country, complained bitterly that the Creeks ran up debts, and then, when they got their annuity, they spent it with the private traders rather than pay their debts. Business got so bad that Hughes laid off the assistant factor. He was convinced that the Creek agent, David B. Mitchell, was in cahoots with the private traders to sell them liquor and undermine the factory. The situation deteriorated, with Hughes and Mitchell trading charges, and in 1819, President James Monroe ordered the Fort Hawkins factory discontinued, for it was a dismal failure.

In 1819, Alabama was approaching statehood. The bill had been reported that January in the Senate, and the constitutional convention met in Huntsville that July. The result was auction fever that saw land going at $49 an acre in Huntsville, and $107 an acre on the Tenessee River.

The receiver of public monies in Huntsville, John Brahan, exhibited an unfortunate tendency to confuse the federal Treasury with his own pocket. When auditors examined his accounts, they found him $78,000 short, a fortune in those days. Brahan sent his resignation to the secretary of the Treasury on June 28, 1819: "I have the mortification to inform you," he wrote, "that there is a considerable deficiency in my cash account."

Such was the nature of territorial government. Washington was too far away. The distances were too great, the mails too slow, the pool of people available for public office too small. They had to make do with illiterate judges, embezzling receivers, profiteering factors, and crooked Indian agents. Under state government, people hoped, matters would improve. Alabama was admitted to the Union on December 14, 1819. It was the ninth state after the original thirteen.

CHAPTER THREE
THE FLORIDA FRONTIER

We have possessed Florida for 16 years but we have, perhaps, as little knowledge of the interior of Florida as of the interior of China.

GENERAL THOMAS S. JESUP

On February 22, 1819, John Quincy Adams, President James Monroe's secretary of state, signed a treaty with Spain's minister, Luis de Onis, that ceded East Florida to the United States. Pretty much the state of Florida as we know it today, the territory changed hands for the paltry sum of $5 million. As usual, there were those who did not think it was much of a bargain, such as the powerful Virginia congressman John Randolph, who said: "Florida, sir, is not worth buying. It is a land of

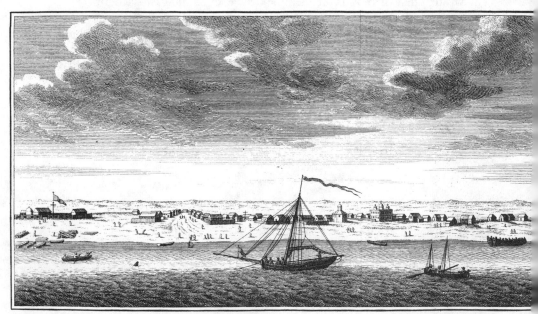

The New York Public Library
In this early view of Spanish Pensacola, the stockaded fort is on the left and the haphazardly built town is on the right. The church to the right of the ship's mast has one cupola, while the governor's house has three.

swamps, of quagmires, of alligators and mosquitos! A man, sir, would not immigrate into Florida. No, sir! No man would immigrate into Florida, no, not from hell itself!"

Randolph's view did not prevail, and Florida passed into American ownership, thanks largely to Andrew Jackson's invasion of the area in 1817. He had stormed in with the Tennessee militia, defeated the Seminoles, and taken Pensacola, frightening the Spanish into selling. When Congress ratified the treaty in 1821, Jackson was named military governor of the new territory in reward for his victory.

President Monroe wrote the military hero on May 23: "I have full confidence that your appointment will be immediately and most beneficially felt. Smugglers and slave traders will hide their heads; pirates will disappear and the Seminoles cease to give us trouble." On this last point, the president was to be proven seriously mistaken.

But for the moment, Jackson had to cope with the customary Spanish foot-dragging that had stalled the Americans in New Orleans and Natchez. It was not until July 1821 that Spain lowered her flag in St. Augustine. In Pensacola, when Spanish troops withdrew from the fort, they took the artillery with them. They left behind a jail too dilapidated to hold offenders and a hospital too filthy to house the sick.

The land archives were in Havana, and as a result people made so many fraudulent claims, Jackson wrote, that "the stranger was accosted in the street and offered a grant for a doubloon." Not being a patient man, his frustration brimmed over that August, and he had the former Spanish governor, José Callava, arrested.

Jackson was not destined to remain long in Florida, for in March 1822, a territory was established and a civilian governor arrived in the person of William P. Duval, who went on to serve six two-year terms. On his heels came an epidemic of yellow fever, also known as black vomit, which killed 300 of Pensacola's total population of 2,000.

Everyone who could leave the infected city did so, just running for the hills and living in huts and tents in the woods. Pensacola became a ghost town. The governor himself was gone for six months and had to be ordered back in March 1823 by Secretary of State John Quincy Adams, "some dissatisfaction having been excited by your absence."

Back on the job, Duval struggled with the land-grant question, for the surveyor general in Havana, Pintado, was demanding extortionate sums for copies of Spanish records. Erasures and misplaced decimal points invalidated the material that arrived, so that a grant of 1,600 acres might read "16,000."

Duval's main concern, however, was for the Seminoles, who at that time numbered about 5,000, many of them in the Tallahassee area, where settlers were pressing in. They were, Duval reported, in a wretched state, digging up miles of country to obtain the brierroot they subsisted on. Harassed by squatters, they were unwilling to farm out of fear they might have to surrender cultivated lands. The search for a way in which the

Seminoles could hold onto their lands and live on an equal basis with the white settlers became the essential Florida predicament, and the main reason that Florida remained a territory for twenty-three years, not achieving statehood until 1845.

In 1823, in the Treaty of Moultrie Creek, thirty-two Seminole chiefs agreed to leave their lands for a swampy 4-million-acre reservation in central Florida. The new location was a huge triangle extending roughly from Tampa on the Gulf to Vero Beach on the Atlantic, with its point at Ocala. As an inducement, the Seminoles were promised an annuity of $5,000 a year for twenty years, on the condition that they remain on the reservation for the period covered by the annuity.

Having found a home for the Seminoles, Governor Duval addressed the matter of fugitive slaves, reporting to Secretary of War John C. Calhoun that more than a thousand were in hiding in Florida. Some cut timber and caught fish for the Havana market. Some joined the pirates operating in the Keys. Some lived with the Seminoles and became members of the tribe.

As the Seminoles grudgingly moved out of the rich farmland around Tallahassee to the swampland south of Ocala, the plantation barons moved in with their slaves to grow cotton and sugarcane. The typical plantation owner felt that the north had no more business discussing the treatment of his slaves than he had meddling in the question of factory labor.

One such owner, Noble C. Jones, shuttled between El Destino and Chemonie, two plantations near Tallahassee that were managed by overseers. Each had several hundred slaves, and illness was widespread, though Noble Jones believed the slaves used their pet ailments, such as "dropsy," to get time off.

From El Destino, Evans the overseer wrote Jones that the slave Mungins was sick all the time for "he will keep his old trade of stealing chickens of nights and eating large baits of them about half cooked." Another unhealthy habit was eating dirt, which some authorities today assert was a way of making up for a mineral deficiency in their diet. "The rest of the black people is well," Evans went on, "except Juner and Little Joe, they eat dirt and are bloated up. I think I have got Joe broken off from eating dirt now and I think I will have Juner cured by another week."

Moxley, the overseer at Chemonie, reported two runaways, whom he had whipped for failing to fill the daily 110-pound quota of cotton. Fearing a similar punishment, four women ran away because they were also short. When they were caught and Moxley prepared to whip them, the brother of one of the women, Aberdeen, picked up an ax. It wasn't a threat exactly, but it made Moxley think twice. Evans himself wrote that Moxley meted out punishment "in too large doses." But Evans added that "negros is this disposition. If they see negros around them idling why they want to do so two [sic]."

Such was plantation life in the early days of Florida Territory, before the Seminoles started raiding and burning. They were unable to survive on their allotted lands, as Governor Duval saw for himself during a thirteen-day visit to the reservation early in 1826. "Nineteen-twentieths of their whole country within the present boundary," he wrote, "is by far the poorest and most miserable region I ever beheld."

To protest their situation, a Seminole delegation trekked to Washington in the spring of 1826. One notable feature of the group's composition was the presence of a runaway slave named Abraham, who served as interpreter and advisor to Chief Micanopy. On May 17, Secretary of War James Barbour received the chiefs, telling them: "Your Great Father does not wish to oppress his Red Children. He has heard of your sufferings, and sent you some help. But he wishes me to inform you that you have had time to plant and gather your crops and by your industry provide your own support."

The people in Washington who handled Indian affairs were discovering that annuities led to a "welfare mentality." If the Indians knew that money and food were coming from the government, they made no effort to plant, and even suspended their hunting. Thus, Barbour preached the gospel of self-sufficiency.

The secretary also advised the delegation against harboring runaway slaves and cautioned them to avoid the curse of drinking. "Let alone the mad water," he said, "and be sober." If they did not like the land on their reservation, he added, they should move west of the Mississippi, where the game was plenty.

But the Seminoles replied that even though they had left their good lands around Tallahassee for the Big Swamp, they did not want to leave Florida, their birthplace. As Chief Charlie Emathla put it, "Here our navel strings were first cut and the blood from them sunk into the earth and made the country dear to us."

Ultimately, the meeting in Washington changed nothing. Depredations continued, settlers were killed, and cornfields were set on fire twenty miles from St. Augustine. Over time, Governor Duval lost his initial sympathy for the Seminoles, remarking in April 1827 that "these people have been indulged so much that they become wanton and insolent. Fed at every white man's house where they called, they mistook humanity for fear, and for kindness and hospitality paid them by robbing their houses and fields and killing their cattle."

Duval saw that the Seminoles were being egged on by the runaway slaves in their midst, and wrote the commissioner of Indian Affairs, Thomas L. McKenney, that "the slaves belonging to the Indians . . . have by their art and cunning the entire control over their masters. The negros are hostile to the white people and are constantly counteracting the advice and talks given to the Indians."

Here was a strange alliance indeed, between America's two disenfranchised races, the red and the black. Bonded in their mutual struggle for land and freedom, this Indian-Negro coalition succeeded in stalling white settlement in Florida for nearly twenty years.

A good example of the Negro leadership was Abraham, born around 1790. He had spent his youth as a house slave in Pensacola. Trained as a valet, and acquiring in the process some breeding and education, he was not your thick-tongued, heavy-footed field hand. In the confusion of the War of 1812, he ran away and joined the Seminoles, becoming a slave of Chief Micanopy. But "slave" was the wrong word, for the Seminoles treated men like Abraham as equals, allowing them to live in their own houses, raise their own crops, and marry into the tribe.

Seminole society amounted to a sort of democratic feudalism. Since they could speak English, and some of them could read and write, the runaways served as counselors. Although nominally an interpreter, Abraham actually functioned as the leader of the Seminole delegation to Washington. Like the Seminoles, the slaves among them fought removal from Florida, fearing that in the process they would be returned to their owners.

Pondering a way to separate the Seminoles from their black allies, Governor Duval proposed giving the Indians the right to sell them. If the runaways knew that the Seminoles might put them up for sale, they would not be so eager to join their ranks.

It sounded like a feasible plan, but the stumbling block was the Seminole agent, Gad Humphreys, who lived on the reservation. Whenever he was asked to recover a runaway slave, he made excuses. He could not find the slave, or the Indians claimed him, or the slave had died. In 1828, after repeated complaints, Indian Affairs investigated Humphreys and discovered that he was himself trafficking in slaves, buying them at cut-rate prices from the Seminoles for his sugar plantation on the Hillsboro River.

Commissioner McKenney informed President John Quincy Adams that Humphreys was conniving with the Seminoles to acquire slaves for his own use, and recommended his removal. He was also charged with pocketing part of the $5,000 annuity meant for the Seminoles, building his sugar mill at government expense, and keeping some of the cattle intended for the tribe. On March 18, 1830, a little more than a year after his inauguration as president, Andrew Jackson appointed John Phagan to replace Gad Humphreys, who went into forced retirement.

With the new president, the humane Jeffersonian promise that "we shall all be Americans" gave way to the Jacksonian caveat that Indians had "neither the intelligence, the industry, the moral habits, nor the desire of improvement" to live among whites. In 1830, the Indian Removal Act made the departure of southern tribes to new lands beyond the Mississippi the law of the land. As it happened, the Louisiana Purchase had added plenty of uninhabited territory where the Indians could be dumped. Jackson argued that moving them west was the humane thing to do, since it would enable them to pursue their way of life far from the white man, "beyond the reach of injury and oppression."

In Florida, the government put considerable pressure on the Seminoles to subscribe to the "advantages" of removal. On May 9, 1832, they signed a new treaty, which provided that a Seminole delegation should travel to

Arkansas to inspect land set aside for them. If the chiefs found the area acceptable, they would agree to move their people there within three years.

Why did the Seminoles sign this treaty? A clue can be found in Article II, which provided $200 for Abraham. In the event of removal, the article stated, Abraham "shall receive two hundred dollars . . . in full remuneration for the improvements to be abandoned on the lands now cultivated" by him. Thus, Abraham had a financial stake in removal, as well as a guarantee that if it took place he would not be returned to his owner.

Escorted by John Phagan, a Seminole delegation of seven chiefs, again including Abraham as interpreter, headed west in October 1832. Starting out by ship from Tampa to New Orleans, they turned up the Mississippi and then the Arkansas to Little Rock. From there, they continued on horseback to Fort Gibson, in today's northeastern Oklahoma, at the confluence of the Neosho and Arkansas rivers.

They reached Fort Gibson in January 1833, and stayed there three months in the dead of winter, examining the site of their new home. It did not look inviting. For one thing, the Creeks were already there, a tribe that the Seminoles did not want as neighbors. As Chief Jumper told John Phagan: "You say our people are rogues, but you would bring us among worse rogues to destroy us."

Nonetheless, they were prevailed upon to sign another treaty on March 28, in which they agreed to removal. Once again, Abraham exerted his influence over his fat and sloppy chief, Micanopy. One of the army officers who observed the slave in various councils commented: "We have a perfect Talleyrand of the savage court in the person of a Seminole negro called Abraham." And like Talleyrand, he was not above taking bribes.

Although the westward journey succeeded in coaxing from the Seminoles an agreement to remove, it was also John Phagan's undoing. When the Indian agent sent his expense vouchers to Washington, his superiors found that some of them were forged. In August 1832, the Treasury Department comptroller, James B. Thornton, wrote Secretary of War Lewis Cass that "of the vouchers exhibited, 12 were found to have been so altered as to increase their aggregate amount $397.50 beyond that expressed in them originally." For the $50 cost of passage on a ferry for an interpreter and seven Indians, Phagan billed the government $100. The trouble with Indian agents was that they started out honest, but so many opportunities presented themselves to cheat the Indians and the bureau in Washington that they often succumbed.

Phagan was replaced by Wiley Thompson, formerly a major general in the Georgia militia, who strove to implement the removal policy. The Seminoles were stalling on their pledge to move west, and in October 1834, Thompson convened them for a serious talking-to, telling them that to remain where they were would spell utter ruin.

When the chiefs caucused among themselves, a young upstart named Osceola spoke out so forcefully against migration that he instantly became the head of the antiremoval faction. "I have a rifle and I have some powder and some lead," he said. "I say we must not leave our homes and our lands."

Wiley Thompson angrily warned the chiefs that if they insisted on staying, their laws would be set aside and they would be hauled before the white man's courts. "If you asked for a crust of bread," he said, "you might be called an Indian dog and told to clear out."

After Thompson's lecture, the situation deteriorated. Osceola emerged as a leader prepared to fight. Using their 1834 annuity, the Seminoles accumulated powder and ball. Osceola traveled to Fort King (at Ocala) in June 1835 to buy ammunition, but the sutler refused to sell. Infuriated, Osceola confronted Wiley Thompson, who had him put in irons and locked up for six days.

Osceola swore revenge, and violence erupted. In August, a soldier carrying the mail was murdered between Fort Brooker (on Tampa Bay) and Fort King. Orange groves and fields of sugarcane were set on fire near St. Augustine. But the Seminole leadership was split, with some chiefs still planning to move. One of them, Charlie Emathla, sold his cattle prior to departure and was on his way home on November 26 when a party of men led by Osceola ambushed him and shot him dead.

All that was needed to start a full-scale war was an incident with the American military, who did not seem alert to the gravity of the situation. As of the first week of December 1835, there were only 536 American soldiers in Florida, stationed in St. Augustine under the command of Brigadier General Duncan L. Clinch.

On December 28, 1825, there occurred two incidents serious enough to make a casus belli. Outside the Fort King palisade, Osceola and his men attacked Wiley Thompson and Lieutenant Constantine Smith in broad daylight as they were taking a postprandial stroll, and killed them. The Indians divided Thompson's scalp into as many pieces as there were participants. Osceola also took his revenge on the sutler who had turned him away, murdering him as he sat with his two clerks in his little house outside the fort.

That same day, a relief column of 8 officers and 100 redlegs (artillery soldiers trained to fight as infantry) was marching on the 130-mile trail from Tampa to Fort King, under the command of Major Francis L. Dade. At eight that morning, as they inched two by two over the narrow trail through the pine woods near today's Bushnell, they were attacked by 100 Seminoles hiding in patches of saw palmetto, the assault led by Chiefs Micanopy, Jumper, and Alligator. Surprised, unprepared, and badly positioned, the Dade column was wiped out except for four survivors. When the Seminoles withdrew, their Negro allies swept in to finish off the wounded and loot the dead.

Three days later, on December 31, came the first pitched battle of the war, when Osceola and 250 men fought General Duncan Clinch on the Withlacoochee River, southwest of Ocala, near Fort Drane. The Seminoles attacked as Clinch was fording the river. He fought bravely, surviving one ball that ripped through his cap and another through his jacket sleeve, but once more a band of Indians routed a troop of army regulars, killing 4 and wounding 19.

These three initial actions in December 1835 ignited a war that lasted seven years. A nation of 17 million Americans, boasting an army, navy, and marine corps totaling about 13,000 men, laid siege to 5,000 Seminoles, of whom 1,500 were warriors.

In some respects, the Seminole War resembled the war in Vietnam more than a century later. For one thing, like other Indian wars, it was undeclared. For another, it was fought by troops on unfamiliar terrain against an enemy on its home ground, well versed in guerilla warfare. The army command at first fought with European tactics of massed formations, sending large columns to thrash about the wilderness ineffectually.

Waged in swamplands not unlike the Mekong Delta, the Seminole War was also notable for its use of naval operations. The Mosquito Fleet was formed to send canoes and flatboats on search-and-destroy missions in the creeks and bayous of the Everglades, much as the navy in Vietnam dispatched patrol ships on operations against the Viet Cong hiding in swamps.

According to naval historians, the strategies of riverine warfare used in Vietnam were developed in the Seminole campaign of the 1830s.

But the most striking similarity between these two conflicts lay in the civilian reaction. The Seminole campaign became unpopular, divided the nation, and was eventually opposed in Congress as a nasty little war of aggression. The longer it lasted, the less support it had. The northern media turned the conflict into a David-versus-Goliath scenario, making a national hero out of Osceola: ten towns and three counties were later named after him.

Florida at the start of 1836 was a very jittery peninsula. Its interior remained a mystery to the white man, a many-stranded necklace of swamps ruled by a disease-ridden climate. The only thing certain about the weather was that it never snowed. In that unknown interior, the military cut the first roads and drew the first maps. And to the bottom of those black-water swamps sank a number of military reputations.

On January 14, 1836, Congress appropriated $120,000 for the campaign and in the next three months added $2 million more. The Seminole war wasn't cheap. Ultimately, it would cost $40 million, eight times the purchase price of Florida. A total of 40,000 American troops were involved (including state militias), and there were 1,500 American casualties. All this to subdue 5,000 Seminoles.

Yet their daring and ferocity made these few Indians seem like a much larger force. On August 23, 1836, forty Seminoles attacked the lighthouse at Key Biscayne, which was manned by two men, John W. B. Thompson and his elderly Negro assistant, Mr. Carter.

On his way from his house to the tower, Thompson saw the Indians land. Sprinting the rest of the way, he managed to bar the door just in time. He and Carter grabbed some rifles, ran up to the second floor, and managed to keep the Seminoles at bay until dark. But Indian bullets punctured the oil tins stored on the ground floor, and the leaking oil caught fire.

Thompson and Carter retreated up into the tower's lantern with a keg of powder, but the rising heat was so intense that it forced them to go outside and lie down on the platform that ringed the beacon. Inside the lighthouse, the heat began to melt the lantern's glass sides. Outside, on the platform, they were subjected to a continuous volley of Seminole gunfire.

Carter was hit seven times and killed, while Thompson got three balls through one of his feet and another in the ankle. Finally, finding the heat unbearable even on the platform, Thompson threw the keg of powder down through the scuttle, intending to destroy the lighthouse and himself. Instead, the keg exploded near the entrance door, collapsing the burning staircase and extinguishing the fire. Lying perfectly still despite the pain of his bullet wounds and burns, Thompson convinced the Indians he was dead. The next day he saw them load his boat with plunder and depart.

That afternoon Lieutenant Thomas J. Leib, captain of the schooner *Motto*, saw from seven miles off Cape Florida that the lighthouse was on fire and tried to beat into the wind toward the cape. At five in the afternoon, he reached the key and landed a party to get Thompson and Carter down.

He tried to throw a line to Thompson on his perch ninety feet above the ground, but that didn't work, and neither did making kites to float the rope up. Finally, he tied some twine to a ramrod and shot it up from one of the schooner's guns. Two sailors scaled the platform bearing canvas and rope, rigged a breeches buoy, and hoisted the wounded man and the dead man down. The *Motto* took Thompson to the hospital in Key West, where he recovered, though he remained a cripple for the rest of his life.

Since the number of American regulars was limited, volunteer companies were raised all over the south, on the theory that misbehaving Indians anywhere and everywhere should be taught a lesson. In 1836, 1,500 Tennessee volunteers arrived in Florida in a jocular mood, and all gave themselves ranks, down to corporal, so that there was only one private, who said: "Gentlemen officers, I am willing to be drilled, wheeled, marched, and counter-marched, I will form a company or platoon, but I object to being divided into sections."

Despite the Tennessee men's good humor, however, the military situation did not improve, and after a year of reversals the war was already unpopular. In 1836, 103 company-grade regular officers resigned, most of them to escape service in Florida. "Why not in the name of common sense let them keep it?" asked the army surgeon Jacob Rhett Mott. In December, the Florida command was turned over to a resolute forty-eight-year-old army veteran, General Thomas S. Jesup.

Meanwhile, in Washington the Florida territorial delegate, Joseph M. White, went to see President Jackson on February 15, 1837, to protest any further draft of men in central Florida. Jackson was then a lame-duck president, serving out the final month of his second term prior to the inauguration of Martin Van Buren in March.

White made his case, arguing that the Florida men had enough to do defending their own frontiers without being subjected to the draft. His words incensed the president, who exclaimed, "Let the damned cowards defend their country." Jackson then launched into an angry tirade, declaring that the people of Florida had done less to put down the war and defend themselves than any other people in the United States. If they had been men of spirit and character, they would have crushed the uprising at once. If those Indians had approached the white settlements of Tennessee or Kentucky, he said, not one would have gotten out alive. In a way, Jackson suggested, it was better for the Florida men to run off and let the Indians shoot them, for that way their widows might find more courageous husbands, and breed up men who would defend the country.

Jackson insisted that there were no more than 600 Seminoles, to which White replied: "Your army and all your generals have been in the field, why have they not conquered these 600 Indians? And what about the Tennesseeans at Wahoo, they apparently had some difficulty in getting their wounded off the field."

At this, Jackson became apopleptic and shouted, "It is a lie!"

"Well, I wasn't there," White said.

"Who knows what they would have done if they had not got out of provisions," Jackson cried.

White thought to himself that the Tennesseeans always seemed to run out of provisions and suffer hunger pangs when they got within sight of the enemy.

With Jesup in charge, the turning point of the war came in 1837, when the general forced the Seminoles out of their hiding places in the Wahoo swamp and along the Withlacoochee (southwest of Ocala) and then sent them scurrying 150 miles south into the Everglades.

On January 27, 1837, Abraham (who had remained loyal to the Seminoles even though he had taken bribes from the army when relocation seemed unavoidable) and about fifty Indians were in the Big Cypress swamp, near today's Naples, when Jesup's men attacked and captured their baggage train. This was a demoralizing blow, for the Seminoles considered the swamps to be their impenetrable domain. As Abraham later recalled, "At the Cypress . . . I lose most everyt'ing, all my powder and blankets, a hundred dollars in silver, my freedom papers, my little boy's pony, everyt'ing."

On January 31, Abraham walked into Gen. Jesup's Big Cypress camp holding a white flag on a small stick. Stopping before the general's tent, he stuck the flag in the ground, made a sort of half-salute with his hand, and waited for the general to appear.

Abraham's boldness led to an eleven-article cease-fire agreement, signed on March 6 at Fort Drane, under which the Seminoles accepted withdrawal to the west. The army set up a relocation camp at Tampa Bay, ten miles from Fort Brooke. The Seminoles had until April 10 to turn themselves in. From Tampa, they would board transports to their new homes.

The chiefs surrendered: Jumper and Alligator and Micanopy. One of the officers who met them reported that "Alligator is a most sensible, shrewd, active and jocose man, worth all the Indians I have seen. Jumper is in decline from pulmonary affection . . . Abraham is a cunning negro . . . who can do more than any other. Micanopy is not the old fool we thought him but actually possessing good sense and exercizing real powers."

Hundreds of Seminoles began to come in. It took time to arrange their passage west; in the interim, the Indians received rations and clothing. Chief Jumper, one of the seven who had visited the new country in Oklahoma, told the army surgeon Samuel Forry that he did not want to go there, for it was nothing but green oaks. "Put us even down upon the capes," he said, "below Charlotte's Harbor. . . . Here we can kindle a fire with pine sticks and dry ourselves. There we would get sick. . . . Here the ground is full of Kontee root. The wood is alive with game. The lakes so abound with fish that our little boys shoot them with bow and arrow."

The March 6 truce stipulated that when the Seminoles migrated west, they could bring their Negroes with them. At first, Jesup intended to comply, writing Joel R. Poinsett, President Van Buren's secretary of war, that "I can have no agency in converting the Army into negro catchers, particularly for the benefit of those who are evidently afraid to undertake the recapture of their property themselves."

But the slave owners denounced the agreement in editorials. "The regaining of our slaves," opined one writer, "constitutes an object of scarcely less moment than that of the peace of the country." Under their relentless pressure, Jesup faltered. When whites demanded to go into the Tampa camp and look for their runaway slaves, he allowed them in, violating the treaty and betraying the trust of Abraham and the Seminoles.

When Jesup changed his position, he did so with a vengeance. In a May 25 letter to Colonel William Selby Harney, commander at Fort Mellon on Lake Monroe, near today's Sanford, Jesup wrote: "I shall send out and take all the negros who belong to the white people. . . . I am sending to Cuba for bloodhounds to trail them, and I intend to hang every one of them who does not come in."

The result of Jesup's reversal was that on June 2, Osceola and Chief Sam Jones, a medicine man who hated the whites, surrounded the Tampa relocation camp with 200 warriors and cleared it out. Between 600 and 700 Seminoles who were about to be moved west vanished into the countryside. Abraham, however, remained a captive in Tampa and, ever the astute tactician, agreed to act as guide to the troops.

Thrust into deep gloom by this setback, Jesup mustered bands of

Creeks, offering them bounties for captured slaves. Thus, the United States Army entered the slave-catching business. The Creeks were paid $20 per captured Negro, and turned the slaves over to their owners. This new arrangement aside, Jesup was not doing so well, and expected to be relieved of his command for failing to conquer the Seminoles.

But then his fortunes changed. The Seminoles were hurting, too, since the fighting gave them no time to plant. In October 1837, Osceola sent word that he wanted to negotiate. Jesup invited him to a council near St. Augustine. When Osceola and seventy-one warriors showed up carrying a large white flag, Jesup surrounded them and took them prisoner. The rules of warfare, he maintained, did not apply to Seminoles. Osceola was expedited to Fort Moultrie, on Sullivan Island in Charleston Harbor, where he died in January 1838.

Jesup's treachery caused a commotion in Washington. The United States believed in itself as the only honest nation in a corrupt world, and here it was rivaling Europe's worst duplicities. Jesup was denounced in the press, and the House called for an investigation. The incident had a bearing on President Van Buren's 1840 defeat at the hands of William Henry Harrison. The Seminole War had become "the dirty little war."

Nevertheless, Jesup pursued his military advantage. He sent seven small forces into the Everglades in the winter of 1837–38, who went about the business of rounding up Seminoles and their Negroes. On Christmas Day, that blunt-spoken veteran of garrison life, Colonel Zachary Taylor, fought the bloodiest engagement of the war in a swamp on the north shore of Lake Okeechobee. Twenty-six of his men were killed and 112 wounded. Present as a guide for American troops, Abraham was released after the battle on condition that he go into the Seminole camps and negotiate for peace.

On March 14, 1838, Jesup reported to Secretary of War Poinsett (who, incidentally, gave his name to the poinsettia, which he brought back from Mexico) that he had taken 642 Indian and Negro prisoners. The Seminoles, said Jesup, had been reduced to "a band of naked savages, beaten, broken, dispirited and dispersed," and the war was all but over.

Jesup's captives were conveyed to Tampa and placed on steamers bound for Fort Pike in New Orleans. Among them was Chief Jumper, who died of consumption on April 18. In mid-May, 1,160 Seminoles and Negroes embarked for present-day Arkansas, but the number that reached Fort Gibson on June 12 was 1,069, the others having died en route.

When Zachary Taylor succeeded Jesup as commander in June 1838, he was not so sure the war was over. Seminoles still lurked in every swamp and hummock, "unsubdued wanderers, armed for destruction." Though a slaveholder and a southerner, Taylor reversed the slave-catching policy and pledged that he would "not aid in depriving the Seminoles of their negros, nor would he do anything that would reduce the latter from comparative freedom to slavery."

Acting perhaps on this pledge, Abraham gave himself up at the head of a group of 196 Indians and Negroes in February 1839. Along with 100 others who had been waiting in the camp, they left Tampa in March aboard the steamer *Buckeye*, which reached Little Rock on April 2. The next day the local newspaper related that "about 260 Seminoles arrived here yesterday from New Orleans on the steamboat *Buckeye* . . . on their way to the country assigned to them in the west. They are a portion of the band who have been bothering our troops in the hummocks of Florida, headed by the negro Abram, who is with the party."

Abraham worked as an interpreter for the Indian agency at Fort Gibson and helped Micanopy and his people adjust to their new life of raising corn, beans, and pumpkins. An Oklahoma newspaper reported him still alive in 1870, "at the advanced age of one hundred and twenty years."

Back in Florida in the spring of 1840, the new governor, Robert R. Reid, informed the legislative council that the Seminole situation was still serious. In February, a mail carrier had been murdered a few miles from St. Augustine. "We are on the verge of desperation," he said. "Men sleep with arms under their pillows. Every neighborhood has its tale of blood."

More bloodhounds had been imported from Cuba, Governor Reid announced, and "why should they not be used? If robbers and assassins assail us, may we not defend our property and our lives even with bloodhounds? . . . Those who are safe from Indian alarms . . . may indulge in gentle strains of humanity . . . were they dwellers in the log cabins of Florida, they would attune their notes to harsher measures."

Reid described a recent example. Mr. Harlan, returning to his cabin in Apalachicola with some friends on January 29, came upon a scene of desolation—articles of clothing strewn outside the cabin, and telltale moccasin tracks. One of the company, searching behind the garden 100 yards off, called out, "Come here, Harlan, here is your wife." Mrs. Harlan was lying behind some logs with her throat cut, the patch of ball sticking to her forehead where she had been shot.

Her eight-year-old son was crumpled near her side, his skull fractured by a pine stick that had been left on the ground next to him. The boy still exhibited signs of life. Harlan dropped to his knees and embraced him, calling "Buddy! Buddy!," and then ran to the corpse of his wife and clasped her in his arms, crying out, "Oh my dear wife!"

Governor Reid quoted the words of the eyewitness who had told him the story: "My heart now assumed a stern fortitude foreign to its nature and I felt like not leaving a single Indian foot to make a track in the ashes of the desolation they had made."

The governor used the grisly account to justify the introduction of bloodhounds, thirty-four of which had been purchased in Cuba for $151 each. With their four Cuban handlers, the dogs were sent to the army post at Garey's Ferry for basic training. This consisted in releasing an Indian prisoner and telling him to go four miles and hide in a tree. The bloodhounds were then unleashed.

The *Savannah Georgian* printed a disturbing letter from Garey's Ferry that called into question the bloodhounds' barbarity: "Eleven of these Florida bloodhounds alias Cuban curs are now at this post, feasting upon their six pounds of fresh beef each day. They have been tried frequently with an Indian prisoner of war . . . but as to their ferocity all is humbug—a child may fondle with them."

Nonetheless, Zachary Taylor had six of the dogs delivered to the 2nd Dragoons. Alarmed, the secretary of war wrote Taylor that the hounds should "be confined to tracking down Indians . . . [and] muzzled when in the field and held with a leash while following the track of the enemy."

When Poinsett's order was made public, it led to outcries from the settlers that the army were a bunch of sissies for muzzling the dogs. In a letter to the *Tallahassee Floridian*, a reader expressed the hope that the unmuzzled bloodhounds would "tear to pieces the red devils."

Although the bloodhound controversy stirred up Congress and the press, the animals turned out to be a disappointment in combat. In the watery Everglades, they lost the scent. General Taylor wrote Governor Reid that he considered them "of no service whatever," and the dogs were discharged from active duty.

The war dragged on. Its main theater, however, had shifted south to the Everglades, giving the rest of Florida a chance to prosper. The war's economic impact was not all bad, for the arrival of thousands of soldiers triggered a building boom. Towns like Tampa sprang up around the forts, and the army built roads from fort to fort. In the 1840 census, the population had risen to 54,477.

In December 1841, more than a thousand men marched into the Great Cypress Swamp. Seventy miles long and thirty miles wide, it was the Seminoles' last stronghold. But the soldiers found only 50 Indians, whom they routed, and in February they headed for the Wahoo Swamp, where two months later they conducted one of the last operations of the war, taking 47 prisoners.

Colonel William Jenkins Worth, now in command of the Florida army, quietly recommended to the War Department that the 300 remaining Seminoles, 112 of them men, be allowed to stay in their Everglades sanctuaries. Thus, military operations came to an end.

In 1842, the little band of Seminole survivors was confined to an area west of Lake Okeechobee. The seven-year Seminole War was over, Florida was pacified, and the path made clear for statehood. On November 25, 1843, Indian Commissioner Thomas Hartley Crawford reported to President John Tyler that "a few Indians remain in Florida, producing no inconvenience by their presence."

Once a territory was pacified, the surveyors were normally the first ones in (after the soldiers and the squatters). But in the case of Florida, one man arrived ahead of the surveyors. His name was Hezekiah L. Thistle.

In its amphibious operations on the Florida waterways, the U.S. Navy had not failed to notice that the country was stocked with abundant stands of live oak, cypress, yellow pine, cedar, mulberry, and other timber useful in ship construction. Florida was one of the finest naval nurseries ever possessed by any nation. Not only was the timber plentiful, it was easily accessible by boat, growing alongside streams or on the seacoast.

Private entrepreneurs had also noted the rich resources of wood. Once Florida was at peace, they lost no time in sending axmen to public lands on missions of pillage and depredation. This illegal cutting finally came to the government's attention. On January 17, 1842, Abel P. Upshur, the secretary of the navy, appointed Mr. Thistle agent for the preservation of public lands, an early form of parks ranger.

Born in New Hampshire, Thistle was a fire-eating Yankee with the authentic crusading spirit. Imbued with his mission, he struck terror into the timber cutters' hearts. Upon arriving at his headquarters in Jacksonville in May, Thistle saw at once that "the great evil" was unsurveyed land claims that went back to the days of the Spanish. There was no way of telling who owned what. Some locations were covered by three or four competing claims.

Squatters based their right of possession on what Thistle called "chimney-corner" surveys, done at a time "when it was well known that a chain was not permitted by the Indians to be stretched upon the land." The Spanish surveyor "would float down the St. Johns in a canoe . . . and he might in some cases mark a tree upon the shore . . . at other times, without going beyond his drawing room, from descriptions furnished by Indian interpreters or Indian negros, he would make plats and receive a high salary."

Since a state of confusion reigned in the St. Augustine Land Office, Thistle decided to run his own surveys in order to establish trespass. To make his way around the interior, he hitched rides on naval vessels.

Thistle learned that a lumber company, Palmer & Ferris, was cutting live oak on public land on the St. Johns river. Tough as whalebone, live oak was well suited to ship's planking. In November 1841, Palmer & Ferris had brought the brig *Nimrod* from New York with a crew of forty and anchored it in the mouth of the St. Johns, near Jacksonville.

Now, in September 1842, Palmer & Ferris had 5,000 cubic feet of timber waiting to be shipped north aboard the *Nimrod*. Thistle was bent on stopping them, but could not find a marshal to serve a writ. The Duval County judge refused to hold a hearing, explaining that the defendants had retained him as their attorney.

Thistle nonetheless notified Palmer & Ferris that he would seize the timber and sell it at public auction on October 20. Palmer & Ferris argued that the timber was destined for the Norfolk Navy Yard and that it had been cut on private land, according to the plats in the St. Augustine land office. The company then rafted the timber to a secret location north of Jacksonville, where the *Nimrod* was to pick it up.

Thistle obtained an injunction from the Superior Court and ordered the deputy collector at St. Augustine not to clear any vessel with lumber on board. Arguing that Thistle was persecuting them, Palmer & Ferris appealed to some of their well-placed Florida friends. They had chartered the *Nimrod* in New York, they said, and the delay in loading the timber was ruining them.

William Duval, Florida's senior statesmen as a six-term governor, backed them up. He wrote Secretary Upshur on December 10 about "the singular and harassing conduct and assumption of power which is now exercized by Mr. Thistle." He was assuming "more than presidential powers," Duval asserted, and sometimes acted in a manner that was "not quite sane." At that moment, he noted, ten suits were pending in the Superior Court docket in St. Augustine concerning his seizures.

The lobbying did not intimidate Thistle. On March 4, 1843, he seized the *Nimrod* and her cargo off New Smyrna, and asked that a court of admiralty be convened to determine the case. Thistle pointed out that the oak on board was insured for $10,000, a sum that showed the cargo's value. It was choice live oak, every stick meant for beams and kelson pieces (timbers bolted to the keel for strength).

On April 18, the case was decided at the St. Augustine Superior Court, which ruled that out of the cargo's seventy-six sticks, sixty-six had been cut on public land. These sixty-six sticks now belonged to Mr. Thistle. In addition, as a penalty, the *Nimrod* was forfeited and sold, along with her tackle, apparel, and furniture.

David Palmer and Darius Ferris, who had grown rich looting public lands, vowed revenge. On June 15, Ferris fell upon Mr. Thistle in Jacksonville's main street and beat him severely. A large number of people observed the scene, though only one interfered on Thistle's behalf. The prevailing opinion seemed to be that if he had winked at what Palmer & Ferris were doing, he could have made several times his salary of $2,000 a year, and saved himself a thrashing.

An eyewitness, the Jacksonville lawyer Philip Fraser, reported to Secretary Upshur on the unequalness of the contest: "Mr. Ferris is a very large, athletic, powerful man in the vigor and prime of life . . . he is much above six feet in height, while on the contrary Capt. Thistle is somewhat advanced in years and rather below the ordinary stature of men. . . . Mr. Ferris made the assault and beat the government agent most cruelly and unmercifully."

Thistle suspected a practical reason for the beating that went beyond revenge: i.e., Palmer & Ferris had plans to remove another cargo of live oak from the Mosquito Lagoon and did not want him interfering. Undaunted, he wrote Secretary Upshur that he was racing there on horseback to head them off "unless my physician says it is too dangerous on account of the wounds I have received."

In July, Thistle seized the ship *Virginia*, branded each piece of timber with the letters *U.S.*, and shipped the cargo to the Norfolk Navy Yard. This particular lot belonged to the firm of Hopkins & Allmand, whose agent, James Boushell, protested that they had bought only girdled trees on land settled under the Armed Occupation Act. Congress had passed the act in 1842 to give settlers the incentive to move to places that were not quite safe yet. Those who accepted the offer could obtain a quarter-section of 160 acres if they cleared it and worked it for five years, and they had permission to cut enough timber to clear the land and build a cabin. In practice, the act enabled squatters who had no intention of staying to come in, cut the timber, and sell it.

In 1843, Thistle made his case to the new secretary of the navy, David Henshaw. He explained that on Lake Monroe, north of today's Orlando, two hundred settlers had taken out Armed Occupation grants without any plan of settling. All they wanted was the profitable wood on the St. Johns River and the principal bayous—these lumber pirates had already stripped the land of its live oak and cedar.

Thistle brought suit against the trespassers, but the St. Augustine land office would not let him examine its archives, which would have allowed him to distinguish public from private land. It seemed that the entire territorial government was in league to obstruct his efforts.

In August 1843, Thistle went to Washington to press the matter further. He wanted $100,000 in damages for the cutting on Lake Monroe and another $100,000 for the same at Mosquito Lagoon. He also requested funds for a schooner to patrol the Florida waters.

Events, however, overtook Mr. Thistle, for in 1843 Florida was approaching statehood. The Missouri Compromise of 1820, pairing Missouri and Maine, held that no slave state could be admitted to the Union unless a nonslave state balanced it. In 1845, Congress twinned Florida with Iowa and admitted both as states. The federal government washed its hands of Florida's timber-cutting operations, and that early conservationist Hezekiah Thistle vanished from the public record.

PART TWO
THE NORTHWEST TERRITORY AND THE MISSOURI COMPROMISE

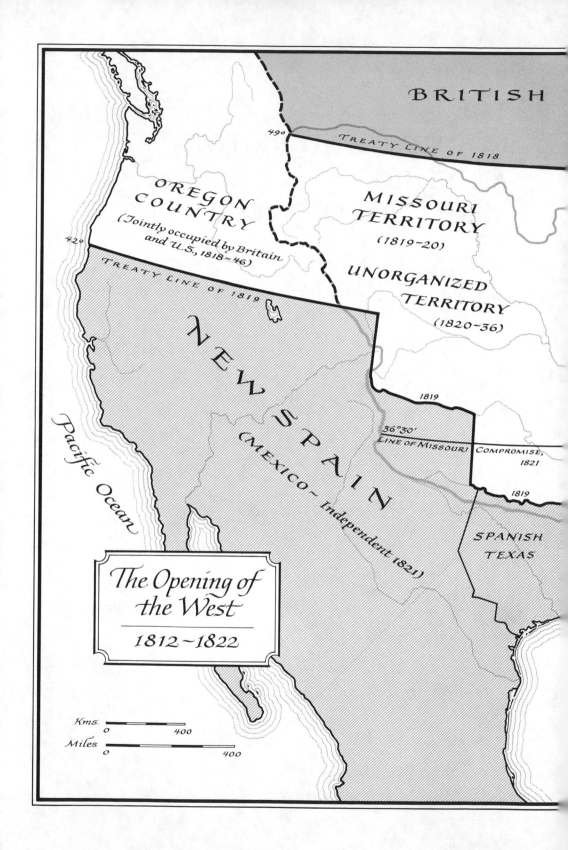

BRITISH

TREATY LINE OF 1818

49°

OREGON
COUNTRY

(Jointly occupied by Britain
and U.S, 1818–46)

42°

TREATY LINE OF 1819

MISSOURI
TERRITORY

(1819–20)

UNORGANIZED
TERRITORY

(1820–36)

NEW SPAIN

(MEXICO – Independent 1821)

1819

36°30'
LINE OF MISSOURI COMPROMISE,
1821

1819

Pacific Ocean

SPANISH
TEXAS

The Opening of
the West

1812~1822

Kms.
0   400

Miles
0   400

NORTH AMERICA

Claimed by U.S. and Britain

N

MAINE (1820)

MICHIGAN TERRITORY (1818–1834)

VT.

N.H.

NEW YORK

MASS.

CONN.

PENNSYLVANIA

N.J.

MD.

DEL.

OHIO

INDIANA (1816)

ILLINOIS (1818)

MISSOURI (1821)

KENTUCKY

VIRGINIA

Atlantic Ocean

ARKANSAS TERRITORY (1819–24)

TENNESSEE

NORTH CAROLINA

SOUTH CAROLINA

MISSISSIPPI (1817)

ALABAMA (1819)

GEORGIA

LOUISIANA (1812)

FLORIDA TERRITORY (1822–1845)

(Spain cedes East and West Florida to U.S. by 1819)

British

Spanish

Boundary of Missouri Territory, 1812–19

Gulf of Mexico

© A. Karl / J. Kemp, 1995

CHAPTER FOUR

THE INDIANA-ILLINOIS FRONTIER

Ahead of him was the log road, the continental sprawling hugeness of America, the fields and farmhouses, the towns. . . . It was a grand country, a country to lift the blood.

WALLACE STEGNER

On Sundays, something hangs in the air, a hallelujah, a skitter of brass, but we can't call it by name and it disappears. . . . It's a crazy feeling that carries through the night; as if the sky were an omen we could understand, the book that, if we could read, would change our lives.

RITA DOVE

The New York Public Library
Chicago in 1820. Today's behemoth was once a hamlet of fewer than one hundred inhabitants. Location was everything—on the Chicago River at the foot of Lake Michigan, surrounded by one of the most fertile prairies in America.

When you think of the Northwest Territory, that land mass of 242,000 square miles, more than twice as big as England, east of the Mississippi and south of the Great Lakes, won not by purchase but by conquest, and comprising the future states of Ohio, Indiana, Michigan, Illinois, and Wisconsin, you might think of it as an iceberg calving.

Pieces were lopped off this great mass to make manageable states in a process that took sixty-one years. In 1787, Congress created "the territory northwest of the river Ohio," specifying that no more than five and not less than three states could be formed within it. But as the territory's eastern fringe along the Ohio River grew more populated, it became apparent that such a vast expanse of land was too much to govern and would itself have to be divided before being made into states.

In 1800, Congress split the Northwest Territory into the Ohio and Indiana territories. Three years later the Ohio part acquired statehood. As the eastern part of Indiana Territory began to fill up, the process was repeated, and in 1805, Michigan Territory was born. Three years later Indiana Territory was divided again with the creation of Illinois Territory, which extended from the Wabash to the Mississippi. These two territories did not become states until after the War of 1812—Indiana in 1816 and Illinois in 1818.

Of the original Northwest Territory, only Michigan Territory remained, out of which Wisconsin Territory was formed in 1836. The next year saw Michigan a state, while Wisconsin kept territorial status until 1846. The conversion of Northwest Territory into states lasted from 1787 until 1846. State-making was a slow business, contingent on settlement and Indian "removal," interrupted by wars, and hostage to the slavery question.

Considered as an abstract process, the long march from territory to state seems almost geometric in its tidiness. In fact, the decision to change boundary lines did not originate in Washington, but with the protests of early settlers too distant from regional centers of power.

In January 1800, for example, the inhabitants of Knox County, on the Wabash River in southwest Indiana, petitioned Congress for a division of the Northwest Territory. They were too far from the seat of Ohio Territory in Chillicothe. They got their wish, and Vincennes became the capital of Indiana Territory, with William Henry Harrison taking the office of governor.

According to the 1800 census, the population of Indiana Territory, including the future states of Indiana, Illinois, Michigan, and Wisconsin, was 4,875. In May 1803, a military post was established in Chicago, and in 1805, Fort Detroit was made capital of the new Michigan Territory. Both forts had strategic locations on the Great Lakes, facing the British on the other side.

In the first stage of territorial government, when a governor and three judges ran things from Vincennes, there were bound to be complaints of neocolonial rule. One of the most common gripes was about the distance to the courts. Settlers sometimes had to travel two hundred miles through the wilderness to have their cases heard. The sheriffs of course were happy to cross the territory's length and breadth to serve papers, since they charged mileage fees. In the words of one plaintiff, they thought of themselves as little lords out to make a fortune from their fees of office.

Once land offices were established, there was the usual chicanery. Nathaniel Ewing, Vincennes's receiver of public monies, got caught red-handed when he tried to rig some land auctions. His scheme entailed bribing prospective buyers not to bid for a particular lot, so that his friends could buy it for him at the government price of $2 an acre.

Henry Hurst, the Vincennes postmaster, wrote to his friend Charles Brent in Winchester, Virginia, that "for a Spanish officer to act in that way is nothing, because everybody expects it of them; but a thing of this kind is never suspected in an American officer." And yet corruption was becoming so widespread that Spanish guile could have learned a few tricks from American honesty.

In 1804, Indiana's territorial government passed into the second stage with the election of a House of Representatives. In 1808, the creation of Illinois Territory defined Indiana as the area wedged between Ohio and Illinois. All the while, Governor Harrison was busy buying land from the Indians in million-dollar batches. In a typical treaty signed at Fort Wayne on September 17, 1809, 3 million acres changed hands.

The sudden loss of their land incited some Indians to action. Captain William Wells, the Indian agent at Fort Wayne, was the first person, in 1807, to warn Secretary of War Henry Dearborn of a rising Indian nationalism led by Tecumseh and his brother the "prophet." Treaties that gave away Indian land enraged Tecumseh, who excoriated the chiefs who had "touched the quill." But his dream of uniting the tribes came to a bitter end.

Where Tippecanoe Creek empties into the Wabash near today's Lafayette, Tecumseh gathered about 1,000 Indians from six different tribes. Exercising his first-strike option, Harrison attacked in November 1811, fighting a battle whose outcome proved indecisive, though the press celebrated it as a victory. When the Indian war got absorbed into the War of 1812, Tecumseh fought on the side of the British. He was killed in October 1813.

By 1815, the war had ended and the area was pacified. Indiana now boasted a population of more than 60,000, and the time was ripe for the next stage. A convention assembled on June 10 in the little town of Corydon, about ten miles from the Kentucky border, to draft a constitution. Lacking any political experience, the forty-three delegates sent a man through the wilderness to Louisville with orders to buy a primer on state constitutions. On his return, the assembly copied some of the articles verbatim from the constitutions of Ohio and Kentucky, and in 1816 Indiana became a state.

• •

In 1822, John Johnson arrived in Indiana from Ohio and bought an eighty-acre tract outside the village of Indianapolis, between the White River and Fall Creek. His son Oliver told *his* son Howard what those early days on a previously unsettled parcel of land were like, and Howard had the account transcribed by the Indiana Historical Society:

"It was just one great big woods. You might think it was a lonesome place to live in but it wasn't to us. Families was big in them days. With 12 of us children there was always plenty of entertainment.

"There was a certain mouldy or woodsy smell to a forest that's hard to describe but to us it was mighty sweet and satisfyin'. When your cabin and well was finished you had a mighty snug and comfortable home. It hadn't cost a cent either.

"In the evenin', Pap would be settin' in his usual place to one side of the fire, chewin' terbacker and spittin' in the fire. He wasn't much to talk to then. Sometimes he would set there by the hour and never say a word to anybody. Us boys would pass the evenin' cipherin' our slates, parchin' corn, mouldin' bullets.

"Mother and the girls would spin and knit. Corn bread was our staff of life. When mother started making wheat bread, Pap fussed around and said he would just as soon skin a hackberry tree and eat the bark.

"Pap made all the shoes for our big family. Sometimes he didn't get to us bigger boys until purty late in the fall. I guess he thought it made us healthy to go barefoot in the frost. On school mornings, we'd heat a clap-board before the fireplace until it was almost charred, stick it under our arm and run thru the forest until our feet began to sting. Then we'd throw the clapboard on the ground, stand on it till our feet warmed, grab it, and make another run.

"The little log mill was mighty essential to the settlers. They ground our corn into meal and I don't reckon we could a got by without corn bread. A trip to the mill had to be made every ten days, and I well remember how I felt when Pap would say, 'Well son you will have to go to the mill today' I'd have what I called mill pains, I dreaded it so. I was always worried for fear the big homemade linen bag that held the corn might catch on a snag and rip open, or the horse would throw me and the bag off.

"One mornin' Pap started me off for the Whitinger mill. I got along all right until I come to a place in the trail where a big tree had blowed over. My horse slipped and made a flounce toward the tree roots and one of them jammed through the bag of corn. Before the thought struck me to plug my old wool hat into the hole, I had lost just about as much corn as the toll would be.

"I told Mr. Whitinger about my mishap and what I could catch when I got home for bein' so careless. 'Now don't worry,' he said, 'Go up to the house and have Mrs. Whitinger give you a needle and thread, and I'll mend your sack while your corn is grindin', and your father will never know the difference'. When I left, he didn't take any toll for the grindin', and I never did forget how good he was in fixin' me up that way.

"I never could make out where the old-timers got all that fightin' spirit. Once when Pap went to vote at Indianapolis, the Whigs had clustered up around the votin' winder and kind of took over matters and wouldn't let the Democrats in. When a Whig come up they would pass him over their shoulders to the winder so he could vote. I reckon Pap's politics sort of worked down into his fists, for when they passed up a genteel-dressed Whig in his long coat-tail in front of Papa, he just grabbed it and yanked back, splittin' it clear to the neck, and the man landed on the ground on his back."

Such were settlement's early days, whose small dramas, drudgery, and delights revolved quietly through the seasons, forgotten by history and Hollywood folklore alike. Heroism didn't necessarily wear a ten-gallon hat. Oliver Johnson doesn't say much about the women, except that they had their particular duties. In sharing the frontier life, however, women proved themselves as capable and as brave as the men.

There was a couple with seven children living west of Lafayette, sixty miles northwest of Indianapolis. The wife, having grown up in Indiana, was used to false alarms about Indians. One time, in the middle of the night, the husband thought he heard Indians coming and jumped out of bed and got out the horse and cart. The wife said she refused to be dragged out of bed at all hours and hurried half-asleep to the fort. She knew that all these scares came to nothing. So the man of the house took the six oldest children and rode off.

Two days later he returned. He found his wife sitting by the spinning wheel, her foot pushing the treadle, as she evened the twine that she pulled from the distaff before the flyers caught it up and spun it into thread. With her other foot she was rocking a sugar trough where the baby slept. On the stove lay a turkey dressed and ready for roasting. A fresh coonskin hung on the wall.

"Mary," the husband grumbled, "why in thunderation have you been using my powder so free?"

"Never mind, Ebenezer, you won't need it," she replied, "for if you hear of an Indian crossing the Mississippi River, you'll be on the go to Lafayette again."

As sure as the Terre Haute land office was selling 640-acre sections at a base price of $2 an acre, wherever settlers lived, circuit-riding lawyers did not lag far behind. Land deals begot litigation, which even then was as American as a girdled tree. Anyone who'd read Blackstone's *Commentaries* could hang up a shingle. The frontier character combined suspicion with gullibility, so that the same person who hired a lawyer over some trifling nuisance was the first to buy the miracle tonic.

When Oliver Smith went west in 1816, he took a coal boat from Pittsburgh down the Ohio past Cincinnati to Rising Sun, Indiana. At that time, Indiana did not have a foot of turnpike road in the state, and no roads at all west of the Whitewater River. Not a bridge to be seen, and five rivers to cross between Cincinnati and Marietta. After his admission to the state bar, Smith moved to Versailles, on Laughery Creek, twenty miles west of Rising Sun. There he hung out his shingle and waited for his first customer.

There was a knock on the door, and a man came in and asked, "Is the squire within? I have a very important case, squire," he went on, "and I have come to fee you." This was music to Smith's ears. The man explained that his neighbor had bored one of his sugar trees without permission. "If he had asked," he said, "he might have bored a dozen of them, and welcome." Smith consulted his Blackstone and saw that the incident presented was a simple matter of trespass.

The court heard the case, and Smith was in the middle of dinner when his client rushed in and announced, "Squire, we have beat him, verdict 12½ cents, here is your fee of $2.50." "Ah," thought Smith, "there's nothing like your first client, your first case, and your first fee."

Smith next moved to Connersville, fifty miles north, where he met Dr. Burr, a root doctor from Ohio. Dr. Burr taught a course in concocting tea from various roots, awarding his students engraved diplomas after three weeks of lessons. Thomas Chinn, the constable, was one of his pupils. When Oliver Smith ran into Chinn in the street and asked how things were going, Chinn replied, "Only tolerable. I lost nine patients last week, one of them an old lady that I wanted to cure very bad, but she died in spite of I tried every root I could find."

Dr. Burr had nailed to the weatherboarding of the town hotel a swamp-lily root almost as big as a man, carved with a face and legs and arms that held a sign announcing JOSEPH S. BURR, ROOT DOCTOR, NO CALOMEL. When the rival physician in town, Joseph Moffitt, who used calomel, called Burr a quack, the root doctor hired Oliver Smith to sue for slander. To mock Dr. Burr, Dr. Moffitt had the town blacksmith make a special root-digging hoe. The case never came to trial, for after graduating a roomful of disciples, Dr. Burr went looking for greener pastures and skipped town.

In 1824, Smith was appointed circuit-riding prosecutor for the Third Circuit in eastern Indiana. He rode from court to court, carrying a dog-eared copy of *Peak's Evidence*. Members of the jury were usually bearded settlers wearing moccasins and side knives. One case involved a man discovered dead in the woods with a broken skull, who had been seen drunk the night before. A jury at the coroner's inquest ruled: "We the jury find that the deceased came to his death by having put too much water in his whiskey, causing him to freeze last night."

Courtroom behavior was spontaneous and unrestrained, for the judges granted the lawyers a wide berth of self-expression. Almost anything went —as in the case of a farmer charged with setting fire to the prairie. Intending to burn only the grass inside his fence, he had started a fire that spread out of control and consumed the haystacks of his neighbor, who finally managed to put it out.

The judge found the man guilty, declaring his offense a grave one. But since the law's purpose was not to punish but to reform, he said, he would fine the farmer the moderate sum of $75. That was quite a lot of money in those days, and suddenly the man's lawyer sprang from his seat in indignation and stormed out, exclaiming: "Jesus Christ! God Almighty! The moderate sum of $75!" as the courtroom erupted in laughter.

Some lawyers gained statewide reputations for their unorthodox style. An attorney named Linder in Vincennes had many imaginative strategies for getting his clients off. A hog thief he was representing leaned over in the middle of the trial and asked what his chances were. "Very slim," Linder whispered. "Shall I take the brush?" the man asked.

"Well," responded Linder, "it is a very warm day, and you must be thirsty, and the water here is about as bad as any I ever drank." Addressing a colleague, he asked, "Anthony, don't you think the water in Kentucky is a great deal better than here?" "Oh yes," Anthony agreed, "much better."

Turning back to his client, Linder said, "If you are dry, go and get a drink." The man slipped out and disappeared. "Linder," the judge said, "your client has cut sticks, and I am inclined to think you advised it." But no action was taken, and such high jinks only added to Linder's notoriety.

Circuit riding offered a good way to get to know the judges and other lawyers, and was thus an entry into politics. It was from this pool of legal talent that men were recruited for state and national office. Oliver Smith, for instance, rose in less than twenty years from the state legislature to the U.S. Senate, that is, from a judicial system in its infancy to an office on Capitol Hill.

In a state like Indiana, which attracted people from all over, there was plenty of room for political differences, some settlers being Yankees and some southerners, some being Whigs and some not. After a while, though, people thought less of where they had come from and more of where they were, which in Indiana in the 1820s was the west—like the man in Terre Haute who said he'd lived long enough in the west to throw off the perversities of the Yankee nature. The west was a transforming experience, just as New England had been.

In Illinois, there had been government of a sort since the inception of the Northwest Territory in 1787. Yet judges for the first Illinois courts traveled no further west than Vincennes, Indiana, where they arrived in June 1790. That was the closest they got to Illinois. In Vincennes, they passed laws concerning the maintenance of ferries and the amount of grain millers should grind. Prairies not part of one's land were to be fired only between December 1 and March 10. The judges set a bounty for killing wolves. They abolished imprisonment for most debts. What was the point of building jails to hold debtors, who could be out working to pay off their obligations?

The 1787 Northwest Ordinance banned slavery, and the French inhabitants, who had come to Illinois long before the Americans, wondered whether they would be able to keep their slaves. Some didn't wait to find out and moved west of the Mississippi to Spanish-held lands.

Years later, after Illinois became a territory, a mountaineer and his wife passed through a town on the Wabash. Asked where he was from, the man said, "Hiwassee purchase, McMinn county, state of Tennessee." And where was he headed? "Going to Missouri," he replied. "Why don't you stay in Illinois?" someone asked. "Don't you like the country?" "Well, sir," he answered, "Your soil is mighty fertile, but a man can't own niggers here, God-durn you."

The bill that established Illinois Territory became law in 1809, designating the Wabash as a natural boundary. That June, Ninian Edwards, formerly chief justice of the Kentucky Court of Appeals, arrived as governor in Kaskaskia, the bucolic territorial capital that was later obliterated by the Mississippi.

Appearing in the middle of the Tecumseh agitation, Edwards wrote Secretary of War William Eustis on July 6, 1811: "Such is the terror produced by actual and threatened Indian hostility that the country exhibits a perfect sense of distress—whole settlements are deserted, and many families are moving from all parts of the territory to Kentucky."

In March 1812, when the population of Illinois was 12,282, the territory got its own assembly and passed into its second stage of government. The war had not only interrupted settlement, but also halted the annuities paid to friendly tribes. When hostilities ended, settlers again ventured in, and in May 1816, President Madison proclaimed the sale of land in Kaskaskia, Evansville (southeast of St. Louis), and Shawneetown (in southeastern Illinois near the Kentucky border). Two years later Illinois citizens celebrated statehood in the streets. Out of a job as territorial governor, Ninian Edwards served in the U.S. Senate, where he vigorously called for legislation that would give settlers easier terms on land purchases.

The single most important issue posed by westward expansion was how public land was to be passed into private ownership. One of the principal ways was through the federal policy of encouraging enlistments and rewarding military service by granting land to veterans.

In 1811, as the country prepared for war with England, Congress passed a law offering soldiers an immediate $16 bounty upon enlistment for five years, plus three months' pay and a 160-acre quarter section when they got mustered out (officers received 320 acres). As more enlistments were needed, other such acts were passed.

To make good on these promises, the government set aside millions of acres in each of the territories of Michigan, Illinois, and Louisiana. Up to 68,500 veterans of the War of 1812 had "bounty lands" coming to them, and at 160 acres a soldier, that added up to 10,960,000 acres.

In Illinois Territory, the military reserved a huge slice of land between the Mississippi and the Illinois rivers. After later additions, the tract rose to 3.5 million acres, all of them entirely surveyed by 1822.

The War Department first issued land warrants in 1817, sending them to the veterans in the mail. After the recipients delivered their warrants to the General Land Office in Washington, they drew their surveyed quarter section in a lottery.

On September 24, 1817, Josiah Meigs, the Land Office commissioner, wrote Secretary of the Treasury William H. Crawford that his office was swamped: "The tickets for the whole of that tract [Illinois] will be in the wheel tomorrow—this office is teazed daily by soldiers, some of them are so insolent and abusive that it is necessary to turn them out."

From October 1817 to January 1819, 17,000 patents were drawn covering 2,800,000 acres. Happy to be home after the war, the veterans often didn't want to go west, so they ended up selling their warrants at the going rate of about $100. As a result, thousands of acres piled up in the hands of eastern speculators, including almost everyone in Congress.

Thousands of veterans, however, did get the itch, making the 1,350-mile trek over the water route from Pittsburgh to the surveyor general's office in St. Louis, where they could pick up a map of their tract, along with the surveyors' field notes, which helped them locate their claim and reduced the number of disputes.

Such clashes arose mainly from the fact that squatters sometimes occupied—preempted—claims to which they had no legal right. These prairie buccaneers became so numerous that they began to form a political constituency, whose demands had to be heard. A strong feeling prevailed in the west that land belonged to the people who occupied it. The squatters had pushed in ahead of surveys, Indian treaties, and land sales. Their argument was that they took all the risks and thus deserved a chance at ownership.

To regulate the squatter situation, Congress passed a preemption act in 1830, allowing squatters who had been on the land at least a year to buy their quarter section before it came up for public sale. In this way, the government inability to control squatting led to a new method of land disposal.

But squatters received no preemption rights to military-tract lands. There were only two ways that such land could be placed on the market: if a veteran didn't like the quarter section he had won in the lottery; or when the government seized land held by nonresident speculators for tax delinquency. In the 1830s, the military land office in Quincy sold off 1,370,000 acres of the Illinois tract for one or the other of these reasons.

Wedged between the Mississippi and the Illinois, the tract's southernmost part was settled first. Named Pike County, it pleased pioneer eyes with its rolling prairies crisscrossed by wooded streams. By 1830, when the county reached a population of 2,400, the settlements on its narrow southern strip broke off to form Calhoun County.

Schools followed children, and courthouses followed crime. In 1822, a man was captured in the woods after stealing a gun. To bring him back to Atlas, the Pike County seat, they tied his feet together and lashed him to the back of a mule. But when they came to the edge of a creek, the gun thief charged his mule into the water, yelling, "I'll go to hell and kick the gate open for you," and drowned.

People in Atlas liked to go by firsts—the first jail built, the first whiskey distilled, the first wheat raised, the winter of the first big snow, and so on. One of the firsts was the first Englishman to settle in Pike County. John Burland, his wife Rebecca, and their five children fled a life as tenant farmers in Yorkshire to realize the dream of working their own farm. They had never in all their lives been more than forty miles from home, yet in the early fall of 1831 they bravely sailed to New Orleans.

In Louisiana, they landed in another world. As Rebecca Burland noted in her journal, "Slavery is tolerated in its grossest forms. I observed several groups of slaves linked together and driven about the streets like oxen under the yoke." The steamboat up the Mississippi took twelve days to get to St. Louis, making frequent stops to chop wood. They continued fifty miles up the Illinois to their destination at Phillip's Ferry (today's Valley City).

Disembarking at the landing and finding the place completely deserted, a wave of discouragement broke over them, and Rebecca burst into tears. Her husband, however, found a cattle path that led to the cabin of Nimrod Phillips and his wife, a squatter couple. Seeing that the Burland children were hungry, Mrs. Phillips offered them the broth from the cabbage she had just boiled.

Rebecca could not help but compare their log cabin to a tidy English cottage. It was far more primitive. Nearly all their possessions were crowded into one room—a bed, a table, chairs, a candlestick made from an ear of corn, and a few tin drinking vessels vied for space with hoes and axes, and herbs suspended from the roof, as well as hams and sides of bacon smoked black. Two guns were mounted over the windows, and honey-filled pots sat under the bed. A small second room held two more beds and a handloom.

An 1820 law allowed land to be sold in eighths of a section—80 acres —at the government price of $1.25 an acre. The Burlands found a squatter named Oakes who had preempted 80 acres and entered them at the land office, and who was disposed to sell his "improvements" for $60. In addition, they would have to pay the full government price of $100 for the 80 acres, since the 1820 law had abolished credit.

Oakes took them around and showed them the boundaries, marked with big stones. He had broken about 12 acres, all ready to be sown, and had planted in addition some 400 sugar maples. The $60 for improvements covered his house and his maple-sugar-making utensils. After paying that and the $100 to the land office at Quincy in exchange for title, the Burlands moved in. The land lay on a sloping hillside near a spring, and their nearest neighbor lived half a mile away. "Everything here bears the mark of ancient undisturbed repose," Rebecca Burland wrote.

The family learned frontier improvisation, making their own furniture —a bench, stools, a table, and beds. Lacking candles, they put a little lard into a saucer and lit a piece of rag for a wick; when the saucers shattered from the heat, they switched to a kettle lid. For soap, they boiled ash and mixed it with pig entrails.

One day John Burland found some horses in his field. He was about to drive them out when a big angry-looking man appeared and snarled, "I intend my horses to be there." When Burland pointed out that the animals were on his land, the man, whose name was Brevet, struck him on the forehead and said there was more where that came from. A known trouble-maker, Brevet soon moved away, much to the relief of all his neighbors.

The Burlands were devout Methodists, but there was no church within walking distance. Though they made do by reading the Bible to-gether, they missed assembling on the Sabbath. Yet even had there been a church, Rebecca Burland didn't like the American sort of service, in which a circle was formed, and everyone held hands and capered about until someone jumped up and, with motions half-convulsive, said, "I feel it." There was too much whimsy in the service, and too little regard for the fitness of the preacher. Rebecca also found that some of the congregation's most rapturous members led far from exemplary lives outside church.

The Burlands began to regret their migration and to long for the comforts of England. Pioneer life was too hard—they had neither beer nor tea. In the winter, even water had to be thawed. Their only hopes were industry and perseverance. John Burland worked harder than he ever had in his Yorkshire tenancy, splitting rails to make fences, hunting quail and rabbit, and getting his maple sugar in, which he sold to Varley the store-keeper at eight cents a pound.

In October came the time to sow, and they had a plow but no oxen. Mr. Knowles, who lived two miles away and worked for hire, agreed to plow and harrow their eight acres of wheat in exchange for Burland's English watch. In November, they measured their first year's progress. It wasn't brilliant, and their children's clothes were in tatters, but at least they had sowed eight acres. Their cow had calved and their first calf had grown into a heifer. They were gaining ground.

One day in 1833, as they cleared more land, John Burland brought one of his daughters to see the fires he had kindled around the trees. Sheaves of wheat lay on the ground close to where the trees were burning. The child got too close and her dress caught a spark. Trailing flames, she ran among the freshly bundled sheaves, and soon the new harvest began to blaze and crackle. Burland saved his daughter, but lost an acre of wheat.

Prices having risen that year, they did so well with the remaining seven acres that they were able to invest $40 with Mr. Varley. With the interest he paid them, the family hired Mr. Knowles to plow more land.

Shortly afterward, their neighbor Mr. Paddock decided to sell his preemption right. He had been working his tract for three years, and the law stated that at the end of his fourth year he had to pay the land office $100 for the 80 acres he occupied. Being lazy, he didn't have the cash, and decided in typical squatter fashion to move further west and preempt again.

Owning about 15 fallow acres plus his house, he calculated a $50 asking price for improvements. But when the Burlands offered 2 cows and 70 bushels of wheat, he accepted, and handed over his preemption certificate (as well as his obligation to pay the government $100 in a year). The Burlands now owned 160 acres.

Once Paddock was gone, a man named Carr with a weasel face and a shifty manner came around asking questions. Paddock's house was a mile away, and caution told them they had better occupy it as quickly as possible, so Rebecca moved in with two of the children.

One afternoon she saw a wagon loaded with furniture approach, bearing Carr, his wife, and two of their children. Carr leaped to the ground and barged in, pushing Rebecca aside. "Well, my dear," he said to his wife, as if Rebecca weren't there, "this is our house, how do you like it?"

As he started to bring the furniture down off the wagons, he informed Rebecca, "We can do without your company pretty well, why don't you be a good neighbor and go home?" But she stood her ground and sent one of her children to get her husband.

When John Burland showed up, Carr brandished a paper from the Quincy land office that certified he had title to the property. "If you intend to spend the night in my house, I'll go and spend the night in yours," he told Burland. Although Quincy was fifty miles away and a three-day ride, Burland realized that the only thing he could do was to go there at once and use his preemption certificate to prove his right.

Rebecca was left behind with the intruders. Carr taunted her with malicious remarks, saying, "Your husband sent you here to get rid of you." The third day of her husband's absence was the Sabbath, and as Rebecca sat reading the Bible to shore up her strength, Carr said, "I will be rid of both you and your cursed religion before long."

Finally, John Burland returned and confronted Carr, telling him that his perjury had been detected. Carr had gone to the Quincy land office, paid for Paddock's land, and sworn there was no improvement on it. His lie voided the purchase as illegal and made Carr liable to a heavy fine.

Carr's confident manner collapsed. Turning humble and obsequious, he pleaded for a compromise, offering to pay the Burlands for the improvements. Burland demanded $80 and took Rebecca home.

Such was the way of the west, with everyone looking to finagle. And yet in spite of their mishaps, the Burlands prospered. A dozen years after their arrival, they had twenty head of cattle, seven horses, and 360 acres of land. What's more, they owned two farms worked by tenant farmers. In Yorkshire, they would still be tenants themselves, earning a meager living on some lord's land.

A small-time farmer of Scotch-Irish descent in South Carolina, George McWhorter owned five slaves who worked his plantation along the Pacolet River in the northwestern corner of the state. One of them was a good-looking young woman from West Africa. George McWhorter "jumped the fence," as the saying went, and in 1777 the young woman gave birth to a boy, half black and half white.

In 1795, when the boy, named Frank, was eighteen, the lure of cheap land drew McWhorter to Kentucky, where he bought 400 acres between the Green and the Cumberland rivers, in an area known as the Pennyroyal Barrens. Four years later, at the age of twenty-two, Frank married another light-skinned slave named Lucy, who was six years older than her husband. Even though she had a different owner, who lived a short distance away in Somerset, husband and wife managed to see each other. Their first child was born in 1800; of the twelve that followed, seven lived to adulthood.

Settlers began streaming into the Pennyroyal, where in 1800 you could buy 100 acres for $20. Slave labor was at a premium, and George McWhorter started hiring Frank out as a laborer and jack-of-all-trades, since he knew him to be hardworking and resourceful. On the frontier, masters and slaves worked together in the fields and marched together against the Indians. For all the brutal disparity between them, white men and black developed the same qualities of ingenuity and self-reliance, each group out of its own conditions. The frontier sparked fires of ambition, although the slave had to overcome not only the wilderness, but his own bondage. Still, nothing was hard and fast in these fluid pioneer settlements. Ways to freedom could be found.

Eventually, Frank worked out a deal with his master (and father) whereby he would pay McWhorter a certain amount of money a year in exchange for time away from the plantation. In effect, Frank was renting himself from his owner. Whatever he earned above and beyond the fixed sum, he could keep. Indeed, McWhorter might have been giving his bastard mulatto son the chance to accumulate enough capital to someday buy his freedom.

The time was 1810, and Frank figured that the United States would soon be at war with England. He made a market analysis: in wartime there was bound to be a rise in the demand for saltpeter, the main ingredient in gunpowder. Having by now lived near the Cumberland River for fifteen years, Frank knew the location of saltpeter caves on the riverbank. Sure enough, saltpeter, which was 17 cents a pound in 1810, jumped to $1 a pound when war broke out.

Frank developed into a small entrepreneur in the gunpowder business, which he was able to do because he controlled his own work schedule, he had access to saltpeter, and the equipment for extraction was simple. All he needed at first was a shovel and a mattock to break up the whitish saltpeter crust on the floor of the caves.

He made the saltpeter right on the spot. First, he leached the dirt in vats and piped the solution into hoppers filled with wood ash. Then he boiled the liquid a second time, separating the impurities from the saltpeter, which percolated through the ash. This was an activity that whites disdained, calling it "nigger work."

Having refined the saltpeter, Frank mixed it with charcoal and sulfur to produce gunpowder. Lexington, eighty miles away and home to six gunpowder mills, was his market. He manufactured an average of four pounds a day and sold it for 50 cents a pound, contributing to the war effort as he made a profit.

In 1815, George McWhorter died. He had wanted to manumit Frank, but didn't put it in his will. McWhorter's legitimate son, Abner (Frank's half-brother), lived in Tennessee, and demanded that Frank pay him $500 for his freedom. When Frank said he didn't have the money, Abner told him just to keep running his late father's plantation in the meantime. He figured it would take Frank a lifetime to raise $500.

But being under no supervision, Frank found ways to siphon off profits. Aside from his saltpeter operation, there are indications he distilled a little whiskey on the side. By 1817, he had amassed enough capital to buy his wife's freedom ahead of his. In that year he paid Lucy's owner, William Denham, $800, and Lucy came to live with her husband on McWhorter's plantation.

Consequently, any children born to the couple after 1817 would also be free, although the four children born before then still needed to be bought out of slavery. Over the next several years, three children were born free: Squire in 1817, Commodore in 1823, and Lucy-Ann in 1825.

Frank went on selling saltpeter, since his absentee owner let him do pretty much what he wanted. At the same time, not wanting to lose a good plantation manager, Abner jacked up the price of Frank's freedom to $800. Maybe he had found out that Frank had paid $800 for Lucy.

Nothing, however, seemed to stop the enterprising slave. In 1819, Frank counted out $800 to Abner McWhorter, and the next year he listed his legal name on the census roll as Free Frank. In less than ten years he had been able to save $1600, a feat nothing less than astounding.

After his manumission, Frank continued to live in the Pennyroyal Barrens and expanded his business interests. But when Lucy's former owner William Denham died in 1819, his son Obediah sued Frank for $212, claiming that his father had once loaned the money to Lucy. Under Kentucky law, a husband was responsible for debts incurred by his wife.

Though Frank knew that the $212 had in fact been paid to Lucy for work done, he also knew he would have a hard time proving it in court. Shrewdly arguing that he and Lucy were still slaves at the time of the so-called debt, Frank pleaded the legal incapacity of slaves to enter into a contractual agreement.

Predictably, the Pulaski County court ruled in favor of Obediah Denham and ordered Frank to repay the $212. But Frank appealed, and in a landmark decision, the Kentucky Court of Appeals ruled in his favor. His argument had been ingenious, for how could chattel borrow money? If Frank and Lucy were guilty, the system that had passed the slave code was at fault. "Not guilty" was the only verdict consistent with state laws.

The Court of Appeals decision encouraged Frank to start buying land, convincing him that the court would also uphold the contractual rights of a freed black in land sales. Between 1821 and 1829, he bought land from the State of Kentucky at $10 per acre, acquiring 759 acres in ten separate transactions, some in partnership. As the only free Negroes in Pulaski County, Frank and Lucy hardly posed a threat to the social order, and thus had no trouble finding white partners, or buying land from whites.

As the owners of a farm, of land, and of a saltpeter business, Frank and Lucy prospered through the 1820s. But the situation of a freed slave had its drawbacks. The two were often stopped, and always had to carry their papers on them to keep from being arrested as fugitives and secretly sold. Not to mention the yassuh-nossuh deference they had to maintain with whites to avoid trouble.

And in that time the attitude in the slave states toward free blacks started hardening. Henry Clay called them "the most corrupt, depraved, and abandoned" of people. Whites applauded the Back to Africa movement, then in its heyday, as a way to get rid of unwanted former slaves. Some whites even bought land on Africa's western coast, which was dubbed "Liberia," and formed the American Colonization Society in 1817 to help free Negroes migrate. More and more of them accepted the offer.

In Danville, a thriving little town forty miles south of Lexington on the wilderness trail, where Frank had an outlet that sold gunpowder to the locals and to passing pioneers, a newspaper called the *Olive Branch* encouraged free blacks to leave for Liberia. When someone asked a local planter his opinion of settlement there, he said, "My Gilbert's a sensible nigger, ask him." Gilbert replied with another question: "Do you reckon there's a place on the face of the earth where they make two crops a year and the white folks ain't took it?"

Free Frank sensed Kentucky's changing atmosphere. Whites now seemed to feel that even free blacks ought to act like slaves. The frontier period was drawing to a close, and with it a certain spirit of openness and generosity. Frank worried about the safety of his property, about how he would support his wife and children in the growing anti-Negro climate.

In 1830, when he was fifty-three, Free Frank decided to move to Illinois. First, however, he had to overcome some legal obstacles. The Illinois legislature had passed a law the previous year stipulating that any free black moving into the state had to post a $1,000 security bond so as not to become a public charge. Ever resourceful, Frank discovered a way around this large capital outlay. He traded some of his land in Pulaski County for a patch of land on the old military bounty tract in Illinois's Pike County owned by Dr. Galen H. Elliott. His status as a landowner was proof that Frank was self-supporting.

Illinois also required a character reference that had to be registered in the county where the newcomer planned to reside. Nineteen citizens of Pulaski County signed references for Free Frank.

In September 1830, he sold his home and what remained of his land for $355 and departed for Illinois with his wife and four of his children—twenty-five-year-old Frank, Jr., thirteen-year-old Squire, seven-year-old

Commodore—and five-year-old Lucy-Ann. The three children who remained slaves, Judah, Sally, and Solomon, had to be left behind in Kentucky.

In 1830, a black family heading west in a heavy canvas-covered "steamboat" wagon pulled by oxen was a far less common sight than gangs of Negro slaves heading south in chains. Free Frank was anxious about slave catchers, also known as "nigger-stealers." Against this contingency he had his freedom papers, but he took along some rifles in case the papers weren't enough. For he knew that the market value for himself and his family was about $4,000.

After a long trip over bad roads, Free Frank crossed the Illinois River into Pike County in the spring of 1831 at Phillip's Ferry, where John and Rebecca Burland would arrive that fall. His land lay fifteen miles from the Mississippi along Illinois's western border. Missouri, another slave state, stretched into the distance across the river. Slave catching was big business, and the law permitted slaveholders to travel across Illinois with their slaves for as long as thirty days.

The Illinois constitution made blacks free but not equal. They couldn't vote or be called as witnesses against whites; they couldn't sit as jurors or serve in the state militia. The children of free blacks could not attend public schools. And measures like the $1,000 bond and the certificate of good character posed formidable obstacles to black settlement.

When Frank registered at Atlas, the Pike County seat, located thirteen miles from his farm, the county population was 2,396. Most of the ex-soldiers who had once lived there had sold their warrants. Frank's land was on Hadley Creek, half prairie and half woods. He had to be careful in marking out his boundaries, for he didn't want some white squatter coming around and disputing his ownership.

At that time, the Illinois gazettes were filled with notices of runaway slaves, accompanied by little drawings of nappy-haired Negroes carrying their belongings in a bag tied to the end of a stick. It would have been natural for people to suspect that this black family living in isolation near the Missouri border was using their home as a refuge for runaways. But in that sparsely inhabited area, settlers worried more about Indians than anything else.

Free Frank and his family soon got down to the hard work of building a new life, clearing land, constructing a cabin, and putting up fences. Frank decided on mixed farming, growing wheat and corn, while on the prairie grass he raised cattle. To bolster his income, he took in stray horses, for which service the county paid him fees. If no one claimed them, the horses were his. Since there was no road from his farm to Atlas, he built one.

In 1835, Frank had saved enough money to buy his twenty-one-year-old son Solomon out of bondage for $550. He returned to his old state to get him, waiting patiently as the emancipation deed was recorded in the Pulaski County records. But two slave daughters and their children remained in Kentucky, owned by the Denhams, Lucy's former masters.

In 1832, a new land act had cut the minimum amount of government land a settler could buy from 80 to 40 acres, payment to be made in full at the time of purchase. With land available in 40-acre parcels at $1.25 an acre, Frank began buying all he could. Deferring the freedom of his daughters still in slavery, he bought 80 acres in 1835 and 280 acres in 1836.

For anyone in possession of 80 acres could start a town. All you had to do was draw up plats showing the streets and alleys and public spaces, and file the plats with the county clerk. But the danger in making these paper towns was that no one would come. If another town started up nearby in a better spot, yours might never get past the blueprint stage.

Free Frank thought the 80 acres he had acquired south of his farm would make a good town location, since it was on the route of a proposed turnpike from Pittsfield, the new county seat, to the federal land office in Quincy. He called it New Philadelphia, had it platted, and began selling lots in 1837. Even though 1837 was a panic year in which banks failed and money was scarce, he sold two lots for $59 each, and four more in 1838 at $60 apiece. In 1839, the new turnpike attracted the first store, a grocery owned by Chester Churchill, who also had a liquor license.

Free Frank proved to be the only black founder of an Illinois town. In contrast to the failed manumission settlements operated by abolitionists, he was a mainstream entrepreneur who succeeded on his own. Frank had not created a settlement for free blacks, but for anyone who could afford a town lot. Capitalism defined his strategy for survival on the frontier. He increased his holdings so that he could live a normal American life and leave property to his children. All he wanted to do was be a part of the system.

There was, however, the problem of his name. Slaves did not have surnames, but Frank felt he needed one to protect his property title and pass it on to his children. In the 1820 census, still feeling the exhilaration of emancipation, he'd listed himself as Free Frank. In the 1830 census he'd used his wife's name, Denham, so that he would be able to trace his children if Denham sold them. Now, in 1836, as the owner of 600 acres, he petitioned the Illinois General Assembly for the right to take a legal surname. His petition was approved. The name he chose was McWorter, a slight variant of his father's name, McWhorter, as if saying "almost, but not quite."

In 1839, a preacher formally married Frank McWorter and Lucy under Illinois law. Frank was asked by the minister whether he promised to cherish and support his wife. "Why God bless your soul," he answered, "I've done that for the past 40 years."

Two years later Frank sold a ten-acre section of his town for $200. Though no more than a crossroads settlement of cabins and a couple of stores, by 1850 New Philadelphia had an interracial population of 58— three black and eight white families. Frank's son Solomon lived there, and started a cabinetmaking business with a white partner. Even that definitive sign of civilization, the post office, made a brief appearance. But when

Hannibal and Naples built its railroad, the route they chose bypassed New Philadelphia, and eventually Frank's town reverted to farmland.

Yet through the selling of town lots, Frank was able to buy the freedom of his last two children remaining on the Denham plantation—thirty-two-year-old Sally in 1843, and fifty-year-old Judah in 1850. Obediah Denham sold them to their father at $500 for each daughter. Judah, the last to be freed, was Frank's firstborn. Frank also purchased the liberty of three grandchildren and his son Squire's wife, Louisa, for a total cost of $4,380. By the time of his death in 1854, at the age of seventy-seven, Frank McWorter had bought ten members of his family out of slavery. In a society that made blacks slaves or Uncle Toms, he refused to be either. He had the gumption to prove his own worth.

The saga of Free Frank ends on a curious footnote. Frank's daughter Sally, whom he had purchased in 1843, had a daughter named Charlotte, also owned by Obediah Denham. But when Obediah's son William tried to buy Charlotte for himself, his father turned William down, saying that he planned to sell Charlotte to someone else.

His father's behavior prompted William to write an intriguing letter to Free Frank's son Solomon in December 1854, shortly after Frank's death. In it, William warned that Solomon's niece was about to be sold outside the Denham family.

"Dear sir," wrote William, "I take my pen in hand this mornin' with sorrow in my hart to let you no that I cannot prevent my father from selling Sharlet. I have kept him from selling hur for too years I can doo nothing more with him if you want hur you had better come quick. . . . I right this unbeknown to my father; you can buy hur for $850 or $900 hur and hur child. I think Sharlet has got as purty a child and as smart as I ever have seen white or black and it is all most white. I feel anctious you wuld come and buy hur the children is all well the male is about to start and I must come to a close. Beshore to comeon right soon. Your friend William Denham."

Aside from suggesting that there was not much difference in education (or lack thereof) between the slaves and their masters, William's letter raises the possibility that he was Charlotte's father. That would explain why Obediah Denham, angry at his son's behavior, wanted to remove Charlotte and her child from the plantation. Indeed, a letter from a white man to a former slave that ended with "Your friend" almost amounted to an admission of kinship.

It was not until 1857, however, that Solomon was able to raise the money to buy Charlotte. By this time, she had two children, and her price had gone up to $993.61. Charlotte and her children were the last freedom purchases made by the McWorters, an antebellum family of black pioneers who overcame the obstacles erected by a society determined to keep them down.

CHAPTER FIVE

THE ARKANSAS FRONTIER

And above all the low chant of their traveling song which the riders sang as they rode, nation and ghost of nation passing in a soft chorale across that mineral waste to darkness bearing lost to all history and all remembrance like a grail the sum of their secular and transitory and violent lives.

CORMAC McCARTHY

In the first twenty years of the nineteenth century, the state-making process followed the territorial model established in the Northwest Ordinance. The only exception was that in the southern states slavery was permitted. Between 1800 and 1820, Congress admitted six states into the Union upon their meeting the necessary requirements—coincidentally, half were free and half were slave: Ohio in 1803; Louisiana in 1812; Indiana in 1816; Mississippi in 1817; Illinois in 1818; and Alabama in 1819.

But when Missouri applied for admission to statehood in 1819, the politics of slavery interfered with the state-making process for the first time.

The Louisiana Purchase had been divided into two territories, Orleans in the south and Louisiana in the north. In 1812, Missouri Territory was formed out of the Louisiana area, and four years later a land office opened in St. Louis.

Slavery had existed in Louisiana Territory under the French and the Spanish, and it persisted in Missouri Territory as many new settlers arrived with their slaves. By 1819, Missouri had attained the population of 60,000 that statehood required, and asked for admission as a slave state. This meant, however, that the Mason-Dixon line west of the Mississippi, separating the slave-free north from the slaveholding south, had to be abandoned.

Until that time, Congress had done nothing to disturb the situation in those states that wished to preserve the slavery that had existed under previous regimes. But the status quo depended on a delicate balance, for in January 1819, when the question of Missouri statehood came before the House of Representatives, there were eleven slave states—Alabama, Delaware, Georgia, Kentucky, Louisiana, Maryland, Mississippi, North Carolina, South Carolina, Tennessee, and Virginia—and eleven free states—Connecticut, Illinois, Indiana, Massachusetts, New Jersey, New Hampshire, New York, Ohio, Pennsylvania, Rhode Island, and Vermont.

The even ratio between free and slave states meant that although the more populous northern states dominated the House, a balance had been achieved in the Senate, with each region wielding twenty-two votes. The admission of Missouri would upset this fragile configuration.

As William Plumer, Jr., a member of the House from New Hampshire, observed: "Many of the southern members openly avow their intention—they say they have now an equality in the Senate, eleven slave-holding and eleven free states, and they are determined not to admit a free state without bringing in at the same time a slave state to preserve the balance. They also throw out many threats and talk loudly of separation."

The Missouri fracas exposed a deepening fault line in the young nation's polity. Forty years before the Civil War, party alignment mattered less than the division between free and slaveholding states.

The House debated the Missouri statehood bill in January 1819, and the sparks started to fly. James Tallmadge of New York offered an amendment providing that no further slaves should be admitted into Missouri, and that all children born to slaves should be set free at the age of twenty-five. The amendment passed in the House, but it produced a congressional crisis. As John Quincy Adams, then President Monroe's secretary of state, noted in his diary: "A motion for excluding slavery from it [Missouri] has set the two sides of the House, the slave-holders and non-slave-holders, into a violent flame against each other."

On January 21, Senator William Pinkney of Maryland, a distinguished jurist, argued that Congress did not have the right to impose restrictions on a state when admitting it into the Union. Such restrictions would make that state less equal than older states and would therefore, he maintained, be unconstitutional. Since older states had the right to uphold slavery, Missouri must have the same right.

Backing up Pinkney's argument with threats, other southern congressmen vowed to dissolve the Union and raise troops to defend the people of Missouri if they were not allowed to keep slaves. The Senate rejected the Tallmadge amendment, and Congress adjourned in March 1819 without resolving the Missouri question.

When Congress took up the matter again in January 1820, the Illinois senator Jesse B. Thomas offered a compromise: Missouri could be admitted as a slave state on condition that slavery be banned in all other states carved out of the Louisiana Purchase north of a latitude of 36°30'. In addition, each slave state would have to be paired with a free state, admitted in tandem. It happened that Maine, long a part of Massachusetts, had applied for statehood. Missouri, Thomas proposed, could be coupled with Maine.

The adoption of the compromise would mean that half-a-dozen territories above the 36°30' line—Michigan, Wisconsin, Minnesota, Nebraska, Iowa, and North and South Dakota—would automatically become free states upon admission to the Union. That would contradict Senator Pinkney's constitutional argument that states should be admitted without restriction. But it also meant that none of these states could be admitted unless a slave state was paired with it. And that in turn would solidly bind the state-making process to the slavery dilemma.

In the furious debate that ensued, Senator Rufus King of New York so bitterly attacked slavery that "the great slave-holders in the House gnawed their lips and clenched their fists as they heard him," wrote John Quincy Adams. President Monroe felt that nothing had ever so threatened the bonds of the Union.

In March 1820, Congress adopted the compromise bill, authorizing Missouri to draft a constitution that placed no restrictions on slavery, while at the same time admitting Maine as part of the package. Missouri's constitutional convention met on June 12, 1820, and Missouri was brought into the Union as a slave state on August 10, 1821. John Quincy Adams presciently remarked in his diary, "I take it for granted that the present question is a mere preamble—a title-page to a great, tragic volume."

The Missouri Compromise prevailed for a quarter of a century. During those years, however, only four territories became states: Arkansas and Michigan were paired in 1836 and 1837, and Iowa and Florida in 1845 and 1846. At that time, the Mexican War and the annexation of Texas made the Missouri Compromise inoperative.

As a by-product of the Missouri Compromise, Arkansas Territory, lopped off from Missouri in 1819, could become a slave state if it so desired. Arkansas, which included the future Oklahoma, had been a county in Missouri Territory since 1813. Before that, when earthquakes in New Madrid, Missouri, had made several thousand settlers homeless in 1811 and 1812, the government offered them warrants for land in Arkansas.

One of those who lost everything in the New Madrid earthquake was John Benedict, who brought his wife and five children to Arkansas in 1812. They crossed from Missouri into northern Arkansas and came to the White River, where Joab Harden ran a ferry consisting of two canoes lashed together with a few split clapboards laid across them. At the river's edge, Benedict cried, "Halloa, halloa, the boat. . . ."

Further south, when the Benedicts reached the juncture of Cadron Creek and the reddish-brown Arkansas River, they broke the first cane to pitch camp. A few other settlers were already there, subsisting like Indians by hunting and trapping.

Benedict bought some land from a squatter named Flanagan, who had decided to move further west. Flanagan was proud of having been a Tory who had fought for the king. He gloated about the rebels he had killed and the houses he had burned down, and announced that he despised the Fourth of July. Benedict took the treasonous talk in stride, for out here the past was indeed a foreign country. Anyway, he soon noticed that all Flanagan cared about were his gun and his dog. When asked, the former Tory said that he agreed with the Quapaw belief that future life was a happy hunting ground.

• •

In 1813, when Arkansas evolved into a county of Missouri Territory, William L. Lovely was assigned as agent to the Cherokees. Writing on August 6, he said of the white settlers, "I am here among the worst banditti; all the white folks, a few excepted, have made their escape to this country guilty of the most horrid crimes and are now depredating on the Osages and other tribes, taking off 30 horses at a time." That was a switch, the whites stealing horses from the Indians.

In 1816, Lovely bought from the Osages a big triangle of land in northeastern Oklahoma. Bounded on the west and south by the Arkansas and Verdigris rivers, the area became known as Lovely's Purchase. The Indian agent clamored for troops to keep the peace and protect incoming settlers, and in 1817, Major Stephen B. Long arrived and built Fort Smith at the junction of the Arkansas and Poteau rivers. Perhaps 2,000 white settlers lived at that time in the entire territory, and there was not a single gristmill. Cornmeal, when it appeared, was ground in wooden mortars.

On July 4, 1819, President Monroe signed an act making Arkansas a territory. Circuit courts were established, and the New Hampshire soldier James Miller was named governor. Though Miller spent much of his time traveling up and down the Verdigris to keep the tribes at peace, white settlers angrily labeled him "a Yankee stickler for legality."

Arkansas was then the most remote frontier, backed up to nominally Spanish Texas, and filling up fast with rough-and-ready types. Reuben Easton, a settler in Cadron Township, wrote Secretary of War John C. Calhoun in 1819 about the difficulties with the Cherokees: "The people is weak heir in number not abel to protect them selves from them they now it & it makes them Sausy and mischievous they are going to & from through our settlements killing up our stock destroying our crops & stealing all our best horses . . . many hardships & deficulties the pore inhabitants heir on the frontier has to incounter. . . ."

Indian affairs were the consuming issue, the question of the day being whether the United States should take sides in quarrels between the tribes. On this point Calhoun was at odds with the superintendent of Indian affairs, Thomas McKenney. On June 29, 1820, Calhoun wrote Governor Miller that "if peace between the Cherokees and the Osages cannot be preserved, the United States will take no part in the quarrel."

McKenney, however, disagreed, writing on August 2, 1821: "The policy of leaving these Indians to settle their own business by murdering one another is exceptional—humanity revolts at it—and our interests are involved in it."

The man in the middle was Major William Bradford, commander at Fort Smith. He reported to Calhoun on August 10, 1821, that he was warning the warriors of both tribes: "You are going contrary to the will of the government, whose wish it is that you should remain at peace. . . . I now say to you that if you shed one single drop of a white man's blood I will exterminate the nation that does it."

"How far I intend to carry these threats into execution is not for them to know," Bradford then went on to confide to Calhoun, "but I will do nothing that will involve the government in a war with either of them." He proved a skilled negotiator, and during his four years of command managed to act as a mediator between the tribes while maintaining Calhoun's policy of neutrality.

But violence could erupt at any time. When hunters and squatters trespassed on their hunting grounds, the Indians fought them off. In December 1823, a hundred Osage warriors suddenly rose from thick canebrake on the Red River, 180 miles south of Fort Smith, and fired on a party of white buffalo hunters, killing four and wounding two. They then made off with equipages, peltries, and thirty horses.

"They will require chastisement before long," wrote Colonel Matthew Arbuckle, the new commander at Fort Smith, for they "are extremely ignorant and faithless, their chiefs are without useful authority, and their warriors are encouraged in dishonesty from infancy."

In 1824, the Quapaws yielded their lands on the Arkansas River for $6,000 and a $1,000 annuity each year for eleven years, and they removed to the Caddo area on the Texas border. But when their new lands on the Red River flooded, they starved. George Gray, the Indian agent on the Caddo prairie, reported in August 1828 that the despairing Quapaws had become unmanageable—they were drunk all the time. He asked for a company of men, as "it is impossible for me as an individual to restrain one or two hundred drunken Indians."

The only official in Washington who spoke up for the Indians, McKenney, was a voice in the wilderness. He wrote Secretary of War James Barbour on April 12, 1828: "It should be remembered how long the Indians have been disappointed in our pledges to them, and how, in fact, the want of confidence arising out of our failure to make them good has produced in them the conviction that we are not to be trusted."

In 1834, one of those Englishmen who regularly came to see how the former colonials were doing with their republican experiment traveled through a number of southern states, including Arkansas. America was an easy target of derision, and there always seemed to be some haughty Brit around to peer down his nose at American manners, American food, American bragging, and American idiom. All the offensive aspects of egalitarianism were smugly pointed out.

The Englishman was George Featherstonhaugh, a geologist trained in precise observation, whose account, *Excursion Through the Slave States*, remains a classic, for all its carping. Traveling with his son through the south, Feather (as I will call him) boarded a coach in Tennessee in which five of the six seats were taken, two of them by a Negro and his owner, a slave trader. Either Feather or his son would have to sit outside next to the driver. Feather approached the slave trader and asked, "Would you mind letting your servant ride on top of the coach so that my son can come inside?"

"I reckon my waiter is very well where he is," the man replied.

The slave trader's name was John Armfield, and he wore a black crepe band on his hat. Feather asked him who he was in mourning for. "Marcus Lafayette," he said [the French soldier had died earlier that year].

"Why," said Feather, "General Lafayette gloried in making all men free, without respect of color, and what are you in mourning for him for? Such men as you ought to go into mourning only when the price of black men falls . . . I shouldn't be surprised if Lafayette's ghost was to set every one of your negros free one of these nights."

At which the Negro servant "boiled over into a most stentorious horse-laugh of the African kind."

Armfield told him to stop laughing. The slave, whose name was Pompey, responded, "Master, I arn larfing at you by no manner of means, I was just larfing at what dat are gemmelman said about de ghose."

Feather and his son crossed from Tennessee into Arkansas on a flatboat, since they had found the ferry unattended. The geologist immediately confided to his notebook that this region was the land of big women. One was six feet two with a dark, bony, hairy face. "I should have taken her for some South American grenadier in women's clothing," he observed.

Approaching the house of a settler, Mr. Russell, Feather noticed two wild-looking boys dragging an ox head through the woods to bait a wolf trap. Then he met Mr. and Mrs. Meriwether, who both talked at the same time. They warned Feather and his son that there were "a heap of villains about," and that further down the Mississippi, at a place called Helena, all sorts of "nigger-runners, counterfeiters, and horse-stealers" were hiding out from the law.

On November 12, they came to a settlement where they were asked, "What goods have you got to sell?" When Feather replied that they had none, a settler asked, "Why what under earth are you if you ain't peddlers?" Apparently, Yankee peddlers were about, ready to stick a clock into every cabin west of the Mississippi.

Three weeks later, heading southwest from Little Rock, Feather and his son reached the Caddo River, where Mr. and Mrs. Barkman lived in one of the first brick houses they had seen. Mrs. Barkman chewed tobacco, smoked a pipe, drank whiskey, and swore like four backwoodsmen. Mr. Barkman heartily approved of Texas, explaining that he had "heern there was no sich thing as a government there, and not one varmint of a lawyer."

The travelers continued to Arkansas's southwest corner, arriving at Fort Towson on the border with Mexican Texas. Since Arkansas criminals routinely escaped into Texas to find refuge under Mexican law, the settlers in Fort Towson had appointed their own magistrate, who was given the Spanish title of alcalde.

Before long, father and son witnessed the apprehension of three fugitives. When the alcalde's wife appeared on the scene, she recognized one of the three as the fellow who had stolen her linen in Arkansas and killed her brother's cow. "I tell you, old Caldy," she said, "if you don't hang these fellows up right off you'll never have another chance. And if you don't, you ain't a going to have a skin left on a cow's back, nor a shift to mine, to all eternity." This alarming prospect sealed their fate, and they were strung up within the hour.

Feather was appalled by the frontier people's low morality and drunkenness. The marshal for Arkansas Territory was one of the famed Rector brothers, who had once monopolized surveying in Missouri. His working day seemed to consist of drinking brandy and gin and playing cards. When his cards didn't come up, he shouted, "Send my soul to hell." Social restraint was not the west's strong point. If Feather took a hotel room and found that black tobacco juice was the only liquid dripping from the walls, he considered himself lucky.

On January 22, 1835, during their return trip, Feather and his son stood at the door of a tavern in Columbia, South Carolina, chatting with some of the planter gentry. Feather asked one of the men if he considered himself an American yet. "My answer," the man replied, "is no sir, I am a South Carolinian."

Feather suggested that the planters would never be as prosperous as the entrepreneurs in the northern states so long as they held men in bondage. The planter argued that the Englishman misunderstood the nature of slavery. In fact, he said, slavery elevated the master's character and made him more vigilant about the welfare of the slaves.

At this point in the conversation, the mail coach drove up. A male slave, who had doubtless been caught running away, lay spread-eagled on the roof, chained at the ankles and wrists. Feather at first mistook the man for a bear on its way to the larder, and only when he drew closer realized that he was seeing a human being.

The geologist got into the coach, reflecting on how the fine theories he had just heard were violated by the reality under his nose. Suddenly, the stagecoach door opened with a bang, and a young white man, fettered and manacled, was bundled into it. He was Bob Chatwood, who had slain a Negro rather than pay him a gambling debt. In the coach, the sheriff's deputy escorting Chatwood passed a bottle around, and everyone took his quid of tobacco out and relaxed. The bottle went around to Chatwood, who was treated like just another passenger. His unpardonable crime, it turned out, was not murder, but playing cards with a slave.

With the advent of Andrew Jackson as president in 1830, the policy of Indian removal was carried out by his secretary of war, John Henry Eaton. Government troops drove the so-called Five Civilized Tribes from their homes in the southern states into Arkansas and Oklahoma.

Betrayed by their venal leaders, the Choctaws in the Treaty of Dancing Rabbit Creek signed on September 27, 1830, ceded nearly 8 million acres in Mississippi and moved to land near Fort Smith. The army's Commissary Department handled their removal. Vicksburg was the gathering point in the fall of 1831 for nearly 4,000 Choctaws who were taken to the juncture of the Red River and the Kiamichi, in eastern Oklahoma.

Passing through their forests, the Indians touched the trunks of trees in a gesture of farewell. They were loaded onto steamboats that took them up the Mississippi and up the Arkansas to Little Rock, and then brought overland 'to Fort Towson on the Red River. Their chief, Mushalatubbee, wanted no missionaries. "We have never received a scholar out of their schools who was able to keep a grog-shop book," he said.

Later that year, 3,400 more Choctaws were removed from Mississippi. Major Francis W. Armstrong, the Choctaw agent, refused to let the Indians go ashore for "indispensable purposes" when the boat transporting them stopped to cut wood. On the tightly packed decks cholera broke out; the Indians were so dispirited that they did not have the energy to bury their own dead.

By 1833, 6,000 Choctaws had completed the journey. That June the Red River flooded and swept away the corncribs of the Indians living on its banks, reducing them to eating the animals they found drowned. Lieutenant Gabriel J. Rains of the Commissary Department tried to give them seventy-eight barrels of condemned pork, declared unfit for the soldiers at Fort Gibson. It was rotten meat, scraped and rebrined and recasked, and the Choctaws didn't want it either, no matter how hungry they were.

When Rains saw that they were grinding up acorns for food, he gave them another batch of pork, this time a hundred barrels of five-year-old meat, "for though these people have refused it in their rations once, they would doubtless be glad to get it, for this is not putrid or spoiled, except by age and salt."

In 1836, 3,000 Creeks were removed from Alabama and deported to Arkansas. Making the winter trek barefoot through eight inches of snow, some Creeks suffered frostbite and others died by the side of the road. They had to be buried, for if their bodies were covered with brush, they were sure to be devoured by wolves. You could trace the Indians' trail from Fort Towson to Fort Gibson by following the square holes squaws had cut into fallen trees, where they had pounded their corn to make bread. By November 1846, 14,000 Creeks had crossed into Arkansas.

With similar matter-of-factness, the Chickasaws were removed from Mississippi, the Seminoles from Florida, and the Cherokees from Georgia. In 1838, General Winfield Scott conducted the enforced removal of the Cherokees. Journeying on foot through the winter months, 4,000 out of 15,000 Indians died. A Georgia colonel said after the Civil War, "I fought through the Civil War and have seen men shot to pieces and slaughtered by the thousands, but the Cherokee removal was the cruelest work I ever knew."

On June 15, 1836, Andrew Jackson signed the bill that admitted Arkansas as the twenty-fifth state. The territorial period, a time of brawls and

duels, of bowie knives (so common they were known as Arkansas tooth-
picks) and buffalo-chasing hunters, was over.

In contrast to the close-lipped frontiersman came the rise of the western orator. Byrd Johnson, the schoolteacher in Van Buren County, north
of the Arkansas River, said of a flood: "The rain came down in torrents, it
ran down in super-abundance, it dislocated our fences and left our crops
exposed to the avaricious appetites of the quadrupeds."

Alfred W. Arrington, who had arrived in Arkansas as an itinerant
Methodist preacher, making stirring temperance lectures once he had a pint
under his belt, soon realized that the law was more lucrative, owing to the
number of crimes of violence. Prosecuting a murder committed by the
outlaw James Foreman, Arrington declaimed: "There on his own floor,
with his household goods around him, his life-blood poured out through 29
dagger wounds sprinkling in crimson baptism the very curtains that hung
around the slumber of his infant children, who were soon to awake orphans
in this wicked world, whose charity was as cold as the pearl-dross of morning dew."

Although a slave state, Arkansas never completely adapted to the plantation economy, and in 1850 remained a frontier area that ranked thirteenth
out of fourteen slaveholding states in the number of its slaves. The mountainous northwest had few slaves, as well as a reputation for being behind
the times, home of Lum and Abner, where coonskins and molasses were
legal tender.

Meanwhile, migrants from adjoining states kept coming to eastern
Arkansas. In Des Arc, a crossing point on the White River fifty miles east
of Little Rock, the *Des Arc Citizen* reported in November 1848: "From
early dawn to late at night the ferrymen are bringing over wagons, stock,
carriages, buggies; also negros and white families of all ages from the prat-
tling babe to the aged sire."

Des Arc seems to have been a community of boosters. In 1859 the
town held a Prairie County Fair, featuring a "negro race," meaning a horse
race with black jockeys run over a five-hundred-yard circular track. Since
this was cotton country, judges offered $10 prizes for the best acre, the best
stalk, the best half-pound, and the best bale. The best peck of goober peas
won 50 cents. The list of prizes was endless: best wagon, horse collar,
plow, cotton scraper, harrow, straw cutter, ox yoke, ax handle, and on and
on.

CHAPTER SIX

THE MICHIGAN FRONTIER

*No more important and interesting story can be found in
the annals of the human race than that of the settlement
across the North American continent.*

SOLON J. BUCK

When Congress declared Michigan a separate territory in 1805, it was a wilderness inhabited by Indians, a few white traders, and the soldiers at Fort Detroit. The British had occupied Detroit until July 1796, and remained a strong and menacing presence at Amherstburg, Ontario, twenty miles to the south. They maintained forward positions on their side of the mile-wide straits, and the Americans at Fort Detroit could see the Union Jack waving across the water on the palisades.

The problem with having the redcoats as neighbors lay not so much in the danger of a direct attack as in the insidious anti-American propaganda the British spread among the tribes, in order to keep their control over the Great Lakes through Indian surrogates.

As the army captain Josiah Dunham, stationed at Detroit, wrote Superintendent of Indian Affairs William Clark in St. Louis on November 3, 1805: "If the Indian is our enemy, it is the [British] trader who has made him so . . . . they fill their ears with stories that enkindle hatred and disgust." According to Captain Dunham, the British told the Indians, "You well know that your American father never sends you goods. None of his children know how to make blankets."

There was some truth in this statement, since the government factory system adopted by the Americans in 1802 offered goods that were demonstrably inferior to those sold by the British. The small, thin American blankets were half the weight of the British blankets. The calico did not hold together. The springs on the traps broke. American factors complained constantly about the shoddy merchandise, while the British used their superior wares to sway the sympathies of the Sacs and the Foxes.

In 1805, Connecticut-born and Yale-educated William Hull arrived in Detroit as governor of the territory. Finding few settlers and no roads, the fifty-two-year-old hero of the Revolutionary War had little to govern. Worrying about the British seemed to be the principal activity.

On the eve of the War of 1812, Hull was promoted to general and placed in charge of the Michigan army. On August 16, 1812, fearing that his food supplies would run out, he surrendered Fort Detroit to the British without a fight. Hull was court-martialed on charges of cowardice and neglect of duty. He was sentenced to be shot, but President Madison reprieved him because of his age and past service.

Thus, the story of Michigan's settlement really begins after the 1812 war, when Hull was replaced as governor by the energetic Lewis Cass, then only thirty years old. Born in New Hampshire, Cass moved to Ohio and got elected to the assembly in 1806. In 1812, he served as a general in the Ohio militia. A year later he was governor of Michigan, where he remained for eighteen years.

In 1814 the war was over, but the British problem wasn't. British agents warned the Indians that the peace would last only a short time and that they should keep a firm grasp on their tomahawks. Cass concentrated on winning over the Indians. On September 3, 1814, he wrote Secretary of War John Armstrong: "The British medals are solid, ours are hollow. This little difference has injured us more in their opinion than any other occurrence."

In 1814, Michigan Territory (which included Wisconsin) had a white adult male population of about 800, facing 2,000 Indian braves, impoverished by the war. Cass reported to Washington in June 1816 that "for a large portion of the year, they subsist on roots, and at one period of the war they killed their children and ate them."

The one way toward rapid settlement was the sale of public lands. But in 1815 the surveyor general of Ohio, Edward Tiffin, reported that Michigan was marshy and unfit for farming. "It is with the utmost difficulty that a place can be found over which horses can be conveyed," said his report. As a result, the military bounty lands marked out in Michigan were shifted to Missouri. A registrar of public lands and a receiver of public monies waited in Detroit, but they had no business to conduct.

In the meantime, British agitation among the tribes had to be countered. In 1815, a Virginia-born officer with a fine record in the 2nd Regiment of Riflemen, Major William Henry Puthuff, was appointed Indian agent on Mackinac Island, a strategic location that controlled the straits connecting Lake Michigan and Lake Huron.

The British had their headquarters forty miles away on Drummond Island, where they distributed presents and traded in furs, encouraging the Indians to rise up against the Americans. The overzealous Puthuff saw spies everywhere. He suspected Elizabeth Mitchell, the Ottawa wife of a British doctor on Mackinac Island, of holding meetings with the Indians. He warned her in October 1815 to stop "her malicious practices" or stand trial. He also suspected her son Daniel of selling the Indians liquor. Daniel Mitchell observed that "there is more of true liberty at Algiers than at present in Michigan."

On Drummond Island, the British officer in charge, Lieutenant Colonel McDonald of the Glengarry Infantry, informed his superiors that "Puttoff [*sic*], their agent for Indian Affairs, actually out-Herods Herod with his frantic violence. With an equal mixture of impudence and falsehood . . . he mentioned having been told that I warned the Indians to grasp firm their tomahawk and be ready to go with me to attack Mackinac in the night!!!!!!!!!!!!"

As the watchful Puthuff maintained a state of high alert, collecting intelligence on British transgressions wherever he found them, the Indians were caught in the middle. Both sides courted them with speeches while their annuities were reduced or eliminated. When the Menomini chief Tomah visited Puthuff on Mackinac Island in 1817, the army trader James Biddle observed that Tomah and his people needed food.

"Damn that fellow," Puthuff said, "why didn't he ask for it, then?"

"I suppose," replied Biddle, "that being a British Indian, he is too proud."

"Well, let him starve then," Puthuff said.

"If all are to starve who are proud," Biddle said, "God help many that I know of, Major."

Tomah's British allies, however, were cutting their costs to finance the Napoleonic wars. Unable to get help from either side, the Menomini chief drank himself to death the following year.

Puthuff also had to contend with unlicensed traders traveling up and down the shores of the Great Lakes, competing with the factory system and offering better goods and prices. While the trader with the most whiskey carried off the furs, the government factors were forbidden to dole out liquor.

As a first step toward regulation, Congress passed a trade act in 1816 allowing only American citizens to obtain trade licenses for use within the United States. But most of the clerks, boatmen, and interpreters were foreign, and trade could not be carried out without them. So the secretary of the treasury issued orders to license foreigners on the payment of a bond, imposing penalties for bad conduct.

William Puthuff saw the new restrictions as a splendid opportunity. When foreign traders came through in 1816, unlicensed and in violation of an act they did not know existed, Puthuff seized their boats and cargo. Upon a payment of $50, Puthuff issued them a license and returned their property.

In July 1816, Ramsay Crooks, John Jacob Astor's field manager for the American Fur Company, went to Mackinac to discuss the seizures. Puthuff told him that he would brook no exceptions. He had set himself up as a one-man licensing bureau for the entire territory. The traders he licensed roamed the lakes, to the surprise of the factors they were competing with.

John W. Johnson, the factor at Prairie du Chien, wrote Thomas McKenney, the superintendent of Indian affairs in Washington, on January 8, 1817: "How Major Puthuff could license traders for this territory is surprising to all Americans here. The blackest characters were permitted and are now trading with the Indians in every direction . . . each trader pays $50."

In October, the acting secretary of war, George Graham, wrote Puthuff to ask who had authorized his licensing activities. The secretary also wanted to know what his Indian agent was doing with the sums paid to him to return the furs he had seized. The government estimated that over a one-year period Puthuff had received $3,200 from the British house of Berthelot & Company and upward of $4,000 from a number of other firms.

McKenney wrote Graham that "his plea is, so I have been informed, that by demanding $50 per license, he should lessen the number of applications! I make these communications with pain."

Puthuff's defense came on October 15, 1818, in a letter to his boss, McKenney: The law on licensing traders, he said, required so much paperwork that he had been obliged to hire a clerk. "I did feel myself authorized to receive the sum of 50 dollars for each license so issued, but never did enforce its collection. . . . This transaction was on my part fair, open, and candid."

Puthuff's superiors were not convinced and dismissed him as Indian agent in 1819. This highly patriotic officer, full of anti-British ardor, had succumbed to the temptation of easy money. After surrendering his job, Puthuff used the capital he had accumulated to open a store on Mackinac Island, which he operated until his death in 1823.

John C. Calhoun, the new secretary of war, upheld the American-only rule in 1818, writing that "foreigners who are odious to our citizens, on account of their activity or cruelty in the late war, are not to be admitted."

Puthuff may have imagined that being in such a remote outpost placed him beyond the reach of the law. The wilderness encouraged a fiefdom mentality, for the government presence in this vast area made up of Michigan and Wisconsin was skeletal at best. And yet the territory was governed. Counties appeared, and courts and judges administered new laws for a new land.

In 1815, the population of Michigan Territory had reached about 5,000. Detroit had one wharf—known as the "public wharf"—while the rest of the waterfront remained in a state of nature. There were five taverns, four lawyers, two doctors, and one road. A rider brought the mail in once a week.

Distances were great, and a thousand-mile canoe trip was commonplace. In the winter, recalled the early Pontiac settler Matthew White, you could walk from Detroit to Buffalo on the ice over Lake Erie. Once when he was staying in a tavern on the prairie, it was so cold in the morning that he couldn't get his boots on. Another traveler advised him to cut some fat off the breakfast fried pork and baste the heel of his stocking and the inside of his boot. In went his foot and on went his boot.

As for the Indians, they danced their begging dance before White's door morning, noon, and night, and came in without knocking. One day his wife was alone in the cabin, and they barged in, wanting to borrow an ax to cut down a bee tree, which she dared not refuse. Returning the ax, they presented Mrs. White with a piece of honeycomb sandwiched between a couple of wood chips. All the Indians wanted was an equal swap, a pail of cranberries for a pail of potatoes. But if they needed flour or salt, the latter costing $10 a bushel, they still insisted on measure for measure.

Then there were the habitual pioneers, who would not stay put. "It is getting too dense around here," they'd tell White. "There is Jones, settled only 10 miles away, and another family is coming to live on the creek, only five miles away. I will not live where my nearest neighbor can leave home in the morning and come to my house and return home the same night."

There were plenty of characters, all right, thought Matthew White. Like the Yankee clock peddler, who could also doctor sore eyes, remove a corn from a man's foot, or a potato from a choking cow's throat, or a splinter from a horse's hoof. His clocks were always $15, and the terms of payment $5 down. But who could buy a clock when there was never any cash money, what with shinplasters (devalued paper notes) and the scarcity of change, so that a silver dollar had to be cut up into eight triangles, each worth a "bit," which was called "cut money." So of course you had those who clipped it.

In the summer of 1836, Matthew White saw his first friction match when O. D. Swift struck a "lucifer" from between two pieces of sandpaper and produced fire. It was years, however, before the farmers could afford them, and they continued to use a hot coal held in tongs to light their candles. At about the same time, the percussion cap replaced the flintlock in rifles.

Dr. Madison, an army surgeon in Green Bay, Wisconsin, had come out west and left his pregnant wife in Kentucky. When she had a baby in the fall of 1820, he started out on horseback with an escort of three soldiers to call on his wife and child. At Two Rivers, they encountered an Indian named Ketawkah who offered to serve as their guide along the Lake Michigan shore as far as Sheboygan.

Soon they came to a small rise, the doctor riding ahead and Ketawkah following two rods (eleven yards) behind. Without warning, the Indian raised his rifle and shot Dr. Madison, hitting him in the neck and shoulders, and then rode off. Fatally wounded, Dr. Madison fell from his horse, moaning, "Oh, why has that Indian shot me—I never did him or any of them injury. To kill me when I was just returning to my wife and my little child which I had never seen—it is more painful than death."

The soldiers chased the Indian and caught him. Why had he done it? they asked. Ketawkah replied that when he saw the doctor at the top of the hill, he thought "he would fire at him to see how pretty he would fall off his horse."

• •

In 1826, George Moran of Grosse Pointe got caught in a rainstorm and stopped at a wigwam where he asked the Indian and his squaw if he could stay the night. When they said they had neither food nor a bed, he elected to stay anyway. Having been assistant paymaster to the Indians at the Detroit agency, he spoke their lingo, and pretended to be asleep in order to hear what they said about him.

"That man," said the wife, "must be a Yankee, for he is very impolite." But then, taking another look at him, she said, "He must be a Frenchman, for he sleeps just like a dog."

The wife told her husband to say that she was sick, and to ask their guest to get some liquor for them. Which the Indian did, and Moran pulled two bits from his pocket and said, "Here, take this, what fools you are to bother me." Hearing Moran speak their language, the wife said, "There, I told you he was a Frenchman."

She went off with a half-gallon kettle to buy some whiskey at Rapp's tavern, and she must have been thirsty, because the inn was a mile away and it was pouring rain. She returned with a full kettle, and they passed it around until they had emptied it. In the morning, the Indian told Moran about his two wives. The first one, from Drummond Island, was no good, she would not drink at all. This one, a Saginaw, was different. She would drink a quart a day, if he let her have it.

Although Article V of the Northwest Ordinance banned slaves in Michigan Territory, the slavery question had a way of intruding everywhere. In Michigan, a controversy arose over some of the runaway slaves who passed through Detroit on their way to Canada.

In 1828, four slaves fled from Cynthiana, Kentucky, and headed north. Their owners, Mr. Thompson and Dr. Shropshire, retained a professional slave catcher named Ezekiah Hudnall, who followed the fugitives through Ohio and Michigan.

In Detroit on December 14, Hudnall caught two of the slaves, Dan and Ben, and put them in handcuffs. But slave catchers attracted little sympathy in Michigan. When the gazettes reported the capture, the news ignited a public outcry. A Detroit man offered $500 for the slaves' rescue. Across Lake St. Clair in Canada, a group of runaway slaves armed themselves and hired a boat.

Hudnall wanted to get out of Michigan fast with Dan and Ben, but in order to do so he had to go before a justice of the peace and present proof of ownership. The JP would then give him a certificate that had to be signed by the governor or, in his absence, the secretary of state.

Fortunately for Hudnall, the Wayne County sheriff, Thomas C. Sheldon, had a reputation for taking bribes from slave catchers. Obtaining the required certificate on December 16, Hudnall brought it over to the State House and delivered it to Secretary of State James Witherell. Instead of signing it right away, Witherell had his son Benjamin tell Hudnall that he would take his own sweet time to transact business.

Forced to wait, Hudnall took Dan and Ben to Grosse Ile, south of Detroit, and made arrangements for a boat that would carry them across the tip of Lake Erie to Sandusky, Ohio. That night Hudnall went off to play cards, leaving the runaways in the care of a man he had hired. The man, who was after the reward, loosened the slaves' handcuffs and let them flee.

Learning of the runaways' escape, Kentucky Senator Richard M. Johnson wrote to Witherell, charging official dereliction. In his reply on April 9, 1829, James Witherell wrote that "the people of Michigan, aware of their obligations to their fellow citizens of Kentucky, interpose no obstacles to the removal of fugitive slaves, but are desirous that agents, claiming slaves for their owners, should furnish well authenticated evidence of their agency, as kidnaping for the New Orleans market has been often attempted." One can see the sides already forming for the conflict still thirty years away.

In 1831, Alexis de Tocqueville and a companion visited Pontiac, "which in 20 years perhaps will be a town." They asked a tavern keeper the way to Saginaw, and he was astonished that they wanted to go that far north, saying: "Do you not know that Saginaw is the last inhabited point this side of the Pacific Ocean? From here to Saginaw, one finds only wilderness and unbroken solitude."

In Saginaw, on the river of the same name about fifteen miles from Lake Huron, a town had grown up around an abandoned fort. A specter haunted the settlers there, a threat worse than Indians, wild animals, or hailstones: blackbirds. Clouds of them lifted up from the marshes, devastating their crops.

Joseph Busby, a town resident, recalled: "Day after day, from daylight until dark, I had to run up and down until I was as wet with dew as if I had been swimming in the river, firing and hallooing at them . . . but on they came, one flock after another. . . . We would take an empty barrel and beat it with a stick, and if we could keep them on the wing they would pass over to the wild rice fields."

It got so bad that in 1835 the Saginaw Board of Supervisors put a bounty of two cents on each blackbird head. Hunters had to present the heads to a justice of the peace, who would then destroy them and issue a county order, which you could take to the store and get 50 cents on the dollar in goods.

There was one particular JP who got all the blackbird business. Instead of destroying the heads, he threw them into his pigpen for his hogs to eat. Then some of the boys would distract the JP by telling him that the major wanted to see him to take a smile (a drink), which he had never been known to refuse. While he was gone, the boys climbed into the pen and repossessed the heads, which they would then sell him a second time. Their self-exoneration consisted in telling themselves that since county orders were worth only 50 cents on the dollar they had to sell each head twice for full payment.

When Jesse Turner arrived in Kalamazoo in 1832, tall hazel bush covered the flats around Arcadia Creek. One day he was standing in front of the town clerk's office when he heard whooping down the trail and saw an Indian running and jumping. The friend he was with had been bitten by a massasauga (a brown and white rattlesnake), and he wanted some whiskey to make him strong, so he could run to Grand Prairie for weeds to cure his friend. Giving him the whiskey, Turner and some other men promised him more if he came back and showed them the weeds, which he did, pounding them into a poultice, and the bitten Indian got well.

The creek bottoms and marshes were full of 'saugas, and Turner killed hundreds with his Jacob's staff while out surveying mill sites. Far from being bloodthirsty savages, the Indians wouldn't kill wolves or 'saugas except in self-defense. But there were some lazy, worthless settlers around who would go looking for Indian canoes to split up, all for pure mischief. And when the Indians trapped for muskrat, they'd steal their traps. The Indian the white man despised was the Indian the white man made.

In 1832, Henry Raymond was town clerk in a hamlet in Wayne County, about ten miles outside Detroit. A fellow came in and asked for a marriage license. Henry didn't have any and admitted that he didn't know what the law required.

"Oh, never mind that," the fellow said. "You know that here in the woods, if we want a thing and haven't got it, we make it." So they put their heads together and drafted the license, which said in part: "Whereas one Joseph Streight proposed to marry one Betsy Bates, and the said people having sworn by the Holy St. John and the Big Horn Spoon there is no legal impediment to the contrary . . . we do pronounce you man and wife."

James Lawrence was twenty-one when he came to the wilderness ten miles south of Coldwater, Michigan, just over the Indiana border, in December 1835. With his father, he cut "the first tree for their first house." In one day, they built a frame twelve feet square, and that night they had a house twelve logs high. Two "land lookers" who had followed their tracks turned up, carrying the ham of a buck one of them had shot. Over a dinner of roasted venison, the four men talked game and range and quarter section.

The visitors left the next morning to seek a home. They soon found one, for there were a million acres lying about unclaimed. Eighty of them could be had by any of Uncle Sam's needy children, provided he had $100 to pay for same.

James and his father went hunting for a shingle tree, but the timber was frozen rock-hard, and they stood the bolts around the fire to take out the frost. Their homemade bread was as tough as their new oak shingles. An Indian came around and they gave him some, and all he said was "No good bret." He picked up his rifle and left. In a couple of hours, he reappeared, dragging the carcasses of two deer, which he drew over the snow as smoothly as if they had been oiled.

Then Mr. Quinn arrived from Ohio with his large family and a few carpenter's tools, and made chairs and spinning wheels and half-bushel measures. He chewed a threepenny paper of "fine cut," cramming his mouth full of the stuff and rolling it around for an hour and then laying it on a stump where he happened to be working. If his supply ran out, he would give his quids a second grinding. His brother once thought he saw a turkey sitting on a log, but it was only Ira's reserve quid of tobacco.

Mr. Quinn's brother-in-law, Monlux, arrived and introduced himself by saying, "I was born in Virginia, the home of presidents." Monlux asserted that what he lacked in "glittering dust" he made up in wealth of family, though he had dust enough to buy eighty acres.

At the first township meeting, Monlux was elected constable and treasurer. He was, however, in the habit of making mysterious disappearances that lasted for several days. One day when James Lawrence went to Monlux's house to pay his taxes, his wife answered the door and said he'd been gone since Monday. She was worried that he might be in the "plenipotentiary."

Monlux and his wife had a son named George Washington, known as Wash, though Unwashed was more like it. Once he was sitting on the board that covered the trough where the buckwheat was rising. The board slipped, and his sister sang out, "Ma, Wash has sot down in the batter." Ma seized Wash by the nape of the neck, kicked him where the batter clung to his person, and whisked him outside. "Stay there," she told him, "till you can larn better'n to set your ass down in the cakes."

The Lawrences had another neighbor, Elmer Bacon, whose wife had fits. He'd race to the doctor five miles away, but by the time they got to her she was all right. When Elmer objected that he was paying the doctor for nothing, she retorted, "Elmer Bacon, 'taint no use talkin', I *can* have fits and I *will* have fits."

After house building, the Lawrences had to cut brush, pile and burn logs, and hold a breaker drawn by seven yoke of oxen. You had to decide real quick on which side of a big oak root to drive the plow. Nor was harrowing after breaking any holiday affair.

As James Lawrence learned from hard experience, the rule for planting corn was:

> *One for the blackbird, one for the crow,*
> *One for the cutworm, and three to grow.*

Michigan started picking up, thanks partly to the opening in 1825 of the Erie Canal, a big ditch that crossed the Empire State and linked the

Great Lakes with the Atlantic Ocean. The territory also attracted quite a few settlers from the south who objected to slavery. By 1835, with the population at 87,000, Michigan stood poised for statehood.

The last hurdle to overcome was the boundary dispute with the State of Ohio over a six-and-a-half-mile-wide strip that included the city of Toledo. Tempers flared, and brawls roiled the border. The statehood process could not be pursued until the Toledo question was solved.

Eighteen thirty-six was an election year. Ohio had two senators and nineteen representatives in Congress, while Michigan had one territorial delegate who could not vote. Martin Van Buren, the Democratic presidential candidate, needed the Ohio vote. A trade-off was proposed in exchange for its support: Ohio would get the Toledo strip, and Michigan would get the Upper Peninsula, lopped off from Wisconsin.

Martin Van Buren carried Ohio and was elected in November, though the Michigan constitutional convention still had to ratify the swap. In the debate in Ann Arbor that December, one delegate said that the Upper Peninsula "isn't worth six cents," while another called the offer "more than princely." Desiring statehood, the convention finally accepted the offer and Michigan was admitted into the Union in 1837, paired with the slave state of Arkansas. Shorn of the Toledo strip, it gained the Upper Peninsula, with its iron and copper mines, washed by Lake Superior to the north and Lake Michigan to the south.

By 1850, western Michigan was seeing settlers. In Oceana County, right on the lake, eight families had built homes. One day a man named Grant turned up in the woods, shot dead. A coroner's jury found that he had been murdered. Someone remembered that one of Grant's neighbors, a widower, had let drop the remark that "if I had such a wife as Mrs. Grant I would be a happy man." On the strength of this hearsay, the man was arrested, and got himself a lawyer, whom he paid in maple sugar, and who had him released for lack of evidence.

In another case, the Oceana magistrate issued a warrant for a man in these words: "Bring him to me forthwith, damn him." A constable of Germanic origin went to fetch the prisoner and escort him ten miles to the magistrate's bench, but the man refused to walk. There came along a loaded team, which the constable impressed into service, addressing the driver thus: "Rufe, you know I'm constable. Vell, I command you by the name of dis state Michigan dat you load off dem shingle-bolts so quick as you can, and carry dis damn ugly cuss to squire Randall's office, so quick dem horses can go dere." Slowly, and sometimes in broken English, law and order came to Michigan.

CHAPTER SEVEN

THE WISCONSIN FRONTIER

*Wisconsin is a young buffalo, and though in a minority,
he roams over his beautiful prairies and reclines in his
pleasant groves with all the buoyant feelings of an
American freeman.*

EARLY SETTLER

A s the territories were formed, offices had to be filled, the governors
often having to take whomever they could get. Not many graduates
of eastern universities followed career paths into the Michigan wil-

The New York Public Library
Cassville, on the east bank of the Mississippi about thirty miles
above Dubuque, was first settled by the Fox Indians. French traders built huts there, and permanent settlers began to arrive in 1827.
The simple house with brick chimneys, the bluffs rising behind
them, the men working on their boat, are in the purest "American
pastoral" style.

115

derness. The qualification for posts like sheriff and justice of the peace was simply the ability to read and write, not necessarily in English.

In 1803, when Wisconsin and Michigan still made up part of Indiana Territory, Governor William Henry Harrison commissioned a French-Canadian Indian trader named Charles Réaume justice of the peace in Green Bay. For fifteen years, this crusty Frenchman, who spoke some English but knew nothing of the law, served as the sole representative of civilian authority in Wisconsin.

Smitten with his own importance, Réaume usually appeared in court wearing a cocked hat and a scarlet coat faced with white silk, its spangled buttons gleaming. Presiding so far from the seat of territorial authority, his authority was absolute. It was pointless to file an appeal.

Wisconsin was then populated with French-Canadian traders married to squaws, so that Réaume dealt mainly with his own people. He usually sided with the traders, and some said that the most reliable witness was a bottle of brandy. This surprise witness having been called by the losing party in a debt case, a rehearing was granted and the judgment was reversed.

In those days, traders could rent a squaw for a designated period of time. Contracts were drawn up that included clauses for good treatment and fidelity. Many of the cases that Réaume heard had to do with breaches of these agreements. When one trader raped a half-breed girl, Réaume sternly ordered him to replace the frock he had torn in the scuffle with a new one. Usually, however, the judge's sentences involved some form of labor on his own farm, such as ten days of ploughing, or cutting and splitting so many rails.

Réaume based his judgments on the precedents he himself had set in other cases. When the trader James Lockwood went to court seeking damages against one of his boatmen who had deserted his post, Réaume declared: "I'll make . . . de man . . . go back . . . to his duty."

"But is there any law on this?" Lockwood asked.

"De law is," Réaume said, "we are . . . accustomed . . . to make . . . de man . . . go back . . . to dere bourgeois" (the French-Canadian term for employer).

In Green Bay, Réaume tried a number of cases in which soldiers had run up debts with traders. Congress had passed a law that "no person who has been enlisted as a soldier shall be liable to arrest or imprisonment for any debt contracted during the term of his enlistment," but Réaume paid no attention to it.

When a soldier owing money was brought to court, Réaume ordered him jailed. "But I don't understand," the soldier said. "You go . . . to de jail . . . and stay dere . . . until you pay . . . de debt," Réaume said, "and you will . . . unduhstand . . . very well."

American soldiers started arriving in Green Bay in 1816, and also established Fort Crawford at Prairie du Chien, at the juncture of the Wisconsin River and the Mississippi. The fort commander, Colonel Talbot

Chambers, showed that American justice could be as arbitrary as the idiosyncratic French variety. Chambers treated the French inhabitants like a conquered people. When the trader Charles Menard was arrested for selling whiskey to the soldiers, Chambers had him whipped and marched through the streets with a bottle hung around his neck, while the army band played "The Rogue's March." Eventually, Chambers was court-martialed and cashiered for cutting his men's ears off as punishment.

Orphaned at the age of ten, Ebenezer Childs grew up in Barre, Massachusetts, about fifteen miles from Worcester. In 1820, at the age of nineteen, he was working in construction at 50 cents a day. One morning the town collector came to see him and told him to pay the so-called "minister" tax of $1.75. For Childs, this amounted to more than three days' wages, which seemed like a lot to hand over to a man who performed no manual labor. Childs insisted he had no money. The collector replied, "Pay or go to jail."

Childs determined to leave the state of Massachusetts and its extortionate laws. That Sunday he crammed his belongings into a pair of saddlebags and rode off on his pony. Taking obscure side roads, he slipped quietly past the church, as cautiously as if he'd stolen a sheep.

As it was, he caught the attention of a tithing man on horseback (since it was a violation to travel on the Sabbath), and the long-spliced Yankee chased the truant all the way into New York State.

Childs made his way to Buffalo and Detroit, finally arriving that summer in Green Bay, where he opened a store. He wasn't supposed to sell whiskey to the soldiers, but when their wives came in to buy sugar, they brought two-quart canteens, which Childs filled, packing the sugar on top.

Childs built a sawmill, which upset the Indians, who trooped to his cabin thirty-strong and looked in the window. "Dogs peep in at windows," he told them, "men come boldly through the door." In they streamed, and accused him of cutting their timber and interfering with their fishing by choking up the river with his logs. They must have their pay, they said. Childs agreed to keep them supplied with food, and both his sawmill and his store flourished. Later he went into the fur trade.

In 1828, the army raised Fort Winnebago at the portage from the Fox River to the Wisconsin by floating logs down the Wisconsin. An Indian village was situated eight miles away. Mail arrived on horseback from Green Bay, 120 miles away. The only stopover between Green Bay and the fort was Rowan's Inn, offering one room to sleep in next to the hogs.

When the army surgeon Dr. Worrel stayed over, Mrs. Rowan told him, "I am dreadful glad you are a doctor, for my children are most rotten with the itch." While cooking the doctor's dinner, she rested a dish of potatoes on the hearth, and her pet pig stuck his nose in it. "Madam," Dr. Worrel said, "I would like to be served before the pig.'

Fort Winnebago created jobs. Twenty-year-old Alexis Clermont, for instance, furnished hay for the horses, earning 75 cents a day and board. Next he worked on the crew of a boat, conveying trade goods from Green Bay to the fort. After that he ran the mail on foot from Green Bay to Chicago, taking Indian trails and traveling with an Oneida brave to split the sixty-pound load.

For food during the two-week trip, they carried two shot bags of parched corn, one hulled, the other ground. This was to fall back on, for they relied mainly on game. They stopped wherever darkness overtook them and slept in the woods, wrapped in blankets. Upon arriving in Chicago, then a hamlet of ten houses, they stayed the night before starting back. The pay was $60 per trip for the both of them.

Caught in a blizzard in March 1839, Alexis became snow-blind and got lost. He was saved by some Indians hauling handmade shingles to Fond du Lac, at the southern tip of Lake Winnebago. They put him on the right track, and he stumbled on a house where a woman lived by herself. Cold and hungry, he asked for breakfast, explaining that he was the mail carrier and would pay her on the way back. "We don't trust," she said.

He went to the next house, also occupied by a woman alone. This time he didn't tell her he was broke. She not only cooked him a meal but mended one of his moccasins. When he finally admitted that he couldn't pay, her eyes blazed and she whacked him with a broomstick. Some time later, he ran into her in a bowling alley in Green Bay, and she demanded 50 cents, half for the breakfast and half for the broken broomstick. Then the steamboats came, and he lost the job.

In 1836, Wisconsin had 11,000 white inhabitants. That year it became the first new territory in a dozen years when Congress sliced it off from Michigan as the last piece of the old Northwest. The Wisconsin Organic Act offered a model for the creation of most of the other trans-Mississippi territories.

During these territorial interludes, the big job was obtaining land cessions from the Indians so that settlers could move in. In the spring of 1836, Lieutenant Alexander S. Howe embarked on a mission to the tribes around Lake Mendota (at today's Madison). He reported on March 25 to Major John Green, commander of Fort Winnebago, that the Indians were in a miserable state because they pawned everything they had to the traders for whiskey. "The Indian gets drunk, broods over his wrongs, and determined to have satisfaction, steals an equivalent from somebody else—and thus commence almost all Indian disturbances."

Major Green called the Winnebagos to council on November 1, to ask them whether they wanted their annuities paid to the chiefs or the families. Dandy, the Indian spokesman, said that the families should receive the money, the implication being that if it was paid to the chiefs they would take the lion's share.

As the next order of business, Major Green recited a list of claims the traders had against the Indians. Each claim inspired an imaginative excuse from Dandy.

About a destroyed canoe: "There was a canoe, but the wind blew it to pieces."

On the horse unpaid for: "It was a young colt, and we won't pay for it."

The story behind the stolen whiskey: "Mr. Jackson shut up a squaw in his store and she did it."

There was really no point in enumerating the claims, thought Major Green, since the Indians always found a reason not to pay them. The major figured that the tribes should have been doing fairly well, since the annuity amounted to $7,000 worth of goods. But the disheartened Indians were bartering it all away for whiskey.

In 1837, Governor Henry Dodge came to Portage to buy the Winnebago lands. Seeing which way the wind was blowing, one of the chiefs, Yellow Thunder, walked into the land office and asked if Indians were allowed to enter. On hearing that they were, he immediately secured forty acres and settled on them, declaring that he would live like a white man.

Charles Cole observed on his arrival in Sheboygan in 1836 that everyone had caught the real estate bug. A Negro rode on a horse through town, ringing a bell and crying, "Now is the time to make your fortune, now's your time . . ." Cole acquired three lots on the river, opened a dry-goods store, and became the town's first postmaster.

In the winter, when no supplies came in, he took a yoke of oxen and a sled and set out for Milwaukee to buy corn, oats, flour, and other groceries from the trader there, Solomon Juneau. One night, Cole was settling down under the stars on his way back when a noise disturbed his sleep. The oxen had broken into the provisions and were filling themselves with corn.

Cole yoked them up at once and attached them to the sled, hoping that by exercising them briskly he could save their lives. They were bloated and overgorged, and one keeled over and died. Hungry Indians, who were all about, took the dead ox and opened him up, removing from his entrails all the undigested corn.

The winters came hard then. Cole once cut the hoops and staves off a barrel of condemned flour that was hard as a rock, pounded it up with a hatchet, and made it into bread.

In 1836 the territory was organized into three judicial districts. Judge William C. Frazier appeared in Milwaukee in June 1837, and his first case was a judgment for debt. The defendant conceded his obligation, but allowed that he was unable to pay it.

"What is your occupation?" Judge Frazier asked.

"Fisherman," the man replied.

"Can you pay in fish?" inquired the judge.

"I don't know but that I could," the man said, "if I had time to catch them."

"You must pay in good fish, we want no stinking fish," Judge Frazier concluded, as he entered a judgment payable in fish, and granted the defendant a twelve-month stay of execution.

Judge Frazier shuttled between the courts of Milwaukee and those of Green Bay, 120 miles apart. In Green Bay, where there was no jail, he sentenced a man to be "banished to the Turkey River." Frazier traveled by steamboat, and since he usually arrived in Milwaukee dead drunk, it became customary to lower him by tackle into a rowboat and paddle him to the landing at Walker's Point. The judiciary had not really changed that much since the days of Judge Réaume.

When Elijah Keyes was a boy growing up in Vermont, his father one day took out an old-fashioned atlas and pointed to the territory west of Lake Michigan. "Boys," he cried, "there's where we want to go, plenty of water-power and timber." They got to Milwaukee in 1837 and headed inland, unable to find even an Indian trail. Traveling fifty miles west to Watertown and ten miles south to Lake Mills, they discovered a floorless shanty roofed with a haystack.

If they had known how hard the life would be, Elijah later reflected, they would have stayed home. That first winter the family ran out of food. Elijah's father, Joseph, sat with his head in his hands, murmuring to his wife, "Olive, I know not where we are to get provisions to live upon." Finally, he left to borrow a few pounds of flour from a neighbor. By the time he got back, night had fallen.

Joseph came in, holding a little bundle in his hands, and said, "Olive, we are ruined." His horse had stumbled and thrown him along with the flour he was carrying into the mud, and the flour was soaked through. But his wife said maybe it wasn't so bad. Opening the bag, she removed the soggy top layer, mixed with mud and water. Underneath was good dry flour.

Their situation improved when the pioneer family learned how to fish, for the stream bottom was literally covered with fish so large you could spear them with a pitchfork. Elijah's father cheered up, surmising, "The indications are that the supply will be fully equal to the demand." They ate fish for breakfast, dinner, and supper. They also got hold of some Hoosier hogs, whose snouts were so long they could reach through fences and root up the third row of potatoes. And yet, in this land of plenty, the unspoken commandment was "This much you can have and no more."

Sometimes it seemed as though food preserved life only for danger to extinguish it. One day Elijah's mother sent the ten-year-old on his pony to a neighbor a mile and a half away for tea and coffee. On the way back, the boy rode right into a dozen Indians in war paint. Half in jest, they made as if to pull him off, saying it was their pony and then allowing him to break away. But as the boy fled, one Indian gave chase until he came up alongside him. He pointed his gun, and the powder flashed in the pan. But there was no ball in the barrel.

In 1806, the United States imported 5 million pounds of lead. In 1842, it exported 14 million. The nation owed its change in status to the lead mines of southern Wisconsin. The southwest corner where Wisconsin touched Iowa and Illinois had been a plenteous resource ever since Julien Dubuque obtained a grant from the Sacs and the Foxes in 1788 "to work the lead mines tranquilly and without any prejudice to his labors."

The most pliable but the least ductile of metals, lead was used by soldiers for bullets and by fishermen for plummets to sink their bait. Builders employed it to frame windowpanes and tighten roof joints and typesetters to make type. Lead combined with tin produced pewter dishes, and it made paint nice and thick.

In 1822, Congress began granting three- and five-year leases on Wisconsin mineral land. The policy for private mining in public areas had been formulated on November 8, 1807, by President Jefferson. In a letter to his secretary of the treasury, Albert Gallatin, he wrote, "I verily believe that leasing will be far the best for the United States . . . one article of it should be that the rent shall be paid in metal, not mineral, so that we may have nothing to do with works which will always be mismanaged and reduce our concern to a simple rent."

One beneficiary of Jefferson's policy was Moses Meeker. Born in New Jersey in 1790, Meeker moved to Cincinnati in 1817 and tried his hand at several businesses. In 1822, he read a notice in the paper announcing that President James Monroe proposed to lease half sections (320 acres) of land on the upper Mississippi where the lead mines were. Interested parties had to post a $10,000 bond and gain the approval of a District Court judge. In addition, the government claimed 10 percent of the lead that was mined.

Having read numerous articles on the richness of the mines, Meeker sent in his bond. Then he recruited a crew of nineteen in Ohio, whom he brought to the mines by flatboat. Catching sight of a steamer loaded with government stores on the Ohio, he shouted to the captain, "Can you take us in tow?" "I cannot," the captain replied; "it is hard work to stem the current."

Meeker and his men arrived on the Fever River on June 1, 1823, and continued upriver thirty miles to a place called Mineral Point. His horses and oxen were on their way, overland via Springfield and Peoria. He asked John Miller, a miner from Hannibal, Missouri, if he could hire some oxen until his arrived, and Miller replied, "You are too much of a Yankee for this country. You cannot hire them, but you can take them as long as you like, and if you want to insult me, you could not do better than by offering to pay for them."

The men lived on their boats for the better part of a year while they built the cabins, furnaces, and stables. Besides Meeker's crew and their families, adding up to 43 persons, only 30 other whites lived in the area.

But some 500 Indians also made their homes there. Though the braves did not work, the squaws proved industrious miners. Their tools consisted of a hoe, an ax, and a crowbar flattened at one end to remove the rocks. Their mode of blasting was to find dry wood and kindle a fire along the rock they wished to break. When the rock was hot enough, they poured cold water over it, producing cracks they pried open. They drew up many tons of mineral dirt with birch-bark baskets attached to rawhide ropes.

In those early days on the Fever River, Indian and white technologies overlapped. Meeker did his smelting in log and ash furnaces, constructed on the riverbank or along the side of a hill. The "eyes" or holes of the furnace received 3,000 to 4,000 pounds of mineral at a time. The fire was kindled, and the molten lead flowed down the sloping flagstone hearth into a basin in front of the furnace.

One day three of Meeker's men got drunk and molested some women in an Indian village. When a brave advanced on them with his gun to drive them away, they snatched the gun and broke it over his shoulders. Then they rushed back to camp shouting "To arms" and calling for an attack on the Indians.

Meeker, who kept the guns locked in a rack, fired on the three drunks. Then, at a powwow with Chief Cattue and 150 Indians, he offered damages in the form of flour, pork, and tobacco, as well as a new gun. The chief wanted him to add a keg of whiskey, but Meeker refused, saying that whiskey had been the cause of the fracas and would only add more mischief. Meeker and the council passed around the pipe and Cattue declared the hatchet buried.

The first winter the miners ran short of food and had to eat spoiled flour and condemned pork. Some of Meeker's men came down with scurvy. The cooks indicated mealtime by hoisting a rag on an upright pole, so that Mineral Point became known as "Shake-Rags."

Endurance paid off. When the word got out that Meeker had smelted 170,000 pounds of lead in his first year, miners started flocking to Shake-Rags. In no time, the rolling prairie, extending for thirty miles, was covered with long-haired miners wearing flannel shirts and heavy boots, accompanied by their corncob-smoking wives.

Soon the creak of windlasses was heard in the land. Once the well-like shaft was dug, the miners positioned a two-handled windlass on posts straddling the hole, using a rope to haul the mineral up through the timbered shaft. Candles set in gobs of clay stuck to the sides of the shaft. After twenty-four hours in the roaring furnace, the molten lead was ladled with an iron dipper into the molds. The "pigs," oblong blocks weighing seventy-five pounds, were stacked like cords of firewood.

Mineral Point developed into the boomtown of early Wisconsin. In 1834, seventeen-year-old Theodore Rolfe journeyed there from Switzerland with his brother Frank and his widowed mother. As it was customary to do, they squatted on some farmland. The following year they heard that preemption rights for their plot were being offered at the Mineral Point land office.

In September 1835, Rolfe rode through the forest carrying the family money in his saddlebags. The leaves were turning, and the vivid colors lifted his spirits. Then Mineral Point's stripped hills came into view, surrounded by piles of dirt and rocks.

Theodore Rolfe knew nothing about land laws, but the helpful registrar, Major John P. Sheldon, explained that he qualified for several "floats." By act of Congress, when two or more parties entitled to preemption rights settled on the same quarter section (160 acres), one party could enter that quarter section, while the other parties could choose unclaimed quarter sections in the same land district, i.e., "floats." Because Theodore had a widowed mother and a brother, the family could claim two floats, which could be used for mill rights or town plats.

Theodore stopped off at Mrs. John Hood's tavern. The place was jumping with land speculators, and he easily sold the floats for $10 each. Now the Rolfes had a farm of their own, and a new set of problems, for that winter, prairie fires burned their stacks of hay and they couldn't feed their stock.

Sick of farming, Theodore bought a wagonload of groceries in New Orleans and shipped them to Mineral Point. At first, the shipping expenses were so high he didn't make a dime, but he persisted, and after a while did well enough to build a brick store.

Meanwhile, the lead furnaces operated around the clock, providing plenty of jobs, and the miners had money to spend. Many of them were Cornishmen, hardened in the mines of England. They didn't like to be paid in paper money—they found metal, they said, and wanted metal back. Two brothers from Galena, Henry and Nathan Corwith, bought a supply of easily negotiable English sovereigns in New York at $4.80 each, which they sold to the mining operators at $4.90. The operators counted the miners' salaries out in sovereigns at $5.00 each. In many a miner's cabin, there was an old stocking under the mattress filled with sovereigns.

In 1840, President Van Buren removed John P. Sheldon from office on charges that the major was using his friends to buy mineral lands that had been withheld from public sale. Before entering land, the buyer had to swear that he did not know it to contain minerals. Sheldon had his friends led blindfold over land to be entered so that they could rightly swear that they had seen no minerals.

To put an end to the widespread fraud and litigation that resulted from claim jumping, Washington finally decided to allow settlers to buy mineral land. Then Mineral Point lost out as territorial capital to Madison, and soon a $140,000 neoclassical dome appeared in the middle of the Wisconsin plain.

The mining country thereafter became quiet and orderly, except for the occasional crime. In 1843, William Coffee was sentenced to hang for stabbing a man to death at a housewarming in White Oak Springs. There wasn't much in the way of recreation then, and on the day of the hanging, sightseers began to arrive at dawn, by wagon, on horseback, and on foot, old and young, men and women, Theodore Rolfe among them. Spectators camped on the hillside, broke open food hampers, and turned the hanging into a holiday.

The push for statehood began in the 1840s. At that time, the territory was inundated with the paper currency called shinplasters, which had no capital to back them. The rates changed so fast you'd fall asleep with $1,000 and wake up penniless. Thus, the people of western Wisconsin insisted on an article in the state constitution that prohibited paper money and recognized only gold and silver as legal tender. The result was that the voters rejected the constitution. But another one, omitting the gold and silver article, passed shortly after, and in 1848 Wisconsin became a state. Five years later Theodore Rolfe was appointed receiver of the land office in La Crosse, to the west and up the Mississippi from Mineral Point.

CHAPTER EIGHT

THE IOWA FRONTIER

How many men since coveted after the earth, that many
hundreds, nay thousands of acres, have been engrossed
by one man, and they that profess themselves Christians,
have foresaken churches and ordinances, and all for land
and elbow-room enough in the world.

INCREASE MATHER

No state embodied the kaleidoscopic nature of territorial development better than Iowa. Until 1812 it was part of Louisiana Territory, the northern half of the Louisiana Purchase. From 1813 until
1821, it was swallowed up by Missouri Territory. Once Missouri was a
state, Iowa-to-be spent thirteen years as "unorganized territory," meaning
that it had no government to speak of. In 1834, this patient patch of earth
was attached to Michigan Territory, and in 1836 to Wisconsin Territory.
Finally in 1838, with a population of 22,859, Iowa attained status as its
own territory, an area that included Minnesota. Eight years later, paired
with the slave state of Florida under the Missouri Compromise, Iowa became the first free state to be carved out of land acquired through the
Louisiana Purchase.

Settlers did their best to adapt to this revolving status. In 1832, during
the years of Iowa's unattachment, William Ross and Matilda Maryan of
Burlington wanted to get married. But there was no justice of the peace.
So they invited along some friends and paddled across the Mississippi in a
flatboat to the Illinois side. There they waited while their friends ventured
into the interior to hunt down an official who had the authority to perform
marriages. Finding one in Monmouth, they brought him back to the river's
edge, where he pronounced William and Matilda man and wife.

In lieu of government, Iowa had troops. In 1833, when squatters
moved west of Burlington, ahead of the land cession treaties, troops from
Rock Island, Illinois, led by Jefferson Davis, were ordered to dislodge them
and burn down their cabins. After their defeat in the Black Hawk War,
however, the Indians had no choice. Negotiations were first conducted
under a big tent at the site of today's Davenport, where the Indians gave
up a strip of land fifty miles wide on the Iowa side of the Mississippi.
Between 1832 and 1851, they sold away all of Iowa for less than 10 cents
an acre.

• •

By 1834, when Iowa was attached to Michigan Territory, circuit-riding judges started making their rounds. That year the celebrated Judge Lynch convened his court outside the blacksmith shop in Dubuque. A discharged soldier, William Hoffman, still in uniform, had been charged with stealing a $20 banknote from his friend and fellow soldier, the Irishman McMurty.

According to the trial testimony, McMurty had come to Dubuque to see his old friend Willy. He told his pal: "Ye's out of the sarvice longer than meself, an' better acquainted with the tricks of the world, do ye be takin' me money and kape it till I gits sober."

Hoffman explained to the court: "I admit he gave me money, and at his request I returned it to him soon after."

"This will not do, old fellow," said Judge Lynch. "You can't pay the 'old soger' here. You must give up the money or take 50 lashes."

A crowd had collected, and people shouted, "Give him a hundred . . . tar and feather him."

"I have not the money," Hoffman insisted. "I am innocent of the charge."

"Give it to him raw if he doesn't fork over," someone yelled.

The prisoner was stripped and dragged to a rise where each of his hands was lashed to the rear wheel of a wagon. A muscular fellow was picked to do the whipping, in ten sets of five. After each set the mob cried, "Score home another five!"

Blood dripped off Hoffman's back. "I am an American soldier," he pleaded, "a native of Kentucky. I beat the drum at Tallahassee and on my breast I carry scars from Bad Axe" (the Wisconsin battle of the Black Hawk War).

At that moment, a tall, rawboned man wearing a white slouch hat and a buckskin shirt pushed through the crowd. Hanging from his belt were a flintlock pistol and a sheath knife. "I say, stranger," the man said. "I mean you with the whip. Suppose you stay your hand till we get better acquainted. . . . I say, if there is any man in this crowd from old Kentuck and ain't ashamed to say so, let him show his hand."

No one raised his hand.

"Makes no difference," the man in the white hat went on. "I am from those parts, and that's sufficient."

Addressing the prisoner, the Kentuckian said, "If you've been guilty of a mean act, acknowledge the corn, and trail from these parts; but if you're not guilty, I'll back you up."

McMurty, the accuser, burst out: "Be the powers that made me, Willy, it's innocent ye are, do yees be batin' him no more, for sure it's a drunken baste that I am not to be rememberin' that he gave it back to me."

Not only was this frontier justice, it exemplified regional solidarity. One Kentuckian strode confidently to the defense of another, in the belief that no Kentuckian would do a low think like stealing money from a friend.

•   •

Along with circuit-riding judges, Iowa had its circuit-riding ministers. In 1840, at Burke's Settlement on the Cedar River, Mr. Morrison, the minister, showed up one afternoon with his wife to officiate at a wedding. Mrs. Burke's son Sam announced their arrival in no uncertain terms.

"Marm! Marm! Here's the elder and his woman. They're nothin' but common folks. She's got a man's hat on and a turkey wing in front of it; his nose is just like dad's, crooked as a cow-horn squash."

From inside the cabin, Mrs. Burke called; "Sam, you run out and grab that rooster, and I'll slap him into the pot. Sal, you quit that churnin' and sweep the floor. Kick that corn-dodger under the bed. Bill, you wipe the tallow out of the chair for the minister's wife, and be spry about it."

Mrs. Burke hurried out of the kitchen in a calico dress, her feet bare, wiping her face with her apron: "How d'ye do, Marm, must excuse my head—hain't had no chance to comb it since last week. Work must be did, you know. Powerful sharp air, hain't it? Shoo there Bill, drive that turkey out of the bread trough. Sal, take the lady's things. Set right up to the fire, Marm. Hands cold? Well, just run 'em in Bill's hair—we kept it long a purpose."

Soon the rooster was cooking in a four-quart kettle hung over the fire. Sal returned to her churn, but upset it, and buttermilk spilled on the floor. "There, Sal," her mother said, "do try to churn a little more keerful. If you are going to be spliced ter-morrow, you needn't run crazy about it."

"I advise you to dry up," replied the bride-to-be, thumping away at the churn.

After supper, when Mrs. Morrison was ready to retire, Mrs. Burke lit a pitch knot and led the way up a ladder into the sleeping loft. "Come on, don't be afraid," she said. "Look out for the loose boards, and mind or you'll smash your brains out against that beam. Take care of the hole where the chimney comes thru." Mr. and Mrs. Morrison spent the night in the loft with four children, all snorers.

Lem Lord, the groom, arrived the next morning, dressed in his grandfather's blue suit, his hair greased with tallow. Clapping Mr. Morrison on the back, he cried, "Now, elder, dive ahead! I want it done up nice. I'm able to pay for the job, do ye hear? Come, father, trot out your gal."

Lem Lord and Sally Burke stood before the minister and made the customary promises. When Mr. Morrison asked, "Will you have this woman?" Lem Lord interrupted and said, "What else did I come here for?"

When Sal's turn came, she answered, "Yaaasss, if ye must know." She then threw her arms around his neck and gave him a kiss that made the windows clatter.

"Now, elder," Lem asked, "what is the damages? Don't be afraid to speak."

"Whatever you please," Mr. Morrison said.

Lem produced a piece of mangy fur. "There," he said, "there's a muskrat's skin, and out in the shed is two heads of cabbage, and you're welcome to the hull of it."

• •

A land rush followed Iowa's rise into the territorial category in 1838. A land office opened in Burlington, and at every point on the Mississippi that had a ferry, wagons were crossing. "Everybody speculating," an eastern visitor reported in a letter home, "nobody raising."

Except for preemption, the land was for sale at auctions. Moneylenders appeared, offering cash at 5-percent-a-month interest. One of those usurers, Ward Lamson of Fairfield, admitted when he was an old man that "when I charged the current high rates I felt like a hog, and I guess that many who paid them thought I was one."

When the Indian cession on the Des Moines River opened up in 1843, whole counties were populated overnight. By the end of the first day of "occupation," with wagons coming in like an invading army, sparsely settled Wapello County had a population of over a thousand.

Arriving in Iowa from Pennsylvania in April 1845, R. B. Groff borrowed a horse at Burlington and rode into the prairie. On seeing a house, he hallooed, and a hand slowly pulled aside the white sheet suspended over the hole that served for a door. A lean, sallow face appeared above a long gray beard.

"Where does this road go?" Groff asked.

"Don't go at all," the lean face said. "Stays here."

"What is up that way?"

"Columbus City."

Groff kept riding, and at dusk found another house. This was Columbus City. A small, unwashed man with a tobacco-stained mouth emerged.

"Can I stay the night?" inquired Goff.

"Yes, sir."

"Have you anything to eat?"

"No, sir."

"Why, how do you do?"

"First rate—how do you do?"

Goff slept on the bare floor in his clothes while his horse grazed contentedly.

Though a movement for statehood began stirring in Iowa in the 1840s, every county in the territory voted against a constitutional convention in the 1842 election. Territorial status was tempting, for the federal government paid all the bills, including the salaries of officials from the governor on down to the fence wardens. Public buildings were paid for, too. There was no taxation, apart from property and county taxes. The men out breaking the prairie knew a good thing when they saw one.

On the other hand, a territory was a political stepchild. It sent no congressmen to Washington and did not have much of a voice in its own affairs. By 1844 there was a change of heart, which translated into a majority for statehood. That October, sixty-six delegates met in the Old State Capitol at Iowa City to draft a constitution.

On opening day, Elijah Sells put forward a resolution to the effect that "the convention be opened every morning by prayer to the Almighty God."

William Chapman seconded, since "the ministers will gladly attend and render the service without compensation."

In the eastern states, where they still had tithing and Sabbath laws, this resolution on prayer would have been routinely adopted. A different mentality, however, prevailed on the frontier, and Sells's proposal provoked a heated debate. Most of the delegates were not politicians but hardworking farmers, who considered prayer a costly frill.

Francis Gehon objected that "it would not be economical, for the convention sits at an expense of $200 to $300 a day, and time is money."

Joseph Kirkpatrick said that although he believed in a "superintending providence, " he did "not want to enforce prayer upon the convention." He added, "Let those who believe so much in prayer pray at home," for "public prayer is too ostentatious."

Elijah Sells responded that he would "regret to have it said of Iowa that she had so far traveled out of Christendom as to deny the duty of prayer."

Ex-Governor Robert Lucas expostulated that not to pray would "give us a bad name abroad."

Andrew Hooton reminded Lucas of Benjamin Franklin, who as a boy asked his father why he did not say grace over the whole barrel of pork at once.

Jonathan Hall perceived a certain hypocrisy at work. He cited the case of a "reverend gentleman" who had fervently prayed for the election of James K. Polk (the Democratic "dark horse" candidate who went on to win the 1844 presidential election). Mr. Hall wanted to know which party was to be prayed for. As for himself, he would pray "that God would lay low and keep dark, and let us do the business of the convention."

Like Elijah Sells, Jonathan Fletcher regretted the opposition to prayer, saying, "I am unwilling it should go forth to the world that Iowa refused to acknowledge a God."

Lyman Evans suggested a compromise: a room for those who did not wish to hear prayers, and another room for those who did.

Stephen Shelleday argued that in supporting the resolution he was expressing the moral and religious feelings of his constituents.

To which Richard Quinton replied that although his constituents were just as religious as Mr. Shelleday's, he did not believe that the moment of religious observance "would change the purpose of the deity, nor the views of the members of the convention." "In the name of heaven," he concluded, "don't force men to hear prayers."

The resolution was postponed, which was tantamount to defeat, by a vote of 44 to 26. There would be no praying at the Iowa convention. The settlers on the western frontier, although they might be sincerely religious, instinctively affirmed the separation of church and state. Far from New England pieties, they were breathing a more democratic air.

Another debate concerned the salaries of public officials. Many of these men, who worked year-round from dawn to dusk for an annual income of maybe $100, were reluctant to vote a $1,000 salary for the state's governor.

William Chapman "desired to pay a fair price for services rendered, but I am not willing to pay a single dollar for dignity. I do not want to have men paid to live as gentlemen with no service to perform."

Stephen Hempstead warned that the convention was "running this thing of economy into the ground." There were men who would take office whatever the salary, but "they will plunder to make it up."

Jonathan Hall said that to pay "such large salaries to our officers is based upon a misunderstanding of the importance of our little state. We are just beginning to totter and not to walk."

William Harrison agreed that "we cannot pay such salaries as does the great and wealthy state of Ohio." Also, he added, "I want the officers to share something of the hardships and privations of our citizens. I would not have them be gentlemen of leisure, talking with their friends, with plenty of money in their pockets."

"Or to ride about in coaches and sport gold spectacles," Sam Bissell chimed in. "I don't want them paid for giving wine parties and electioneering the legislature. They should walk from their residence to their office, as other citizens."

Here was the purest expression of the ethic of equality: elected officials should mirror the values and the standard of living of those who elected them. In a democratic society, holding office should not be a license for a showy way of life.

The delegates to the Iowa convention were not only drafting a state constitution but defining a community's shared sentiments. These were men who fiercely believed in the Declaration of Independence and government by the consent of the governed. But what would this free state's policy be on the question of admitting Negroes as citizens on the same footing as whites?

The assembly referred the matter to a select committee. One of the related issues the committee had to consider was the propriety of a constitutional provision banning Negroes from settling in the state of Iowa.

After deliberation the committee drafted its report, which said that all men were created equal, including black men. This was, the report went on to say, an abstract proposition, which "becomes very much modified when man is considered in the artificial state in which government and society place him."

The question was, "Would the admission of the negro as a citizen tend in the least to lessen, endanger, or impair the enjoyment of our government institutions?"

The answer was: "However your committee may commiserate with the degraded condition of the negro and feel for his fate, yet they can never consent to open the door of our beautiful state and invite them to settle our lands. The policy of other states would drive the whole black population of the Union upon us. The ballot box would fall into their hands and a train of evils would follow that in the opinion of your committee would be incalculable . . . idleness, crime, and misery would come in their train, and government itself would fall into anarchy and despotism."

The report concluded that "the people of Iowa do not want negros swarming among them," which expressed the feelings of the settlers, who were opposed to black neighbors in any form, either as free men or slaves. And yet the proposed article barring Negroes from the state was not included in the constitution, for the delegates feared it might compromise their admission to the Union.

The convention adjourned on November 1, 1844, after sitting for twenty-six days, and submitted a constitution to Congress that December. Since Florida had been waiting six years for a free-state companion, the pair were quickly admitted under the terms of the Missouri Compromise. This was the first time that two states were coupled in the same bill. Congress passed the legislation in February 1845 and President Tyler signed it in early March (Polk had not yet been inaugurated).

The Florida constitution sanctioned slavery, while Iowa's provided that "neither slavery nor involuntary servitude, unless for the punishment of crimes, shall ever be tolerated in this state." On account of boundary disputes, the 1844 constitution was rejected by the people of Iowa. Another convention gathered in 1846, and Iowa was admitted to the union in December of that year.

New Jersey–born James Lyon was the curious sort, who liked to eavesdrop on conversations. On the Mississippi steamboat, while traveling through Iowa in 1855, he heard one man say to another: "I'm sorry, but the Indian has to go. His civilization is a dream." In a Davenport dry-goods store, he listened as a farmer declared: "There's a new kind of cane to make sugar. . . . They call it Chinese and it's guaranteed to grow wherever corn will grow. Just think of that! No more of that brown New Orleans stuff, so wet you can take most of it up with a blottered paper, and what's left is mostly sand."

Lyon crossed the Mississippi into Illinois and came to the farm of a sheepherder, who asked: "You from Ioway? Couldn't have come from nowhere else on that trail. . . . Did Indian Trotter fetch you over? Mighty good boatman, even if he is an Indian, but he's some white they say. . . . We're some crowded right now, but you can sleep near your ponies."

The sheepherder wanted to talk politics: "I'm a Democrat, a Douglas Democrat, but I do wish he had let the nigger question alone. His squatter sovereignty will make war in every new state—is making war in Kansas right now. I hate rowdies and border ruffians. I'm getting tired of this slave-hunting business anyhow, even if Henry Clay did vote for it.

"I have two boys who wanted to go to Ioway," the sheepman went on, "but they have the Kansas fever now. . . . The trouble with Kansas is some like a prairie fire, all hands can put it out at the start, but if you wait till the wind gets hold, nobody knows where it does stop."

"Iowa is the land of promise," Lyon said.

"The land of promises, you mean. Ioway has a crowd of people, they are too many at once. . . . Most things are uncertain, but sheep are sheep. They don't cost nothin', they just are. You can count 'em and you know what you've got. But Ioway promises are nothin'."

That evening after supper, the sheepherder took his guest outside. On the prairie at night, the moonlight seemed to flood the ground like an overspreading stream, until every rising twig or blade of grass cast a shadow. It made the kettles and pans by the shearer's wagon glint, and it lit with a strange metallic sheen the hair of the dogs lying silently beside it.

The sheep were in their fold, and a dozen men sat around the camp-fire. The talk was of Kansas.

"Make it Kansas and we'll go," one man said. "I'd shoot an Indian on sight, but maybe a shot at a border ruffian would do just as well."

"You!" said another. "You wouldn't shoot a rabbit. You can beat any ram in the herd in a foot-race—proved it yesterday."

"If those people in Kansas keep on playin' Indian," the first man re-plied, "burnin' farmhouses and killin' folk, I think there's a call for some old-fashioned straight shootin'."

"If there's a neighbor-fight," an old shearer opined, "the sheriff, if he's any account, can stop it. The United States will have to stop the Kansas row. Backfirin' won't help anymore, the thing's gone too far, but if it ain't stopped pretty soon, herdsmen is gonna have wool to give away."

"What you talking about?" another shearer interrupted. "Don't you know war helps the wool market? Did year afore last, when those Russians and English got at it. [The Crimean War broke out in 1853.] War is good for business. I'm for war, I am."

"I'm for stoppin' it right now," the old-timer countered.

"Wait till after shearing, dad," said the man who thought war was good for business, "and we'll all go down and see it through."

PART THREE
THE LEAP TO THE PACIFIC,
THE COMPROMISE OF 1850,
AND
THE KANSAS-NEBRASKA ACT

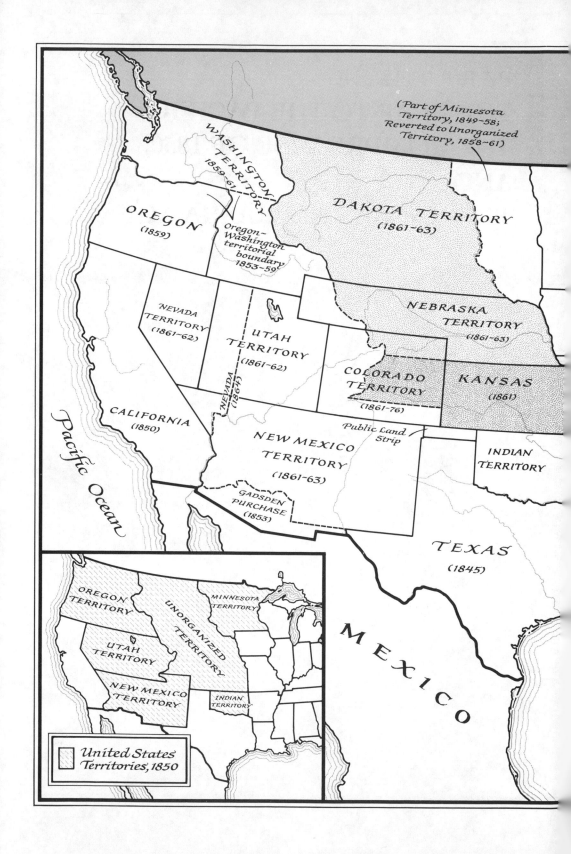

(Part of Minnesota
Territory, 1849–58;
Reverted to Unorganized
Territory, 1858–61)

WASHINGTON TERRITORY 1859–61

OREGON
(1859)

Oregon–
Washington
territorial
boundary
1853–59

DAKOTA TERRITORY
(1861–63)

NEVADA
TERRITORY
(1861–62)

UTAH
TERRITORY
(1861–62)

NEVADA
(1864)

NEBRASKA
TERRITORY
(1861–63)

COLORADO
TERRITORY
(1861–76)

KANSAS
(1861)

CALIFORNIA
(1850)

Pacific Ocean

NEW MEXICO
TERRITORY
(1861–63)

Public Land
Strip

INDIAN
TERRITORY

GADSDEN
PURCHASE
(1853)

TEXAS
(1845)

MEXICO

OREGON
TERRITORY

MINNESOTA
TERRITORY

UNORGANIZED
TERRITORY

UTAH
TERRITORY

NEW MEXICO
TERRITORY

INDIAN
TERRITORY

United States
Territories, 1850

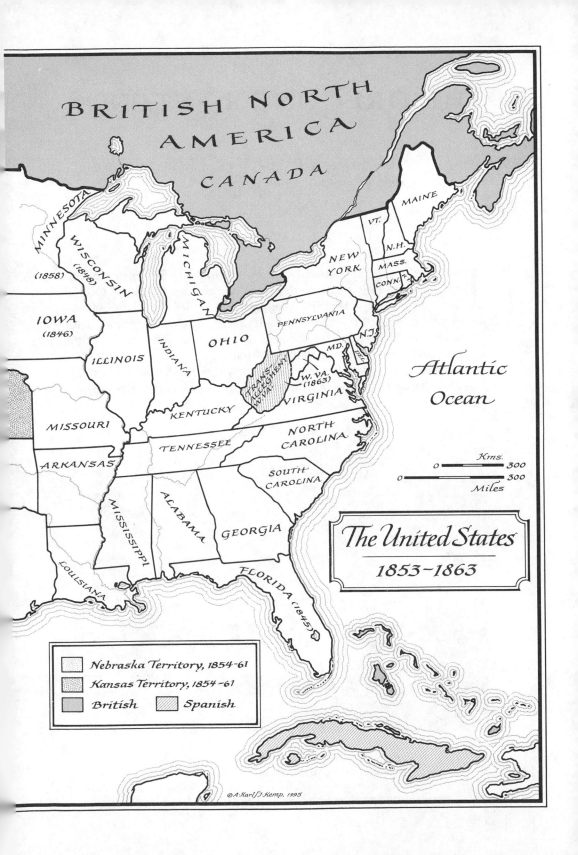

BRITISH NORTH

AMERICA

CANADA

MINNESOTA (1858)

WISCONSIN (1848)

MICHIGAN

MAINE

VT.

N.H.

NEW YORK

MASS.

CONN.

IOWA (1846)

ILLINOIS

INDIANA

OHIO

PENNSYLVANIA

N.J.

MD.

DEL.

MISSOURI

KENTUCKY

TRANS-ALLEGHENY

W. VA. (1863)

VIRGINIA

Atlantic Ocean

ARKANSAS

TENNESSEE

NORTH CAROLINA

SOUTH CAROLINA

Kms. 0 — 300

Miles 0 — 300

MISSISSIPPI

ALABAMA

GEORGIA

LOUISIANA

FLORIDA (1845)

The United States

1853–1863

Nebraska Territory, 1854–61

Kansas Territory, 1854–61

British   Spanish

©A·Karl/J·Kemp. 1995

CHAPTER NINE
THE OREGON FRONTIER

*I went to Oregon because the thing wasn't fenced in and
nobody dared to keep me out.*

EARLY SETTLER

In 1844 the country elected James Polk president. One of the planks
in the Democratic platform that year was the annexation of Oregon
Territory. Senator William Allen of Ohio coined the phrase "Fifty-
four Forty or Fight" to express the idea that the United States' Pacific
boundary should extend to the northern latitude of 54° 40'—that is, all the
way up the western coast of Canada to Russian Alaska.

Looked at that way, Oregon Territory was twice the size of Texas. It
included British Columbia and the present states of Oregon, Washington,

The New York Public Library
Built in 1843 in southwest Wyoming, Fort Bridger soon became an
important relay station on the Oregon Trail, where pioneers could
repair their wagons and buy supplies. The mountain man James
Bridger charged high prices, but threw in free advice.

and Idaho. Long claimed by both England and the United States, this vast expanse was jointly occupied under the terms of an 1818 treaty. In practice, though, the British ran things because they had facility of access, Oregon Territory being a southward continuation of British Canada.

But in 1844 the expansionist Democrats made "Fifty-four Forty or Fight" their battle cry, and Polk was voted into office with a mandate to take the territory even if it meant war.

Rather than settling Oregon, the British used it as a fur-trapping preserve, holding a virtual monopoly until American trappers figured out a way to cross the Rockies. The British Hudson's Bay Company built posts along the river routes. The man in charge was John McLoughlin, a six-foot-seven-inch Irishman also known as "the king of Oregon." He ruled over a kingdom seven times the size of England that had a single-crop economy. That crop was beaver, or "hairy money," as the trappers liked to call it.

From his base at Fort Vancouver (today's Vancouver, Washington), opposite the confluence of the Columbia and the Willamette, McLoughlin sent out trapping parties as far east as Idaho and as far south as California.

The Americans naturally wanted a piece of the action. On the other side of the Rockies, in 1822, an innovative St. Louis entrepreneur named William H. Ashley launched a company to engage in the fur trade and ran an ad in several St. Louis papers, asking for a hundred enterprising young men to ascend the Missouri River. Among the recruits were Jedediah Smith and James Clyman, who would gain a certain notoriety as mountain men.

In September 1823, Ashley sent a small force of his best men, including Clyman and Smith, to explore an overland route across the Rockies. They drifted up the Missouri into South Dakota, then turned west along the White River, and into Wyoming and the Powder River country.

The expedition reached an encampment of friendly Crows on the Wind River, near today's Dubois, Wyoming, with whom they wintered, hunting buffalo and drying the meat into jerky. Spreading sand on a buffalo robe, Clyman drew a map with a twig, and the Crows showed them how they could circle the south end of the Wind River Range and find an open pass through the Rockies. On the other side, the Crows said, they would see a river teeming with beaver.

In February 1824, the Clyman-Smith party headed south along the mountain range's eastern base, down to the Sweetwater River. There they crossed the Continental Divide, a sinuous barrier of mountain crests extending from Canada to the Mexican border. On one side of the Divide, the rivers ran east into the Mississippi and the Rio Grande, and on the other side they ran west into the Columbia and the Colorado. Its geographical oddity was that from points so close together streams should flow in opposite directions to destinations so far apart.

The way through this wall of mountains was the South Pass, a broad and flattened cavity on the continent's spine at 7,500 feet. Shivering like aspen leaves, it took them two weeks to traverse the pass. The wind blew so fiercely it blew the trapper's fires out, and they had to eat their meat raw, while the horses ate snow. But they had found the gateway across the Rockies and into the Pacific northwest, a feat comparable to Champlain's discovery of the Great Lakes. Trappers competing with the Hudson's Bay Company for the rich beaver grounds of the Oregon Territory would be the first to use the pass. Later came the emigrants on the Oregon Trail.

For the next fifteen years, American trappers threw down the gauntlet to the British in Oregon, establishing an American presence there a decade ahead of the settlers and two decades ahead of any government. Under the joint-occupation agreement, American trappers could not be excluded. Without realizing it, they were the point men of Manifest Destiny.

In April 1825, William Ashley joined his crew on the Green River. He divided the company into four beaver-catching teams that headed off in different directions, while he and seven men went exploring in bullboats down the Green into southern Wyoming and Utah.

Ashley made arrangements "to rendezvous for all our parties on or before the 10th of July next" on the tributary of the Green soon to be known as Henrys Fork, which flowed down from the Uinta Range in Utah into the Green at today's Utah-Wyoming border.

Although this "rendezvous" seemed like a fairly routine matter, it was in fact an arrangement that introduced a wholly new type of trapping operation. Instead of buying furs from Indians, Ashley was relying on freelance trappers who were paid by the pelt rather than getting a fixed wage. These trappers, however, were months away from their base in St. Louis. It was impractical to bring them back with their furs after every season. But neither did Ashley like the idea of building expensive permanent posts, that in any case would have to be manned by trappers who would be better employed in the field.

Thus was born the system of the "rendezvous." Once a year, at a designated time and place, Ashley's supply train arrived from St. Louis to buy the trappers' furs and sell them whatever they needed. The Missouri businessman had hit upon a way to keep his trappers in the Rockies year-round, for the rendezvous quickly became the sole institution the mountain men respected.

The annual conclave grew into a great Rocky Mountain gathering, combining aspects of a carnival, a souk, a hoedown, and a rodeo. The site of choice was a grassy meadow by a stream, ringed with trees, and providing enough room for several hundred trappers and as many or more Indians. The designated time usually fell in July, when the trappers began riding in, many of them accompanied by their squaws. Soon the meadow was dotted with tents and wigwams.

It was a time of amiable mixing between trappers and Indians, of yarn telling around the campfire, of men mending moccasins, playing cards, and swapping horses. In these enchanted mountain clearings, as the grass waved in patterns on the meadows and the wildflowers bloomed under clear summer skies, the trappers waited for the supply train. When the pack mules appeared, the guns began to fire and the festivities started in earnest.

Then Ashley ordered the bales of merchandise ripped open. The trappers did their buying for their one shopping spree of the year, paying with beaver worth $3 a pelt. Ashley's prices were outrageous—for inferior tobacco that cost him 10 cents a pound, he charged the trappers $2—the idea being that the trappers would remain constantly in debt.

The proceedings reached their climax when the whiskey kegs were bunged and a saloon was improvised under a tent. The trappers, who had gone dry during the long months on the beaver streams, bought whiskey at $5 a pint and proceeded to get riotously drunk. Then they started playing pranks, arm wrestling, and quarreling over Shoshone beauties.

At the first rendezvous on Henrys Fork on July 1, 1825, Ashley collected $50,000 worth of fur, a sum that was definitely worth his trouble. Two years later he brought the first wheeled vehicle over the South Pass— a cannon on wheels, a four-pounder. Three years after that, in 1830, the supply train arrived in ten mule-drawn wagons. And so the rendezvous was established for the trapper as every holiday rolled into one, where he could attain the full expression of his robustly independent personality.

The mountain-man style consisted of making light of both skills and mishaps. These were men who could trap and skin a beaver, light a fire in a blizzard, kill a bear, build a cabin. They could do anything with a horse or a gun. Mike Fink could "sky a copper" and shoot the tail off a pig without hurting it. But mountain men took their accomplishments in stride, just as they did their close calls. If you had an encounter with a bear, the thing to say was, "Why that bear didn't seem a bit wild."

The dangers of mountain life bred an untrammeled individualism. These were men removed from all governance, two thousand miles away from the nearest American court, unrestrained by law or religion or any other socially inhibiting agency. All prohibitions were cast aside—although an unspoken understanding existed that murder was in poor taste. The elements and the Indians were the only boundaries on free will. If the snow was four feet deep, if there was no game, if the Indians were on your trail and you were out of ammunition, you maintained your good cheer. The mountain man Joe Meek joked about playing cards in the winter with three other men and using a frozen corpse for a table.

Extreme situations were the rule. Meek explained how he had once kept from starving: "I held my hands in an anthill until they were covered with ants, then greedily licked them off." Pain was deflected by humor, as when Jim Bridger, having lived with a three-inch iron arrowhead in his back for three years, had it removed by the missionary Dr. Marcus Whitman. The reverend wondered aloud why the wound had not gotten infected. "Meat jes don't spoil in the mountains," Bridger said.

The missionaries' arrival signaled the beginning of the end of this brief and wondrous era of unlimited personal freedom. The missionaries, and after them the emigrants, brought religion and family values into the trappers' pristine environment, upsetting the balance of their mountain morality.

When Whitman and another reverend, Samuel Parker, appeared in the spring of 1835 with the supply train at the rendezvous on the Green River, their presence put a damper on the trappers' fun. Whitman decided to hold a Sunday service. The trappers were attentive until a herd of buffalo came into view in the valley. Suddenly, every man went for his horse and saddle, without waiting for the benediction.

When the men returned with twenty buffalo, noisily rejoicing, the Reverend Mr. Parker rebuked them for breaking the Sabbath. The trappers reflected that it would have been better had he not done so, and better yet had he not followed his chiding by eating heartily of the tenderloin.

Events seemed to be conspiring to terminate the trappers' boisterous self-reliance. The men had overhunted and beavers were getting scarce. Other companies had followed in Ashley's wake, and the trappers now outnumbered the pelts. By 1837, desperate mountain men were stealing from their suppliers and deserting after running up debts. In 1840 settlers started crossing the Rockies, and the party was over.

Seeing the lay of the land, the trapper Robert Newell said to Joe Meek: "Come, we are done with this life in the mountains—done with wading in beaver dams and freezing or starving alternately. The fur trade is dead and it's no place for us now. Let us go to the Willamette and take farms. What do you say, Meek? Shall we turn American settlers?"

"What suits you suits me," Meek replied, and they headed down the Columbia and began tilling the soil in the Willamette Valley. So died the era of unfettered mountain capitalism. In 1845, two British soldiers visited Joe Meek on his farm and asked him in a spirit of raillery, "Have you seen any wonderful transformations in nature?" "I reckon I have," he replied. "When I came to this country, Mount Hood was a hole in the ground."

When Ashley's men found the South Pass and began catching beaver along the Green River, they entered land that the Hudson's Bay Company was already trapping. As in a proxy war, the Anglo-American struggle for the Oregon Territory was fought by rival companies of trappers. The two sides never engaged in direct combat, but carried out a campaign of dirty tricks and harassment through Indian intermediaries.

From 1825, when Jedediah Smith's party went west of the Rockies, until 1840, when American settlers began coming to Oregon in significant numbers, this sub rosa warfare continued. The Americans received no instructions or support from Washington, but knew that their competition with the British had a patriotic dimension.

The Hudson's Bay Company under John McLoughlin, on the other hand, formed a deliberate policy of badgering the Americans. McLoughlin appointed as his "brigade" leader Peter Skene Ogden, a wilderness-hardened commander born in 1794, the son of Tory parents. Between 1824 and 1830, McLoughlin sent Ogden out on annual expeditions in the Snake River country of eastern Washington, Idaho, and Utah. Ogden's mission was to overhunt the beaver and create a "fur desert" between United States territory and the eastern approaches to the Columbia River. This would discourage the intrusion of American trappers as well as the subsequent entry of settlers, thus keeping the Oregon country British.

Ogden's first foray into Snake River country in 1824–25 resulted in a confrontation with American trappers. He started out from the Hudson's Bay Company's Flathead post on the Columbia River accompanied by a clerk, 2 interpreters, 70 trappers, their wives and children, 372 horses, and 364 beaver traps. Pushing into Idaho and northern Utah, he got as far as today's Huntsville, where he caught 600 beaver.

On May 25, 1825, Ogden's brigade was camping on the Weber River (in today's Utah county of the same name). A party of twenty-five to thirty Americans led by the independent trapper Johnson Gardner rode up the valley with colors flying and bivouacked within a hundred yards of the British tents. The next day Gardner strode into Ogden's camp and boldly told the Hudson's Bay leader that he was trespassing on American territory. Ogden replied that they were both in territory jointly governed by Britain and the United States. (In fact, they were in Mexican territory, which went as far north as the 42nd parallel, the border between Idaho and Utah).

But Gardner, thinking he was on home ground, commanded Ogden to take his men and "return from whence you came without delay." Ogden responded that he would be glad to do so upon receiving an order to that effect from his government. If that was the case, Gardner warned, the British remained at their own peril.

Gardner did not follow up his threat, and on July 17, 1826, Ogden returned to his home base on the Columbia, laden with 3,800 beaver and otter skins. He had ascertained that the area south of the Snake River, where the Americans were, was now stripped of beaver. The expedition had exceeded all expectations.

Ogden had by now developed several strategies for getting rid of his American rivals, and felt "fully justified in placing every impediment in their way." One tactic was to trap female beavers about to litter, thus destroying their young before birth.

The indefatigable Ogden was off again in September 1826, this time plunging straight through Oregon and into northern California, where he trapped on the Klamath River. But on this trip the beaver proved shy, and the winter came hard. In February 1827, Ogden confided to his journal: "This life makes a young man sixty in a few years. Wading in cold water all day they earn 10 shillings per beaver. A convict at Botany Bay [the site of a penal colony in Australia] is a gentleman at ease compared to my trappers."

During another expedition in 1829, Ogden gave his name to a landscape feature, Ogden's Hole (today's Huntsville, Utah). On this occasion he had in his brigade quite a few Indian auxiliaries, as well as his own Indian wife, who had taken their baby along.

That February at Ogden's Hole, the Hudson's Bay brigade came face-to-face with a party of American trappers headed by Joe Meek. To Ogden's annoyance, the Americans immediately set to bartering with the Indians for furs, drawing them away and offering them whiskey.

The two groups had camped in close proximity. One day Ogden's horses stampeded, and several galloped away in the direction of the Americans, among them the horse belonging to Ogden's wife, with her baby strapped to the saddle.

The mother followed her horse into the American camp. As she did so, she spotted one of her husband's packhorses, loaded with beaver, which had also strayed with the herd. She mounted her horse, holding the bridle with one hand, as with the other she took hold of the packhorse's halter, then started out of the camp with both horses.

"Shoot her, shoot her!" cried some of the American trappers. But others shouted, "Let her go," and "She's a brave woman," and "I like her pluck." As the trappers argued, Ogden's wife escaped with her baby and the company's furs.

Ogden went on his sixth and final expedition in September 1829, advancing as far as central California. By this time he felt "like a ball on a tennis court." He was also experiencing diminishing returns, for he came back to Fort Vancouver in July 1830 bearing a mere 1,300 furs. Weary of his vagrant life, he accepted a transfer to British Columbia.

Ogden's departure did nothing to lessen the rivalry between British and American trappers, who continued to butt heads like the local bighorn sheep. The conflict abated only when the beaver ran out and the settlers started coming in, tipping the scales in favor of an American Oregon.

After winning the 1844 election with his 54° 40' slogan, President Polk backtracked in 1845, offering the British the 49th parallel as the boundary between Canada and the United States. After much waffling, England accepted. The Treaty of Washington, signed on June 15, 1846, gave the United States the part of Oregon Territory below the 49th parallel; that is, the future states of Washington, Oregon, and Idaho. The main reason England was willing to give up this territory was the decline of the fur trade, caused by years of trapper rivalry.

The settlers didn't wait for the government in Washington to sign a treaty with England. They embarked for Oregon as soon as it was feasible. What set their wheels rolling was the discovery of a low meadow in a mountain range, followed by William Ashley's demonstration that wagons could be driven across the Rockies.

Marcus and Narcissa Whitman built their mission on the Walla Walla in 1836, and soon the settlers followed. A bill to establish Oregon Territory was introduced in the Senate in February 1838, and though the legislation took ten years to pass, the westward movement was on.

Families gathered in the Missouri River towns of Independence, Westport, and St. Joseph, all their possessions squeezed into the cubic footage of a cloth-covered wagon. Everyone left with hopes of a bright future, not realizing the length or difficulty of the trip, although they had the prudence to travel in groups.

In the makeshift villages where the trains formed, people exchanged helpful hints: Store your food in sacking, not in barrels. Pack the butter in the center of the flour and the eggs in cornmeal. Take along a tin reflector to bake bread. Get plenty of one-inch rope to lower the wagons into ravines. Give your oxen two shoes to the hoof. Start from St. Joe instead of Independence to avoid paying the ferry over the Kansas River.

And then it was yoke up and move out, as the wagon trains formed on the banks of the Missouri. Chance had brought people together who had in common the desire to move, and during the four-month journey there took place every conceivable human event from birth to death. From one to the other, it was sometimes but a few hours, or a few miles. In the morning a child died of the croup and in the evening a child was born.

There was no one great peril, but a hundred vexations: wagons overturned, axles broke, cattle ran off. A boy fell and a wagon ran over his legs. The biggest killer was not cholera but carelessness, such as handling firearms in jolting wagons. If you came to an Indian village, the villagers were all over you, panhandling. At night, the settlers drew their wagons in a circle, driving the cattle inside and pitching their tents outside, more to pen the cattle in than as protection against the Indians. About their odyssey, the pioneers liked to say, "The freeness of the plains brings forth the full manhood."

On May 14, 1842, Elijah White, a Methodist missionary and doctor of medicine, was in Elm Grove, twenty miles south of Independence. His wagon train consisted of 114 settlers, 18 wagons, and innumerable horses, mules, and cattle. There were also a great many dogs. White thought they would be a nuisance, using up scarce food and water on the prairie, and likely to go rabid. By a two-thirds vote, the settlers decided to kill the dogs, and there followed a chaotic scene, with the men firing, and the women and children crying, and the doomed canines yelping and running. But, reflected White, better dead dogs than dead cattle.

In June, the eighteen covered wagons reached the South Platte, and the earth trembled as they thundered over the plain. In one of those all-too-common freak accidents, a pioneer named Bailey passed behind a wagon just as its owner pulled on a blanket. A casually placed rifle discharged, hitting the young man and killing him.

On the Sweetwater River, they dried buffalo meat in the sun. The air over the South Pass, in early August, was cold and damp. On the Green, the settlers realized they were moving too slowly and jettisoned their excess

goods. By mid-August, they had reached Fort Hall in Idaho (today's Poca-
tello), situated in the middle of a green plain. These forts served the function of later highway rest stops, places where the emigrants could fill up
their wagons with supplies, water their teams, relax and freshen up.

Captain Grant, Fort Hall's commander, was a professional pessimist
who told the emigrants that they would not be able to take their wagons
across the Blue Mountains in Oregon. Taking him at his word, White and
the others abandoned their wagons and continued on horseback. On August 23, White left the main party and pushed ahead, reaching Marcus
Whitman's Walla Walla mission, and was soon joined by the others.

Back east, there was talk of "Oregon fever." The *Iowa Gazette* wrote in
April 1843: "The Oregon fever is raging in almost every part of the Union.
Companies are forming . . . and will make a pretty formidable army. This,
if nothing else, will compel Congress to act upon the matter."

On the Blue River below Kansas City, the sixty wagons to be led by
Peter Burnett began to assemble in early May of 1843. Pursued by creditors, Burnett had no reason to stay in Missouri and was attracted by the
donation bill then before Congress (free land to spur settlement). On May
22 the emigrants elected him captain, along with a nine-member council.
The next day at 4 A.M., the sentinels fired their rifles for reveille. Smoke
from slow-kindling fires floated on the morning air. Men made sure there
were no stray or stolen horses. After breakfast the pioneers struck their
tents, loaded their wagons, and yoked their teams. At seven the "pilot"
gave the command "To Oxen!" and off they went, in four-wagon platoons,
to the crack of whips.

Marcus Whitman was on this journey, heading back to Walla Walla
after lobbying President Tyler in Washington to take action on Oregon's
status as a territory. When they got to Fort Hall, the glum Captain Grant
delivered his usual sermon on leaving the wagons behind. He pointed to
the abandoned wagons from the year before and said it was impossible to
take wagons the rest of the way. But Whitman knew better, and told the
others that with all the women and children they would never make it on
horseback, and that besides, wagons and cattle were essential to men expecting to live as farmers. The emigrants followed his counsel, and they
made it, establishing the feasibility of taking wagons to Oregon. This gave
rise to the "Whitman saved Oregon" version of events.

Born in England, John Minto came to Pittsburgh in 1840 at the age of
eighteen. The young man so admired America's commitment to personal
freedom that a reading of James Fenimore Cooper's *The Pioneers* inspired
him to cross the Rockies. In 1844 he took a job as a deck hand on a steamer
to St. Louis. From there he traveled to Kansas City, where he heard that a
party of emigrants was assembling fifteen miles to the north, at Weston,
and that families were looking for single men to help on the trip.

In Weston, Minto teamed up with twenty-five-year-old Willard Rees of Ohio and they went to see a fellow named Morrison, who needed hands. Morrison told them: "I will haul your trunks, board you, have your washing and mending done, and you will give me your help in getting my family and effects to Oregon."

The bargain was sealed. Morrison handed Rees a gold coin and said, "Take this money and ride to the mill at St. Joe and buy nine barrels of flour, and—Nancy, how much corn have we in the house?"

"Oh, a right smart chance," his wife replied.

"Well, get three hundred pounds of cornmeal. I reckon that will last as long as it will keep good."

Rees went on his way, and Morrison's wife declared, "Wilson, you'd feel queer if that man should serve you a Yankee trick and go off with your horse and your money."

The truth was, Nancy Morrison didn't really want to go to Oregon. She was leaving too many friends and relatives behind.

Originally from Kentucky, Robert Wilson Morrison had been farming near St. Joseph for years. After marrying a Missouri girl and having a sizable family of three girls and three boys, he had suddenly decided to pick up and move on. It was simply a matter of selling the farm and packing two wagons.

On the eve of their departure, Nancy Morrison's brother came around to say goodbye. "Well, Wilson," he asked, "why are ye goin', anyhow?"

"I allow that the United States government has the best right to that country, and I am going to help make that right good," Morrison said. "Then, I am not satisfied here. There are few things that we can raise that will pay for shipment to market—tobacco and hemp are about all, and unless a man keeps niggers—and I won't—he has no even chance with the man who owns slaves."

"There's Dick Owen, my near neighbor," Morrison continued, "has a few house slaves and a few field hands; they raise and make about all his family eats and wears and a surplus besides. I'm going to Oregon where they'll be no slaves and we'll all start even."

No one had ever heard Morrison talk at such extended length before, but that was how he felt and he wasn't about to change his mind.

At the emigrant camp, people voted for Cornelius Gilliam, who claimed to have risen to the rank of general in the army, to command the train. The election barely mattered to John Minto, for they were on the trail at last, and he was absorbed in his workday. On the night of June 30, a guard fired his gun, and Captain Shaw, the officer of the day, told Minto, "The boys are getting very careless, John," which they agreed was due to Gilliam's lack of authority. The general did not believe in the importance of drill, nor did he have a plan in case of Indian attack.

On July 4, the settlers were sitting around the campfire in the evening, talking about conditions in Oregon. One man said there would be plenty of money there. Minto disagreed, saying they'd have to depend on what they raised and the game they killed.

"No money there, John?" an old Virginian asked. "Why man alive, John, money grows thar!" "Yes, and feather beds grow on bushes," Captain Shaw added.

On July 11, as he drove the lead team up the Platte, across Nebraska, Minto heard the sound of buffalo. Looking ahead, he saw a vast herd ascending the hill. At the head of the train, General Gilliam called from his wagon for his horse, flung himself in the saddle, and yelled, "You boys with the teams, camp where there is wood and water, and you that can get horses and guns, mount and follow me." Minto wanted badly to be in on the chase, but since he was in the lead, he had to see to campsite selection.

Gilliam and the other hunters killed fourteen buffalo. They foolishly let the animals lie out on the plain all afternoon, and when they returned to gut them found that the meat had rotted under the July sun. "What a waste," reflected Minto. Captain Shaw said he would not continue serving under this so-called general who had been so headstrong and unreflecting, galloping off after the buffalo without first looking to see whether any Indians were about.

The next day a meeting was held, and the emigrants questioned Gilliam's competence. Several wagon owners said they wanted to strike out on their own. Trying to assert his authority, Gilliam said he would "hang upon the nearest tree the man who dares to leave the company." At this, Daniel Clark broke in, saying, "If any of you men intend to go to Oregon, come on, I'm going." Gilliam mocked him, saying, "That's all the sense he has." And yet Dan Clark had forded the swollen streams better than any man in the company.

The following morning when Gilliam got up, he spotted a settler with a rifle making for the foothills. "Going hunting without leave?" he roared. "I'll—" His wife restrained him: "Now, Neal, be careful." Gilliam gestured toward the campfires and said: "They may all get to Oregon as they can, without me. I'll have nothing more to do with them."

After the July 12 meeting, the train split up into three independent companies, whose leaders were Gilliam, Morrison, and Captain Shaw. By July 30, Morrison's company had reached Fort Laramie in eastern Wyoming, at the juncture of the Laramie and the North Platte. While they stayed at the fort a few days, Minto went out to visit a nearby Sioux camp, but came upon only twenty lodges and a few men.

Some time later Minto was at work behind his wagon when Mrs. Morrison hailed him from the campfire. She was standing across from three Sioux squaws, trying to keep from laughing. "John," she said, "if I understand these women correctly, they think you belong to me, and want to buy you for a husband for that one in the middle; they offer six horses." While the bemused Minto looked on, Mrs. Morrison signaled to the Indian women with her hand that the young man was not for sale.

On August 30, Morrison's group arrived at Fort Bridger, in Wyoming's southwestern corner. The mountain man Jim Bridger had built a trading post on Blacks Fork of the Green River, right on the Oregon Trail.

Here Wilson Morrison traded his plow irons and a cow for flour, while John Minto traded his double-barreled gun for some deerskins.

On September 1, the party came to the Divide between Blacks Fork and the Bear River. As he fished for trout, Minto saw a contest between a falcon and a hare. You would have thought the hare did not stand a chance, but each time the falcon swooped down in a blur of talons and wings, the hare found some sagebrush and bunched itself up into a ball. After several dives, the falcon flew off with an angry scream.

At the border between Wyoming and Idaho, some Indians offered Minto a gallon tin pail heaped with ripe blackberries, the high point of the trip. At Fort Hall, on the left bank of the Snake near the Portneuf, Captain Grant was still sounding off. A Baptist minister, Reverend Cave, asked the captain if the emigrants could get to the Columbia River with wagons.

"It's just about a year since a lot of people came here and asked me the same question," Grant said. "I told them no, that we found it difficult to pass the narrow trails with our pack ponies. They went on, just as if I had not spoken a word, and the next thing I knew they were at Fort Walla Walla. You damned Yankees will do anything you like."

The Oregon Trail was by now well known to the Indians, who regarded the passage of the emigrants as an opportunity to improve their standard of living. As soon as the Morrison wagons approached the Columbia, it was like running a gauntlet of thieves. On the Umatilla (near today's Pendleton) in Cayuse country, Morrison's prize mare was stolen while he slept in his wagon.

On October 14, the settlers halted at the mouth of the Deschutes, only ten miles from The Dalles. Here the trail wound up a steep hill and they had to double the teams. But Indians hiding in the woods drove off an ox. Mr. Morrison gave the reins to his wife and took off in pursuit. When the Indians saw a woman driving a team, one of them rode alongside the wagon and tried to push the lead ox over a steep embankment. Mrs. Morrison thrashed him with her whip, and the Indian raced away with a cry of pain.

As suddenly as it began, the journey came to an end. Morrison settled in Clatsop County, on a farm twelve miles from Astoria, at the mouth of the Columbia. John Minto went to work in a nearby sawmill, and in 1847 married Morrison's fifteen-year-old daughter. One of his motives may have been that married couples were entitled to double the donation grant, or 640 acres. The Mintos found some land on the coast and began to farm. Eventually, they bought a cow; Minto's wife complained that the Indians would come and drink the milk right out of the pail. But here in Oregon, on his own land, John Minto felt for the first time that he was an American. Still wearing the Scottish cap he had brought with him across the Atlantic, he dwelled contentedly among his fellow settlers, who did not question his right to be one of them.

On a summer morning in 1845, the editor of the *Democratic Review*, John L. O'Sullivan, penned a column for the July–August issue containing two words that are still title chapters in American history books: Manifest Destiny.

The idea that the United States should stretch from the Atlantic to the Pacific oceans and from Canada to Mexico was not self-evident. Some statesmen, such as John Quincy Adams, believed that "the United States and North America are identical." But others, like the influential Massachusetts senator Daniel Webster, said, "I would not vote one cent from the people's treasury to place the Pacific coast one inch nearer than it is now."

In his editorial, O'Sullivan asserted that the American claim was "but the right of our manifest destiny to overspread and to possess the whole of the continent which Providence has given us for the development of the great experiment of liberty and federative self-government." The argument rested on a curious form of circular reasoning: By what right did we continue to spread out? By the right of Manifest Destiny. And how did we come by that right? Why, it was our Manifest Destiny.

For years, settlers who had never heard of Manifest Destiny had been going west. But the catchy phrase served as a good horse to pull the wagon of expansion. The advent of the steamboat also pushed things along, as well as Samuel Morse's invention of the telegraph in 1844. Manifest Destiny became the bible of an ambitious new ideology, though in the case of Oregon and Texas, the faithful had not waited to hear the sermon.

What it boiled down to was that America was an equal-opportunity acquirer, whether by force of arms in Texas, by purchase in California, or by negotiation in Oregon. As a state requiring security, as a government looking to provide cheap land for its citizens, and as a new nation that aspired to become a continental power, it was simple pragmatism for the United States to extend from sea to sea. Providence was tacked on to make a number of highly practical reasons seem foreordained.

As it happened, 1846, the year that followed the launching of the Manifest Destiny concept, was also the year of the Great Migration into Oregon and the year of the war with Mexico. America had been given its Manifest Destiny shot, and it seemed to take.

One of those who left for Oregon in 1846 was a twenty-three-year-old Boston Brahmin and recent Harvard graduate by the name of Francis Parkman, who did not go to settle but to observe. In particular, he wanted to observe the Indians; the migration was for him an irritating sideshow.

From notes taken on his westward journey, Parkman wrote his first book, a fascinating first-person reportage called *The Oregon Trail*. But in it he betrayed the prejudices of his background and class, for he saw the frontier not as heroic but as squalid; the landscape not as majestic but as demoralizing; the Indians not as noble and oppressed, but as a "ragamuffin horde"; and the settlers not as decent folk but as "moronic scoundrels."

Parkman's opinions may have been colored by his own physical condition. He was a sickly individual forcing himself to be a man of action, and the traveling made him unwell. An assiduous student of his own poor health, he habitually listed in his journal the various medications he had to take.

To the emigrant train he saw assembling in May on the Missouri, the snobbish Bostonian preferred the company of a group of traveling Englishmen. On June 14, when one of the wagon-train people came to Parkman's camp looking for a stray, he noted with comical hauteur, "A true specimen of the raw, noisy western way. 'Hullo boys, where do you water your horses?' This was his form of address."

On June 15, they reached Fort Laramie. A weary Parkman found the place crowded with "rude and intrusive" emigrants who were "constantly asking questions, and refusing to credit the answers."

"Where are ye from, Californy?" one of them asked Parkman.

"No."

"Santy Fee?"

"No, the mountains."

"What yer been doin' thar? Tradin'?"

"No."

"Trappin'?"

"No."

"Emigratin'?"

"No."

"What have ye been doin' then, God damn ye?"

At the same time that Parkman was enjoying his journey west in the spring of 1846, a twenty-four-year-old Swiss peasant named Heinrich Lienhard bought a wagon in St. Louis with four friends for $50. Harnessing their oxen, they crossed Missouri and joined a wagon train at Independence.

At the emigrants' camp, a servant girl approached the five bachelors and asked who was doing their wash. Lienhard answered that they did it themselves. She offered to do his gratis if he gave her the soap, but her mistress appeared and said, "Lucinda, leave that be, I'll see that you have enough work for us without doing the wash for other people."

On May 12, when they had thirty wagons, the settlers waded into the undulating prairie. Whips cracked, wheels rumbled, and Herman the Alsatian (one of the five in Lienhard's wagon) moved his plug of tobacco from one cheek to the other. They walked in hip-high grass and slept in damp clothes.

After a few days, Lucinda left her employers and married eighteen-year-old Alfred Harlan. The wedding night, however, was not a success, and the next day they wanted nothing to do with each other. It was whispered that Alfred was upset, having discovered that Lucinda was not a virgin.

The days revolved around assorted mishaps. One of Lienhard's cows calved, but they had to slaughter the calf because it could not keep up. The mother refused to move from the spot where she had last seen her calf, and they had to tie her to the wagon and pull her along.

When Judge Morin, who had been elected captain of the train by acclamation, turned out to be a martinet, a meeting was held. Speaking in his own defense, the judge said, "Look here, I wanted to do what was right . . . my life is your life. . . ." The vote went against him, and he spoke up again: "Go to hell, you damned fools." Later, Lienhard overheard Mrs. Morin in their wagon: "Didn't I tell you, you fool you, it serves you right."

As they approached the Platte, the grass got shorter. Every day they observed herds of buffalo grazing on the other side of the river. One morning the cry went up, "Indians in great numbers." Waiting inside the circle of wagons, the settlers clutched loaded rifles. The Indians came closer, and Lienhard watched one snatch a vest out of a wagon. A man inside yanked it back and knocked the Indian down. When the Indian saw armed men behind the wagons, they left.

In their party was a skinny widow and her two children. She owned a small wagon drawn by a team of light oxen and driven by a man of about forty who was passing himself off as her second husband. In the middle of the night, when everyone was sleeping, the young men on watch heard strange noises. One after the other, they crept quietly up to the widow's wagon, and then compared notes.

A short time later, the "husband" left the train. He could no longer stand it, he told his friends, after driving the wagon all day he wanted some rest at night. Now the widow had to drive the wagon herself. She approached the five bachelors, saying, "I should think that since there are five of you with only one wagon, one of you could be spared to take care of a helpless, deserted woman."

When she singled out Zins (one of the five), he explained, "You see, I is a poor fellow, I got only one ox. So if I gets a woman, I puts her under the other yoke." They all laughed, and the widow retorted, "Laugh as much as you please, as long as I get a husband." But none of the five volunteered.

On reaching Fort Laramie, the widow said she would go no farther, since she could not drive her wagon alone. One of the emigrants, Mr. Wright, offered to take her in his, but Mrs. Wright approached the issue from a different perspective, saying, "If you take this person along, I'll stay here." Wright threw up his hands: "I see that I cannot be of help to this woman."

The arrival of the wagon train coincided with Francis Parkman's stay at the fort, and he noted the incident in his journal on June 26: "One woman, of more than suspected chastity, is left at the fort, & Bordeaux [the trader] is fool enough to receive her." Three days later Parkman mentioned the widow again in a letter to his father: "A party that passed yesterday left at the fort a woman who it seems had become a scandal to them. . . . She is now lodged among the squaws of the traders in a most pitiful situation. . . . She is left alone among the Indian women, and the half-savage retainers of the company."

The widow's fate has been lost to posterity, though we know what happened to Parkman—he returned to Boston and became a famous historian. The five bachelors joined a division of the wagon train on its way to California, and headed south from Wyoming into Utah.

At the Great Salt Lake on August 16, Lienhard saw a parcel of clothes flung out of the Harlan wagon. Stout, blond Lucinda followed in tears, dragging herself through the grass with her bundle in her arms. Finally, one of the wagons took her in.

On August 28, in northeast Nevada, some Shoshones appeared. Seeing that one of the settlers had a pipe, they asked for a smoke. "These dirty Indians are not going to smoke my pipe," the settler said. Lienhard and the others could see that the Indians were displeased by the man's gruff manner. One of the women quickly filled a pipe of her own, lit the bowl, and motioned to one of the elderly potbellied Shoshones. The Indian took ten big pulls, blowing the smoke out through his nostrils. Then he handed the pipe to his equally big-bellied companion, who puffed away and passed it on to two old squaws. To Lienhard they looked like two old sows who had wandered into a mudhole.

Traveling west along the Humboldt River, the emigrants had almost run out of food when they came upon some Indians who offered them grasshoppers to eat. The Germans in the party let go with their "Donnerwetters!" Eventually, they crossed into California and reached Sutter's Fort, where Lienhard took a job working for his fellow Swiss.

Eighteen forty-eight was the year that Oregon became a territory. Two Oregon bills had previously been brought before Congress but got snagged in the politics of slavery. When the southern senators discovered the proposed legislation banned slavery in the territory, they blocked it.

Thomas Hart Benton, the senator from Missouri, made himself the champion of the Oregon question. Although he was from a slaveholding state, he did not believe that slavery was feasible for Oregon. What were they going to do, he asked, transport slaves thousands of miles over the Oregon Trail, or on ships around the Horn?

A third bill, when it came before the Senate in 1848, also prohibited slavery. Again the senators from the South were up in arms, arguing that Congress could not pass any law that prevented people from moving to the territories with their slaves.

It seemed absurd to Benton that the slavery question should prevent the formation of a territory where in fact slavery did not exist. "We read in the Holy Writ that a certain people were cursed by the plague of the frogs," he said. "You could not look upon the table but there were frogs, you could not sit down at the banquet but there were frogs, you could not go to the bridal couch but there were frogs! And here, we can have no measures proposed, without having this pestilence thrust before us. Here it is, this black question forever on the table, on the nuptial couch, everywhere."

Benton's oratory proved persuasive, but when their amendments got voted down, the southerners resorted to a filibuster. They treated their

colleagues to all-night speeches recounting the biblical creation, Eve's conversation with the snake, and the fall of man. Apart from this effort, Senator Andrew Pickens Butler of South Carolina accused Benton on the Senate
floor of leaking the substance of secret sessions to a reporter. Butler called
Benton's conduct "dishonorable."

The hot-tempered Benton sprang to his feet. "You lie, sir!" he cried.
"You lie! I cram the lie down your throat!" These two venerable solons,
both white-haired and in their sixties, were restrained by other legislators
from doing violence to each other.

"I will see you, sir, at another time and place," Butler said.

"Yes, sir," replied Benton, "but take notice that when I fight, I fight
for a funeral."

When the third Oregon bill came to a vote on August 13, 1848, it
passed, and Oregon became a nonslave territory. Manifest Destiny was
stronger even than the politics of slavery. Benton told J. Quinn Thornton
of the Oregon Provisional Government, who was an interested observer of
the proceedings: "I did not blame Judge Butler so much as I did that
scoundrel Calhoun [John Calhoun was Butler's fellow senator from South
Carolina] who, while egging on Butler, sat there looking as demure as a
whore at a christening."

Besides becoming a territory, the other event in 1848 that transformed
Oregon was the discovery of gold in California. It had a powerful ripple
effect. An agricultural community Arcadian in its simplicity, Oregon was
touched with the finger of Midas. The initial consequence was a population
depletion far greater than the human loss caused by the Indian wars. Two-
thirds of the able-bodied men in the territory headed for the California gold
mines.

All other activities came to a halt. Crops were not harvested, grain was
not ground, lumber was not sawed. Souls went unsaved, for even the
missionaries succumbed to gold fever. Explaining to his superiors why he
had left his Oregon station for California, the Baptist Ezra Fisher wrote: "I
went to the mines principally to raise something to give my family the bare
comforts of life."

The lure of gold seemed to dissolve society's most dependable rou-
tines. The *Oregon Spectator*, the first newspaper published west of the Rockies, failed to go to press from September 7 until October 12, 1848. On its
return, the editor apologized, saying: "The gold fever which has swept
about 3000 of her officers, lawyers, physicians, farmers, and mechanics
from the plains of Oregon into the mines of California, took away our
printers also—hence the temporary non-appearance of the *Spectator*."

In 1849, however, the miners started coming home, some disappointed
and some rich. The inflow of gold brought prosperity, and Oregon basked
in the optimism of high wages and paid debts. Gold gave life to commerce.
Towns sprang up. The rivers bustled with boats awaiting supplies for the
mines. For farmers and lumbermen, it was a seller's market.

So much gold poured into Oregon that a coinage act had to be passed, which established the dollar value at $16.50 an ounce. The territory used its own gold coins, decorated with a beaver. But the downside was that all thought and effort seemed focused on getting rich.

By 1850, the American population of Oregon was around 12,000. A few settlers still came "the Horn around," but most came "the plains across." They put down roots fast. When an 1848 immigrant asked for a night's lodging from a settler who had crossed the year before, he was told, "Come out and see my garden truck. I've got a right smart chance of potatos, cabbage, peas, and wheat."

The Donation Act of September 1850 gave away land in Oregon Territory before the federal government had acquired title to it from the Indian owners—"Indian giving" in reverse. Because the act granted 320 acres to bachelors and 640 acres to married couples, a spate of May-September unions occurred, as husbands three times the age of their thirteen-year-old brides signed up.

By the time sixteen-year-old Harriet Clark and her forty-year-old husband took the Oregon Trail in 1851, the once bone-shaking journey had become a pleasure trip, a smooth road all the way. The two brought chickens along so they'd have fresh eggs. Harriet always remembered the trip as one long picnic, gathering berries and wild onions at every stop.

When they reached Salt Lake City, where the Mormons had settled, they sat in the adobe tabernacle and listened to some strong anti-U.S. sermons. One man said he wished Zachary Taylor was in hell begging bread, and everyone cheered.

The woman sitting next to Harriet told her, "If I had known of this two-wife business I would never have come." Then she started crying, and said her heart was broken because her husband had gone that morning to be "sealed" (wed) to a sixteen-year-old girl.

Oregon waited eleven years to advance from territory to state. The government in Washington was so far away it seemed like a mirage. With their long habit of self-rule, Oregonians even chafed under the minimal territorial government. Nonresident appointees arriving after a seven-month sea voyage were considered aliens and openly derided. People didn't like territorial laws such as the sheriff's power to sell property to pay for back taxes.

The opinion prevailed, however, that territorial laws were preferable to state laws. Opponents to statehood argued that it would bring increased taxes, as opposed to the federal funding they now enjoyed. The advocates of statehood said that it would bring Oregon congressional representation, which would deliver a railroad.

The referendum on statehood appeared on the ballot three times, and three times a majority voted it down. Meanwhile, the folks north of the Columbia River were energetically sending petitions to Congress setting forth their desire for a separate government. Acceding to their wishes,

President Millard Fillmore signed a bill creating Washington Territory in March 1853.

In Oregon the change of heart toward statehood finally came as a result of the Dred Scott case. On March 6, 1857, the Supreme Court decided that the slave Dred Scott had no right to sue in a federal court because he was not a citizen of Missouri or of the United States. Slaves were a form of property, the court reasoned; thus the Constitution protected the right of their masters to own them. Congress had no authority to abolish slavery in the territories. The Court in effect was declaring the Missouri Compromise —stipulating the admission of a free state for every slave state—unconstitutional.

For Oregon, the message of the Dred Scott decision was that a territorial legislature had no authority to ban slavery. Only a state could do that. Even proslavery Oregonians did not want slavery thrust upon them by a Supreme Court decision. The people of Oregon quickly swung over to wanting statehood. In June 1857, another referendum on framing a constitution passed, 7,617 to 1,679.

When the constitutional convention met in Salem on August 17, though, there was a real danger that it would introduce slavery. The many settlers who had been given donation grants needed labor urgently and had a curiously ambivalent attitude toward slavery. As they put it, "I shall vote against slavery, but if it carries I shall get me a nigger."

Consequently, the slavery issue overshadowed all others as the delegates hammered together a state constitution. In printed and spoken word, proslavers argued the need for cheap labor. Antislavers replied that one free white man was worth two slaves. Slavery would cost more than it would bring in benefits, for runaway slaves would find asylum with the Modoc and Klamath Indians and incite the tribes to war, as they had done in Florida. The debate proceeded along practical rather than moral lines.

The men drafting the Oregon constitution ultimately sidestepped the slavery dilemma by ruling that it would be dealt with in a separate election. The constitution did, however, disqualify Negroes and Chinese from voting. It was adopted on November 9, 1857. The results of the slavery election proved to be more ambiguous. Though the people of Oregon rejected by a wide margin the right to own slaves, they also approved a proposal to exclude free Negroes and mulattoes from the territory.

This murky tangle of freedom and restrictions led to a protracted debate in Congress and delayed Oregon's statehood for over a year. To complicate matters even more, the territory was a long way from the 60,000 people required for statehood in the Northwest Ordinance. At long last, however, President Buchanan signed the admission bill on Valentine's Day, 1859, and Oregon became a state. It was just in time for the Civil War.

CHAPTER TEN

THE CALIFORNIA FRONTIER

Dust always blowing about the town,
Except when sea fog laid it down,
And I was one of the children told
Some of the blowing dust was gold.

ROBERT FROST

The New York Public Library
San Francisco before the gold rush was a collection of sparsely
populated whaleback hills fronting on a natural harbor. Two wide
streets, Clay and Washington, run down to Montgomery, on the
bay. Among the points of interest are the Calaboose, William
Leidesdorff's City Hotel, the Howard & Mellus Store, Sill's Blacksmith Shop, and Captain John Paty's adobe house.

The settlement of California was Spain's last major colonial venture in the New World. In 1769, Father Junipero Serra and his fellow Franciscans joined a military expedition heading north from Baja California and founded Mission San Diego. Between 1769 and 1823, the Franciscans built twenty-one missions in the side valleys off the Pacific coast, as far north as San Francisco.

To protect the missions, the Spanish built four military posts, or presidios, in San Diego, Monterey, Santa Barbara, and San Francisco. The soldiers rounded up the Indians and resettled them around the missions, where they were baptized by the friars and taught farming and carpentry.

Before the Spanish arrived, an estimated 300,000 Indians lived in California, 80,000 of them in what became the mission strip south of San Francisco. Owing to a pleasant climate and plentiful natural resources, this area contained the highest population density of Indians in North America.

The missions soon turned into coercive fiefdoms, which prospered thanks to the mass of unpaid labor. The Indians came to loathe the peonage of mission life, not to mention the floggings administered for insubordination. They sometimes rebelled. More often, they ran away. A few friars were poisoned by their house servants.

Each mission had its squad of soldiers, who routinely raped the Indian women. The friars had no leverage to discipline the soldiers, upon whose protection they depended. But when the Indian women aborted the unborn children of rape or strangled them at birth, the prolife Franciscans were outraged.

The friars' zeal to put a stop to abortions gave rise to some truly bizarre events. According to the deposition of Lorenzo Asisara, a neophyte in the Santa Cruz Mission, the following incident occurred in 1791:

One of the Franciscans, Father Ramon Olbes, noticed that two Indian women had scratched each other's faces in a fight. Inquiring into the cause of their quarrel, he was told that one had children while the other did not. Olbes sent for the childless woman's husband, and through gestures, asked him why it was so. The husband pointed to the sky to signify that only God knew the reason.

Olbes summoned an interpreter, who asked the husband if he slept with his wife. When he nodded, Olbes had the couple placed in a room and instructed them to perform coitus in his presence. The husband refused. Olbes then commanded him to show his penis and prove that it was in proper working order.

Afterward, the friar sent the husband to the guardhouse in shackles. He turned to the wife and, through the interpreter, asked why her face was scratched. She said the other woman had attacked her out of jealousy. Olbes wanted to know if her husband had been sleeping with the other woman. She said he had.

Olbes now suspected that the woman was guilty of aborting her pregnancies, and asked, "Why don't you bear children?"

"Who knows?" the woman replied.

Olbes took her into another room and proceeded to examine her genitals, as if he were a gynecologist for the Inquisition. The Indian woman resisted and grabbed the cord at the waist of his robe. Biting through the heavy sleeve, she buried her teeth in his arm. Olbes cried out, and the interpreter rushed in to help him subdue the woman.

At Olbes's orders, the Indian woman received fifty lashes. He then had her shackled and locked in the nunnery. He had one of the mission carpenters carve a wooden doll in the form of an infant, and commanded the woman to carry it in her arms for nine days, as though it were a child. He also made the husband wear cattle horns on top of his head, the Spanish sign of the cuckold (though in this case, the husband had cuckolded the wife). As the man was marched daily to mass from jail, the other mission Indians mocked him. All this was part of the friars' program to prevent abortions and infanticides.

What could not be prevented was the astonishing death rate among the Indian population as a whole. During the mission period the number of Indians living between San Diego and San Francisco declined from 80,000 to 18,000, mainly because of disease. As the anthropologist Alfred Kroeber put it, "the Fathers . . . were saving souls only at the inevitable cost of lives."

With the Spanish ousted from Mexico in 1821, California became Mexican and the missions went into a period of decline. The Franciscans were discredited for having sided with Spain in the struggle for independence. Departing Spanish priests were not replaced. Funds to maintain the missions dried up.

In 1833, the anticlerical Mexican Congress secularized the missions, which was tantamount to closing them. The church lost title to the lands, and sometimes it passed to the baptized Indians, who often sold their acres for a few bottles of brandy.

One way or the other, the Indians were dispossessed, and wandered about like vagrants. Much of the land ended up in the hands of wealthy ranchers. By 1845, 9 million acres of mission land had been sold off in eight hundred substantial grants.

By then, 7,000 Mexican settlers had found a home in California, many of them soldiers or the descendants of soldiers. Rarely had an army career provided such a golden opportunity. Abandoned mission buildings were put to various uses. Some became Mexican garrisons. At the Carmel Mission near Monterey, a kiln was converted into a crematorium for dead dogs. The citizens of Monterey stripped the tiles from the friars' residence, and the adobe walls returned to mud.

American interest in California started with Yankee merchants out of Boston. They developed the so-called triangular trade—ships carrying manufactured goods sailed around Cape Horn to the Pacific northwest coast and California. There they sold their goods and loaded up with seal-skins and otter to sell in China, bringing Oriental imports like tea back to Boston.

Richard Henry Dana, who shipped out as a sailor, provided an eyewitness account in *Two Years Before the Mast*, published in 1840. When his ship the *Pilgrim* arrived in Monterey harbor, the boats were lowered and the men clambered in. Resting on their oars in the swell, just outside the surf, they waited for a wave to bring them in. Catching the top of the wave, they raced toward land with the speed of a racehorse, as the sterns pointed skyward, and shot up on the beach. The dry steerhides they had come for were waiting for them neatly stacked on the beach and folded in half, stiff as boards. The sailors, wearing thick woolen caps, carried them on their heads down to the boats.

Trading aboard ship lasted for a week, as the inhabitants came out in their own boats. The *Pilgrim* was a floating general store, dispensing everything from Scotch whiskey to Chinese fireworks. Dana, a twenty-two-year-old Harvard graduate, did not think much of the locals. "The Californians," he wrote, "are an idle, thriftless people and can make nothing for themselves. The country abounds in grapes, yet they buy bad wines made in Boston and brought round by us, at an immense price."

Some of these American traders settled in Monterey and in the little Mexican harbor town of Yerba Buena, later renamed San Francisco. In the 1830s, with the opening up of the Oregon Trail, emigrants began arriving in California from the east. One of the first was the Swiss adventurer John Augustus Sutter.

Born in 1803, Sutter married a rather strict and overbearing woman when he was twenty-three. They had four children, and Sutter opened a dry-goods store in a town near Bern. As he piled up debts the urge to escape his creditors and his wife got the better of him and he fled to America, arriving in New York in 1834.

Sutter went west to St. Louis, where he joined a trading expedition on its way to Santa Fe. As part of starting a new life, he invented a heroic past for himself, claiming to have served as a captain in the Swiss Guard of King Charles X of France. In Westport (part of today's Kansas City) in 1838, Sutter managed to latch on to a fur-company wagon train headed for the Rockies. At the annual rendezvous, some trappers Sutter met took him to Fort Vancouver. On a whim, the footloose Helvetian bought passage on a ship to the Sandwich Islands (Captain Cook's name for Hawaii), and stayed there four months.

On July 1, 1839, accompanied by eight Kanakas, Sutter sailed into the magnificent harbor of Yerba Buena and anchored in the bay. But a Mexican officer came on board and told him: "This is not a port of entry. You cannot land here, you must go to Monterey." So off he went to Monterey, where he made friends with Governor Juan Alvarado. Again on a whim, he asked for a grant of land on the Sacramento River, which he had never seen. The governor amiably told him to go and make his selection, and then come back to Monterey to receive both his grant and his Mexican citizenship.

Returning to Yerba Buena, Sutter paid a call on General Mariano Vallejo, who was stationed in Sonoma, to keep the West Coast secure against the Russian presence there. Vallejo told him there was plenty of fine land closer to the bay, such as the Napa Valley. Sutter said that he preferred to be on a navigable river. His real reason was that he wanted to put some distance between himself and the Spaniards. "I noticed," he said, "that the hat must come off before the military guard, the flagstaff, and the church, and I preferred a country where I could keep mine on."

From Sonoma, it was only some fifteen miles to the coast. There the Russians owned a depot called Fort Ross at Bodega Bay (in today's Marin County), perched atop a seventy-foot precipice overlooking the Pacific. Sutter went to have a look and was warmly welcomed by the urbane commander, Alexander Rotscheff, who gave him a tour of the twin-towered quadrangular fort.

A model for the settlement Sutter was soon to build, Fort Ross was manned by 130 Aleuts sent down from Alaska. The purpose of this south-ernmost Russian outpost was to serve as a granary for the czar's Alaskan stations, where nothing grew. Besides the granaries, the fort held work-shops, an onion-domed chapel, and redwood huts for fishermen and hunt-ers. Down on the beach, Sutter saw a wharf, a tannery, and a boat shed. In the fields that lay along the plateau, the Russians grew their indispens-able barley and wheat, with the help of paid Indian labor.

In August 1839, Sutter and his Kanakas, plus nine hired men, as-cended the Sacramento in a small, two-masted boat propelled by sail and oar. Two flatboats loaded with supplies followed. From San Pablo Bay, they sailed into Suisun Bay and found the mouth of the Sacramento, a wide, placid river in the summer, though high mud coats on the trunks of the sycamores lining its banks told of spring floods. The men noticed bunches of feathers tied to overhanging branches, which the Indians had left as offerings to the gods who had granted them good fishing.

When Sutter finally came to the juncture of the Sacramento and the American, he took the latter river past tule-covered lagoons as far as the boats would go and then he landed. After putting his supplies ashore, he summoned all hands and told them he was sending the schooner downriver the next day and those who wanted to leave could, for he wanted no discontented workers. Six sailors quit, and he was left with eight loyal Kanakas, a Belgian, a German, and an Irishman.

Moving inland a quarter of a mile from the landing, Sutter found some high ground and commenced building, first grass huts in the Hawaiian style, then adobe covered with tule. He was launching a kingdom on a shoestring, and there followed a series of "please to send me" letters to San Francisco merchants as the schooner shuttled on its shopping trips.

When the Indians came for presents, Sutter offered them bags of

Hawaiian sugar and blue beads from Sitka. Then he fired his cannon at a target to impress them with the big bang. At first, the Indians were troublesome, prowling around at night with weapons hidden under the blankets Sutter had given them. But the trouble stopped when he started using a "work-against-goods" system. He had the blacksmith make tin coins with a hole in them; one coin meant one day's work. The coins could be used to buy goods at the store, so that they put their energies to constructive purposes.

Soon the Indians learned the use of the plough and the whipsaw. By 1840, Sutter had 600 men working in the fields, and four or five oxen a day had to be slaughtered to feed them. He harvested 40,000 bushels of wheat a year, most of which he sold to Fort Ross. He also owned 12,000 head of cattle, 2,000 horses, and 15,000 sheep.

Sutter named his fiefdom in the wilderness New Helvetia. His nearest white neighbor lived in the Napa Valley, a hundred miles away. "I was everything," he later recalled, "patriarch, priest, father, and judge. I had church bells from Fort Ross which were rung at funerals, and also by the night watch as on a vessel at sea." He officiated at weddings and burials, and sent out punitive expeditions when Indians attacked his farms or stole his cattle.

Sutter set about changing the habits of the Indians, not on principle like the Franciscans, but in a practical way. For example, because polygamy was the rule, the chiefs had acquired so many wives that no women were left for the young men. So Sutter asked all the men to stand in a row, and all the women to line up facing them. Then he told the women to step forward one by one and select a husband. Only the most important chiefs were allowed to keep two wives, since Sutter had two.

In 1841, Sutter erected a fort protected by walls two feet thick and eighteen feet high. Built out of adobe bricks, it encompassed five acres. On the bastions, twelve cannon were mounted. Inside the walls stood barracks, workshops, a bakery, a mill, a smithy, and a blanket factory. A tannery, its odors wafting over the walls, lay outside the fort. It had taken Sutter four years to erect his tiny kingdom. When in 1841 he finally had time to go to Monterey to pick up his Mexican citizenship and sign his land grant, it came to thirty-three square miles, or about 49,000 acres.

The ships' captains who brought up supplies and saw Sutter's mix of workers, which included Kanakas, Indians, Mexicans, runaway slaves, mountaineers, and deserting sailors, said, "My God, how can you manage with such a crew of rascals?" "I get along with them fine," Sutter said, "because I give them nothing but water to drink." But when Sutter built a distillery for his needs and those of his visitors, he himself became a heavy drinker.

In July 1841, Alexander Rotscheff approached Sutter with an intriguing offer. It had been decided in St. Petersburg to vacate Fort Ross. Having exterminated the seal and the otter, the Russians had not found a substitute resource to pay for the fort's upkeep. There was also friction with the Mexicans next door.

As a result, Fort Ross was up for sale. Rotscheff did not want to sell to Vallejo, who had on one occasion insulted the Russian flag. Therefore, he offered the fort and all its contents to Sutter for $30,000. The deal included a twenty-two-ton launch, the cannon, and even the soldiers' uniforms. Sutter could hardly refuse, and a contract was drawn up in French, whose first words read, "With the consent of the Emperor of all the Russias. . ."

Sutter felt that he was dealing directly as one emperor to another. By this time he was printing passports for the inhabitants of New Helvetia, which the Mexicans honored. Sutter himself often wore a gold-braided Mexican uniform, and when notables came, he hoisted the Mexican colors and fired a salute.

The emperor of New Helvetia paid $2,000 down on the fort, putting up land as collateral for the rest. In the months to come he transferred from Fort Ross to New Helvetia 1,700 head of cattle, 940 horses, 900 sheep, 49 ploughs, 29 rakes, 43 harnesses, and a glass greenhouse.

The Mexicans, who had claims on Fort Ross, were not pleased. Sutter's one-time sponsor, Governor Alvarado, called him "an ungrateful villain." From Sonoma, General Vallejo harassed Sutter every way he could, stopping his men and inspecting the cattle he brought from the fort.

In 1841 emigrants began trickling over the mountains on horseback and on foot (but not yet in wagons). Sutter's houses were soon crowded with hungry, destitute Americans. Very few of the pioneers owned more than their teams. That winter he often had to go out and rescue them in the snow. A few of them he hired, like his clerk and right-hand man, the inestimable John Bidwell, formerly a schoolteacher in Missouri.

In 1842 and 1843, hundreds of emigrants came through, for Sutter had accidentally chosen a highly strategic site, right on the route from Nevada to California. He welcomed them all, while hoping to stay neutral as friction grew between Mexico and the United States. In Monterey, a new governor arrived, Manuel Micheltorena, whom Sutter quickly made his ally.

But in spite of his penchant for nonalignment, Sutter was about to be thrown into international intrigue. On March 8, 1844, he saw two men on horseback approach the fort wearing the Scotch caps of the Hudson's Bay Company. The men were Captain John C. Frémont and his guide Kit Carson, and the caps were a ruse.

Frémont, who had some surveying experience, had in 1842 been sent by the U.S. Topographical Bureau on the first of four expeditions across the Rockies and into Oregon Territory. When he shot the rapids of the Platte River, he lost much of his equipment and nearly lost his life.

On the second expedition to the Columbia River in 1843, Frémont had gotten himself in hot water from the start, for he had taken along an army howitzer without permission. With twenty-five men and a hundred horses, he defied a ban on Americans entering California, and crossed the Sierra Nevadas in five feet of snow. He lost horses in snowdrifts and his starving men had to eat the mules. In February 1844, he reached Carson Pass (west of today's Woodfords, California), which by boiling water he computed to be at 9,338 feet (the higher the altitude, the longer it takes water to boil).

Below Frémont and his party lay the Sacramento Basin. A pathetic procession of skeletal men leading skeletal horses descended into the valley. Frémont and Carson rode ahead, looking for Sutter's Fort. On March 8 they found themselves face to face with a short, stout, mustachioed man of forty, whose fringe of blond hair circled a bald head too large for his body. A pair of round, doll-like blue eyes regarded the two travelers.

"I have heard of you and knew you must be in this direction somewhere," Frémont told Sutter. The captain acted a little high-handed, demanding rather than asking, as his men came straggling in, that they be given room and board. Sutter offered what he had and sent for more. Soon Indian girls entered bearing fresh trout and salmon, venison and bear meat, followed by salad and fruit. It was a welcome change from mule stew. Frémont was impressed by the order and industriousness of Sutter's domain, which equaled in size several Swiss cantons together.

Frémont wanted thirty horses, thirty mules, and thirty saddles, as well as clothing. Ready to comply, Sutter started his forge going day and night shoeing the captain's horses. He charged everything at cost, taking payment in the form of an order on the U.S. Topographical Bureau. "No one else in California would have trusted him for a dollar," Sutter later said. He did what he could for the captain, who in Sutter's opinion took favors for granted. He was still the neutral Swiss, trying to stay on good terms with both the Americans and the Mexicans.

When Frémont left on March 24, Sutter was not sorry to see him go. There were by now about four hundred Americans in the valley. Frémont had talked to some of them, forming a strong impression of Mexico's shaky hold on California, and returned to St. Louis in August 1844.

Relations between Mexico and the United States had hit a low point. In 1844, Congress was debating whether the Republic of Texas should be invited to join the Union. In California the Mexicans suspected that American settlers wanted a second Texas and that Sutter supported their cause.

At this point there was a rebellion of Mexican generals against Governor Micheltorena. These uprisings were not unusual in California. As Richard Henry Dana had observed ten years earlier, "Revolutions are matters of constant occurrence. . . . They take muskets and bayonets, and seizing the presidio and the customs-house, divide the spoils and declare a new dynasty."

Catching wind of the plot, Sutter saw the chance to defend his ally the governor, while becoming the military hero he imagined himself to be. Raising two hundred men, he declared himself "Commander in Chief of the Forces of the River Sacramento," and set out to fulfill his lifelong dream of glory on the battlefield.

The strategy of these Mexican revolts consisted of simulating combat in order to win by bluff. Sometimes a mule or two were killed. Sutter joined Micheltorena at San Luis Obispo. The governor had such a bad case of piles that he could not sit on his horse, but had to be transported to the scene of battle in a kind of buggy. The rebel general, José Castro, had stationed his troops around Los Angeles, a hamlet, as Sutter explained in letters, that was "near San Diego."

On February 19, Sutter's men came face-to-face with General Castro's troops at Cahuenga Pass, north of Los Angeles. But when the Americans Sutter had among his mounted riflemen saw that there were also Americans under Castro's command, they refused to fight. As a result, Micheltorena was defeated and dispatched into exile and Sutter was taken prisoner. A few days later he swore allegiance to the new regime under Governor Pío Pico and was sent home. He got back to the fort on April 1, out $8,000 and 150 horses on account of a futile, comic-opera war.

In the meantime, Polk had been elected on an expansionist platform, which included statehood for Texas and the slogan "Fifty-four Forty or Fight." With Texas about to become a state, the Mexicans were wondering what was next on Polk's agenda.

In Washington, the administration felt that war with Mexico was inevitable. Thus, in the spring of 1845, John Frémont was sent on his third expedition, this time under the sponsorship not only of the Topographical Bureau but also of the War Department. Officially, however, he was an engineer on a scientific mission to survey the Rockies and the Sierra Nevadas.

But if that was the case, why did he need sixty armed men, including sharpshooters outfitted with the finest rifles obtainable? A kind of Trojan horse, Frémont's scientific mission could be converted into a military force if and when the time came.

In August 1845, Frémont arrived with his company at Bent's Fort on the Arkansas River in Colorado. In the fall of that year, the Mexicans offered to buy Sutter out for $100,000, hoping to garrison the fort with soldiers who could stop the American migration. Tempted by the six figures, Sutter asked for time to think the deal over. "What will the settlers in their valleys do if you abandon them to the Mexicans?" John Bidwell asked. Sutter declined the offer.

On December 9, Frémont revisited Sutter's Fort, again demanding mules and supplies. A month later he marched to Monterey and met with the American consul, Thomas Larkin. When he continued his march southward, the alarmed Mexicans ordered him out of California. Frémont's response was to occupy a high point called Gavilan (Hawk's) Peak, twenty-five miles from Monterey, build a log fort, and raise the American flag. But he left after three days, heeding Larkin's warning that the Mexicans were about to attack.

Frémont headed north for Oregon on March 9, 1846, and stopped at Sutter's Fort on March 21. Sutter had no idea what the captain's comings and goings meant. But when he heard some time later that Frémont had bought stolen horses from the Indians 120 miles north of the fort, he began to suspect the engineer's integrity.

Frémont was in Oregon when war with Mexico broke out in May, and he at once headed south, calling his reentry "the first step in the conquest of California." The captain's presence incited American settlers to acts of rebellion. On June 14, 1846, about thirty-five greasy-haired men in leather hunting shirts seized Sonoma. The settlers unpacked an unbleached cotton cloth five feet long and less than a yard wide, and sewed a single red flannel strip on the bottom. In the upper left-hand corner, they outlined a five-pointed star in ink and painted it red. Then they depicted a bear facing the star on its right side. Under the star and the bear appeared the words CALIFORNIA REPUBLIC.

The settlers took a few prisoners, notably the mutton-chop-whiskered Vallejo and his brother. They were held at Sutter's Fort, where Sutter had them dine at his table. This did not sit well with Frémont, who rode to the fort and told Sutter: "You do not know how to treat prisoners."

"Yes I do," Sutter replied, "for I have been a prisoner myself." Yet he added: "Take charge of these men, for I want nothing further to do with them."

Frémont, however, commandeered the fort and ordered Sutter to enter the service of the United States as a lieutenant of dragoons at $50 a month. The Mexican War lasted only a few months. When it ended in January 1847, Frémont was appointed governor of California. After the splenetic engineer quarreled with other officers, he was recalled and sent to Washington for a court-martial, but Polk pardoned him.

Henrich Lienhard, the Swiss bachelor we last saw on the Oregon Trail sharing a wagon with four friends, arrived at Fort Sutter in mid-October 1846 and tossed his hat in the air with joy. An Indian scalp dangled from the gatepost, and as he entered the fort, some soldiers accosted him and urged him to enlist. The Mexican War was on, and Lienhard ebulliently joined the boys in blue. Soon he was marching off to San Jose.

After the war he returned to the fort and full employment when Sutter made his fellow Swiss the overseer. Sutter by this time was a morning drinker, and when Lienhard arrived with the daybook, he was already at the whiskey bottle. Once during dinner Sutter smashed an entire set of dishes in a liquor-driven rage. On many an occasion Lienhard had to undress his boss and put him to bed.

To some extent Sutter's drinking was a by-product of his fame. Visitors by the score came through wanting to meet the celebrated founder of New Helvetia, who invariably invited them in for a drink. When he'd had a few, he started telling war stories: "At Grenoble, I received a bayonet wound in the leg. Our major noticed the blood running down my white trousers and called 'take him back to be treated.' But I told them to go on." Lienhard had heard that one so many times he almost believed it.

Most of all Lienhard disapproved of the Indian girls who were constantly at Sutter's beck and call. The older Sutter got, the younger the girls, some a mere eleven years old. "Everyone knew," Lienhard wrote in his memoirs, "that Sutter was a typical Don Juan with women. In addition to the large number of Indian girls and women in his harem, there were also in the fort many Indian loafers who rarely worked, but were fed and nicely clothed because their wives received special consideration from the master of the fort."

Sutter always said, "I, Sutter, am the law." Another of his favorite remarks was "I will do anything to be honored." Lienhard lost all respect for his chief, who had become a sodden braggart. Having seen the sober trading post degenerate into a den of iniquity, the disillusioned overseer left California in 1850.

After the war made California part of the United States, emigrants streamed into the new territory and business boomed at Sutter's Fort. In 1847, needing to expand the scope of his activities, Sutter started building a gristmill on the American River, about four miles above the fort. He got a good fall of water by damming the river and digging the "race" (or ditch for providing water power to turn the wheel).

By the end of 1847 everything had been put in place—four pairs of millstones, wheels, and a building. The gristmill was six weeks away from completion and Sutter predicted that he would soon be grinding wheat for the entire Sacramento Valley.

In August 1847 some eight hundred Mormon men who had been sent to Salt Lake City to fight in the California war came by Sutter's domain on their way back to Utah. About eighty of the group stayed to work at Sutter's so that they could buy horses and cattle to take home with them. Sutter assigned thirty-four of the Mormons to putting up the gristmill, and on November 30 they raised the frame. He had never seen better workers.

Sutter also needed a sawmill, and had in his employ a mechanic from New Jersey, James Marshall, who said he could build one. He was a quarrelsome fellow, but Sutter humored him. Marshall found a site in Coloma, about forty miles away, on a stream alongside a pine-clad hill. Though it lay outside the boundary of Sutter's grant, meaning that the lumber would have to be rafted down the American River, Sutter trusted his man and told him to go ahead.

In a lashing rain on the afternoon of January 24, 1848, a soaking-wet and mud-splattered Marshall entered Sutter's office next to the guardhouse. He asked to see Sutter alone in the big house. Why, Sutter wondered, had Marshall come forty miles on horseback in a hard rain? He knew it couldn't be for provisions, which had been sent up the day before.

Marshall followed Sutter inside the house, gasping and looking like a madman. When they were inside, Marshall asked if the door was locked, and Sutter went and turned the key, wondering why all the mystery.

"I want two bowls of water," Marshall said.

Sutter rang one of the six different bells he had for clerks and servants, and the water shortly appeared.

"Now I want a stick of redwood," Marshall said, "and some twine, and some sheet copper."

"Why do you want all those things?" Sutter asked.

"I want to make some scales," Marshall said.

"But I have scales in the apothecary's shop," Sutter said.

Sutter left for a moment and returned carrying the scales. Marshall pulled from his pants pocket a white cotton cloth that he carefully unrolled on the table. Sutter saw a small pile of tiny grains, some as minuscule as a pinhead, others the size of a pea.

"I believe this is gold," Marshall whispered, "but the people at the mill laughed at me and said I was crazy."

"We will soon see," Sutter replied. Ignoring the scales, he dropped the gold in a bowl of water along with some silver dust and the gold sank to the bottom, outweighing the silver.

Sutter pulled the *American Encyclopedia* off a shelf and riffled through the pages. After a while he pronounced, "I believe this is the finest kind of gold."

Marshall said that the millrace was too shallow at the lower end and the water dammed up against some gravel bars. It washed back against the flutter wheel and prevented it from turning. To deepen the race, the men had to blast the exposed rock, and Indians dug up the hefty pieces and hauled them away.

Every evening Marshall routinely raised the dam gate and let the water flow through to get rid of as much sand and gravel as possible. In the morning he closed the gate, shut off the water, and examined the race to see what still needed to be cleared. One morning as about a foot of water ran through the ditch, Marshall caught sight of something shiny. He climbed down and scooped it up. Every night's washing laid bare another little yield.

For some reason, when he rode to the sawmill the next morning with Marshall, Sutter felt depressed. He sensed that the discovery of gold would be a curse, and that it would ruin him. But he surrendered to his destiny. Marshall took him to the millrace that the workers were deepening to ten feet, digging through sand and gravel. Sutter told them to stop and let the water through. When the water had flowed awhile he ordered the channel dammed up again.

The water and loose dirt ran off, revealing a scattering of little yellow flakes on the muddy bed of the ditch. Sutter picked up a few, and Marshall and the Mormon workers handed him some more. Sutter told the men that it was gold all right but to keep it quiet until he got his gristmill going.

A few days later, when Sutter had to send another wagonload of provisions to the sawmill, he made the mistake of manning the wagon with the Swiss teamster, Jacob Wittmer, rather than one of his Indians. Wittmer was a friend of the cook at the sawmill, Mrs. Wiener, and when he got there, he hailed one of the cook's sons. "We have got some gold," the boy cried. The teamster laughed. Mrs. Wiener appeared in a doorway and said, "Well, you need not laugh, it is true." To prove it, she gave him a gold flake.

When Wittmer returned to Sutter's, he headed straight for the store outside the fort kept by Sam Brannan and George Smith. Aside from Sutter's, this was the only retail shop in the valley.

One of the store's rules was no credit for whiskey, which was not the best article to be sold on time. Wittmer was miserably dry. Upon entering the store he walked up to the counter where he had been so often refused, and called for his poison.

"You know very well whiskey means money," George Smith told him.

Wittmer proudly displayed his gold flake. "That is money," he said. "It is gold."

The secret was out. George Smith couldn't wait to tell—among other people—his partner Sam Brannan, a Mormon who happened to be away at the time collecting tithes for the construction of a temple from Mormon workers in the area. He pocketed the money, got himself excommunicated, and moved on to San Francisco, where he became a leading citizen.

News of gold led to an invasion of the Sacramento Valley, which to Sutter was as bad as a plague of locusts. His workers departed for the hills, leaving the tanning vats full of rotting leather. And so it went in the shoe shop, the saddle shop, and the smithy—all instantly vacated.

In March, an item appeared in a San Francisco paper. By May, eight hundred miners were in the hills panning for gold. Easy riches attracted riffraff and the stealing began. They stole the bells out of the main house and the gate weights from the gate. Sutter cured his salmon in barrels, and they stole the barrels. There were no laws, and Sutter's men had deserted, and he had no way to keep people out. He never finished his gristmill. There was a saying that a thief would steal anything but a millstone but they stole the millstone.

In September 1848, William Grimshaw was on a boat heading up the Sacramento on his way to Sutter's, having come from New York upon hearing the news. Arriving at his destination, he made fast to some sycamores and instantly realized that the famed fort had been turned into a supply depot for miners. It was a busy scene, with carts raising dust, and Indians bartering bits of gold for blankets. A wrinkled trapper was shaking a bag of gold, saying, "I guess this beats beaver skins."

When Grimshaw introduced himself, Sutter hired him as bookkeeper, since all his people had left for the mines. Grimshaw kept a ledger with running accounts for "Welsh Sam," "Dancing Jim," and a number of other miners. In those days no one ever asked the price of anything. When John Fowler gave an oyster supper for some of his friends, he paid $144 for a dozen two-pound tins of Baltimore oysters, and he paid without a murmur.

The blacksmith charged an ounce of gold ($16) for shoeing one shoe. Joseph Wadleigh arrived from the East Coast with a supply of tin plate and a set of tools, and hammered out tin pans at an ounce apiece. Sitting at his desk before his ledgers, Grimshaw could hear the tinner's tap-tap-tap all day long and into the night. Pans being as indispensable to the miner as a pick and shovel, Wadleigh soon made a fortune and went home.

In the spring of 1849, Grimshaw balanced the books and sent $50,000 in gold dust to San Francisco. The dust was poured into buckskin sacks, then nailed up inside a strong wooden box and delivered to the captain of a launch. "I doubt if we went through the formality of taking a receipt," Grimshaw later recalled. "Although we had no government, no courts, no judges, no sheriffs, no churches, no preachers, and no taxes, never before or since has there existed a community where every man's rights were so protected."

But despite the sudden boom, Sutter's fears were founded. Life after gold was precarious. The basement of the big house was turned into a bar and gaming den patronized by horse thieves and swindlers, where stabbings and shootings were commonplace.

So many squatters invaded his land that Sutter declared bankruptcy in 1852. Twelve years later a grateful California legislature voted him a $250 a month pension, which could not even begin to pay his debts. Once the lord of a vast domain, Sutter became a pleader before the U.S. Congress for relief. Eventually, he moved to the Moravian village of Lititz in Lancaster County, Pennsylvania, and it was there that he died in 1880.

News of California gold spread as quickly as an ignited trail of gunpowder circling the earth. Every day Horace Greeley ran a two-column "Golden Chronicle" on the front page of the *New York Tribune*. On December 5, 1848, President Polk told Congress: "The accounts of the abundance of gold in that territory are of such an extraordinary character as would scarcely command belief were they not corroborated by the authentic reports of officers in the public service."

In London and in Sydney, Australia, paperboys called out the news on street corners. In Canton it was told by ship captains. The news radiated with the brightness of the nuggets themselves. Was there a single person on the planet who had not heard it?

And so they came to California from every land on earth, it seemed, attracted not so much by the certainty of wealth as by the sense of possibility. Here was a chance, open to all. In the new gold-rush economy, there were a hundred ways to make money, and not necessarily by finding gold.

Soldiers and sailors who happened to be in the vicinity got a jump on everyone else by deserting. Alfred Green, a volunteer soldier stationed in Los Angeles, decamped for the mines the minute he heard the news in March 1848. He and five fellow soldiers expropriated three of Uncle Sam's two-wheeled carts, drawn by Uncle's horses, and loaded them up with Uncle's provisions.

The six men headed for the foothills of Placerville, about thirty miles east of Sacramento, and started panning. They were collecting about $120 worth of gold a day, split six ways. Downstream, some Indians were panning, and when they quit, in the evening, they stopped to admire Green's brightly colored necktie. Would he sell it? He would. They went off to one side and made up a little parcel from the gold they had panned that day and exchanged it for the necktie.

Despite extra sentries placed on gangways and forecastles, with two at each cathead, men-of-war and merchant ships docking at San Francisco soon lost their crews. A vessel would hardly be a month in port before three-fourths of her sailors were gone.

J. P. C. Allsopp, a Louisiana-born sailor whose ship sat anchored off San Francisco in December 1848, later recalled: "I saw a launches' crew coxswain at the moment the boat reached the landing place jump ashore and make tracks for the sand hills. . . . Even warrant officers took 'leg bail,' and the sentries ran away from their posts, taking their muskets with them. California is full of the descendants of runaway sailors who, cured of their passion for salt water, made excellent farmers. . . . Crews had to be made up of worthless landlubbers who did not know the difference between the maintack and the futtock shrouds."

Allsopp himself shortly demonstrated a preference for dry land over water. San Francisco then looked like a soldier's camp, covered with tents. Seeing the crowds and the lack of accommodations, he opened a boarding-house on Clay Street. He fitted out the bunks the way they used to be in the steerage of the old Blackball liners, and charged $2 a bunk. A code of regulations was posted in various parts of the building:

> No Fighting Allowed on the Premises.
> Gambling Strictly Prohibited After Midnight.
> Men Are not to Turn in like the Georgia Major,
> Booted and Spurred.

John Currey followed his star to California in 1849 via the Isthmus of Panama. Travelers disembarked on the Atlantic side, and natives charged exorbitant rates to pole them up the insect-ridden Chagres River in cramped boats. Then they caught a mule train down the Pacific slope through the jungle. All too often baggage was lost or stolen, and all too often travelers had to wait for days in the jammed and unsanitary sinkhole of Panama City before boarding a northbound steamer.

When Currey arrived in San Francisco, there were twenty wooden houses and a thousand cloth tents scattered in the sand hills. He was a lawyer, and found business aplenty—admiralty cases, real estate closings, ejectments for forcible entry, litigation on mercantile contracts, and some foreclosures.

Real estate speculation focused on land north of Market, east of Kearny, south of Pacific, and on to the bay. South of Market a series of hills rose up like haystacks. North Beach was the populated part of the city. Lots later worth half a million in the center of town were sold at auction for three and four hundred dollars. The auctioneer sold them so fast it made your head spin.

When Alex Todd arrived in San Francisco in 1849, he saw a long line in front of the post office at the corner of Pike and Clay. Upon further inquiry, he learned that there was no postal service of any kind to the mines, or even to the tent cities of Sacramento and Stockton. The miners had to come to San Francisco to pick up their mail.

Alex Todd decided to start a letter express to the mines, charging a

The New York Public Library
In San Francisco after the gold rush, long lines formed daily in front of the post office at the corner of Pike and Clay. The window was opened at 7 A.M., and $25 in gold dust would hold one's place in line. In the "Faithful Representation," two lines have formed for general delivery, one for box delivery, and one on the far right for newspaper delivery.

dollar for every letter. After offering to kick back a quarter per letter to the San Francisco postmaster, he was sworn in as a clerk. Soon he had a list of a hundred customers.

On Todd's first visit to Stockton, some merchants told him they had something they wanted freighted to San Francisco. He went into Bell's store to see what it was—a lot of gold dust packed in bags. Stuffing the bags into a keg labeled BUTTER, he delivered them to Lord & Company in San Francisco. He carried something like $200,000 worth of dust, for which he charged a shipping fee of 5 percent. On arrival he picked up a load of mail for the return trip.

His client list grew until he sometimes had two thousand letters on a trip. When the steamers docked in San Francisco, he went aboard before the passengers got off and bought all their New York newspapers, which were many months old. Sometimes he collected as many as a thousand, which he sold to news-starved miners for a half-ounce each ($8).

It wasn't long before the miners started asking Todd to hold on to their gold dust, and his express service turned into a banking business. He charged his depositors half a percent a month. All the security the miner had was a receipt. Todd's net profit from holding the dust was $1,000 a day.

But as his business expanded, he had losses from fires and robberies. He wasn't robbed on the road but by his own clerks. In 1852 a "confidential" clerk in Stockton stole $70,000. Another clerk in Mariposa embezzled $50,000, and one in Mokelumne Hill took $40,000. They handled so much gold dust that some of it stuck to their fingers. When the clerk at Mokelumne Hill was caught, he committed suicide.

As for fires, there was no fire insurance. All you could do was jump and hope for the best. Todd jumped out of the bedroom window above his burning office in Stockton in May 1850 with no clothes on. When the flames had been extinguished, he dusted himself off and went back to retrieve his safe from the ruins.

For a while, Alex Todd had the postal express field to himself, but employee theft caused his early retirement. Other companies sprang up, and all were eventually absorbed by Wells Fargo after it began operations in 1852. Todd himself sold out to Wells Fargo a year later, but no one could take away from him that he had been the first, in the glorious era of hand-stamped letters, of big bags of gold dust carried on packhorses like barley, of old newspapers worth their weight in gold, and of racing to catch the Panama steamer.

In the 1840s, China began to open up to the outside world. During the Opium War (1839–42), the British established a trading presence and obtained the cession of Hong Kong. In 1840 the Chinese signed a trade treaty with the United States. Then, in the 1850s, China fell into a period of anarchy called the Taiping Rebellion, which ravaged seventeen provinces and killed 20 million people.

In 1848, American ships landing at Chinese ports had brought news of California gold. In the midst of China's social and political breakdown, thousands wanted to leave. Chinese entrepreneurs formed the so-called "Six Companies," which carried shiploads of emigrants to San Francisco as contract labor. They traveled in Six Companies ships, were met on the dock by a Six Companies agent, and were given Six Companies equipment and sent to the mines.

In 1849 a miner reported "crowds of Chinese, bound for the diggings, under gigantic basket-hats, each man with a bamboo laid across his shoulder, from each end of which was suspended a collection of mining tools, Chinese baskets and boxes, immense boots, and a variety of Chinese 'fixins.' . . . All speaking at once, gabbing and chattering in their horrid jargon, and producing a noise like a flock of geese."

Usually, the Chinese bought worked-out and abandoned claims. Here was a great opportunity to unload supposedly worthless mines on the "celestials," as they were called (China being known as the Celestial Empire). But a lot of these old claims still had gold in them for those persistent enough to get at it. The Chinese were painstakingly thorough, and left not an inch unworked. They did not have a "millionaire mentality," and were satisfied with a few dollars a day.

Anti-Chinese feeling grew with their numbers. The foreign-miner license tax that Congress passed in 1850 charged $20 a month for permission to prospect. But that measure did not stop the inflow, for by 1852, 21,000 Chinese were living in California. That year Chinese camps on the American River were attacked and destroyed, and the miners were warned that they would be shot if they came back.

President Polk announced on May 11, 1846, that the nation was at war with Mexico. In August he sent a message to Congress asking for $2 million to pay for the campaign. Seizing the opportunity, Pennsylvania congressman David Wilmot offered an amendment to the money bill that any territory eventually acquired from Mexico should be slave-free.

Polk wrote in his diary for August 10 that it was "a mischievous and foolish amendment. . . . What connection slavery has with making peace with Mexico is difficult to conceive." The amendment died with the bill, and both houses passed another bill for $3 million in March 1847 without the Wilmot proviso. But the question of whether Congress had the right to ban slavery in the territories remained alive and festering in the minds of legislators.

On February 2, 1848, a week after gold was found at Sutter's Fort, the defeated Mexicans signed the Treaty of Guadalupe Hidalgo, giving up California and New Mexico Territory for $15 million. The United States now owned plenty of Pacific frontage in addition to the incomparable harbor of San Francisco. Mexico, on the other hand, lost half its territory and gave up forever the chance to become a great power. With the Mexican cession and the Oregon Territory, Polk the Great Acquirer almost doubled the nation's surface, adding 1,204,740 square miles to the 1,787,888 he had started with when he came to power.

But rapid territorial expansion in a sectionally divided nation carried a price tag. It was left to Polk's successor, the victorious general (and slave owner) Zachary Taylor, to pay it. The admission of slave and free states in tandem mandated by the Missouri Compromise in 1820 had remained in force until the acquisition of Texas in 1845. A slave state admitted to the Union without any territorial interlude, Texas briefly skewered the delicate legislative design, bringing the total number of states in 1847 to 15 slave and 14 free. The admission of Wisconsin in 1848 restored equality, but the balance remained more fragile than ever.

Because the gold rush of 1848–49 had brought 80,000 miners into California, the new acquisition was seriously in need of state and federal government. Therefore, Zachary Taylor began pressing for California statehood right after his inauguration in March 1849. But the mood of Congress favored debate on the issue of slavery in the territories. Did Congress have the power under the Constitution to ban slavery in territory acquired from Mexico? This question, held in abeyance for almost thirty years by the Missouri Compromise, was now examined again.

In the meantime, California wanted instant statehood without going through the territorial hiatus. When the military governor, General Bennett Riley, arrived in April 1849, the people pressured him to call for a constitutional convention. Assenting to the popular will, he did so on June 3. The forty-eight delegates elected included some of the principal actors in the drama of conquest, such as John Sutter and Thomas Larkin. That September they gathered at Monterey in a two-story yellow sandstone mansion known as Colton Hall.

With the exception of eleven ranchers from the south who didn't want to pay state taxes, all the delegates favored statehood. Thus, using the Iowa constitution as a model, they quickly drafted one for California. Among its articles was a provision surprisingly advanced for the time: A married woman would have the right to own property in her name.

Even more surprising, considering the fact that a number of the delegates hailed from slave-owning states, the article banning slavery was adopted without a murmur of protest. This had a lot to do with the practice of mining, which was based on the labor of free men. Anyone could go to the mines with pick and shovel and start digging. The miners already didn't think much of the Chinese and Mexican workers, and they sure didn't want slave owners coming into the diggings with their slaves.

As Walter Colton, the Vermonter who had built Colton Hall, explained it: "The cause which excludes slavery from California lies within a nutshell. All here are diggers, and free white diggers won't dig with slaves. . . . They won't degrade their calling by associating with slave labor."

World traveler Bayard Taylor was visiting California at the time of the convention, and wrote that "here, lawyers, physicians, and ex-professors swing pick-axes . . . LABOR IS RESPECTABLE." Free miners didn't want slaves coming in and destabilizing the mining economy. Even the southerners wanted to protect the profession of mining from slavery.

The only point of dispute turned on the future state's eastern boundary. In the end, the assembly sensibly decided on the natural boundary of the Sierra Nevadas. When they had completed their draft, on October 13, 1849, the elated delegates felt as though they had fashioned the blueprint for Creation itself. Theirs was a state with gold-veined mountains and 750 miles of ocean frontage. Swinging his sword, Sutter proclaimed, "Gentlemen, this is the happiest day of my life."

Two senators, John Frémont (who had returned to California and made a fortune in gold) and William M. Gwin, were sent to Washington, but Washington was not ready for them. Besides California, Congress was entangled in the formation of Utah and New Mexico territories and the retrieval of fugitive slaves.

Henry Clay, the senator from Kentucky, known as the Great Compromiser for pushing through the Missouri Compromise, proposed grouping all these matters before Congress in one piece of legislation called the "omnibus bill." The package failed after eleven weeks of debate in the Senate in the spring and summer of 1850. "The Omnibus is overturned," declared Senator Thomas Hart Benton of Missouri, "and all the passengers spilled out but one." That one was Utah Territory.

On the Fourth of July, 1850, a discomfited President Zachary Taylor listened to patriotic speeches for two hours under a hot sun while cooling himself with iced milk. "Old Rough and Ready" succumbed to gastroenteritis and died on July 9, at the age of sixty-five. He was succeeded by his vice president, Millard Fillmore. The legendary orator and statesman Daniel Webster became Fillmore's secretary of state.

In the Senate, Stephen A. Douglas of Illinois, chairman of the Committee on Territories, believed that each western territory had to settle the question of slavery in its own way. Congressional imposition of slavery or nonslavery, he argued, was a violation of the territories' rights. What gave other sections of the country such as north and south, Douglas asked, the authority to regulate slavery in the west?

As the thirteen colonies had once fiercely maintained, Douglas declared unfounded any law passed by Congress affecting a people who lacked congressional representation. He formulated the doctrine of popular sovereignty, which held that the territories be permitted to decide such issues themselves, as California had done in its constitution.

The Mississippi senator Jefferson Davis responded that popular sovereignty in California amounted to "the will of the conglomerate mass of gold-hunters, foreign and native." The southern senators reaffirmed the position that they possessed the right to go into any state and reclaim their fugitive property.

But Douglas shrewdly gathered up the remains of Clay's omnibus bill and crafted it into five separate bills. These passed with astonishing speed, owing to Taylor's death, the senators' weariness, and Douglas's skill at finding a slightly different majority for each bill.

The legislation making Utah a territory got voted through on August 1. When the admission of California as a free state came under consideration on August 13, Jefferson Davis and nine other senators objected to California's bypassing the territorial stage, which they hoped would have given its inhabitants more time to appreciate the benefits of slavery. To back up their point, they threatened to break up the Union. Yet the bill passed that very day, and California became a state, permanently destroying the balance in the Senate between slave and free states. President Fillmore, whom historians generally refer to as Taylor's "dim and forgotten" successor, signed the statehood bill on September 9, which remains a legal holiday in California.

Two days later the bill making New Mexico a territory became law. New Mexico and Utah were now poised for admission as states with or without slavery, according to whatever their constitutions prescribed. On August 26, the southerners got their due with the passage of the Fugitive Slave Act, a decree that was denounced by the north and ushered in a period of slave hunting and the kidnapping of free blacks. The flurry of legislative wheeling and dealing ended with a fifth bill abolishing the slave trade in the District of Columbia.

When the dust settled, the Compromise of 1850 represented a triumph for Douglas. By cleverly navigating the passage of each bill, the thirty-seven-year-old Democrat achieved a temporary truce in which neither side had surrendered to the other without getting something in return. The Compromise effectively delayed secession and Civil War for another decade. The Northwest Ordinance's ban on slavery gave way to Senator Douglas's doctrine of popular sovereignty.

By 1850, California had more than 200,000 inhabitants, and probably half of them were miners. The work was arduous but not complex since nature had done the preliminaries, with water eroding the rocks and washing the gold down mountain streams. Since there were at first no state laws on claims, the miners made up their own. Each camp had its rules on the size of a claim and the way to work it.

They had a wonderful phrase in the mines, which was, "Have you seen the elephant?"—meaning "Have you got any life experience?" At a trial in Placerville before a jury of miners, the plaintiff's lawyer announced that he would read from Blackstone, volume 2, page 124.

One of the jurors said, "No, you needn't, we don't submit to any of Blackstone's laws here."

"No, nor Mexican neither," added another juror.

A third juror expressed his agreement by standing up and shaking himself and making sounds that were somewhat like the cry of a humpback whale.

The lawyer for the other side had seen the elephant. He said he knew better than to think that laws of any kind existed in Placerville, and particularly the accursed laws of Mexico. The jury found for the defendant—a white man—against the plaintiff, who was a greaser (Mexican) and had a lawyer who quoted Blackstone.

A Boston native, Ed Morse took off for California in 1850, at the age of seventeen. Though six feet tall, he was pale and thin, and when he reached the mines near Marysville, he had trouble finding work. "Oh yes," they told him, "we've work for a man but not for a boy."

After a while he landed a job on a wing dam (in a side channel of a gold-bearing stream), wheeling barrows full of dirt from the bottom to the top of the bank. The river gold shimmered in fine little flakes like fish scales, and the owner was clearing $5,000 a day. When the packtrain brought food from Marysville, the men fought for the privilege of paying a dollar for an onion.

One of the pump men got dysentery from drinking bad river water and died. Ed Morse replaced him, pumping on the platform in the broiling sun. It got so hot that he, too, slaked his thirst from the river and got sick. They fetched a doctor from Cedar Bar who advised Ed to apply some thick fried flapjacks to his abdomen. The physician charged an ounce of dust per visit and kept returning until Ed's supply ran low. Ed now weighed a hundred pounds, but finally a Spanish woman cured him with tea from the leaves of the manzanita bush (an evergreen shrub).

Ed next headed for Nevada City via Pitt Hill and Rough and Ready. He found work in the Slate Range prying apart slabs of slate—crevicing— and washing out the dirt and panning what they thought was gold dust. Then an old miner passed through and told him, "Why you damned fool that is nothing but mica."

Born in New York City in 1825, Lemuel McKeeby left for California in 1850, traveling overland to Placerville. His sole possessions were a frying pan, a coffee pot, a blanket, and $40 in cash. Knowing nothing about mining, he teamed up with a few other fellows. They went to a store that outfitted miners and bought a rocker (a cradle for washing ore) for $30, a shovel for $10, and a pick for $5. Ten dollars more got them a wooden bucket to carry dirt, a tin dipper, and a pan.

Loading the equipment on their backs, they set out for Nevada City, rumored to be the new El Dorado. The town offered four saloons, which aside from drinks served mainly flapjacks. In one place the cook boasted that he could throw his pancakes up the chimney, run around outside, and catch them in his pan.

That June, Lem saw someone being flogged for theft. They took his shirt off and went at it, each lash raising welts. At one point the prisoner called the whipper by his first name and asked him not to strike so low.

Lem thought the man was getting what he deserved, for each cabin door hung open and pans of gold dust were left lying in the bunks because miners trusted each other.

Lem then moved to Railroad Hill in Yuba County and put together a company that brought water to the miners by ditch. But another company formed upstream and diverted the water from Lem's creek. For miners, water rights were a burning issue.

One day Lem was on his way to his ditch when he met some men who said they'd broken his dam. "Well, I'm going to fix it," he said, "and you four big cowards can watch me do it."

A few days later he was served with a summons to appear before Judge Barber in Marysville and show cause why he should not be punished for contempt of court. The bewildered Lem lost the case. Later, he heard that Cowen, the other group's leader, was boasting that he would "law" McKeeby to death, until he got Lem's water claim and with it his last shirt. As sore as he was, Lem knew the fix was in and there was nothing he could do.

So he picked himself up and in the spring of 1855 went to live in Sebastopol (named after the city in the Crimea besieged the year before for 349 days). There luck and his claim paid off. Soon he was hiring miners at $5 a day, and drawing gravel and water through "Long Toms" (troughs to separate gold ore). Only once did he catch a miner stealing. When they cleaned the Long Toms, they found thousands of dollars' worth of gold that had fallen between the boards. Lem collared one of his men pocketing the amalgam and hauled him off to the sheriff in North San Juan.

By 1856 the mining portion of California had begun to find a place in society. Schoolhouses and churches sprang up and miners wore boiled shirts on Sunday and dropped gold dust in collection plates. Dances were held, and that was where McKeeby met Miss Caroline Sampson, a school-marm. Before long he married her. Selling his interest in the Sebastopol mine in 1863, Lem moved to Carson City, Nevada, and became a judge. He died in 1915, at the age of ninety.

When J. D. Borthwick arrived in San Francisco from London in 1851, he found that some of the streets had actually been planked. Where there was no planking, the mud remained ankle-deep. The streets of Chinatown were dense with long-haired Celestials studying bills that told them where the best rat pies were to be had. All over town, wall posters announced that Shing Sing or Wong Choo did the washing and ironing at $5 a dozen.

Since the hotels were full, Borthwick stayed in a dormitory, six beds to a room. When he went to the office in the morning to pay his dollar, an old miner was there weighing out his gold dust and said to the proprietor: "Say now, stranger, do you do nothin' else but just sit thar and take a dollar from every man that sleeps on them beds?"

Borthwick visited Placerville and liked the equality in the mining camps, where each man could make as much money as his neighbor, depending on his luck and hard work. Placer mining seemed like the fulfillment of democracy, a profession open to all, with no diploma required.

The only way to distinguish oneself in the mines was through intrinsic merit. It was not as in countries with stratified classes, where people from different stations when thrown together held a secret contempt for the others. Here, what you saw was pretty much what you got. People did not trouble to hide their true natures. There were no pinchbecks; every man was the genuine article. One knew that no hidden agenda lurked behind the hearty goodwill.

And even though this was close to a classless society, it also encouraged an individuality of manner, for since one could not be singled out because of status, one had to affirm oneself by force of personality. Perhaps most important of all, there were no class barriers to prevent seeking out those whose company one most enjoyed.

David Anderson was an unemployed actor who appeared in San Francisco in 1851 and got a job as stage manager in a theater. After a while he recruited a troupe of actors and took them to the mines to perform the classics. In 1851, Anderson and his company settled in Placerville and built a small theater in a tenpin alley.

The miners bought their ticket with their single crop. Every evening Anderson stopped by the box office and weighed the receipts—a saucer full of dust. Wishing for saucers galore, he went to Nickerson's saloon one Saturday night to drum up more business and gave an impromptu performance. After losing a few hands of three-card monte, he jumped up and cried out: "I am damned if I ain't ruined, my wife and children are in New York, and the last dollar I had has gone in that infernal game."

Downing his drink he declaimed, "I am going to hell and you shall all go with me." He walked up to the big potbellied stove in the middle of the saloon and threw in a pinch of powder. This was followed by a flash, and a stampede of players upset the tables and jumped out the doors and windows. Money lay all over the floor and the games were a mess, and not everyone thought it was funny.

Anderson traveled the rough mining roads with his scenery packed on mules. One of his actors, Ned Bingham, had twins, whom his wife carried in baskets on horseback. After the discovery of silver in Nevada, the troupe did standing-room business. The miners would pay almost any price to get in. Once there was so much competition for the best seat in the house that Anderson auctioned it off for $1,200.

Because of the region's high number of stabbing deaths, *Hamlet* was tremendously popular. Anderson always played Polonius, and one evening in Dogtown, Nevada, when he was staggering around on the stage after having been run through by the unstable prince, an elderly woman sitting in the front row cried out, "What a shame it is to bring a poor old man like that up into the mountains."

• •

In 1851, Louise Clappe was traveling in California with her husband, Dr. Fayette Clappe, who abruptly decided that a practice in the mountains would be good for his health. That was that. The Clappes went off to a mining camp at Rich Bar on the North Fork of the Feather River, north of Marysville, and spent a year there, at the Empire Hotel. Louise seems to have adapted to the rough miner life rather well, even though she described herself as "a shivering, frail, homeloving little thistle."

Much of her time was spent studying the mores and vocabulary of the miner subculture. The miners worked the "bars," which were made up of gravel and water-worn boulders. In the miner language, if you put someone in a bad position, you "got the deadwood in him." If you wanted to borrow something, you said, "Have you got a spare pick-axe about your clothes?"

Louise saw two men quarreling in the street, and heard one say, "Only let me get hold of your beggarly carcass once, and I will use you up so small that God Almighty himself cannot see your ghost." She overheard a miner at Rich Bar comment on another miner's spouse: "A wife of the right sort, she is. Why she earnt her old man nine hundred dollars, clear of all expenses, by washing. Such women ain't common, I tell you."

She spoke to a miner who had lost his horse. He told her how he had asked a Mexican in the hills for help. "The cross old rascal pretended not to understand his own language," the miner recounted, "though I said as plainly as possible, 'Senor, sabe mi horse vamos poco tiempo?,' which perhaps you don't know, means 'Sir, I have lost my horse, have you seen it?' Mexicans ain't kinder like our folks—somehow, they ain't folksy."

On October 29, 1851, Little John, the Swedish waiter at the Empire Hotel, was arrested for stealing $400 in gold dust from his employer, Curtis Bancroft. It was only when he heard someone say, "Little John's over at the Humboldt bucking away large sums at monte" that Bancroft began to suspect him.

Little John appeared before a judge and jury even though there was no way to identify gold dust. When he was asked where he got the money to gamble, he said his father had sent him $500 from Stockholm. Where was the letter that came with the money? He had lost it. Little John was sentenced to thirty-nine lashes and deportation.

Now and then a "lucky strike" or an "excellent prospect" gladdened the miners' hearts, but most of the time they felt sorry for themselves. Louise also felt they were by nature jingoistic and racist. She often heard them describe Mexicans as "half-civilized black men."

With all the excitement of mining-camp life, Louise Clappe felt that she had seen the elephant. But revelations kept coming. One of Louise's neighbors asked to borrow a teaspoon because she had guests. "Since you're entertaining, why not take them all?" she asked. "Oh no," the woman said, "my guests would think I was putting on airs. One is enough. They can pass it around from one to the other."

"Really," Louise Clappe concluded in a letter to her sister Molly, "everybody ought to go to the mines, just to see how little it takes to make people comfortable in the world."

It wasn't until after California became a state that the first Vigilance Committee appeared in San Francisco, in 1851. The promise of gold had attracted bands of Australian criminals called "Sydney ducks." In the absence of an effective police force and criminal court system, the Vigilance Committee was the citizens' response to a crime wave.

There were about two hundred vigilantes enrolled under the leadership of William T. Coleman. They were summoned when needed by the bell of the Monumental Fire Engine House. Their rooms were situated on Battery Street between Pine and California, and sometimes served as cells. They hanged a few men on Market Street, from a derrick normally used to hoist goods from vessels.

Most of the vigilantes were professional men and merchants, respectable members of the community. James Dows, a liquor-store owner, joined after burglars blew open his safe in the winter of 1850–51. Among the first to sign up was Dr. Beverly Cole, whose job it was to pronounce men dead at hangings. He also visited the committee's prisoners in their cells.

One of the jailed men in 1851 was Alfred Green, the army deserter who ran off to the gold mines in 1848. He had moved to San Francisco, where he opened the first racetrack. Arrested on suspicion of fencing stolen goods, Green was put next to the cell of a man named Brace, who had been sentenced to hang for murder. A thief by profession, Brace had been captured in the loose chaparral at the southern end of the bay. When Dr. Cole visited Brace in his cell, the prisoner told the doctor that nature had intended him to be a thief and a pickpocket. To prove it, he wriggled out of his handcuffs and then slipped them back on, much to Dr. Cole's surprise.

On the morning of Brace's execution, Green heard his neighbor talking to himself in his cell. "See old hand what you have brought me to. Yes, but there is no blood on it. But then you stole. You are guilty only of petty thefts, thank God. Why do they want to hang poor Brace, who never harmed anybody?"

Coming to see Brace for the last time, Dr. Cole found him in a state of extreme agitation. He gave the condemned man an ounce of brandy at ten o'clock and another at eleven. At noon the doctor occupied his position near the scaffold. Brace approached the gallows with another man, named Heatherington, who was also being hanged. Heatherington insisted on giving a speech to the spectators to explain his actions. Fortified by the brandy, Brace turned to Heatherington and said, "Shut up, damn you, I'm going to hell and I want no delays." When the men were cut down, Dr. Cole examined them to make sure they were dead.

Things eventually quieted down in San Francisco, and the first Vigilance Committee disbanded. But in 1856, when a rigged election put James P. Casey on the Board of Supervisors, the crooks took control of the city once again. James King, the crusading editor of the *Daily Evening Bulletin*, courageously exposed Casey's criminal activities. On May 14, 1856, Casey raised a Colt navy revolver and gunned King down in the street.

Dr. Cole was summoned to the scene and stanched King's shoulder wound with a small surgeon's sponge. King died four days later. The killing gave birth to a second Vigilance Committee and Dr. Cole signed up in a warehouse near North Point.

The committee went straight to the county jail and removed Casey from the sheriff's custody. They tried him at their headquarters on Sacramento Street—known as Fort Gunnybags because it was fortified with sandbags. Shortly afterward, Casey was dangling at the end of a rope and Dr. Cole was on hand to verify his decease.

Another time they went out after a man named Maloney, who had been arrested by the police and was under the protection of Chief Justice D. S. Terry of the California Supreme Court. When a group of vigilantes led by Sam Hopkins barged into Judge Terry's office to grab Maloney, the judge drew a Bowie knife and slashed Hopkins across the neck.

Dr. Cole was called to the engine house on Jackson Street where Hopkins had been brought, and found him sitting on a chair, bleeding to death. He laid Hopkins out on the ground and attempted a ligation of the carotid artery, but it was twilight and he could not see too well. For three weeks, Hopkins was nursed by vigilantes, and no one was more eager for his recovery than Judge Terry. Hopkins got better, while Terry had to stand trial.

After 1856 there were no more vigilance committees, but those who had been a part of it never forgot the early days. As the vigilante John Manrow put it, "Even after we broke up, we were always listening for the tap of the bell."

THE MINNESOTA FRONTIER

Seeing the land for that moment before mule and plow altered it right up to the water's receding edge, then back into the river again before the trawlers and cruisers and cutters became marooned. . . . Back onto the Old Man, shrunk once more into his normal banks, drowsing and even innocent-looking, as if it were something else besides he who had changed, for a little time anyway, the whole face of the adjacent earth.

WILLIAM FAULKNER

The New York Public Library
Built on a plateau at the junction of the Mississippi and Minnesota rivers, Fort Snelling was then the westernmost outpost of settlement. The fort was also the headquarters for the Indian agency, which explains the teepee village below it and to the left.

Freed black, with cymbals at heel,
An ex-slave who thrivingly danced
To the ring of his own clashing light
Through the thousand variations of one song . . .

JAMES DICKEY

In Minnesota the first settlers were soldiers. Whereas other territories called in the military to oust squatters, here the squatters followed the army. For years the troops remained in splendid—if tedious—isolation at the junction of two great rivers, hundreds of miles from the nearest settlement.

Minnesota Territory was a hybrid. The triangular section wedged between the Mississippi and the Wisconsin border made up part of the old Northwest, while the rest constituted the northernmost part of the Louisiana Purchase. Situated at the approximate geographic center of the North American continent, Minnesota sent out river systems in all directions, ultimately serving as the riparian equivalent of a railroad yard.

Its 11,000 lakes nourished three great systems: The Mississippi rose in Lake Itasca and flowed south; the Red River coursed north into Canada's Lake Winnipeg; and in the east, the Lake Superior highlands offered access to the Great Lakes–St. Lawrence system. Thanks to its river routes, Minnesota presented a northern gateway both to the American west and to British Canada.

After the War of 1812, Congress cut back the large standing army to a peacetime force of about 10,000 regulars. This left more than enough men to pursue an aggressive policy in zones of former British presence. In 1817, John Calhoun became secretary of war under president Monroe. In his seven-year term of office, he deployed the army as a wilderness police. "With judicious conduct on the part of our officers," he wrote, "it is believed that our North Western frontier will be rendered more secure."

Calhoun's idea was to build forts on strategic river routes. Someone reminded him that in 1805, Lieutenant Zebulon M. Pike had bought nine square miles of land from the Indians at the juncture of the Mississippi and Minnesota rivers. Losing no time in pursuing his plans, Calhoun ordered the 5th Regiment of Infantry to that remote strip of Minnesota land in the fall of 1818.

Starting from Detroit in May 1819, traveling by boat from Lake Huron to Lake Michigan, and then from the Fox to the Wisconsin and up the Mississippi, Lieutenant Colonel Henry Leavenworth and his 98 men did not reach their destination at the mouth of the Minnesota until August 24.

Despondent over the difficulties of travel, Leavenworth wrote Major General Jacob Brown, chief of the army's Northern Division, that the territory he had seen so far seemed not worth settling, and that a garrison in Minnesota could not "do any good to our country." The Indian agent Thomas Forsyth agreed that this upper country was "not fit for either man or beast to live in."

Still, the colonel had his mission and finally chose a site for a log stockade on low ground along the right bank of the Minnesota. In summer, half the men fell sick from bad water and squalls of mosquitoes. In the subfreezing winter, wild storms lifted the roofs off cabins, and scurvy and dysentery spread through the ranks. Men who went to bed at night in apparent good health were found dead the next morning. "I can safely say," wrote Leavenworth, "that I never witnessed nor experienced more severe duty."

Spoiled provisions sold by swindling contractors were largely responsible for illness. Often, bread arrived covered with two inches of mold. The brine from pork barrels was drawn in St. Louis to lighten the load on the river trip, and water was added before reaching the fort to mask the fraud, and the men ended up eating rotten pork.

Christmas came, but Colonel Leavenworth was not in a festive mood: "The mercury is 10 below zero and the ink freezes in my pen while I write. . . . The dysentery yet rages. Death's details for pest hill are too heavy." By the spring of 1820, thirty soldiers had died, nearly one-third of his force.

Fearing spring floods, the colonel moved the survivors to high ground. But he disliked his assignment so much that he asked for a transfer to Florida to fight the Seminoles. He didn't mind combat as long as it was in a warm climate. In mid-August 1820, he was relieved by Colonel Josiah Snelling, after whom the still unbuilt fort would be named.

Then thirty-eight and round-faced, Snelling was soon dubbed "Prairie Dog" by his men for his coloring and quick temper. He arrived on September 5 with his wife Abigail, who was pregnant with their fourth child. Five days later he presided over a groundbreaking ceremony for the new fort, a projected diamond-shaped structure perched on a bluff overlooking the two great rivers, like a castle on the Rhine.

Like early settlers everywhere, the soldiers hewed timber, burned lime, dug for coal, made shingles, quarried stone, and hammered together log barracks, all the while standing guard against the Indians. By 1825, the fort was finished, "reared as if my magic in the forest wilds," in the words of the Indian agent.

Thus, Minnesota's early history was written in the log books of a single outpost. The northwesternmost military fort in the United States, Fort Snelling lay far in advance of the line of settlement. It was the only point on the map beyond Prairie du Chien, Wisconsin, and the closest large town was St. Louis, seven hundred miles away.

Regular army soldiers formed the vanguard of Minnesota settlement for almost twenty years, with the usual component of slackers, drunkards, and immigrants just off the boat. Snelling deplored the quality of his men, writing that "the last detachment of recruits from New York were the greatest vagabonds I ever saw. . . . I have almost been inclined to think that the best men are kept on the seaboard and this post made a kind of Botany Bay for the reception of those who can live nowhere else."

In his efforts to discipline the ruffians, Snelling came to be known as a bit of a tyrant. The real tyrant, though, was the weather. The only supply route, the Mississippi, was closed from November to April. The seasonal supply problem sometimes brought them to the edge of starvation. Correspondence with Washington took from three to six months. When Snelling ran out of forms, he wrote his post returns on cartridge paper.

The spring thaw brought supplies, visitors, mail, newspapers, and in 1823, the first steamboat. It also brought flooding. Every year the Mississippi burst its banks, inundating the rich bottom lands and drowning cattle. In May 1826, Snelling wrote a fellow officer "that the whole country in front of the garrison is a lake. All our boats were lost. . . . Not a plow or a spade has yet been put in the ground nor a seed sown."

The reference to planting was an indication that Snelling was turning his frontier troops into farmers and ranchers in order to make the fort self-sufficient. Since they were never attacked, he employed his troops to grow vegetables and keep herds of cattle. The men cut hay for their stock and chopped wood for their fires. Like the settlers, they battled against nature's sieges. Severe winters killed their cattle; marauding blackbirds destroyed the corn crop; and the fort's well, quarried through solid limestone, went dry.

Most of the officers were West Point graduates. Snelling, who had come up through the ranks, described them as "green," with "scarcely sprouted beards." Garrison life gave them bad habits and fort morale deteriorated from not rotating the troops. Drinking led to quarrels and quarrels led to duels, which Snelling permitted as an outlet for general frustration.

Martin Scott, the son of a poor Vermont farmer, arrived at Fort Snelling as a lieutenant in 1821. Born in Bennington in 1788 and promoted through the ranks, he was snubbed by the West Point graduates, who said he lacked polish.

The haughty West Pointers soon formed a cabal to make life miserable for Scott so that he would ask for a transfer, or resign his commission. But no one dared to insult him directly, since that would have led to a duel. Scott was a dead shot, who could throw two potatoes in the air and put a bullet through both.

Lieutenant Scott asked the post surgeon, Dr. John Gale, what he should do. "Either resign or challenge the first one who insults you," Gale told him. There were no volunteers until Lieutenant Keith, a Virginian and a practiced duelist, agreed to add Scott to his list of "affairs of honor."

In the officer's mess one day, Lieutenant Keith went up to Scott and said, "I hear you Vermonters are as yellow as the corn you feed your pigs." Keith soon received a challenge. The one officer who had not joined the cabal agreed to act as Scott's second.

At sunrise on the appointed morning, the principals and their seconds repaired to the field. As the seconds tossed a coin for position, Keith remarked in a loud voice: "I will shoot the damned Yankee through the guts."

Scott had intended to fire in the air, for his opponent was consumptive and already half-dead. But on hearing Keith's boast, he realized that he was defending his life. Scott said to his second: "I will shoot him through at the first button of his coat." The second handed him his pistol and the lieutenant drew a bead on a nearby tree stump, to make sure his hand was steady.

Time was called, the word was given, and both pistols cracked in the morning air so close together that they sounded like a single shot. Keith staggered and dropped to the ground, blood pouring from his mouth and nose. A bullet hole stained his coat, just above the top button.

Sustained by pride, though hit in the gut, Scott walked out of the ravine with a firm step. The ball had passed through his body, nicking his spine. When he reached his room, he fell unconscious on the floor. Both men had been true to their word. Amazingly, both survived.

When he was in a condition to go to mess again, Scott sat down and declared, "Anyone who insults me will promptly be called to the field." There were no takers, for he had forced the respect of his fellow officers.

Scott was promoted to captain in 1828 and to major in 1846. By then he was commanding a regiment in Monterey during the Mexican War. In September 1847 the brave duelist met his death at the battle of Molino del Rey, leading an American charge against a heavily defended building. This time the bullet caught him in the chest.

The most troublesome aspect of Colonel Snelling's duties was the Indians. The two tribes who did business at the fort, the Sioux and the Chippewas, were always at war. Fortunately, the Indian agent, Lawrence Taliaferro, proved to be capable and trustworthy.

Tall, lean, and swarthy, Taliaferro was descended from a Genoese family that had come to Virginia in 1637. He spent twenty years at the Indian agency outside the walls of the fort, reappointed six times by three different presidents (John Quincy Adams, Andrew Jackson, and Martin Van Buren).

The Sioux chief Little Crow called the agent "No Sugar in Your Mouth" because of his plain speaking. Taliaferro was the foe of the fur traders who cheated the Indians and sold them whiskey; when he caught them, he canceled their licenses and confiscated their wares. Indians came from great distances to smoke a pipe with Taliaferro and obtain some of the goods he doled out, such as powder, tobacco, and blankets. The agent's power lay in providing or withholding assistance. "I have had more than 1,400 Indians on visits to this agency during the month past," he wrote on one occasion, "and all with grievances of some sort to redress."

Taliaferro acted as mediator between the Indians and the soldiers, as well as between quarreling tribes. His fairness put him in great demand. He complained that every time a hog wandered away from the fort he was called in. Among other conflicts, he once arbitrated a dispute between an army officer and a young Indian accused of killing the officer's pointer dog on the prairie.

More important, Taliaferro weaned away the tribes from their allegiance to the British. In two years he collected thirty-six portraits of George III and twenty-eight Union Jacks. He also tried to get the Indians to respect the Sabbath, finally convincing them that the white man had a "medicine day" when they should not come to the fort.

When the Sioux murdered a white trader, Taliaferro asked them to turn over the murderer. If they refused, he warned, they would be cut off from agency favors. Again, when the Sioux killed seven Chippewas, Taliaferro demanded that they surrender the guilty. But that did not prevent the Sioux from periodically making trouble. The only thing to them better than firewater was an enemy's blood.

In 1827, Colonel Snelling gave up his command. The intemperance of his men had driven him to drink. His vigor and judgment failed him, and public displays of drunkenness sapped his authority. In addition, he was caught "borrowing" money from the commissary and charged with embezzlement. He left Fort Snelling in October, one step ahead of disgrace, and died less than a year later in Washington, worn out by his years in the wilderness.

In May 1833, Dr. Nathan S. Jarvis put down his bags at Fort Snelling and began a three-year stint as army surgeon. A New Yorker, Dr. Jarvis found himself 1,200 miles from home. However, he looked forward to his new assignment and to the discovery of an unknown country. From the fort's parapet, Jarvis could see the winding Minnesota and the Mississippi running between verdant sloping banks. Five miles upriver were St. Anthony's Falls, the nation's mightiest after Niagara.

The only thing wanting, thought the doctor, was society. The garrison made up the entire white population for hundreds of miles around. Only two steamboats a year came to Snelling. First you heard the puffs and then you saw the boat edging round the bend. Though its docking was an occasion for rejoicing, the boat carried its share of misery. Lieutenant Hunter, hailing the arrival of the mail, opened his letter to learn that his father had died.

Most of the time the soldiers were secluded from the world like exiles. Once in a while, stragglers passed through, like the lone fellow paddling against the current in a log canoe who said he wanted to see the country. Then in July 1834, two young missionaries arrived, Samuel Pond and his brother Gideon, sinewy six-footers from Connecticut, aged twenty-six and twenty-four.

Off the pair went, wrote Jarvis, "to take up their abode with a band of Indians and live like them on boiled corn with grease or tallow, or dog's meat, or roasted ground-hogs, or raccoons." Language was the barrier, and the Pond brothers went on a deer hunt with their Sioux band in October to improve their vocabulary. But Samuel Pond still found himself unable to convey an abstract idea. "I cannot preach Christ crucified," he said.

As a visitor to the mission put it, "Mr. Pond has long been yearning to see inside of an Indian. He has been wanting to be an Indian, if only for half an hour, that he might know how an Indian feels, and by what motives he may be moved."

At the fort, Jarvis succeeded in persuading the Sioux to take his medicines. It was a great improvement over their tribal doctors, whose cure was to rattle a gourd filled with birdshot over the patient while blowing on a kind of whistle.

Bored and lonely, Dr. Jarvis wished he had a wife. It was such boredom, he knew, that motivated the men to desert. One soldier was sentenced to a hundred lashes of a cat-o'-nine-tails on his bare back in the presence of the entire command. With his skin the color of a ripe blackberry, he was then marched down to the river to the tune of "The Rogue's March" and drummed out of the service.

In June 1836, Dr. Jarvis left Fort Snelling to serve under General Edmund Gaines in the Seminole War. For three years, he had been "secluded from the world and its attractions," but did not regret his time spent on what was then the northwest frontier.

The steamboat upon which Dr. Jarvis embarked at Fort Snelling in June 1836 brought his replacement, Dr. John Emerson, who was accompanied by a skinny forty-year-old slave named Dred Scott. Born in 1795, Scott had originally belonged to a Virginian, Peter Blow, who moved to St. Louis in 1827. There Peter Blow died in 1831, and Dred Scott became the property of his daughter Elizabeth, who eventually sold him to Dr. Emerson. In 1834 the doctor was transferred to the fort at Rock Island in the free state of Illinois. In 1836 he was sent to Fort Snelling, at that time situated in the free territory of Wisconsin.

Slaves were permitted in army forts, and there were already a number at Fort Snelling. Most belonged to Taliaferro, who had inherited them from his family in Virginia. He rented or sold them to the garrison officers as house servants.

Dr. Emerson bought from Taliaferro a pretty mulatto girl named Harriet, who was said to have broken many a heart. Dred Scott fell in love with Harriet and married her the year of his arrival, 1836. As justice of the peace, Taliaferro performed the ceremony.

In 1838, Dr. Emerson returned to St. Louis. He died in 1844, leaving Dred Scott and his wife Harriet and their two children Liza and Lizzie to his widow, Irene Sanford Emerson. Mrs. Emerson moved to New York, leaving Scott and his family with the sons of Scott's original master—Henry and Taylor Blow.

Henry Blow was a lawyer, active in the antislavery movement. Knowing that Dred Scott had previously lived in Illinois and Wisconsin—a free state and a free territory—Blow decided to use him as a test case on the rights of slaves. The lawyer's argument was that the years Dred Scott had spent in free areas made him a free man. The larger issue was whether Congress could prohibit slavery in the territories, as it had done in the Misouri Compromise of 1820.

The case was listed in the Missouri court docket as *Scott, a Man of Color* v. *Emerson*, although by this time Scott had been sold to Mrs. Emerson's brother, John F. A. Sanford, who lived in New York. During the trial, Scott stayed in the custody of the St. Louis sheriff. Occasionally, the lawman hired him out for jobs.

The lower court ruled that Dred Scott was a free man. But the Missouri Supreme Court reversed the decision in 1852, holding that because Scott had voluntarily returned from free territory, he remained a slave in Missouri.

Henry Blow filed a new suit in the federal courts, seeking a Supreme Court ruling on Dred Scott and on the larger question of slavery in the territories. In the momentous decision rendered on May 6, 1857, each Supreme Court judge wrote a separate opinion. About the only point a majority agreed on was that a slave could not be a citizen, and thus did not have the constitutional right to sue in a federal court.

The Supreme Court endorsed the proslavery point of view, and Dred Scott returned home in bondage. By now he was over sixty years old, and allowed that he was "puzzled by all the fuss they made in Washington." In the end, the passage of a slave at Fort Snelling was a minor episode that helped kindle a major conflagration.

Until the Treaty of 1837, under which the Sioux gave up a large triangle of land at the intersection of the Mississippi and St. Croix rivers, Minnesota had been all Indian country. In 1839 squatters started arriving in the Fort Snelling neighborhood from failed Canadian settlements. Months later, the fort's commanding officer, Major Joseph Plympton, razed their cabins and told them to move a few miles downriver.

That same year, some of the lands vacated by Indian cession east of the Mississippi, across from St. Anthony's Falls, were thrown open to settlement. Major Plympton received a letter to that effect one winter evening. Confiding the news to Captain Martin Scott, the major proposed that the two should leave at dawn to make preemption claims in the newly opened strip.

Franklin Steele, the enterprising fort sutler, got the news in the same mail and decided not to wait until morning. He and a friend, Norman Kittson, loaded a wagon with boards, straw, nails, potatoes, and other edibles, and headed for the falls five miles away.

Unloading the wagon by starlight, the pair nailed the boards into a kind of shack. Then they made holes in the snow and placed potatoes at intervals in the frozen ground. Their work done, they slept on straw, covered with buffalo robes.

In the morning, Plympton and Scott came along and accepted an invitation into the makeshift hut for breakfast. While the coffee boiled over a fire, Steele showed his guests his fine crop of snow-capped potatoes. When he got back to the fort, he proved up his claim, which gave him access to the water power on his land.

The American mania with being first began with preemption claims, where minutes mattered. First to the North Pole, first on the moon, first in sales or stolen bases, first like Lindbergh or Miss America. It's all a throwback to the need to be first on the land.

By 1848, the squatters expelled from the immediate vicinity of Fort Snelling had formed a rough frontier village of several hundred shacks and shanties, called St. Paul. It was around then that James Goodhue, a native of New Hampshire and a graduate of Amherst, resolved to become Minnesota's first journalist.

In 1849, Goodhue shipped his presses by river to St. Paul. That May he brought out the first issue of the *Minnesota Pioneer*. An army officer named Richard Johnson visited the newspaper office on his way to the fort and saw that an old hen had made her nest in a corner.

"Are you planning to raise your own poultry?" Johnson asked.

"The old fool is sitting on two brickbats," Goodhue replied, "but should she hatch out a brickyard it will be just what we need."

Minnesota was part of Wisconsin Territory, but when Wisconsin became a state in 1848, Minnesota was cast adrift, in a kind of limbo, without courts or government. The residents met on August 4, 1848, and drafted a petition to Congress for admission, but in Washington there was some skepticism about Minnesota's readiness.

As Joseph M. Root, a member of the House from Sandusky, Ohio, put it: "When God's footstool is so densely populated that each human being can only occupy two square feet, then, but not till then, will a white man go to that hyperborean region in the Northwest, fit only to be the home of savages and wild beasts."

But Stephen A. Douglas, chairman of the Senate Committee on Territories, thought otherwise. He pushed for an act of Congress to make Minnesota a territory. It passed on March 3, 1849.

Henry Hastings Sibley, who had come to Minnesota in 1834 as the agent for the American Fur Company, was voted in as delegate to Congress. He used to say: "I was successively a citizen of Michigan, Wisconsin, and Minnesota territories without changing my residence from Mendota" (just outside St. Paul). But there wasn't much a non-voting territorial delegate to Congress could do for his constituents, beyond organizing mail routes, Indian affairs, and land offices.

Alexander Ramsey, the first governor, arrived in St. Paul on March 4 and started the machinery of government turning. He assigned judges to the new court districts, some of them deep in Indian territory; conducted a census; arranged the election of councilmen and eighteen members of the assembly; and formed counties and county seats.

A Pennsylvania Quaker, Governor Ramsey visited Fort Snelling in 1850. When Major Woods, the officer in command, told him he was entitled to a salute and a review of the troops, Ramsey, a pacifist, declined both. "Is there anything I can do to show my respect for the chief executive of Minnesota?" Woods asked.

"Have you any hard cider made from corn?" Ramsey inquired.

The major broke out the old brown jug. After a few swigs, the governor pronounced it as good as Pennsylvania cider made from rye.

By 1849, Fort Snelling was no longer in Indian country, for the Sioux and the Chippewas had moved west. Nor was it any longer on the frontier, since Fort Ripley had been built a hundred miles up the Mississippi. Surrounded by settlers, its functions had become mainly ceremonial.

A product of pure improvisation, territorial government showed a healthy contempt for the lessons of the Old World. In 1849, William D. Phillips, the district attorney for Ramsey County, was arguing a case in court when his counterpart, a lawyer from the east, dropped an allusion to Demosthenes. Phillips pounced: "The gentleman may be a classical scholar; he may be as eloquent as Demosthenes; he has probably ripped with old Euripides, socked with old Socrates, and canted with old Cantharides [Spanish fly, the aphrodisiac]; but, gentlemen of the jury, what does he know about the laws of Minnesota?"

"It was a jumble, but we all got through," recalled Charles Flandreau, a lawyer in the territorial days. "One old party used to say, 'Don't worry, you will get through the world, I've never known anyone to stick.' "

Born of Huguenot parents in 1828, Flandreau studied law in Massachusetts and went west in 1853. In the valley of the Minnesota he found a young Scotsman living alone who asked him to be his partner. "I am a lawyer," Flandreau said, "how can I live where there are no people?"

"Why that is the easiest part of it," the Scotsman replied. "We can hunt for a living and I have a shack."

The first winter, using a dead pony for bait, they shot forty-two wolves from the back window of the shack and sold the pelts for 75 cents each. Later Flandreau briefly served as the Indian agent for 7,500 Sioux, summing up his experience by saying, "You might as well attempt to put a hoe in the hands of a deposed monarch of France as to make a husbandman of a Sioux warrior."

Going back to lawyering, Flandreau in 1855 walked 120 miles through two-foot-deep snow from St. Peter on the Minnesota to Winona on the Mississippi to adjust some claims. Another time he paddled 150 miles down the Minnesota to oppose a motion, sold the canoe for $3, and walked home.

One of Flandreau's cases obliquely raised the issue of church and state. Bill Smith, who lived in Le Sueur, above St. Peter on the Minnesota River, was charged with vandalism. A picket fence separated his house from the Presbyterian church next door. Churchgoers hitched their horses to Smith's fence and the animals would then nibble the heads off the pickets. After a while the irate Minnesotan instructed his son to cut the halters of any teams found tied to his fence. He was acquitted by a non-Presbyterian jury.

With Indian lands opening up, the territorial years, from 1849 to 1858, were a time of rapid growth: dozens of towns sprang up on principal rivers. In 1855, when the first million acres of surveyed lands were offered for sale, a veritable invasion occurred. St. Paul filled up in a flash, and people camped out in the street. Once the government extended preemption rights to squatters on unsurveyed lands, the invasion turned into a stampede.

Daniel Johnston, age twenty-three, arrived in St. Paul in 1855, and a year later accepted a job from a land company that owned five townsites on the Red River. His task was to survey and occupy the towns to prevent preemption, for which he received expenses plus a small share in the company.

Hearing that another group was trying to get there ahead of them, Johnston advanced his departure to the last day of 1856 in the middle of a severe winter, accompanied by a cook, two guides, four ox-team drivers, the superintendent John Moulton, and two sleds. As Johnston put it, they didn't mind starting out in inclement weather because there was no "get left" in any of them.

The five towns in question lay 125 miles west of St. Cloud, which was seventy-five miles northwest of St. Paul. Upon reaching St. Cloud, Johnston's party hit unburned prairie and had to break a path through eight-foot snow drifts. On the burned prairie the snow was usually blown down to a three-inch crust that cut the fetlocks of their cattle.

The days were much alike, shoveling snow off strips of unburned prairie. When they saw that the necks of three oxen had begun to gall, they changed the bows and wrapped them in soft cloths. On January 23, 1857, a blizzard doused their fire and blew down their tent. "Spread out the bed and get into it quick," shouted the guide Pierre Bottineau. The "bed" was a fifteen-foot-long wool comforter padded with quilted cotton batting three inches thick, intended to cover all nine men. The wind howled through the treetops and they shivered in wet clothing. Six inches of snow drifted onto the comforter. It was cold at first, but eventually they steamed up.

At 3 A.M., Dan heard the half-breed guide singing in Chippewa as he attempted to start up the fire from live coals. When the sun rose on January 24, 1857, it was flanked by two brilliant sundogs. The cattle were growing weak. Cut by the ice crust and inflamed by the subzero temperatures, their ankles had swollen to the size of teakettles. The animals stained the snow with blood at nearly every step. They were thirty-five miles from their destination and the guides said the best thing to do was push on.

On January 29, they came to the junction of the Bois de Sioux and Otter Tail rivers, where they were platting their first town, Breckenridge. Luck was with them, for a herd of buffalo was basking on the prairie, in a bend of the Otter Tail. The animals' heads were plunged into the snow to get at the dry grass. As protection against wolves, the bulls fed outside, while the cows and calves huddled in the center.

The guides crawled toward the herd through eighteen-inch-deep snow, drawing in close. Smelling the men's wolfskin caps, the buffalo snorted and stamped the ground but kept feeding. When the guides fired, the startled buffalo jumped and raised their heads, but seeing nothing, they went on eating.

On January 30, Dan Johnston and John Moulton tried to survey the Breckenridge townsite, but the wind blew so hard they couldn't keep their chain straight. It was discouraging, but "the million in it" kept them going. While they worked, the guides hunted, and by February 1, the party had a ton of buffalo packed in ice.

By this time they were short of flour. When it ran out, they started eating the cornmeal intended for the cattle, putting the cattle on tree browse, which was tough on man and beast. Soon one of the oxen could not get to his feet and had to be shot. In March six oxen died while they waited for Moulton to return with supplies. On April 10, Dan shot an otter but the meat was so oily and fishy that, as hungry as they were, they threw it out for the wolves. Moulton finally arrived on April 17, chilled to the bone after practically swimming across the prairie through snow and slush.

Two days later Dan and English Billy (the cook) were sent to hold the first town below Breckenridge. Again they encountered some buffalo. With dinner on his mind, the cook fired once and fired twice, but his quarry moved slowly away and out of sight. Billy grabbed his gun by the barrel and swung it over his head. "I'll break it," he said, "damned if I don't."

"Better think four times before you do that," Dan said. "There aren't many extra guns out here. Anyway, your priming's wet. Reload and we'll get that buffalo yet."

"Get that buffalo," Billy replied with a sneer, "he's half way to Pembina by now" (Pembina, the northernmost county of Minnesota Territory, lay on the Canadian border).

"Reprime your gun and we'll crawl up the bank and see about it," Dan said. At the top of the bank they saw the buffalo, both fired at once, and he went down. "I could put three of my fingers into the hole our balls made through his heart," Dan said.

At Breckenridge, Dan Johnston had two hundred lots for his share, but the railroad built its station so far away that the land was worthless. Cured of townsite speculation, Dan returned to St. Paul and became the editor of the *St. Anthony Express*, a public-spirited newspaper that dispensed neighborly advice to its readers: "Keep litter off the streets, improve your lots with shrubbery and fences, and build in good taste, back from the sidewalk."

On December 24, 1856, the Minnesota delegate to Congress, Henry M. Rice, introduced a bill to allow the roughly 150,037 people of the territory to frame a state constitution. In January 1857, the House Committee on Territories cobbled together its own bill, which passed by a vote of 97 to 95.

This halfhearted welcome to the federal family must be seen in its political context. California's admission as a free state under the Compromise of 1850 had broken the free-slave balance maintained since 1820 by the Missouri Compromise. After California, the Union consisted of sixteen free and fifteen slave states and the southerners in Congress naturally fought the admission of any more free states.

Specifically, the southerners blocked efforts to organize Nebraska Territory, which sat north of the notorious 36° 30′ line. To break the deadlock, Senator Stephen A. Douglas of Illinois proposed to divide the territory into Kansas and Nebraska. The settlers living there would decide whether or not they wanted slaves, under the Douglas doctrine of squatter sovereignty. Since the territory happened to be too far north to grow crops requiring slave labor, Douglas expected both its new halves to go antislave.

The Kansas-Nebraska Act passed in 1854, repealing the Missouri Compromise and leaving the issue of slavery up to the inhabitants of the territories. One of the consequences of squatter sovereignty was that militants from both sides of the slavery issue flocked to Kansas to claim it as their own. Open warfare broke out in 1856, and soon Bleeding Kansas became the curtain raiser for the north-south war.

The disorder in Kansas also resulted in the collapse of the Whig Party, which tottered to its grave. In its place there rose a new party, the Republicans, an amalgam of Free-Soilers, antislavery Whigs, anti–Kansas-Nebraska-Act Democrats, abolitionists, and Know-Nothings.

Yet another consequence was Abraham Lincoln's return to politics. He had served one term as a Whig congressman and then had gone back to the practice of law in Springfield. But the Kansas-Nebraska Act roused him, and in October 1854, in Peoria, Lincoln gave his first speech denouncing slavery. It must not spread into the territories, he said. The question of slavery in those areas was the business of all the people, not just those in Kansas and Nebraska.

And where did all this leave Minnesota? When the Senate Committee on Territories reported its own statehood bill on February 18, 1857, southern senators objected. Minnesota, they argued, included land from the old Northwest, but failed to observe one of the Northwest Ordinance's basic provisions—not fewer than three nor more than five states could be made from that region. The limit of five states had already been reached, the gentlemen from the south pointed out: Ohio, Indiana, Illinois, Michigan, and Wisconsin.

Why, the southerners asked, should the five-state provision be violated when the provision banning slavery was so strictly adhered to? The northerners replied that the strip of eastern Minnesota belonging to the old Northwest, between the Wisconsin border and the Mississippi River, was just "a little gore of land." The bulk of the proposed state was made up of land from the Louisiana Purchase.

When the Senate debated the bill in February 1857, Senator Albert Brown of Mississippi raised the issue of settlers in Minnesota Territory who were not yet U.S. citizens. "There may be in this territory," he said, "Norwegians who do not read one word of English. . . . What a mockery and what a trifling with sacred institutions it is to allow such people to go to the polls and vote."

William H. Seward, the antislavery senator from New York, responded that Texas had been admitted as a slave state without having a single United States citizen.

The bill passed in the Senate 31 to 1, the hold-out being John B. Thompson of Kentucky, who said: "I am not as a southern man going to help them bludgeon us. I am not going to put into their hands the club with which to cleave down a brother. . . . Soon the name of Minnesota will occur more often on the statute books than the name of the Lord God in the 20th chapter of Exodus, and a Minnesota senator will land here with all the pomp and circumstance of a bashaw with three tails."

Thompson concluded that Minnesota Territory should be governed "as Great Britain rules Afghanistan, Hindostan and all the Punjab, making them work for you as you would work a negro on a cotton or sugar plantation."

The Minnesota "enabling act" got through both houses in February 1857. Lame-duck president Franklin Pierce signed it a month before the inauguration of Democrat James Buchanan.

Everyone assumed that the Democratic Congress would admit the new state without delay. But Minnesota became embroiled in the battle over Kansas. In 1857, the situation had reached such a point of lunacy that two legislatures were operating there: one proslavery in Lecompton and one antislavery in Topeka. In Lecompton, the lawmakers passed a proslavery constitution at the end of the year. That document came before the Senate in February 1858, at the same time as the Minnesota constitution.

Predictably, the southerners wanted Kansas admitted as a state before Minnesota entered on the free side of the ledger. "Do Republican senators hope to have two more senators on this floor to aid them in the exclusion of Kansas?" asked Senator Brown of Mississippi.

Brown also trotted out his old noncitizen argument: "All you have to do is catch a wily Indian, give him a hat, a pair of pantaloons and a bottle of whiskey, and he would then adopt the habits of civilization and be a good voter."

In the House, Francis Preston Blair of Missouri said of the Minnesota vote to ratify their constitution, "At one of the precincts, one pair of breeches was obtained and 35 Indians were successively put into it and in that way it was ascertained they had adopted the habits of civilized life."

Blair's efforts were of no avail. The Lecompton constitution, although approved by the Senate, went down to defeat in the House. Kansas statehood would have to wait, and the southern senators relaxed their resistance to Minnesota. By May 11, 1858, the Minnesota bill had been passed by both houses, and Minnesota became the thirty-second state—and the seventeenth free state. To mark the occasion, one of the St. Paul newspapers carried the following headline:

O GLORIOUS DAY!
MINNESOTA'S A STATE!

PART FOUR
THE CIVIL WAR STATES

CHAPTER TWELVE

BLEEDING KANSAS

> *We cross the prairie as of old*
> *The pilgrims crossed the sea,*
> *To make the west, as they the east*
> *The homestead of the free.*
>
> > *"Emigrant's Song"*
> > *(to the tune of "Auld Lang Syne")*
> > JOHN GREENLEAF WHITTIER
>
> *You take the sinners away from the saints, you're lucky*
> *to wind up with Abraham Lincoln.*
>
> > Hud *(the movie)*

In May 1854, Congress passed the Kansas-Nebraska Act, and President Franklin Pierce signed it. A political unknown, Pierce had emerged as a compromise candidate at the Democratic Convention of 1852, and went on to win the election.

To placate the south, Pierce brought in the proslavery extremist Jefferson Davis as his secretary of war. Rumor had it that in the matter of states' rights, Davis had considerable influence over his suggestible chief.

In the southern view, Kansas was the key to restoring the legislative balance that had been broken by the admission of California as a free state in 1850. The territory held no less of a burning interest for the antislavery side. Thus, when the Kansas-Nebraska Act ordained in 1854 that the residents of those territories should decide for themselves whether or not they wanted slavery, both factions sent their partisans to populate Kansas and win it to their cause.

As Senator Charles Sumner of Massachusetts put it, "Squatter sovereignty puts freedom and slavery face to face and bids them grapple." But the nation waited anxiously to see whether the two sides would grapple with ballot boxes or with guns. The south held two advantages: the proximity of the slave state of Missouri and the fact that Jefferson Davis controlled the army and had the president's ear when it came to territorial appointments. Whenever he could, Davis used the men and means at his disposal to advance the proslavery cause in Kansas.

One of the first to grasp the importance of numbers was the Worcester antislavery educator Eli Thayer, who said on March 13, 1854, as the issue was still being debated: "Let us settle Kansas with people who will make it free by their own voice and vote."

Acting on his own advice, Thayer drew up a charter for the New England Emigrant Aid Company. Conceived as a crusade against "slave power," the plan, approved by the Massachusetts legislature, aimed to send antislavery militants to Kansas to build free-state towns and form a free-state party. To attract volunteers, the company offered to pay for the $25 fare from Boston to Kansas City.

The first principle of the Emigrant Aid Company was "Slavery must not secure another foot of the public domain." To that end, the company hired Charles Robinson, a man of action who had once led a squatter uprising in Sacramento. His job was to explore Kansas Territory and choose a site.

In July 1854, Robinson arrived at a green valley that unfurled before a hill on the Kansas River, thirty-seven miles west of Kansas City. Robinson called the place Lawrence after Amos Lawrence, wealthy backer of the Emigrant Aid Company. The first party of twenty-nine emigrants soon appeared, bringing to this legislative Armageddon the Puritan principles of duty and service, and a belief in the primacy of moral values over expediency. On September 9, 114 more New Englanders followed. Soon Lawrence was a thriving tent community, its washtubs and log tables out in the open air. Some soft-slippered, kid-gloved people who did not take to frontier life went home, but those who stayed saw the rise of the first free-state town in Kansas, along with the first prairie Sabbath and the first prairie grave.

Initially, the only problem the citizens of Lawrence faced was claim jumpers. Missourians came and squatted on land that had already been surveyed and claimed by the Lawrence people. Once, when Robinson and some of his friends confronted a group of interlopers, it looked like there might be a gunfight. His men asked Robinson if they should shoot to kill or aim over their adversaries' heads. "I would be ashamed to shoot at a man and not hit him," Robinson said. But the claim jumpers departed without firing a shot.

Aside from Lawrence, Kansas consisted of 50 million acres of grassland and two forts, Leavenworth and Riley. The question of who was going to live on that grassland remained as open as the land itself. For aside from the free-staters in Lawrence, the settlers in Kansas in 1854 were mostly proslavers from neighboring Missouri, where three out of four people had southern ancestors, and about one family in eight owned slaves.

As Preston Brooks intoned on the floor of Congress, "It will be found that Missouri is nearer to Kansas than Boston." And just as in New England Eli Thayer was promoting antislavery migration, in Missouri the proslavery activists rallied under the banner of Senator David Rice Atchison. He was rabid on the subject, telling Jefferson Davis: "We are organizing. We will be compelled to shoot, burn, and hang, but the thing will soon be over."

Atchison formed an outfit called the Blue Lodge. Its members wore a bit of hemp in their lapel buttonhole, a reminder that hemp was used to make nooses. Their password was the phrase "Sound on the Goose." Every man was judged by his soundness on the goose, meaning his proslavery convictions.

Before long, gangs of "border ruffians" began riding into Kansas and raiding free-state settlements. On October 4, 1854, E. D. Ladd of Lawrence wrote the *Milwaukee Sentinel* that "the Misery-ans have taken down and removed the tents of our squatters and burned down the cabins, while the owners were absent."

Three days later the first governor of Kansas Territory, Andrew H. Reeder, arrived in Leavenworth. In its territorial period, between 1854 and 1861, Kansas Territory would have six governors, almost one a year. Trying to govern Kansas was like sitting on a hornet's nest.

A Pennsylvania lawyer, Reeder was not necessarily sound on the goose. The first order of business was sending a territorial delegate to Congress, and Reeder called for a November election. Any free white male twenty or over and an actual settler could go to the polls. The border ruffians saw their chance to go to Kansas and stuff the ballot boxes. If New England abolitionists could vote in a Kansas election, they figured Missourians had the same right.

On election day, November 29, the Blue Lodge organized day trips to polling places. Their invitation to cross the Missouri into Kansas and vote read "Free ferry, a dollar a day, and liquor." About 1,700 Missourians availed themselves of the opportunity. The election judges were persuaded, sometimes at gunpoint, to let these armed nonresidents cast their ballots. The little town of Douglas, for example, with 50 legal votes, cast 283. It was no wonder that former Indian agent John H. Whitfield, a thick-tongued Tennesseean, won election by a wide margin and set off for Washington to defend proslavery interests.

Not everyone in Missouri shared the opinion that participation in a Kansas election was a civic duty. Tom Thorpe, who farmed out Platte City way, said, "They been a jawin' me, wantin' wagons, but I don't subscribe to such doins. . . . I'm no abolitionist, I tell you, I'm pro-slave, I'm dyed in the wool and can never be made a free-soiler. But this going over there to vote ain't right."

Governor Reeder agreed. In fact, the Missourians' proslavery zeal converted him into a friend of the free state. In preparation for the March 1855 election of a territorial legislature, he ordered a census on January 22 to protect against voting fraud.

One of the census takers he hired was James McClure, who had been in Kansas only a few months. Reeder ordered him into the 6th and 7th districts, warning the young man that those areas were crawling with pro-slave ballot stuffers.

Early in February, McClure got a horse, a revolver, and a rough map and set out for Fort Riley. It was a cold damp day, with a fine snow blown by a chill wind. Unfortunately, he couldn't find any roads, or anyone to count. He was getting discouraged when he saw smoke. Riding closer, he saw some Indians around a fire and beat a hasty retreat. They weren't included in the census.

In the 6th District, McClure tallied up 83 persons. Then he proceeded to the settlement called Hundred and Ten, where Fry McGee, who headed the proslavery movement in the district, owned a saloon.

McClure went in and stood a round of drinks. "Are you sound on the goose?" McGee asked. When McClure introduced himself as a census taker, McGee replied, "You're an abolitionist, one of Reeder's spies." McClure assured him that he only wanted to collect information.

"No damned Yankee is going to spy around this place and take names unless it's under my supervision," McGee said. But the proslavery leader grew easier to deal with when he got so drunk he had to be carried home.

McClure spent the night in a vacant cabin and obtained his data the next day from a free-state man. Hundred and Ten had 52 inhabitants, but in the November election for a delegate it had cast 607 votes.

When the Kansas census was completed on February 28, 1855, the total was 8,501: 2,905 voters, 408 foreigners, 151 free Negroes, and 192 slaves. The rest were women and children.

In March 1855, eleven-year-old Dewitt Goodrich was traveling by wagon across Missouri with his father, who had decided to flee from the "Wabash shakes," as the fever was known in Indiana. Stories of fair Kansas had put the emigration bee in his bonnet.

One evening in camp, when Dewitt was fetching water at the spring with a bucket, he saw a teenaged girl pass swiftly by on a horse, followed by a Negro boy of about ten who was carrying her bonnet and had a hard time keeping up.

A man rode up and dismounted. "When you are through watering," he said to Dewitt, "I'd like to borrow your bucket and get this boy to water my horse." Seeing that he was the only boy there, Dewitt started walking toward the spring when the man said, "I did not mean you. I meant this boy." And he pointed to an elderly "darky" about seventy years old. Dewitt could not understand why an old man should be called a boy.

In New York, Ralph Waldo Emerson gave a speech in which he said: "I know that slavery will go at last, and go with tattooing and cannibalism. . . . The thoughts of the mind are the emancipators of slaves."

In Missouri, people made ready to vote in the March 30, 1855, Kansas legislative elections for twenty-six members of the House and thirteen Council members. On March 10 the *Western Argus* ran this advertisement: "Election in Kansas—the ferry that never stops. . . . We keep two good boats, and when one can't run the other can. All who wish to be in Kansas in time to vote, go to the landing and you will not be disappointed."

Came the day, and the ferries at Weston and Westport could not handle the crowds. Thousands of Missourians armed with rifles, pistols, and bowie knives crossed the river to vote. In Lawrence, they came a thousand strong, wearing white ribbons in their buttonholes to distinguish themselves from the settlers. When one of the election judges asked a border ruffian, "Do you plan to make Kansas your future home?" he replied, "It's none of your business." Though Lawrence had 369 legal votes, 1,034 were cast.

Arriving in Leavenworth on election day, William Hutchinson of Randolph, Vermont, saw roads crowded with Missouri voters returning home in their two-horse farm wagons, holding a gun in one hand and a whiskey bottle in the other, shouting, "We've made a clean sweep." A ragged crew, in his view, that had just enslaved Kansas.

In a territory with a voting population of 2,905, 6,038 ballots had been cast, 5,247 of them proslavery and 791 free-state. Most of the free-staters disdained to vote in the rigged election. On April 2, Charles Robinson wrote Eli Thayer, asking for two hundred Sharps rifles and a couple of field pieces.

Governor Reeder reported that "Kansas has been invaded by a regular organized army, armed to the teeth, who took possession of the ballot-boxes and made a legislature to suit the purposes of the pro-slavery party."

Reeder ordered new elections in six disputed districts. In response, the editor of the *Brunswicker* in Brunswick, Missouri, opined: "This infernal scoundrel will have to be hemped yet." On May 17, William Phillips, a Leavenworth lawyer who had officially protested the validity of his district's election, was abducted from his home by fourteen Missouri men and taken across the river to Weston. They rode him on a rail for a mile and a half, and then put him up for sale at a mock auction. A clowning Negro acted as auctioneer and sold the lawyer for a dollar. Fifteen months later, on September 1, 1856, border ruffians murdered Phillips in his home.

The "pukes," as the eastern press called the gangs, operated in Kansas with impunity, aided and abetted by proslavery sheriffs and judges. The law itself encouraged these men to shoot, hang, drown, and tar and feather their opponents.

In May 1855 the Emigrant Aid Company started sending rifles to its people in Lawrence and Topeka so that they could defend themselves. In June, the free-staters held a convention in Lawrence to repudiate the "bogus" legislature.

Reeder's strategy was to convene the legislature in a place far from the intimidating presence of the "pukes." The governor had bought some land 125 miles from the Missouri border, where he planned to build a town called Pawnee and make it the territorial capital. This would have the dual effect of isolating the legislature and creating a boom in building lots.

Reeder ordered the thirty-nine legislators to convene in Pawnee in July. "And the governor says he don't go in for real estate on the side"— such was the greeting among lawmakers arriving in the as yet unbuilt town of Pawnee. Since there were no accommodations for them, they slept on buffalo robes and cooked their food by the side of a log. After four days in the wilderness, they voted unanimously to repair to the more civilized location of Shawnee Mission, near Fort Leavenworth.

In the meantime, Governor Reeder's real estate speculation had come to the attention of his superiors in Washington. He was removed from office on August 15.

That same month, in order to halt the spread of a free-state settlement in Pawnee, Jefferson Davis enlarged the borders of the Fort Riley Reservation to encompass the new town.

One of the Pawnee settlers was Lemuel Knapp of New York, who had come to Kansas under the auspices of the Emigrant Aid Company. In August he and the other settlers were told to leave, since Pawnee was now military land.

In November, Knapp was still there. One morning soldiers arrived and tore the roof off his cabin. Rain and snow poured in and that night his children's hair froze on the pillows. They moved to Ogden, just outside the reserve, but Ogden was proslave, and Lemuel Knapp had to endure all sorts of petty persecutions. He was kept dancing attendance on the bogus courts as a witness or a juryman. One of his ponies was stolen and another was shot, and his woodpile was set on fire.

The systematic harassment of antislavery settlers gave a strong impetus to the movement for a free-state government that would challenge the "bogus" Lecompton legislature. Making things worse, Wilson Shannon, a former governor of Ohio who was considered sound on the goose, arrived in Lecompton on August 10, 1855, as the territory's second governor, replacing Reeder.

The free-staters of Lawrence and Topeka now moved to form an alternate government. A constitutional convention was held in Topeka and drafted a constitution that banned slavery in Kansas after July 4, 1857.

On December 15, 1855, the Topeka constitution was adopted. On January 5, 1856, state officers were chosen and Charles Robinson was elected governor. These developments represented a total breakdown of the territorial system: Kansas now had two competing state governments. A fraudulently elected proslavery legislature sat in Lecompton, while in Topeka a free-state legislature deliberated in defiance of federal authority.

The situation had spun out of control. Governor Shannon wrote President Pierce: "It is vain to conceal the fact—we are standing on a volcano." In his message to Congress on January 24, 1856, the president endorsed the "bogus" Lecompton legislature and called the Topeka movement an act of rebellion.

•   •

In the winter of 1855–56 the southern states mobilized their resources to send volunteers to Kansas. On December 6, the *Montgomery* (Alabama) *Mail* announced the sale of "forty likely negros" by "a friend of ours" to raise funds to send three hundred emigrants westward. Such was the belated southern response to New England's Emigrant Aid Company.

In April 1856, Albert Morrall, a clerk in a Charleston dry-goods store, joined a company that called itself the Palmetto Guards. Under the command of Captain Frank Palmer, thirty men had signed up to go to Kansas and reinforce the border ruffians. Charleston ladies wove them a flag, a crimson banner displaying a single white star and bearing the words SOUTH CAROLINA on one side and SOUTHERN RIGHTS on the other.

Reaching St. Louis, the Palmetto Guards took the steamboat to Kansas City. On the boat were two well-dressed young men who looked and sounded like Yankees. That evening after it got dark, passengers heard a commotion on the forward deck. One of the Yankees had his back to a column, and Captain Palmer stood before him shaking his fist and crying, "Damned abolitionist!"

The Yankee calmly replied that education for the Negroes would bring great benefits. A crowd of Palmetto Guards closed around him and threatened to throw him overboard. Soon the second Yankee, wearing a short cloak thrown over his shoulders, came on deck from the stateroom area and pushed toward the rail.

The steamer's whistle blew. As the boat drew close to the bank near a woodyard and sailors threw out the planks, the two Yankees darted out a side gate and onto the shore. A few moments later several Palmetto Guards ran out of their staterooms shouting that their wallets had been stolen.

During the spring of 1856, Missourians again poured into Kansas Territory and arrested free-state men on sight, whether they were riding on the prairie or traveling on steamboats. In Atchison, the Palmetto Guards seized Pardee Butler, pulled him into a grocery store, and stripped him to the waist. Then they tarred him, covered him with a coat of cotton wool for want of feathers, tossed him into his buggy, and set him adrift on the prairie.

In Lawrence, rifles arrived from the east in crates labeled BIBLES and men drilled in expectation of attack. Frederick Law Olmsted, the landscape architect who designed Central Park, sent the free-staters a brass howitzer, which had to be fetched in Kansas City.

On May 21, Sheriff Sam Jones led a force of 800 men and five cannon, including assorted border ruffians and the Palmetto Guards, into Lawrence. He was accompanied by Senator David Atchison and a U.S. marshal to dole out arrest warrants on long-standing charges. Under the pretext of also gathering information for a grand jury presentment for treason, the operation really aimed to sack Lawrence, citadel of insubordination.

Inside Lawrence, Thomas Bickerton was using slugs of type from the newspaper *Herald of Freedom* to make cannonballs for the howitzer. He had

18 men in his company, drilled so they could fire five times a minute. But when the mob appeared, the Lawrence Safety Committee decided that resistance was useless and ordered him not to fire. That reminded Bickerton of a Nantucket boat steerer he had known who always wanted to hit a whale easy, lest the harpoon should madden him. Disgusted, he replied, "Gentlemen, I'll go out home; you can give up the howitzer just as well without me."

Albert Morrall, in charge of the Palmetto Guard cannon, aimed it at the Free-State Hotel, built by the Emigrant Aid Company. He warned the people inside that he would start firing in thirty minutes. One of the charges in Sheriff Jones's indictment was that the hotel presented a threat to public safety because it had been fortified with portholes and breastworks. Morrall fired thirty cannonballs at the stone building, but failed to bring it down. After emptying the cellar of wine and liquor, the border ruffians burned it to the ground.

Sheriff Jones's men destroyed the *Herald of Freedom* and *Free State* presses as nuisances, and threw their type into the Kansas River. Then they looted the town.

On the night of May 24, 1856, in reprisal for the sack of Lawrence, the abolitionist fanatic John Brown committed his infamous massacre at Pottawatomie Creek, near Dutch Henry's Crossing in Franklin County. Five proslavery settlers were murdered. This spread consternation among the border ruffians, murder having been until then a proslave monopoly. In June civil war raged through the territory.

On June 17, 1856, the Republican Party held its presidential convention in Philadelphia. The main plank of its platform was a free Kansas. In Washington three days later, the House voted on the admission of Kansas under the Topeka (free-state) constitution. The bill faltered, 107 to 106.

On July 4, the free-state legislature assembled once again in Topeka's Constitution Hall. Under orders from Jefferson Davis, Colonel Edwin V. Sumner (later a noted Union general) marched down Kansas Avenue at the head of five companies of dragoons and set up two cannons aimed at the building where the legislature sat. Gunners stood by holding lighted matches. As roll call began inside the hall, Sumner entered and ordered the lawmakers to disperse. He added as they left the building that he found his duty on this occasion the most disagreeable of his military career.

As the Missouri senator Thomas Hart Benton told a colleague: "You blame Pierce, sir, don't blame him, he has nothing to do with Kansas. Jefferson Davis holds him as a nurse holds a sucking baby."

In August and September the free-state militia took the offensive, attacking and taking a number of proslavery towns, such as Franklin and Hickory Point. The free-state general James Lane devised a frontier tactic for capturing a log blockhouse. Piling hay onto a wagon, he set the load on fire and pushed the small inferno into the loghouse where the proslavery men were entrenched.

Thomas Bickerton participated in the assault on Franklin and burst into the post office with his men, looking for the ardently proslavery postmaster Samuel Crane. "Oh, don't shoot my husband," Mrs. Crane begged. "He deserves to die," one of Bickerton's men said. "He is a great villain." "I know it," Mrs. Crane replied, "that's just the reason I don't want him shot." Thanks to this wifely logic, Crane was spared.

On September 14 a free-state militia known as the "Lawrence Stubbs," led by Colonel J. A. Harvey, laid siege to Hickory Point. Inside the fortified blacksmith shop were twelve men, including Albert Morrall, one of the few Palmetto Guards who had not been captured in skirmishes since the sack of Lawrence.

Morrall and the others saw a load of hay rolling toward them and they fired under the wagon at the legs of the men pushing it. Jumping onto the tongue, the free-staters set fire to the hay and escaped through the smoke. By the end of the battle one proslaver had been killed and four wounded; three free-staters were hit in the legs.

Overwhelmed by events, Governor Shannon resigned in August and was replaced by John Geary, the six-foot-five former mayor of San Francisco. Finding the territory overrun with armed bands, Geary helped restore order by mustering the militias on both sides into U.S. Army service.

On November 3, 1856, Americans went to the polls to elect their fifteenth president. Franklin Pierce had lost the Democratic nomination to James Buchanan, largely because of the mess in Kansas. The vote was 1,927,995 for Buchanan and 1,391,555 for Republican John Frémont (whose slogan was Free Soil, Free Men, and Frémont). The voters cast 864,523 ballots for the third-party candidate Millard Fillmore. Without Fillmore as the spoiler, Buchanan might not have won.

On a cold January night in 1857, William Coffin, Benajah Hiatt, and Eli Johnson arrived in Atchison, Kansas, and trudged along a hog track through deep snow to a settler's cabin. They were Pennsylvania Quakers who had met in Indiana and had decided to join the free-state movement in Lawrence.

A rough-looking man with a great shock of untidy hair came to the door and told them to "light and tie your horses to the stack." Inside, a fire roared in the hearth, in front of which lay two large dogs. Between the hounds a lank and sallow-faced woman sat smoking a short-stemmed corncob pipe. She kicked the dogs out of the corners and sliced a few pieces of fat side meat. Then she made some corn dodgers by mixing meal and water, and brewed some strong coffee, smoking and talking all the while.

"I have no sass to give you," she said, "as we have no sass hole." (Missouri and Kansas settlers called all vegetables sass, or sauce, and dug a hole under the cabin floor to preserve them through the winter.)

The three Quakers were wondering what side of the slavery question their host was on. After they had eaten, he said, "Now, gentlemen, you'ns are tired, but mebbe you'ns would like to jine our family worship; we'ns allers has family worship."

His piety told them that he was a free-state man. This he confirmed, adding that his name was Oziah Judd, late of Lockport, New York. He took a well-worn Bible down from the shelf and they all knelt.

"Thank you for this cold night, O Lord," Oziah Judd said, "and send it a little colder."

"Why do you want it colder?" Coffin asked.

"One more cold night would send the Missourians home to care for their slaves," Judd replied.

Oziah Judd's prayers were not answered. Like Pierce, President Buchanan supported the southern wing of the Democratic Party and used his patronage to crush the free-staters in Kansas.

Amid the turbulence, Governor Geary resigned in March. His successor was Mississippi-born Robert Walker, a distinguished jurist, who had been secretary of the treasury in the Polk administration. When he swore his oath as Kansas's fourth territorial governor on May 24, 1857, Walker promised both factions fair elections.

On June 9, the free-state legislature met in Topeka, passing laws as if their counterparts in Lecompton did not exist. On June 15 delegates were elected in Lecompton for a constitutional convention. Although Kansas had 9,251 voters, only 2,071 voted for the delegates. This meant that the free-state men, who still abstained on principle, could have won the Lecompton election.

For more and more immigrants kept arriving to swell the free-state ranks, while neither the border ruffians nor the southern militias became settlers. In the north, pulpit and press broadcast the free-staters' perils. Money was raised, and a tide of newcomers from the north poured around the ineffectual barriers raised by the proslavers on the rivers.

On September 7, 1857, the delegates assembled at Lecompton to draft a constitution. The proslavery faction's convention happened to overlap with the October election of a new Lecompton legislature. Governor Walker hoped that this time all the voters would take part in the election and that the ensuing legislature would be accepted by all. On September 16 the governor assured the people of Kansas that the upcoming vote would be fair to both factions.

On October 5 and 6, for the first time, an honest election took place in Kansas Territory, thanks to the governor's firmness. Walker sent federal troops into fourteen precincts with orders to prevent the border ruffians from voting. Any returns deemed patently fraudulent were rejected.

McGee County, a Cherokee reservation not open to settlement, delivered 1,200 proslavery votes. At the Oxford precinct in Johnson County, "a paltry hamlet of six houses, including stores," the polling place sent in a manuscript roll fifty feet long containing 1,628 names. Walker threw out these and other such returns on October 19.

With the border vote discounted, and the free-state people now voting, the free-staters captured both houses of the legislature. In the House, they held a majority of 24 to 15; in the Council, nine free-staters had been elected and four proslavers. The proslavers complained that the "sneaky abolitionists" had cut loose the ferry boats at some of the landings so they could not be used on election day. That was just fine with Governor Walker. As a result of his courageous stand, however, Walker received so many death threats that he left the territory on November 16. The Virginia lawyer J. W. Denver took over the gubernatorial reins.

The proslavers had not yet given up. Their last chance lay in the Lecompton constitution, which delegates had drafted and approved in September. If they could get it recognized by Congress as the lawful constitution of the state, Kansas would be proslavery. But to do that the constitution had first to be submitted to a popular vote, which they knew would mean its defeat.

So they thought of a stratagem to finesse the vote. Instead of proposing the entire constitution, they offered only the article permitting slavery. Voters were asked to cast their ballots for the constitution "with slavery" or for the constitution "without slavery." Either way the constitution would be approved. If "without slavery," that meant that the slaves already in the territory would not be interfered with. In this way the proslavers would preempt any attempt to constitutionally forbid slavery in toto.

Obviously, to the free-state men, voting on the slavery article alone was a lie, a cheat, and a swindle. On December 2, 1857, a free-state convention in Lawrence denounced the Lecompton constitution and urged free-staters to stay away from the polls. But five days later, in his message to Congress, President Buchanan endorsed it.

The new legislature, controlled by the free-staters, sat for nine days in December and considered a strategy that would cancel the Lecompton single-article trick. On December 17 the lawmakers passed an act submitting the entire Lecompton constitution to a popular vote, to be held on January 4, 1858.

But prior to that, on December 21, came the vote on the slavery article: 6,226 voted for the Lecompton constitution "with slavery," and 569 for "without slavery." On that day, the Pennsylvania Quaker William Coffin was assigned by the free-state leaders in Lawrence to observe the vote in Kickapoo, a precinct with 160 votes. Yet there was little he could do when some armed Missouri men rolled a cannon and aimed it at the polling place while they cast 900 votes.

So many elections were taking place in Kansas that one squatter predicted native Kansans would be born with attached ballot boxes. On January 4, 1858, voters rejected the entire Lecompton constitution by 10,226 to 162 (this time the proslavers abstained).

Nonetheless, the Buchanan-supported Lecompton constitution went on to Washington for congressional approval, despite the fact that it had not been ratified by a popular vote. This stuck in the craw of even some southern congressmen. Senator James Henry Hammond of South Carolina pronounced it "disgusting."

The proslavery party had lost at the polls to the superior number of free-state settlers, but this was ignored in Washington. On February 2, President Buchanan recommended that Kansas be admitted to the Union under the Lecompton constitution. "Kansas," he said, "is at this moment as much a slave state as South Carolina and Georgia."

The Lecompton constitution won approval in the Senate but got defeated in the House, where a compromise bill proposed by William H. English of Indiana passed in April. The bill provided for a bizarre referendum in which Kansas would vote, not on the constitution, but on accepting a land grant of 5 million acres. If the voters accepted the grant, Kansas would automatically become a state under the Lecompton constitution. If they rejected it, statehood would be postponed until Kansas acquired a population of 97,000. In yet another election, Kansans were asked to vote on the English bill in August 1858. In effect, it represented the last gasp of the proslavery movement.

By the summer of 1858, most Kansans had come to ignore the proslavery courts still operating in Lecompton. In Linn County, Captain James Montgomery organized a squatter's court that had its own free-state laws. A secret antislavery order was formed, the "Wide-Awakes," which many army officers joined. The troops at Leavenworth were disaffected and did not want to be used to enforce the "bogus" laws.

That July a Lecompton marshal named Campbell and his deputy came into Linn County to arrest some free-staters. After stopping in the hotel in Mound City for dinner, they continued on, but Captain Montgomery and some of his friends caught up with the marshal on the open prairie, ordering him to halt.

"Boys," said Campbell, "I am a United States marshal, and to arrest me is a very grave crime, punishable by death."

"Shut up and dismount," Montgomery snapped, "and turn over your arms."

The marshal and his deputy surrendered two nice new navy revolvers. Montgomery tore their warrants up and relieved them of a list of friends they had planned to stay with, which he did not tear up. Making the pair sign an agreement not to return to Linn County, he sent them off on foot after removing their boots.

Montgomery was not a man to take lightly. In May, he had addressed a large outdoor meeting after the Marais des Cygnes massacre, when departing southern militiamen rounded up eleven men at random, lined them up before a firing squad, and cut them down. "It's crimes like this," Montgomery said, "that will free the slaves." He raised an arm over his head and cried: "You can count on the fingers of one hand all the years that slavery has to live."

August arrived, and with it the vote on the compromise English bill, linking the Lecompton constitution to a land grant. On August 2, every voter in Dragoon Creek, a town that did not yet have a school, went to the polling place four miles away near today's Harveyville, twenty miles south of Topeka. The creek was high, and there was no bridge, so they cut some elms to get across. Indefatigable in their opposition to the proslavers, Kansans rejected the English bill by a decisive vote of 11,300 to 1,788.

In September 1858, Governor Denver resigned, the first of five governors who had not been pressured to leave by threats. On November 19, the sixth and last governor of Kansas Territory, Samuel Medary of Ohio, took the helm.

Besides dramatizing in microcosm the slavery struggle, Kansas illustrated the proposition that there was a west as well as a north and a south. Western interests at times diverged from the interests of the other regions. Slavery failed in Kansas, while free labor flowed in. The plantation system did not work well in the west. But neither was Kansas a replica of abolitionist New England. Not all free-state Kansans cared about the fate of the Negro. Some just didn't want plantation owners and their slaves coming in and competing with free men for cheap land.

In 1859 the burgeoning Republican Party took over the free-state movement in Kansas. What had been an improvised, grass-roots crusade became the agenda of a legitimate political party.

On January 3 the fourth Lecompton legislature assembled and adjourned to Lawrence, for that body was now made up mainly of free-state men who repealed the "bogus" laws and called for another constitutional convention. On June 7, 1859, thirty-five Republicans and seventeen Democrats were elected as delegates to a constitutional convention in Wyandotte (today's Kansas City), which ran from July 5 to 29.

Inspired by the Ohio constitution, the Wyandotte document banned slavery but denied Negroes the vote. It was ratified by the people of Kansas on October 4, by a vote of 10,421 to 5,530.

In December 1859, Abraham Lincoln spent three days campaigning in Kansas Territory. It was largely over the Kansas issue that Lincoln had become a Republican in 1856. He believed that since the territories were places where poor people could go and better their condition, those regions should be kept free of slavery.

A year earlier Lincoln had contested the senate seat of the "Little Giant," Stephen A. Douglas, the champion of squatter sovereignty. In his speeches Lincoln drove home the inconsistency between squatter sovereignty and the Dred Scott decision, which ruled that Congress could not exclude slavery from the territories. In this context he declared that "a house divided against itself cannot stand. I believe the government cannot endure permanently half slave and half free."

Lincoln lost the election. But as a result of his debates with Douglas, he gained national recognition and heard his name mentioned as a presidential hopeful for 1860. This was why he visited Kansas, speaking in the Kansas-Missouri border towns of Elwood, Troy, Atchison, and Leavenworth.

On December 1, 1859, at Elwood, Lincoln shrewdly showed himself to be no John Brown abolitionist but a moderate on the slavery issue when he said: "People often ask, 'Why make such a fuss about a few niggers?' I answer by saying that slaves constitute one seventh of our entire population. . . ."

On December 3, the Doniphan County settler Albert D. Richardson went to Troy to hear Lincoln. It was boastful to call Troy a town: It had a shabby frame courthouse, a tavern, and a few shanties. In December, it was freezing cold. The wind off the prairie swept through the cracks in the buildings and cut travelers' faces like a knife.

Though distractions in Doniphan County were few and far between, no more than forty people were sitting in that bare-walled courthouse when Lincoln and his party arrived, wrapped in buffalo robes.

Richardson watched a long-limbed, angular man of fifty rise from behind a rough table and begin not to declaim but to talk. He seemed to be all head, hands, feet and legs, and the lines that would give his face majesty were yet to come.

Lincoln argued the question of slavery in the language of the average Illinois farmer. Accustomed to high-flown rhetoric, Richardson thought, "If the people of Illinois believe this is a great man, they must have some very peculiar ideas."

And yet in spite of himself, he felt drawn in by the closeness of the argument, which had the solid, consistent strength of a blacksmith's chain, forged and welded. Lincoln was fair, he didn't distort or misrepresent the views held by Douglas and his allies. Quite the contrary, he stated their position with more strength than they could have done themselves.

Then, however, he modestly inquired into the soundness of his opponents' views. Whenever he heard a man vow to adhere unswervingly to the principles of the Democratic Party, Lincoln said, it reminded him of "a little incident in Illinois: a lad, plowing on the prairie, asked his father in what direction he should strike a new furrow."

"His father said, 'Steer for that yoke of oxen standing at the further end of the field.' The lad started up, but just as he did, the oxen started also. He kept steering for them and they continued to walk. He followed them all around the field and came back at the starting-point, having furrowed a circle instead of a line."

After his speech, which was well received even though he was not well known in Kansas, Lincoln went into a back room of the courthouse kept warm by an old box stove and joined some young men in talk. It was a cold night, but no one wanted to go for wood and miss what the lanky candidate had to say.

Several sacks of Patent Office reports from Washington were lying on the floor and began to serve as fuel. Someone asked, "Mr. Lincoln, when you become president, will you sanction the burning of government reports by cold men in Kansas Territory?"

"Not only will I not sanction it, but I will cause legal action to be brought against the offenders," Lincoln said, his feet propped against the stove and his chair tilted back. No one there could tell whether he was kidding.

Although the Kansans had adopted a constitution, the process of statehood was still being held up by southerners in Congress. On April 11, 1860, the House voted to admit Kansas under the Wyandotte constitution, but the measure failed in the Senate.

At the Republican Convention in Chicago from May 16 to 18, Lincoln was nominated on the third ballot. He entered the campaign with the Republicans united, the Democrats divided, and four candidates in the field.

Born in 1833, David P. Hougland came to Kansas City, Missouri, in April 1857 with $3.75 in his pocket and a good kit of tools. Someone directed him to Gillis House, "four dollars a day or ten dollars a week." He figured he'd better go by the week, and then he asked who the best carpenter in town was.

Mr. Johnson, they said. Going by Johnson's shop, Hougland found him looking at some plans and asked, "Do you want a hand?"

Johnson glanced up. "Do you have a set of tools?"

"I do."

"Send your chest up and start in the morning. If you suit, I'll give you $2.50 a day."

Hougland saved his pay and soon claimed a quarter section on the Missouri border. He put up a plank house and returned to Kansas City. But the next time he went out to his land, he found that his cabin had burned to the ground.

When Hougland brought out a load of lumber to rebuild his new home, he saw a covered wagon standing on one corner of his spread. A man from Weston by the name of Ducate galloped down with four or five other men, all armed, and told Hougland to leave.

The next day Hougland came back with eight men to Ducate's seven. In the ensuing parley, Ducate called one of Hougland's men, Tom Vaughn, a liar. Vaughn drew his gun and fired, but missed, and Ducate and his men rode off.

Hougland got himself an Allen revolver and slipped it into his saddlebags. A few days later he had two sides of his house up and was driving nails when Ducate rode up, a pair of revolvers stuck in his belt and a double-barreled shotgun in his hand. Ducate dismounted and said, "Get off my land."

Hougland spoke to him pleasantly. But just then Ducate's horse pulled up his picket pin and wandered off, making Ducate look around. Hougland drew his revolver and made Ducate drop his gun. He never saw the low-down claim jumper again. Hougland found, however, that he could not hold his claim and continue working as a carpenter at the same time. So he sold it for $75, as unambivalently as he had once defended it.

In May 1860, when Lincoln announced, Hougland said he'd vote for him and commenced to boost his candidate. That did not make him popular in the heart of border-ruffian country in the slaveholding state of Missouri.

Hougland now lived in the vicinity of Pleasant Hill, about fifteen miles southeast of Kansas City. On November 2, 1860, the night before the election, someone slipped a note under Hougland's door warning that anyone who voted for Lincoln would be tarred and feathered.

On election day, Hougland went to the polling place at Pleasant Hill, where you voted through the window of a tailor shop. Instead of dropping your ballot directly into the box, you had to hand it to the volunteer at the window, Fount Freeman.

Hougland took his copy of the *Missouri Democrat*, cut the Republican ballot out of the paper, and passed it over. "How do you vote?" Freeman asked.

"There is my ticket," Hougland said.

"It is a damned black Republican ticket!" Freeman exclaimed. He was so angry that he dropped the ballot on the floor and stomped on it.

"Pick it up, Fount," one of the clerks said. "It has to be counted."

As Hougland got on his horse, one of the men on the sidewalk called out, "How did he vote?"

Fount stuck his head out the window and said, "It was a damned black Republican vote."

The men standing in line shouted and shook their fists as Hougland rode off. He later heard that John Duley, the town bully, said that if he ever caught Hougland in Pleasant Hill he would whip him within an inch of his life.

Several days afterward, Hougland had occasion to go to Jim and Andy Allen's store in Pleasant Hill. As he filled his order, he noticed Andy's face suddenly grow pale. Turning around, Hougland saw John Duley standing in the door, casually cracking jokes with some fellow outside.

His business finished, Hougland tapped Duley on the arm and said, "Please let me pass." Duley made room, but as Hougland went by, he felt a hand come down on his shoulder. "See here," Duley said, "I understand you have threatened my life."

"I don't threaten men I don't know," Hougland replied.

"I am John Duley, a little the best man in town," Duley said, "and you can't come here."

"That may be," answered Hougland, "but don't you put your hand on me when I do come." Going to his horse, Hougland mounted and rode away.

Some days passed, and Hougland was on his knees at his front gate running a screw into a hinge when he heard a soft whistle, saw something hit the gate, and heard the pop of a rifle. The sequence of sensations seemed to verify the theory that a ball discharged from a gun travels faster than the report. The ball had skinned his ear and shaved his sideburn.

Then the newspaper in Harrisonville, about ten miles south of Pleasant Hill, published Hougland's name on a list of "Lincoln's Hirelings." So it came as no surprise when in May 1861, two months after Lincoln's inauguration, Hougland received an anonymous letter, which said, "Sir, we consider you one of our worst enemies, and deem it our duty to notify you and yours to be gone by 11 o'clock this day, or the consequences to you and yours will be evil."

He showed the letter to his wife Sarah, who said: "We won't go. We have a good double-barreled shotgun, a rifle, two revolvers, and there is also old Bucephalus" (their musket, which they had named after Alexander the Great's warhorse). "It is good for twenty of them the first shot."

"All right," Hougland said. "Barkis is willin'." (Here was a frontiersman who had read *David Copperfield*.)

At Pleasant Hill, some of the boys were discussing Hougland. One of them, Larkin Skaggs, who later joined Quantrill's raiders, said, "I don't want a better job than killing that damned nigger lover." Then he rode off to find his man.

When Skaggs arrived at his house, Hougland was armed and waiting, and asked, "Larkin, what will you have?"

"A friendly chat," Skaggs said. His nerve failed him and he was soon gone.

But the next day the parents of Hougland's Missouri-raised wife came by and said that his situation was desperate. In Pleasant Hill they were talking about setting fire to Hougland's house and killing husband and wife. Sarah's parents were so emphatic that for her sake Hougland decided to leave.

Loading Sarah and the baby into a wagon, Hougland headed south on the Harrisonville road when a little boy who often played at their house waved at them to stop. "Don't go that way, Mr. Hougland," he warned, "four men just went that way, and I heard them say they was going to kill you on the prairie."

Hougland thanked him and turned down another road. The family spent the night with a Covenanter (Scotch Presbyterian) who told them, "Our denomination don't take no part in politics."

"Well," Hougland said, "if you think slavery is wrong, then you should take part."

The next day, near Olathe, about ten miles into Kansas, another family took them in during a storm. The wife took one look at the fugitives and exclaimed, "You must have been run out of Missouri."

"That is what's the matter," Hougland replied.

In the morning, they drove into Olathe. Stopping their wagon on the south side of the square, they inquired about renting a house. There were none to be let. A man walked out to the wagon, introduced himself as F. S. Hill, and asked, "How did you come to be in this shape?"

"I voted for Lincoln in Missouri, and that was all," Hougland said.

"Drive into my barn," said Hill. "There is room for your horse and wagon, and I will see if I can't get you a house in the morning."

In the meantime, there was a vacancy for the family at the Olathe Hotel. When they first got to their rooms, Sarah threw her arms around her husband and kissed him. "I feel better than I have for a year," she said. "I feel as though I could get up and shout."

The Houglands remained in Olathe for the rest of their lives, driven off their land and forced to leave their home because a man had exercised his right to vote. In 1905, when Hougland gave his recollections to the Kansas State Historical Society, he said: "I have always been glad that I cast my first vote for a Republican president. Slavery was no corner-stone to build a nation on."

During the Buchanan administration's final months, Kansas statehood marked time. But when Congress reconvened in December 1860 after Lincoln's election, the Kansas admission bill was reintroduced.

A four-month interim then existed between election in November and inauguration in March, which invited trouble. And this time the biggest trouble the country had yet known broke out. South Carolina seceded on December 20, 1860, followed by Mississippi on January 9, 1861, Florida on January 10, Alabama on January 11, and Georgia on January 19.

By the time the Kansas legislation came up for a vote on January 21, five southern states had given up their seats in Congress. Without their opposition, the bill making Kansas a state passed easily in the Senate on January 21 by 36 to 16. One week later it sailed through the House by 117 to 42.

Not only the breaks in the southern ranks delivered Kansas into the Union, but the looming spirit of the new Lincoln administration. Yet it was Buchanan who signed the bill on January 29, 1861, making Kansas the thirty-fourth state. Entering as a free state, and one of the most Republican in the country, Kansas furnished the Union Army with 20,000 men— eighteen white and two black regiments. Considering the turmoil of Kansas's territorial period, no state motto could be more appropriate than the one that was chosen: *Ad Astra per Aspera*—To the Stars Through Difficulty.

CHAPTER THIRTEEN
THE WEST VIRGINIA DILEMMA

In our scouting expeditions in West Virginia, we found little farms in secluded nooks among the mountains where grown men assured us that they had never before seen the American flag.

GENERAL JACOB D. COX

The New York Public Library

One of the by-products of the Civil War was prisoner-of-war camps. Some of the 211,000 Union soldiers captured by the South were sent to this camp in Salisbury, North Carolina. Here they are shown in 1862 in one of the earliest representations of the game of baseball. The pitcher is winding up to throw the ball, while a man on first base is stealing second, holding his army cap in his hand. The players in the field are bare-handed, and the crowd of military and civilian spectators is much too close to the diamond.

If the Civil War's blood-soaked cloud had a filament of a silver lining, it was the enhanced state-making ability of the Lincoln administration. Thanks to the absence of southern legislators from Congress, three states joined the Union between 1860 and 1865—Kansas in 1861, West Virginia in 1863, and Nevada in 1864. In addition, four new territories were formed: Dakota, Colorado, Nevada, and Arizona. Congress banned slavery in all four.

However, only one change in the map of the United States resulted from the Civil War. That was the creation of the state of West Virginia, which did not even exist as a territory before breaking away from Virginia. Stretching from the Atlantic Ocean to the Ohio River, Virginia was divided by the Alleghenies. The third of the state that lay west of the mountain chain presented a completely different character from the tidewater plantations in the other two-thirds.

Mainly pioneer farmers and lumbermen, the mountaineers who lived in trans-Allegheny Virginia felt alienated from their mother state. They were underrepresented in the Virginia legislature, and neglected in terms of roads and other services. The easterners ran the state government, even though by 1830 the population had reached almost equal numbers in the two sections—362,745 in the east and 319,516 in the west.

In 1859, West Virginia served as the site for an incident that helped ignite the Civil War, polarizing the nation along pro- and antislavery lines. In West Virginia's eastern panhandle, along the Potomac River and across from Maryland, there was a national arsenal where 90,000 guns were stored, and an armory able to manufacture 1,400 muskets a month.

The arsenal and armory sat in the little town of Harper's Ferry. On October 16, John Brown and his followers launched their famous attack. Two days later, 10 of the 23 raiders lay dead, 5 had escaped, and the remaining 8, including Brown, had been captured. Refusing to plead insanity at his trial, Brown was found guilty—along with other counts against him—of killing 3 of his hostages. At 9 A.M. on Friday, December 2, in a field outside Charlestown, West Virginia, they hanged him.

Though Virginia, as a slave state, had common interests with the seven cotton states that seceded from the Union between November 1860 and March 1861, for the moment it stayed where it was.

Anti-Lincoln sentiments, however, received free expression in the eastern Virginia press. The *Richmond Daily Examiner* reported on February 28, 1861, that when Lincoln was introduced to the Virginian George W. Summers, the president said; "I have hearn tell of you for a long time occasionally."

The paper's Washington correspondent described Lincoln as being "marked by a vulgarity and awkwardness which, if he were a black man in Virginia, would exclude him from the rank of household servants, and by an extremity of cowardice which would make him unwilling to go on errands at night by himself." Such were the images of Lincoln constantly held up for the contemplation of southerners.

Virginia governor John Letcher, who had been elected in 1859 thanks to western support, called for the election of delegates to a convention in April 1861 to decide whether Virginia should secede. In mid-April, the 152 delegates met in Richmond. By then, however, events had catapulted the nation into war.

On April 12, after Lincoln had sent a fleet carrying provisions to relieve the blockaded garrison at Fort Sumter—in Charleston harbor on a sandbar overlooking the sea—the Confederate batteries opened fire on the fort. On April 13, after thirty-four hours of bombardment, the fort surrendered. The encounter proved to be the opening salvo of the Civil War, and each side claimed that the other had started it.

On April 15, Lincoln called for the states to supply 75,000 militiamen in defense of the Union. Such was the atmosphere in which the delegates in Richmond voted on the question of secession. Lincoln's request for troops to fight their southern brethren raised the temperature to the boiling point. One of the convention members spoke with a pistol on the desk in front of him.

On April 17, 88 members to 55 adopted the ordinance of secession, and a popular vote ratified the measure in May. Virginia joined the Confederacy (as did Arkansas, Tennessee, and North Carolina), which moved its capital from Montgomery, Alabama, to Richmond, a city of 40,000 and a hub for five railroads.

Of the 152 delegates who attended the Richmond convention, 47 came from the western mountain region. Of these, 32 voted against secession. West Virginia found itself in the peculiar position of having to secede from Confederate Virginia if it wanted to remain within the Union.

Possessing only between 2,000 and 3,000 slave owners out of 300,000 inhabitants, West Virginia did not feel, geographically or socially, a strong kinship with the secessionist south. Also, wedged as it was between north and south, the region was bound to become the cockpit of war. West Virginia's best chance lay with the Union's twenty-three states and 22 million people, rather than with the eleven-state, 9-million-strong Confederacy (which included 3.5 million slaves).

The West Virginians lost no time disassociating themselves from the Old Dominion. A hundred delegates representing thirty-four western counties attended a convention in Wheeling from June 11 to 25, 1861. On June 13 they declared their part in secession to be null and void and expressed the desire to muster soldiers for the Union and to form a new state that they called Kanawha.

On June 19, the delegates voted for a "Reorganized Government" consisting of a governor (Francis H. Pierpont), two U.S. senators (Waitman T. Willey and John S. Carlile) and two members of the House (Jacob B. Blair and William G. Brown). Washington immediately recognized the

"Reorganized Government" as the legitimate, nonsecessionist government of Virginia, and the Congressmen were seated.

It wasn't long before West Virginia's fears of becoming the first battleground were confirmed. The war's first important action in the field took place on June 3, 1861, at Philippi, West Virginia. There about 3,000 Union men routed a Confederate force one-third their size that had been burning railroad bridges along the line of the Baltimore & Ohio. In July other battles were fought at Rich Mountain and Corrick's Ford (near today's Parsons).

Confederate troops now occupied the valley of the Kanawha. They held Charleston, too, but in those early campaigns the city changed hands half a dozen times. Union general Jacob D. Cox crossed the Ohio at Gallipolis into the upper Kanawha valley and took Charleston for good on July 25.

In his reminiscences General Cox credited the Methodist circuit-riding ministers with penetrating West Virginia's remotest recesses to preach the Union gospel. "In our scouting expeditions," he wrote, "we found little farms in secluded nooks among the mountains where grown men assured us that they had never before seen the American flag, and whole families had never been further from home than a church and country store a few miles away. From these mountain people several regiments of Union troops were recruited."

By the end of 1861, Union troops had almost undisputed control of trans-Allegheny Virginia. In the meantime, West Virginia continued its determined course toward statehood. Another convention in Wheeling that August called for a constitutional assembly in November, whose delegates would be elected in October.

But how could the Lincoln administration allow a province to secede from a state when it was itself battling the secession of eleven states? Lincoln's attorney general, Edward Bates, conveyed the government's quandary to the Wheeling convention on August 12. Making West Virginia a state, Bates wrote, would violate the constitution. The West Virginians could no more declare themselves separate from Virginia than other states could declare themselves out of the Union. This was the wrong time to be introducing novel theories of government, Bates concluded.

Ignoring Bates, the October plebiscite voted to create a new state by 18,408 to 781 and sent 53 delegates to the constitutional convention. When the delegates met at the Wheeling Federal Building on November 26, 1861, a debate immediately erupted over the name of the new state.

State-naming was one of those appealing postcolonial ceremonies, where the namers did not have to be guided by deference to the English royal family, but could choose a topographical feature or the area's Indian heritage.

Kanawha had been proposed, but was meeting resistance. As Mr. Parker pointed out, "We already have a county of Kanawha. . . . Now if we have the name of the state of Kanawha, the county of Kanawha, and the post office at Kanawha court-house, we will get into confusion."

But Mr. Battelle replied: "We are forming a new state. I for one would want a new name, a fresh name. . . . I oppose the striking out of the name of Kanawha."

To which Mr. Willey responded that "Kanawha . . . is a very hard name to spell" (laughter). "I think the rose would smell sweeter by some other name."

For Mr. Sinsel, no name existed but Virginia, "which makes me think of the virgin queen who swayed the scepter of England with so much glory and renown."

Mr. Brown, however, pointed out that "the virgin was not above suspicion. . . . History tells of dalliances not to the credit of the virgin. . . . I only regret that our old mother state has been caught in dalliance, from which we are trying to rid ourselves by a division of our territory."

Picking up on this reference to Virginia's secession, Mr. Van Winkle asked, "Why must we be so servile to Old Virginia, now that we are casting off our fetters?" He favored Kanawha, "one of the most euphonious names with which I am acquainted. . . . Almost every letter in it has a soft and musical sound."

In the end, it was Mr. Stuart's viewpoint that carried the day: "From my heart I love the name of Virginia. A familiar name, a name I have listened to ever since I was able to speak . . . is West Virginia. Something attaches to the name that ennobles us in the eyes of the country."

The final vote was 30 for West Virginia, 9 for Kanawha, 2 for Allegheny, and 1 each for Augusta, Potomac, Columbia, and New Virginia (8 of the 53 delegates did not vote).

Far more important than this amusing episode, though, was the delegates' statement about slavery. On that explosive subject the constitution explicitly said, "No slaves shall be brought, or free persons of color be permitted to come into the state for permanent residence." Existing slaves in the new state, however, would remain slaves.

The issue of the new states' borders brought the delegates' expansionist ambitions to the surface. Originally, West Virginia was to be made up of those counties west of the "sky-kissed summits of the Alleghenies," in the words of one delegate.

But since the rebel legislature in Richmond was in no position to object, the delegates decided that by adding a few eastern counties they could encompass the route of the Baltimore & Ohio railroad, which stretched from Baltimore to Wheeling. Capturing this plum was the key to economic growth. And so it was that West Virginia instantly grew an eastern panhandle consisting of seven counties east of the Alleghenies—thereby assuring that the new state could collect taxes from and enjoy the services of the B & O railroad.

As a result, West Virginia ended up with one of the strangest shapes of any state in the Union, resembling a splayed frog with its hind legs sticking out. One leg represented the northern panhandle between Ohio and Pennsylvania. The other indicated the thicker eastern panhandle, which crossed Virginia as far as the Potomac, with Maryland on the other side. The body of the state was outlined by the five hundred peaks of the Allegheny ridge to the east and the Ohio River to the west, and at the southern end was a border with Kentucky. In its final form, West Virginia absorbed 35 percent of Virginia's territory.

Forty-eight counties west of the Alleghenies voted on the constitutional referendum that took place on April 3, 1862. The vote was overwhelmingly pro-statehood, 18,862 to 514.

In Washington, where the thirty-seventh Congress sat in session, Waitman T. Willey, one of the senators from West Virginia (and a Methodist lay leader) asked the Senate to take up the admission of West Virginia as a state. His request was referred to the Committee on Territories. For the remainder of 1862, Congress, the president, and his cabinet grappled with the propriety of West Virginia's admission.

Attorney General Bates continued to argue that the Wheeling "Reorganized Government" represented only a small part of Virginia. To insist on statehood, he said, "was nothing less than attempted secession, hardly veiled under the flimsy forms of law."

Many senators also raised objections. As Senator Lazarus W. Powell of Kentucky put it: ". . . I do not believe it was ever contemplated by the Constitution of this country that less than one fourth of the people constituting a state should in revolutionary times like these form themselves into a legislature and give their consent to themselves to form a new state within the limits of one of the states of this Union." In other words, this was a secession inside a secession.

But Lincoln had a lot more than the vexing problem of West Virginia on his mind. Shocked by the carnage at Antietam in September 1862, he decided that the time had come for a preliminary proclamation of emancipation. On September 24, he published a document promising freedom to all persons held as slaves in territories that remained in rebellion one hundred days after that date. Emancipation ensured the death of slavery in the event of a northern victory.

While Lincoln made his proclamation, the West Virginia statehood bill, having passed in the Senate in July, came up for a vote in the House on December 9. It passed, 96 to 55.

On December 15, two days after the carnage at Fredericksburg, Senator Orville H. Browning of Illinois delivered to Lincoln a copy of the West Virginia statehood bill. Though radical Republicans supported the statehood movement, Lincoln still believed that the bill represented grave constitutional problems.

The president asked Browning how long he could hold on to the bill before approving or vetoing it. Ten days, Browning told him. "I wish I had more," Lincoln said. Then he instructed each of his six cabinet members to answer these questions: "1st is the said act constitutional? 2d is the said act expedient?"

Lincoln received numerous letters and telegrams from West Virginia saying that a denial of statehood would ruin the Union cause there. But he continued to question the legitimacy of a "Reorganized Government" as an agency for the creation of a new state.

On December 31 three of the four West Virginia congressmen, concerned about the president's delay in acting on the bill, visited the White House: Senator Waitman T. Willey and House members Jacob B. Blair and William G. Brown.

Lincoln said he was glad to see them, for the members of the cabinet had come down on the statehood question three for and three against. He then read a paper that the West Virginians knew the president had written himself, though he did not say so. When he had finished, Willey said, "This is by far the ablest paper of all."

"Yes," Lincoln said. "I suppose you think it is the odd trick."

"It is the trick we want," Blair said.

Lincoln invited them to explain their reasons for creating this new state. It was the outcome of half a century's growth, Willey replied. Most slaves were in eastern Virginia. Only about 10,000 were in the trans-Allegheny part. There was in fact no similarity between the two regions. The discussion went on for hours. To make or not to make a state.

The West Virginians left the White House still unsure of which way Lincoln would go, though he invited them to drop by on the morrow. The next morning, the first day of the New Year 1863, Jacob Blair arrived at the White House early. Lincoln greeted him by showing him the bill and asking, "Do you see that signature?" It read: "Approved, Abraham Lincoln."

The problem for the president had been the legality of secession. For a state to be formed from another state, the constitution required the consent of the mother state's legislature. In the case of West Virginia, the legislature of the "Reorganized Government" had given its consent. But could this legislature be said to represent the state of Virginia? It was a body chosen in an election in which the majority of the qualified voters had not participated.

But these Virginia voters were in open rebellion against the Union. It was absurd, Lincoln reasoned, to defend their rights over the rights of voters who had cast ballots to remain in the Union. Upholding Virginia's objections to West Virginia's secession would in effect be tantamount to rewarding Virginia for treason.

If a majority deliberately repudiated its rights and duties, it could not complain when a minority continued to exercise those rights. "Can this government stand," Lincoln wrote, "if it indulges constitutional construction by which men in open rebellion against it are to be accounted, man for man, the equals of those who maintain their loyalty to it?"

"It is said," he went on, "that the admission of West Virginia is secession and is tolerated only because it is our secession. [But] there is still difference enough between secession against the constitution and secession in favor of the constitution."

Of course, Lincoln also had practical reasons for bringing West Virginia into the Union camp. "We can scarcely dispense with the aid of West Virginia in this struggle," he observed. "Much less can we afford to have her against us, in Congress and in the field."

Finally, admission of the new state would turn that much slave soil into free soil, establishing "a certain and irrevocable encroachment upon the cause of rebellion."

On April 17, 1863, West Virginians voted for statehood 27,749 to 572. On June 20, West Virginia became the thirty-fifth state, and the twenty-fourth state in the Union, to which it contributed an estimated 25,000 soldiers. When Virginia returned to the Union in 1867, it had to accept the amputation of her trans-Allegheny province as a fait accompli.

CHAPTER FOURTEEN
THE NEVADA FRONTIER

In Nevada, you can live as you please, dress as you please, eat as you please, make money as you please, lose it as you please, die where you please and be buried where you please.

MARTHA GALLY, *homesteader*

The New York Public Library
When silver was found in Nevada in 1859, on the eastern slope of Mount Davidson, at more than 6,000 feet, Virginia City sprang up. The mining community was laid out in tidy rows on the steep slope. The border inset gives a good idea of commerce in the instant city: the Pioneer Drug Store; a newspaper, the *Territorial Enterprise;* and the usual services for miners, an assay office, a recorder's office, a searcher of records, and a Wells Fargo Express office.

At the close of the Mexican War in 1848, Nevada was a desert separating Utah and California, ribbed by a hundred mountain ranges and covered with sinks and washes left by vanished lakes. Plants needing little rainfall grew there, such as yucca, agave, mesquite, and creosote bush.

In Nevada's early days, stations for the mail route from Sacramento to Salt Lake City attracted small clusters of settlers, and California-bound wagons created a demand for supply centers along the trail.

One of the first settlers was Ohio-born Thomas Knott. Returning east from California in 1853, he came into the Carson River valley. So much snow had fallen that he camped at the head of the valley, where the river gurgled out of the mountains. The fine flat of pine timber growing there caught his eye. At the end of May 1853, when a packtrain was able to cross the mountains, Knott had his mill irons brought over, as well as a blacksmith anvil, tools, and a mill crank that weighed 190 pounds. From abandoned immigrant wagons he gathered four hundred iron wagon tires to build a sawmill. In July, he started to cut lumber, which he sold in Salt Lake City.

But Salt Lake City was four hundred miles away. Since Nevada was attached to Utah's Great Salt Lake County, the settlers in Carson Valley griped that they had to go four hundred miles to get a deed notarized. Inaction from Utah provoked squatter meetings, and eventually the settlers incorporated themselves as Carson County.

Nevertheless, the scattered Nevada settlements stayed under Mormon rule until 1857. That was the year when the Mormon leader Brigham Young, threatened with the invasion of 6,000 federal troops, summoned all the Mormons home to defend Salt Lake City. Though esteemed as wilderness breakers of a high order, who not only broke it but kept it broken, the Mormons were not much liked because they had too much of an "us against them" mentality.

With their departure, only two hundred settlers remained in Carson Valley. But in June 1859, on the eastern slope of Sun Mountain, thirty miles north of Carson Valley, miners found the solid gold and silver ledge of the Comstock Lode. The irony of Nevada was that the most barren landscape had yielded the greatest wealth.

Overnight, miners were lining up at the Virginia City assay office, maker and breaker of dreams. Soon the California-bound wagons were changing direction, and California miners were bringing to this new venture their habits and techniques.

Virginia City was where Nevada began. And thanks to the $300 million in gold and silver that eventually got chipped and blasted out of the Comstock, the territory was hustled into early statehood. In this case, it wasn't the number of people that counted, but the number of taxable dollars.

You didn't find surface placer mining in streams here as in California. Buried deep in the mountains in veins mixed with other minerals, Nevada silver required elaborate equipment to be mined and processed. The enterprise cried out for trained engineers who could shore up a shaft with square-set timbering and who knew enough not to skimp on safety. The minimum explosive charge had to be used, and ventilation was essential. The list of dangers was a long one.

One definition of gold mining was "the sudden acquisition of wealth without work" but that was not the case in Nevada, where mining was labor-intensive and called for a large capital outlay. Calls for more capital were known as "Chinese dividends." A poor mine was "barren as a mule." An oft-heard saying was "Nobody cooks hares till the hares are caught," meaning—Get your ore!

When employees stole ore, that was known as "high-grading," while going for surface veins to make a quick profit was called "picking the eyes out of a mine." "Ore in sight" meant ore exposed on three sides, while a worthless body of rock lying within a vein was called "a horse." After examining a vein, the engineer Clarence King once shot back this telegram: THE MINE IS A PERFECT LIVERY STABLE.

Experts knew that samples could not determine the value of a mine. When someone asked the California mine operator John Gashwiler for his opinion of a mine based on some gold ore samples, he answered that "you might as well show me the hair from the tail of a horse and then ask me how fast the horse can trot." Nevada mining was a multifaceted industry, in which the cost of extraction had to be computed along with labor costs and smelting fees.

Having shaken off the Mormon grip and become a boisterous and prosperous frontier mining society, Nevada gained territorial status in 1861. The rich diggings prompted Congress to look favorably on the region's application, even though the 1860 census showed a total population of only 6,857.

On July 7, Nevada's first territorial governor, James W. Nye, arrived in Carson City. He brought along as his secretary Orion Clemens, another loyal Republican. Orion's kid brother Sam tagged along as secretary to the secretary.

Governor Nye had a new census taken, which showed a population of 16,374, and growing fast. He then called for an election on August 31 to name nine Council members, fifteen members of the House, and a delegate to Congress. In the light of Nevada's later destiny as the state of legalized gambling, a few words from Nye's address to the legislature on October 2 are worth quoting: "I particularly recommend that you pass stringent laws to prevent gambling. Of all the seductive vices extant, I regard that of gambling as the worst."

The territorial legislature promptly divided Nevada Territory into nine counties and ordered the construction of a jail. Around that time, Sam Clemens took the pen name Mark Twain, and later wrote that in the legislature's first session, it passed so many private toll-road franchises that "the ends of them were hanging over the boundary line everywhere like a fringe."

Twain later worked as secretary to one of Nevada's first senators, William M. Stewart. One day when the senator was out of town, Twain wrote the following letter in reply to a request for a post office from a crossroads settlement called Baldwin's Ranch: "What the mischief do you suppose you want with a post office at Baldwin's ranch? It would not do you any good. If any letters came there, you wouldn't read them . . . and such letters that ought to pass through with money in them, from other localities, would not be like to get through, and that would make trouble for us all. No, don't bother about a post office in your camp. . . . It would only be ornamental folly. What you want is a jail, a nice substantial jail. I will move on the matter at once." Upon his return, Stewart fired the budding satirist.

On the heels of the miner, scribbling out his claim on a scrap of paper, stuffing it into a tobacco can and burying it under a rock, came the doctor, the newspaperman, and especially the lawyer.

The mining engineer Louis Janin, who worked in Virginia City in 1862, wrote his brother Henry: "I never knew of such a quarrelsome, law-loving people as the Nevadians. There seem to be half a dozen claimants to each piece of property, and each must go to law about it. We peaceful citizens think the lawyers keep up the dissensions, especially in mining claims, and often sigh out the wish they were all hung."

Typical of the carousing newspaperman was Alfred Doten. Arriving in Virginia City in 1863 with his carpetbag and his little mutt Kyzer, he took a job at the *Virginia Daily Union*. Doten hailed from Plymouth, Massachusetts, and had Mayflower ancestors on both sides of his family, but in Nevada he shed his Puritan origins and adapted wholeheartedly to boomtown convivialities.

Doten was assigned to cover the brothels and saloons where news items might be gathered, and attend the music halls and melodeons that offered entertainment ranging from Chinese jugglers to performances of *Hamlet*.

He kept a detailed diary of his daily activities, which conveys the ups and downs of the Comstock life with a wonderful immediacy. Doten seldom went to bed before three in the morning, often too drunk to remove his boots. He covered murders and mining accidents, fires and felonies. On the disaster beat, there was never any shortage of copy.

Since most of the miners carried weapons, the slightest dispute could lead to a shoot-out. In Pat Mulcahy's saloon on C Street, Ben Ballou caught a bullet in the forehead just over the left eye after a small spat with Bill Sheppard. When Sheppard was acquitted, he took the jury and two hundred friends to the International Hotel for a treat.

At the Nevada Foundry in nearby Silver City, a fire broke out. Having scrambled to the roof for safety, Jim Ryan, the bookkeeper, yelled down to

Jason Showers for help. When Showers said he was sick, Ryan called him a "damned son of a bitch" and added, "I'll take care of you later." But Showers beat him to it. He came to the foundry later in the day and shot Ryan in the back of the head.

Aside from shootings, the most common cause of death and injury was mining accidents. The superintendent of the Ophir mine in the Comstock Lode lost his life when a thirty-pound lump of clay slicked off from the side of the shaft and fell forty-five feet, breaking his neck. In the Bonner shaft, a greenhorn took a misstep going down an iron ladder and dropped eighty feet to his death. As he fell, his body struck the other miners lower on the ladder, but they managed to hang on.

Outside another mine, two men stood drilling a boulder by the side of the road prior to blasting it. A wagon rolled by, and the man holding the drill tried to tell the man with the hammer to stop striking until the wagon had passed. As he put his hand over the top of the drill, the man with the hammer gave one last blow, smashing his imprudently cautious companion's knuckles.

Such mishaps were an everyday occurrence, as were fires. During a performance at the Music Hall in Virginia City by the Corrigan Brothers (who parodied the Corsican Brothers), a footlight burst and the kerosene caught fire, streaming across the stage. One spectator tried to extinguish the flames with his hat, but they ran down into the audience through cracks in the stage and six hundred spectators stampeded for the exits. In less than half an hour, the Music Hall was cinders.

Another conflagration started when a man using a candle to hunt bedbugs on his wall ignited the wallpaper. Soon the firemen went on strike over salary cuts and marched up A Street with their caps on backward. This town of combustible frame houses didn't waste much time in restoring their wages.

In their own way, the firemen showed a commendable civic-mindedness. When Julia Bulette, a popular "nymph du *pavé*" (one of the many monickers for whores), was found strangled in her bed, Engine Company No. 1 (of which Julia was an honorary member) handled the funeral arrangements. Sixty firemen and a marching band led the cortege, which included sixty carriages bearing the grieving sisterhood. At Flower Hill Cemetery the mourners heard a heartfelt sermon extolling Julia's many virtues.

Julia's murderer, John Milliean, was caught when he tried to sell a silk dress of an unusual design that was known to have belonged to the victim. In his room police found Julia's trunk, filled with her furs and jewelry. Milliean was tried and hanged.

Though lynchings were rare in Virginia City, one almost took place at the satellite community of Gold Hill. There, Mrs. de Gaston had hired a diminutive Negro man named Joe Scott to cook and do chores around the house. One day she came home and found him with her eight-year-old daughter. He had the little girl lying on her back on a box with her skirt up, and he was standing between her legs trying to force himself into her. The child was lying perfectly still, neither resisting nor objecting. When Mrs. de Gaston ran outside and called for help, Joe Scott tried to flee, but some men caught him and dragged him up to the top floor of the Gibson & Cross saloon.

Twenty citizens held a lynch trial and ruled that Mrs. de Gaston should be allowed to flog Joe Scott to her heart's content. Hauling Scott to Mrs. de Gaston's kitchen, they stripped off his shirt and tied him to a chair. A large, strong woman, Mrs. de Gaston delivered two hundred lashes, whipping the man until she got tired, then resting, then whipping him again. Scott's back was a row of bleeding welts, and he begged for mercy, but she pressed on with her task. After she finished, the townspeople took Scott out the back way and let him go, reasoning that the child had not been injured since there had been no penetration.

The bright side of Virginia City was its cornucopia of amusements. Alf Doten seems to have enjoyed them all. Attending a prize fight four miles from town, Doten stood in a crowd of 1,500, taking notes: "Round 7, Cooper made a clever carom on Foy's conk, drawing claret in profusion. . . . Round 50 was well contested. Cooper got in a low blow called foul, but the fight went on. . . . After 64 rounds & two hours & 28 minutes, Cooper's seconds threw in the sponge. Both men were badly disfigured. The purse was $105."

At night Alf went to see Ross & Carlo's knife-throwing act at Maguire's, or a minstrel show, or Señorita María and her fandango, which was interrupted by a shower of coins thrown onstage by appreciative miners. Evenings often ended at the brothels, where Alf spent hours talking and drinking with the girls, concluding his diary entries by noting the presence of "a little bit of jollification."

Alf's transacted dalliances grew fewer and fewer after he began an affair with the wife of an old friend from Plymouth, Ellis H. Morton, who rented him a room. In his diary, Doten recorded his 526 encounters with "Mrs. M.," devising a simple code in which he substituted the letters v, w, x, y, and z for the five vowels.

Ellis Morton was often away on mining business. One day Doten noted (in the decoded version), "Morton rose early at 5—I slipped into his place and did some fucking." Another time Doten wrote: "Turned in with my love bud. When I was fucking her we thought we heard Morton—I accidentally popped out as I went off spent over her arse. She didn't get off at all. Too much in a hurry."

But usually, Doten enjoyed "the best fucking on the face of the earth —Heavenly." "I came home at 9 this evening and me and my love went to bed and had one of our best fucking matches—We felt each other's cocks all we pleased and then she got on and fucked me bully and I lying on my back. I got my gun off in that position."

The romance ended when Mrs. Morton left her husband and went to San Francisco. Eventually, Doten married and had four children, moved to Gold Hill, and bought the *Gold Hill News*. He got stout from eating and drinking, and became the most influential newsman on the Comstock. Alf Doten died in Carson City at the age of seventy-four, leaving to posterity an unexpurgated account of the bachelor life in Virginia City during its heyday in the 1860s.

Even before its territorial organization was completed and without congressional consent, Nevada rushed headlong into statehood, driven forward by the mine owners who wanted their interests protected by the federal government. In Washington, where he was fighting an expensive war, President Lincoln saw the advantages of statehood for a territory rich in gold and silver.

A constitutional convention sat in Carson City from November 3 to December 11, 1863. Trouble arose when the delegates introduced a provision authorizing the legislature to tax all property, including mines. The mining interests protested, arguing that unproductive ventures would be taxed as well as mines containing rich deposits. On January 19, 1864, the people of Nevada voted against the constitution by 8,851 to 2,157.

But this reversal only occasioned a short delay in the statehood movement, which was by now receiving plenty of encouragement from Washington. For on January 1, 1863, Lincoln had produced his Emancipation Proclamation, a decree granting freedom to slaves in states that were then in rebellion. Nevada could play a part in protecting this crowning event of the war.

Although it did not free a single slave, the proclamation brought thousands of runaways within Union lines and into Union ranks, thus helping to end the war. The recruitment of black troops, Lincoln believed, was the heaviest blow dealt to the rebellion. By the time it was over, black Union soldiers numbered 180,000.

The Emancipation Proclamation derived from the president's war powers, conferred on him as commander in chief in a time of armed rebellion. When the war ended, however, the danger was that Congress might repeal Lincoln's emergency measure. Wanting to protect the proclamation against repeal or repudiation, Lincoln decided to have it enacted as the Thirteenth Amendment to the Constitution, for which he needed a two-thirds vote in both houses of Congress, and ratification by three-fourths of the states.

The addition of Nevada to the Union would bring Lincoln a step closer to the required majority of states, and possibly put him over the top. As the president confided to his assistant secretary of war, Charles A. Dana, the former managing editor of the *New York Tribune*: "I am very anxious about this vote. . . . It is going to be a great deal closer than I wish it was. . . . Here is the alternative: that we carry this vote, or be compelled to raise another million, and I don't know how many more men, and fight no one knows how long. It is a question of three votes or new armies."

If only three votes were needed, Nevada could help. On February 9,

1864, Senator James R. Doolittle of Wisconsin introduced a bill to enable Nevada to draft a constitution and become a state. One condition of the Doolittle bill was that Nevada must come in as an antislave state. Going up to both houses of Congress, the bill encountered some opposition because of Nevada's meager population. Most of the resistance came from the New York and New Jersey lawmakers.

And so it was that the New York delegation was asked to help appoint a collector of customs at $20,000 a year for the Port of New York. And so it was that the New Jersey delegation was given its choice of two tax collectors for their state. And so it was that the Nevada statehood bill passed. Lincoln, who was not above using patronage when it counted, signed it on March 21, 1864.

Even so, some Nevadans still opposed statehood. In an editorial on July 26, 1864, the *Humboldt Register* wrote: "DON'T WANT ANY CON-STITUTION that's what's the matter. The Humboldt world is dead-set against engaging to help support any more lunk-headed officers and if we undertake to support them without taxing the mines, we'll run hopelessly into debt."

This turned out, however, to be a minority view, for 10,375 voters ratified the constitution in September 1864, with 1,284 voting against it. Eager to attain statehood before the presidential election in November, Nevada wired the entire constitution to Lincoln at a cost of $2,416.77. At that time it was the longest telegram ever sent.

Lincoln proclaimed Nevada the thirty-sixth state on October 31, 1864. A week later he won a second term. Nevada voters went heavily for the Lincoln–Andrew Johnson ticket.

In the meantime, the Thirteenth Amendment had been winding its way through Congress, finally passing in the Senate on April 8, 1864, by 38 to 6. But in the House on June 15, enough Democrats voted against the amendment that it failed to get the required two-thirds majority. Most of the nays came from the "Don't mess with the Constitution" contingent, though there were also some from border states that did not want slavery abolished.

In the 1864 election, however, the Thirteenth Amendment appeared as a plank in the Republican Party platform. Having won the election, Lincoln had a mandate for the amendment's passage into law. In addition, so many Republicans had been swept into office on his coattails that they now controlled two-thirds of the House.

On January 6, 1865, when debate on the amendment reopened in the House, the Democrats had a change of heart. Their depleted party was starting to have second thoughts about being viewed as the party of slavery. The chance for a new image now presented itself. As the new York Democrat Anson Herrick put it, the party could now "rid itself at once and forever of the incubus of slavery."

Thus, on January 31, 17 Democrats voted for the amendment, and it passed by 119 to 56. The only remaining hurdle was ratification by three-fourths of the states.

At about that time the newly elected Nevada senator, William M. Stewart, reached Washington and went to see Lincoln. The president told him: "I am glad to see you here. We need as many loyal states as we can get, and in addition to that, the gold and silver in the region you represent has made it possible for the government to maintain sufficient credit to continue this terrible war. . . ."

One of the thirty-sixth state's first actions was to help abolish slavery by voting to ratify the amendment. Charles A. Dana later wrote: "I have sometimes heard people complain of Nevada as superfluous and petty, not big enough to be a state; but when I hear that complaint, I always hear Abraham Lincoln saying, 'It is easier to admit Nevada than to raise another million soldiers.' "

No more soldiers had to be mustered, for on April 9, Lee surrendered to Grant at Appomattox. On April 14, Lincoln was shot while attending the theater. When he died the next day, Alfred Doten noted in Virginia City, "The news cast a pall over all. . . ." The boomtown was draped in mourning, flags stood at half-mast, bells tolled for hours, and even the saloons were closed. "No secesh dared shoot off his mouth," Doten wrote. Two men at Gold Hill who said they were glad Lincoln was six feet under were clapped in jail. Vigilantes seized the pair and and whipped them with a "black snake" that drew blood. Each one was made to wear a placard that said TRAITOR TO HIS COUNTRY.

With the end of the war, the Confederate states returned to the Union. Needing passage by twenty-seven of the thirty-six states, the amendment was ratified by December 1865, thanks to the boost of eight ex-Confederates, and added to the Constitution: "Neither slavery nor involuntary servitude, except as a punishment for crime whereof the party shall have been duly convicted, shall exist within the United States or any other place subject to their jurisdiction."

THE NEBRASKA FRONTIER

*Beyond the pond, on the slope that climbed to the
cornfield, there was, faintly marked in the grass, a great
circle where the Indians used to ride . . . whenever one
looked at this slope against the setting sun, the circle
showed like a pattern on the grass; and this morning,
when the first spray of snow lay over it, it came out with
a wonderful distinctness, like strokes of Chinese white on
canvas. The old figure stirred me as it never had before.*

WILLA CATHER

Nebraska State Historical Society
Circa 1886, Solomon Butcher photographed John Curry and his
wife in front of their sod house near West Union, Nebraska. Among
their proud possessions, all brought out for display, are a birdcage,
a Christmas wreath, and a sewing machine, while the roof of boards
and sod is decorated with antlers.

In 1834, two Presbyterian missionaries, John Dunbar and Samuel Allis, headed west from Boston to set up a mission among the Pawnee Indians in what is today Nebraska. At that time, Nebraska showed up on maps as part of Indian Territory west of Iowa, Missouri, and Arkansas.

Under the Indian Removal Act of May 28, 1830, passed during Andrew Jackson's first term, the tribes were shoved westward. Jackson, the former Indian fighter and Tennessee frontiersman, considered removal the only solution to the "Indian problem." The act quickened the pace of forced migration. The Shawnees and the Ottawas were moved out of Ohio in 1831, and the Kickapoos were ousted from Illinois in 1832. Whenever a tribe was targeted for relocation, it received solemn assurance that the new lands were its own "as long as the waters run and the grass shall grow."

The Indians' destination was a large "Indian Territory" west of the Missouri, a space that created de facto segregation between red man and white. In 1834, Congress approved an Indian Trade and Intercourse Act, which provided safeguards for the relocated tribes. White squatters were rigidly banned, the ban to be enforced by the army. Trading was allowed only under federal license.

By 1840, a "permanent Indian boundary" stretched from the Gulf of Mexico to the Great Lakes. Besides Nebraska, Oklahoma, Kansas, and parts of Iowa, Minnesota, and Wisconsin had become Indian Territory, supposedly for good. Of the Indians who had lived east of the Mississippi, only 12,000 remained. Ninety thousand had crossed the Father of Rivers to join the 250,000 already living in the west.

In government circles a genuine conviction prevailed that the "permanent Indian boundary" could be maintained. After all, so much land was available elsewhere. West of the boundary, the Indians could work out their destiny, hunting buffalo and living their desultory life. No one then considered that settlers could not be indefinitely bottled up east of the Missouri, and that little by little Indian territory would be whittled away.

One of the oldest Nebraska tribes, the Pawnees lived in villages on the Platte River, sustaining themselves by hunting. Theirs was the rolling prairie land, the ancient domain of the bison.

In the 1830s, the Pawnees began to kill buffalo for robes to sell to traders, leaving the meat for wolves, but they soon found that each season they had to travel farther to find the herds. They also depleted their lumber by feeding cottonwood bark to their horses in winter, thus killing the trees.

In 1832, thousands of Pawnees died of smallpox. In 1833, the tribe gave up a large tract of land for $1,600 in trade goods and a twelve-year annuity of $4,600. Every year they went to the Indian agency at Bellevue, a few miles south of Omaha, to collect their annuity.

The agency's main task was to wean the Pawnees away from their nomadic hunting habits and make farmers out of them. Through treaties and annuities they became wards of the state. In this task, missionaries could also play a part by living with the tribes and trying to "educate" and convert them.

In July 1834, Dunbar and Allis arrived at Fort Leavenworth, Kansas, where the Indian agent, Major Dougherty, told them they were rash to venture among the wild and treacherous Pawnees. Reaching Bellevue, the two missionaries set out on foot for a Pawnee frame-lodge village of about 2,000 people on the Platte, a hundred miles away. "They are very accommodating," Dunbar noted, "borrowing and lending almost everything they have without any hesitation."

The Pawnees loved their nomadic life, and spent five months a year on the hunt. The Indians made it clear to Dunbar that they did not wish to live like the white man. When they were not hunting or making war, "they smoke, talk, feast, sing, and lounge away the time." Dunbar found them "abominably lazy." The women did all the work. They dressed and sewed the buffalo skins for tent covers, cut and carried wood, planted and hoed, made the fires and cooked the food, bridled and unbridled and saddled and unsaddled the horses. And when the ground thawed in the spring, you could see the squaws digging for potatoes. To Dunbar, the female members of the tribe were "mere slaves."

As for harvesting souls, the missionaries' crop was meager, for "their minds are dark as midnight with respect to the eternal realities." At the same time, Allis felt, it was a mistake to come right in and start force-feeding them Christianity and telling them their own beliefs were wrong. "I had as lief the Indian should smoke and paint his face," he noted, "as Christians to indulge in a thousand unnecessaries." The important thing, the missionaries agreed, was to teach the Pawnees to farm and nudge them toward the sedentary life.

In 1838, matters took a turn for the better when the new Indian agent, Major J. V. Hamilton, sent the mission fifty-two plows with harnesses. The following year a government blacksmith arrived. The results were discouraging, however, for the Pawnees sold all but six of their plows. Farmers were needed to show them how to plant, and Allis volunteered. While he taught the tribe to farm, he could throw in a little Scripture.

Dunbar in the meantime tried to convince the scattered Pawnees to regroup in one village where they could work their fields. They agreed but took their time about choosing a site. When Dunbar tried to prod them in the spring of 1840, they told him that the chief was away and that "he is like your president, we can do nothing without him."

Dunbar and Allis had been pleading for reinforcements from Presbyterian headquarters, and in 1840, George B. Gaston arrived as their assistant. He turned out to be a holier-than-thou backbiter, who wrote his superiors on the "board": "I wish the board would give us their opinion of Mr. Dunbar and Mr. Allis keeping so many cattle, as it requires such a great deal of time to take care of them that it appears to me missionaries ought to spend in a different and more useful manner."

At last, in July 1841, the Pawnees selected a spot on the north bank of the Loup River, twenty miles from its junction with the Platte, and began to build their new homes. Around then, Major Hamilton was replaced as Indian agent by Major Daniel Miller. Coming from the slave state of Missouri, Miller privately referred to Indians as "red niggers." Yet Hamilton had been all talk, Allis thought—he built castles in the air and lacked firmness with the Indians. As a result, traders sold the tribes illegal liquor, and intemperance reigned, "and to add Satan to sin, black pepper is sometimes used to give the infernal stuff a more fiery taste."

Major Miller, Dunbar reported, was "a thorough-going man who intends to do his duty to the letter. He has commenced a vigorous warfare with the whiskey traders. . . . He gives them no quarter but lets the law take its course." Finding a keg of rum among some traders camped five miles from the mission, Miller axed it to splinters. Three Pawnee chiefs stood aghast at seeing two gallons of alcohol seep into the ground. But they finally laughed and said it was good. Miller fined the traders four hundred packs of buffalo robes, which he sent to the Indian Affairs Office in St. Louis.

Fulfilling the terms of the 1833 treaty, Miller sent the Pawnees fourteen yokes of oxen in 1842. He also appointed four farmers to teach and assist the different Pawnee subtribes: George Gaston with the Tapages, George Woodcock with the Grand Pawnees, James Mathers with the Loups, and Mathers's son Carolan with the Republicans.

Allis now worked as a teacher and built a schoolhouse. He translated hymns into Pawnee and had his pupils sing them. But attendance fluctuated with the hunting season, an unfortunate hiatus, since the students were making good progress in reading and writing. Nor would they remain in school past the age of sixteen, when they became braves.

Old conflicts also got in the way of missionary efforts. On June 27, 1843, the Sioux raided the new consolidated village and killed some of the best men in the tribe. Seventy Pawnees were either killed or captured. The Sioux burned their lodges to the ground and stole their horses.

The survivors seemed to turn to their new life with a greater resolve. They now had four ox teams breaking the prairie, and they planted a hundred acres of corn. Even the first chief blistered his hands using a spade. Ditches and sod fences were built around the village to fortify it, and the chiefs asked for two hundred rifles and ammunition.

Dunbar felt he was getting somewhere when a chief told him that white people seemed more active and cheerful on Mondays after the Sabbath, while the Pawnees simply labored from day to day. "It is hard," said the chief. "We drag out life—not enjoy it."

Dunbar may have thought that he was making progress. But Gaston continued to bad-mouth his boss in letters to the board. One of his charges was that Dunbar would not let him use an idle team of the mission's oxen to draw a load of potatoes, which "lie exposed to the light fingers of these savages."

Why did Dunbar keep so many head of cattle, Gaston asked, which did nothing but destroy Indian corn? Why did Dunbar spend most of his time tending to his own property, to the detriment of religious instruction? In every letter Gaston complained—that Dunbar could not speak the Pawnee tongue, that he was as sociable as a hermit—while hastening to add, "I am not writing to find fault."

Yet one thing was sure: Although the Pawnees were now planting, they were doing less well than they had done as hunters. Dunbar had never seen them so destitute. They came to him and said, "My father, I am poor, have pity on me, give me a bite to eat, an ear of corn, or a potato, and I will go."

Events were unfolding that Dunbar could not control. In 1844, companies of emigrants began to pass through the Pawnee hunting grounds on their way to Oregon, driving off the buffalo. On their summer hunt, the Pawnees had to go so far to find the herds that most of the meat had been eaten by the time they got back. And while they pursued the buffalo, the weeds gained on their corn.

To make matters worse, some of the whites who worked with the Indians were acting more savagely than the so-called savages. Unfortunately, the sort of men employed as farmers for the tribes were often the castoffs of society, Dunbar thought. They had not come because they wanted to help the Pawnees, but because they were unemployable elsewhere.

James Mathers, who had appeared at the mission in 1842 with his wife and two sons, caused the most problems. His way of teaching the Indians was to treat them harshly, and whip them when they stole. He flogged an Indian girl so badly for taking food that she almost died. In early September 1844, Mather's son Carolan found an Indian helping himself to some corn and shot him in the back. The charge of duckshot injured his intestines. Major Miller backed Mathers in his punitive conduct, claiming in his reports that Dunbar and Allis had poisoned the minds of the Indians.

Early in October 1844, another assistant to the missionaries arrived. Timothy Ranney went to see Major Miller when he passed through Bellevue. Miller read Ranney a critical assessment of Dunbar and said he was anxious to have him removed. After a few days at the mission, however, Ranney became convinced that Miller's charges were bogus.

When the Pawnees preferred charges against Mathers and his son, Miller had no choice but to call a council at the village on October 9. When the day came, he opened the proceedings by asking the chiefs to speak out fearlessly. "Tell me just how you feel," he said.

One of the Tapage chiefs got to his feet and said: "My grandfather [the president] has sent men to work here which have no sense. There is one there [pointing to Mathers] and one there [pointing to Gaston] who do nothing every day but whip us. I would be glad if these two men would go away."

Then the Loup chief stood up and began to speak: "Our grandfather

asked us to come here [to relocate] and now we have nothing to eat. . . .
Those men plow more for themselves than for us. I want to tell the truth:
my men always get the timber over their heads when they go that way
[pointing at Mathers]. That is why I ask you to take him away. I expect the
young men will kill him and then I will be blamed as I am chief."

The man who had been blasted with duckshot was brought before the
assembly so he could show his wounds. Miller asked him what he was
doing when he was shot. "I was getting something to eat," he said. Major
Miller got all red-faced and blustery, and said, "How dare you go into the
field."

At this, the Loups rose in a body and walked out. Miller ordered them
to stop, but they kept going. Then he turned to the Indians who remained:
"You must always expect to be poor if you steal. I feel bad to see him shot.
But if the Pawnees stay out of the fields and don't steal they won't get shot
and the white people will not whip them."

A long silence followed. Finally, the Tapage chief stepped forward
and said, "I wish my father would tell those men to throw away their bad
hearts."

But Miller replied: "Tell them that it is good that the white people
should whip them if they steal. . . . White people also are whipped when
they steal." If the Pawnees mistreated a white man, the major warned,
their grandfather the president would send his war chief with soldiers as
numberless as the grass of the prairies and their big guns would destroy
their village.

Miller's words so disheartened the Tapages that they also rose as one
and left the council. Dunbar had attended many such conclaves, but he
had never seen one end this badly. If Major Miller's aim had been to
provoke the Pawnees, he could not have done better.

After this episode, Major Miller started to harass the mission in earnest. Early in 1845 he removed the government interpreter and discharged
Samuel Allis as a teacher.

That spring, as the result of another Sioux raid, the Pawnees could
not grow any corn. In the winter, they were afraid to hunt. Seeing the
Indians begging by day and stealing by night, Dunbar decided to give
away his reserve of four hundred bushels of corn. But he knew that if he
handed over the food without conditions, the Pawnees would return the
next year expecting more.

So whenever a Pawnee received some corn, Dunbar asked for an ax or
a hoe or a buffalo robe in return. In this way he tried to avoid establishing
a precedent of charity. He planned, he said, to return what the Indians
gave him.

But Miller got wind of the transaction and immediately charged Dunbar with violating the Trade and Intercourse Act, which forbade missionaries to trade with Indians. The major put Dunbar in the humiliating position
of having to plead guilty to violating the letter of the law.

Miller, however, soon got his comeuppance. In June 1845, Major

Thomas H. Harvey, the Superintendent of Indian Affairs in St. Louis, accompanied Miller to the Pawnee village. Major Harvey was known to harbor kind feelings toward the "red man," and to show interest in his improvement. At the village Harvey told the Pawnees to speak without reserve about the white men in their midst.

When the Pawnees voiced their grievances against Miller, Harvey called on the major to justify the course he had pursued. This was vexing to Miller, who in the end had to make a public apology. Such an admission of guilt did not please Superintendent Harvey. Major Miller remained on the job no longer than it took for Harvey to exchange letters with the Bureau of Indian Affairs in Washington. On January 12, 1846, he was replaced by John L. Beans.

On August 20, 1845, the Pawnees had returned from their summer hunt carrying a good supply of meat. But while out on the prairie they had fought with the Otoes (a Sioux branch) and both sides suffered casualties. Looking for revenge, a band of Otoes galloped by the mission. As Mrs. Allis walked at sunset by a thicket of tall reeds, she saw a head rise above the reeds and a rifle leveled at her. Two balls whizzed by her and struck the Allis house.

Dunbar began to worry that the Sioux marauders were closing in. He was also concerned about the safety and behavior of his two oldest sons, eight-year-old Jacob and six-year-old Benedict. They had too much of the Indian about them. While Dunbar was converting the Pawnees, they had converted his children. Deciding to send his sons back to the United States, Dunbar made arrangements for them to attend boarding school in Massachusetts.

In the fall of 1845, the Pawnees settled their score with Mathers's son Carolan when a Loup chief shot and seriously wounded the young man. Mathers then killed the chief. Carolan lingered until November, and on his deathbed he said to his father, "I consider you responsible for this."

Mathers was finally removed from Pawnee country. As a parting shot, he made wild accusations against the missionaries in his report to Major Harvey. But Harvey did not forward the report to Washington. "If I had," he wrote Dunbar, "I would deserve a scolding from Mr. Crawford" (the commissioner of Indian Affairs).

In 1846, the Sioux repeatedly attacked the mission. One day, as Allis and the blacksmith sat talking on a log, Sioux riders dashed by and fired a ball that passed between them. One warrior aimed at the blacksmith's head but did not fire, as if saying, "I'll get you next time."

The mission had become unsafe, and the missionaries abandoned it in June and went to Bellevue. Large numbers of migrants were now coming through on their way to Oregon and California. The ill-disposed Pawnees harassed the pioneers, stealing from them what they could. Watching the covered wagons crisscross the Pawnee lands, Dunbar knew he was witness to the beginning of the end of Indian Territory.

With the evacuation of Dunbar, Allis, and Ranney, the mission was terminated. It had lasted eleven years. In the end, the trio's efforts came to nothing, for the Pawnees were eventually driven from their village by Sioux raids.

Allis believed that by trying to help the Pawnees he and his colleagues had contributed to the tribe's demise. Every year the situation had gotten worse instead of better. And now that the missionaries were gone, Allis suspected that the Indian agents would all the more easily be able to steal from annuities and cover their tracks. Bad Indians, he felt, were made by bad white men.

The territorial annexations of the 1840s obliterated the very concept of an Indian Territory west of the Missouri that would keep Indians and whites segregated. Texas was annexed in 1845, Oregon ceded by the British in 1846, and California and the southwest surrendered by Mexico in 1848. With the Gadsden Purchase of southern New Mexico and Arizona in 1853, the continental United States assumed the borders that it has today.

All these new territories and states in the west and southwest dissolved the "permanent Indian frontier." The annexations also nearly doubled the country's Indian population. Jefferson Davis, the secretary of war in 1853, noted that the nation's land surface had increased by a million square miles, and that the Indian population had grown from 240,000 to 400,000.

Settlements now sprang up to the west as well as to the east of Indian country, which was no longer a useful buffer separating the United States from foreign lands, but an isolated section of the Great Plains encircled by a ring of states and territories, and a zone of transit for westward-bound emigrants. Vast numbers passed through, killing the buffalo and destroying the timber and the grass.

There was an urgent need to regulate this traffic, and to keep the Plains Indians from attacking wagon trains. On February 27, 1851, the Senate appropriated $100,000 for treaties "with the wild tribes of the prairies."

One type of treaty called for the purchase of lands in Indian Territory. Thus, on July 23, 1851, at Traverse des Sioux on the Minnesota River, the eastern Sioux signed away their lands in Iowa and Minnesota for an annual payment of $68,000 over fifty years. The government assigned them to a reservation on the upper Minnesota, ten miles wide on each side.

The other type of treaty negotiated permission from the tribes to build roads and military posts. At Fort Laramie on September 17, 1851, the major prairie tribes agreed to let the United States start construction on their lands, in exchange for a ten-year, $50,000-a-year annuity. In July 1853, a similar treaty was signed at Fort Atkinson, on the Arkansas River in present-day Kansas, with the Comanches, the Kiowas, and the Apaches. Indian country was going fast. The "permanent Indian frontier" started to evaporate like a river in the desert.

•   •

While treaties were being signed in western forts, pressure mounted in Congress to carve out of Indian country territories that could become states. The architect of that policy was Stephen Arnold Douglas, the Little Giant of Illinois, who had the unstoppable momentum of a steam locomotive. The steadfast apostle of Manifest Destiny, Douglas proclaimed: "I would make this an ocean-bound republic."

Douglas's efforts on behalf of Nebraska started as early as 1844, before the Oregon and California questions had been settled; his initial sponsorship coincided with the rolling of the first wagon trains over the Oregon Trail. As John Quincy Adams, the Illinoian's colleague in the House, noted in his diary for December 11, 1844; "Douglas wanted to introduce a bill to establish a territory with a strange name." No one had heard of Nebraska, or had any idea where it was. But Douglas said he wanted to "serve notice on the Secretary of War to discontinue using the territory as a dumping-ground for Indians."

In 1847, Douglas jumped from the House to the Senate, where he served on and eventually won the chairmanship of the Committee on Territories. He also moved his home to Chicago, by then a city of 17,000, which he saw as the railroad hub between east and west. His primary concern became the route of the transcontinental railroad, which he firmly believed should go through Chicago and westward via Iowa and Nebraska.

The northern route Douglas envisioned, however, had to cross the "Great American Desert"—or, as it was still known, "Indian Territory." Such a path did not seem feasible until the area was settled. The southern route, on the other hand, would traverse already settled areas in Texas and the southwest.

In order to strengthen his argument for the northern route, Douglas was desperate to get a Nebraska bill passed. But while he focused on western expansion, the rest of Congress was mired in the slavery issue. Nebraska was above the line established by the Missouri Compromise, and southern congressmen did not want any more free states.

For Douglas, slavery was nothing but a distraction from the main job of making a coast-to-coast America. He had his eye on the great railroad from Chicago to the Pacific, which would bind the distant shores of a mighty nation. What was Nebraska but an Indian reservation blocking the way? "It is utterly impossible," he said, "to preserve that connection between the Atlantic and the Pacific if you are to keep a wilderness of two thousand miles in extent between you."

But southern objections could not be satisfied. Southerners became for the occasion the staunch defenders of Indian rights, waxing eloquent about treaty guarantees, and federal promises that the tribes would not be disturbed again. Where, the southern lawmakers demanded to know, would the 60,000 Indians who lived there go? How could a territory be created before the Indian titles were extinguished?

In response to these objections, George W. Manypenny, who had taken over as commissioner of Indian Affairs on March 4, 1853, began vigorously pursuing a policy of acquiring title to Indian lands. By 1856, the commissioner had signed fifty-two treaties and the Indians had given up 13 million acres of land. Manypenny had the disagreeable task of visiting the tribes to tell them that they would have to move once again. In Nebraska the Omahas and the Pawnees ceded most of their acreage and were transported to reservations.

Back in Washington, Douglas realized that the only way to pass a Nebraska bill was to finesse the slavery issue. The way to do it, he decided, was to invoke the Compromise of 1850, which provided that Utah and New Mexico territories could be admitted with or without slavery, leaving the inhabitants to decide the issue for themselves when they voted on a constitution.

The same arrangement, Douglas figured, could be applied to Nebraska. Northerners would not mind, for they would realize as he did that slavery could not flourish on the Great Plains. Douglas needed a way to patch together a Democratic majority in both houses of Congress, at a time when the Democratic Party was a collection of leaderless, warring factions. The answer was squatter sovereignty—essentially state's rights prior to statehood.

Of course, since Nebraska was above the 36°30' line, allowing the possibility of its becoming a slave state effectively repealed the Missouri Compromise. To the abolitionists who accused him of caving in to slavery, Douglas responded that he was not repealing the Missouri Compromise but ignoring it. Put the quibbling behind you, he said, these people will not want slaves. To those who argued for Indian treaty rights, he retorted that "you cannot fix bounds to the onward march of this great and growing country. You cannot fetter the limbs of the young giant."

And so it was that Iowa senator Augustus C. Dodge introduced a bill for Nebraska Territory in December 1853. It went to the Committee on Territories chaired by Douglas, who rewrote the bill to include a proposal for the creation of two territories, Kansas and Nebraska, in both of which the question of slavery would be determined by the residents.

The Senate passed the bill on March 3 by a vote of 37 to 14; on May 25, Douglas's prize document made it through the House, 113 to 100. When President Pierce signed the legislation on May 30, 1854, Douglas boasted: "I passed the Kansas-Nebraska bill myself." He was right to the extent that he alone had found a way to hold together a Democratic majority. But he underestimated the reaction in the abolitionist press, which accused him of selling out to slavery.

Concurrent with the act's passage, Congress divided Indian Territory at the 37th parallel, the border between Oklahoma and Kansas. The land south of the border, in what would become Oklahoma, was left to the Indians. North of the border, where the land was divided into Kansas and Nebraska, Indian country was finished.

Nebraska—a vast area including much of Colorado, the Dakotas, Montana, Wyoming, and Idaho—had been allotted as a permanent home for the tribes. But the thrust of westward expansion pushed all that aside. In the 1850s, the Indian Territory policy gave way to the reservation system.

Senator Douglas's triumph came on December 2, 1863, when Peter Dey, the chief engineer of the Union Pacific, got a telegram in Omaha announcing that President Lincoln had fixed the start of the transcontinental railroad "on the western boundary of the state of Iowa, opposite Omaha." The road would go through Chicago after all.

As soon as the Kansas-Nebraska Act was passed, squatters trickled into Nebraska under the 1841 preemption law and claimed 160 acres. They lived like prairie dogs in dugouts made of three-foot-long sod bricks. The roof always leaked, and wives fried pancakes on the stove while their husbands held umbrellas over their heads.

Omaha took shape across the Missouri from Council Bluffs, Iowa. The first legislature assembled there on January 16, 1855, in a single room, sitting at schoolboy desks, some whistling, others with their feet on the desk in front. Things moved fast in the territory. The same issue of the *Nebraska Palladium* that reported the arrival of Silas Strickland from Tennessee carried a notice that he was announcing his candidacy for election to the territorial House of Representatives.

In a spirit of abandon, the second territorial legislature licensed five banks "of issue," meaning that they were allowed to print money. This worthless currency became known as "stump-tail money." The story was told of a steamboat captain who pulled up to a woodyard and called out, "Is your wood dry?" From the yard came "Yep." "What is your wood worth?" "What kind of money do yer tote, Cap?" "The best in the world, the new Platte Valley Bank." "If that's so, Cap, I'll trade cord for cord."

When the Bank of Nebraska at Omaha closed its doors, the sheriff's writ of execution listed the following assets: "Thirteen sacks of flour, one large iron safe, one counter, one desk, one stove drum and pipe, three armchairs, and one map of Douglas County."

Nobody ran credit checks or asked for references, for everyone was a newcomer:

> Oh, what was your name in the States,
> Was it Thompson or Johnson or Bates?
> Did you murder your wife or fly for your life,
> Say, what was your name in the States?

In 1855, the territory's first census put Nebraska's population at 4,494. By 1860, it was 28,841. Then came the Homestead Act of 1862, which brought in the second big wave of pioneers. Entire Nebraska counties filled up in a season or two. In the United States, between 1863 and 1900, a total of 141,446 Homestead entries were put in for about 19 million acres of land. But only half of these entries were carried through to the final patent.

A free farm did not necessarily mean a successful farm. The trouble with the Homestead Act was that it encouraged failure by requiring too little. It was a vote of confidence in human nature—here, take this land, it won't cost you a cent, and make something of it. Dig a well, build a shack, grow some crops, and it's yours.

No allowance was made for human frailty, for the unqualified and the unequipped, for bad luck or born losers. Half the homesteaders went bust. Sometimes things turned out even worse. In January 1886 near Tryon, Nebraska, south of the Dismal River, George Klein came home to find his wife and three children lying dead on the floor of their sod house. Overcome by the hardship and loneliness of their prairie existence, his wife had given her children gopher poison and then swallowed it herself. A neighbor said: "If she could a had even a geranium . . . but in that cold shell of a shack . . ." The solitude of the prairie could stun a person. With no trees, the range of vision traveled to the distant horizon line; and above, the sky was a motionless expanse.

On balance, however, it's hard to quarrel with the indiscriminate generosity of the Homestead Act, which offered the landless the fulfillment of ownership. The system worked fairly well, except for the aggravation of contested claims. Every town in western Nebraska had shysters who got rich on land disputes.

In Rushville, C. C. Akin specialized in defrauding homesteaders. But they got their own back. One day a bunch of angry settlers yanked Akin out of his hotel and tarred and feathered him. As one of the participants, Jules Sandoz, said after that incident, "Not much money changing hands on bogus contests any more."

On the heels of the Homestead Act, the transcontinental railroad broke ground in Omaha in 1863. With the railroad came a third wave of settlement. There were jobs for graders and track layers. Tons of stones needed to be quarried for bridges and piers. Millions of cords of lumber had to be cut for ties and wood-burning locomotives. The credo of the arriving settler was: How can I make money? Let me count the ways: I can string telegraph wire; I can lay track; I can outfit settlers; I can repair wagons.

Supply and demand worked here not as an abstract economic principle but in everyday practice. Andrew Murphy at 14th and Howard saw the wagons coming through and opened a repair shop. He also shoed horses. The sign above his door said:

ANDREW MURPHY

PRACTICAL

HORSE SHOER

The railroads became real estate agents, selling the right-of-way land the government had given them, offering easy credit and low prices, for every settler on railroad land was a potential customer. The railroads hauled livestock for free and provided seeds to plant crops—all to attract settlers.

It was the Sioux City & Pacific Railroad, which crossed Nebraska along the Elkhorn River, that devised the slogan "Free Homes for the Millions." John Ross Buchanan, the general passenger agent, recalled: "That was my slogan or rallying phrase. . . . It headed every circular, folder, and poster I ever issued, and I issued them by the millions. . . . In every possible publication, in black, blue, and red ink, in English and German was this sentence: FREE HOMES FOR THE MILLIONS—the storybook call of free land."

The town of Beatrice in 1863 had one hotel—the Pacific House—as well as one general store called Klein & Lang on the corner of Second and Court. The Smith brothers put their bank in one half of a shack, while a watchmaker set up his business on the other side. Outside town there was a sheep ranch, but no road; the ranchers steered their wagons to town right across the prairie.

Two young Mennonites. Peter Jansen and his brother, John, had started the sheep ranch, building a corral and a shed and obtaining their fuel from the Indian reservation. They also planted crops, proving that farming on the tableland could work.

One time Peter Jansen brought a wagonload of valuable breeding sheep through Beatrice and spent the night at the hotel. He kept his flock in the livery-stable corral across the street, and sat up all night with his dogs to watch over them. When he trudged back to the hotel in the morning to wash up, he overheard Major Wheeler, the stagecoach man, say: "That boy's all right. A boy who sits up all night with a few sheep will certainly succeed." Near the ranch Jansen often met Indians who were not bashful about asking for "tobac." He told them to "puckachee," to move on.

In 1863, the painter Albert Bierstadt visited Nebraska on one of his western trips. The son of a German cooper, Bierstadt was born in the Old Country in 1830 and came to America at the age of two. He made his reputation as a painter of the American west, when that region was still largely uninhabited and unknown. His slick and monumental canvases offered a grandiose and reassuringly banal version of the wilderness. Yet he based his depiction on direct observation, for he traveled thousands of miles in difficult conditions to make sketches and photographs of his subjects. But his pictures conveyed so little sense of the inherent menace of the landscape that they looked like blown-up postcards.

A master of hype, Bierstadt took his paintings on traveling exhibits to major cities. People lined up and paid admission to see the twelve-by-seven-foot *Storm in the Rocky Mountains*, or the ten-by-six-foot *Last of the Buffalo*. The artist's works sold for what were then princely sums—$25,000 and up—and his popularity broadened and grew. Like some frontier Warhol, though, Bierstadt saw his reputation soar and then come crashing down. He was the master of what one modern critic has called "the opportunistic sublime."

In 1859, Bierstadt joined a survey party and made his first trip to the Rockies. Returning with a trunkful of buffalo robes, Indian blankets, feathers, and moccasins, the painter hung the souvenirs in his New York studio. One visitor felt as if he had entered "the depot of a fur trader."

On May 4, 1863, Bierstadt left New York with his writer friend Fitz Hugh Ludlow for a second trip west. They caught a train to St. Joseph, Missouri, and hopped on the stagecoach at Atchison, Kansas. The coach headed northwest into Nebraska and the Platte River valley, on the old Oregon Trail.

At Fort Kearney on the Platte, the pair met the superintendent of the Overland Trail, Mr. Munger, who told them that herds of buffalo had been reported at the fork of the Republican and Kansas rivers, near today's Junction City, Kansas. The herds were on their summer migration to the plains north of the Platte. This seemed to Bierstadt like a splendid sketching opportunity. Munger suggested they stop at Comstock's ranch on the Little Blue, about thirty miles southeast on the Nebraska-Kansas border, and offered to accompany them.

That June evening they found a corral and a loghouse in a clump of tall cottonwoods. Ansell Comstock, a compact man of sixty-three with grizzled wiry hair, answered the door holding a lantern. Over supper Comstock related that he was from Rochester, New York, and had lived in Michigan, Wisconsin, Minnesota, and Texas. He had been driven out of Texas, he said, by the corrupt manners of the slavocracy.

His aim was always to live beyond the reach of society, for he disdained fine gentlemen and town meetings. This seemed to be a family trait, for Comstock's eldest son George said, "I cannot breathe free in sight of fences; I must be able to ride my horse where I like." The rancher's livestock and horses roamed free over the thick grass, which provided an inexhaustible supply of winter feed and saved him the trouble of mowing and stacking.

A widower, Comstock had a family of twenty living under one log roof, and they were practically self-sufficient. In the morning he went out with a spade over his shoulders and crossed a log bridge to his vegetable patch. Antelope were plentiful within an hour's ride. Bierstadt and Ludlow slept rolled up in blankets in a loft and breakfasted on buffalo.

The next day a party of eleven left by saddle horse and farm wagon for the Republican River thirty miles away. Bierstadt carried along his stool, an umbrella, a large color box, and some sketching paper, which he pinned to a wooden board. The artist and the hunters forded the Little Blue just across from the ranch and set out over the trackless plain. Ludlow carefully noted the prairie flowers, the ground poppies and prairie roses.

At the Republican, they shot an antelope and cut off its head so that Bierstadt could sketch it. After they made their camp, Ludlow went stalking buffalo with the guide, John Gilbert. Three miles out, they hid in some bushes near a draw and tried to flank a bull, but they fired and missed. "Cuss his tough hide," Gilbert said. "Why didn't we shoot him in the first place, instead of trying to creep round? Then we'd had a good tongue for supper at least. Now we hain't got nothin' . . . I don't believe in throwin' a chance that's close to you for a maybe ten miles off."

Instructing Ludlow in the ways of the prairie, Gilbert said that the herds kept sentries posted and it was hard to get by them. The jumbled human/beast imagery struck the writer, who began recording examples of animal metaphors. When one man said he'd lost his lariat, another noticed it on the ground and said, "If it was a snake it would bite you." When one of Comstock's many children showed up streaked with dirt, Comstock scolded, "Aren't you ashamed to sprain the flies' legs that light on your face?"

The next day a herd was reported to be grazing on top of the bluff. "Now boys," said Bierstadt, "is our time for fun. I want to see an enraged buffalo. I want to see him so bad that he will bellow and tear up the ground." He packed his sketching equipment in Munger's buggy, and followed the four men who rode off to stampede the herd—Munger, Gilbert, Ludlow, and Ben Holladay. As they climbed a ravine to the top of the bluff, they spotted the buffalo sentries, who pawed uneasily, lashed their sides with their tails, and stretched their necks.

In the lead, Munger watched as hundreds of buffalo whirled around —"like as if they had springs in 'em," said John Gilbert—and trotted away. Suddenly, Munger and Ben Holladay surprised as big a bull as ever trod the plains, and they stopped him with shots from their Colt revolvers.

"Bring along your painter," Munger shouted. As the buggy carrying the famous artist rolled toward them, Munger and Holladay kept the bull at bay in a grassy basin.

Jumping from the buggy, Bierstadt opened the big blue umbrella and planted it in the ground in less than a minute. He sat under it on his campstool, his color box on his knees, his brush and palette in his hands, and a clean board pinned to the cover of his color box.

Munger's old giant had been shot in half-a-dozen places, but stood his ground. Great spurts of blood came up through his shaggy coat. He was too badly hit to keep up with the herd. At every plunge he was headed off by a turn of Munger's bridle. He stamped a circle twenty feet in diameter, flattening the grass, but would not lie down, though blood mixed with white foam flowed from his nostrils. His breath made a rushing sound like a blacksmith's bellows, and his sides heaved, as if he were no longer breathing with his lungs, but with his entire body.

Munger and Ludlow circled the bull to attract his attention for the painter's benefit. One rider advanced his horse and menaced the bull with his weapon. The old giant lowered his head until his thick beard swept the dust. Behind an immense fell of hair his eyes glared red. Drawing in his breath with a painful hiss, he charged. A twist of the rein drew the horse out of harm's way and the bull's horns hooked air.

Though the massive humped body held six bullets, the bison stood unflinching. "It was," Ludlow later wrote, "the first time I had ever seen moral grandeur in a brute." For fifteen minutes the two riders taunted the expiring bull as the artist's eye followed and his hand sped over the paper.

Now the animal was close to exhaustion. The blood streamed faster from his wounds, but he showed no sign of surrender, and in his eyeballs there was the glint of revenge. Bierstadt applied the finishing touches and then asked his two helpers to put an end to the creature's misery. Munger and Holladay rode closer, with guns drawn. They fired, aiming for the heart. When the smoke lifted, a hole the size of a saucer streamed blood from the buffalo's side.

But he would not fall. He swiveled on quivering legs. He stiffened his tail. And, summoning all the life left in him, he made a final charge in the direction of the man who had been sketching his death. Bierstadt saw the mortally wounded bull bearing down on him, snorting foam and blood, and ran so fast that, as George Comstock put it, "his coat-tails stuck straight out and you could have played a game of euchre on them."

Ten feet from Bierstadt the buffalo's strength gave out. He tumbled to his knees, made one last effort to rise again, and pushed himself up on one leg. And then with a great groan he fell on the trampled turf and the anger in his eyes glazed over. Even in death they remained wide open, as if releasing the last of their animal power.

The men stood in awe and turned away. Ludlow observed the black moving mass of the buffalo herd extending without a break to the horizon's edge. There must have been hundreds of thousands of them. Finally, writer and artist returned to Comstock's ranch and resumed their westward journey when the stage came through.

It was not until 1889, twenty-six years after sketching the wounded bull, that Bierstadt painted *The Last of the Buffalo*—a newsworthy subject, for at that time there was an outcry over the buffalo's imminent extinction. But instead of showing white hunters slaughtering the herds, Bierstadt painted an Indian hunting party coming in for the kill—already an anachronism. In his rendition, long lines of buffalo try to flee up a river, chased by Sioux riders naked to the waist. The foreground shows a massive bull locked in combat with a mounted Indian. The bull has impaled the white pony, which is rearing up on its hind legs as the rider sinks a spear into the animal's rump. The painting's unintended irony was that both hunter and hunted were doomed.

Throughout its territorial interlude, from 1854 to 1867, Nebraska kept getting whittled down. With the absence of secessionists from Congress, the Civil War years provided a window for the creation of new territories. Organized in 1861, Colorado Territory reduced Nebraska by 16,000 square miles. Then came Dakota that same year, which further diminished Nebraska by another 229,000 square miles, and in 1863 the creation of Idaho Territory advanced the process further. Then in 1864, Montana was carved from Idaho, and in 1868, Wyoming Territory was formed from parts of Dakota, Idaho, and Utah.

In January 1865, the Nebraska legislature applied to Congress for statehood. An enabling act was passed and delegates to a constitutional convention were elected, but most of them opposed statehood, fearing higher taxes. In his message to the legislature on January 9, 1866, Governor Alvin Saunders chided Nebraskans for their shortsightedness. "Nevada," he said, "with a much less permanent population than Nebraska, has already become one of the independent states of the Union."

Heeding the governor, the legislature drafted a constitution without the election of delegates, which Nebraskans approved on June 2, 1866, by 3,938 to 3,838, a very slim margin in a very small vote. Nebraska entered the Union as a free state, though suffrage was restricted to free white males. On March 1, 1867, President Andrew Johnson made Nebraska the thirty-seventh state, covering an area only one-fifth the size of Nebraska Territory.

Two years later the Nebraska legislature passed a law to encourage people to plant trees, offering a tax exemption of $100 a year for each new acre planted. On the prairie, trees could become an obsession. J. Sterling Morton, an Omaha entrepreneur, had a picture of an oak tree appearing above the legend "Plant Trees" painted on his carriage door, engraved on his letterheads and envelopes, and cut into the ground glass of his office entrance.

Everything that happened out on the prairie was magnified into a scale that required the qualifier "great." The Great Prairie Fire of October 1871 jumped the Loup River "as easy as a jackrabbit jumpin' a road," leaving a trail of cindered haystacks. The Great Storm of April 1873 blew freezing sleet and snow so thick that a man driving his wagon couldn't see the horses hitched to it. People in sod houses burned baskets of 10-cent corn to keep from freezing.

As for Andrew Murphy, the Practical Horse Shoer, he converted in 1899 to automobile repair. What was an automobile but a wagon with a combustion engine? By then Omaha had become the "Porkopolis of the Plains." The boom attracted retailers. The Hayden Brothers, for example, employed three hundred clerks in their general store. W. R. Bennett asked shoppers to "turn a nickel loose in Bennett's." For that nickel you could buy five dozen clothespins, a box of checkers, or a baseball bat. Jonas Brandeis, a Czechoslovakian immigrant, opened the Fair Store in 1881, introducing the charge account, illuminated display windows, and helium balloons that snowed coupons on an unsuspecting populace.

Every house in Omaha had a front porch. Alice Towne Deweese, who grew up there, believed the front porch was formative of the American character. The porch was not quite inside, and not quite outside. On spring and summer evenings, every other family sat out on its porch, observers and actors in the same spectacle. Visits were informal, because people didn't have to be asked in. Everyone had a view of passing carriages and firetrucks pulled by big dappled gray horses straining at their harnesses.

Night brought on the soft, high-pitched whine of the katydids. People relaxed and began to tell stories. In that interval before bedtime, a child could learn something of the hidden lives of his parents. The front porch fostered an unseen and unconsidered knitting together of the family and the community.

CHAPTER SIXTEEN
TEXAS AND THE CATTLE FRONTIER

Swing the other gal, swing her sweet! Paw dirt,
dogies, stomp your feet!
Ladies in the center, gents round run, swing her rope,
cowboy, and get you one.

Square-dance call

What it comes down to is that the America of the pioneer
has been made subjective by us. The endless rolling back
of the frontier goes on within our heads all the time. We
are the updated Daniel Boones of American inner-space.
. . . Always moving the big wagon-train of great new
possibilities, always crashing on.

SEYMOUR KRIM

National Archives
In 1900, in the town of Langtry, a bearded Roy Bean, saloon owner
and justice of the peace, conducted his court on the front porch
with a rifle within reach. It was said that he once fined a dead man
$40 for carrying a concealed weapon.

In twenty years, between 1820 and 1840, Texas changed hands several times. For centuries, the area had been a part of Spain's American empire but remained a wilderness, with three outposts and a population of 4,000. Texas was run by the familiar Spanish triad of the missions (which helped to keep the Indians in line), the presidios (whose soldiers stepped in when the missions failed), and corrupt governors (who made money on supplies for the soldiers).

Texas was attached to Mexico, and in 1821, when Spain recognized Mexico's independence, the Mexicans, just as the Spanish had before them, invited Americans to settle there. They offered free land, a better deal than Americans could get in their own country. By 1830, more Americans than Mexicans were living in Texas.

The Mexicans soon discovered that by putting out a welcoming hand to the Americans they had grasped a bear by the tail. The thrust of Mexican legislation was abolitionist, but the Texans were slaveholders who ignored the local laws against slaves and against further immigration. All this led to the well-known events of the Texas revolution of 1835 and the establishment of the Republic of Texas a year later.

In 1840, the Republic of Texas was a frontier community of 40,000, including slaves. Desiring annexation by the United States, but rebuffed because of slavery, Texas teetered on the edge of bankruptcy. To attract settlers, the republic in 1841 passed an act granting 640 acres to each head of a family and 320 acres to a single man, as well as larger grants to people bringing in settlers on the *empresario* model.

The burning issue in the 1844 election was the annexation of Texas. The debate brought some new players onto the political stage. When the Democratic Convention in Baltimore nominated James Polk to head the ticket, the Whigs asked one another, "Who is Polk?"

The candidate was a protégé of Andrew Jackson, with a long political career in the House and as governor of Tennessee. In the south, a movement bearing the slogan "Texas or Disunion" had been launched. In the north, the abolitionists were lobbying against annexation, and seemed to be going against the national interest by blocking expansion. Thus, if you were for annexation, you voted for James Polk. If you were against it, you voted for Henry Clay.

The plodding and colorless Polk beat the charismatic Clay by 38,000 votes. Congress admitted Texas as the twenty-eighth state on December 29, 1845, bypassing the territorial interlude. But Mexico did not accept the annexation of Texas. When President Polk, who insisted on the Rio Grande as the Texas boundary, sent General Zachary Taylor there to show the flag in January 1846, skirmishes broke out with Mexican troops.

Polk declared war and invaded Mexico. General Winfield Scott captured Vera Cruz in March 1847 and Mexico City that September, ending the war. In February 1848, the Treaty of Guadalupe Hidalgo placed the Texas boundary at the Rio Grande and delivered California and New Mexico to America for $15 million. Through the combined strategies of conquest and purchase, America extended itself to the Pacific. This was not exactly Jefferson's "empire of liberty." It was more like imperialism at full throttle, with Polk as the American conquistador.

The annexation of the slave state of Texas, however, upset the balance created by the Missouri Compromise, making the ratio in 1846 fourteen nonslave to fifteen slave states. This opened up a debate in Congress over slavery in the western territories. The danger was that slavery in the west would cut off the access of settlers to land, for the ordinary settlers could not compete with slaveholders, who had the free labor of blacks. As one politician put it, the question "is not whether black men are to be made free but whether white men are to remain free." Thus the Republican Party established itself on the principle of keeping slavery out of the west, and Lincoln won the presidency on a platform that pledged to carry it out.

But not before the crisis came to a massively destructive head. In 1861, Texas seceded from the Union over the issue of slavery. It joined the Confederacy on March 2, and provided the south with about 60,000 men. But there was not much fighting in Texas, which served mainly as a conduit for supplies from Mexico. However, the last land battle of the war took place at Palmito Ranch near Brownsville, on May 13, 1865, more than a month after Lee's surrender. There, beside the mouth of the Rio Grande, in a *beau geste* finale, a band of diehard Texans inflicted heavy losses on a Union unit.

In 1865, Texans returned from the war to a sparsely populated state that had few roads, less than a hundred miles of railroad track, and nebulous areas designated on maps as "rolling table lands" and "salt plains." But Texas had never ceded its public domain to the federal government, which other states handed over upon graduating from territorial status. And it also had its own land policies, which favored the raising of cattle. In Texas, a man could graze a large herd on state-owned prairie without owning a single acre himself.

When American settlers moved into Texas in the 1820s, they adopted the methods of the local Mexican cattlemen for herding and handling cattle. Texas became cow country. Ranching developed on a large scale and the free public land served for grazing rather than for crops. All the ranchers had to do was brand their cattle, ride the range, and find a market.

In 1842, settlers in Mexican Texas opened a "beef trail" to New Orleans, running overland to Shreveport and down the Red River to its junction with the Mississippi. Cattle were also moved north into Missouri, but they carried ticks that gave the local animals "Texas fever," and quarantine laws soon were passed to keep the longhorns out.

In 1860, Texas had a population of 504,215 human beings and 3,533,767 head of cattle. Came the war, and a market for the cattle opened up in the feeding of Confederate soldiers. The herds were driven across Louisiana to Vicksburg, until Grant took Vicksburg in 1863. Then New Orleans also fell to northern forces. Union control of the Mississippi, patrolled by gunboats, halted cattle driving from Texas.

As the market dried up, the number of cattle increased. So the Texans went out on the range with a wagon and an ax and skinned the animals for their hides, selling them at a dollar apiece.

Texan troops coming home in 1865, ragged and defeated, found the range crowded with fat, mature cattle. The ranchers were broke, the Confederate currency they had collected for their beef now used by schoolchildren as page markers in their textbooks.

Texas had about 5 million head of cattle roaming wild; but without a market, the longhorns were not even worth rounding up. It was said that a man's poverty was estimated by the number of cattle he owned. The great forces unleashed by the Civil War, however, were about to provide the buyers Texas needed.

Over the years in Washington, there had been various proposals to offer free land to settlers. These attempts had been blocked by southern congressmen, who feared that free land would lead to the formation of more nonslave states. But with secession and the departure of those congressmen, a homestead bill was introduced, passed, and signed by the president on May 20, 1862.

The bill offered 160 acres of land free of charge, except for a $10 filing fee, to American citizens over twenty-one. The only condition was that they had to live on their quarter section for five years. Lincoln aimed through the Homestead Act to create a class of prosperous small farmers, and so it did, distributing millions of acres and creating 372,659 farms.

American Heritage Center, University of Wyoming
Surrounded by Indians, his horse lying on the ground with an arrow in its hide, the lone cowboy is about to make his last stand, six-gun drawn. The theme of the lone cowboy overcome by superior forces was so frequently portrayed that one can only wonder how the Indians were vanquished.

After May 1862, while the war raged in the south, thousands of settlers traveled to Kansas, Nebraska, and the Dakotas to claim their quarter
section. They moved into the Great Plains, an area that for years had been
considered uninhabitable. The underpopulated Plains states and territories
competed to attract them. When Kansans warned settlers that Dakota was
barren, the Dakota newspaper editor Moses K. Armstrong replied in 1864
that the area around the recently built Fort Dodge in western Kansas was
"a prairie where the cows give blue milk and the wind whips the long-tailed
pigs to death."

Kansas, for example, had 10,400 farms in 1860; by 1870, the number
had more than tripled, to 38,202; and in 1880, it more than tripled again,
to 138,561. Not all of these farms were homesteads, for there were other
ways to obtain land, but the free quarter-section exerted a powerful attraction.

Along with the Homestead Act, the expansion of the railroads proved
to be another boon to the Texas cattle market. Wanting to spur construction, Congress gave the Illinois Central a right-of-way through public lands
in 1851, granting the company alternating square-mile sections on either
side of the road. The government held on to every other section, putting
them up for sale at $1.25 an acre, and calculating that the number of settlers
the new rail line brought in would more than compensate for the land given
away to the rail company. Completed in 1857, the seven-hundred-mile-
long Illinois Central was a huge success, resulting in thirty-seven towns
and attracting thousands of settlers.

In the ensuing scramble to build railroads with grants-in-aid, a total of
176 million acres of public land passed into the rail companies' hands, more
than the area of Texas. In each case, the government kept alternate sections, creating a checkerboard pattern of public and private ownership.

As this construction boom picked up momentum, the Civil War began
—the first war in which railroads played a decisive role. By 1861, 31,526
miles of track had been laid, two-thirds of which were in Union hands.
The trains in the south were old stock, poorly maintained. Thanks to the
railroads at the service of the Union Army, large troop units could move
from one strategic position to another in a matter of days, and food and
ammunition soon followed.

When General Sherman captured Atlanta in the summer of 1864, his
army of 100,000 men and 35,000 animals was kept supplied by a single-
track road that originated 500 miles away, in Louisville. Civil War historians consider that the south's limited access to railways was in no small
measure responsible for the Confederacy's final collapse.

The building of a transcontinental railroad was also the result of the
Civil War, for secession put an end to the quarrels over the northern or
southern route. It was on July 1, 1862, that Lincoln signed the Pacific
Railroad Act authorizing the continuation of existing lines through to California.

The Union Pacific was promptly incorporated. It aimed to build from the western border of Iowa to the California-Nevada line, where it was to meet the Central Pacific, which would build eastward from Sacramento. For each mile of track, Congress offered the companies 6,400 acres of land, plus a loan of $16,000 to $48,000, depending on the terrain. Investors still hesitated, so Congress doubled the land grant, and capital began to come forth.

The Railroad Act had been amended to allow both lines to build until they met. That added the element of a race, since the company laying down the most track won the biggest subsidy. Consequently, the companies wrangled on where to meet, and it took another act of Congress to join them up at Promontory, Utah Territory, on May 10, 1869.

Along with the settlement of the prairie, brought about by the Homestead Act, and the westward push of the railroads, came an increased demand for beef. Cyrus Hall McCormick had invented a mechanical grain cutter in 1831 that was taken up by prairie farmers; when McCormick's reaper made extensive wheat growing possible, much midwestern cattle land became farmland. It took three or four years for cattle to mature, whereas wheat was an annual cash crop, which now required less labor than raising stock.

During the war, with a million and a half Union soldiers in the field, the demand for beef rose. Chicago, already a railroad hub, became the entrepôt for the slaughtering and shipment of cattle. There had been small stockyards in Chicago since 1837, but as the railroads began to converge there, shippers could send live animals as well as packed meat.

It soon became apparent that Chicago needed one large central stockyard where all the animals could be assembled. The Union Stock Yard and Transit Company took the initiative, buying 320 acres of land on open prairie four miles from downtown, so as not to be enveloped by the mushrooming metropolis.

On June 1, 1865, construction started on 500 pens covering 60 acres. The entire area was lined with three miles of water troughs into which flowed half a million gallons a day from the Chicago River, and ten miles of feed troughs filled with corn and hay.

By 1868, the stockyard had grown to 2,300 pens that spanned 100 acres, capable of handling 21,000 head of cattle and 75,000 hogs. The pens were divided into four shipping and receiving yards, each one assigned to a particular railroad. A loop of track circled the pens so that trains could load and unload at their yard.

It was at the Union Stock Yard, on land once covered, like the city next door, with tallgrass prairie, that east met west. It was here that a longhorn raised on Texas grass was fattened on Illinois corn and turned into the sirloin that landed on someone's plate in New York or Boston. Actually, the slaughtering and packing of beef was not at first a major activity. Most of the cattle ended up being sent out on the hoof, transferred at the stockyards to east-bound trains. As late as 1871, less than 4 percent of the cattle arriving in Chicago was packed there. Packing was for pork, which could be salted or smoked.

In terms of the market for cattle, there was an interesting conjunction of events: In the east, a growing demand for beef; in Texas, an equally great supply; and in Chicago, the facilities to pack the cattle or ship it east on the hoof. The question remained: How were the Texas ranchers going to get their cattle to Chicago?

They were slowly wising up to the situation, as they ruminated over the Confederate defeat and hung around saloons exchanging war stories. E. C. Abbott, known as Teddy Blue, heard a veteran say in 1865: "I was coming down the road and I met a damn blue-bellied abolitionist, and I paunched him [shot him in the gut]. And he laid there in the brush and belched like a beef for three days and then he died in fits, the bastard."

The first task for the Texans was rounding up the herds that had been roaming the range in their absence, in the splintering canebrake of the Llano hills, in the blackjack thickets east of the San Antonio River, in the tangles of mesquite and chaparral on the upper Rio Grande, and in the *brasada* between the Rio Grande and the Nueces. The *brasada* was the worst jungle in cow country, a dense brush full of thorny vegetation that was perilous to man. In addition, due to years of neglect, the cattle had reverted to an undomesticated state. As Colonel Henry Dodge put it, "the domestic cattle of Texas, miscalled tame, are 50 times more dangerous to footmen than the fiercest buffalo."

Jim Cook rode with the brushpoppers (as they were called), signing on with Ben Slaughter in 1865 to round up wild cattle in the *brasada*. In Dogtown, the capital of brush country on the Frio River, Cook joined Longworth the *caporal* and ten Mexicans. The method was to bring a decoy herd into the thick growth of spiky brush and wait for the wild cattle to follow the decoys into a corral.

Cook's pony, a trained cow catcher, made him pull leather, and he wore heavy boots and gauntlet gloves against the brush. Cook hunted the wild longhorns over a hundred-square-mile area, until one day he accidentally stampeded the decoy herd. When the *caporal* said unkind things about his mother in two languages, the brushpopper quit.

After rounding up and branding the cattle, the men had to take them north into Missouri or Kansas to a town with a railhead, where they could be sold and shipped to Chicago. The bottom line was that a steer that cost $4 in Texas sold for $40 in Kansas.

In 1866, Bill Jackman came back to Uvalde from the war and asked Cood Adams for employment. Cood told him, "I am getting Mexicans for $12 and board." Jackman signed on and helped round up the cattle. When he asked what brand to gather, Cood said, "Bring everything you find regardless of brands."

Soon they were off on the trail drive through Indian Territory (Oklahoma) into Kansas. Entering Kansas, they found some nice running water, but the nesters had plowed a furrow on each side of the trail and posted signs that said KEEP YOUR CATTLE INSIDE THESE FURROWS OR BE PROSECUTED.

On seeing the signs, the cowboys were enraged. Givens, the trail boss, said to Jackman: "Bill, suppose we put our herds into that fine grass and water." When the cattle smelled the water, they ran toward it, but soon there appeared some nesters astride their old mares, armed with double-barreled shotguns, who demanded that they turn the cattle back. "We cannot stop them," Jackman said.

The nesters went for the law and Jackman had to remove the herd to high ground. He knew who the judge would side with, for on another occasion he had been arrested on someone's land and brought before a judge. The Dutch landowner said, "Judge, this here is the fellow vot told me to go to hell mit a pistol." "This seems to be a very aggravated case," the judge told Jackman. "I fine you $100 and costs."

With so much cattle roaming over the Texas range, it was a propitious time for rustlers. Born a slave east of San Antonio, James Cape was forced to join the Confederate Army and fought the Yankees at St. Louis, where he was wounded in the shoulder. The doctor told him, "If the bullet had went three inches to the right, it would have cut your jugular and then I wouldn't be needing to tend this wound."

Cape was sure he was going to Gloryland, but he survived and went back to Gonzales County. There he was offered a job at $15 a month. Most of the ranchers, being southerners, hated "free niggers," but hired them anyway because they worked cheaper than white men.

Cape soon realized that his boss, Mr. Ross, was a rustler. He could already feel the rope around his neck and see the buzzards flying around his head, and told Ross he wanted to go home. Ross said: "James, when I'm ready for you to go I'll tell you, and if you try to leave before then I'll put daylight through you."

So Cape volunteered for a cattle drive north. When the critters smelled water ten miles away, he later recalled, they'd rush to get there. And when the streams ran swiftly, the cattle were swept too far downstream to make the landing. They had a "stomp" in a storm, and the rustlers had to wait for lightning to flash to see where they were. When the storm stopped, the men fired into the faces of the stampede leaders and the herd settled down and started circling. In Kansas City, Ross gave Cape ten dollars and told him to have a good time, but he took off and found another job.

Many of the attempts to reach a railhead in eastern Kansas or Missouri in 1865 and 1866 failed because of the hostility of the nesters, still dreading Texas fever, and because of gangs of Jayhawkers (unemployed free-state veterans of the Kansas-Missouri border war) who exacted tolls and otherwise harassed the cattlemen.

In 1866, James Daugherty crossed into Kansas with his herd and found a buyer in Fort Scott, in Bourbon County on the Kansas-Missouri border. Twenty miles south of Fort Scott, a band of Jayhawkers rode up and shot one of Daugherty's men in the saddle. They told him his cattle were infested with ticks and argued among themselves whether to hang him or not. Since he was only nineteen, they let him go. Driving at night alongside a guide, Daugherty got his herd to his buyer at Fort Scott. It seemed to him that the Jayhawkers were nothing but rustlers using ticks as an excuse to steal cattle.

In eastern Kansas and Missouri, the drovers ran up against armed mobs who spat in their faces, tied them to trees, whipped them, and stampeded their cattle. On the trail from Texas to Sedalia, a town in central Missouri that had a railhead where the herds could be shipped to St. Louis over the Missouri Pacific, nesters and Jayhawkers barred the way. Nor could the Texans resume shipping from New Orleans, which was still recovering from the war. So how were they supposed to get their cattle to market?

In Springfield, Illinois, a young cattle broker named Joseph McCoy had an idea. In 1865, there were no lines west of the Missouri, but construction crews for the Kansas Pacific had begun to push the track into the mixed-grass prairie west of Kansas City. By 1867, the Kansas Pacific was operating as far as Salina, 180 miles west of Kansas City.

McCoy's plan was to build a cattle depot with a railhead west of the settled areas the nesters were blocking, "to establish a market where the southern drover and the northern buyer could meet on equal footing, and both be undisturbed by mobs or swindling thieves." As it turned out, his idea launched a migration that populated the west, created the legend of the cowboy, and saved Texas from bankruptcy, as well as converting it from a southern to a western state.

McCoy approached the leading railroad men but found them lacking in vision. In St. Louis in 1867, he called on the president of the Missouri Pacific and found a cigar-chomping lout who told him: "It occurs to me that you haven't any cattle to ship and never did have any, and I sir have no evidence that you ever will have any . . . therefore, get out of my office." McCoy was also turned down by the Kansas Pacific at Salina.

Undeterred, he chose as his site "a small dead place consisting of a dozen log huts and one saloon"—Abilene, twenty miles east of Salina, in the Smoky Hill valley. Covered with thick grass, the place was a depressed, nondescript little crossroads where the saloonkeeper sold prairie dogs to eastern tourists as a curiosity.

There McCoy built a stockyard for 3,000 cattle out of posts made from railroad ties. He also put up a three-story hotel with an office for himself. He was taking a big risk, for as yet he had no railhead, but he figured that if he could fill his pens with cattle, the trains would follow.

McCoy sent agents to Texas and Oklahoma to promote Abilene, instructing them "to hunt up every straggling drove possible." Following the cow trails, the men overtook the herds and convinced the drovers that they would get a warm welcome in Abilene.

Only when cattle began to crowd his yards did the Kansas Pacific build a spur line to Abilene, using cull ties. From Abilene, the cattle were shipped to St. Joseph, where McCoy had signed a contract with the Hannibal & St. Joseph to carry the product to Chicago.

On September 5, 1867, the first shipment of twenty cars left Abilene for Chicago, and McCoy watched the iron horse chug down the Kaw valley bearing its trainload of cattle. Though pleased, he still had to overcome the reputation of the lean and ungainly longhorns, which were said to be as palatable as prairie wolves. They were also known as "the butcher's nightmare: eight pounds of hamburger on 800 pounds of bone and horn."

Demand in the east was such, however, that Abilene soon started doing a tremendous business. It became the point where the railroad intersected with the cattle trail, and in 1868, 75,000 head were sold there. Ever the impresario of beef, McCoy sent live buffalo bulls to Chicago and held roping demonstrations at the fairgrounds.

As a destination for the Texas cattle drives, Abilene lasted until 1872. It was done in by its own success, for other Kansas trail towns on other railheads, wanting to get in on the action, began to compete. In the spring of 1871, the Atchison, Topeka & Santa Fe completed a line to Newton, sixty-five miles south of Abilene, which became a rival depot, closer to the Oklahoma line. By 1872, Wichita, even further south, was flourishing.

At the same time, the westward-moving trains brought in more settlers. The rail companies acted as colonizing agencies, making deals with groups and selling entire towns. But once they started growing crops, the farmers took umbrage at the thousands of head of cattle annually barging through their lands, and at the lawlessness of the trail towns. The old conflict between the nester and the drover moved west with the railroads.

Texas produced only about 20 percent of the nation's cattle, but drew the lion's share of attention because of the drama of the trail drives. The most popular route for driving Texas cattle to Kansas railheads was the Chisholm Trail, originating near San Antonio and running north through Waco and Fort Worth to the Red River, the border between Texas and Oklahoma. It then continued across Oklahoma on a fairly straight south-north line past the present towns of Duncan and El Reno. Crossing the border into Kansas at Caldwell, the trail finally proceeded past Wichita and Newton to Abilene.

In April 1869, William Slaughter was hired as trail boss to take 4,500 head of cattle to Abilene. He traveled through wide-open country, not a fence in sight, and he and his men soon crossed the Brazos above Waco. The river was so wide and deep that when the cattle piled in all you could make out was a sea of horns.

One night, approaching the Red River, the herd stampeded. The drovers soon saw that some Indians had cooked up a ruse to gain possession of their *remuda* (reserve of horses). And as every cowhand knew, a trail drive was only as good as its *remuda*.

Then, just as the weather turned fine, and the cattle stayed quiet, and Slaughter and his men began to tell each other that cattle driving was just about the easiest job they knew of, a storm blew up and the cattle put on a big show, and it took three days to round them up.

Once they had forded the Red River, they were in Indian Territory until they crossed the Kansas line. Montague, Texas, was the last town they would see until Caldwell, Kansas. On the other side of the river, thousands of Indians made their homes. To get through, the drovers had to pay a toll in steers.

The Indians approached with a "How John! No cara swap horses? Dimme Cartuches!" These Indians had to be watched around the clock. Lots of times Slaughter didn't pull off his boots for three days and three nights. There were days when he would have given five dollars for half an hour's sleep. He mixed chewing tobacco with spit and rubbed it into his eyelids to stay awake.

And most of the cowboys were getting only $30 and grub, never thinking of time and overtime, or shorter hours and more pay. Slaughter had his share of it, going hungry, getting wet and cold, going to sleep on herd and losing cattle, getting cussed out by the boss, scouting for strays, trying the sick racket now and then to get a night's sleep.

At the Canadian River, the bank on the far side rose six feet above the water and 116 head could not get out and started milling around and drowned. On the other side of the Canadian, they went out looking for a place to camp and came across a little clump of trees where they saw a man hanging by the neck with a sign that said "death to the one who cuts him down." They did not cut him down.

Then on the Salt Fork of the Arkansas River, large herds of buffalo thundered through, and the drovers had to send men ahead to keep the bison from stampeding the herds. Slaughter saw more buffalo in that herd than he had ever seen of any living thing, unless it was grasshoppers in Kansas.

When they crossed into Kansas, they discovered that a dozen range cattle had gotten mixed with their herd. Slaughter saw two men riding around the herd with one of his hands, and when they left, the hand came up and said, "Those men are butchers and they said they would give us $300 for those range cattle and not want a bill of sale." But Slaughter said he could not do that, he would look for the owners. They reached Abilene in late June and sold the cattle for $25 a head.

In 1870, when George Sanders was seventeen, he hired with Monroe (Dunk) Choate to take a herd to Abilene. Someone asked Choate what he thought of taking along a seventeen-year-old kid. "His age is all right," Choate said, "if he has the staying power, but most kids are short on sleep and generally sleep on the watch."

They reached Abilene, where they found plenty of buyers and sold the cattle off fast. The grangers, who had no fences, asked the cattlemen to bed their cattle on their property so they could use the chips for fuel. One evening George noticed men and women in buckboards going to different herds and begging the trail boss to stop on their land. The farmers squabbled over the herds, and the cowboys encouraged the row. One of the trail bosses said, "Down in Texas, if you gave a man dry dung he would fight you, but here in Kansas they will fight you to have it." The grangers figured that 1,000 head would leave enough chips on the ground in one night to yield 500 pounds of fuel. But that attitude soon wore off, and a couple of years later they didn't want the drovers around.

As Teddy Blue recalled, you'd be leaning against the bar in San Antonio and one of the bosses would come up. "Want to go up the trail?" "What outfit?" "Olive outfit. Thirty dollars a month and found." As the saying went, when they found you, they expected to find you in the gap (the saddle).

Teddy Blue remembered the low rumbling noise along the ground, of cattle running at a dead run with cutbanks and prairie-dog holes all around them. It sure was a pretty sight to see the herd strung out for almost a mile, the sun flashing on their horns. Eleven men made up the crew: two point men, two on the swing (riding back and forth), two on the flanks, two drag drivers in the rear, the trail boss, the *remuda* man, and the cook. To be a cook, you had to convince your boss that you could boil water without burning it.

After a day on the trail, the men would come off herd, the dust half an inch thick on their hats and piled like fur in their eyebrows and mustaches. The boss had to ride his tail off hunting for water and then spreading the herd along the river's banks. The men would drink it, too, and say, "I ain't kicking, but I had to chew that water before I could swallow it."

In those days, all the cattle in the world seemed to be heading north from Texas. You could stand on a hill and see seven herds behind you and eight in front of you, and the dust from seventeen more. In a hailstorm, you'd cover your head with your saddle, and there'd be dents in the saddle. Once during a storm, Old Matt Winter whipped off his hat and shook it at the sky, shouting, "All right, you old bald-headed son of a bitch up there, if you want to kill me, come on and do it!"

"I believe I would know an old cowboy in hell with his hide burnt off," Teddy recalled. "It's the way they stand and walk and talk. See that droop to his shoulders? He got that coming up the trail riding on three joints of his backbone."

When the war ended in 1865, George Hindes of Pearsall, southwest of San Antonio, returned to find his cattle stolen or otherwise scattered to the four winds. Starting over, he had gotten 1,500 head together by 1872, and started up the trail to the Red River, which was wide, muddy, and swift. But a hundred miles from the Kansas line, the drovers butted into a band of Osages who demanded a good beef out of each and every herd.

About fifty of what George thought were their ugliest bucks came to his camp. He told them to pick one out fast, for he was in a hurry. The sharp-eyed chief picked a fat, high-grade steer that weighed about 1,500 pounds. He was about to shoot the animal when George said that one was a favorite of his. But it was no use, the Indian shot him before George could say scat, and in less than ten minutes they had him skinned, cut up, and packed on ponies.

Seeing what had happened, Hinde's friend John Redus began pushing his herd pretty lively. When the Osages called on him for a beef, he tried to give them a crippled steer, and George watched as 100 braves strung their bows and loaded their guns and rode full tilt into Redus's herd, scattering about 1,000 good beeves to the winds and killing 100 or more right there on the prairie.

As the railroads moved west, bringing more nesters as well as new railheads, other cow towns took Abilene's place. In 1872, Dodge City, on the Arkansas river in southwestern Kansas, became the quintessential cow town, free from the nesters' inhibiting presence.

Dodge City attracted a lively mix of buffalo hunters, railroad construction gangs, and cowboys. The last arrived after months of hard work and bad food on the trail, without liquor or recreation, their wages burning a hole in their pocket. They were like carnivalgoers after Lent. Now it was their day to get shaved and their night to howl.

Andy Adams recalled that before they reached Dodge City the trail boss gave first-timers a little lecture: "Don't ever get the impression that you can ride your horse into a saloon, or shoot out the lights in Dodge. . . . I want to warn you to behave yourselves. Wear your six-guns into town, but leave them at the hotel. And when you leave town, don't ride out shooting. Omit that."

Andy found that much of the saloon talk was about business. He overheard a rancher say: "I'll not ship any more cattle to your town until you adjust your yardage charges. . . . Your stockyards want to charge me 20 cents a head and let my steers stand out in the weather."

There was also a certain amount of bragging about sharp practices. "I was selling a thousand beef steers one time to some Yankee contractors," Andy heard a cattleman say, "and I got the idea that they were not up to snuff in receiving cattle out on the prairie. I was holding a herd of about three thousand and they had agreed to take a running count, which showed that they had the receiving agent fixed. We were counting cattle as they came between us, my foreman and I, and I had lost count several times but guessed at them and started over, and when I thought about nine hundred had passed us, I cut them off and sang out, 'Here they come and here they go, just an even thousand by gatlins.' "

• •

At their peak, the buffalo roamed the short-grass plains from Canada to Mexico "in numbers numberless." The herds during the 1840s were estimated at 25 million, and travelers reported their wonder at coming upon an interminable dark tide upon the landscape, the sound of their hooves like rolling thunder.

The opening of the overland trails led to the killing of buffalo by migrants and soldiers. A market developed for robes, and Indians began noticing a decline in the herds. But it was after the Civil War, as the railroads opened up their western routes, that large-scale buffalo hunting erupted. Sportsmen could ride a train west of the Missouri and fire at buffalo herds through the window of their compartment.

In 1870, Philadelphia tanners found methods to turn the stiff hides into supple leather, and the wholesale destruction of the buffalo got under way. The Union Pacific, finished in 1869, split the buffalo into two distinct herds, north and south. Pre- and post-industrial west overlapped when mounted Indians and grazing buffalo could be seen side by side with railroads on the open prairie.

By 1878, the herds had been decimated. A buffalo census in 1889 disclosed a shocking statistic: Only 1,091 buffalo remained in the entire country.

As Teddy Blue recollected, buffalo slaughter was a dirty business, and the cowpunchers and buffalo hunters didn't mix much. By 1875, there must have been 5,000 hunters and skinners on the northern plains. They worked in pairs. Two hunters rounded up a herd and shot all the buffalo they could. Two skinners followed in a wagon and took the hides.

Riding the prairie, you'd find lots of skeletons with pieces of hide still sticking to them. It was all a put-up job on the part of the government, thought Teddy Blue, aimed at controlling the Indians by getting rid of their food supply. As for the hunters, they were dirtier than the animals they hunted. In saloons, the last man to catch a louse and show it paid for the round of drinks.

The disappearance of the Great Plains tribes' principal source of meat did make it easier to keep the Indians on reservations. The scarcer the buffalo, the more the Indians depended on federal beef rations. By 1871, 250,000 Indians were living on reservations west of the Mississippi. Indian agents warned the tribes that leaving the reservation would mean no more supplies. By 1875, the Indians had been reduced to submission while the buffalo were on their way to extinction.

The beneficiaries were the cattlemen. They moved into the old buffalo range from Texas to Saskatchewan, where the grass, without buffalo to chew it, had grown rank and luxuriant. When the ranchers discovered that they could winter their cattle without feed on the northern plains, they drove Texas longhorns into the grasslands of Nebraska, the Dakotas, Wyoming, Montana, and Colorado, right up into the foothills of the Rockies. In the winter months, the cattle pawed through the snow to the succulent grass beneath.

With the extinction of the buffalo came another rise in the demand for beef, not only because of the change in the Indian diet, but on account of new developments in the shipping of beef from Chicago.

Only half the body weight in a steer could be turned into usable beef. The rest,—the bones, joints, entrails, and gristle,—were of course inedible. But when steers were shipped east on the hoof, the freight charge was for the animal's entire weight. The way to save 50 percent on the cost of freight was to slaughter the cattle in Chicago and ship the fresh beef east, but the hitch was spoilage. In 1868, the Detroit packer George H. Hammond designed a sort of icebox on wheels and sent 16,000 pounds of fresh beef to Boston. This initial success led Hammond to build a plant outside Chicago, at today's Hammond, Indiana, on the Calumet River, to harvest ice. By 1873, he was doing a million dollars' worth of business a year.

Two years later Gustavus F. Swift arrived in Chicago from Massachusetts, where he had worked in the meat business since the age of fourteen, starting as a butcher's helper. In 1877, Swift tried shipping dressed beef east. Since he had no refrigerated cars, he shipped in midwinter, leaving the freight-car doors open.

But dissatisfied with seasonal shipments, Swift hired an engineer to design a refrigerated car that would improve on Hammond's model. One of the problems with Hammond's method was that the ice often touched the meat, freezing and discoloring it. To avoid such mishaps, Swift's engineer placed boxes filled with ice and brine at either end of the cars. That chilled the air over the boxes, which was then circulated in pipes over the meat.

By 1880, Swift was using half-a-million tons of ice a year, traveling as far as the lakes of Wisconsin to chop up their frozen surface. Along the eastward-running track from Chicago, he maintained stations to replace the melted ice during the four-day trip to New York City. In 1883, for the first time, more dressed and slaughtered beef was shipped east than cattle on the hoof. Swift incorporated his business in 1885 with a capital of $300,000. When he died in 1903, the company was worth $25 million.

Thanks to the refrigerated rail car and the open range vacated by the buffalo, America became a nation of beefeaters. Lucky cattlemen could also procure lucrative contracts to provide beef to Indians, for by 1880 the government was buying 500,000 head a year for the reservations. As the song went:

> Oh, you'll be soup for Uncle Sam's Injuns;
> It's beef, beef, beef, I heard them cry.
> Git along, git along, git along little dogies,
> You're going to be beef steers by and by.

. .

The boom in beef ironically brought the end of the cattle drive. The open range moved north, the meatpacking industry moved west, and the railroads moved south, making the drives from Texas to Kansas obsolete.

The era of the cattle drives lasted roughly twenty years, from 1866 to 1886. During that time, when the route from San Antonio to the Kansas cow towns made up one vast stretch of rich grassland, about 8 million head of cattle were driven north and sold.

Even if new methods of transportation and the rise of western packing plants had not occurred, the trail drive would have been doomed. For the cattle ranchers' system depended on the use of the public domain for grazing. Texas cattlemen kept their longhorns on public land and the trail drivers took them on their long trek to market over public land. The government raised no objections so long as the range remained open to all and the land was not wanted by settlers.

Then the railroads came in, selling off their federally granted land. The nesters followed and bought up land that had been used for grazing. As a result, the cattlemen themselves started buying land, to protect the range and keep the nesters at bay.

But the problem with that was fencing. In the west, old-style rail fencing was impractical because wood was scarce and the surfaces to be fenced were vast. There was one burning issue in those days, constantly discussed in local papers: how to make cheap fencing.

In De Kalb, Illinois, a prairie farmer named Joseph Farwell Glidden inadvertently came to the rescue. One morning in 1873, Glidden found that his cattle had broken down the smooth wire fence around his pasture. In repairing the fence, he took some of the staples that fixed the wire to the posts and twisted them around the wire to make sharp burrs.

That at least is one version of how barbed wire was born. Another has Glidden making the barbs to protect his wife's flower beds from dogs. It appears more likely that Glidden attended a county fair where one of the exhibits was a strip of wood studded with thin wire nails called brads. The strips were intended to be hung from smooth wire to keep the cattle in.

Impressed by the device, Glidden took it one step further by placing barbs on the wire fence itself at regular intervals. Adapting an old coffee mill, he turned the crank to twist the wire around the barb and hold it in place.

On November 24, 1874, Glidden took out patent 157,124 for his invention. Other inventors received patents for different kinds of barbed wire, and Glidden was in litigation until 1892. But in the meantime, he cornered the market, designing a machine to make the stuff and building a factory. He figured there must be a market for it out west.

The cattlemen were skeptical at first. As the Texas stockman A. H. Pierce put it: "It jest won't do! The cows will jest run into that Glidden wire and cut themselves. Know what that means? Screw worm! Every open cut means screw worm trouble. It will ruin thousands of heads."

But Glidden sent salesmen through Texas to demonstrate the safety of his "bob" wire. Sure enough, hardware stores soon began to stock it and ranchers began to buy it, and Glidden started shipping his product west by the trainload.

The miles of four-strand barbed-wire fences that eventually covered the prairie spelled the end of the open range, the cattle drives, the long-horns, and the cowboys. The new invention also quickened the nesters' march over the plains. A trail driver wrote in 1874, the first year barbed wire was on sale, that "now there is so much land fenced in that the trail is little better than a crooked lane. . . . These fellows from Ohio and Indiana have made farms, enclosed pastures and fenced in water holes until you can't rest. . . . They are the ruin of the country. They have destroyed the best grazing land in the world."

There was a song for that, too:

> They say that heaven is free range land,
> Goodbye, goodbye, O fare you well,
> But it's barbed wire for the devil's hatband,
> And barbed wire blankets down in hell.

Not only the nesters, but the ranchers as well were enclosing their land. Fencing off large grazing tracts, the cattlemen often forgot the distinction between land they owned and public land. The fences put an end to mingled herds. The ranchers introduced blooded stock and the longhorn became a museum piece. So much land was fenced that the trail drivers could not get through, and the cattlemen were forced to patronize the railroads which came right to their door.

It was also the end of the cowboy because his duties changed. He now had to mend fences that kept the cattle in instead of taking the herds on their eight-hundred-mile trek. Or he served as a checkline rider, keeping the cattle back from the fence. Instead of finding streams for his steers, he had to grease the windmills that drew water up from the water table that lay one or two hundred feet underground. Instead of spending months on the trail, he stayed on the ranch. Instead of adventure, ranching became strictly business. "Between barbed wire and railroads," wrote the cowboy W. S. James, "a cowboy's days were numbered."

Some resistance to barbed-wire fences arose from owners of small herds who were ruined by the end of open grazing. They went around cutting fences to try to preserve the free range. In the absence of regulations, the cattle barons had fenced in public water holes and well-traveled public roads. So these infuriated Texas Luddites bragged that wherever they saw a man putting up a fence they were right behind him, cutting it. The situation got so bad that some nesters pulled down their wire and rolled it up to keep it from being destroyed. Finally, on February 25, 1885, Congress passed a law barring interference with settlers.

The illegal enclosure of government land posed a more serious threat. Having begun in 1875, the land-grabbing reached such proportions that complaints poured into the General Land Office. The areas involved were not small—one was 60,000 acres, while another cattleman had enclosed 250 square miles. Something had to be done, and in August 1885, President Grover Cleveland issued a proclamation ordering the removal of illegal enclosures. The pseudo-homesteading of ranch hands to increase their employers' property was also banned.

Then came the blizzard of 1886, when freezing rain encased the buffalo grass the cattle depended on for winter feed. Hundreds of thousands of range cattle died of exposure and starvation. The open-range industry never recovered from that notorious winter. In the spring, an army of homesteaders streamed west in covered wagons, invading the range along a thousand-mile front.

At its peak, the open range occupied more acreage than the nations of western Europe, extending as it did from Canada to Mexico and from the Missouri to the Pacific. A nation unto itself, the range could claim its own geography, borders, dialect, and customs—all emanating from a single purpose, the raising of cattle.

Its leading citizen was the cowboy, who became a folk figure of more durable proportions than the logger, the forty-niner, the mountain man, or the soldier. In essence, however, the cowboy was no more than a cattle attendant, as such people exist all over the world, from those who tend yaks in Central Asia to the *gardians* of the Camargue or the gauchos of Argentina.

But this "ordinary bow-legged human," whose actual span of activity on the trail drives was a fleeting twenty years, has been buried under a heavy tonnage of pulp and celluloid. Having outlasted all other contenders in the legend playoffs, his persona obviously contained strong imagery, but what was the reality?

First of all, the cowboy appropriated the usages of the range's prior occupants, the Spanish. His costume, borrowed from the Mexican *vaquero*, seems picturesque only to noncowboys, just as knights in armor seem picturesque only to nonknights, or Cossacks to non-Cossacks. The garb was in fact highly functional and prosaic in the extreme. "Why the bandana?" asked cowhand Henry Young. "It was used as a towel, a bandage, to protect the eye from sun glare and to keep the rain from dripping down your neck and chilling the fins. The big hat was the proper conk cover in the sun and chaps in brush country protected the legs."

Second, the cowboy came into prominence after the Civil War, when the time was right for a hero wearing neither blue nor gray. A figure worthy of admiration, who rose above sectional differences, was needed to unify the nation. The cowboy fit the bill, belonging neither to Dixie nor to Yankeeland, but to the far-off and emerging west.

Third, he was a textbook example of the west as democratic leveler, for he was judged on performance, not on where he came from or what he had been before. A curious part of this leveling process on the range was the unimportance of last names. On a trail drive you might find "Busted Snoot" Johnny and "Two Bits Ranch" Johnny and several other Johnnys. Nicknames were the rule, so that a man with smallpox scars on his face might be known as "Sand-blast Pete." When a trail boss said, "That's Bill Adams. That's his name. It's the name he's using now," he was really saying that when a man became a cowboy, he reinvented himself. Everyone started out on the same footing.

The cowboy was just another rural outdoor employee, working with cattle instead of sheep or crops. But the physical demands of his job appealed to an America that took pride in its agrarian roots and still believed in the Puritan work ethic. The reality that gave birth to the legend was one of conquering obstacles through physical skills. For although he was an animal tender, the cowboy was not stationary: He had to take the herd on a difficult voyage over a long distance where he was likely to encounter adversaries. This overland journey, often undertaken in bad weather under dangerous conditions, had the makings of an epic—and a man on a horse lends himself to epic treatment better than a man on foot.

In the abstract, life on the range sounded tempting. The cowboy had the run of the land and spent his time outdoors, in contrast to the dingy offices and sweatshops of the urban east. Mobile and unattached, he appeared to be master of his destiny. His roof was the sky and his pillow was his saddle. As presented in song and story, he exemplified a degree of personal freedom that other Americans strove futilely to attain.

In fact, however, the cowboy led a utilitarian, no-frills existence, a grim adaptation to landscape and longhorns. The drudgery of his tasks did more to define him than high deeds. Far from being the loner riding into the sunset, he invariably labored as part of a team. On the trail drive, a cowboy was never alone. He was as tightly hemmed in by the collaborative demands of his work as a soldier in a barracks or a sailor aboard ship, aside from those brief periods of release when he reached the cattle terminal. Few professions kept a man on duty night and day for weeks and months at a time.

Freedom in the west meant free public land for grazing, free water, free timber for fencing and building, and freedom from regulation. But the cowboy was the captive of a hundred rules connected with his work. One reason why some men chose to be cowboys was simply that they were drawn to a highly regimented environment where someone constantly told them what to do.

Out of the cowboy experience came a distinct vernacular. The language developed from the nature of the work, as did the language of mining or river travel (from which Mark Twain got his pungent and watery name). When a man "sold his saddle," it meant that he'd betrayed a trust, or become destitute, or gone crazy—in other words, it meant the ultimate in irreversible bad luck.

The cowboy idiom was usually pithy, often humorous, and sometimes self-mocking. Henry Young recalled: "I wasn't bigger than a pint of cider, and I started to chin with the livery stable fellow—where can a fellow get a job? What can you do? Anything anyone else can. He sent me to see the boss, the wife was cooking supper and said light and cool your saddle. I could smell the chuck cooking and that got my tapeworm real excited."

Although uneducated and supposedly monosyllabic, cowboys had a gift for expressing themselves. A cowhand arriving at a ranch at three in the morning, only to be awakened by the breakfast bell at five, remarked: "A man sure can stay all night quick at this place." Three things merited respect on the range, they said: a cowboy who could stay awake all summer and catch up on his sleep in the winter; a good trail cook; and a cattle brand that wasn't doctored.

The cowboy vernacular was partly derived from working with others and having to remain on good terms with them. A cowhand at the chuck wagon would wryly comment, "This bread is all burned but gosh! That's the way I like it," because you could not afford to be on bad terms with the cook. And as with other hard-pressed groups, the cowboy's habit of making setbacks more bearable by joking about them became second nature.

The subtext of much cowboy colloquy consisted of a sort of tactful obliqueness. One of the rules of conversation was to make it possible for each sentence to be the last. Thus, when a young hand arrived at the start of the drive without a hat, the trail boss didn't ask him "Where's your hat?" —which would have required a reply—but said merely, "I've seen a few tenderfeet go bare-headed in the sun," which could be left at that. Cowboy conversation could be as subtle and as weighted with hidden meaning as negotiations between ambassadors.

Cowboy psychology also had its dark side. The profession attracted its fair share of misfits and weirdos, some of whom bordered on the pathological. On a trail drive to Kansas, the young brushpopper Jim Cook had to contend with another fellow in the outfit, Jack Harris, whose habit it was to ride alongside Cook, draw his six-shooter, cock it, aim it, and ask: "Are you the sheriff that is looking for me?" Then he would flip the revolver and offer the butt to Cook, explaining, "I'm tired of fighting, take my gun." As Cook reached out his hand, Harris quickly reversed the pistol, aiming the barrel at Cook's face and saying, "Just for practice." After a while, Cook got fed up and told Harris to stop before his finger slipped and he fired for real.

The trail boss, Mac Stewart, was another eccentric. Seeing a rock or a piece of wood lying on the ground, he would get off his horse and carve something on it with his knife. When Cook, who was riding behind him, finally stopped one day and picked up a rock that had been the object of the trail boss's attention, he saw an inscription saying: "This is the skull of Mac Stewart when he was a buffalo."

One day, Mac and Cook had to bring the mess wagon over the Red River on a raft. For some reason, Mac had taken off his boots, and as the raft neared the bank, one of the boots rolled off into the rushing water. Mac started cussing and snatched his other boot and hurled it in the river after the first. The nearest place to buy boots was Camp Supply in Indian Territory. In the meantime, Mac had to ride barefoot, and soon his feet were bleeding.

But forget about lost boots and hailstorms, stampedes and Indians. For one brief and glorious moment, there existed pure, free, open-range ranching, with trail drives over unfenced and empty land that belonged to the cowboy, though he owned none of it. After that came barbed wire and windmills, cattle wars and sheep wars, and the irreversible advance of the nesters. But the dream of freedom lives on in the legend of the cowboy, which is at its heart a haunting elegy for a way of life that in retrospect seems felicitous only because it disappeared so quickly.

PART FIVE
THE PARTISAN LOGJAM

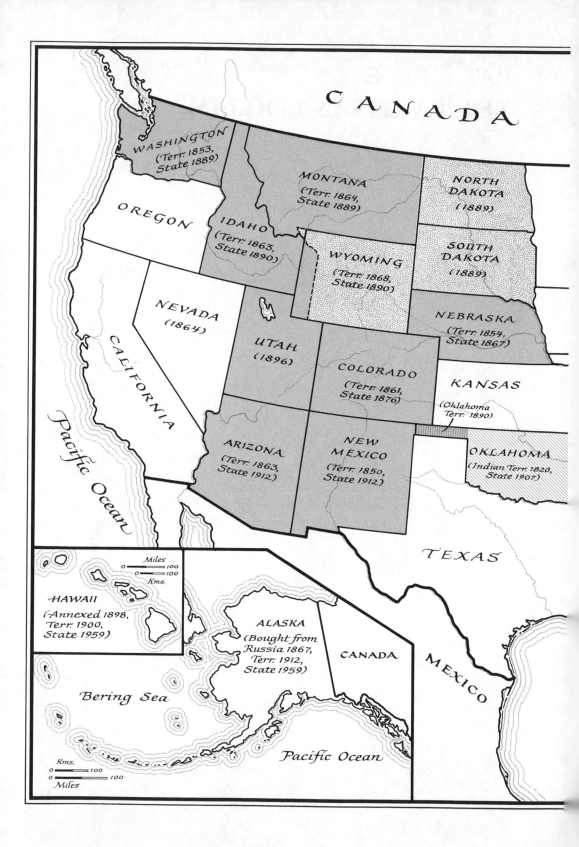

The United States

1864 to Present Day

Dakota Territory, 1864–68
Indian Territory, 1820–1907
Other U.S. Territories
as of 1864

Atlantic
Ocean

Kms.
0 ——— 300
0 ——— 300
Miles

© A·Karl/J·Kemp. 1995

CHAPTER SEVENTEEN

THE COLORADO FRONTIER

*I'm scouting, getting the feel of the land, the way
the fields step down the mountainsides hugging their
battered, sagging wire fences to themselves as though
both day and night they needed to know their limits.*

PHILIP LEVINE

In 1858, "argonauts" found rich veins in the unexplored ranges of Colorado, folding westward like granite pleats. The people who had long argued that the stony spine of the Continental Divide harbored vast deposits of gold and silver turned out to be right. Soon the area, then part of Kansas Territory, got its first surge of newcomers.

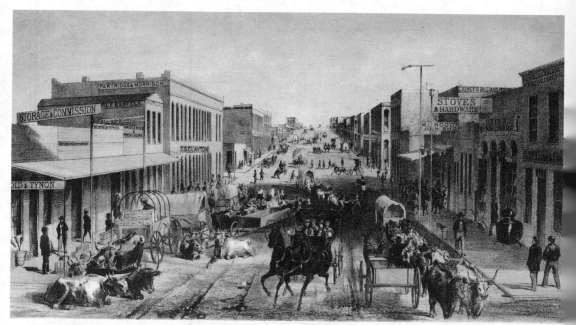

The New York Public Library
Denver's busy F Street in 1866 was as yet unpaved but had plank sidewalks. Men in top hats and women in hoopskirts shared the urban space with high-stepping horses and dozing cattle.

Denver and other little embryo towns sprouted in the no-man's-land triangle between the Santa Fe and Oregon trails, serving as supply depots for the miners. Pike's Peak, seventy-five miles south of Denver, attracted a swarm of prospectors in 1859. Many of these became "Go-Backs," who returned with zero ounces of gold. A sign on a wagon cover in Denver in 1859 said THIS OUT FITT FOR SAIL. Others, however, struck it rich.

Mr. and Mrs. Henry Tabor passed through Denver in 1859 and went mining up in the Sawatch Range at 14,000 feet, where the town of Granite is today. Henry Tabor sawed some lumber to make sluice boxes, and they found plenty of gold, but it was mixed with black sand and they didn't know how to separate it.

"Really," Mrs. Tabor recalled, "the women did more in the early days than the men. There were the sick to take care of, and many unfortunate men were shot by accident."

By May 1860, the couple had $7,000 in gold dust, so they opened a store. Tabor was postmaster, and his wife kept the express-company books, weighing the gold the miners took out of the gulch. "I never saw country settled with such greenhorns as Colorado," she said. "Many of them did not know one thing about weighing gold."

Once they had roads, it took them only four days to go to Denver. Mrs. Tabor would go on horseback accompanied by her husband because they didn't trust the express. Carrying the gold on her person, she reasoned that highwaymen wouldn't dare search her. "In some places," she recalled, "it was so steep we had to hang on to our horses' tails, it was all they could do to get up the grade."

Evelyn Silverthorn was twelve when she came to Denver in May 1860 with her parents. The family rented a house at Fourteenth and Lawrence made of rough unpainted board; white muslin covered the windows. One day when some Indian women had gathered in front of the house, Evelyn's mother decided to get some moccasins for little brother, who had stepped on prickly pears.

As her mother negotiated the price in the dining room, Evelyn stayed in the bedroom. She crawled under the bed, watching the open door to make sure the squaws didn't steal anything. Soon a squaw looked in, saw Evelyn's new sunbonnet on the bed, and tucked it under her blanket.

After the trade of sugar for moccasins, Evelyn crawled out and said, "Mother, one of the squaws took my sunbonnet." Her mother asked the women if this was true and they all denied it. Evelyn pointed out the guilty one, but the squaw vigorously shook her head. Her mother took hold of the squaw's elbows and raised them until the sunbonnet fell from the folds of her blanket. The Indian woman quickly went out into the street. Mrs. Silverthorn followed and started to box the thief's ears, but passersby gathered and said, "Oh don't, Mrs. Silverthorn, we will all be killed."

•   •

In 1861, when secession cleared Congress of southern Democrats, Colorado became a territory. Absorbing pieces of Nebraska, Wyoming, Utah, and New Mexico, the area formed the large rectangle occupied by the state today, 300 miles north to south, and 400 miles east to west, for a total of 66,718,000 acres. Since much of that acreage belonged to the Indians, the process of extinguishing title by treaty soon began.

When an act of Congress in 1862 extended preemption rights, settlers moved in and claimed their quarter sections of unsurveyed land. Four notched logs laid in a square on the ground would guarantee a preempted quarter section for a year. "They were as respected by newcomers as if they had been a square of infantry," wrote one Colorado historian.

Among the thousands of settlers who moved to Colorado in 1862 were Emily and David Witter. They boarded a train at Indianapolis, which took them as far as Eddyville, Iowa, on the Des Moines River. Then they headed west toward Omaha in a light wagon with a feather bed in the back for the children. There was no bridge yet over the Missouri, but as it was winter, they crossed on ice that was getting soft. They made it, but the children caught the measles, and that held them up for three weeks.

Having left the "States" for the "plains," they resumed their journey on the Elkhorn military road. On the first night, two big Indians came by their camps and asked for biscuits. When Emily Witter gave them some, they said: "Good Squaw." A Pawnee helped them over the ice at the Loup Fork of the Platte; when the Witters asked "How much?" he said "Thread and needle," and Emily gave him a spool of thread and some needles.

At the Platte, some pioneers ahead of them took the wrong ford. The Witters saw a load of wood disappear in quicksand as the frantic settlers cut the mules loose and swam to shore. What with mishaps big and small, it took a month to cross five hundred miles of plains. Tired and homesick, Emily Witter perked up at her first sight of the Rockies—they looked like silver and gold piled up in the sunlight. The Witters reached the mountains the first week of April, and the sun was so bright they rubbed lampblack on their cheeks to prevent sun blindness.

The higher they went, the longer they had to wait for their food to cook—an hour to boil potatoes. The snow was so deep that David Witter had to walk in front of the team with two long sticks to try and find the road. In May, they reached Hamilton, in northwestern Colorado on the Williams Fork of the Yampa River, where Witter had been appointed postmaster. About twenty miners lived in the log-cabin village. Each of them carried a little buckskin bag filled with gold dust, which Emily weighed on the post-office scales. Once a week husband and wife would wash the sweepings off the office floor and collect a little pile of gold dust.

In the summer of 1864, the Witters got the wagon ready to go to Colorado City for the session of the territorial legislature, although they had heard that the Indians were up in arms. The Cheyennes and Arapahos had been attacking wagon trains along the main trails. The situation got so bad that service was interrupted on Ben Holladay's coach line. At Plum Creek, war parties had caught ten wagons and murdered nine settlers. Every ranch between Fort Kearney and Julesburg, people said, had been abandoned. But when Governor John Evans pleaded for federal troops, he was told, "Don't you know there's a war on?"

In November, Colonel John Chivington, a Methodist preacher and Indian hater, took 750 men to Fort Lyon, near the junction of the Arkansas and Purgatoire rivers in southeastern Colorado. Thirty miles northeast of the fort was a camp with 500 Cheyenne, mostly women and children. Chivington instructed his men: "Kill and scalp all, big and little; nits make lice." About 200 Indians were killed, which led to further violence. The war finally burned itself out in 1865. Two years later, federal troops transported the Cheyennes and Arapahos to a reservation in western Oklahoma.

Emily Witter, seeing the Indian wars from a settler's point of view, said: "Do you wonder I have no love for the Indians? I saw where whole corrals made of wagons had been burned, nothing remained but the wheels and the graves of those killed."

In March 1864, with President Lincoln coming up for reelection, Congress passed an enabling act to go ahead with Colorado statehood. Colorado was expected to vote Republican, and Lincoln needed the votes. But in the territory, considerable opposition to statehood arose, since it would bring conscription, as well as higher taxes. Voters rejected a proposed constitution by 4,672 to 1,520.

But in 1865, Colorado tried again, and in September, with the war over, this second constitution passed by the narrow margin of 155 votes. The legislation then went to Washington, but the timing was bad, for Congress was locked in battle with Andrew Johnson, who had succeeded Lincoln after his assassination in April 1865.

A self-educated Tennessee tailor, Johnson had served as governor of his state and in both houses of Congress. When the Civil War came, he refused to join the Confederacy. His loyalty to the Union made him Lincoln's choice as vice president in 1864, when the president was looking for a "War Democrat" to balance the ticket.

As president, however, Johnson's leniency toward the south embittered the radical Republicans in Congress. In 1866, Congress was still denying readmission to the southern states unless they accepted the equality of Negroes. When the lawmakers voted to admit Colorado, Johnson bridled. Feeling that no new, sparsely populated states should be admitted while the old southern states were kept out, the president vetoed Colorado statehood. Twice in two years, efforts to make Colorado a state failed.

In 1867, the Union Pacific continued to advance, from North Platte, Nebraska, to the northeast corner of Colorado at Fort Sedgwick, where Lodgepole Creek ran into the South Platte. An army regiment was assigned to protect the railroad. The regimental surgeon was a young man from Pottsville, Pennsylvania, Dr. Henry Parry, who wrote letters home to his father, Judge Edward Owen Parry.

"I observed," Parry wrote from North Platte on May 16, "that in every establishment the persons behind the counters attended to their customers with loaded and half-cocked revolvers in their hands. Law is unknown here, and the people are about to get up a vigilance committee."

Under a broiling sun, the regiment marched 106 miles from North Platte to Fort Sedgwick. The prairie land was as level as a floor, with not a tree or a bush or even a stick of wood in sight. When one man grumbled, another said: "Who wouldn't be a soldier and tramp the prairies? Do you want to spend all your summers on Governor's Island [off Manhattan]?"

The soldiers guarded the work gangs on the track, and every ten or fifteen miles stood a little bulletproof adobe house where a few men with plenty of ammunition could hold off one hundred Indians. At that time, however, the Cheyennes were on the warpath, and they had cleared all the adobe stations between North Platte and Sedgwick. Every day stages were attacked, and Dr. Parry saw six- and eight-horse stages fly by at full gallop, their fiercely mustached drivers armed with four Colt revolvers in their belts and clutching a Henry rifle between their knees.

In June, Dr. Parry's regiment reached Fort Sedgwick, an outpost that covered half a square mile on the south bank of the South Platte, midway between Denver and Fort Laramie. A few days later, Indians killed two men and injured five in a raid near the fort. Dr. Parry had the opportunity to treat his first arrow wound. They were worse than bullets, he thought. "Those beautiful descriptions of Indian characters by Washington Irving and Fenimore Cooper," he wrote, "are outrageous misrepresentations. In war, cruelty and torture are their chief study."

What the plains tribes needed, Dr. Parry believed, was a tremendous thrashing, for they laughed and hooted at the infantry. They boldly rode within range of the muskets, then ducked under the bellies of their ponies. The only reason they left the telegraph lines alone was that they were convinced the Great Spirit walked on the wires.

By June 23, the track had been laid to within a mile of Fort Sedgwick; workers and soldiers cheered when they heard the whistle of the engine and saw its dark bulk come puffing toward them. To Dr. Parry, inspired by a sense of America's westward mission, the clouds of smoke seemed to spell C-I-V-I-L-I-Z-A-T-I-O-N.

A. K. Clarke came west in 1868 as a telegraph operator for the Union Pacific in Denver. A few years later he found some good grazing country near Deer Trail, thirty miles east of Denver, on the middle fork of Bijou Creek. He bought some cattle, started a ranch, and built a dugout house on the bank of the creek. One of the earliest ranches in Colorado, Clarke's place fronted a grove of cottonwood saplings half a mile long.

As it turned out, the grove served as a favorite Indian·camping ground.

Clarke had just gotten settled down with his cattle when Piah and his band of Utes appeared at the lower end a quarter mile away. In the morning, the squaws knocked on his door, wanting sugar. In the evening, Clarke could hear the Indians chanting and dancing until midnight.

Time passed, but the Utes showed no sign of breaking camp. The grass was getting short, because they had so many horses. Clarke decided that he must go and ask Piah to move on. Piah said, "This old Indian campground for long, long time. You move."

"Indian ponies eat all the grass," Clarke said. "You move over on Willow Gulch, about two miles, good grass, plenty water for Ute ponies."

"No," replied Piah. "You go Willow Gulch. This old Ute campground."

Clarke felt that his generosity and patience were being taken advantage of. "You move," he said, "or I will write Thompson" (the Indian agent). But Piah stood his ground.

Clarke sent off the letter, and a week later came the reply from Thompson saying that Piah had to move camp.

"He say that?" Piah asked.

"Yes," said Clarke, "and here is the letter."

Piah could not read, so Clarke read it to him.

"All right, Ute go," Piah said. The next day the Indians broke camp and left, trailing their teepee poles behind their horses. Piah relied on the agent for permits and annuities and could not afford to disobey him.

William Jackson Palmer was a railroad man, but in the Civil War he commanded the 15th Pennsylvania Volunteer Cavalry. After the war, he migrated west and helped build the road from Kansas City through Denver to Cheyenne.

In 1870, Palmer struck out on his own and launched the Denver & Rio Grande, a railroad that served the mining communities in mountainous areas. After traveling to Wales and studying the Festiniog Railway there, Palmer had decided that a three-foot-wide track would be practicable in steep and winding areas that were closed to the four-and-a-half-foot broad-gauge lines.

Congress granted Palmer right-of-way, and construction began in March 1871 on the first seventy miles of track between Denver and Colorado Springs (where there were no springs). Using Westinghouse air brakes to control the speed on steep grades and sharp curves, the Denver & Rio Grande became as safe as driving a coach over flat land.

By June 15, 1872, the track had reached Pueblo, 118 miles from Denver. Soon the line extended to the coal mines of Canon City, and eventually to Durango and Silverton. The Denver & Rio Grande poked through the Rockies with 1,600 miles of three-foot track, climbing higher than any other railroad—9,383 feet over La Veta Pass in the Sangre de Cristo Mountains. In the winter, they kept the trains going with the aid of steam-driven rotary snowplows.

William Walk, a railroad engineer from Lexington, Missouri, worked on the Canon City–to–Leadville run through the mountains in 1873. They'd build a while and run out of materials and then wait for more rails and ties. Putting down the road from Gunnison to Delta through the Black Canyon, they had to watch for landslides. Every engine carried dynamite to blast rocks too heavy to be rolled off the track.

Walk also piloted the Montezuma, one of the three narrow-gauged locomotives that Palmer had ordered from the Baldwin works in Philadelphia. "There was a sweet little engine for you," he recalled. "She was perfectly balanced, not top-heavy, and took the curves like a piece of tangent track, yet she never so much as spilled a drop of water from a glass set in any of the windows of the cab."

"Some of the early towns I went to were nothing but mudholes. I watched Creede [a mining town in the San Juan Mountains, near the Continental Divide] grow from a patch of willows to a city of thousands in six months. It was downright dangerous to run an engine from Wagon Wheel Gap to Creede during the mining excitement, for people would use the right of way as a sidewalk. I had to keep two men in the cab, one on each side, to watch the track so no one was hit. People paid absolutely no attention to the oncoming train."

One night Walk made the run from Salida to Pueblo in the No. 2 locomotive as a storm was coming up. It was such heavy going that it took him five hours to go forty miles. Stopping at Cotopaxi, about twenty miles from Salida, Walk wired Pueblo and warned them not to let the No. 1 locomotive leave Salida. He watched as the operator sent the message and put it on file.

The following week the company president, E. T. Jeffery, summoned Walk to the Pueblo office. "Bill," he said, "I'm disappointed in you. You were the last one to come over that track in the No. 2. Why in hell didn't you report the condition? No. 1 went in the river. Why did you let her go out?"

Ed Gray, the chief dispatcher in Pueblo, denied receiving Walk's wire, although a check with the depot showed that the message had been sent. Further investigation revealed the wire hanging on a hook beside Ed's desk, which he soon vacated. Two months later Ed asked for reinstatement and Jeffery said, "There's just one man who can get you back on the payroll, Bill Walk." But Walk said, "No! He hasn't got enough wrinkles in his belly yet." Six months later he relented.

Sometimes the water in the canyon rose two or three feet over the tracks. The roadmaster would wade ahead with a long pole to test the depth. The water always put out the fire in the firebox, but the head of steam was enough to carry the engine through.

Bill Walk believed in hunches. Once, when he was about a day out of Salida, something told him to stop and he did. Dave Muse, the conductor, although fed up with Bill's hunches, agreed to walk around the curve just ahead. He came back white-faced. "If you'd gone around that curve," he said, "you'd have cracked her into six thousand tons of rock. Half the cliff has dropped on the track."

The company offered Walk a promotion, but he didn't take it. He liked the call of the throttle and the open track. Eventually, he had a heart attack on the job and realized that his train days were over.

John Taylor was born in Paris, Kentucky, in 1838, the son of slaves. "As soon as I was big enough to mock a man at work I was sent into the corn and tobacco fields," he recalled. "I was raised on the handle of a hoe until I was 23. Then I became a runaway nigger" (in 1861).

In 1864, Taylor enlisted in the first Negro regiment formed by the Union Army in Kentucky. The regiment was the first to enter the city of Richmond after its evacuation by Confederate forces. Upon Taylor's discharge in 1865, "There was nothin' for me to do, 'cept wage-hand around the cotton fields. And I sho didn't like that. Maybe I was lazy, 'cause I'd got fatted up in the army."

He would have reenlisted, but "I fell in love with a yella gal, Caldonie." When he worked in the fields, however, "I couldn't forget my soldier days." In 1867, he did reenlist and spent three years on the Texas frontier. In Tucumcari, New Mexico, he was camp cook.

Mustered out of the army in New Mexico in 1871, John Taylor moved across the border into southwestern Colorado. There he lived with the Utes, hunting and trapping and taking a number of Indian wives. "I married those gals the Indian way and I was divorced the same way," he said. "Divorce is easy. You do somethin' your squaw don't like, she picks up your saddle and throws it out the hogan [earth-covered dwelling] and you're divorced."

Taylor never became a member of the Ute tribe, explaining, "I'm a free man, I ain't no ration Injun. Massa Abe proclaimed us free, and I fought for that freedom too."

Eventually, he married a woman with a homestead, which he inherited when she died. The homestead was chosen as the site for the town of Ignacio (southeast of Durango, in today's La Plata County), and Taylor was paid $5,000 for the land. He joined an association of settlers who had come to Colorado before 1880, the San Juan Pioneers, and lived well into the twentieth century. In 1917, he dyed his hair and tried to reenlist once again, but the army told him: "You're a Civil War veteran, you're too old for this one."

Taylor died in 1934 at the age of ninety-six. Led by his widow, Kitty Cloud, the townspeople of Ignacio followed his coffin in falling snow to the Indian burial ground. Walking in the procession were bandy-legged cowboys, paunchy sheepmen, the Ute chief Buckskin Charlie, whites, Mexicans, and Indians, but not a single black man on that gray winter morning stood by the side of the open grave.

• •

In 1875, Jim Barker was elected justice of the peace in El Paso County, south of Denver. His first case was a complaint from a traveling missionary, Elder Slater, who said his one-eyed mule had been stolen by the mountain man Zimri Bowles. Mike Irving, the constable, had arrested Bowles as the mountaineer was easing the mule down the steep slope of Mad Gun Mountain, his lariat neatly tied around the animal's tail.

The evidence was conclusive, and Barker sentenced Zimri to a year in the territorial penitentiary. "An' now, Zim," Barker added, "seeing as how I'm about out of things to eat, an' as you will have the cost [of the court] to pay, I reckon you'd better take a turn among the foothills with your rifle and see if you can't rustle up some meat before night."

Which marketing duty Zim performed, bringing in a black-tail fawn and a rabbit. The next day Constable Irving escorted Zim through the mountains to the penitentiary at Colorado Springs. They arrived loaded with a deer, two antelopes, and a small cinnamon bear, which they sold to the warden.

The constable then handed the warden a note from Jim Barker, which said: "I sentenced Zim officially to one year in the Colorado prison, and hated to do it, seeing as Zim once stood by me like a man when the Injuns had me in a tight place. . . . My wife Lizzy, who is a kind o' tender-hearted critter, come and leaned her arm on my shoulder and says, 'Father, don't forget the time when Zim with his rifle covered our cabin from Granite mountain and saved us from the Arapahoes.'. . . . So I changed my mind as follows: seeing the mule had but one eye, you can let Zim go at about six months, and sooner if the Injuns should get ugly." The warden told the constable that he could not receive the prisoner, and Zim was released.

Thoughts of Colorado statehood had to be deferred during President Ulysses S. Grant's scandal-ridden two terms (1869–77). Crooks surrounded the president, and corruption tainted the Republican Party. The bucks stopped at the Oval Office.

In 1875, Congress passed an enabling act for Colorado in anticipation of the 1876 election, when the Republican candidate would presumably win Colorado's three electoral votes. On July 1, 1876, Coloradans ratified a constitution, 15,443 to 4,062. It granted the vote to Negro males but not to women. Statehood came on August 1, 1876.

By then, Rutherford B. Hayes, the three-term governor of Ohio, had been nominated on the Republican ticket. Running against Samuel J. Tilden, a reformist Albany lawyer, Hayes won by the margin of one electoral vote even though Tilden had a majority of 250,000 in the popular vote. It was a textbook example of a stolen election, which Hayes would have lost without Colorado's three votes.

By chance, Colorado statehood coincided with the country's hundredth anniversary, leading the *Denver Weekly Times* to comment on July 5, 1876: "We celebrate the progress of the hundred years and the good start the men of 1776 gave us. Here in Colorado we do more. We celebrate our emancipation from parental control and discipline, and step into the family of states on equal footing with all."

That year Denver's Fourth of July parade commemorated both statehood and the Centennial. The men of the Colorado Commandery rode in front on jet-black horses, their officers on pure white ones, followed by a marching band, the Governor's Guard, the masons and the pioneers (a little straggly as to step), Scandinavians and Germans, Odd Fellows in purple uniforms, the Erie Brass Band; and Lady Liberty, in the person of Miss Neoma Hagerty, who sat under an awning holding the young republic in her lap, driven by a bewigged and powdered coachman.

Then came the Grand Car of the Union, two large transfer wagons lashed together and drawn by six white horses. Under its canopy in the first section sat thirteen married women symbolizing the original states, the one from Virginia dressed up like Martha Washington. The second wagon carried young ladies from distinguished families, each representing one of the thirty-eight states, again including the original thirteen. The youngest, sixteen-year-old May Butler, was Colorado.

The Irish-Americans followed, and after them the Red Cross Champions, the Knights of Pythias with their red plumes and black uniforms, and the hook-and-ladder companies, their horses and carts a mass of roses. Last in the procession came a long-haired bearded man who drove a team of elk harnessed to a buckboard out of which rose a five-foot-high aspen.

A gust of wind at Cherry Creek bridge lifted the canopy over the float of the thirty-eight states, leaving the young ladies exposed to the blazing July sun. The parade ended in Denver Park with an afternoon picnic. Thirteen toasts were drunk to, among others, Washington and Lincoln, Womanhood, and the Law of the Land. Then in the cool of the evening a display of skyrockets and Roman candles enchanted the crowd.

Once a barren plain where jackrabbits hopped and yucca grew, Denver was now a city of 35,000, with plank sidewalks and little horse carts that bounced over the unpaved streets. Sprinkling carts fought a daily battle against the dust. Charpiot's was the hotel for "swells," and the markets sold bear meat. You couldn't find a single building over three stories. Pigtailed celestials wearing blue-black tunics, flapping trousers, and white-soled slippers delivered their newspaper-wrapped bundles of laundry in large wicker baskets. A sign on a door exemplified the bustling Denver spirit: GONE TO BURY MY WIFE. BACK IN HALF AN HOUR.

By 1876, the Atchison, Topeka & Santa Fe had laid its tracks as far west as Pueblo, and the Denver & Rio Grande had pushed over the Sangre de Cristo Mountains to Alamosa, making Denver a railroad hub. Thanks to its mining operations, Colorado had turned itself into a frontier industrial state. Martial law in Leadville was declared not because of an Indian massacre, but a miner's strike.

Fred Vaille arrived in Denver in 1876 to secure the telephone franchise for Colorado (the infant's first wail had been heard on March 10 of that year in a hookup between Boston and Cambridge). Vaille canvassed Denver, resolved to install a telephone exchange if he could sign up 125 subscribers. He put a telephone on a stand in the window of his office, but people were slow to respond to something they could find no use for. Some held back to see how many would sign up, since it all depended on the number of people you could call.

By February 1876, Vaille had 161 subscribers and set up a switchboard over Conrad Frick's shoe store at 1514 Larimer. Monday, February 24, was announced as opening day, and one newspaper described the telephone as "the new system of galvanic muttering machine."

Each subscriber received a black walnut backboard holding all the necessary equipment: a single-stroke bell; a crank turned by hand to throw the subscriber's set into the line; a button to ring the bell at the central office; and a receiver that doubled as a transmitter. You put the piece to your ear and then to your mouth, passing it back and forth more or less quickly depending on the speed of the conversation.

Vaille found subscribers in the countryside, and soon Colorado had exchanges in Georgetown, Boulder, Gunnison, Colorado Springs, and Pueblo. Out beyond Denver, there was still open range for cattle; when the telephone poles went up, the cattle found them excellent substitutes for trees, and used them to scratch their sides on, sometimes knocking them over. The twilight of the open range had overlapped with the dawn of the party line.

Anyone who worked for the telephone company had to hear a litany of complaints, from people who said "It's nothing but a toy" to millionaires who didn't want charity calls. Dry-goods stores frowned on customers calling for "a spool of thread at once." Ditto grocers: "Send me a cake of yeast right away." Doctors didn't know whether it was a blessing or a curse, with patients keeping them on the line about their stomachaches— at least they saved on house calls. But eventually it appeared that the telephone was here to stay.

In 1876, La Junta, on the Arkansas River in southeastern Colorado, functioned as the hub where the freight from New Mexico arrived. It had saloons and dance halls and a hotel in the form of fifteen boxcars on a side track fitted up for sleeping. The only thing wanting was a graveyard.

In March, John Chambers, a fiddler in the Bronco dance hall, died of consumption. They buried him in a plot on the edge of town and erected a marble headstone to mark the first death in La Junta. But the local boys worried that the grave looked lonesome and wondered how long Chambers would have to wait for company.

One night in Ed Silk's saloon, Rufe Edwards left a poker game to see about a rumpus in his dance hall next door. In his absence, Tim Shea of Dodge City took a stack of blue from Edwards's chips and mixed them in with his own. When Edwards returned, he looked at his stake and asked,

"Who has them blues?" But no one replied and he broke the game up in a rage.

Tim Shea wanted a drink, but no one would serve him. So he started to shoot at the feet of a kid called Cherokee Charlie, shouting, "Get behind that bar and give me a drink." The kid said, "If you spoil my boots it will cost you $35." Then he went behind the bar and put a glass and a bottle in front of the gambler, who laid down his gun and poured. The kid grabbed Shea's gun and said, "If you drink that it will be your last."

Shea was led out of the bar, meek as a lamb, but the next morning he was back looking for his gun. "I am going to kill Rufe Edwards and light out for Deadwood," he said. Edwards, who had followed him into the saloon, shot the unarmed man dead.

At the coroner's inquest, Mexican Joe showed up wearing Tim Shea's overcoat, which was too big for him and hung to the ground. He served on the jury that voted "killed in self-defense." Everyone thought the fiddler would at last have company, but a woman arrived who claimed Tim Shea's body and took him away.

A few weeks later a kid came into Billy Patterson's saloon. When he was refused a drink on account of his age, he shot and killed the bartender, George Harrington. The local boys buried George in the grave they had dug for Tim Shea, and John Chambers finally had a neighbor.

The Utes, who were in Colorado long before the white man, still occupied much of the western part of the state. In 1868, the United States signed a treaty with three Ute bands giving them 16 million acres, almost the western third of Colorado. In 1873, the treaty was revised and the Utes ceded 4 million acres in exchange for annuities of $25,000 a year. Pushed west and then south, and under the supervision of three Indian agencies, they still had 12 million acres along the White and Uncompahgre Rivers, and on the border with New Mexico.

In 1878, the government appointed Nathan S. Meeker agent to the White River Utes in northwestern Colorado. Ohio-born, Meeker was an abolitionist, a poet, a correspondent for Horace Greeley's *New York Tribune*, and a devoted agrarian socialist. In 1870, he had gone west to found a colony, buying 16,000 acres of railroad land on the Cache la Poudre River from the Denver Pacific.

Since alternate sections belonged to the government, he acquired those too, "to prevent uncongenial neighbors." He ended up with 60,000 acres at an average price of $3.33 an acre, which he paid for with the $150 membership fees of future colonists. Each member of the Union Colony, as it was called, got a tract of land and a lot in the town of Greeley.

The colonists, mainly from states east of Ohio, started arriving in May. By June 1870 the population in the tent city of Greeley had reached 460. The land was high, rolling treeless prairie at an altitude of 5,000 feet. Water for their crops came from the river via thirty-six miles of irrigation canals.

The Union colonists brought the Puritan spirit to northern Colorado. Upright and religious, they were mostly temperance people who took the evils of alcohol seriously. As one of them put it, they felt "an emancipation almost as great as that enjoyed by the slaves" at not having to associate with drunkards. No Germans with their lagers and loud songs, no Irish with their whiskey and red faces, no rum-soaked city trash. When one rash outsider tried to open a whiskey shop, the townspeople burned it down. A proposal for a billiard hall was brusquely rejected.

In Denver, fifty-two miles south of Greeley, the feeling was "Let them run their town as they wish." Though the colony was a success, and its population grew to 1,200, its founder did not prosper. Meeker's newspaper, the *Greeley Tribune*, went bust and he found himself deep in debt. So in 1878, when he was sixty, Meeker jumped at the chance to earn the steady income of an Indian agent. He would create a Union colony among the Utes.

When Meeker arrived on the White River in May, he found that the agency was a cluster of log buildings at the edge of the wilderness, twelve miles from the main Ute village in the Powell Valley. He decided to move the agency to the village, and rebuilt it in a spot where the Utes pastured their horses, near 3,500 acres of tillable land. The Utes considered this an intrusion. But when they objected, Meeker told them that the Indian commissioner in Washington, Edward A. Hayt, would get "heap mad" when he found out.

In July, Meeker was joined by his sixty-three-year-old wife, Arvilla, and his twenty-year-old daughter Josie, a graduate of Oberlin. Two assistants also arrived: Frank Dresser and Shadrack Price (the latter had a sixteen-year-old wife). Tall and attractive, her ash-blond hair cut short, Josie began studying Ute customs, but when she brought home a pair of moccasins, her father told her: "You are here to teach and not to learn."

The Utes were hunters and horsemen, whom Meeker sought to turn into farmers against their wishes. To them, the agency was just a place to get rations and annuity goods that were routed their way via the railroad station in Rawlins, Wyoming, two hundred miles to the north.

With his complete indifference to the Utes' long-established way of life, and his conviction that he was the agent of their salvation, Meeker did not make himself popular. His method was to hold back their rations to incite them to work. On December 24, 1878, he wrote Colorado senator Henry M. Teller that "in a year or so . . . I shall propose to cut every Indian to bare starvation point if he will not work."

In the spring of 1879, Meeker reported to Commissioner Hayt that he had planted eighty acres fenced with cedar posts and barbed wire. But the Utes kept roaming off the reservation on summer and winter hunts and stood accused of setting forest fires. Frederick Pitkin, the Colorado governor, said they had burned millions of dollars worth of timber and were intimidating miners and settlers (though others said that railroad tie-men had started the fires in their camps).

Meeker knew the source of the trouble: it was horses. As he wrote the Bureau of Indian Affairs in his 1879 mid-August report, the White River Utes, who included some known horse thieves, probably had 4,000 horses. Wandering about on their mounts, they had no interest in planting. They used good tillable land for pasture, and instead of plowing spent their time organizing horse races. They even built a racetrack on agency grounds. Idleness and gambling were the result.

Meeker discovered that Johnson, the Ute medicine man, was stealing water from the schoolhouse for his ponies. Fed up with the tribe's riding and racing, Meeker ordered Shadrack Price in September 1879 to plow a parcel of land where the Utes had their corrals. The Utes said they needed that ground for their horses. On September 8, Meeker wrote Hayt, "They would listen to nothing I said, and since if they could drive me from one place they could drive me from another, I ordered the plows to run."

Price started plowing, but (in Meeker's words) "two Indians came out with guns and ordered him not to plow. . . . I directed the plowing to proceed . . . the plowman was fired upon from a small cluster of sage-brush, and the ball passed close to his person. They have had free rations so long," Meeker went on, "and have been flattered and petted so much, that they think themselves lords of all."

On September 10, Meeker confronted Johnson on the agency steps and told him in the heat of argument: "You have too many ponies. You had better kill some of them." A big man, though no longer young, Johnson lost his temper, picked Meeker up, and flung him against the hitching rail.

Meeker's telegram that day to the Bureau of Indian Affairs said I HAVE BEEN ASSAULTED BY A LEADING CHIEF . . . AND INJURED BADLY, BUT WAS RESCUED BY EMPLOYEES . . . LIFE OF SELF, FAMILY AND EMPLOYEES NOT SAFE . . . WANT PROTECTION IMMEDIATELY.

Fort Steele, twenty miles from Rawlings, Wyoming, and two hundred miles from the agency, was the nearest military post. On September 24, the Fort Steele commander, Major Thomas Tipton Thornburgh, set out at the head of three companies of cavalry (about 200 men) and a twenty-five-wagon supply train.

Five days later, the thirty-five-year-old West Pointer and his troops crossed Milk Creek, the northern boundary of the Ute lands, twenty-five miles from the agency. They rode right into an ambush. The Utes killed Thornburgh and 9 of his men and captured 43.

At the agency that Monday, September 29, a hint of October breathed down from the mountains. A new week had begun and there was much to do. The new storehouse for the winter harvest needed roofing. Coal for the winter had to be dug from the mines in the canyon. Forage for the milk herd had to be stored.

But that afternoon 25 armed Indians led by Johnson and another chief called Douglas surrounded the agency building and started firing. The women fled into the milk house and locked the door. Meeker and 7 others were killed, while Mrs. Meeker, Josie, and Mrs. Price were taken prisoner.

Allowed to go back into the house and get some things, Mrs. Meeker saw her husband stretched out on the floor with a bullet hole in his forehead. She bent to kiss him and then they pushed her outside. The Indians looted the agency buildings and burned them to cinders. Tying a chain around Meeker's neck, they dragged him behind a pony over the agency grounds. When they were finished, they jammed an oak barrel stave into his mouth, forever silencing the obstinate do-gooder whose disregard of Ute traditions and tactless insistence that he knew what was best for them had led to the massacre.

Drunken Utes carried off the women to Douglas's camp a few miles away, where they were kept for twenty-three days. Arvilla and Josie Meeker and Mrs. Price were treated as squaws belonging to the chiefs. As Josie later related in a deposition, Chief Pah-sone took her while the other squaws were in the tent. "A good many times," she said, "I pushed him off, and made a fuss, and raised a difficulty." But the other squaws gestured to her to comply, which would place her under Pah-sone's protection.

Arvilla Meeker was put "under the protection" of Douglas. She said in a statement: "It was made known to me that if I did not submit I would be killed or subjected to something of that kind . . . the women made all the motions of a fire and burning. Douglas I had connection with once, and no more, I was afraid he had disease." As for Mrs. Price, she was shared by Johnson and another chief, both of whom "outraged" her.

On October 21, the Utes gave up their captives to a special envoy from Secretary of the Interior Carl Schurz, General Charles Adams, who interrogated the women. At first, they were reluctant to talk. When Adams asked Josie how she had been treated, she said, "Well, better than expected." "Did you suffer any indignities?" he asked. "Oh no, Mr. Adams," she replied, "nothing of that kind."

It was not until she was examined by a woman doctor in Denver that Josie poured out what had happened. Perhaps she was too modest to discuss such matters with a man. Or perhaps, after three weeks of captivity, she had begun to adapt to and identify with her captors.

Mrs. Price, however, had no qualms about telling Adams that she had been raped by two Indians, and added: "I want the privilege of killing them myself."

But part of the deal for turning over the captives was that the authorities would arrest only Douglas, who spent some time in Leavenworth. In his report to Carl Schurz, Adams said: "I don't think Mr. Meeker understood these Indians. . . . He thought he could succeed in forcing them to accept the situation as farmers. . . . They told him that the other agents had tried it and failed and why should he attempt it? His answer, they said, was that he was a farmer and they were not."

The Meeker massacre was convenient to whip up Colorado public opinion for a "Utes Must Go" campaign. The objects of wrath were not only the White River Utes responsible for the killings, but the Southern and Uncompahgre bands as well—about 4,000 Indians in all. As the *Denver*

Times put it on October 15, 1879, "Either they or we must go. And we are not going."

Forces were soon at work to extinguish the Utes' title to Colorado lands. In January 1880, the House Committee on Indian Affairs held hearings on the "Ute Indian outbreak." And that June, Congress passed a bill removing the Utes to a reservation in Utah at the junction of the Green and Duchesne rivers.

In August 1881, the White River Utes left Colorado under military escort on a thirteen-day march along Indian trails to their new homes in Utah. About 1,400 Indians, driving their sheep and goats, their teepees rolled up on the backs of ponies, moved along the Yampa and over to the Green. In June 1882, the government opened the vacated Ute lands to settlement. Soon farms and ranches dotted the valleys and new communities sprang up all along the rivers.

One fine spring day in 1885, R. E. Arnett was out digging postholes on his ranch near Sterling, on the Platte River in northeast Colorado, when he looked up and saw smoke puffing out of the pipe of his dugout stove. Returning to the dugout, Arnett found dinner on the table, and a fine-looking stranger who said, "I thought I would come in and stay a few days, if that's all right with you."

"I'll be glad to have you, "Arnett said. "I don't see a man out here often." In those days, people left their doors unlocked and passing cowboys made themselves at home.

Over dinner, the stranger said, "I am headed for Canada. I have been bootlegging to the Indians and Uncle Sam is on my trail."

He'd been arrested, he said, and the sheriff had taken his six-guns but overlooked his pillbox (a small, four-barreled derringer). Although handcuffed and forced to ride a horse with a rope around his neck, he'd managed to work the derringer out of his shirt pocket. He moved his horse up even with the sheriff's, leaned over, stuck the derringer down the ear of the sheriff's horse, and fired. The horse fell, pinning the sheriff's leg. The prisoner jerked the rope away and rode off to find some friends who filed the handcuffs off and gave him a fresh mount. The sheriff rounded up a posse to chase him, but he got away.

He had once belonged to the Texas Rangers, Arnett's guest said, and had gone out on a posse himself that was hunting the outlaw Charlie Bass. The lawmen spread out in different directions, and he stopped at a spring to eat his lunch. He heard a noise down the trail, and when he looked up, he saw a man leading a horse that was walking on three legs. The man had two guns leveled at him and said, "I believe you are one of those damned Rangers. If I was sure, I'd kill you."

"No," he said, "I'm just looking for antelope."

"That looks like a good lunch," said the man with the lame horse, "and I'm going to help you eat it."

The man helped himself, and said: "That is a good-looking horse you have and he is shod. I have a good horse but he is tender-footed. When he gets a chance to rest his feet they will grow out and you will have a real horse."

When the Ranger got back to camp leading the lame horse, the captain asked, "Where did you get that old cripple?"

"Oh, I traded it with Charlie Bass," he said.

"Why didn't you arrest him?" asked the captain.

"I didn't like the looks of the guns he kept pointed at me," the Ranger said.

He quit the Rangers and got a claim of five hundred acres of the finest land that ever lay out of doors. And now Uncle Sam would get it.

After about ten days, the stranger said, "Well, I'll be moving toward Canada now. I have had a real rest and I will never forget your hospitality."

Arnett felt sorry to see him go. He was good company.

Bill Burt started out in the medicine-show business in 1888 with the Big Sensation Company. Throughout Iowa, Nebraska, and Colorado, Big Sensation sold a line of cure-alls from established firms, such as Hamlin's Wizard Oil. Burt belonged to the Lyceum Four, a quartet that wore Prince Albert frock coats, pin-striped trousers, wing collars, high silk hats, and pearl-gray spats over patent leather shoes. Between songs, they delivered the sales pitch, crying out "Just another bottle, doctor" as a refrain to be repeated by the crowd.

Big Sensation had twenty-eight people on the payroll, including a twelve-piece brass band. Everyone doubled "on canvas," pulling up the tents and so on. The large tent housed five hundred canvas chairs facing the stage; behind them rose a thousand circus seats or bleachers. Hung across the front of the small tent was a banner announcing THE KING OF THE FORCEPS. The king had a queen—she did the holding and he did the pulling. During the show, fifteen-minute intermissions were devoted to the extraction of teeth. Any aching molar was removed without charge and supposedly without pain. The horns blared and the drums banged to drown out the screams.

After the show, the tent went down and the Rock Island or the Colorado Central would have the Big Sensation in another state by the next day. In Thurman, Iowa, however, the King and Queen of the Forceps broke a man's jaw, and Big Sensation was held up until they settled.

Bill Burt left Big Sensation in 1890 for Shaker Remedies, a top-of-the-line outfit offering medicines compounded from formulas devised by the Shaker community in Lebanon, Pennsylvania. After four weeks each in Pueblo and Colorado Springs, they pitched their tent in Denver on an open lot.

Each miracle cure had its own "lecturer" and "qualified physician." One old hawker had a profound superstition about the first bottle sold—it had to be sold from the stage by him personally, or the efforts of his agents circulating through the audience would come to nothing.

He would look over the audience and describe in a stage whisper the exact person who would buy the first bottle. Then he told the story of the helpless infant or beloved parent who had passed away, adding, "I don't mean to say this remedy would have saved the poor unfortunate, but I will say that had a bottle been in the house it would have prolonged that life until the doctor arrived."

Then he pointed his finger at the chosen buyer and yelled, "And won't YOU give a dollar to save a life by buying this bottle?" In a flash, the crucial first bottle passed from the stage into the hands of the lucky buyer, and the agents fanned out while the audience was still warm.

At first, the entertainers sang psalms dressed in Shaker bonnets and brown one-piece Shaker gowns. But they failed to please on the open lots, so the company engaged other artists. No salary was too high for a performer who could hold the crowd. The lecturers kept up the Shaker window dressing, wearing their buttoned-to-the-neck frock coats and high-crowned bell-shaped hats, both in Shaker brown.

The qualified physicians assumed a starchy dignity. Their spiel brimmed with thee and thou, Brother and Sister, and exhortations for correct living and proper food. But on one occasion, a Punch-and-Judy show was finishing up when the qualified doctor came out and started his pitch, only to be interrupted by a squeaky voice that said, "Quit kidding, doc, they ain't your brothers and sisters."

Eventually, Bill Burt got tired of the medicine-show business, married a girl in Denver, and opened a hardware store.

Surveying had started in 1785 after the Land Ordinance marked out the seven Ohio ranges, and was still going on in the twentieth century in the Colorado Rockies. In 1902, H. A. Sumner headed a surveying party employed by the railroad west of Leadville, by then a mining district of two thousand claims with whimsical sobriquets like "Tingle Tangle," "Bank Statement," and "Dante's Inferno."

The surveyors worked at 10,000 feet, and as one of the men put it, "The altitude here is so high you don't find any bedbugs." So many things could go wrong in the mountains. Every line sight meant cutting down aspen and lodgepole pines, and more timber meant more axmen and thus more tents. The food intended for the surveyors was mistakenly sent to Boulder. Ask the men who opened the trails, slipped on damp rocks, and sprained their ankles, to go without.

It was bad enough hearing the coyotes howl at night or seeing the fresh tracks of a mountain lion in the snow. But you also had to make your contour maps accurately and get your reports in on time. And then headquarters sent you out a two-legged tripod. And now they were at the tunnel section. Twenty-eight tunnels in less than ten miles would have to be bored.

Contractors were interested in making bids until they came on site. "Why it's just impossible to get steam shovels onto the work site," they said. And at that elevation, all the new members of the party started gasping for breath.

In 1905, Sumner was in the mountains north of Leadville, surveying the Gore Canyon. Its ragged granite walls soared almost vertically to 3,000 feet. How could you survey an almost vertical canyon?

You had to adopt the rappelling techniques of mountain climbers and send men down the face of the cliff with ropes around them. A man was lowered to a certain point and then he drove sixteen-inch steel pins into the crevices. After that, they floated logs down the Gore River to the spot where the man had hammered in the pins. Men at the top of the cliff hoisted the logs with ropes to the level where the man with the pins was. He then fastened the log to the pins with a wire rope five-eighths of an inch in diameter.

Once he had fastened the log at both ends along the cliff wall, a man could stand on it and continue fixing logs to the wall until he had a foot bridge running horizontally along the cliff. The engineer was J. J. Argo, and the men on the cliff were known as "Argo's squirrels." One of them stepped out onto a log that slipped off a slackened wire and dropped a few hundred feet into the swiftly running river. He survived to tell the tale.

Surveying remained as hazardous as it had been in colonial times, and had its share of fatalities. E. A. Meredith, a workaholic in charge of the survey work in the Rockies, visited the Gore Canyon site in 1905 during the spring flood season, when the water was still icy cold. A gust of wind blew his hat into the river, and as he fished around for it with a stick, he fell in off the slippery rocks.

By the time the men pulled him out, he had caught pneumonia. They sent him to Denver in a caboose, but he died somewhere near Georgetown.

CHAPTER EIGHTEEN

THE DAKOTA FRONTIER

Here was a wide open and unskimmed country where a
man could hew his own line and not suffer for his
independence. . . . There was something remote and clean
and active in the prairie wind and the flat country leaning
westward.

WALLACE STEGNER

O n the prairie, the Missouri River served as the crooked axis of
settlement, forming the border between Iowa and Nebraska, then
running across the Dakotas into Montana. Along this winding

The Taft Museum, Cincinnati, Ohio
In 1881, the painter Henry Farny visited Fort Yates in Dakota
Territory, on the Missouri River, where he observed the Indian
Long Day listening at a telegraph pole so that he could tell his
fellow Indians that he had heard spirit voices over the wires. This
would, he hoped, make him eligible to become a medicine man.
Long Day borrowed the white man's technology to maintain the
continuity of his own culture, but in Farny's painting he is listening
forlornly to the sound of his own demise.

avenue of empire, whoever arrived first had the edge—provided he had the brains to figure out the way things worked.

In the 1850s, the unsettled area between Nebraska and Canada was dotted with forts and trading posts. In 1855, an army captain stationed at Fort Randall, on the Missouri at the Nebraska line, resigned his commission. His name was John Blair Smith Todd, and he was a classic example of the "phase capitalist," who understood the different stages of economic opportunity in a new wilderness region.

Captain Todd left the army to form a trading company with a fellow officer from St. Louis, Colonel Daniel Marsh Frost. Their main office was in Sioux City, Iowa, but in 1857 they built a small post fifty miles up the Missouri, at today's Yankton, South Dakota.

In the course of trading with the Indians, John Todd became involved in government negotiations to obtain Indian land cessions. The government wanted a big triangle of land in the southeast corner of South Dakota, between the Big Sioux and Missouri rivers. But the Yankton Sioux, who owned the land, refused all offers.

Spurred by the recent townsite booms in Iowa and Nebraska, the enterprising Todd offered a helping hand. With the assistance of squaw men who had some influence in the tribes, he arranged the cession of 14 million acres at a cost of 12 cents an acre.

The treaty was signed in 1858, when Todd brought the principal Yankton chiefs to Washington. As a reward, Todd & Frost were given options to buy land at a low price, and they formed the Upper Missouri Land Company. The trading company and the land company worked hand in hand. Licensed traders picked sites for trading posts where they knew towns were likely to rise, thus situating themselves in the best locations before the area opened to settlement.

By the time Congress ratified the Yankton cession, in February 1859, the land company had already occupied eight townsites, including Yankton, Vermillion (twenty miles downriver from Yankton), Elk Point (ten miles from Sioux City), and Smutty Bear's Bottom, which no longer exists.

In 1859, two thousand Sioux remained in Yankton, showing no inclination to move. When their treaty goods arrived by steamboat that July, the Indian agent, A. H. Redfield, told the tribe that the goods would be distributed at the reservation site. The Indians broke camp and started up the Fort Randall military road to their new home. Shortly afterward, the Upper Missouri Land Company took possession of Yankton.

The next step was attracting settlers. Todd & Frost marked off town lots and penned brochures that described the Dakota winter as "exceedingly pleasant" and told of two-hundred-pound Missouri River catfish.

But Dakota's anomalous position in the territorial quilt posed an obstacle to settlement. For half a century, Dakota had existed only as the outlying region of other territories, belonging in turn to Michigan, Iowa, Wisconsin, and finally Minnesota. When Minnesota gained statehood in 1858, Dakota fell into limbo, unattached and devoid of status. Lacking a government, Dakota urgently required territorial organization, especially now that land companies were establishing townsites. But when Dakota settlers petitioned Congress in 1858, north and south were too busy digging "the bloody chasm."

At that time of no government, Dakota had three settlements worthy of the name: Yankton, a bunch of shacks in the treeless prairie, bisected by a muddy track grandly called Broadway; Sioux Falls, founded by the Dakota Land Company, which consisted of a little stone house with a hand press that turned out a weekly called the *Dakota Democrat*—it printed a number of appeals to those unfortunate enough to still be living outside the Dakota limits, who were invited to hasten at once to that favored land where the earth needed only to be "tickled with a hoe to laugh with a harvest"; and Pembina, in the northeast corner of today's North Dakota, on the Red River just south of the 49th parallel (the border with Canada), a customs port and fur-trading center, most of whose inhabitants were French Catholic half-breeds.

All three outposts were waiting for the boom that would send settlers swarming in, and all three sent petitions to Washington asking for congressional action to organize Dakota as a territory; the Pembina petition was written in French.

In 1861, Captain Todd went to Washington and circulated a petition for territorial recognition to help break the logjam in Congress. It didn't hurt that he was Mary Todd Lincoln's cousin. Two days before Lincoln's March 4 inauguration, Congress passed a bill granting territorial status to Nevada, Colorado, and Dakota. Once again, the departure of southern legislators had made it possible for Congress to ignore the question of whether those territories should or should not permit slavery. The bill was signed on March 3 by President Buchanan, who gave up the Oval Office to Lincoln the next day.

When William Jayne, Lincoln's friend and family doctor from Springfield, arrived in Yankton as governor on May 26, Dakota's territorial period began. It would last for twenty-eight years. The territory, including North and South Dakota, as well as most of Wyoming and Montana, had a white population of 2,401 in the first census.

Yankton, known as "Captain Todd's town," became the territorial capital of what was still mostly wilderness. During its sixty-day first session in March 1862, people dubbed the territorial legislature "the Pony Congress," because of the long treks on horseback members of distant counties had to make to attend.

Among the laws passed in March were a number of divorce bills for the legislators' friends. The business only took as long as the time required to read letters from the plaintiffs. In one epistle, a wife called her husband "no better than a wooden man." Among other laws enacted, one barred Indians from leaving the reservation without the written permission of an Indian agent—which later contributed to the Sioux uprisings.

Yankton had not been designated the territorial capital for sentimental reasons. Its leading citizens knew that funds for territorial expenses, ear-marked by Congress, would flow into the capital, and that they would help disburse such monies. In Yankton's case, the funds included (by 1872) $60,000 a year for the courts, $70,000 for surveys, $20,000 for the legislature, and $15,000 for federal salaries, plus the cost of post offices and other public buildings, troop supplies, and annuities for 30,000 Indians.

Thus, the territorial mentality became a colonial satrap's mentality. The men who had organized the land companies now sought territorial offices so that they could tap into federal funds. Their interest naturally lay in maintaining the territorial status quo rather than in pressing for statehood.

With Yankton as the capital, many political plums fell into the waiting hands of its leading citizens. When Congress appropriated funds for a road from Sioux City to Yankton, territorial officials, who were also the local businessmen, cheered.

In spite of all this finagling, or perhaps because of it, Yankton stagnated. It was less a capital than a campsite for traders, trappers, and land agents. There it sat, in the middle of gently rolling country covered by a thick sod of tall plains grass. The Ash Hotel was notable for its dirt floors, its blanket partitions, and its bed sharing.

After the 1862 Homestead Act, Dakota lost out in the contest for settlers because it was last in line, with the least to offer. Dakota's eastern and southern neighbors—Minnesota, Iowa, and Nebraska—spread unattractive rumors about their rival. The Minnesota newspapers ran headlines such as these:

ANOTHER SURVIVOR
OF PLAGUE–STRICKEN DAKOTA
REACHES TOWN

or

POOR DAKOTA CRIPPLE
LOSES BOTH LEGS AND AN ARM
DURING WINTER STORM

The negative advertising went something like this: "Why, Dakota's no place for a white man. It's drought in the summer and blizzards in the winter. And if you get a good crop, the grasshoppers will get to it before you will. And if the grasshoppers don't get you the Indians will. No one in Dakota dies a natural death."

In 1862, when Frank Trumbo was eleven, his parents left Nebraska and settled in Vermillion, where the first Dakota land office opened on July 16. A thousand Sioux had set up camp in the willows near the town, which had a population of 150. That August, news came of a massacre in Minnesota, and more settlers arrived, fleeing for their lives.

Frank's parents died two years later. He went to work in a store in town to earn enough money to buy cornmeal, the staple diet of his eight younger brothers and sisters. They were lucky, thought Frank, that the water they mixed with the meal to make bread was free.

Later he married and took a homestead. Then the grasshoppers attacked and left his fields as barren as though they had been swept by flames. They even ate the binder twine on sheaves of grain, and they chewed the wooden handles on the pitchforks and stripped the bark off the 1,500 cottonwoods Frank and his wife had planted that spring.

When his wife began to cry, Frank said, "What are you crying about, you ought to be thankful they left us the barbed wire fence and the mortgage." When the insects took a sabbatical, drought, hog cholera, and low prices for farm products took their place. Finally, Frank had enough and sold the farm.

In 1862, the rush of prospectors to the gold mines of Montana and Idaho led Congress to authorize armed escorts for emigrant trains. In 1864, Captain James Liberty Fisk commanded a train of one hundred wagons traveling from St. Paul to Virginia City, Montana (forty miles southwest of today's Bozeman).

Fisk had a troop of fifty men, including a cavalry detachment and a mountain howitzer, to guard 165 emigrants. One of the pioneers was John Larned, who had invested $15,000 in a stock of hardware to sell the miners, and his son, Horatio.

They started out on July 15 and by mid-August had reached Fort Rice on the Missouri, twenty miles south of Bismarck in today's North Dakota. There Fisk departed from the trail to blaze his own way to the mines, saying that he had no fear of the Indians, a bit of bravado that made the emigrants shake their heads in dismay.

On September 3, about 160 miles west of Fort Rice, they were passing through a valley's deep ravines in pouring rain when they were attacked by a band of Dakota Sioux. Seven men lost their lives. The Indians made off with two headquarters wagons, one containing several Springfield rifles with 5,000 rounds of ammunition, and the other carrying kegs of whiskey.

Jefferson Dilts, the scout, rode to the upper part of the gulch to strike the Indians on their flank. They later found him with three arrows in his body, surrounded by six dead Indians. The next day they started up again, expecting another assault, and it came. Drunken Indians shook their rifles in the gullies and ridges, smoking cigars thy had found in the whiskey wagon. Fisk used the twelve-pounder to clear the way, loading it with spherical case shot.

On September 5, as the number of pursuing Indians increased, Fisk decided to stop and make a stand. Soldiers and emigrants formed a semicircle of wagons before a shallow ridge. A band of Indians perched on a hill a third of a mile away fired into the camp. A party of soldiers attacked and took the hill, leaving on it a guard of ten men, including Horatio Larned.

Fifteen volunteers were dispatched to Fort Rice for reinforcements. While they waited for relief, several hundred Indians gathered on the hills. One morning a brave descended with arms outstretched, holding a stick in one hand, which he plunged into the ground. Then he beckoned for someone from the parapet of wagons to join him and sat down.

Lieutenant Mitchell ventured out, and Indian and white man shook hands, and a pipe was lit. From the cleft of the stick, Mitchell took a letter written by Mrs. Fanny Kelly, who had been captured by the Dakotas on July 12. "They say for soldiers to give 40 head of cattle," Mrs. Kelly had written with the point of a bullet. "They say they will not fight, but don't trust them. . . . Give them nothing till you can see me for yourself."

Fisk could not give the Indians forty oxen, a loss that would have left him stranded. But he offered his best saddle horse and a team hitched to a wagon loaded with presents. The Indians refused. They said that by ransoming Mrs. Kelly at the fort they could obtain enough provisions to last the winter.

On the fourteenth day, just when Fisk had decided to move on, a soldier looking through his field glasses saw in the distance ten men with blue overcoats. It was the relief column. Protected by the reinforcements, the wagon train returned to Fort Rice, at that time garrisoned by Confederate prisoners of war who had been released from northern prison camps on condition they serve on the frontier. While refusing to take up arms against the Confederacy, they had no objections to fighting Indians.

Horatio Larned later got a job as an Indian trader and stockman. In 1866, he bought a hundred head of cattle in Sioux City, Iowa, which he had to escort through hostile Indian territory, to Fort Rice, 480 miles away. At Fort Sully, twenty-eight miles north of Pierre, South Dakota, Larned visited the Indian camp with presents and spent the night as the guest of Chief Porcupine.

Larned hired Porcupine and an Indian escort to help him take the cattle to Fort Rice, figuring that Porcupine would provide protection from other Indians. During the trip, Porcupine told Larned how three winters before he had fought some white men in wagons at the edge of the Badlands. The whites had piled up some earth in front of the wagons so the Indians could not get at them. Porcupine said he had ordered a white woman they held prisoner to make a talking paper that he tied around a stick and took close to the white camp, planting the stick in the ground.

"And all you had on," Horatio interjected, "was a feather in your hair, a belt breech clout, and some moccasins . . . and moreover, I saved your life at the time."

How was that? Porcupine asked.

"One of the men in the little fort at the top of the hill was mad at you because your people had killed his brother, and he had his rifle cocked and sighted when you were putting that stick in the ground, but I took it away from him."

Porcupine put his hand over his mouth the way Indians do when they are astonished, but said nothing.

A few days later, Porcupine asked Larned for his rifle to go hunting. Larned let him have it, but when Porcupine didn't return, he wondered if the chief had absconded with his weapon. At sunset, Porcupine came in with an antelope slung over his shoulders. They reached Fort Rice with every animal accounted for. Major Galpin told Horatio that having Porcupine along was as good as an insurance policy.

Pleased with his presents, which included a handsome shirt, Porcupine took the steamboat home. When Horatio saw him off, the chief said: "I did the best I could. There is no split in my tongue."

Two years later, in 1868, Horatio Larned was in charge of the trading post at Fort Berthold, a North Dakota reservation for 3,000 Mandans, Arikaras, and Hidatsas. A party of Indians came in to trade buffalo hides. One of them, Drag-the-Stone, spotted Horatio and went up to him, smiling and leaning his elbows on the counter.

"I was going to kill you once," he said, "when you had those cattle on Blue Blanket Creek. We were going to wipe you out, but Porcupine came out to see us and said he had promised to get the cattle to Fort Rice and he would do it or die."

The next time Horatio saw Porcupine, he mentioned Drag-the-Stone, and Porcupine said: "You saved my life once and I did not know it." Then he laid his long forefingers side by side. "That is the way we are now," he said.

The friendship between a red man and a white man was repeated on a larger scale with the government's shift to a peace policy in 1868 after a period of intermittent Indian warfare. At the treaty of Fort Laramie in April, the Sioux, Cheyennes, and Arapahos agreed to move to a reservation west of the Missouri River that was in effect the western half of today's South Dakota. In counterpart, the government recognized the country in northern Wyoming as "unceded Indian territory" on which no whites could settle.

Before the railroads, Dakota settlements were far apart, the only roads prairie trails, the typical town a one-street Nowheresville with a general store, a feed barn, a post office, and a row of hitching posts. Statehood depended on population growth, and a growing population depended on railroads. But by 1870, not a single line of track had reached the meager 14,181 white inhabitants of Dakota, even though it had been a territory for nine years.

It was not until 1873 that the Dakota Southern from Sioux City to Yankton became the first railroad to enter the southern part of Dakota Territory. Puffing into Yankton came that harbinger of better times, the steam locomotive.

The railroads not only made Dakota, but created an alliance between territorial officials and railroad promoters. For if a train came through a town, that town's fortune was made. Soon the railroads had lobbyists in Yankton during the Assembly sessions, able to bribe the entire territorial legislature into doing their bidding.

Dakota's greatest asset was the Northern Pacific, which went from Duluth, Minnesota, to Tacoma, Washington. In 1869, the Philadelphia investment banker Jay Cooke had raised $4 million to get construction for the line under way. Workers broke ground near Duluth in March 1870, while the western end got started at Kalama on the Columbia River, thirty miles north of Portland.

By 1871, the road was open on a straight line across Minnesota to Fargo, North Dakota, where the Northern Pacific crossed the Red River. After Pembina, that made Fargo the nucleus of settlers in North Dakota. The first settlers were known as the "end-of-the-track gang," because they pushed just ahead of track construction in search of locations to put up their tents. Their settlement was called "Fargo on the Prairie," while the area where the saloons and dance halls were got the name "Fargo in the Timber."

When H. E. Crofford and his wife came to Fargo in April 1871, men were still building the Northern Pacific bridge, so the couple crossed the Red in a small flatboat. To them, the growing track looked like a black thread running west to the horizon. The grass that year shot up two feet high, and the prairie chickens were so plentiful that when the Croffords came home from a drive they found their wagon wheels dripping with egg yolk. Swarms of grasshoppers ate the sides off their tent and then they chewed the linen coat off Mr. Crofford's back while he was mowing. It was a regular nightmare. They couldn't keep the grasshoppers out of their tent or their bed.

The Croffords started a hotel, and soon Fargo had a general store, a harness shop, and two or three saloons. As soon as the bridge was completed and goods could be shipped to market, everyone started building and planting. The railroad gave Fargo its heartbeat. J. B. Chapin, a saloonkeeper, bought a tract of several hundred acres and raised a bumper crop of "Number One Hard"—no one back then said "wheat." The valley became known as the granary of the world.

By June 1873, construction of the Northern Pacific had been finished up to Bismarck. But the company's bond sales were falling while building expenses rose. The cost of buying up competing outfits such as the St. Paul & Pacific and the Oregon Steam Navigation Company added millions to the deficit. The problem with railroads was that until they completed the track no money came in. In 1873, Cooke floated $9 million worth of bonds, but sold only $2 million worth, a discrepancy that sank Jay Cooke & Company and put the Northern Pacific into receivership with 555 miles of road completed. Construction stopped at Bismarck on the east bank of the Missouri.

•   •

There came a time when the Plains Indians could no longer retreat. The Pacific northwest was settled. All that remained for them was the Great Plains and the Rockies, and the white man was in both places. The census results turned out to be the Indians' worst enemy. In 1870, the white population of the United States was 38 million. The Sioux could fight the visible enemy, the soldiers and settlers, but not the invisible enemy—the forces of expansion originating in the east, like railroad bonds and immigrants off the ship.

In 1868, the Fort Laramie Treaty had given the Sioux half of today's South Dakota. Their portion included the Black Hills, which were actually mountains 5,000 to 6,000 feet high, with dramatic rock formations rising out of the middle of the prairie, creased by shadowy ravines, cooled by the shade of pine trees, and watered by innumerable streams. Known to the Indians as Pah Sappa, the Black Hills were ringed by "hog-backs," steep narrow ridges like the walls of a fortress. The narrow canyons that the rivers had cut offered the only way in. If there was one place on the continent where settlement would never take hold, this seemed to be it.

The rumor spread, however, that the Black Hills were gold hills, and in January 1873 the Dakota Legislative Assembly asked Congress to fund a scientific exploration there.

The Black Hills also came to the notice of Lieutenant General Philip Sheridan. A famed Civil War cavalry officer, "Little Phil" commanded the Military Division of Missouri, a jurisdiction that included Dakota Territory. Caustic and unyielding, Sheridan was credited with the remark, "The only good Indian is a dead Indian."

In 1874, Sheridan decided to build a post at the foot of the Black Hills, "to better control the Indians making raids toward the south." He ignored the fact that in doing so he would be violating the Fort Laramie Treaty, which stipulated that no white man should "pass over, settle upon, or reside" on land set aside for the Indians.

In the summer of 1874, Sheridan sent Lieutenant Colonel George Armstrong Custer on a reconnaissance of the Black Hills under a treaty provision that authorized agents of the government to enter the reservation. One of Custer's instructions was to report on the mineral wealth of the area, where gold had been found by Indians as well as whites.

On July 2, Custer left his headquarters at Fort Abraham Lincoln, across the river from Bismarck, at the head of ten companies of cavalry, two companies of infantry, 61 Indian scouts, three Gatling guns, an artillery piece, and a hundred wagons pulled by six-mule teams. He also brought along a number of civilian auxiliaries, among them a botanist, a geologist, a zoologist, a paleontologist, and two gold miners. He led about 1,200 men in all, including musical accompaniment from the 7th Cavalry band, which consisted of 16 men on white horses playing "The Girl I Left Behind Me."

With guidon pennants flying, they proceeded southwest over alkali flats, churning dust as they went. The thermometer stood at 101, and there was no shade. Custer drove his men thirty miles a day; he measured the distance by using an odometer strapped to the wheel of a cart to count the revolutions, which were converted into miles.

Theodore Ewert, the bugler for Company H, rode his gray horse Monkey and played "Boot and Saddle" and "Stand to Horse." Now twenty-eight, he had been in the cavalry since the age of fourteen, and was still a private. In the journal he kept, he maintained the aggrieved disposition of the "grunt" who feels a healthy contempt for his officers.

All Custer wanted, Ewert wrote, was "more fresh laurels." What did he care about "the hardships and dangers to his men" and "the probable loss of life"? Why, he used the hospital tent for his dining room. When Private Cunningham got so sick that he fell off his horse, the three expedition doctors were too drunk to help, and Cunningham died "through the neglect of men claiming to be doctors . . . who only managed to drink the brandy [kept] for the use of sick soldiers."

They trudged along the eastern borders of Montana and Wyoming and on July 13 crossed cactus-covered flats, a misery for the horses, said Ewert. Cactus needles pierced their fetlocks and the trail was spotted with their blood.

On July 30, they reached the Black Hills. The miners went to work, looking for veins of gold-bearing quartz and probing the creek beds. The soldiers joined in, prospecting with tent pins and pothooks. By the first of August, the miner Horatio Ross had collected enough gold dust to fill a small bottle.

Custer wrote a dispatch saying that "gold has been found in paying quantities. I have upon my table forty or fifty small particles of pure gold, in size averaging that of a small pinhead, and most of it obtained today from one panfull of earth." Cautiously, he concluded: "Until further examination is made regarding the richness of the gold, no opinion should be formed."

Custer's scout, Lonesome Charley Reynolds, sped across the prairie to send the dispatch from the nearest telegraph station, at Fort Laramie, arriving there on August 8. On August 13, he galloped into Sioux City, Iowa, where the reporters got hold of him. That resulted in headlines such as this one in the Yankton newspaper:

STRUCK IT AT LAST!
RICH MINES OF GOLD AND SILVER
REPORTED FOUND BY CUSTER

On August 30, Custer led his men back into Fort Lincoln, his long hair flying. "He wanted to be first," wrote Private Ewert. "Here I am! . . . I have discovered gold! I am a big chief! . . . Here is George Armstrong ready to have his noble brow entwined by laurels!"

By the time Custer was back from the 1,205-mile round-trip expedition, Dakota had contracted a bad case of gold fever. When prospectors started scrambling to the Black Hills, the army kept them at bay. On September 3, 1874, General Sheridan ordered General Alfred Terry, who commanded the Department of Dakota, "to use the forces at your command to burn the wagons, destroy the outfits, and arrest the leaders" of parties trespassing in the Black Hills.

In fact, most of those caught were simply escorted off the reservation. That was not a very effective deterrent. In 1875, hundreds of miners invaded the Black Hills, hoping to avoid the army and the Indians. John E. Maxwell wrote the *Faribault* (Minnesota) *Republican* on April 7, 1875: "At Yankton you can get off the [railway] cars and get into a boat or a wagon and in a few days you are in a region where there is gold. . . . The only reason why these hills are not now already occupied . . . is in order to gratify the whim of a few miserable savages, who ask that this beautiful country may remain idle . . . and who cost the country immense sums for their annual support."

By October 1875, an estimated three hundred miners were laboring in the hills. One of them, Charles H. Jacobs, observed on October 20: "Once in a while a party is caught and brought back, but each report of rich diggings found there raises two or three more parties, who will risk almost anything for the sake of securing a good claim."

In November, Jacobs was in the mining camp of Custer City. He had come through with some wagons to the Spotted Tail Indian Agency and then walked ninety miles, eluding the soldiers by traveling at night off the road. On Iron Creek he found forty men at work, each taking out two to eight dollars a day. The gold was there if you wanted to work for it. "Those coming here expecting to find it sitting around in bags labeled with their names on it," noted Jacobs, "or nuggets chasing them around begging to be picked up, generally go right back."

Philip Wells was the son of a Minnesota trader who had married a Sioux woman. As a boy, he went to the Black Hills with his father, who was killed by a band of Sioux. Philip was captured and spent several years with the tribe, coming to know the area well. Upon his release, he became a hay contractor at the Standing Rock Reservation.

In 1857, a company of men asked Wells to take them to the Black Hills, offering him $150 a month for two months. "They want a man who can evade the Indians and the soldiers," a friend warned, but the money was too good to pass up.

Near Kadoka, east of the Badlands, Wells saw a dapple-gray horse off the trail. A loose horse on the plains belonged to whoever could catch it, but Wells's packhorse was too slow for the chase. Besides, Wells noticed that the horse had trouble turning its head. Sensing something wrong, he slackened his pace.

But one of the other men in the party dashed after the dapple-gray. A shot rang out and he fell dead to the ground. A second man behind him was also hit and dropped down, mortally wounded. An Indian who had been hiding in the tall grass, holding the horse by a lariat around its neck, jumped on the decoy and raced off.

When Wells reconnoitered, he caught sight of some soldiers and realized that news of his group's movement had been carried up the Missouri by steamboat and that the cavalry was looking for them. The men hid in the valley of the White River until the soldiers had left, but Indians raided their camp and stole their horses. They had to continue on foot eighty miles to Rapid City.

Needing a stake to buy supplies and having only two dollars among them, the men gave the money to Wells so that he could join a poker game in one of the shacks. After he had won seven dollars, his backers punched him in the arm so he would leave the game and they could get something to eat. But Wells was on a roll and stayed in the game, drawing a full house kings high. Another player drew only one card, and when he flipped it over, he acted highly pleased. But Wells knew that only a full aces high or four of a kind could beat his kings.

So Wells bet every cent he had and the other man raised him by his last twenty. Wells had run out of cash himself and could not call the raise, but didn't want to give up a winning hand. So he said, "I can send you back for your buckskin sack" (of gold dust), "but I will call you." He put his cards down and slowly reached into his pocket as though getting his wallet. The man who had raised him sprang up cursing and slammed his full house tens high on the table while Wells raked in the pot. He had won forty dollars, and his boys pulled him away from the game.

As miners formed camps in the Black Hills, the government made efforts to buy the region from the Sioux. In September 1875, commissioners went to the Red Cloud Agency on the White River, just over the Nebraska line, to negotiate. Sitting Bull and Crazy Horse refused to attend, but on September 20 the commissioners sat in council with Red Cloud, the spokesman for the Teton Sioux, and other chiefs.

The mood of the council was contentious. One chief complained about short beef rations. "No doubt," he said, "each steer was weighed twice and called two." Another objected to calling the United States "Our Great Father." "I never called anybody Our Great Father but God," he said. The missionaries had provided him with a defense against federal paternalism.

Red Cloud said he wanted enough money for the Black Hills to feed several generations of his people. The commissioners proposed $6 million but the talks were inconclusive. In their report, the spurned commissioners said that if the Indians continued to refuse, "the government should withhold all supplies not required by the treaty of 1868," an agreement that guaranteed rations for four years only.

After the failed September council, President Grant indicated to the secretary of war, W. W. Belknap, that Dakota prospectors should be given the green light. General William Tecumseh Sherman, commanding general of the army, wrote that if miners streamed into the Black Hills, "I understand that the president and the Interior Department will wink at it."

A crisis started to brew: In the fall of 1875, bands of disgruntled Sioux left their reservations to go buffalo hunting in the "unceded Indian territory" in northern Wyoming and Montana. Hostile Sioux under Sitting Bull began roaming in the Powder River country.

The Bureau of Indian Affairs sent couriers who ordered the wandering Sioux to report to their agencies by January 31, 1876. The government expected the Indians to travel two hundred miles in the dead of winter over frozen ground, without grass for their ponies or food for themselves.

When the Sioux missed the deadline, Secretary of the Interior Zachariah Chandler turned the matter over to Secretary of War Belknap "for such action as you may deem proper." Two days later Belknap replied that he was taking immediate measures "to compel the Indians to remain upon their reservations."

General Sheridan mounted an operation into the "unceded Indian territory" in March 1876 to trap the disobedient bands. The operation lasted through June and led to a number of engagements in Montana Territory. Everyone knows the legendary climax: the battle of Little Bighorn. And everyone knows the story: Custer divided his troops; the Indians outnumbered and surrounded him; the flamboyant general and 269 of his officers and men were killed.

Custer's defeat shocked the nation. Public opinion ran strongly against the Sioux, whose refusal to return to their reservations seemed to pose a threat to white society. But though the Indians could win a battle, they were not organized to conduct long-range warfare. They had no commercial or industrial base, no source of food and forage to keep an army in the field, and depended on the enemy for their weapons and ammunition. The bands broke up and carried on the struggle in raids and skirmishes.

In August 1876, Congress amended the Fort Laramie Treaty of 1868, giving the Sioux a choice between ceding the Black Hills or having their rations cut off. It was sign or starve, and in 1877 the Sioux signed a new treaty, under which they relocated to reservations in Indian Territory.

Disdaining to sign, Sitting Bull feared that if he surrendered he would be killed, and wondered where he and his people could turn. "We have two ways to go," he said. "The land of the Grandmother, or the land of the Spaniard." The former was only a couple of hundred miles away, and in May 1877 he sought asylum in Canada with 1,000 of his people.

The Canadians would not permit American soldiers to cross the border and capture Sitting Bull. But neither would they give the Sioux a reservation or supply them with rations on a regular basis. Though the Indians were free, and had no agent to obey, they had no food, and Canada was even colder than Dakota. In the spring, when the Sioux hunted buffalo, they had to compete for dwindling herds with Canadian tribes.

In 1880, Sitting Bull's people began to drift back into the United

States and surrender at Indian agencies. They turned in their guns and added their names to the rolls at Rosebud, Pine Ridge, and Standing Rock. The three reservations were home to about 14,000 humbled Sioux.

Sitting Bull held out until July 19, 1881, when he surrendered at Fort Buford on the upper Missouri at the border of Montana and North Dakota. He brought with him the remnants of the Great Sioux Confederacy—200 ragged and emaciated Indians. For two years, he was interned at Fort Randall, on the Dakota-Nebraska line, as a prisoner of war. In May 1883, the army sent him to the Standing Rock Reservation.

The villains in all this were not Sitting Bull or George Armstrong Custer, but the settlers and their relentless takeover of places "the Indians don't need."

In July 1878, T. E. Cooper was driving the Episcopal minister R. R. Goudy to an appointment in southern Minnesota, and the talk turned to the failure of the wheat crop that year. Cooper was all but wiped out. "I should think," Goudy said, "that a man like you, sir, who have met with reverses here, would push out into northern Dakota, as it is the most promising place within the limits of the United States for men to acquire an independence."

"No Dakota for me," Cooper said. "I crossed the entire territory, from east to west, with an ox team in 1864, in a train of 123 wagons drawn by 246 pairs of oxen in pursuit of the precious metal in the Rocky Mountains, and I am free to say that I would not give the shadow of a lamb's tail for all the Dakota dirt we passed over. Oh! no, Mr. Goudy, I could never think of going to Dakota to make a home."

"Well, sir," Goudy replied, "I have been out there on three occasions, and you would be surprised to see the push and enterprise that is going on along the line of the Northern Pacific Railway. You must remember that it is 14 years since you crossed those plains. Lands are going to be valuable out their right soon, and five years from now they'll be worth as much as these farms we are now passing."

Letting Goudy convince him, Cooper pulled up anchor from the old Minnesota moorings where he'd been for twenty years. He left in August 1878, taking a two-horse hack the ten miles from Fisher, Minnesota, to Grand Forks, North Dakota, and crossing the "Raging Red" in a little ferryboat. Grand Forks was then a hamlet of 200. Cooper was pursued by four or five real estate people, who tried to get him to go and look at "splendid locations."

Cooper drove to his claim near Manvel, about fifteen miles north of Grand Forks, taking the old Fargo and Winnipeg stage road across the Turtle River. While looking for a spot to build his home, he put up with Mr. McKinzie, who told him, "I believe you understand prairie land. Look around for a few days."

Cooper did look around, sold his Manvel claim, went north to an area east of Park River, and located on a spot he called Grafton, for he planned to plant a nursery and work at grafting fruit trees. He also became postmaster. His salary was 70 percent of the sales on stamps.

Linda Slaughter, the wife of the post surgeon at Fort Rice, which was twenty miles south of Bismarck, saw it all—Little Bighorn, where the victors became the vanquished, for Sitting Bull's triumph sealed the doom of the Sioux nation and they were all turned into blanket Indians.

After Little Bighorn, the army built Fort Yates on the Standing Rock Reservation to keep the Indians in check. In 1880, Father Stephen was named Indian agent. Part of his job was to provide government beef to the Indians. But his employees, in cahoots with the beef contractors, weighted the scales to cheat the government. Holes were drilled in the scales and filled with molten lead, thereby increasing the weight of the beef, as well as the profits of the contractors. The drilling was done in a blacksmith shop in Bismarck, and the weights were carried to Fort Yates by an employee of the Indian agency.

Linda Slaughter by then was teaching elementary school in Bismarck, and the daughter of one of the Indian agency employees was one of her favorite pupils. One day the little girl came to school in tears, saying that her father had fled into the Black Hills. The authorities were looking for him because he knew the name of the blacksmith who had bored the crooked weights.

It chanced that about that time the commander at Fort Yates came to visit Linda and her husband the major and expressed his disappointment that the detective he had hired could not find out who had fixed the weights.

"Why I know who did it," Linda blurted out, and told him the blacksmith's name, without thinking that the man's wife was her friend.

Worrying whether she had done the right thing, she sought advice from her old friend Colonel Sweet, a lawyer for the beef contractors. "The husband of a friend of mine," she said, "has been detected in a crime against the government and will soon be arrested. Would it be wrong of me to go and tell his wife about it?"

"Why certainly," Sweet said, "that would be assisting a criminal to escape justice."

"In that case," said Linda, "I won't tell Mrs. Oliver that her husband has been found out in the bored weight case at Standing Rock."

Colonel Sweet almost fell off his chair. That night Oliver and his wife were on their way to Canada.

Thomas Riggs, a Protestant missionary at the Cheyenne River Agency, accompanied a band of Dakota Indians on their last buffalo hunt in the winter of 1880–81. Their circumstances had turned the Indians into hunters of tongues and hides, wasters of resources, and the herds were disappearing. White sportsmen helped to hasten the decline, thanks to the breech-loading rifle. And of course there was the phenomenal stupidity of the animal itself.

In December, sixty Indians, all veterans of the battle of Little Bighorn, assembled at the town of Bear Creek with forty women and a few children. Several inches of snow covered the ground. They headed west along the Moreau River and, not far from the Slim Buttes, saw the first buffalo. Two scouts sallied out the next morning, after taking an oath of office by placing the palms of their hands down flat on the ground. Each scout rode his second-best horse, saving his buffalo runner for the hunt.

Riggs asked Chief Touch-the-Cloud what the scouts would do if they saw no buffalo. "If they have nothing to tell," he said, "they will not come back until after dark. Even the dogs of their own tents will not know when they return."

When the scouts returned before sunset, the camp went wild. Riggs saw them appear from opposite directions on a ridge a mile from the camp. The chiefs gathered facing west, brushed the snow from the ground in front of them, and knelt on one knee. Lighting a pipe, the tribal crier handed it to the scouts as they jumped from their horses.

"You who are no longer children," the crier said, "tell me if you have seen anything of prowling dog [wolf], or flying bird [buzzard] or feeding animal [buffalo]. Tell me truly and make me glad." When the scouts said they had seen buffalo, the whole camp shouted, "Ha-i, ha-i." Then the crier asked for more details: "And beyond that . . . and beyond that."

The next morning, December 24, was gray and cold; the hunters went out with blackened faces in deep snow. They soon spotted the buffalo, but the herd was small. The Indians said they were tired of venison and porcupine and badger and longed for the meat of former days. Some of them were sitting astride the horses they had ridden against Custer.

Suddenly, they shot off as if in a race, the ropes knotted around their belts tied to the bridle to keep them from losing their horses in a fall. Riggs's horse caromed off the other horses, and his heavy Remington was in his way. At the head of the valley, they saw the herd. The startled buffalo made little upward tail movements as they broke into a lumbering gallop.

The hunters came to the edge of a steep-sided, flat-bottomed stream and watched as the buffalo climbed out on the opposite side, trying to escape. A sheet of ice under the snow brought down about twenty horses, and the others had to help them out.

The Indians in the lead began to fire. They carried bullets in their mouths and poured the powder by guesswork from their horns, rapping the rifle butt sharply on their thighs to settle the charge.

The first run killed fifty buffalo. The leaders did not stop but went ahead to shoot more, while those on slower horses dismounted to cut and skin the animals and then pack the meat for the trip back to camp. Little Bear killed a buffalo with his bow, in the way of his fathers. His strength was so great that the steel-pointed arrow pierced the buffalo and came out the animal's other side.

That night the fires crackled and the pots boiled. They had provisions for four weeks but were out twelve, and ran out of sugar, coffee, and flour. For six weeks, they ate nothing but plain meat, and after a while no salt. The worst was running out of tobacco. Little Bear cut up his old nicotine-stained pipe stem, shaved the pieces thin, and powdered them in the palm of his hand to smoke in a borrowed pipe. "I can stand hunger and thirst," he said, "but without tobacco I am dead."

They killed about two thousand buffalo on this final winter hunt, with its clear-cut and invariable ritual of chase and shared spoils. It was the conclusion of a tradition of thought and form and action handed down through the generations. The hunting camp was a movable social unit and the crier its recognized spokesman. All that was gone now and would never come again.

By 1877, the twin catalysts of the gold rush in southern Dakota and the Northern Pacific running across northern Dakota had brought in enough settlers to qualify the territory for statehood. A disparity existed between north and south, however, for in 1877 the northern half of Dakota Territory held only seven of the thirty-six seats in the territorial assembly.

In addition, no serious statehood movement had yet formed, largely because the people in power wanted to maintain the territorial system that was proving so lucrative for them. This was the heyday of the "territorial ring," a type of political machine in which public officials allied with Indian agents and Sioux traders embezzled funds destined for the reservations.

The territorial ring awarded contracts to local merchants and farmers, providing an infusion of capital into the economy. But you had to belong to the club to profit from the corruption, in the same way that immigrants in eastern slums tried to better themselves through corrupt political machines in the cities.

In 1877, Rutherford B. Hayes took the presidential oath after winning the election by one electoral vote. The reformer Carl Schurz became Hayes's secretary of the interior and tried to clean up the rotten Indian agencies. In March 1878, troops marched into four Sioux agencies in Dakota and told the agents to leave at once.

The most blatantly crooked of the Dakota Indian agents, Henry F. Livingston, went on trial in 1879. Among other charges, he stood accused of holding on to 5,000 pounds of tobacco that belonged to the Indians. In the middle of his trial, he won election to the Yankton Board of Education. The Yankton oligarchy had decided to show support for one of their own.

Though the federal government paid Dakota's bills, many Dakotans resented Washington's interference in local matters and territorial rights, including the right to steal from the Indians. Livingston was acquitted. Retried in 1880, a friendly jury of his peers acquitted him again. On its own turf, the territorial ring had more power than the federal reformers.

• •

While the Department of the Interior tried in vain to clean up the venality, the Northern Pacific started up once more under new ownership. The key player was Henry Hilgard, who came from one of those Bavarian families that produced a pastor and a jurist in each generation. As a young man, he quarreled with his father, changed his name to Villard, and sailed to America in 1853 at the age of eighteen. He spoke no English, but caught on fast, eventually finding work as a newspaper reporter. Villard made a reputation as a Civil War correspondent, getting scoops on major battles. After the war, he got into railroading, where he rose with spectacular speed. He bought a controlling interest in the Northern Pacific and the board elected him president in 1881.

By 1882, crews were laying track in Montana, despite the exorbitant cost of grading, bridging, and tunneling. The company disbursed $4 million a month for the main and branch lines. Ever the optimist, Villard went on the road visiting construction columns, changing locomotives where the track was uncompleted, the way pony express riders used to change horses.

A gap of four hundred miles stretched between the eastern track on the upper Missouri near today's Bozeman, Montana, and the western section at Clark Ford near the Idaho-Montana line. Villard crossed the gap by buggy, driving through the high grass that divided the eastward-running Missouri headwaters from the westward-running Columbia. Here lay an immense unexplored region, he thought.

In Portland, Villard had to build a passenger station and a decent hotel. He also had to construct a bridge over the Willamette, and set up machine shops, freight houses, roundhouses, and docks—the outlay came to $3 million. This was heroic capitalism, involving new companies, new bond issues, and always hovering on the verge of bankruptcy.

In 1883, the route came to completion. Villard made the inaugural trip in a special train loaded with dignitaries—European ministers, congressmen, governors—and they traversed the country over virgin tracks, often not seeing a human habitation for hundreds of miles.

On September 3, the entourage stopped in Bismarck to lay the cornerstone for the state capitol. The guest of honor, an object of great curiosity to the VIPs, was Sitting Bull, who had been granted leave from the reservation by the secretary of the interior. Now that the Sioux were defeated, Sitting Bull had been transformed into a folk hero. Also, a band of two hundred Crows had gathered there, right on the railroad line. Villard knew that he would never see such a spectacle again.

Villard spoke and then Sitting Bull, who had been escorted to Bismarck by a soldier-interpreter. The legendary chief rose, but instead of reciting the speech that had been prepared for him, he said in his own language: "I hate you. I hate all the white people. You are thieves and liars. You have taken away our land and made us outcasts." The interpreter, however, read the prepared remarks, and everyone applauded.

The train continued on to Goldcreek in western Montana, where it was to meet another train coming from the Pacific coast. There the last spike would be driven. The ceremony took place on September 8, but instead of using a golden spike, they brought over the first spike driven down for the Minnesota division way back in 1872. After a track-laying demonstration, cannons were fired as Villard swung the hammer and delivered the final blows.

After that, the train sped on across the territories of Idaho and Washington, finally reaching the terminal at Tacoma. Villard marched at the head of a procession from the station to Commencement Bay and gazed out over the waters and at the peaks of the Cascades in the distance to the east, and he thought: "I have conquered the West without firing a shot."

In the 1880s, once the land in the more easterly states had been grabbed up, Dakota experienced a boom. Settlers poured in, giving the parallel movements of statehood and division into north and south a new urgency. But there remained an Old Guard of territorial single-staters led by the venal Nehemiah Ordway, a former New Hampshire state senator who was appointed governor in 1880, when Dakota's population was 75,000.

Ordway promptly made his son George the territorial auditor, and gave a New Hampshire crony a lucrative contract to build the penitentiary at Sioux Falls. In 1883, he decided to move the territorial capital from Yankton to Bismarck. Opposing the removal became a way for people to fight Ordway and the territorial ring, as well as an expression of support for division and statehood. In Yankton, the resistance to removal was such that some of the territorial departments, such as the Treasury and the Supreme Court, refused to move. The end result was two capitals, located in cities four hundred miles apart.

The confusion generated by a divided government led to a growing dislike of the territorial system. Meant to be transitional, it had lasted since 1861. Dakota now had a large population, which resented living under the tutelage of the federal government. The territorial hiatus had come to signify corruption and carpetbaggers like Ordway.

An increasing number of citizens wanted division and statehood, which would bring a rise both in population and property values. In 1882, a movement started up to make the southern part a state and the northern part a territory. But the political configuration in Washington presented an obstacle. That year Chester Arthur became president after James Garfield's assassination. Although Arthur was a Republican, a Democratic majority sat in the House, while the Senate was evenly split, 38 to 38.

The congressional blocking of new states that had gone on before the Civil War over the slavery issue now continued on account of party rivalry. The Democrats opposed Dakota statehood because Dakota voted Republican. The new state would add two Republican senators to Congress, and four if it divided into two states.

Fed up with the bickering in Congress, Dakotans resorted to do-it-yourself statehood. In September 1883, a convention met in Sioux Falls and drafted a constitution that Dakotans adopted on October 20 by a vote of 12,336 to 6,814. But when Senator Benjamin Harrison of Indiana proposed a bill for Dakota statehood in February 1884, the legislation passed the Senate but not the House. The Democrats argued that Dakota had acted illegally in voting on a constitution without an enabling act, and anyway, "Why rush new states into the Union? With 38 states already, what is the need of dividing up a territory across which there is no natural dividing line?"

This debate raged from 1883 to 1888. Now and then, the Republicans waved the bloody shirt, as when a Republican senator said, "Shall 20,000 scarred veterans now residing in Dakota, who marched through the burning sands and miasmatic swamps of the South to put down a wicked rebellion, stand with bared heads and beg their old opponents in arms to be admitted to the Union they helped save?"

In 1883, Governor Ordway appeared before a grand jury, charged with selling county commissions to the highest bidder, but the jury refused to indict. A year later he was again summoned before the law, indicted for more corrupt practices in office, but he got off on a technicality. Finally, President Arthur intervened and removed Ordway in 1884.

Later that year Grover Cleveland became the first Democratic president to be elected since James Buchanan in 1856. Dakota saw its chance for statehood diminish under a Democratic administration.

In September 1885, however, Dakotans once again took matters into their own hands. A second constitutional convention gathered in Sioux Falls, and this time the vote was 25,138 for and 6,527 against. Once again, Senator Harrison introduced a bill, in January 1866. And once again, congressional Democrats accused Dakota of acting improperly. Senator George Graham Vest of Missouri even declared that Dakota was in a state of rebellion. For all that, on February 6, the bill passed the Senate, 32 to 22. But over in the House, the Committee on Territories refused to report it and the bill died.

In 1888, another presidential election year, the Republicans included statehood for North and South Dakota on their platform, making Dakota a national issue. Their candidate was Benjamin Harrison, who defeated Grover Cleveland in November. The Republicans triumphed, winning a majority in both houses of Congress.

The lame duck fiftieth Congress convened on December 3 and took up an omnibus bill to admit five new states—North Dakota, South Dakota, New Mexico, Montana, and Washington. The southern senators wanted New Mexico as a sectional counterbalance to the Dakotas. Before leaving the Senate, Benjamin Harrison said of this balancing strategy: "Can we not get rid of this old and disreputable mating business? It grew out of slavery."

In the final struggle over the omnibus bill in January 1889, Congress dumped New Mexico when it was pointed out that 100,000 New Mexicans could not read or write or speak English. The admittance of the remaining four states would not upset the congressional balance of power, since Washington and Montana were Democratic while the Dakotas were Republican. In February 1889, the omnibus bill was passed. President Cleveland signed the bill on February 22 with a quill pen; the quill had been plucked from the wing of an eagle killed in North Dakota.

The following year, the 1890 census reported the population of South Dakota as 328,808 and that of North Dakota as 182,719, for a total of 511,527 Dakotans, one-third of them foreign-born.

The motto *E Pluribus Unum* (From the Many, One) appeared on the seal of the United States, picked in 1776 by John Adams, Benjamin Franklin, and Thomas Jefferson. The Dakotas' polyglot population of Scandinavian, German, Russian, and middle European immigrants exemplified that ideal.

On February 26, 1898, Richard Dolwig and his family left their village in Hungary, traveled by train to Berlin and Bremen, and boarded a steamer for the United States, arriving in Baltimore on March 15. Dolwig registered with Customs and bought six tickets for himself, his wife, and his four children to Dickinson, North Dakota, via Chicago, on the main Northern Pacific line. To his surprise, he could find no first-, second-, or third-class carriages. From the window as they approached Dickinson, he saw horses grazing in deep snow. When he stepped off the train, the snow rose up to his knees.

Now for the first time since leaving Hungary, Dolwig felt discouraged, and overcome by a sense of strangeness. Having come to a desolate land, he knew no one he could speak to. The friend who had written Dolwig to join him in Dakota was not at the station. The Hungarian looked disconsolately out at the bleak, snow-covered flatland before him. He could barely make out the line between earth and sky, and the freezing wind that whipped across the plain chilled his bones. Truly, this was an American Siberia.

A man came up, speaking German. He said that Dolwig's friend had not been able to meet him because the roads were impassable. "If you like you can stay with me," the man said.

Dolwig had the Old World reticence that does not like to accept hospitality from a stranger. But his wife and four children stood beside him, shivering.

"But do you have room for us all?" he asked.

"I will make room," the man said, "because when I came over from the Old Country, I too was glad when someone sheltered me."

CHAPTER NINETEEN

THE MONTANA FRONTIER

Montana is what America used to be.

> *Phrase on a belt buckle*
> *in a western-apparel store*

The territory of Montana stands as a tremendous land as yet virtually untapped. Already planetarily famous for its wealth of ores, Montana proffers further potentialities as a savannah for grazers and their herds, and where the hoofed kingdom does not obtain, the land may well become the last great garden of the world. Elbow room for all aspirants will never be a problem, for Montana is fully five times the size of all of Scotland.

> *IVAN DOIG*

The New York Public Library
First called Last Chance Gulch when gold was found there in the summer of 1864, the mining community was renamed Helena after Pumpkinville, Squashtown, and Tomahawk were voted down. In 1865, Helena was one year old and already thriving, with one- and two-story houses dotting the valley and farms off to the left.

In 1850, Montana was as wild as when Lewis and Clark had been there almost a half century before. Yet a single fact ruled the region's destiny: that the Missouri's headwaters, intermittently navigable nearly up to the river's source at the Three Forks, provided a means of access for the white man.

By mid-century, however, no settlers or missionaries had come to Montana, and a dozen Indian tribes continued to roam over hunting grounds rich in game. The only white presence consisted of fur traders, who built posts at strategic points along the Big Muddy. Fort Union, begun in 1829 by John Jacob Astor's American Fur Company, was completed in 1834, on the Missouri a few miles above its juncture with the Yellowstone.

In 1834, Astor sold out to another outfit, Pratte, Chouteau & Company, who took over Fort Union and its satellite posts, while also building new ones. In 1850, Fort Sarpy opened for business 150 miles up the Yellowstone from Fort Union, below the mouth of the Rosebud, in eastern Montana. These isolated ventures, thousands of miles away from centers of population, rarely saw the steamboat arrive with mail and news from the United States. The Missouri froze four months a year and company agents lived in daily contact with the Indians.

Unlike settlers, the fur traders did not want the Indians' land, and unlike missionaries, they had no desire to improve or convert the tribe. The traders' only motive was profit, and the requirements of commerce established a sort of crude etiquette between red man and white.

It was not good business for the traders to alienate their source of pelts. At the same time, however, order had to be maintained, and infractions such as pilfering punished. The traders came to consider the Indians not as an abstract and inimical entity, but as individuals with qualities and faults. They knew that a Payute was different from a Crow, and that one Crow was different from another. The usual shorthand about some essential Indian nature proved worthless when dealing with particular Indians on a daily basis over long periods of time.

The traders also admired the Indians' skill with horses and their endurance—in winter men rode bare from the waist up, and children played naked in the snow. The women were sturdy in childbirth, never taking a day off from their work. The men's sight and sense of navigation were uncanny. An Indian could shoot twenty arrows into the tall grass and find every one.

But each trader also had his least favorite tribe. For Edward Denig, the chief clerk at Fort Union from 1849 to 1856, it was the Arikaras. They never combed their hair, he said, which provided an excellent pasture for vermin. On any fine day, a visitor to their village could see hundreds of men with their heads in the laps of their wives, who picked off enormous crawlers and put them in their mouth until they collected a mouthful the size of a walnut and spit it out.

Nevertheless, these posts became centers for authentic white-Indian social groups, not only because the Indians traded there, but because the company men took Indian wives. For Indian men, squaws existed as commodities to be traded like furs. For the traders, an Indian wife not only relieved a life of tedium but helped forge useful alliances with tribal clans.

What one of the traders called "the rutting business" was indeed a business, involving drawn-out negotiations over a squaw's worth. One of the "squaw men" committed an amusing malapropism when he recorded in his journal: "Committed fortification today." The squaws who lived with traders adapted to white ways. Some wore ball gowns on special occasions, and one learned to play cribbage. Intermarriage served as only one of the ways that whites and Indians began to accept each other's value systems. The traders saw, for instance, that what appeared to be Indian indolence was in fact work habits of a different frequency.

In 1855 at Fort Sarpy, amid its stockade of cottonwood logs and flat-roofed houses and stables, a visitor would be met by the bustle of a sur-rounding Indian encampment, the din of voices, the beat of drums, the strokes of an ax, the crash of a falling tree, the whinny of horses, the bark of emaciated dogs scrambling over a bone. Two Crow girls might be harnessing a wolfhound to a travois, while others picked berries among the shrubs.

Inside the fort, one of the clerks, James Chambers, would be recording his usual complaints in his journal. Isolation and hard winters turned many of these men into grumblers. Chambers resented his boss Robert Meldrum, the chief trader, for going native. Meldrum dressed like an Indian and said he would rather speak Crow than his mother tongue. But Chambers thought his superior was too lenient and faulted him for his "prodigal liberality." When the Crows came in to celebrate a victory over the Black-feet, and Meldrum gave a squaw ninety strands of beads, Chambers re-buked him, saying, "You might have saved them and traded them for robes."

The fort teemed with loafers, sponging and thieving, "filling their gut and receiving presents." That, too, Chambers noted, was Meldrum's doing. Supposedly an authority on the Crows, the chief trader did not realize they had to be treated firmly. Once Chambers himself caught Meldrum's Crow wife stealing sugar. Taking her by the arm, he led her away, and she started crying.

That was another major annoyance at Fort Sarpy, thought Chambers —woman trouble. Mose, a black employee, had an Indian wife who ran off with a young Crow. Chambers found him being consoled by another employee, a Virginian known as Big Six.

"Oh, Six," said Mose, "you do not know how I loved that woman. I worked for her, cooked for her, washed for her."

"Perhaps your color does not suit," Big Six said.

"What do you mean?" asked Mose. "I am lighter than an Indian. And what about our son, who is light-skinned?"

"Oh," said Six, "doubt exists about your being the father. The child's hair is straight and yours is wool."

"Don't trifle with the feelings of a man in misfortune," Mose said. "White folks have no feeling for a man of color."

Mose then announced: "No, sir, I'se done, I washes my hands clear of the strumpet." But several days later he filled his pockets with sugar and coffee and went out looking for his wife, whom he brought back to the fort.

Then Big Six took up with "a dirty little lousy slut that was offered to me last fall," as Chambers put it. "I enquired of her mother what she received for her she told me one horse, one gun, one chief's coat, one indigo blanket, two shirts, one pair leggings, six and a half yards of bed ticking, 100 loads of ammunition, 20 bunches of beads, 10 large plugs of tobacco, and some sugar, flour, etc. . . . Oh, said the old crone, I am rich now."

In winter, the days were dull, no trade went on, and time hung heavy. To pass it, Chambers and Big Six shot at targets for money. On April 5, Chambers won $2.50—"the target was a small pup tied up at one hundred yards. I shot and struck puppy and beat Big Six."

In the spring, business picked up. They bought buffalo robes and beaver, deer, and elk in exchange for goods that came from all over the world—little bells and mirrors from Leipzig, clay pipes from Cologne, beads from Italy, calico from France, and guns from England.

The trader had plenty to do, drying and packing skins, skinning and butchering buffalo for meat, making little repairs about the fort, sawing planks for a boat. In August, news reached them that the Crows and the Blackfeet had fought. The report described one of the casualties as a "knapper"—that is, someone who had been scalped but not killed. The word was also used for scalp, as in "take care of your knapper."

On November 7, the Crows traveled to Fort Sarpy to collect their annuity. It should have been a congenial occasion, but one Indian displayed the utter unpredictability that marked the tribes by shooting one of the fort employees, a Dutchman, for no apparent reason. The other Crows told Chambers they hoped he would not censure the whole nation for the faults of one bad man. To make amends, they brought the wounded Dutchman a present of sixty-two robes.

Then the winter descended upon them again, and the rivers iced up. On January 3, 1856, the temperature fell to 34 below zero, and horses and oxen froze to death. The fort filled up with Crow loafers who came in for coffee (a Crow could smell coffee five miles away, said Chambers) or lay on the floor snoozing with the dogs.

When the Indians left in February, Chambers called it "glorious news" and hoped "never to see their snouts again." Among the worst offenders were Rotten Tail, who cheated the traders out of thirty robes, and Four

Dances, a disagreeable rascal who stole everything he could get his hands on. To make matters worse, the Crow chief, Bear's Head, let his people do what they pleased, so that "the bucks are raping the squaws in broad daylight in every corner and indeed seemed to prefer witnesses to the operation."

"On the whole they may be put down as the Horrid Tribe," wrote Chambers, although he admitted the existence of a few good Indians. Dogs Head "is the best Indian on the Upper Missouri," he wrote. Old Grey "gives all his robes to the fort." The traders did not believe that the only good Indian was a dead Indian. They believed in two kinds of Indians: those who had furs to sell and those who did not.

After the fur traders came the miners. In the summer of 1862, sizable gold deposits were found along the bed of Grasshopper Creek, in southwest Montana. The town of Bannack sprang up, expanding to a population of 300 by the fall. In May 1863, prospectors found "color" at Alder Gulch, seventy miles east of Bannack. One rich strike followed another, settlements arising in such a scattered and haphazard fashion that the area became known as "14-Mile City."

The miners at Alder Gulch at first lived in brush "wickiups," dugouts, and caves in the rocks. Later in the year, a town went up nearby called Virginia City. This district held the richest gold placer deposits ever found, yielding $30 million in gold in three years.

The combination of gold and the absence of government led to a period when only the outlaws were organized. Montana was another one of those large western areas that kept being attached to one territory and then another. First split between Dakota and Washington territories, it was after March 1863 part of Idaho Territory, which also included Montana and Wyoming. The capital was Lewiston, which lay three hundred miles from the mining camps of Montana through snow-clogged Rocky Mountain passes.

This vacuum of authority offered boundless opportunities for outlaws. In Bannack on May 24, 1863, the smooth-talking Henry Plummer was elected sheriff. Plummer also happened to be the leader of the "road agents" (as the highwaymen were called) who preyed on gold shipments and stagecoaches.

The turning point in this bandits' Arcadia came with the people's trial of George Ives, a henchman of Plummer's in Virginia City. Ives was tried in December 1863 before a miner-judge. In spite of threats from the outlaws, a jury of twenty-four miners returned a guilty verdict in half an hour, sentencing Ives to be hanged. Ives, who was charged with murder, pleaded for time to write his mother and sisters in the United States, but one of his guards said, "Ask him how long he gave the Dutchman." Then they strung him up.

Ives's trial led to vigilante groups that broke the power of the road agents. They appointed officers and drew up bylaws, one of which stated,

"The only punishment that shall be inflicted by this committee is death."
Vigilantes inflicted punishment frequently in 1864, when they hanged
twenty-two road agents, five in one day.

It became a part of vigilante folklore to pass on the hanged man's last
words, which probably improved in the telling. When they stood Plummer
on the gallows he had built as former sheriff, he said, "Now, men, as a last
favor, let me beg that you will give me a good drop."

Boone Helm, one of the many Confederate soldiers who had headed
west to the mines, shouted, "Hurrah for Jeff Davis! Let her rip."

Bull Bunton declared, "All I want is a mountain 300 feet high to jump
off of."

Jack Gallagher asked, "How do I look, boys, with a halter round my
neck?" He wanted one last whiskey, and toasted the vigilantes: "I hope
forked lightning will strike every strangling villain of you."

The prize, however, went to George Shears, who said: "I am not used
to this business, never having been hung before."

Montana miners felt a dire need for a separate territory east of the
Bitterroot Range on today's Idaho-Montana line. In Alder Gulch, they
raised $2,500 in gold dust to send to Washington a lobbyist named Sidney
Edgerton, who had been appointed chief justice of Idaho Territory. Edgerton came from Ohio and had served in the House of Representatives from
1859 to 1863. Presumably, he knew his way around the capital, and started
east in mid-January 1864.

It happened that James M. Ashley, the chairman of the House Committee on Territories, also from Ohio, was a friend of Edgerton's. Ashley
soon introduced a bill to create Montana Territory, which sailed through
both houses of Congress and was signed by President Lincoln on May
26. Montana's gold deposits, "in such a mercenary age as ours," reported
Edgerton, helped get the legislation passed.

Sidney Edgerton became the first governor of a territory that exceeded
in size the six New England states and would remain a territory for a
quarter of a century. The new authorities had their work cut out for them.
When the first jury was convened in December, the jurors had to be taught
the legal names for crimes, such as "larceny" and "mayhem."

Lyman Munson, a graduate of Yale Law School, was named one of
three Supreme Court judges in Montana Territory. He took a steamer from
St. Louis for Fort Benton in January 1865, covering 3,000 miles in fifty
days. The river was swarming with buffalo. Some of them got entangled
in the sternwheel and ripped out the buckets.

It was 140 miles by prairie schooner to Helena, then called Last
Chance Gulch, a rip-roaring camp of 3,000, with ox and mule trains clog-
ging its streets. Now that the courts were in place, the question was how
to end vigilantism. In a conference with the two other judges, Munson said
that their first duty should be to stop nocturnal hangings and restore law
and order.

But one of his colleagues replied: "I am content to let the vigilantes go on, for the present. They can attend to this branch of jurisprudence better than the courts—besides we have no secure jails in which to confine criminals."

The other judge chimed in: "If we attempt to try one of those road agents in court, his comrades will get him clear."

The first term of Munson's court commenced in August 1865. He vowed in his charge to the grand jury that there would be no more midnight trials and secret executions. The next day three suspicious-looking men came to see him and said that his remarks were exciting considerable comment. When they asked about the language he had used, Munson told them they could find a transcript of his remarks in the clerk's office.

Things were changing. Now, when a crime was committed, the perpetrator was arrested, indicted, and tried. If convicted, the judge sent him to prison in Virginia City, the territorial capital. But when the governor was absent, which was often, and when the secretary who replaced him was drunk, which was oftener, the convicted criminal received a pardon.

On one occasion, a defendant pardoned in Virginia City returned to Helena swearing to take revenge on the witnesses who had testified against him. The man arrived in Helena at 9 P.M. An hour later he was surrounded by vigilantes who hanged him with his pardon in his pocket.

That was the unexpected result of Judge Munson's first murder trial. The second trial took place in August 1866. Munson sentenced the defendant to hang, but President Andrew Johnson commuted the sentence to life imprisonment, to be served in Detroit. On his way there, the man escaped. There were bound to be a few glitches during this period of transition from vigilante rule to lawful procedure.

William T. Hamilton moved to Fort Benton in 1864, at a time when tons of supplies were arriving by steamboat for the miners. Finding no hotel, Hamilton started one, a log house with a cook and a Negro waiter. He bought an old stove for $50, borrowed tin plates and cups from fur-company agents, and charged a dollar for a meal. Then he got himself some steers and opened a butcher shop, selling beef at 25 cents a pound.

In 1865, Hamilton was named sheriff of Chouteau County, an area as big as the state of New York. One day Governor Thomas Meagher, who had replaced Edgerton, asked Hamilton to go out to Indian country and persuade the Crows and the Gros Ventres to come to Fort Benton for a council. Presents for the Indians were arriving by steamboat.

"We want you to bring in the tribes," Meagher said.

"How can I?" Hamilton asked. "I have to look after my eating house and the butcher shop. I have two prisoners on hand and no jail to confine them." But the governor assured him that he would assign a deputy to take care of his sheriff's duties, as well as find an assistant to handle Hamilton's business. So the reluctant lawman left in August 1865, accompanied by a Piegan guide.

THE MONTANA FRONTIER 323

The Crows dwelled at Medicine Springs, ninety miles east of Fort Benton. Hamilton forded the Missouri at Arrow Creek, reached Medicine Springs, and followed the lodgepole trail to a big band of Crows situated on the Musselshell, which ran into the Missouri from the south.

Hamilton gave the chief an important-looking letter from the governor, sealed with wax and stamped with an eagle. But the chief did not want to go to Benton. He said his ponies' feet were tender, and that they would find no buffalo on the way.

Pursuing his mission, Hamilton headed north to Beaver Creek, looking for the Gros Ventres village. Unlike the Crows, the Gros Ventres agreed to attend the council. The next day Hamilton left with Bear Wolf, Star Robe, and two subchiefs.

The tribes started coming in, and eventually 3,500 Indians assembled at Fort Benton, including Gros Ventres, Piegans, Bloods, and Blackfeet. On September 20, the steamboat unloaded the gifts and the council began. The clerk read the treaty on a roll of paper, and then interpreters repeated it in two Indian languages. It took fifteen minutes to get through one sentence.

Hamilton reflected that the commissioners in Washington had about as much sense of the Indians as an Apache did about ancient Rome. It was useless to present Indians with this legal jargon of "the party of the first part" and "the party of the second part," and "for and in consideration of." So he and the clerk condense the treaty from forty sheets of paper down to one.

The Indians agreed to cede their land south of the Missouri and move to a reservation to the north, located between the Missouri and Milk rivers. But the treaty was never submitted to the Senate for approval. When Hamilton saw the way the Indian agent, Gad E. Upson, talked to the Indians, he decided that "he knows as much about Indians as I know about the inhabitants of Jupiter." For the Blackfeet, though, treaties proved to be irrelevant. Tribal resistance ended in 1870 with an army massacre in the Marias River.

In the fall of 1862, Nathaniel Pitt Langford, a twenty-year-old New York–born lawyer, came to Montana on Holladay's stage line from Atchison, Kansas, by way of Denver and Salt Lake City. The trip to Helena took twenty-two days and the only stops were the changing stations fifteen miles apart. Every day they would pass the eastbound coach heading for Atchison, which usually had a wounded or a dead man aboard.

Langford went on to Bannack seeking his fortune as a miner, and soon joined the vigilante association. A mulish sort of man, with a high forehead, a full beard, and deep-set eyes, the young lawyer had no patience for the riffraff that the mines attracted. In his view, some people came to work, and some came to profit from the work of others.

In 1866, Langford was named the territory's first tax collector, based in the capital, Virginia City. This turned out to be a difficult assignment,

a little like being fire chief in hell. For the rough-and-ready mining communities had no intention of paying taxes. Langford was about as popular as
influenza.

It was in the nature of the population to be rebellious: Langford estimated that four-fifths of the miners were openly declared secessionists.
That was an exaggeration, though the region abounded in Confederate
sympathizers. Virginia City had first been called Varina in honor of Mrs.
Jefferson Davis, and there was a Jeff Davis Gulch and a Confederate
Gulch. These place names were straws in the wind. At Bannack, Langford
had seen a "Secesh" flag flying. In fact, Montana attracted extremists of
both camps, who lambasted each other in the newspaper columns, the
"nigger lovers" against the "arch traitors."

But to Langford, each little mining community seemed to be under
rebel rule, the saloons packed with good ol' boys quick to buy a hospitable
drink, but less than eager to pay taxes. He hardly knew where to start. He
didn't even have any tax forms, which he had to borrow from the collector
in Utah. It was small consolation that he only had to collect property taxes,
income tax being nonexistent in the territories.

When Langford posted notices, about a dozen men arrived at his office
to say that although they believed in paying taxes, many others they knew
did not, and would not pay. What was he going to do about the delinquents? Did he really think he could collect without the help of a regiment
of soldiers? By twos and threes they came and advised Langford "as a
friend" not to press the matter. One spoke to him more bluntly: "I owe no
allegiance to any government but that of Jeff Davis, and you needn't expect
to collect a tax from me."

When the deadlines on the notices passed, Langford found more than
a hundred delinquents. He put up another notice: SEIZURE IF NOT PAID
WITHIN TEN DAYS.

The warning brought in half the delinquents. Langford announced
that the rest would be indicted. His friends asked him to "let it pass for this
time," but Langford said, "I was sent here to collect U.S. taxes and I will
do it or resign."

When the court was in session, he had the delinquents indicted, asking
the judge to fine them five cents and costs. Two of the culprits paid him a
visit and started cussing him out. "Don't say another word in my office,"
Langford said, "or I'll thrash you as you've never been thrashed before."
When he caught a man tearing down one of his posters, he had him arrested
and hauled into court, where the vandal had to pay a fine for hindering a
revenue officer.

Aside from property taxes, a $10 license had been imposed on miners,
which they refused to pay. There was also a licensing fee for traders. Each
time a new mining town sprang up, so did unlicensed traders, selling goods
from wagons and eluding the authorities. Forced to hire assistants who
could canvass the mining camps, Langford found that the expense of collection exceeded the amount collected.

But he pushed on, posting notices in the camps. A few days later, a committee of five miners appeared before his desk. If he tried to enforce the license fee, they said, there would be bloodshed. All five were "secesh." But as they left, one of them hung back to tell Langford that he had been coerced into joining the committee.

"I suppose you were forced into it by your neighbors." Langford said, "just as General Lee was forced into the rebellion."

"I suppose so," the man replied. "I don't suppose you could hope for greater success in resisting the law than General Lee obtained."

A few days later Langford and his assistant collector, Mr. Cross, went to German Gulch, accompanied by a United States marshal. The miners there refused to pay, and Langford had many of them indicted. In the street, a hostile crowd gathered. One of the miners became so abusive that the marshal sent him in handcuffs to the Madison County Jail seventy-five miles away. The experience frightened Mr. Cross so badly that he resigned.

The Montana tax district was vast. The mining-camp circuit alone extended to 1,400 miles. Langford posted hundreds of notices in the various gulches, but the miners tore most of them down. He had 400 miners indicted and issued 600 distress warrants against the property of delinquents. But miners were not the only danger. Indians killed Langford's brand-new deputy, Frank Angevine, making off with $40 in revenue stamps.

It seemed to Langford that overwhelming forces had teamed up against him. Montana was a godless country, where two hundred murders had been committed but not one killer convicted. The law didn't exist, and not one day went by without a shooting or a knifing. You might as well, he thought, have applied to the emperor of China for redress. He knew there was a price on his head. But *they* knew that he was not going to cave in.

People were afraid to travel, since road agents infested the trails. Langford couldn't find anyone willing to carry money, and besides, he couldn't ask the deputy collectors to take all the risks. He had to go himself, even though every time he did he expected a road agent, disguised with mask and blanket, to spring out of ambush and shove a shotgun in his face.

Langford had to proceed as if in enemy territory. He could not follow procedure and announce where he would be on what day. When he needed a horse, he sent a friend to get one and instructed him to give the stablehand the wrong destination. The friend would ride out of town, where Langford would meet him. Langford made thirty trips that way between Virginia City and Bannack.

He also made repeated tax-collecting visits to the small gulches and outlying mining camps accessible only by bridle paths, chalking up many thousands of miles. In 1867, he stopped at all the gulches and camps in Deer Lodge County west of Butte. One day he arrived in the little town of Silverbow and met up with the deputy he had stationed there. Langford had on him about $12,000, $5,000 of it in gold dust. At $18 an ounce, that meant a seventeen-pound sack of dust. He and Murphy, the deputy, planned to leave the next day for Helena, about fifty miles away.

When they went to the stable to get their horses, they noticed four men lurking about, but Murphy said they were only miners slinking around because they wanted to hide the location of their claim. The stableman said the four were going to Bear Gulch, in the opposite direction from Helena.

Langford and Murphy saddled up and rode out. At a bend in the trail two miles out of Silverbow, they came to a log cabin. Four horses stood hitched in front and four double-barreled shotguns were leaning against the wall beside the door.

"Great Caesar!" Murphy said. "There they are. We are in for it now."

It was a cabin saloon and the saloonkeeper invited them in for a drink. They declined.

"Well come in anyway," he said, "and surprise your bowels with a glass of cold water."

They were about to dismount when the owners of the four horses came to the door—the men they had seen in Silverbow. Langford and Murphy slowly rode off, debating what course to pursue.

"If my horse was as good as yours," Murphy said, "I'd take the chance and go on, but this little cayuse would soon be run down."

"I wish you had a strong horse," Langford said, "for I don't like taking the risk alone."

"Sorry," Murphy said, "but you can see for yourself it would be madness."

Langford rode on alone at a steady trot. At the crossing of a trout-filled stream, he halted, hoping to meet a fishing party. Finding no one about, he continued on, listening for friendly voices as he passed through a valley covered with dense willow thickets. Reaching the base of a tall, steep hill, he looked behind him and saw four horsemen approaching at a gallop, a few hundred yards away.

Langford's horse Ned was the best four-miler in the Bitterroot Valley, where he'd been raised. Langford had once ridden him ninety miles from Virginia City to Helena in one day. As soon as he got over the crown of the hill, he tightened the girth and urged Ned on to top speed, even though boulders studded the trail.

By the time the road agents got up the hill, Langford had a mile lead. But they began to gain on him and came so close he could hear the labored breathing of their horses. He thought of throwing the sack of gold dust into the bushes, for Ned was carrying in excess of two hundred pounds. But Ned strove on and one by one the road agents' horses wore out. That evening Langford got to the town of Deer Lodge. He stabled Ned, and the next morning took the coach to Helena.

In 1870, Langford joined an expedition to the little-known headwaters of the Yellowstone in southern Montana. The group of nine plus four attendants, led by General Henry D. Washburn, surveyor general of the territory, left Helena on August 17.

On the night of September 20, they made camp at the confluence of the Firehole and Gibbon rivers. Some of the men proposed buying quarter sections of the magnificent landscape, knowing it was sure to become a source of great profit. Others suggested they all collaborate on a real estate venture.

But one member of the party, Judge Cornelius Hedges, said that no one should privately own such an extraordinary natural phenomenon. He argued that the area should be set aside as a national park, an idea he had already discussed with another member of the expedition, the surveyor David E. Folsom. The others agreed to help promote the scheme.

Eventually, it was Langford who became known as the "John the Baptist" of the national park concept, writing articles and going to Washington to do a little missionary work. In 1872, Langford helped to draft the act that Congress passed on March 1, creating a protected area.

Yellowstone became the world's first national park, its 3,468 square miles teeming with wildlife on volcanic plateaus that averaged 8,000 feet in altitude. Yellowstone boasted such phenomena as 10,000 geysers, fossil forests, eroded lava flows, and an obsidian mountain. The notion that spectacular sites should be set aside and managed by the government for the enjoyment of the people is considered today to be one of the United States' major contributions to planetary thought, and it all started with a few Montana men talking around a campfire.

The 1870 census undercut Montana's expectations. Only 20,595 persons dwelled in the huge territory, where at rare intervals you could see a clearing ground around a woodyard, but never a scythe or a reaping hook following the axes. Aside from the miners, white men worked as wolfers, trappers, and Indian traders.

One of the traders was Peter Koch, who had a post at the mouth of the Musselshell River, consisting of a gun shop, two saloons, and a few cabins. Along the riverbank, Koch had driven in a row of stakes, hanging an Indian skull atop each one for decoration.

Koch carried out trade with the Crows and the Gros Ventres in the old way. The Indian came in followed by his squaw, staggering under the weight of half a dozen buffalo robes. Then he threw the robes on the counter one by one, calling out what he wanted in exchange—sugar, coffee, tobacco, flour. The staples were measured out in a tin cup one by one and poured into a corner of the squaw's skin dress.

"Tail" was thrown in, a tip to the Indian based on the volume of trade. The trader could well afford the bonus, since his profits were exorbitant. Three cups of coffee bought a robe, and a red three-point Mackinaw blanket was worth three robes. A necklace of blue beads, which had cost the trader 16 cents, could buy a robe worth $15 retail.

The traders sold what passed for whiskey in violation of the law. It was vile stuff made from raw alcohol, rank chewing tobacco, red peppers, Jamaica ginger, and black molasses, all mixed together and boiled. The penalty for distributing the rotgut was that drunken Indians would ride by yelling insults: "You miserable dirty white dogs, you are here with your cattle eating our grass, drinking our water, and cutting our wood. We want you out of here or we will wipe you out." Then they fired their rifles over the merchants' heads. The traders couldn't keep horses, which the Indians would steal, or cut hay, which they would burn.

Besides the Indian trade, Koch went out wolfing, heading into buffalo country with a partner and plenty of strychnine, which they sprinkled over buffalo carcasses. When the poisoned carcasses were frozen hard, you could get a hundred wolves with a single buffalo, and each wolfskin was worth $3.

The country was alive with wolves, but sometimes the Indians made it too dangerous to leave the fort. The tribes hated wolfers, for many of their dogs were poisoned when they moved camp through baited country. In retaliation, the Indians cut up the wolfskins or stole wolfers' horses to make them "set a-foot." You could always tell wolfers because they fried their pancakes in wolf fat, saying it gave them a better flavor.

By 1878, Nathaniel Langford had given up tax collecting to become a bank examiner. In June of that year, he had to go to Santa Fe on business. The cashier of the Second National Bank in Helena, by now the territorial capital, asked him to take a large quantity of gold and currency to Denver. Langford agreed and proceeded southward from Denver to Santa Fe in a stagecoach.

Forty miles from Santa Fe, they were passing some isolated hills known as Wagon Mound Buttes when a man jumped from the bushes, raised a double-barreled shotgun, and aimed it directly at Langford's head. "I want that treasure-box," he said.

"There is no treasure-box on this run," Langford told him. "I haven't had a treasure-box for more than two months, for you fellows have run the road to suit yourselves."

"I know better than that," the gunman said, "and if you don't throw out that box, I'll shoot the top of your head off."

He held the gun so close, Langford could have touched it.

"Oblige me by holding your gun a little out of line with my head," Langford said. "I can even read the *New York Herald* ad you're using for wadding."

"Just give me that treasure-box and you won't be hurt."

Langford handed him the way packet and suggested he see for himself. The gunman looked through it and returned it, demanding angrily: "Any passengers aboard?"

"There is a man inside," Langford said, "but he's not a passenger, he's the company blacksmith."

"That's played out," the gunman said. "I want that man."

He rattled the coach door and woke up Stewart, the blacksmith, who slipped a small roll of greenbacks into his shoe. When his search yielded only one Mexican dollar, the road agent said, "You son of a bitch, what business have you got traveling through this country with no more money than that?"

Stewart said that as the company horseshoer, his bills were paid on the road and he didn't need to carry cash. The road agent examined Stewart's hands, which were hard and callused, saw his box of tools, and returned the Mexican dollar, as one working man to another.

Then the gunman threw the leather way packet into the sagebrush, exclaiming in disgust: "No passengers, no treasure-box, no nothing. This is a hell of an outfit." For ten minutes, he searched the rear boot and the mailbags. Finally, he said, "Well, I guess you'd better drive on."

Mexican Charley, the driver, gathered the reins, but Langford said, "Hold on, Charley, I want my way packet."

"You can't have it," the road agent said.

"I can't go without it," Langford said. "The company will discharge any messenger who loses his way packet."

Sympathetic to the trauma of unemployment, the road agent stepped into the sagebrush, picked up the way packet, and handed it to Langford.

In 1879, the Montana legislature sent a petition to Congress asking for statehood. Then the 1880 census showed a population of 39,159. That same year, the Northern Pacific reached the Montana line—and in December 1881, the Utah & Northern Railroad reached Butte, capturing the mining trade, though it was too cold for a spike ceremony.

Ignored by Congress and left out of national politics, Montana drafted a constitution on its own, which was adopted on February 9, 1884, 15,506 to 4,266.

But in March 1885, when Grover Cleveland was inaugurated, the Democrats controlled the House but not the Senate, which resulted in the blocking of all state-making on partisan grounds. Four years later the Republicans returned to power when Benjamin Harrison was elected to the White House. With majorities in both houses, the Grand Old Party could take their time and create whatever states they wanted.

In this dilemma, the Democrats of the 50th Congress decided to act while they still had control of the House, in order to give statehood to Democratic as well as Republican territories. Knowing the futility of opposing Republican Dakota, William Springer of Illinois, Democratic chairman of the House Committee on Territories, developed an omnibus bill that paired off Democratic Montana and New Mexico against Republican Washington and Dakota. But Dakota was divided in two and New Mexico got dropped.

When the omnibus bill came up for debate in the House in January 1889, Montana delegate Joseph K. Toole made the case for his territory— it had a surplus in its treasury, its population was largely American-born, and the limitations of territorial government were obstructing progress. The bill passed. President Cleveland signed it on February 22, 1889, less than two weeks before Harrison's inauguration.

In July, another constitutional convention met in Montana. In one memorable speech, the mining millionaire W. A. Clark, who was presiding officer, had this to say about mine-produced pollution in Butte: "The ladies are very fond of this smoky city because there is just enough arsenic in the air to give them a beautiful complexion. . . . It has been believed by all the physicians of Butte that the smoke is a disinfectant and destroys . . . the germs of disease."

On October 1, 1889, a vote of 24,676 to 2,274 approved the constitution, and on November 8, President Harrison proclaimed Montana the forty-first state. After twenty-five years as a territory, it became the "Treasure State."

The superintendent of the census said in his bulletin for 1890: "Up to and including 1890, the country had a frontier of settlement, but at present the unsettled area has been so broken into by isolated bodies of settlement that there can hardly be said to be a frontier line. In the discussion of its extent, the westward movement, etc., it cannot, therefore, any longer have a place in the census reports."

Bureaucratic fiat abolished the frontier. But tell that to the cattlemen and the sheepmen in Montana and other western states who were fighting over grass. In 1880, Montana had 428,279 cattle and 279,277 sheep; in 1890, 513,687 cattle and 1,238,029 sheep; in 1900, 333,541 cattle and 3,047,745 sheep. In twenty years, the number of sheep increased more than ten times, while the number of cattle steadily declined.

From the start, bad feelings festered between the two groups of animal tenders. The cattlemen, part of the horse culture that gave the west its legendary aspect, looked down on the plodding sheepmen who worked on foot. It was the dashing cavalier, skilled and high-spirited, versus the humble herder, often foreign-born. The cowboys could not find anything noble about overseeing thousands of bleating sheep, until in doing so the herder began to look and smell like one of his flock. The cowboys called the shepherds "mutton punchers" and "snoozers," while referring to the sheep as "stubble jumpers" and "hoofed locusts."

In addition to this caste contempt, the cattleman had sound economic reasons for resenting the sheepmen. Sheep required much less of an investment than cattle. One sheepman and two collies could handle 3,000 sheep, taking the docile animals over long distances. They cropped the short grass left by cattle and ate weeds that cattle wouldn't touch.

Cattlemen called the sheep "tramps," and complained, "They just drift around in search of good feeding ground, regardless of the interests of anyone else." They said the sheep killed grass by eating its roots, and that they stank so badly that cattle would not feed where sheep had been.

The sheepman defended the animal that gave him employment: "He feeds me, he clothes me, and he takes only what nature provides in abundance to grow and reproduce." What a wondrous beast, fleece-bearing and meat-producing. Each year the annual crop of lambs nearly doubled the size of the flocks; yet all they wanted was water and grass. In the winter the flocks stayed in the sheltered lowlands, giving birth to their lambs in the spring. Then they moved to mountain meadows for the summer, going back down in October.

Each year the wool was sheared and shipped to eastern markets. The animals grew a new coat, while the wethers (castrated sheep) were marched to railheads and feedlots to be turned into mutton. As long as the open range lasted, the sheepmen prospered. But as the range started to contract because of the influx of homesteaders, the cattlemen used vigilante tactics to get rid of their woolly rivals.

In 1885, masked intruders set sheep camps on fire. Several attempts were also made to poison the flocks with saltpeter. In Butte Valley, eight armed men broke into a corral and shot up the sheep, while in the Tongue River Valley, ranchers stampeded horses through the flock.

In December 1900, on the banks of Bear Creek thirty miles from the Custer battlefield, cowboys clubbed to death 3,000 sheep while holding the herder at gunpoint. The sheep killers fell in behind herds of wild mustangs so their trail could not be traced. During the slaughter that night, "alibi dances" were held at several ranches.

Although the Wool Growers Association offered bounties for the killers' capture, none of the Bear Creek raiders were ever identified or prosecuted. O. C. Cato, sheriff and cattle rancher, said he had found the bloodstained clubs and would arrest the first man who claimed one.

In a Powder Valley saloon at a stage stop, a cowboy was drinking at the bar one afternoon when a herder and his collie came in. "This is no place for a dog," said the cowboy, who drew his gun and shot the collie. As he fired, the herder drew and seconds later both men lay dead on the floor.

The clash between cattlemen and sheepmen generated considerable violence in the western states; scores of raids; 40 or 50 men killed; and 50,000 sheep shot, clubbed, poisoned, dynamited, and "rimrocked" (stampeded off a cliff). The true cause of it was the change in public land use, from grazing to farming.

Overcrowding led to the end of the open range. By 1907, the range was gone, eaten up, with millions of acres settled. The cattle herds now grazed on private land, while the sheep were forced into remote canyons and lowland deserts unfit for farming.

Many Montanans still remembered the days when the bunch wheat grass grew twenty inches high, covering the prairie and waving like golden grain, and you could ride with your feet in the stirrups dragging through it.

CHAPTER TWENTY

THE WASHINGTON FRONTIER

The ends of the earth are ever the points on a map that colonists push against, enlarging their sphere of influence. On one side servants and slaves and tides of power and correspondence with the Geographical Society. On the other the first step by a white man across a great river, the first sight (by a white eye) of a mountain that has been there forever.

MICHAEL ONDAATJE

Was there ever national blunder so great, ever national crime so tremendous, as ours in dealing with our land?

HENRY GEORGE

The National Archives
Five loggers sit with their arms crossed on the stump of an enormous red cedar they have just cut down near Deming, Washington. These logger snapshots were not unlike those of hunters on safari photographed with their kill.

When Washington joined Montana and the Dakotas in statehood, thanks to the Omnibus Act of 1889, it had been a territory for longer than any of them, since 1853. Before that, Washington was part of Oregon Territory, created in 1849. As gold made Montana and South Dakota, lumber made Washington. The northwest corner of the United States was carpeted with forests that went back to prehistoric times.

The logical place to start logging was Puget Sound, an arm of the Pacific sheltered from storms and strong currents by the Olympic Peninsula and Vancouver Island, reached via the Juan de Fuca Strait between those two land masses. Since there were no roads, lumber could not be carried overland and had to go by the water route.

A vast and protected deepwater harbor, Puget Sound was backed by fine stands of Douglas fir that grew right down to the water's edge. The trees rose to a height of two hundred feet, in pure stands with branchless trunks, centuries old. The story was told about two loggers counting the rings on the stump of a tree they'd just cut; when they got as far back as the pilgrims, they gave up.

Puget Sound offered a providential setting for the cutting and shipping of lumber, and soon the Sound was dotted with small artisanal operations like Henry Yesler's on the site of Seattle. In those early years in the 1850s, all a logger needed was eight to ten yoke of oxen and the necessary saws, axes, and chains. Labor, gravity, and water did the rest.

The greatest expense was preparing a "skid road," which consisted of peeled logs that were laid every five feet across a path through the timber down an incline. The skids were slushed with dogfish oil so that the newly cut logs could slide over them, their descent sounding like distant thunder.

A chute dropped the logs into the Sound when the tide was in. They then floated in harbor corrals constructed of long sticks linked by chains, until they could be turned into planks and piles in the adjacent steam sawmill. "Logs on the pond" meant that a lumberman's financial standing was respectable.

Seattle prospered, shipping a dozen cargoes of lumber to San Francisco in 1854. When the sawmills did well, so did the townspeople, from the bark peelers to the sawdust wheelers to the chief sawyer. In the early days, the lumber towns with their sawmill next to the wharf were little fiefdoms, with no government around to interfere. There was timber for the taking on public land, without restriction. "No one can find fault with them but Uncle Sam," said a visitor, "and he is far distant."

Soon modest individual efforts gave way to companies backed by San Francisco investors. At Port Blakely on the southern end of Bainbridge Island, Captain William Renton, who had lost his right eye in a mill accident, built a modern mill for $80,000. Andrew Pope and his partner William C. Talbot started the Puget Mill Company at Port Gamble, along the tip of the Kitma Peninsula, with a capital of $30,000. Pope and Talbot were "full of energy and push," said a contemporary, and by December 1855 had thirty-eight saws in operation, running day and night.

• •

In 1852, about 4,000 settlers were scattered over the part of Oregon Territory that lay north of the Columbia River. Not all of them worked as lumbermen, for farmers had also settled in the valleys close to the Columbia. Distant from the seat of government, these far-flung inhabitants felt neglected and drafted a petition asking Congress to form a new territory north of the Columbia River.

As it happened, the people and government of southern Oregon were not opposed to this breakaway movement. They felt that by consenting to reduce the size of the huge territory (which included the present states of Oregon, Washington, and Idaho), they would increase their own chance for early statehood.

Joseph Lane, Oregon's delegate to Congress, lobbied for the division. The bill for separation passed both houses of Congress, and in February 1853, in the last days of his term, President Millard Fillmore signed the organic act that made Washington a territory. It would remain a territory for thirty-six years, while Oregon became a state in 1859.

In March, Fillmore was replaced by Franklin Pierce, a veteran of the Mexican War. Pierce picked a fellow officer named Isaac Ingalls Stevens to be governor of the new territory, a man who had been first in his class at West Point.

A pugnacious James Cagney type with a large head on a short bandy-legged body, Stevens was known for impulsive decisions and a marked inability to get along with his colleagues. The benefits of territorial status soon became apparent through congressional appropriations—$20,000, for example, for a two-hundred-mile road from Steilacoom to Walla Walla. Stevens himself put in for $5,000 to buy books for a library, believing as he did that knowledge was the great leveler, because it leveled upward.

Stevens also had the job of Superintendent of Indian Affairs, which made him the key figure in the implementation of the government's reservation policy. In 1854, Congress appropriated $45,000 for negotiations with the tribes in Washington Territory, intending to extinguish Indian titles and open the land to settlement.

Between December 1854 and July 1855, Stevens and his negotiating team went on a whirlwind tour of six tribal councils. In December, the Nisquallis and Puyallups agreed without objection to the treaties' terms. In exchange for 2.5 million acres between the Cascade mountains and Seattle, the Indians received three reservations of 1,280 acres each, plus a cash payment of $3,250 for moving expenses. The government also guaranteed them annuities for twenty years, not in cash but in items beneficial to the tribes.

Up and down Puget Sound Stevens went, signing treaties and making frequent use of the father-child analogy. At a council on January 25, 1855, an old Skakomish chief startled Stevens when he expressed his opposition: "I don't want to sign away all my land," he said. "Take half of it and let us keep the rest. . . . I don't like the place you have chosen for us to live on. I am not ready to sign the paper." But the next day the chiefs convened again. They wanted the goods and knew they had no leverage, so they signed.

In February, Stevens arrived at the mouth of the Chehalis River, in southwest Washington. Here the chiefs objected to mixing several tribes on one reservation. Stevens had banned liquor from the council, and when on February 28, the Chehalis chief Carowan showed up drunk, the governor lost his temper and tore up the document that described Carowan's status as a chief. Stevens left without a treaty. It was his first setback.

In May, Stevens called an important council of the eastern tribes in Walla Walla. On May 29, 1,800 Indians attended, but again protests rose from the ranks. "Goods and earth are not equal," said the Walla Walla chief Peu Peu Mox Mox (Yellow Serpent). "I do not know where they have given land for goods." But Stevens sweetened the pot, and signed treaties with the Yakimas, the Cayuses, the Umatillas, the Nez Percés, and the Walla Wallas.

In July, after winning over the Flatheads and the Blackfeet, Stevens boasted that 11,300 of the 15,000 Indians under his jurisdiction had signed treaties. While he was still in Blackfoot country, however, the Yakimas rose up in anger at prospectors who had invaded their lands, killing eight of them in August. Then on September 23, Andrew Bolon, an unpopular Indian agent, turned up on the banks of the Columbia with his throat slit.

These murders could not go unpunished. The army had to be called in. General John E. Wool commanded the 1,000-man Army of the Pacific, with jurisdiction over a huge expanse of land, from Utah to the Pacific and from Mexico to Canada. With such a small number of men at his disposal, Wool tended to believe that the Washington settlers were at fault in their troubles with the Indians.

Wool also blamed Stevens's shotgun treaties for not protecting Indian interests. He had to follow orders, though, and in October dispatched 102 men under Major Granville O. Haller to arrest Bolon's killers. At Toppenish Creek, the troops met a large party of Yakimas. In the ensuing fray, Major Haller suffered five dead and seventeen wounded.

From Puget Sound came a clamor for retaliation. The *Pioneer and Democrat* in Olympia wrote, "We trust they will be rubbed out—blotted from existence as a tribe." Volunteer units quickly formed, long on verbiage and short on training.

In November and December, regulars and volunteers invaded Yakima country and drove off the Indians. On December 5, 1855, a party of Oregon volunteers captured Yellow Serpent and 40 warriors as the Indians rode up carrying a white flag to parley. The next day the prisoners were shot as they resisted guards who tried to bind their hands. The Oregon men scalped Yellow Serpent and skinned his body. Then they cut off his ears and preserved them in alcohol. Volunteers drank toasts from the jar they had placed his ears in.

Stevens called for a vigorous winter campaign. But General Wool put his foot down, charging that the volunteers' sole function was to fill the pockets of the war profiteers who sold them supplies.

In mid-January 1856, Colonel Silas Casey arrived in Steilacoom with two companies of the 9th Infantry. When Stevens asked him to hand over arms for the volunteers as well as provide twenty-five tons of oats for their horses, Casey refused. He ordered that two companies of volunteers be placed under his command and the rest sent home.

When the Indian war dragged on, Stevens blamed the drawn-out conflict on a lack of cooperation from General Wool and Colonel Casey. They were not backing his policy of isolating the friendly Indians and crushing the troublemakers. Seeing himself as "a father punishing his children to make them good," Stevens felt all the more aggrieved.

In the spring of 1856, aiming to prosecute the war more effectively, Stevens declared martial law in Pierce and Thurston counties, the Tacoma-Olympia area at the southern end of Puget Sound. Critics at once accused him of overstepping his authority. Only the legislature, they said, could suspend civil rights and habeas corpus and declare martial law. Not even the president of the United States had that power.

Stevens had arrested three half-breeds, charging them with giving assistance to the Indians. In May, he ordered that they be tried before a military tribunal. But on May 5, the Third District Court in Steilacoom opened for its spring session, and Federal Judge Edward Lander appealed to Stevens to let justice take its normal course in district court.

Two days later, when Lander took his seat at the bench, one of Stevens's men arrested the judge and took him to Olympia, along with his clerk and court records. The lawyers who happened to be in district court that day were astounded. They had seen some pretty outlandish courtroom tactics in their day, but arresting the judge topped them all.

This was in fact a breakdown of the territorial system. A governor appointed by the president had suspended civilian government and obstructed the operation of a federal court. The Steilacoom lawyers sent letters to Congress and President Pierce, accusing Stevens of "a most despotic assumption of authority."

Backtracking in view of the rising opposition, Stevens had Judge Lander released and drafted a defense of his conduct. But the Steilacoom attorneys wrote Secretary of State William Marcy that Stevens was acting like "a diminutive Napoleon." They urged that he be removed from office.

On May 12 in the Second District Court in Olympia, Judge Lander, sitting in for an absent colleague, issued a writ of habeas corpus for the arrested half-breeds. Two days later he ordered Stevens to present himself and explain why he was defying the writ. Upon which a band of Stevens's volunteers smashed in the courthouse's bolted door and took Lander into custody for the second time that week.

As these events unfolded, public opinion increasingly turned against martial law. When Stevens set May 20 as the date for the half-breeds' court-martial, the growing anti-Stevens faction issued a statement declaring that "military despotism is as hard to bear as it was in 1776."

It finally dawned on Stevens that he might be wrecking a brilliant career. On May 25, he released Lander and the half-breeds and revoked martial law. The three accused men appeared before the Second District Court, where their case was dismissed. In July, Judge Lander cited Stevens for contempt and fined him $50, but Stevens exercised his gubernatorial powers and granted himself a pardon.

On September 12, Stevens received a severe reprimand from Secretary of State Marcy, but President Pierce allowed his fellow Mexican War veteran to remain in office. Although the martial law fracas had its farcical elements, it involved the right to retain civil liberties, the separation of powers, and the question of civilian rule in wartime—issues that would again be put to the test during the Civil War.

The guessing game on Puget Sound was which of the mill towns would grow into cities. Charles Prosch bet on Steilacoom, having been sold on the town by Captain Lafayette Balch, who in 1851 had taken a donation claim on the site. Balch platted the land, sold town lots, and built a saw-mill. In 1858, he talked Prosch, an experienced printer, into coming there and starting a newspaper to help promote Steilacoom in its rivalry with Olympia.

When Prosch arrived in February with his wife and three sons, Steilacoom still had more Indians than whites. The only industry, lumber, employed most of the townspeople. A man hauling piles from timber to water with three yoke of oxen could make $30 a day. As for Indian labor, it could only be counted on until May, when the Indians disappeared into the forest to pick berries.

Prosch published the *Puget Sound Herald*. He did his best to refute the calumnies that were retailed about Washington Territory, such as the following in the California *Guide and Register:* "We are informed that it is not a very desirable climate to live in, as it rains almost incessantly six months a year."

What an odious lie! Prosch fumed. The sun shone aplenty on Puget Sound, interrupted only by an occasional gentle drizzle. The weather was in fact extremely pleasant, neither too hot nor too cold. Prosch received numerous inquiries as to the possibility of getting to Washington Territory by rail. The answer, unfortunately, was no, and this was the principal reason for the slow increase of the population. In 1858, the inhabitants of the Puget Sound area numbered about 4,000. When steamers brought the mail, they dropped off one bag for the entire area.

Another reason for zero growth was the lack of women. It required all the towns on the Sound to muster enough females to make up four sets in a dance. The steamer puffed from town to town, collecting them. In an editorial entitled "A Good Wife," Prosch observed: "There is probably no community in the Union with so large a population of bachelors. We have no spinsters." In 1859, he wrote a piece titled "The Scarcity of White Women," explaining that "the proportion of white men to white women is about 20 to one. . . . Sooner or later, the tide of female emigration will set in."

In 1861, a young man showed up in Seattle who would do something about the woman shortage. A born promoter, twenty-two-year-old Asa Shinn Mercer hailed from Princeton, Illinois (fifty miles north of Peoria), and had just graduated from college. Mercer's uncle, a judge in Seattle, was involved in a project that year to build a territorial university. The lucky nephew, freshly matriculated, became the new college's president. The position proved to be less grand than it sounded, for all the classes were in one room, and after the second term the university closed, owing to dwindling attendance.

Temporarily unemployed, Asa Mercer focused on the woman problem. It was said in Puget Sound that "men are wondrous cheap and women are so dear." They were dear because of, among other things, the Donation Act of September 27, 1850. Passed to encourage settlement in remote Oregon (which then included Washington), the act allowed an unmarried man to claim 320 acres, while giving a man and a wife the right to 640. A few land-hungry men married squaws, but this was frowned on as bad for the moral tone of the community.

Seeing that Seattle had a large contingent of discontented and hard-drinking bachelors, Mercer felt sure that an increase in women would supply a civilizing influence. "I had been taught to believe," he said, "that practically all the goodness in the world came from pure-minded women."

In New England, where the Civil War had cut down so many husbands, there languished thousands of widows who might be persuaded to seek a new life in the west. Mercer talked the prospects over with Governor William Pickering, who offered plenty of encouragement but no funds. So the young man collected contributions from prospective husbands to finance a trip to Boston, and left in 1862 on the seven-thousand-mile journey across the Isthmus of Panama.

On this initial trip, Mercer recruited schoolteachers. Quite a few agreed in principle, but when the day of departure came, only eleven showed up. On May 28, 1863, the Seattle Gazette saluted the arrival of "eleven accomplished and beautiful young ladies who have been added to our population."

In 1865, Mercer left on a second recruiting mission, this time for a larger catch. Since the round-trip by schooner cost $500 plus expenses, not to mention the women's fares, he contracted with a number of bachelors who paid him $300 each against the promise of a wife.

When his steamer came into New York Harbor in April 1865, Mercer decided to travel to Washington and pay a call on President Lincoln. As a five-year-old boy in Illinois, Mercer had once been bounced on the president's knee. He now hoped to make use of this connection to ask Lincoln for a ship to carry his prospective brides from New York to Seattle. At the close of the Civil War, hundreds of vessels lay idle and thousands of seamen remained on the payroll.

Reaching his New York hotel on the morning of April 16, Mercer encountered black crepe on all sides, and read a bulletin in the lobby announcing Lincoln's assassination at Ford's Theater. Everyone was in shock, and for the moment Mercer felt at sea without a compass.

Collecting his wits, he went to Washington anyway, and called on the commander in chief of the Union Army, General Grant. Mercer figured that the general, who had been stationed at Fort Vancouver on Puget Sound as a young officer in 1852, might respond to the woman problem, since he had not brought his wife to the fort and was said to have taken consolation in drink.

"Sit down, Mercer," Grant told him, "and read the morning paper until my return. I am going to the White House to meet President Johnson and his cabinet and will bring your matter to a head one way or the other."

Half an hour later Grant reappeared. As he walked in the door, he said to one of his aides, "Captain Crosby, make out an order for a steamship, coaled and manned, with capacity to carry 500 women from New York to Seattle for A. S. Mercer, and I will sign the same."

Armed with Grant's order, Mercer went to Boston to recruit passengers. Calling himself a female-emigrant agent, he ran ads in newspapers and issued nearly five hundred tickets for the trip. Then he returned to Washington to call on the crusty quartermaster general, Montgomery C. Meigs. But right in line in front of him was a man who had furnished a horse to the Union Army. He had already been paid twice and was applying for the third time, but Meigs recognized him, flew into a rage, and had the man arrested.

It was an inauspicious time to present Grant's order, and Meigs said, "There is no law justifying this order and I will not honor it."

Weeks passed, and Mercer was about to leave Washington when he got a letter from Meigs. The quartermaster general wrote that he had ordered a special appraisal of the 1,600-ton propeller-driven *Continental*, a steamer built in 1862 and requisitioned during the war to carry troops to New Orleans. He stood ready to waive the requirement that the ship be sold at public auction if Mercer could pay $80,000. This was a giveaway, said Meigs, considering that the *Continental* was a brand-new ship worth $250,000.

Sitting in his room at the Merchants Hotel, Mercer gazed out the window and wondered where he would find $80,000. He had not been wondering long when a card arrived from Ben Holladay. A shrewd operator, Holladay had built a transportation empire that ranged from the Overland Stage Company, which ran 260 coaches over 3,000 miles of western roads, to the California, Oregon, and Mexican Steamship Company.

The card said: "I understand the government offers you the *Continental* for $80,000 and that you have not the money. If you will let me have her I will fit her for the trip and carry your people to Seattle at a nominal figure." Holladay wanted the *Continental* for his steamship route to Mazatlán, Mexico.

Mercer felt like a drowning man catching at a straw, since without Holladay's intercession, he would have had to cancel the trip. He immediately signed a contract with Holladay's lawyers to provide 500 passengers from New York to San Francisco. Later he regretted not having insisted on a clause that would have allowed the first 150 passengers to be carried free, while requiring each additional passenger to pay $100.

For by the time he left for Boston to gather his flock, the eastern press had seized on the humorous aspects of the project, and the headline writers were having a field day: HEGIRA OF SPINSTERS, PETTICOAT BRIGADE, WIVES FOR THE WIFELESS, CARGO OF HEIFERS, MERCER'S SEWING MACHINES, FEMALE FREIGHT, VOYAGE OF THE VIRGINS, and so on.

Was it a "Mercer-nary Cargo," wondered the *Springfield Republican*, adding: "It may well be doubted whether any girl who goes to seek a husband is worthy to be a decent man's wife." The most scurrilous article, appearing in the *New York Herald*, warned that the women leaving for Seattle would be turned into whores.

As Mercer feared, the bad press undermined his plans. Four-fifths of his 500 recruits canceled, and Mercer had to inform Ben Holladay that he had only 100 passengers. "In that case our contract is void," Holladay said. But since the ship was heading for the Pacific anyway, he agreed to transport Mercer's maidens at the going rate.

On January 16, 1866, the *Continental* left New York for its three-month voyage around the Horn, carrying about 100 women. Among the passengers was a reporter for the *New York Times*, Roger Conant—known as "Rod"—who kept a journal. In the first few days, many of the women suffered seasickness, but after a while they became accustomed to the rolling of the ship and swarmed over the decks like a hive of bees.

Mercer, who did not want his wards to associate with the ships' officers, distributed yarn to keep them occupied. Conant found one young woman knitting socks and asked her if she intended to marry when they reached the territory. "I did not come out for that purpose," she said, "but if I receive a good offer I shall take the matter into consideration."

Flirting was a problem, and Captain Charles Winsor complained that his men were neglecting their duties. On moonlit evenings, certain young officers could be seen on deck with their arm curled around a girl's waist. When the second engineer sat beside a girl who was sewing and tried to sneak his arm around her, she jabbed it with the needle. "Ouch! What made you do that?" he asked. "Your arm was not in the right place," she replied.

On February 3, they crossed the Equator. The officers ribbed the ladies they would get a visit from Old Father Neptune, and the ladies retorted that they were ready for him. One of the women held up an infant belonging to another passenger and exclaimed, "Oh my little darling I wish you was mine!" To which an officer said, "I know of only one way to get them," which caused her to rush below.

Later in February, they stopped in Rio de Janeiro, where Mercer was invited to call on the American consul and his wife with six of his emigrants. On their return, Conant asked one of the six if she'd had a good time. "Not very pleasant," she said. "The consul's wife was very cold and stiff in her manner toward us and seemed to think we were a lot of marriageable stock fit for anybody's pickings. I wish that I had not gone."

As the *Continental* proceeded down one coast of South America and up the other, the ladies grumbled about the length of the voyage and the toughness of the navy-issue wafers called hardtack. "I paid twenty dollars for this pair of teeth before I left Lowell," said one, "but if I have got to keep on eating this stuff I shall not have a tooth left in my head by the time I reach Seattle."

Approaching San Francisco in April 1866, Mercer realized he had to raise funds to lodge his ladies in hotels and pay for their transportation to Seattle. He called in a widow named Mrs. Berry and asked her for a note for $250, assuring the woman that her intended husband would be glad to reimburse her. "Oh, Mr. Mercer," she said, "do you think anybody up there would be willing to marry me?"

"Certainly," Mercer said. "There is a nice old farmer who lives near me, who wants a wife, and he promised to take whoever I brought."

"If that is the case, I will give you my note for any amount, if you promise to recommend me to him."

"I picked you out on purpose for him," said Mercer, handing her the note to sign.

When Conant saw Mercer leaving the widow's side, he asked, "How much did you gammon Mrs. Berry out of?"

"Only $500," Mercer said, laughing.

Some of the other women he called in signed notes, and some did not. One woman said, "I'll see your head in the bottom of hell before I give you one red cent."

On April 24, the ship passed through the Golden Gate and anchored off Folsom Street. The curious lined the wharves, and a number of men rowed out in boats, asking to come aboard. The next day the ladies went ashore to their hotels, the Fremont and the International. In shop windows, they saw cartoons making fun of them. One showed the *Continental* surrounded by small boats filled with men, their arms extended toward the ladies, who stood at the ship's taffrail waving handkerchiefs. In another, a man ran at top speed as a large party of ladies pursued him close behind. The papers were full of articles about the visitors, one quoting a San Francisco dowager who said, "Of course, no *respectable* woman came on the *Continental*."

Couples in want of maids came to the hotels, trying to hire Mercer's brides by painting a dismal picture of Washington Territory. When fifteen ladies defected, Mercer quickly made arrangements to sent the rest in bunches of ten to forty on lumber boats to Puget Sound. Conant went along, and put up at Seattle's Occidental Hotel, a two-story, Swiss-chalet-type building.

Seattle was a clearing in the forest, a mile long and a quarter mile wide. Logs floated in the bay. Indians beached their canoes along the shore. Crows dropped clams on the rocks to break the shells. The refrain Conant heard around town was, "I don't see what Mercer brought all those women up here for when there is nothing for them to do."

By this time, the western papers had got hold of the story, and were turning the "Mercer Belles" into objects of ridicule. The articles showed how the masculine west viewed women, portraying them as not much better than cattle. Indeed, the *Idaho World* compared the Mercer enterprise to a cattle auction: "Walk up fellers and select your gal! Here's Betsy Jane, has good teeth and warranted kind in harness. How much for Betsy? Sold to Jack Longhead for $500. . . . The next animal, fellers, is a blue-eyed Yankee gal named Jerusha Ann, heavy on the hug, and warranted to last a life-time. . . . Wake up fellers! Sold to the daredevil Tom for 50 ounces of dust. Here's a stunner, Tabithia Marier, a pine-gum lunch will last her a week, and if not sold will be thrown ashore."

Relatively milder remarks, such as the *Walla Walla Statesman*'s comment that Mercer's women "are in search of a market for their kisses," also stung the new arrivals. It was not surprising that the women became reluctant to conclude the matches that Mercer proposed. The promoter had not escaped his own net, for on July 15 he married Miss Annie E. Stephens of Baltimore, capping a romance begun aboard ship.

When a number of Puget Sound bachelors who had paid Mercer for a bride came to collect the ladies he had picked for them, the women, feeling humiliated, would not even speak to their prospective mates. The men left empty-handed, muttering darkly about Mercer for bringing women "that wasn't on the marry." The first five to be thus disappointed were Humbolt Jack, Lame Duck Bill, Whiskey Joe, White Pine Joe, and Bobtail Bob.

Another hopeful, a young man who had a little farm nearby, went to pick up his bride at her hotel. "How are you, Ma'am," he said. "I'm the feller what paid Mercer $300 to bring you out for a wife. I suppose you are as willin' to get married this afternoon as any other time, as I must be home by sundown to milk the cows and feed the pigs."

"Sir, she said, "you are either an impertinent fellow or you are laboring under a delusion. You did not send $300 to bring me out. I paid my own passage. If you gave Mercer $300 you have been badly sold by him."

"All I want is a wife, if you are willing," the young man said.

"I do not wish to marry," she said.

"Well, if you didn't come out to get married, what the deuce did yer come out for?" the young man muttered as he left.

Then another farmer arrived at the Occidental, who wished, he explained, to take two or three of the ladies out to his farm on approval. He would, after a test period, pick the lucky bride. The ladies responded without enthusiasm.

Mercer realized that it was not so easy to match people up. The women had a say in the matter and were not chattel to be bartered. Some, however, did find husbands. Sara Robinson married the storekeeper David Webster on May 27, and the newlyweds rented a small house. Sara loved Seattle's lush greenness, and the way the roses bloomed at Christmas. Some living expenses were high—potatoes at a dollar a bushel—but smelts were so plentiful at the foot of Pike Street that they could be caught with pins.

There were all sorts of odd-seeming matches. Mary Martin, forty, got hitched to John Tallman, twenty-five. Miss Griffith, a factory girl from Lowell, married a lumberman from Olympia worth $100,000. Sara Wakeman, a widow with an elderly mother and three active young sons whose necks she was often on the point of wringing, wedded Zeke Washburn, an old backwoodsman who lived on the White River.

As for Asa Mercer, he moved to Wyoming, where he died in 1917, at the age of seventy-eight. If he had written a résumé, it would have read like this: Teacher, surveyor, college president, commissioner of emigration, legislator, justice of the peace, insurance agent, shipper, author, editor of a livestock journal, farmer, commercial agent, World's Fair commissioner, tourist guide at Yellowstone, and footloose dreamer.

United States Attorney John McGilvra arrived in Puget Sound in the summer of 1861. Verifying his suspicions that the mills were cutting on government land, he indicted Josiah Keller, a partner in the Puget Mill Company, and several others. Keller wrote that he had been "indighted for $10,000, which if we are eventually convicted for, the fine will be three times the amount. . . ."

But McGilvra, who had political ambitions, soon decided that "a vigorous prosecution" of lumbermen would force the sawmills out of business and damage the territory's prospects. The men he indicted in 1861 pleaded guilty to stealing government timber, paid a modest fine, and spent one day in jail. One of them, Edwin G. Ames, of the Puget Mill Company, explained how the prisoners walked into the jail escorted by the sheriff and the judge, broke open a box of cigars, had their smoke, and walked out, "having satisfied the law."

The ambitious McGilvra, it seems, took bribes. Cyrus Walker, a partner in the Puget Mill Company, wrote on January 17, 1863: "Mr. McGilvrey [sic] is evidently in the market and I think he puts too high a price on his services."

McGilvra proposed a rate of "stumpage," requiring the loggers to pay for the timber they cut on public land. In Washington, the land commissioner, J. M. Edmunds, agreed that "it would be better to accept [stumpage] as a basis for compromise than to go into the courts." A fee of 50 cents per 1,000 feet was assessed, and the government was now in the logging business.

McGilvra collected the fees, relying on stumpage figures submitted by the mills, which he never questioned. He had in fact become a part of the fraud he was supposed to suppress. Then in 1865, McGilvra became a land speculator, in partnership with Cyrus Walker—a gamekeeper turned poacher.

In the meantime, the stumpage rate swung widely from 25 cents to $2.50 per 1,000 feet, depending on the influence of the lumber lobby. It was estimated that by the late 1870s, about $440 million worth of lumber had been stolen from public land, the Puget Mill Company being at the top of the list of the principal thieves. In 1875, the land commissioner wrote fatalistically that "the perpetration of innumerable frauds" is "among the traditions of this office."

The question of lumber theft took a bizarre twist when the Northern Pacific began putting down track in Washington Territory. For each mile of track laid, the Northern Pacific obtained from the government a forty-mile strip of land on either side of the track. This was granted as usual in alternate sections, so that every other strip was preserved as public land.

Hoping to include as much timber as possible in the land grants, the railroad directed its engineers to lay the track on the route from the Columbia River to Puget Sound through the most heavily timbered areas. In Washington Territory, the Northern Pacific ended up claiming 7.7 million acres, including 2 million acres of timber.

The timber companies in their illegal cutting operations did not distinguish between the public and private strips in the checkerboard pattern the government land grants created. They just took what they could. Since the Northern Pacific would not get title to its timbered land until it was surveyed, the company feared it would by that time be stripped bare. Thus, to protect its own interests, the railroad threw itself into the battle against the illicit removal of timber on public land. In April 1871, J. W. Sprague of the Northern Pacific instructed the railroad's Puget Sound lawyer, Hazard Stevens (son of Isaac), to do what he could to stop the stealing.

Captain B. B. Tuttle, the federal timber agent in western Washington, was widely believed to be on the take. Despite the flagrant evidence of the Puget Mill Company's wrongdoing, Tuttle never raided their camps. Nevertheless, Stevens hired Tuttle at a generous salary to assist in his investigation. Stevens's main impediment was the United States attorney, Leander Holmes, worthy successor of McGilvra in hindering rather than enforcing the prosecution of timber thieves.

Two powerful capitalist interests locked horns—the railroad and the lumbermen—as the government's local representative sat on the fence. Leander Holmes refused to help Stevens find violators but loaned him a deputy U.S. marshal armed with a stack of blank subpoenas to serve on persons who knew about timber theft.

Stevens and Tuttle toured the Puget Sound logging camps in August 1871. For once, Tuttle did what he had been hired to do, seizing logs cut on public land and ordering witnesses to appear in court. The two men also operated along the Hood Canal, on the eastern side of the Olympic Peninsula, where lumber camps crowded the banks. Driven by a stiff breeze, their small steamer coasting over the whitecaps, Stevens and Tuttle confiscated the logs tied together in rafts for delivery to the sawmills. By the end of 1871, Tuttle had recovered 3 million feet of illegally cut logs, one-fifth the total amount of legal timber cut on public land in that year.

Sprague wrote Stevens on August 9, 1871: "I am much pleased with your efforts in timber matters. . . . You are making it lively for the timber thieves."

Tuttle sold the logs he had seized at public auction. The loggers, who still had to fill their orders, arranged not to bid against each other; but Stevens sent his own people to the auctions to run the prices up.

Bitter though they were against the Northern Pacific, the lumbermen stopped horning in on the railway's turf. The railroad succeeded where the government had failed, helping to put an end to the era when public timber could be cut at will. When Carl Schurz became Secretary of the Interior in 1877, he sent special agents from Washington to investigate fraud, rather than rely on the local timber agents and the U.S. attorney, who were in the pay of the loggers.

But in 1878, Congress thought up yet another bonanza for the loggers, the Timber and Stone Act. The bill's intention, as announced by Senator Aaron Sargent of California, was to "make an honest business of lumbering." Instead, because the legislation was so full of loopholes, it became the principal vehicle for fraudulently assembling large amounts of land.

The act made claims final in sixty days. It required neither proof of residence nor intent to improve the land. In Olympia, lumber companies hired agents to round up sailors and working stiffs and march them in to file their claims. They received from $50 to $125 for a day's work. When you added the fees for perjured witnesses and the cost of the land ($400 for 160 acres at $2.50 an acre), the lumbermen could boast that "our lands cost us on average less than $600 for a claim."

Authorities estimated that three out of four timber and stone claims filed in Washington Territory were fraudulent, and the General Land Office temporarily suspended the program twice, in 1883 and in 1885. But when federal agents started nosing around getting affidavits from dummy entrymen, bribery was once again the answer.

In the summer of 1883, the Department of the Interior sent agent T. H. Cavanagh to Puget Sound to investigate abuses under the Timber and Stone Act. When the lumber companies found out that Cavanagh was a friend of H. G. Struve, a prominent Seattle lawyer, several mills paid Struve to use his influence. Soon the word came down that "the agent can be fixed."

William Talbot, the senior partner of the Puget Mill Company, railed against the "thieving" government agents who blackmailed honest timber claim owners. Economic growth was the bible of this entrepreneur, who believed that healthy, income-producing fraud should not be encumbered by government interference.

The manipulation of the land laws by the large Puget Sound mills was so successful that soon it became hard to find prime trees that could be felled directly into saltwater harbors. In January 1884, an official of the Puget Mill Company wrote that "the timber contiguous to the Sound is nearly exhausted. The part remaining is such as was passed by in recent years."

But the company did not have to worry, because by 1892 it had acquired 186,000 acres of land. Rail lines were built into the logging camps to haul the logs out. Lumber production, 1.7 million feet in 1880, soared to ten times that in 1890. The company started trading on an international scale, buying eighty-nine lumber ships. Soon Australian ships cleared for Melbourne and Chilean ships bound for Valparaíso were sailing into Puget Sound. Logging was the territory's most powerful economic and political force. It was also the principal promoter of statehood.

The bill chartering the Northern Pacific had been signed by Lincoln on July 2, 1864, and it turned 40 million acres of public domain over to the railroad. Some people called it the biggest real estate giveaway in American history.

On that very day, Job Carr celebrated his fifty-first birthday. This fourth-generation Quaker had enlisted in the 26th Indiana Infantry Regiment at the age of forty-eight, after the bombardment of Fort Sumter. Wounded twice, at Shiloh and Stone River, he was about to be discharged, and was entitled to 320 acres of public land.

Carr had read that the Northern Pacific would terminate at Puget Sound, so he decided to go there and scout locations. On a canoe trip with friends along the shores of Commencement Bay, he spotted the Point Defiance peninsula, admiring its high banks and its creek trickling through the trees into a pond. "I raised on my feet and exclaimed Eureka! Eureka! and told my companions there was my claim."

By January 1865, he was building a cabin on the future site of Tacoma. His two grown sons, both Civil War veterans, joined him in 1866 and took claims adjoining their father's.

Other men, drawn like Job Carr by the prospect of the Northern Pacific, began arriving in Commencement Bay, including the Kentucky-born promoter Morton Matthew McCarver. In the west, they said, you could find two kinds of men: the "stickers" who stayed on the job, and the "short-stakers" who jumped from employment to employment. McCarver belonged to the latter category. At sixty-one, after an eventful life of roaming the west as a gold miner, real estate speculator, Oregon apple grower, and Idaho storekeeper, McCarver saw Commencement Bay as his last chance. Settling the terminus of the Northern Pacific would be like striking the Comstock lode.

Job Carr sold McCarver 160 acres, which had cost Carr nothing but the filing fee, for $1,600. Placing all bets on his expectation of the railroad, McCarver platted a town called Tacoma and sold lots. The old boomer penned some of his most alluring promotional copy: "I can frequently with my bare hands throw out enough smelts to supply a camp of 50 men." He found investors and bought 280 more acres. Tacoma, McCarver promised, was the place "where the iron of the rail will meet the salt of the sea."

By 1869, Tacoma had a lumber mill and a post office, with Job Carr as postmaster. By 1870, a school and a stagecoach line to Olympia had cropped up, but still no railroad. Seattle and Olympia were also in the running as terminals. Seattle was closer to the open ocean and reachable over the lowest mountain pass, Snoqualmie. The drawback for Olympia was its harbor, where mud flats forced steamers to come in at high tide. Tacoma's trump card was that the eastern capitalists backing the Northern Pacific wanted the line to go through Portland, and Tacoma was closer to Portland than Seattle.

By 1872, the contenders had been narrowed down to Seattle and Tacoma, where McCarver's group now owned 1,200 acres and had 1,500 more under option. On June 30, 1873, the Northern Pacific site commissioners wired in code to General George W. Cass, president of the railroad, that they "unhesitatingly decide in favor of Tacoma." The triumphant Tacomans took to the street, chanting: "Seattle! Seattle! Death rattle! Death rattle!"

McCarver felt that finally, after a lifetime of failure, he had struck the mother lode. But ten years would pass before the railroad actually arrived, for in 1873 its principal backer, Jay Cooke, went bust. The track had been laid as far as Bismarck going west and Kalama going east, but a 1,500-mile gap yawned between the two points. It would not be filled until 1883.

In 1881, Henry Villard took control of the Northern Pacific, and in September 1883 the final spike pierced the ground at Goldcreek, Montana. And then down the grade and into the Tacoma station came the wood-burning locomotive loaded with VIPs, and Tacoma's fortune was made.

In the 1870s, the settlers of Puget Sound were getting tired of living under the territorial system, an arrangement they considered little better than colonialism. They wanted a representative form of government, with governors and judges elected by the people rather than appointed by the president.

But Washington did not yet have the requisite population. The general rule stipulated that a territory had to have enough people to elect a representative to the House under the federal ratio, which was 125,000 persons per representative. Washington Territory in 1880 had a population of 75,116. However, the requirement was loosely enforced, and Nevada had attained statehood in 1864 when its population was well under the necessary figure, thanks to its silver and gold mines.

Acting on its own, the territorial legislature called a convention at Walla Walla in the summer of 1878 to draw up a state constitution. That October voters ratified the document by a vote of 6,462 to 3,231. But when the legislature next asked Congress to pass an admission bill, Congress did not act, because of party alignments.

The Democratic blockade broke in 1888 with the election of Benjamin Harrison, giving Republicans a clear majority in Congress for the first time in ten years. With deferral futile, the lame-duck Congress passed the omnibus bill granting statehood to the Dakotas, Montana, and Washington.

Thus, in 1889 a second constitutional convention assembled during the summer, meeting in Olympia on July 4. The delegates numbered forty-three Republicans and twenty-nine Democrats—farmers, stockmen, bankers and merchants, a couple of doctors, a couple of teachers, a preacher from North Wales, and quite a few lawyers.

Exerting their muscle, the timbermen tried to block a move to give ownership of tidelands to the new state. Resisting these demands, the convention affirmed public ownership. This constitution had a reformist bent, and included an antimonopoly clause that expressed the Washingtonians' fear of lumber trusts. It also contained an article specifying that no money be spent for religious worship in schools, as well as one prohibiting corrupt solicitation.

The constitution was ratified, and J. W. Robinson, a territorial lawyer, was appointed to take it to the nation's capital and receive from President Harrison the proclamation making Washington the forty-second state. In September, Robinson met with President Harrison and Secretary of State James G. Blaine, who came from the lumber state of Maine. Blaine asked Robinson, "What is the greatest quantity of merchantable timber you have known to be on, say 160 acres?"

Robinson replied, "I represented a timber claimant in the land court in which witnesses testified that his quarter-section contained 36 million feet of first-class merchantable timber."

"Well," Harrison interjected, "that much timber could hardly grow on 160 acres."

"Mr. President," replied Blaine, "that would depend upon how high it grew."

CHAPTER TWENTY-ONE

THE WYOMING FRONTIER

> *We're going to give you a fair trial, followed by a first-class hanging.*
>
> > *The vigilance committee*
>
> *We're building a country out here, and there's no place for weakness.*
>
> > *OWEN WISTER*

Wyoming became a territory in 1868, patched together from a big piece of Dakota and small pieces of Idaho and Utah. Before that, it was a thoroughfare rather than a destination. Wyoming's South Pass offered the only way through the Rockies. Thousands of settlers bound for Oregon and California funneled through the three-mile-long, 7,550-foot-high pass, stopping in Wyoming only to camp at night and graze their cattle. Straddling the Continental Divide, Wyoming did not appear as a place to linger, but a natural boundary to be crossed.

Wyoming's only residents were Indians, mountain men, and soldiers garrisoning the forts on major rivers. It would take the twin enterprises of the telegraph and the railroad to bring large numbers of people to Wyoming. Ribbons of rail and lattices of wire strung on poles would eventually wrap the continent into a national unit. If the railroads abolished distance, the telegraph eliminated the four time zones, reducing communication between east and west from weeks to seconds.

The first intercity telegraph line, covering the forty miles from Washington, D.C., to Baltimore, had been completed in 1844. It immediately transformed journalism, by providing transmission of "spot news" from that year's political conventions. By 1852, competing companies had built a 15,000-mile wire grid across the east and midwest. Many of these small outfits were absorbed by the Western Union company in 1856.

The Western Union, as its name indicated, aimed to complete a transcontinental line from San Francisco to New York and sent agents across the country to man the stations. That was how Oscar Collister came to Wyoming. Born in Ohio in 1841, Oscar was a cross and sickly child, small in stature; as a grown man he weighed but a hundred pounds. As a boy, Oscar caught every fever around, including the telegraph fever. His ambition was to join Western Union, and he worked without pay as a messenger until he was promoted to night operator at seventeen.

In 1861, the company sent Oscar to the western wilds at Deer Creek, a hundred miles west of Laramie, near today's Rawlins. There connection with the California telegraph would finish the transcontinental line—at first a solitary wire run along a string of forts.

Usually, telegraph offices were located in railroad depots, but in Wyoming, Oscar arrived years ahead of the railroad. Deer Creek was a trading post run by squaw men in log cabins. At that time, the Pony Express carried the mail from St. Joseph, Missouri, to Sacramento, California, on a route through Laramie, the South Pass, Salt Lake City, and Carson City. Inaugurated on April 3, 1860, the mail service lasted only a brief eighteen months, becoming redundant when workers joined the two telegraph lines on October 24, 1861. Eight years before the Union Pacific locomotives touched cowcatchers at Promontory Point, Western Union and the California lines had completed a transcontinental telegraph.

But that momentous occasion still lay in the future when Oscar Collister arrived at Deer Creek in June 1861. Soon afterward, Bond, the regular Pony Express rider, came through. He was known to be short-tempered and quick on the trigger. Bond made a pronouncement concerning Lincoln's inauguration that Oscar knew to be false. When Oscar told him so, Bond drew his gun. But he turned to the chief trader, Bissonette, and said, "I don't want to kill a damn tenderfoot who don't know no better." Oscar realized that he had to learn the ways of the west. You could not contradict an armed man, no matter how wrong he was.

It didn't do to contradict your boss either, so Oscar kept his mouth shut when Ed Creighton, the line chief, came through, took one look at him, and asked, "What prompted them to send out a spindly kid like you?" Ed had come out to locate trouble on the line. Oscar found that time hung heavy, except when there was line trouble.

Deer Creek had been an Indian agency under Major Twiss, who lost his commission with the expiration of the Buchanan administration in 1860. But as Twiss had adopted the habits of the country, taking a squaw wife and fathering several half-breed children, he continued to live in the area. Someone told the major that Oscar played chess, and a friendship began. When the war news came over the wire, Oscar passed it on to the major, whose knowledge of military matters put events in perspective.

The Civil War was a windfall for the telegraph business. The government built 14,000 miles of lines for military use, and turned them over to the Western Union after the war. So cozy was the relationship between government and telegraph company that General Thomas E. Eckert, the assistant secretary of war under Lincoln, eventually joined Western Union in a high managerial position. But for Oscar, in charge of 250 miles of wire, the Civil War meant Indian trouble.

That summer of 1861, Indians brought the line down west of the Sweetwater Bridge. Carrying a gun and a saber almost as long as he was, Oscar rode forty miles north to Casper and then forty miles west to Sweetwater Crossing, locating the place where a Sioux party had cut the line. They had taken quite a lot of wire, which they used as arm bracelets. Oscar sent some men from Fort Laramie with a military escort to fix the damage.

Oscar later heard that when some of the Sioux who had cut the line got sick, their medicine man told them it was because of the wire bracelets, which he ordered them to bury. The Great Spirit protected the talking wire, the shaman explained, and the Great Spirit had avenged its desecration. In the next two years, the telegraph operators were the beneficiaries of this belief, for the Indians did not touch the wire. As Oscar put it, "The Indians are almost as superstitious as the witch-burning founders of the city of Boston."

The winter of 1861–62 was severe and monotonous. Oscar boarded with the traders and did not appreciate their squaws' cooking. But one of the unmarried squaws made him a pair of buckskin moccasins bearing his initials in various colored beads. When Oscar offered money for her work, she refused. Her name was Bright Star. She often came to Oscar's office, quietly watching as he read the Morse paper tape and tapped out forty words a minute on the clicking key.

One afternoon in November 1863, Bright Star came into his bunk with her chaperone, who asked Oscar if he wanted her for his squaw. Oscar replied with the common term of the country, "When the grass is green," and was immediately hugged and kissed. But fate intervened, and Oscar was told that he was being transferred to Salt Lake City. He was alone in his bunk meditating on the future when Bright Star came in. She pulled on his coat and led him behind the building. Then she told him that in a dream she had seen him shot in the back with an arrow. She had seen both of them in the Happy Hunting Ground. He must leave quickly, she said as she mounted her pony and rode away. Two days later Oscar left for Salt Lake City.

At Fort Reno, built in 1865 at the Bozeman Trail crossing of the Powder River, one of the high points of garrison life was the arrival of the mail, which a rider brought from Laramie in a padlocked bag.

In 1866, Lieutenant Clarke was on duty one day when the mail came. He unlocked the padlock, spread a blanket on the ground, and emptied out the contents. Then he assigned two men to sort out the letters for Fort Reno and throw the others addressed to points west back in the bag.

One of the men, Private A. B. Ostrander, said as he got down on his knees: "This is a nice thing for us to be doing, handling everybody else's private letters."

"What's the matter with you?" asked Lieutenant Clarke.

"Well, this mail ought to be put up separate in Laramie," Ostrander said. "They could save one bundle for us and one for each post above, then all we'd have to do is take out our own bundle."

"Shut up and go to work," Clarke said.

"That would make four bundles to leave Laramie with," Lieutenant

Kirtland said. "One for Bridger's Ferry [Fort Bridger, on Blacks Fork, in the southwestern corner of Wyoming], one for Phil Kearny [a fort in the Bighorn foothills on Piney Fork, in northern Wyoming], and one for C. F. Smith [a log and adobe fort in southern Montana, at the Bighorn Crossing of the Bozeman Trail, ninety-one miles northwest of Phil Kearny]. And they would vary so much in bulk that Van [the mail carrier] would find it hard work to balance the sack on the back of his horse."

"He always has three or four soldiers for an escort," Ostrander said. "One of them could carry a sack to help him out."

"The mail carrier is sworn in by the government," said Kirtland, "and is responsible for it. He gets ten dollars a day and no one else is allowed to handle the bags."

Clarke growled his assent and Ostrander relented, although he thought: "If a soldier isn't allowed to carry a locked bag of mail, how is it that two enlisted men are allowed to handle each individual letter? I give up." So he sorted the mail—officers on one side of the blanket and enlisted men on the other—divided the letters by company, and handed them to the orderly sergeant.

After the Union Pacific was incorporated in 1862, it took the construction crews a while to get going. Starting in Omaha, they had laid only 40 miles of track by the end of 1865. In 1866, however, they completed 260 miles, and in the fall they reached North Platte, Nebraska. In July 1867, they dipped into Colorado at Julesburg for a few miles before continuing westward into Wyoming.

A floating population in the thousands followed the railroad, made up of laborers and their parasites (gamblers, saloonkeepers, and prostitutes), and they turned supply bases into instant towns. Julesburg, which in June 1867 had a population of 40 men and 1 woman, grew to 4,000 people in one month. For a short time, this city of tents became known as "the Wickedest City in America." Its canvas saloons were called "whiskey ranches."

The Union Pacific laid out a town, left an agent in charge of selling the lots, and moved on. Some towns put down roots, and some died. But the track pushed on. For the railroad, the marching order went like this: surveyors first, graders second, and third the *Frontier Index*. For along the way, the railroad had picked up a movable newspaper, which followed the crews along the grade, publishing two issues a week from wherever they happened to be.

This "press on wheels" lasted roughly two years, as the railroad crossed southern Wyoming. It was the brainchild of two brothers from Virginia, Fred and Leigh Freeman, who managed to promote their pro-Confederate and anti-Reconstruction views while printing the Union Pacific's house organ.

The Freeman brothers, who had fled the south at the end of the War Between the States, migrated to Kearney, Nebraska, where Leigh found work as a telegraph operator. In 1865, they started publishing a four-page paper at Kearney on an old-time hand-roller press, using hand-spiked typography and a six-column format. But the brothers quarreled with the officer in charge of the military reservation and had to leave town.

When the grading crews moved to North Platte in the fall of 1866, the *Frontier Index* moved with them, the Freemans carrying the press in a wagon driven by three ox teams. Soon North Platte became another one of those "hell on wheels" towns, with nine saloons.

What fit the frontier better than a newspaper that advanced with it? The *Frontier Index* provided semiweekly accounts of the building of the railroad, as well as reports on life in the depot towns, ads and notices, national news and 'Secesh' editorials. The *Index* described itself as "The Pioneer paper of the Plains—of the successive terminal towns of the Union Pacific Railroad. . . . It is found in the reading rooms of every town throughout the West!!!! . . . As the emblem of American liberty, the *Frontier Index* is now perched upon the summit of the Rocky Mountains; flaps its wings over the Great West, and screams forth in thunder and lightning the principals [sic] of the unterrified anti-Nigger, anti-Chinese, anti-Indian party—Masonic Democracy!!!!!!!!!!!"

The paper claimed a circulation of 15,000 throughout the West. It *was* a curiosity, unique in the history of journalism, moving by wagon every few weeks to an advanced point on the grade, but its immediate audience consisted of the curious mass of people for whom following the railroad had become a way of life.

Once a site was designated as a division point and a depot, it employed multitudes. Aside from workers to grade and lay the track, the company contracted crews to cut thousands of cords of cedar and aspen for the wood-burning locomotives. Hundreds of men went out and chopped wood, and the hills were stripped of trees as though a barber had given them a shave.

Hundreds more were retained to dig fireguards on both sides of the track. Because live coals dropping from engines sometimes caused range fires, Congress decreed that the railroads must plough six-foot strips along the tracks to prevent fires. In addition a thousand men had the job of keeping the track open in winter.

Thus, a mobile mass of job seekers trailed behind the grading crews, providing a readership for the *Frontier Index*. Its earliest extant issue, dated Julesburg, July 26, 1867, was printed on wrapping paper. A note on page 3 explained: "The Index is one day behind time, on account of waiting for our printing paper to come, but we are . . . compelled to issue on brown wrapping paper or none at all."

An editorial written in the standard inflammatory style denounced "the smelliferous skullduggery being played by the niggerpoolists." The editors apologized for having written in a previous issue that a certain place was "contagious to the waters of the Platte." The *Index* abounded in colorful expressions, such as this one intended to convey skepticism: "Hey, doctor, how did you get that petrified log to swim like a pine cork?" Under the headline MISCELLANEOUS ITEMS, the editors ran stale jokes, like the one about the Irishman who had never eaten corn on the cob. Finding some on his plate at the boardinghouse, he handed the cob back to his landlady and asked, "Would you be so kind as to put some more beans on the stick?"

Such was the *Frontier Index*, a folksy, racist, and irreverent sheet that appeared with every few miles of newly laid track. Railroaders lived in their long, narrow world, bounded by the right-of-way fence, and thought in terms of miles between divisions. The paper reported their progress, as the flatcars loaded with ties came to a stop, and sweating men lugged and laid them on the prepared grade. From another car, they slid off pairs of rails, each one twenty-eight feet long and weighing 560 pounds. They placed the rails in position on the ties, where gaugers, spikers, and bolters squared them and pounded them into place. Men swinging steel-headed mauls drove in the spikes, three blows to a spike, ten spikes to a rail, and four hundred rails to a mile.

In November 1867, the railroad arrived in Wyoming. The company had chosen Cheyenne as a supply depot, and the town soon had a population of 6,000. In April 1868, the *Index* was publishing in Laramie, reporting on April 21 that "the town is only a week old, and there are already a thousand lots taken." When Laramie was two weeks old and had two thousand inhabitants, the paper announced that it was destined to become "the half-way Chicago between Omaha and Salt Lake City."

The Freeman brothers took up the cause of Laramie versus Cheyenne, the latter town being home to a rival newspaper called the *Leader*. They pointed out that the *Index* was movable while the *Leader* was "dead stationery." "The press on wheels . . . will be the advance guard of the new commonwealth and all croakers and one-idea organs such as the Cheyenne squirts had better lie low or they will get scooped."

In May 1868, when Ulysses S. Grant was nominated for president at the Republican Convention in Chicago, the *Index* said he was "too much nigger for us." The paper began to refer to him routinely as "Useless Slaughter Grant," and castigated "the seven-year nigger agitation which has brought us as a nation to the door of anarchy and ruin."

In September, it was "off for Bear River" on the Idaho line, where the old overland stage route came through. Bear River City grew into another "hell on wheels." There was little law of any kind, and gangs of outlaws roamed the town. On October 30, the *Index* reported that "last Friday somebody went crazy with bad whiskey and opened a promiscuous fire from a pistol."

A vigilance committee formed and placed the following ad in the *Index* on November 3, signed "All Good Citizens": "The gang of garroters who are congregated here from the railroad towns to the east are ordered to vacate the city or hang within 60 hours from this noon."

The *Index* supported the vigilantes, who lynched three outlaws and locked up some unruly graders. As a result, on November 20, a big gang of "shovel men" from the grading camp stormed into Bear River City to deliver their brethren from jail. In the ensuing riot, they set fire to the *Frontier Index* office and destroyed the plant. Escaping any way he could, Leigh Freeman rode out of town on an ox.

Years later, in an article in the *Butte City Union*, Leigh Freeman recalled the riot of November 20, 1868, writing that "our office was burned to a grease spot, and the type ran down the hillside in a molten mass." But in its short life span, the *Frontier Index* was a lively and controversial presence on the Wyoming frontier.

Child of the telegraph and the railroad, Wyoming began to attract settlers a couple of months before the Union Pacific reached Cheyenne in November 1867. It was still part of Dakota Territory, but the distance from Cheyenne to Yankton was 350 miles. In October 1867, the *Cheyenne Leader* called for a separate territory, saying, "Dakota is a slow coach; we travel by steam."

Dakota was not averse to dumping Wyoming, and the Yankton legislature wrote Congress urging that it be made a separate territory. By July 1868, the Wyoming territorial bill had passed the Senate and the House. On July 25, President Andrew Johnson signed it into law.

In 1870, the new territory's first census gave Wyoming a population of 9,118 in an area of 98,000 square miles. Though the population kept growing, most of the settlement in the 1870s was restricted to towns along the Union Pacific track. That made sense because the railroad was the territory's biggest employer. Besides track construction, it also owned coal mines in Rock Springs, repair shops in Cheyenne, and rolling mills in Laramie.

By comparison with such wealthy neighbors as Nevada and South Dakota, Wyoming was impoverished, since it had no precious metals. Nor was it much good for farming, for there was little arable land, insufficient rainfall, an average elevation of 6,700 feet, and a short growing season. Good grazing land, however, made it suitable for cattle.

In 1869, territorial officials arrived in Wyoming's capital of unpainted plank houses and unpaved streets, Cheyenne. On December 10, the first territorial legislature passed "An Act to Grant to the Women of Wyoming Territory the Right of Suffrage and to Hold Office." At that time, Wyoming had one woman for every six men, and people considered the act a publicity stunt to attract more females. As the *Cheyenne Leader* put it: "We now expect at once quite an immigration of ladies to Wyoming." By March 1870, the *Leader* complimented the legislators of "a shrewd advertising dodge. . . . A cunning device . . . for notoriety."

In 1870, Eliza Stewart, a schoolteacher in Laramie, was told by Sheriff N. K. Boswell, "Miss Stewart, you have the honor of being the first woman ever called upon to serve on a court jury." Eliza was thirty-seven, and had come to Wyoming the year before. She sat on a mixed grand jury of six women and six men, and when Chief Justice Howe addressed them as "ladies and gentlemen of the grand jury," she felt a distinct sense of elation.

"What an event!" she thought. Within twenty-four hours, King William of Prussia had cabled congratulations to President Grant. The jurors served for three weeks, in cases that involved horses and cattle theft, illegal branding, and murder. Eliza felt sure that the presence of women had inhibited the male jurors in their chewing and drinking.

In 1871, the second legislature tried to repeal the women's suffrage law. In the upper house (the Council), C. K. Nuckols, a Democrat, pointed out that since women promised to obey men in the marriage ceremony, "I think you had better abolish this female suffrage act or get up a new marriage ceremony to fit it."

Another Democrat, W. R. Steele, said: "This woman suffrage business will sap the foundations of society. Women will get so degraded as to go to the polls and vote and ask other women to go. A woman can't engage in politics without losing her virtue. No woman ain't got no right to sit on a jury nohow, and every lawyer knows it. They watch the face of the judge too much when the lawyer is addressin' 'em. Let's at least prevent any more of 'em from gettin' the vote, and save the unborn babes and the girl of sixteen."

Opponents of the new law deployed other arguments: women's suffrage increased the cost of political campaigns by making it necessary to provide carriages at every polling place; the women ignored the party system and voted on the candidates' personal morals; if women voted differently from their husbands, it would make trouble in the family; men could pay off the $2 poll tax by doing road work, but women did not have that option.

The legislature voted for repeal, but the governor vetoed it. There were no more attempts to interfere with women's suffrage, which was carried into the Wyoming constitution when the territory became a state, known as "the Equality State."

In 1876, Jesse Knight went to Minnesota to fetch his bride, Mary Hezlep, and bring her to Evanston City, on the Idaho line in the southwest corner of Wyoming Territory. Arriving on the westbound train, which then traveled at thirty miles an hour, the couple stayed the night at the Mountain Trout Hotel and were the guests of honor at a charivari (a mock serenade for newlyweds).

The next day Jesse carried his bride across the threshold of his old homestead and introduced her to his bull terrier, Gummus, who had been trained to guard gold against marauders when Jesse was a prospector.

"Gummus, this is Mrs. Knight," Jesse said. "She has come to live with us, and whatever she says to us we must do. We must take very good care of her, and never let anyone hurt or bother her. Do you understand that, Gummus?" The dog raised his eyes and blinked.

"All right, Gummus, go and make friends with her." Gummus went over and rested his dark and drooling jaws in the bride's lap.

Jesse Knight worked as the district clerk when court was in session in this sagebrush-covered town at 5,000 feet elevation. One night, while Jesse performed his official duties, a bleary-eyed man barged into the cabin.

"Hi sweetheart," he said. "No, you needn't call your husband, I saw him leave a while ago. You're alone and I'm coming in."

"I'll call the dog," Mary warned.

"That's what they all say," the man replied. "I ain't afraid of no damn dog."

Mary said one word: "Gummus." The dog had been taught to go for the throat, and only her hand hooked into Gummus's collar saved the intruder's life.

Mary had learned on her father's knee: "The fault, dear Brutus, is not in our stars, but in ourselves, for we are underlings." And she wasn't going to be an underling. She had a long, hard winter ahead of her, but she told herself, "If the Chinese down the river can make vegetables grow, so can I."

In 1878, T. S. Garrett arrived at the Wells Fargo office in Denver. Stopping by Grove's gun shop to clean his Spencer carbine, Garrett found himself in the midst of a discussion about firearms. One man was saying that he could outrun all the sixteen shots in a Henry rifle, while another declared that he wouldn't take a Spencer as a gift. Joining in, Garrett bet a $10 hat that with the seven bullets in his gun, he could knock out seven knots on the pine boards of a corral at thirty yards in less than twenty seconds.

He won. One of the fellows in Grove's that day, part owner of a bull train, observing Garrett's prowess, offered him a job hauling freight to Laramie. He later taught Garrett the saying "You are never safe from Indians except when they are in sight."

Once in Wyoming, Garrett found a job with an outfit that used ox teams to freight supplies to government posts on the plains. There was good money in hauling because it was dangerous work, owning to frequent Indian attacks.

One of the fellows on the wagon train did nothing but grumble—they never started early enough or drove late enough, they never made camp in the right place, that sort of thing. When Garrett caught a jackrabbit and cooked it, the grouch said, "Why I'd just as soon eat crow as jackrabbit."

"Well," Garrett said, "it seems to me an agreeable change from pancakes straight, and I guess I'll take a chance and finish it."

They were camped on the Little Sandy one evening, south of the Wind River Range and west of the South Pass. Suddenly, a wild-looking Indian decked out in war paint and feathers rode up on a fine horse, carrying a Winchester and a six-shooter, and leading a young mule.

"How," Garrett said, "where you catchie mulie?"

"I stole him, by God," the Indian said, "can't you speak English?"

The wagon train was taking a load to Fort Washakie, an outpost maintained for the protection of the Shoshones on the Wind River Reservation.

They had to make their way through snow so deep that it took fourteen days to go the fourteen miles from Lost Soldier Creek to Crook's Gap. Eight mules drove the big Studebaker wagons, but since there was nothing to feed the mules, the men gave the animals the paper targets that were piled on top of the wagons and destined for shooting practice at the fort.

When they got to Washakie, the quartermaster sergeant refused to unload the wagons. Lieutenant Elting, the quartermaster, came up and asked: "Why don't you unload the freight?"

"Look at the condition of it," the sergeant said.

"What do you expect them to do," said the lieutenant, "haul it back to the railroad? Put this freight in the warehouse."

Garrett went to the office with the lieutenant, who told the clerk to write out an affidavit. "What's the excuse?" the clerk asked.

The lieutenant said: "Bad roads, bad snow, bad bridges. Make out a good strong affidavit. These men are 31 days late and their freight is in terrible condition."

If it had been left up to that fool of a sergeant, Garrett thought, they would be on their way back through the snow to the Union Pacific line at Rock Springs.

Born in Illinois in 1850, Edward Day Woodruff became a doctor and headed west in 1880 to Lander, Wyoming, in the Wind River Mountains. He started right in with Jack Parker, who owned the saloon and had cancer on his lip where he held his pipe. No sooner had Woodruff cut it out than Jack started smoking again. Eventually, the saloonkeeper had to have the whole right side of his face cut away.

Woodruff also served as an expert witness in murder cases. The nearest court was in Rock Springs, 100 miles south. Court was in session under a big tent. Since everyone chewed tobacco, it had to be adjourned from time to time so a man with a shovel could come in and turn the earth.

Woodruff stayed in Rock Springs after the court session ended to doctor the coal miners. For ten years, he was in the employ of the Union Pacific Coal Company. He had his bailiwick all to himself, because the nearest doctor was in Rawlins, 150 miles away. But the Rawlins doctor, a rambunctious type, came to Lander one day to confront Woodruff and said: "You're poaching on my territory. Get out or I'll run you out."

"I do not believe," Woodruff replied, "that it is part of professional ethics for one doctor to treat another as you are treating me. This is a virgin territory, after all, open to all comers. No man is running me out of town and as long as I'm here I intend to make good."

But the Rawlins doctor considered Lander as part of his practice. He had friends among the Molly Maguires, a violence-prone labor group operating in the coal mines, and he asked them to help him "run that tenderfoot out of town."

One morning two brawny Scotsmen barged into Woodruff's office.

The doctor had to order them out at the point of a gun. Another time he saw a row of Mollies sitting on an embankment across the street from his office. A law had been passed that you couldn't buy whiskey during certain hours without a doctor's prescription, and Woodruff heard the men on the embankment bet they could get one from him. He caught one Molly saying to his companion, "Go get a prescription from that tenderfoot doctor."

When the fellow came in, Woodruff met him gun in hand. He made the Molly sit there and sweat it out for a couple of hours while his friends downstairs waited. When Woodruff finally let the man go, the others jeered him hot and heavy.

After that, the doctor's problems with the Molly Maguires ceased, for they said: "Aw, you can't bluff that tenderfoot out of town. Of course you can kill him, but it's kind of handy to have a doc around."

The Union Pacific coal mine at Rock Springs was all-white until 1875, when the miners struck. They were getting a dollar a ton and demanded $1.25. The Union Pacific brought in Chinese miners and the striking white miners lost their jobs. The Chinese were shipped in by the carload and given work while the frustrated strikers watched.

After 1875, more Chinese were laboring in the mines than whites. Every man worked for the same pay under the same terms. But since the Chinese were in the majority, their refusal to join the union guaranteed the failure of any strike action. As a result, the pay dropped to 74 cents per ton. Many were the white miners' grievances—the Chinese bribed the pit bosses for better locations, they said, and the company used rigged weights.

In 1885, 331 Chinese and 150 whites were employed at the pits in Rock Springs. Most of the latter belonged to the Knights of Labor, who backed Chinese-exclusion legislation.

David Thomas was a mine boss at the Number 5 mine. On September 2, 1885, he noticed that at the next mine over, Number 6, Chinese workers had been assigned to stalls previously promised to whites. These stalls were moneymakers because the coal was easily accessible. Thomas resented the mine superintendent, Jim Evans, for giving the Chinese preference at a time of white unemployment.

When two white miners found Chinese in their stalls that morning, a fight broke out that spread to other stalls and then to other mines, as men attacked each other with picks, shovels, drills, and tamping needles. Half an hour later the white miners left the mine and marched up and down Front Street, shouting, "White men fall in." At 2 P.M., a mob of armed miners set out for Chinatown.

"I was standing at No. 5 tipple" (an apparatus for tipping and unloading coal carts), Thomas said, "when I saw a mob form, with rifles, shotguns, and revolvers. They stopped for a moment at the railroad crossing. A shot or two were fired at the Chinese who came out of their dugouts and shacks. More shots were fired at the fleeing Chinese, and the mob set fire to Chinatown."

The enraged mob slaughtered twenty-eight Chinese. Union Pacific had hired the Chinese for their docility, and this same docility made them easy targets. Thomas was friendly with an old laundryman, Ah Lee, who lived in a dirt dugout with a board roof. Ah Lee had bolted his door, but the rioters broke in through the roof and murdered him. Thomas knew the man who had pulled the trigger and asked him, "Why did you kill poor Ah Lee?"

"I had to, Dave," the man said, "he was coming at me with a knife."

"Oh," said Thomas, "is that why he was shot in the back of the head?"

Thomas observed a housewife step over the body of a dead Chinese and steal packages of laundry he had laid aside for delivery. That evening he walked over to Chinatown and saw the flames from forty burning houses light the faces of the rioters in the street. The next morning, touring Chinatown, he noticed blackened bodies lying in smoking cellars.

A week later, on September 9, troops arrived to escort the Chinese back to their ruined homes. While waiting for their houses to be rebuilt, they were lodged in boxcars. Soon the Chinese returned to work, and the Union Pacific fired forty-five whites for taking part in the riots. But when the court asked men in Rock Springs to serve on a grand jury, they declined, saying, "I don't think my back is bulletproof."

In 1888, the *Cheyenne Sun* opined that it was time to agitate for statehood, "as it seems to take several years of hard knocking at the door." That November, Benjamin Harrison was elected president and Francis Warren, a longtime resident of Wyoming, was reelected governor. Warren promoted statehood in June 1889 and called for a constitutional convention.

Times had changed. By 1889, the buffalo had ceased to roam and the Indians had been steered onto reservations. The stagecoaches and the prairie schooners gathered dust in museums. Mule teams disappeared, along with mule skinners cracking their blacksnake whips. The Sunday Sabbath crossed the Missouri, invading the Rockies, and a district judge on the Green River in Wyoming, William Ware Peck, shocked everyone by having an Episcopal minister open the court with a prayer. The population hovered around 60,000 in the 1890 census.

Attended by elected delegates from the ten existing counties, the convention met in September 1889 in Cheyenne and drafted a constitution that included women's suffrage. On November 5, it was ratified by 7,272 to 1,923. The low turnout did not help the cause of statehood, but the territorial delegate, Joseph M. Carey, presented the constitution to Congress and arranged for its consideration by the House, which approved it on March 26, 1890. The Senate approved the document on June 27. On July 10, President Harrison signed the statehood bill, making Wyoming the forty-fourth state.

• •

Wyoming didn't have the ethnic tensions that bedeviled Arizona and New Mexico, but it did have bears. And no account of Wyoming would be complete without a bear story. Hank Mason had a ranch in northeastern Wyoming, seven miles east of Gillette. One day in 1898, walking along Donkey Creek with his Winchester, he saw some familiar tracks.

As he stepped around a fallen tree, an enormous bear rose up thirty feet away. Hank fired, hitting it in the shoulder, but the bear kept coming. When he tried to reload, his gun jammed. So he turned to fight the bear, who proceeded to get Hank's head in his mouth, while he guarded his face with his elbows, which were reduced to pulp. When Hank fell and played dead, the bear walked away. After a while, he tied his wounds with his shirt and started for home. But the bear heard him and came back.

Hank clambered to the top of a quaking aspen, but the tree was too short. The bear reached up and snagged him by the heel, pulling him down and tearing the skin off his foot. The bear hurled Hank to the ground and put Hank's head in his mouth and crushed his skull. Hank passed out and the bear just left him there. The men who found the nearly dead rancher counted thirty-three bites, but Hank survived to tell the tale.

They found the bear, too, and shot him. He measured nine feet long. A taxidermist stuffed him, and he turned up as an exhibit at the Omaha State Fair.

CHAPTER TWENTY-TWO

THE IDAHO FRONTIER

The Indians survived our open intention of wiping them
out, and since the tide turned they even weathered our good
intentions, which can be much more deadly.

JOHN STEINBECK

The whole nation had been footloose too long, Heaven had
been just over the next range for too many generations.
. . . How did a tree sink roots when it was being dragged
behind a tractor? Or was an American supposed to be like
a banyan tree or a mangrove, sticking roots down
everywhere, dropping off rootless appendages? Could you
be an American, or were you obliged to be a Yankee, a
hill-billy, a Chicagoan, a Californian? Or all of them in
succession?

WALLACE STEGNER

U nlike the rest of the United States, Idaho was first settled from the
west, not the east. After 1860, the rumor of gold brought a swarm
of miners from the Pacific, and it was not until 1864 that a large
Confederate influx from Missouri redressed the balance. In the meantime,
while thousands of Americans were killing each other in the War Between
the States, in Idaho thousands were rushing from creek to creek to get rich.

The advance man for this frenzy of gold-seeking was Elias Davidson
Pierce. A native West Virginian, he arrived in the Idaho panhandle in 1852
to trade with the Nez Percés. Trading goods for horses, Pierce won the
Indians' respect by being honest and strict and by learning their language.
"I never romanced nor took any hand in their kind of sport," he wrote in
his reminiscences.

"The course I pursued," he said, "gave me a wonderful influence over
them." The Nez Percés told him that in the mountain creeks running into
the Clearwater River, shiny metallic chips could be found. Under the guise
of trading, Pierce went on a prospecting trip in February 1860. On February 20, he was panning in the Clearwater off a gravel bar, and when he
washed the pan, he saw color.

"I knew then," he wrote, "that I had the shaping of the destiny of that
country and that I could flood that entire region with good reliable men at

my own option." In March, he went to Walla Walla, only seventy miles away, to get outfitted. But on his return to Lapwai, the Nez Percé village where he had his trading post, the subagent Charles Frush asked Pierce if he had permission to travel through the reservation. Without replying, Pierce kept riding. Frush trotted alongside him, insisting that he must have a pass. "I would just as soon have that much brown paper," Pierce said. But not wanting Frush to follow him, Pierce remained in Lapwai.

Andrew J. Cain, the Indian agent, warned the Nez Percés that the discovery of gold on the reservation would flood the whole country with whites. When Pierce went back in August with ten prospectors he had recruited in Walla Walla, Indian guards patrolled the trails that led to the streams.

Pierce and his people spent a month and a half ducking the patrols. Once they reached the gravel bars on the reservation's upper borders, the Nez Percés left them alone. Finally, in Orofino Creek, the men got their first glimpse of gold. Pierce wrote, "I never saw a party of men so much excited; they made the hills and mountains ring with shouts of joy."

Pierce and his party rode back to Walla Walla on October 21 with several hundred dollars' worth of dust. When they displayed their loot in old Preston & Merrill yeast powder cans, the sight caused quite a commotion. Though some people feared that an influx of miners would start an Indian war, the *Portland Times* gave Pierce extensive publicity. Its editor, Alonzo Leland, would soon leave for the mines himself.

Determined to build a permanent camp on the edge of the reservation, Pierce obtained equipment from a mining company and a "flour stake" from a mill against future pay dirt. When he led another party to the Snake River in November, he ran into Andrew Cain, who urged the Indians not to ferry the prospectors across. But they liked Pierce's trade goods better than they did Cain's advice.

By December, eight cabins had been built on the site of Pierce City, on a tributary of the Clearwater. While waiting for the snow to melt to begin placer operations, they sawed lumber to make rockers and sluice boxes, which would separate the heavier gold from the gravel by a washing process.

Idaho was still part of Washington Territory, and the territorial legislature, in anticipation of a gold rush, created Shoshone County in January 1861, in the Clearwater area. Sure enough, the miners swept in and staked their claims—1,800 by mid-April 1861. By June, Pierce City had a population of 3,000. Walla Walla, the point of departure, was full of pack animals, and not a pick or shovel could be had at any price.

At the town of Orofino, barefoot miners paid $20 for gum boots. At the general store, the conversation turned on gold: "Yes sirree, $250 a day to the hand." "Jacob Weiser washed out $4000 in four days with one rocker." "This is the best thing since California." At the mouth of the Clearwater, where it ran into the Snake, the tent city of Lewiston went up as an outfitting station.

Andrew Cain gave up his obstruction tactics, for the word came from his boss, B. F. Kendall, the superintendent of Indian Affairs in Washington Territory, that "to attempt to restrain miners would be, to my mind, like attempting to restrain the whirlwind."

The surge of miners created a number of lucrative ancillary activities. At Lewiston, the old mountain man William Craig started a ferry across the Snake and the Clearwater, pulling in $400 a week. Arriving at Craig's Ferry in 1862 in a mule-drawn wagon, Mr. and Mrs. Theodore Schultz found 500 men with their freight and horses and mules standing in line waiting to cross. The Schultzes were told they would have to wait a week because of the backup.

"Those rascally ferry and bridge men were the curse of the country," Mrs. Schultz later recalled. "They charged 50 cents to cross a mule over a narrow creek."

A devout Irish Catholic, Mrs. Schultz was a purposeful woman almost six feet tall, packed into a powerful frame. She went down to the riverbank to find the head ferryman, and told him, "I want to cross."

The ferryman showed her his list. "I don't want to see your list," she said. "I want to get over the river."

"You must wait a week or more," he said.

"I'll not," she said, "I'll eat my supper on the other side, with the help of the holy virgin, and if you take us across, I'll pray for you all my life, so I will."

To her surprise, the blarney worked, and the ferryman took them over. The first woman in the Millersburg camp, Mrs. Schultz saw men take out 50 ounces a day and walk away with 50 pounds of dust. She started a boardinghouse, charging $2 per meal, and her main complaint was that gold dust got into everything.

In 1862, reports circulated of other strikes in the Salmon River area. More mining towns went up, such as Florence and Elk City, both sites benefiting from a flume nine miles long that brought water to the diggings. These mines were located well within the Nez Percés reservation, but no one seemed to mind.

In March, Alonzo Brown left his home in Roseburg, Oregon, to go to Florence. Traveling to the Salmon River and then up the river to a trail, he found himself in a dark basin at an altitude of 6,000 feet, surrounded by a meadow of tall marsh grass. The gold lay only a few inches under the turf in the little meadows and blind gulches of this great, bleak, wintry basin that had not been peopled since coming fresh from the Creator's hand. Now a field of white canvas tents covered it end-to-end.

Horses could not go the last sixteen miles into the basin. The men had to carry everything on their backs. Little Slate Creek, the halfway mark, was the campsite for 150 men. A contingent of Rebs had arrived, and Brown heard one discussing the war with a Union man. When the Reb erupted with "old Abe the nigger lover," a fight would have started if some of the older men hadn't quieted them down.

In the mining camps, where it took a while for news to arrive, every Civil War battle was fought a second time. Passions were intense, and Brown witnessed north-south disputes almost daily: "Have you heard the news?" "What news?" "New Orleans has been taken." "It's a lie, a damned Abolition lie. All hell couldn't take New Orleans." "No, but the Yankees did."

In the winter, the snow fell in piles six to twelve feet deep. You'd see men walking in single file, led by one who wasn't yet snowblind, with the blade of a shovel under his arm, and the man behind him holding another blade, and so on.

Miner and mining excitement made Idaho, and Lincoln declared the area a territory on March 4, 1863. Absorbed in the Civil War, Congress held back troops and let the young territory fend for itself, except for the building of Fort Boise in July 1863 at a crossroads of the Oregon Trail. A town went up next to the fort, and became a supply source for miners.

Boise revived the rip-roaring spirit of the mining towns in Nevada and California. For Boise miners, it was said, there was no such thing as bad whiskey. They called their home brew "tangle-leg" or "tarantula juice." Two of the favorite toasts were: "Here's nuggets in your pan," and "Let the hide go with the hair."

An ode to Boise prostitutes appeared in the local paper: "Ye pining, lolling, screwed-up, wasp-waisted, putty-faced, consumption-mortgaged and novel-devouring daughters of fashion and idleness, you are no more fit for matrimony than a pullet is to look after a family of fifteen chickens."

When J. M. McConnell got to lawless Boise in 1863, each man seemed to carry his life on his belt. McConnell homesteaded on the Payette River, where he kept horses. One day in 1864, he recognized a horse in the Boise stable that had been stolen from his corral a week before. The stable proprietor told him that one Gilke, owner of a restaurant, had placed the horse there.

Gilke told McConnell that John Kelly, the famous California violinist, had given him the horse as a present. McConnell looked up Kelly, who refused to explain the horse's provenance. McConnell said the horse had been stolen from him and that the man Kelly had got it from was perhaps the thief.

"You wouldn't tell him so," said Kelly.

"The hell I wouldn't," McConnell replied, "show me the son of a bitch."

Friends advised McConnell, however, that the only way to retrieve his horse was to hire a lawyer and sue, which he did. After paying for the issuance and service of papers, as well as the lawyer's fee, it cost him $70 to get back a $50 horse.

When he recovered his property in front of the stable, a dozen "follow-ers of the road" (outlaws) were hanging about, wearing buckskin suits, sporting ivory-handled revolvers, and enjoying the discomfiture of those they referred to as "vegetable men."

"Gentlemen," McConnell said, "I want to make a little speech before I say goodbye."

"Fire in, stranger," one of them said.

"I can catch any damn horse thief who ever marked these prairies, and the next one who steals a horse from me is my injun. There will be no lawsuit about it."

No one said anything, but a few days later some men raided McCon-nell's ranch and made off with five horses and four mules with a total value of $2,000.

Seeing that the thieves had taken the Brown Lee trail, McConnell rounded up a couple of ranch hands and rode off in pursuit. After a hard ride, they surprised four horse thieves at their camp and shot them dead. One of McConnell's men was wounded, but McConnell recovered his horses and mules.

The leader had gone to Payette. McConnell followed, finding him already in custody of the sheriff, who had arrested the man for buying supplies with bogus dust.

"Give him a hearing and discharge him," McConnell said, "I want him dead or alive."

The man was acquitted and turned over to McConnell, who took him to Boise, where a court convicted and sentenced him.

After that incident, some of McConnell's neighbors asked him to join them in a compact for mutual protection. They formed the Payette Vigi-lance Committee, aimed at ridding the country of horse thieves, bogus dust operators, and road agents. In all cases, the committee held a trial by jury. A first conviction brought a notice to quit the country within twenty-four hours. A second brought a whipping, and a third a hanging—three strikes and you're out.

In January 1865, the Payette vigilantes moved on the Washoe Ferry outfit on the Snake River, four miles above the river's confluence with the Payette. Under the cover of the ferry operation, the bandits were able to learn the movements of packtrains and stagecoaches. They had built a house on each side of the Snake. The one on the Oregon side was a small wooden fort.

The vigilantes crossed over a river packed with cakes of ice. One man went up to the blockhouse and asked to be ferried across, pretending to be nearly frozen. When he was let in, the others pushed in behind, before the outlaws had a chance to grab their guns hanging on the wall. The Payette vigilantes captured six bandits without firing a shot.

The Stewart brothers, Alex and Charlie, were sentenced to hang at noon on January 17 on the stage road, and the other four were ordered to leave the country. McConnell felt sorry for the Stewart boys, fine-looking, convivial young men not nearly as bad as those who'd been deported. He took Alex Stewart aside and said he would help the brothers escape, "Not because I think you're innocent, but you're young and this may be a lesson to you. But don't ever come back."

That night a blizzard blew the snow into every nook and cranny. McConnell got two horses saddled and hid them in the willows by the river. Though he knew he'd be shot if he was found out, he let the prisoners slip out and told them to git. Then he went to the barroom and kept everyone busy with songs and bunkum speeches while the Stewart brothers galloped across the sagebrush hills to Oregon.

But a couple of months later, Alex Stewart made the mistake of showing up again in Boise. When McConnell heard about it, he got on his mule and rode the thirty-five miles from his place into town. He found Alex in a boardinghouse behind the saloon. "I thought you had some sense," McConnell said, "but you are a damn fool."

"Well," said Stewart, "it looked hard for a man to be run off his property."

"That is not the question. I told you I would let you go if you didn't come back. Now you better be gone within 24 hours, or the chances are you won't live another 24."

Stewart left. But after a number of incidents chasing outlaws, McConnell decided that one day his number would be up if he stayed in Idaho, so he moved to Humboldt County, California.

The problem of appeasing and governing newly annexed areas that did not meet the criteria for statehood went back to the dawn of the republic. Wait-listed territories chafed under a system they considered neocolonial.

Territorial status had one advantage, however—the federal government paid the bills. It paid for the legislature, including the costs of printing, rental of halls, utilities, and stationery. It paid for the federal courts, including the judges' salaries. It paid for roads, for troops, and for public buildings.

But the biggest expense was Indian Affairs, a large bureaucracy that employed agents, clerks, farmers, teachers, and soldiers. Indian policy had evolved over the years, but its underlying aim always remained the same: to move the Indians out of the way of advancing settlers, and to explain the move by saying, "This is what is best for the Indians."

At the Walla Walla Council on May 29, 1855, Governor Isaac Stevens concluded treaties with the Umatillas, the Yakimas, and the Nez Percés. The agreement guaranteed that, once on their reservations, the tribes "would never again be disturbed while the sun shone or water ran."

But in 1863, under the pressure of the mining invasion, the Nez Percés signed away nine-tenths of their reservation, or 6,932,270 acres, at eight cents an acre. Many of the chiefs refused to sign the new treaty, declaring that the government had not honored the old one.

One of these chiefs was Joseph, who made his home on the Wallowa River, in the land of winding waters in northeast Oregon, near the Idaho line. In 1875, the government threw the Wallowa region open to homesteaders and assigned a five-man commission to parley with young Chief Joseph, whose father had died in 1871.

Joseph told them: "In the treaty councils, the commissioners have claimed that our country has been sold to the government. Suppose a white man should come to me and say, 'Joseph, I like your horses, and I want to buy them.' I say to him, 'No, my horses suit me, I will not sell them.' Then he goes to my neighbor and says to him, 'Joseph has some good horses. I want to buy them but he refuses to sell.' My neighbor answers, 'Pay me the money and I will sell you Joseph's horses.' The white man returns to me and says, 'Joseph, I have bought your horses and you must let me have them.' If we sold our lands to the government, that is the way they were bought."

This was a pretty good summary of what went on in treaty negotiations. But the commissioners remained unmoved. They decided that Joseph's band should be relocated to the Lapwai Reservation on the Clearwater and receive 1,200 acres (as opposed to their 1 million acres in the Wallowa country).

In May 1877, the government gave Joseph a month to bring his people to the reservation. He asked for an extension so that he could round up his cattle in the dozens of hidden valleys. It would also, he explained, take time to cross the Snake, whose waters were raging in the spring thaw. The extension was denied. Officials told Joseph that if he and his people missed the deadline by one day, troops would be sent after them.

Joseph came in, losing several hundred head of cattle on the Snake. He camped on the Idaho side of the river. Soon after, other nontreaty bands joined his. Tension and resentment ran high, and three young braves who had been drinking whiskey went out and killed four whites.

Fearing he would be blamed, Joseph took his people south to White Bird Creek, which empties into the Salmon. On June 15, Captain David Perry and two companies of the 1st Cavalry, totaling about 110 men, rode after him. With half as many warriors, Joseph routed Perry's force, killing 34. From the field of battle, the Nez Percés recovered 63 rifles and plenty of ammunition.

Knowing he would be hotly pursued, Joseph led his band east, across the Bitterroot Range and into the buffalo plains of Montana. They dipped into Yellowstone Park, then headed north, hoping to get to Canada. In late September 1877, thirty miles from the border, Colonel Nelson A. Miles caught up with them. For four months, over 1,300 miles, Joseph's Nez Percés had fought a retreating action. But now some of his bravest warriors were dead and his people exhausted. He surrendered, speaking his memorable words, the terse requiem of a dying people: "From where the sun now stands, I will fight no more forever."

The army settled Joseph and his 418 Nez Percés in a malarial part of

Indian Territory (Oklahoma). When the government allowed them to return to Idaho in 1885, only 268 remained alive.

After the Civil War came the era of Christian reformers in Indian
Affairs. The reformers assumed that progress depended on turning the
Indians into farmers. Education and religion, they believed, would facilitate the transition. Desiring a massive reorganization of the Bureau of Indian Affairs, President Grant in 1869 asked religious groups to help run
the agencies and reservations. Grant created a ten-member Board of Indian
Commissioners, made up of reformers, whose mission it was to promote
"peace and civilization."

Essentially, the peace policy—known at the time as "piety or bullets"
—aimed to move the Indians onto reservations under religious supervision.
Congress wanted them to be self-sufficient, thus placing the tribes in a
double bind. First they were relocated, and then they were expected to
survive "by their own exertions."

At the Fort Hall Reservation, on the Snake River above today's Poca-
tello, Agent W. H. Danilson struggled to feed 1,300 Indians on rations for
half that number. At the Lemhi Reservation, between the Salmon and
Lemhi rivers, Agent John A. Wright received 78 cents per Indian per week.

On the Nez Percé Reservation, there had been missionaries since 1836,
when Henry Harmon Spalding established a Presbyterian foothold. By
1871, churches held services in Lapwai and Kamiah, seventy miles to the
east, causing disputes between the missionaries and the Indian agent over
who was in charge of what.

In 1873, Sarah McBeth arrived as a teacher in the Lapwai school. A
year later, Spalding died and she succeeded him. Sarah had already served
among the Choctaws in Oklahoma and felt deeply that she had a special
call for working with Indians. Thin-lipped and unsmiling, slight and pale,
her long hair parted down the middle and gathered up in a severe bun in
back, Sarah fervently believed in the necessity of breaking the chiefs' power
and raising the moral tone of the people.

Efforts at acculturation seemed to be modestly successful among the
Nez Percés. At the Lapwai school, students were more than usually willing
to attend, perhaps because the Indian agent, Charles Monteith, withheld
rations from the parents of absent children. Attendance reached seventy-
five in 1883, and a year later, Monteith announced that apprentices could
now run the grist- and sawmills.

In 1879, Sarah's younger sister Kate came to Lapwai to help her. The
two women worked for the Presbyterian Board of Foreign Missions, and
they both moved to Kamiah, where the Bureau of Indian Affairs had contracted with the board to operate a school for girls. Kate McBeth described
the Kamiah situation in her journal as "a mix-up of heathenism, white
men's vices, and religion."

The Nez Percé language had no word for "husband," she noted, and
"a woman who would not, even when hungry, steal a piece of bread, would

think it nothing more than fun to steal a man, or husband, from another woman." She found that "tripping and stumbling into sin was a common occurence. . . . Of course the church must forgive the penitents to the seventy times seven!"

The sisters made the male Indians wear pants cut from flour sacks, the result being that they walked around with the word "Idaho" printed on their rear ends in large letters. If the men wanted to enter the schoolroom, they had to wipe the paint off their faces. Sarah learned the Nez Percé language, and the Indians had a good laugh at her expense when she dug potatoes out of the grave (ta-me-kash) instead of out of the field (ta-ma-ne-kikt).

In 1884, the McBeth sisters decided to do something about the Fourth of July, which the Nez Percés had turned into a two-week pagan carnival rife with gambling, drinking, and fornication. The horse racing and wife swapping had to stop.

The sisters thought of introducing a counterholiday to keep the Indians from temptation. Why not a nice picnic, the kind they used to have on the banks of the Ohio when they were girls? The Indians could have it on the banks of the Clearwater. But how to explain it to them? A picnic made no sense to people who spent all their time out of doors. It would be hard to convince them that eating by the side of the river was a special treat.

The sisters enlisted the support of Robert Williams, the first Nez Percé minister, who suggested they do it "when the berries get ripe . . . the blackberries and huckleberries." So one Sunday, Williams announced a picnic to his flock. They would take food and spend the day at a spring on the mountain ten miles away. "It is just like the Fourth of July," he told his perplexed parishioners. "Poor things, how much they need to know yet," Kate wrote in her journal.

The first Kamiah picnic was set for July 4, 1884. A week before the holiday, a bad omen made its appearance: two large rattlesnakes turned up in the woodshed. Sarah told Kate: "You had better not talk about them, the people will say the medicine man sent them here."

Kate dreaded the long and arduous horseback ride up the mountain under the broiling noonday sun, but she had to go, because Sarah lacked the strength to make the trip. Reverend Williams had issued a general invitation, and all the church Indians came. They reached a sloping arbor along the side of a rocky hill, where the incline was so steep there was hardly enough level ground to unpack their hampers.

Somehow news of the snakes had got out and men and women came up to Kate to inquire about particulars. Nodding to each other with knowing looks, they said, "It is the work of the Te-Wats" (medicine men). Kate laughed it off, but they said it was not a good idea to laugh at the Te-Wats.

All in all, however, the picnic seemed to be a success. The men went to kill the beef for the barbecue, and the women busied themselves in the arbor, laying out places. The Nez Percés liked the free food, and approved of the occasion as an improvement over the normal working day. Kate went from one group to the other, finding everyone in a holiday mood.

Then several pistol shots abruptly rang out. Some of the young braves had brought along liquor, and one of them, Alex, was drunk. Tom Hill, the tribal police chief, tried to arrest Alex; when the young man resisted, Tom shot him. Another Indian, named Nine Pikes, came to Alex's help and was also shot, and lay dying of his wounds.

Reverend Williams pushed his way into the melee, crying: "Stop! Leave our picnic grounds, you police!"

Kate saw Alex, in leggings and flowing hair tied in a ponytail, stumble to the stream, stopping every few steps. At the edge of the water, he fell to the ground, dead. "There was a great hollering to get away from him," she wrote, "for they have a superstition that if one looks upon one shot with a gun or pistol, he will die."

The aroma of roasting beef filled the air, but the sky clouded over and rain whipped down, making the barbecue sputter and fizzle. Women gathered up their cakes and pies and their hungry whimpering children. The long winding descent toward home began as the rain turned to hail. Kate forded the river under a barrage of hailstones and emerged wringing wet, her sunbonnet sticking to her face.

Troubles darker than the mountain storm were gathering at the reservation. The omen of the snakes had come true, and the Te-Wats had struck. The killing of the two Indians brought out some of the underlying tensions. The Indian agent, Charles Monteith, for some time had been lobbying the commissioner of Indian Affairs to have the McBeth sisters removed "for repeatedly interfering with reservation affairs." He accused the sisters of turning the church Indians into an aristocracy, who felt superior to the blanket Indians. He used the incident at the picnic to recommend their expulsion from the reservation.

At the end of August, Sarah McBeth left Kamiah for Mount Idaho and never came back. She said she had been ousted for teaching the Indians the Declaration of Independence. Kate was ordered to Lapwai, where she felt herself to be "a kind of state prisoner." The shootings led to a full investigation, and in December, a grand jury indicted Tom Hill for murder and he stood trial in Mount Idaho (about thirty miles south of Lapwai). A jury found him guilty of "justifiable homicide."

Christian reformers wanted to integrate the Indians into American society and turn the "heathens" into good citizens. By giving each Indian a piece of land, many of them believed, they could break up the tribal hierarchy and destroy the influence of the chiefs and medicine men.

In 1887, Congress passed the Dawes General Allotment Act, sponsored by Senator Henry Dawes of Massachusetts. Under the act, reservation lands would be parceled out among Indian households, and the surplus sold and opened to settlement. The government would stand back and allow private property to exert its magic influence.

But as the House Committee on Indian Affairs put it, "The real aim of this [allotment] bill is to get at Indian lands and open them to settlement. If this were done in the name of greed, it would be bad enough; but to do it in the name of humanity and under the cloak of an ardent desire to promote the Indian's welfare by making him like ourselves, whether he will or not, is infinitely worse."

Nevertheless, many reformers genuinely believed that the allotment policy would prove to be the Indians' salvation. It was the same old story: by getting the tribes to give up hunting and fishing for farming, and by conferring on them certain advantages of citizenship, such as the vote, the Indians would cease being outcasts in their own country.

One of these true believers was Alice Fletcher, the daughter of a New York lawyer, born in 1838. Active at first in the temperance and feminist movements, Alice went on to Indian reform. She became an anthropologist, studying the customs of the Plains Indians, measuring their heads with calipers, and presenting papers to Harvard's Peabody Museum. Alice backed the Dawes allotment plan, and when it became law, the government sent her to the Nez Percés Reservation in Idaho to help implement the new policy. Her task was to survey the reservation land, take a census of the Indians living there, and assign specific plots to individual Indians.

Alice Fletcher arrived in "the queer little sunburnt town of Lewiston" on May 30, 1889. Then fifty-one, she was short and plump, and had a forceful, tenacious nature. Her friend E. Jane Gay, who had been a nurse in the Civil War, accompanied Alice to Idaho as cook and photographer, referring to her as "Her Majesty" on account of Alice's no-nonsense manner and supposed resemblance to Queen Victoria. In the wilds of Idaho, Alice Fletcher and Jane Gay took on what was considered a man's job. The frontier dissolved a good many conventions, including those concerning women's roles in society.

As it turned out, the allotments got bogged down in reservation politics, and Alice and Jane spent four years in Idaho. Between 1889 and 1893, they lived on the reservation from April to November, returning each winter to their little house at 214 First Street in Washington, D.C.

In June 1889, the pair went from Lewiston to the reservation headquarters at Lapwai, where Alice got her first inkling of the difficulties ahead. Resistance to the allotment policy had been raised from all sides. The white ranchers opposed it because allotment meant they would lose their right to free grazing on reservation land. The Indian agent, Charles Monteith, knew that the policy would put him out of a job, because the reservation would cease to exist. And the chiefs saw that they would lose their prestige, for once each Indian had his plot of land, they would all be equals.

Alice Fletcher's only ally was the surveyor, Joe Briggs, a 260-pound, broad-shouldered Vermonter, whose first words to her were, "I was not aware that you were a lady." Briggs got busy recruiting Indian chain men to survey the reservation's 800,000 acres, an obstacle course of canyons, gulches, and rocky wastes.

Soon a delegation of cattlemen came to see Alice. They had 10,000 head of cattle eating reservation grass, and made it clear that they did not intend to stop grazing. Why couldn't the Indians, they asked Alice, be located in the canyons? Alice replied it was her sworn duty to place them on the best land, so that they could become self-supporting farmers.

The men hung about, chewing their plugs, with vehement expectorations. Alice assured them that better times were coming under the reign of law. "Law!" a cattleman exclaimed. "What do we want with law? We done as we wanted to and ain't got no use for law." As they mounted their horses, one of them muttered, "Why in thunder did the government send a woman to do this work? We could have got holt of a man." They sounded out Briggs, who told them that from the look of Miss Fletcher, "Everything will have to be done on the square."

Alice wanted to explain the allotment policy to the Indians. But when she asked Monteith where they were, he sullenly replied, "Oh, they're all about." Getting nowhere, she decided in July to move her operation to Kamiah. There, too, at first, she met with a cool reception. Her interpreter was threatened with violence if he remained in her service.

But Alice persevered and held a meeting for the Indians in the Kamiah church. "You will have 160 acres," she explained. "Your boy, being 18, will have 80 acres, and the little girl will have 40 acres—that's 280 acres."

An elderly headman rose and asked: "How is it that we have not been consulted? Who made this law?"

The judge of the Indian court, whose job would be abolished under the allotment plan, said, "We do not want our land cut up in little pieces."

"I have come to bring you manhood," Alice said, "that you may stand up beside the white man in equality before the law."

She asked them to get themselves registered. "The women must come also," she said. "Every man, woman, and child in the tribe must have land. It is their inheritance."

But even the apparently simple task of making a list of reservation residents, Alice saw, required great patience and tact. A Nez Percé was not supposed to speak his own name, and therefore you could not ask him what it was. You had to deduce his name from the maze of family relationships. When Alice asked about grandparents, they told her, "All our fathers' uncles are our grandfathers, and all our mothers' aunts are our grandmothers."

Joe Briggs was also having problems, climbing up and down canyons in 110-degree heat. Despairing of his workers' slow pace, he realized that "you can't hurry an Indian," and he had to buy them hobnailed boots because they cut their moccasin-shod feet on the rocks. He couldn't use the compass, because "the needle hugs the earth—there's too much mineral in the ground." When he started navigating by the sun, the headmen, to sabotage his work, set forest fires that darkened the sky. As if this were not enough, the white cattlemen followed him around, urging him to put the Indians in the ravines.

But Briggs won the Indians' confidence by being straight with them. When one said, "I want this land," he said, "Not if I can help it. You'll starve to death on that land. Sagebrush on it." Another said, "This is my land. I grew up here." "Do you want to start a rattlesnake farm?" Briggs asked. Nine times out of ten, they took his advice. Later an Indian who had ignored him came back and told him: "I got bad land, all alkali, no good for grain, no good for nothing. What I do now?"

"Guess you'll have to marry that woman who picked it out for you," Briggs said. "That woman married already," replied the Indian. "Then you'll have to eat alkali," Briggs said.

Slowly, Alice also began to win the Indians' trust. Each day she convened a court to decide claims disputes. They called her "the measuring woman." In Lewiston, the cattlemen held an "indignation meeting," and voted to ask the territorial delegate to have Alice fired. One rancher complained that she had described them as "buzzards sitting on a fence waiting for the old horse to die."

Alice and Jane left in November 1889—their cabin was unheated and the Idaho winter was fierce—and returned in May 1890. That summer Chief Joseph, who had come back to Idaho, visited Alice, but would not take an allotment. "It was good," she said, "to see an unsubjugated Indian. One could not help respecting the man who still stood firmly for his rights."

There was in fact a split between those who took allotments and those who refused, the older men who held to their right to roam at will over the reservation. The deeper reason for their opposition, Alice knew, was their fear that equally held land meant an end to tribal hierarchies. All she could do was explain the benefits of the new arrangement, over and over again.

In 1891, Alice's third year on the reservation, some Indians still resisted. In her absence, the Indian agent had tried to undermine the program by saying that she was cutting the land into little three-cornered pieces. So she had to go around repeating that 160 acres was not exactly a garden plot. Briggs, in the meantime, was discovering the cattlemen's dodges, the illegal timber cutting, the diversion of streams, the continued pasturing of cattle.

The breakthrough came in November 1891, when the Bureau of Indian Affairs issued an order that no Indian could go hunting unless he had an allotment. All of a sudden, the Nez Percés started clamoring for their portions. When Alice and Jane reappeared in June 1892, in their fourth and final year, the Indians asked for wire fencing, thinking it was a direct line to citizenship.

By the time Alice and Jane left in November 1892, the 1,400 Indians on the reservation had been settled on good bottomland along the Clearwater and its tributaries, between Lewiston and Kamiah. At Lapwai, Alice and Jane said goodbye to Kate McBeth, who said, "Come and visit." "Oh no, I cannot," Alice said, "the people would all want their allotments to change at the first sight of my face."

The Nez Percés allotments occupied about 260,000 acres, leaving 540,000 acres of surplus land on what had once been their reservation. After Alice's departure, three commissioners came to buy the extra acreage. "What are we going to do with our cattle and horses?" the Indians asked. They had no choice but to sell, though, and gave up the surplus land for $1,626,222, or $3 an acre.

In the fall of 1895, three men guarded by an escort of soldiers brought the payment for the land to Lapwai. Allotment Indians were summoned to the agency courtyard, where an officer read off names on the list, and men came up one by one to receive their checks. The representatives of seven banks stood by, accepting deposits.

The government opened the surplus land to settlers on November 18, 1895. Eventually, a dozen towns rose up on the reservation. In principle, Indian allotments could not be sold for twenty-five years, but in practice ways were found around the ban. The Indians who sold and went through the money ended up as farm laborers, picking hops or pulling beets.

The principal result of the Dawes Act nationally was that in 1881, Indians held 155,632,312 acres of land, and in 1900 they held 77,865,373 acres. By the time Congress repealed the act, in 1934, they were down to 48,000,000 acres.

Idaho's population in 1890 was 88,548. In the territory's twenty-seven years, twelve men had served as governors, and six of these carpetbag governors had served less than a year. One of them, Caleb Lyon, was accused of embezzling $40,000, which he said he had lost on a train.

Besides corrupt or absent officials, the people of Idaho had to contend with Mormons in the south, who had come up from Utah. Voting as a bloc, they held the balance of power in territorial politics from 1872 to 1882, creating anti-Mormon feeling that targeted polygamy.

In the 1880s, anti-Mormon fever ran high, and federal legislation barred polygamists from voting or holding office. A politically ambitious United States marshal, Fred T. Dubois, used the Mormon issue in Idaho to discredit the Democrats, with whom the Mormons usually sided, and to build up the Republicans. In the 1884 legislative elections, voters unseated the Mormons in their stronghold, Oneida County.

The next year, Idaho passed a test-oath measure under which a man, if challenged, had to swear under oath that he did not belong to the Mormon church. If he refused, he could not vote or serve in the legislature. Mormons as a result went underground and ceased to be a political force in Idaho. In 1890, the Supreme Court upheld the test oath, ruling that it was constitutional for a state to determine its internal voting qualifications.

Fred Dubois, who had been a student orator at Yale, was elected territorial delegate to Congress in 1890. The voters gave him a mandate to push for statehood. Idahoans chose delegates to draft a constitution, which they speedily approved. In Washington, a Republican Congress was eager to welcome new Republican states. Speaking for Idaho before the Senate, Dubois said, "She will be no laggard in the never-ceasing onward race."

The statehood bill passed the House on April 3, and on July 1, it breezed through the Senate by voice vote. "It came so quickly at the close," Dubois said, "that I hardly knew the child was born."

On July 3, 1890, Dubois and the clerk of Congress took the statehood bill to the White House. President Harrison and Secretary of State James G. Blaine were cordial in their congratulations. "Mr. President," Dubois said, "I wish you would put off signing this bill until tomorrow. Our people almost unanimously wish to become a state on the Fourth of July."

"Very well," Harrison said, "I will do what you wish. But let me call your attention to this fact—the star of a new state goes on the flag of the United States on the Fourth of July following the date of admission to the Union. If I wait until tomorrow, the star of Idaho will not be on the flag for another year. If I sign the bill today, your star goes on the flag tomorrow."

"Sign the bill now," Dubois said. "I want the star of Idaho on the flag tomorrow." Idaho became the forty-third state on July 3, and Fred Dubois was one of the new state's first U.S. senators, and had a town named after him.

The *New York Post* commented: "Another mining camp becomes a state . . . the Republicans in Congress thus add two more votes in the Senate for free silver coinage and against sound money." To which the *Salt Lake Tribune* replied: "New York be blowed. . . . They are a set of slaves who wait for some English or German banker to take snuff before they sneeze."

The admission of Idaho marked the end of the frontier period in the Pacific northwest. Idaho provided the missing piece in the puzzle linking the Rockies to the Pacific, lying as it did between Washington and Montana in the north, and Oregon and Wyoming in the south. It had fought off the Mormons, who made up one-fourth of its population, and rejected a separatist movement that wanted to attach the panhandle to Washington state.

And on December 29, 1890, while Alice Fletcher was still in Lapwai, U.S. troops massacred the Indians at Wounded Knee, South Dakota. It was the last major confrontation between the army and the tribes. Indian resistance to white settlement on the western plains ended the year that Idaho became a state.

PART SIX
THE PROBLEM STATES

CHAPTER TWENTY-THREE
THE UTAH FRONTIER

Far out in the desert to the north dustspouts rose wobbling
and augered the earth and some said they'd heard of
pilgrims borne aloft like dervishes in those mindless coils
to be dropped broken and bleeding upon the desert again
and there perhaps to watch the thing that had destroyed
them lurch onward like some drunken djinn and resolve
itself once more into the elements from which it sprang.
Out of that whirlwind no voice spoke and the pilgrim
lying in his broken bones may cry out and in his anguish
he may rage, but rage at what? And if the dried and
blackened shell of him is found among the sands by
travelers to come yet who can discover the engine of his
ruin?

CORMAC McCARTHY

The National Archives
This was Salt Lake City in 1870, with its orderly layout and wide,
tree-lined streets and the Wasatch Mountains in the background.

Mormonism is at once an irreconcilable Christian heresy and the most typical American theology yet formulated on this continent.

A. LELAND JAMISON

Born in Norwich, Massachusetts, in 1810, Louisa Barnes moved with her parents to Winchester, New Hampshire, and attended the Female Academy. One of her classmates, Rebekah Pratt, had a seafaring brother named Addison. Rebekah often turned the pages of her map book to trace his course over the briny deep.

When Addison returned home between voyages, Louisa sensed an attraction between them. Nurtured over a period of time through correspondence, the epistolary romance led to marriage in 1831. Addison and Louisa Pratt settled down in the Buffalo, New York, area, finding a farm near the town of Ripley, which lay along Lake Erie close to the Pennsylvania line. Addison alternated farming with navigating the Great Lakes routes.

In 1832, Louisa's sister Lois arrived for a visit, but soon fell ill with consumption. Louisa heard that a sect in a neighboring town, calling themselves the "Latter-Day Saints," believed in healing the sick by faith. But when the Presbyterians in Ripley told her that they were impostors and deceivers, she did not pursue it. To her great sorrow, Lois died.

In the winter of 1835, another sister, Caroline, came through with her husband. It turned out that they had both been converted to the Latter-Day Saints. They were on their way to Kirtland, Ohio, outside Cleveland, where the sect had its new headquarters, and the story they told Louisa was nothing short of amazing.

A young man named Joseph Smith from Palmyra, New York, near Rochester, known for discovering buried treasure, had been visited by an angel, who gave Smith the location of some buried gold tablets.

Locating the plates on the side of a hill near the village of Manchester, Smith found on them inscriptions in a mysterious language. He claimed that he could decipher the text, and produced a translation of what he termed "The Golden Bible." According to this scripture, America had first been inhabited by a Hebrew tribe, which divided into two branches, the Nephites and the Lamanites. The latter, cursed with dark skin for their wrongdoing, destroyed the former, and survived to become known as Indians.

In March 1830, Joseph Smith published his translation in an edition of 5,000 copies, calling it *The Book of Mormon*. Word quickly spread that God had revealed to Joseph Smith the blueprint for a return to authentic Christianity. The time was ripe for Smith's revelation, for many were troubled by the tumult of an expanding America. Western New York, a region that had attracted thousands of immigrants following the Erie Canal's completion in 1825, had become a hotbed of revivalist sects. The fires of revival had swept through so often that people referred to the area as the "burned-over" district.

Against an "every man for himself" frontier ethic that was creating as many casualties as success stories, Mormonism offered the acquisition of spiritual grace. Mormonism converted the frontier experience into religious terms—instead of free land and a better life, attainable salvation. Just as Andrew Jackson, elected in 1828, proclaimed that the common man could hold office, Joseph Smith in 1830 affirmed that every Mormon could be saved. The millennium, the Second Coming of Christ, the kingdom of God, were at hand. The living and the dead would be reunited, and peace and harmony would reign.

Hearing all this, Louisa Pratt thought: "It is too good to be true." But she was still grieving over her sister Lois, and the promise of an end time in which the dead would be resurrected caught at her heart. The pledge of an egalitarian salvation also presented a more attractive prospect than forbidding Calvinist beliefs in original sin and predestination.

In 1837, Louisa and her husband decided to join the Mormon faith. Joseph Smith and his followers had by then begun the odyssey that would take them across the country, from western New York to Kirtland, Ohio, to northwestern Missouri, and then to Nauvoo, Illinois.

On their way to Nauvoo with their four children, the Pratts stopped at a coach station. There a tattered-looking woman stole two dollars from Louisa's satchel. "She shall see the time," Louisa said, "when she will need money and cannot get it." Such a sentiment expressed the core of the Mormon faith: that both righteous and unrighteous conduct would eventually get their just deserts.

In Nauvoo, Addison Pratt worked on the temple for a dollar a day and board. By this time, the Mormons, with their unstoppable dynamic fervor, were sending missionaries abroad. In 1843, the sect's leaders called on Addison Pratt's seafaring experience and sent him to the South Seas. Louisa would not see her husband for five years, and she entered a state of virtual widowhood.

By 1844, the Mormons had become unpopular in Illinois. In June, 1,500 armed men assembled outside Nauvoo, and to calm things down, Joseph Smith and his brother Hiram surrendered on riot charges. On June 27, masked men murdered the Smiths in the Hancock County Jail at Carthage.

When violence continued to flare, the Mormons decided to look for a place of refuge. In 1845, the government published John C. Frémont's report on his exploration in the Rockies, which included a map that showed the Wasatch Range in Utah and the Great Salt Lake. The accompanying description said: "The bottoms are extensive, water is excellent, timber sufficient, soil good and well adapted to grains and grasses. . . ."

Brigham Young, Joseph Smith's successor, saw the report, and liked what he saw. "The watchword was Go!" Louisa Pratt wrote in her diary. Yet she wondered whether she would be able to make the trip, alone with her four children. When she asked why those who had sent her husband to the ends of the earth did not prepare her for a perilous journey, she was told: "Sister Pratt, they expect you to be smart enough to go yourself without help, and even to assist others." Such was the core of Mormon strength: to be united in self-reliance, with no tolerance for slackers.

The ninth of eleven children, Brigham Young had grown up in a marginalized family in western New York, as had Joseph Smith. He came to Louisa and said: "The oxteam salvation is the safest way." Such was the language of the Mormons: Every decision was couched in the rhetoric of salvation. Before the faithful waited an appointed place, a hidden place, where they could escape "the desolation and wickedness" of the United States.

Companies formed, made up of 100 families each. Young left in February 1846, heading the first group of 1,800 in 400 wagons, and crossed the frozen Mississippi into Iowa Territory. Journeying during the cold, wet season known as "between hay and grass," the wagons made slow progress. Young stopped for a while at Sugar Creek, nine miles from Nauvoo.

Leaving in a later train, Louisa Pratt rode horseback and helped drive the stock. She noted that one of her cows "had nothing of the gathering spirit," a reference to the Mormon practice of asking converts to give up the non-Mormon world and "gather" with the saints. The captain of her company came by and remarked, "That cow is no Mormon."

The companies behind Young were strung out along the entire breadth of Iowa. Wagons sank in mud, sometimes covering less than half a mile a day. On June 14, they reached the Missouri, "sprawled like a serpent in the sun." When Louisa's turn came to cross, her wagon slipped off the ferry into deep mud. But the companies made it to the other side, coming upon a sloping tableland six miles north of today's Omaha. At the top of the rise, they found thick woods, with no place to pitch a tent, and mosquitoes beyond endurance.

The Mormons wintered there, building a log-cabin and sod-house town with a population of 3,483. Louisa Pratt paid $5 for a sod house, but the damp did not suit her, and she suffered fever, scurvy, and swollen legs. That winter, 600 Mormons died, succumbing to maladies ranging from malaria to black leg scurvy. But they held to their faith. One time when Louisa had run out of food, Sister Rockwood said, "You do not seem much troubled." "Oh, no," Louisa replied, "I know deliverance will come in some unexpected way."

In April 1847, when fodder for draft animals grew green on the prairie, Brigham Young and a pioneer company of 143 men, 3 women, 2 children, 3 slaves, and 72 wagons rolled out of Winter Quarters. Without professional guides, they headed for the Great Basin, leaving behind 4,000 persons, including Louisa Pratt.

On July 7, Young reached Fort Bridger in southwestern Wyoming.

Jim Bridger, the old mountain man who had explored the Great Basin, told them: "If you stop in Salt Lake Valley your people will perish. I will give you $1,000 for the first ear of corn you raise there."

On July 24, the pilgrims emerged from Emigrant Canyon, a forty-mile-long desert valley surrounded by mountains. The Great Salt Lake shimmered below them. They had reached their destination, an area so inhospitable that it was occupied only by Indians called "Diggers," who spent their time in the food quest, digging for roots and making snares for rabbits.

The Mormons found themselves on the eastern edge of the Great Basin, an enclosed region bounded by mountains. To the west, the Sierra Nevadas formed a "rain shadow," blocking rain-bearing winds from the Pacific, so that the basin had an annual rainfall of ten inches, barely enough to support semidesert vegetation. The soil was mostly infertile and tainted with alkali. From west to east, a series of mountain ranges wriggled irregularly northward like a bunch of caterpillars, separated by wide desert valleys, their floors reaching as high as 6,000 feet. On the eastern fringe rose the Wasatch Mountains, a spur of the Rockies that the Mormons had crossed and left behind them.

The Great Basin was a throwback of creation, a tub without a plug. None of the water from its rivers flowed out to sea. Instead, it ended up in lakes that turned to salt because they had no outlets. The Humboldt River in northern Nevada, for instance, drained into a closed basin called the Humboldt Sink, a lake in western Nevada with an intermittently dry bed. In northern Utah, the Great Salt Lake served as a catchment basin for the rivers flowing down from the mountains that ringed it; in fact, it resembled an inland sea, a vast bowl of soup rich in minerals that yielded half a cup of salt for every quart of water. Other rivers in the Great Basin didn't even reach lakes, but simply disappeared in the sand.

It was fitting that this closed geographic system, long regarded as an obstacle to westward expansion, was being settled by a people who wanted to create a closed social system, separate from the rest of America.

Sam Brannan had taken 235 Mormons from New York to California around the Horn in the *Brooklyn*. On reaching San Francisco, he set out to meet Brigham Young, finally catching up with the Mormon leader on the Green River in Utah in late June. When they came to the Great Basin, Brannan said, "For heaven's sake, don't stop in this godforsaken land, nobody on earth wants it, come on to California, a land of sunshine and flowers."

Brigham Young said: "Brannan, if there is a place on earth that nobody else wants, that's the place I'm looking for." Utah was then a dormant province of the former Spanish empire, now belonging to Mexico, though uninhabited by Mexicans. A no-man's-land, as far from Washington as Plymouth had been from London.

They started laying out Salt Lake City in ten-acre blocks. The High

Council divided the city into nineteen wards, distributed land, and issued building permits. Canals were carved out of solid limestone in the flanks of mountains, each farmer contributing the labor that entitled him to enough water to irrigate ten acres.

The High Council also functioned as a court, sentencing criminals to the whipping post. John Nebecker, one of the judges, recalled that the penalty for stealing was restoring fourfold. "There was one case brought before me," he said, "where a man who kept a dog stole some biscuits from his neighbor and the neighbor borrowed a shotgun and shot the dog. I gave the man who had lost the biscuits the full benefit of the law—namely, 16 biscuits."

In May 1848, Louisa Pratt left the banks of the Missouri for the mountains in a train of six hundred wagons. In the Platte River buffalo country, she saw large herds marching as orderly as a company of soldiers. Then it was two weeks along the Sweetwater River in Wyoming and miles without seeing a tree. She wrote of Frances, her second daughter: "It is her greatest pride to have people come to her to borrow fire, and praise her for being the lark of the company."

On August 20, Louisa could see the Salt Lake, and started dreaming of green corn and cucumbers. Instead, her husband was returned to her, back from the South Seas. Man and wife had to learn to know each other all over again. Just when they had begun to recover their former intimacy, Brother Young decided to assign Addison to another mission. "My heart shrank from the repetition of past trials," Louisa wrote. In a state of utter discouragement, she went to Sister Young and said, "If I am left again, I shall choose another man."

"I do not believe you would," Sister Young replied. "You have been faithful so long. You are not in earnest."

"I am more than half so," Louisa said.

Her daughter Frances said, "Mother, I will stay and let you go, rather than you and father should part."

In response to Louisa's entreaties, the Council deferred Addison's departure, but then summoned him to help pilot an emigrant train of non-Mormon forty-niners to California. Louisa confided to her diary: "Now I am fully reconciled to say adieu."

Frances said: "Oh mother, it sounds too willing. Do change it a little!" Accordingly, Louisa wrote: "I must try to be resigned."

When Addison left on October 4, 1849, Louisa lost her self-control, and wept and made a scene. That night a young man in her husband's party returned, and said they were detained at Cottonwood due to a lame ox.

"Why did not Mr. Pratt come himself?" Louisa asked.

"He did not wish to have the parting scene repeated," the young man said.

Louisa gave the young man a note for her husband that read, "Had you returned yesterday, it would have given me greater joy than your presence did after a five years' absence."

That winter she heard that Addison, having reached California, was to be sent again to the South Seas. "Another five-year widowhood!" she thought to herself, and sank into despair.

"I found my spirit growing rebellious, imagined my trials greater than any other woman's ever were."

"I imagined my companion was glad to go from home because I could not always manage to please him."

Finally, she resolved that the only thing to do was wait for the will of the Lord. Soon after, the Council told her to go and join her husband. And she did, spending many fruitful years in the South Seas as a Mormon missionary.

By the time Louisa Pratt left Salt Lake City, the Great Basin was no longer a no-man's-land. The Mexican War had ended in early 1848, and under the Treaty of Guadalupe Hidalgo, signed on February 2, 1848, the southwestern boundary of the United States was extended to the Rio Grande. Utah became a part of the territory ceded by Mexico.

The Mormons lost no time creating the squatter state of Deseret, adopting their constitution and forming their government. They had not waited for permission from Congress. Thus, in 1849, when they sent a delegate to Congress, Almon W. Babbitt, armed with a petition for statehood, he was not seated.

Inaugurated in March 1849, President Zachary Taylor led the opposition to Utah statehood. Babbitt reported that when he went to see Taylor, the president "tried to reason with me in relation to the absurdity of the Mormons asking for a state." On July 7, 1849, Babbitt wrote Brigham Young that Zachary Taylor had said "before 20 members of Congress that he would veto any bill passed, state or territorial, for the Mormons; that they were a pack of outlaws, and had been driven out of two states and were not fit for self-government."

A year later, Zachary Taylor died, and the outlook for Utah brightened. In the Compromise of 1850, Congress admitted California as a free state, while making Utah and New Mexico territories that would decide for themselves whether they wanted slavery. Thus, on September 9, 1850, Utah became a territory. President Millard Fillmore, who was not as rabidly anti-Mormon as his predecessor, named Brigham Young governor and appointed a full slate of territorial officials.

Utah was called a territory, but in fact it operated as a separate country with home rule. The territorial system, which had worked reasonably well since its adoption in the Northwest Ordinance of 1787, broke down in the Mormon nation. The Mormons were too far outside the mainstream. Their belief that God spoke directly to the leaders of the church was blasphemous to Protestants. Their first loyalty was to their church and not to their country, which did not make them good candidates for citizenship. And they permitted polygamy, a practice that most Americans found morally repulsive. For all these reasons, the Mormons were not deemed ready for statehood, and Utah would remain a territory for forty-six years.

The Mormons themselves were ambivalent about statehood, making repeated petitions to obtain it while aiming always to remain self-sufficient and apart. In the beginning, they were lucky, for in 1849 thousands of gold seekers came through, pumping cash into their economy.

As Louisa Pratt put it, "The whole gentile world came rushing to the gold mines." The prospectors' teams were jaded and their wagons broke down. They wanted fresh animals and pack saddles. It was a fine chance for trade. The Mormons called the Gold Rush "the Harvest of '49." Plenty of Mormons also took part in the "three-cornered trade": Utah produce in exchange for miners' dust, to pay for goods from the United States.

The trader Alexander Topponce paid for goods in dust, or "Lincolnskins" (greenbacks), or "Jawbone" (credit), or merchandise. When he went to Mormon settlements to buy cattle, he took the local bishop with him. Topponce and the bishop would meet a Scandinavian with a little herd who proudly said, "Dees haar bees my cattle, Beeship." The bishop would advise him to sell so that tithing accounts could be settled, and so that his children could get new clothes and make a decent appearance at meetings. Then the herdsman would say, "Aw! Aw! Das is all right." Topponce then trailed the cattle to Salt Lake City and sold them at a 100 percent profit, slipping a kickback to the bishop.

The attraction of the Mormons' novel American religion in distant places like Scandinavia can be attributed to the land policies that still existed in much of Europe. In the 1850s, three-fourths of Denmark's emigrants to the United States were Mormon, converted by missionaries. They came from their compact villages on the sandy Jutland Peninsula, a flat and treeless landscape like a North Sea version of Utah where the inhabitants lived in huts and slept on the floor on straw. In Jutland villages, half-a-dozen gentry owned all the land and the social distance between proprietor and tenant yawned as widely as it had in the Middle Ages.

After being conscripted into the army when they came of age, young Danish men spent their entire lives slaving for the gentry without anything to call their own. Their escape to America transformed them. And so the Jutland emigrant Christian Nielsen established himself in Utah and sent a letter to his village on April 27, 1856. Nielsen reported that he was a miller in Sanpete County. The Indians were friendly but dirty, he said, and sold their children as slaves. One Indian wanted to trade him his squaw for an ox. In three years, Nielsen had become the owner of two town lots and twenty acres of ploughland. He believed in the Mormon God, who noted every sparrow's fall. And he signed his letter "Emigrant of 1853," a plain fact that was as good as a nobleman's title.

And what of Jens Hansen of Spanish Fork, who accumulated fourteen wives and twenty-three children, the wives sitting at supper in descending order of age while the daughters waited on table? And what of the Danish weaver who was dumped in the Tithing Yard in Salt Lake City clutching a handful of green corn tossed from a basket, penniless and bewildered and alone, though his pounding heart told him that he was on the threshold of a better life? And what of the Jutland boy backtrailing 150 miles to find a stray cow, and of a Danish frock coat traded for a windowless cabin, and of the first feel of the plow, and of holding the deed in your hand? Here was an entire unwritten history of Scandinavian tenant farmers raised to the property-owning class, a history of small actions and individual purpose.

Mormon self-reliance extended to seldom calling on federal troops to put down Indian hostilities. The Mormons conducted their own Indian relations, based on peacemaking and conversion. They tried adopting Indians, but that didn't work too well, for however often the Indians were given baptisms and new shirts, they never became "white and delightsome," as Brother Young had promised.

A lot of the adopted children died of the measles, and a few ran away and rejoined their tribes. Since some young men did not want a squaw wife and could not find a white wife, they remained unmarried.

Priddy Meeks bought a three-year-old girl, who was called Lucy, and when Lucy reached maturity, she gave birth to a bastard daughter. The man responsible, who everyone thought would marry Lucy, shot himself just before his child was born. Perhaps he chose to die rather than marry an Indian. Or perhaps he could not face the Mormon penalty for his sin—confession and apology before the entire congregation.

Lucy went into seclusion and lay in bed with her face to the wall. She said it had been a mistake to suppose that she could be a white girl. She said she wanted to join her own people, and that night she died.

The Indians were Utes, one of the poorest tribes. They had no horses, wore rabbit-skin blankets, and had been reduced to begging from the Mormons. Elizabeth Wood Kane wrote: "They have the appetite of poor relations, and the touchiness of rich ones . . . the Mormon women are tired out, baking for their masters, while the squaws hang about the kitchens watching for scraps like unpenned chickens."

Apart from their begging, the starving Utes sold their children. Hanna Leavitt Terry recalled that "once when the Indians were hungry, they sold Susie to father. The Indian lay down a blanket and father poured wheat on it as long as any would stay without rolling off. . . . Susie was about five years old. Father kept her five years and let Brother William Pulsipher have her for a span of oxen."

This buying and selling of Indian children in Mormon families resulted in heartbreak and maladjustment. They fitted in nowhere. Susie never married but had three children. When she was brought before the church to answer for her sins, she said, "No white man will marry me, and I cannot live with Indians. But I can have children, and I will have them."

• •

The non-Mormon territorial officials who arrived in Utah in 1850 clashed with the Mormons, for Brigham Young was governor and it was he who doled out the patronage. Controlling the probate courts, the Mormons turned them into a separate court system. Unable to govern, the territorial officials went back east.

When Brigham Young publicly proclaimed the practice of polygamy in August 1852, the issue became part of the congressional debate over slavery and states' rights. If states could decide for themselves whether to keep slaves, the same ought to be true of keeping wives, it was argued.

In 1854, congressional debate raged over the Kansas-Nebraska Act, a bill that proposed to allow those two territories to determine whether or not they wanted slavery. If Kansas and Nebraska entered the Union on those grounds, northern senators argued, then Utah should be admitted as a state even though it practiced polygamy. In 1856, John C. Frémont ran unsuccessfully for president on the Republican ticket on the platform of abolishing the "twin relics of barbarism, slavery and polygamy."

In 1857, with Mormons in open revolt against territorial courts and officials, President Buchanan named a new governor of Utah, who declared martial law. Twenty-five hundred men, one-sixth of the entire U.S. Army, marched on the territory. The so-called Mormon War, although remembered as "Buchanan's blunder," was notable mainly for an absence of fighting. In the spring of 1858, Buchanan offered an amnesty.

Though he never held political office again, Brigham Young continued to rule Utah as president of the Mormon Church and accepted the presence of an army of occupation, which remained until 1861, when it was called away on more pressing matters.

The Mormons welcomed the Civil War as the long-awaited American collapse. Brigham Young told the saints in 1863 that the United States "is going to pieces, and it will be like water that is spilt upon the ground that cannot be gathered." The Mormons hoped that north and south would destroy each other "like Kilkenny cats." When that happened, they would take over the country and establish their rule.

But the hoped-for collapse did not occur, and after the war the outcry against polygamy gathered strength, preventing statehood for another thirty years, and maintaining the perception of Utah as a willfully incompatible and un-American entity.

Utahans watched as later territories acquired statehood—Oregon in 1859, Nevada in 1864, Colorado in 1876, Montana in 1889, Wyoming and Idaho in 1890. Some of these states had fewer inhabitants than Utah. In 1890, for example, when Utah had a population of 208,000, Idaho became a state with 84,000, and Wyoming with 61,000.

But Utah remained a territory. As Mark Twain put it, quoting a non-Mormon settler: "There is a batch of governors and judges, and other officials here, shipped from Washington, and they maintain the semblance of a republican form of government—but the petrified truth is that Utah is an absolute monarchy and Brigham Young is king."

Polygamy was the great stumbling block to statehood. At first, the Mormons kept the practice secret. On July 12, 1843, in Nauvoo, thirty-seven-year-old Joseph Smith privately dictated his revelation concerning plural marriage, which a few church elders practiced discreetly. Hosea Stout, the Mormon police chief at Nauvoo, recorded in his diary the nights spent with his second wife as being "on patrol guard."

But in the rough informality of Winter Quarters on the Missouri, polygamy came out into the open. Fifty-two-year-old Patty Sessions found it hard to accept her husband's second marriage to the younger Rosella, and wrote in her journal: "He has lain with her three nights. She has told him many falsehoods and is trying to have him take her to Nauvoo and then to Maine and leave me for good."

Polygamy had to be kept quiet while the Mormons lived within the monogamous United States (although rumors from time to time leaked out, fanning anti-Mormon feelings). But once they were in Utah, Brigham Young made polygamy official on August 29, 1852. The question was, why did the Mormons insist on polygamy, which made them pariahs in American society? By discarding it, they could have made themselves acceptable, and saved themselves from years of persecution. Instead, they stubbornly clung to it.

From the Mormon crucible, there surfaced many reasons for taking more than one wife, chief among them the "Old Testament" explanation. The Mormon leaders claimed they were simply emulating Hebrew patriarchs of the early Christian church, like Abraham. Was it not said in Exodus 21:10 that if a man "take another wife, he must not reduce the food of the first or her clothing, or her conjugal rights?"

Detractors, however, held to the "lecher" explanation. Beset by strong sexual drives that his wife could not satisfy, the charismatic Joseph Smith dreamed up polygamy in order to avoid guilt-inducing clandestine affairs, reconciling his hormones with religious law.

A more widely applicable variant was the "biological" explanation: Monogamy was contrary to human nature. Unlike women, a man could father children by a number of different wives at the same time. This led into the "procreation" explanation: A strong Mormon society needed numerous children, who could be produced in polygamous marriages. Later research, though, uncovered that plural wives had fewer children than they would have had with a single husband.

In fact, a minority of Mormon men practiced polygamy, probably about 10 percent. The elders regarded taking more than one wife as a reward for long service in the church. It could not occur without permission from Brigham Young, as well as the first wife's consent. A certain level of affluence was required to maintain such large families, which introduced a crude element of eugenics, the idea being that the more prosperous a man was, the more suitable to beget many children and improve the race.

But in the end, polygamy was the product of a pragmatic American religion, a set of beliefs that had to meet the challenge of a large community's survival in the Utah desert. The community had to be trained in a spirit of obedience and self-sacrifice; a high moral standard had to be maintained. The Mormons knew of the debauchery of other frontier communities, knew how freedom often led to license and individualism to rebelliousness.

In the straitlaced Mormon society, tobacco and alcohol (and even coffee and tea) were banned. But polygamy, which outsiders considered barbaric, was encouraged because it strengthened community ties, creating a web of kinship relations among the settlers and maintaining the unity of the family.

Instead of being a form of sexual excess, polygamy was an added constraint that required large doses of fair-mindedness and patience from husbands and wives. For the men, the practice transferred the task of governing from the community to the family and gave rise to a patriarchal hierarchy.

Polygamy also made possible a "clean" society free from adultery and prostitution. The "best little whorehouse in Utah" did not exist. In Utah, said a Mormon elder, there was "no adultery, whoredom . . . brothels, street walking, venereal diseases; no child murder (abortion) and other appendages of female ruin."

Offering yet another way of subordinating the ego to long-range goals, polygamy, like temple building, was a group effort that purged the community of the evils that plagued monogamous societies. The political cost of polygamy to the Mormons was so great that the advantages to the community had to be even greater.

Nevertheless, the Mormon leaders developed elaborate justifications for plural marriage. Asserting that polygamy conferred benefits on women, Mormon theology held that a woman without a husband would find the gates of heaven closed when she died. Mormon men married many women, even women in old age, to help them get through the gate. Marriage represented the passport to the millennium. Women had to be "sealed" with their husband in this life, for no marriages would be performed in the afterlife.

But many Mormon wives endured plural marriages in a spirit of plainly agonized self-sacrifice. Women talked among themselves, exchanging grievances. One told Eliza Snow that sharing her husband caused her so much distress she thought she would die. "Such graves are strewn from Nauvoo to this place," Eliza Snow replied. Another explained the way she had survived: "Your comfort must be wholly in your children." A third advised, "Make yourself indifferent to your husband."

Married to a Mormon elder, Jane Snyder Richards was extensively interviewed in 1880 by the historian Hubert Howe Bancroft. Born in Watertown, New York, in 1823, Jane Snyder became a Mormon at the age of

The National Archives
A rare photograph of Mormon wives with their children, shown at a dairy in Mormon Lake, Arizona Territory, in 1887.

seventeen. Three years later, in 1843, she wedded twenty-one-year-old Franklin Richards, and they were sealed "for time and eternity."

When they had been married eight months and Jane was pregnant, Franklin came to her and said he "wanted to make a crooked road straight." He wished to marry seventeen-year-old Elizabeth McFate. Jane felt so crushed that Franklin waited three years until she finally agreed "to let another share my pleasures," as she put it. Jane told him: "I can yield on anything but the children. But I would like to wring the neck of any other child that calls you papa."

Elizabeth visited Jane and said, "I don't know how we are going to get along, but I will try and not make you miserable, Mrs. Richards." "Don't call me Mrs. Richards, call me Jane," she replied. "I won't quarrel, whatever happens," Elizabeth promised. In their house in Nauvoo, Elizabeth had the upper story and Jane the lower. They got on well, sharing household duties. If one washed, the other cooked.

When Jane had a toothache, Elizabeth offered to take her daughter for the night so that Jane could sleep undisturbed. The next day Elizabeth explained the real reason: "I didn't want you to feel I should want Franklin to stay with me while you were suffering." Thus, there came to exist among plural wives a complicity that remained hidden from their husbands, a world of feminine understanding, subtle and recondite. On an emotional plane, a more durable affinity may have existed between wives than between spouses.

Elizabeth and Jane normally took turns spending the night with Franklin. A cross word rarely passed between them, though once when Elizabeth caught chills and a fever after going outdoors barefoot, Jane called her imprudent. "Who does that concern the most?" Elizabeth replied. In situations without privacy, the Mormon watchword of "Mind Your Own Business" could still be invoked.

Richards was away so often on his missions to England that Jane was glad for Elizabeth's company, and learned to live comfortably without him. But Elizabeth died of consumption on the way to Utah. During the trip, while her husband was absent, Jane gave birth to a girl, who died. Then her oldest daughter also died, and Jane said that "I only lived because I could not die."

In 1849 in Salt Lake City, Franklin was appointed one of the Twelve Apostles. He took two more wives—Jane's sister Sarah, and Charlotte Fox. Franklin told Jane that he married only because his religion demanded it, and not out of lust. Procreation, not pleasure, was the aim. This may sound like balm for a resentful wife, but it's undeniable that the arrangements of polygamy stifled romantic love. How could there be wife wooing when each polygamous household was a collective? For the wives, marriage represented a duty, a kind of religious penance. For the husbands, the negotiating skills of a Jefferson or a Madison were required to maintain a semblance of impartiality.

One example of how the arrangements of plural marriages could blow a tempest into every domestic teapot was given by Jane Snyder Richards. By 1852, Franklin Richards had a total of six wives, including Jane. Everything had to be done in sixes, including the number of gifts he brought home from a mission. But when, in the interest of fairness, he gave each wife the same sweater, or the same bonnet, Jane let him know that none of his wives took pleasure in a duplicate of what the others had.

So the next time Franklin came back from England, he brought six shawls, each with a different design. But that created the problem of who should have first choice. Jane saw the shawl she liked, but as the senior wife, entitled to first pick, she deliberately deferred to the others. This was not an act of selflessness, she later realized, but a hidden form of pride. She told the other wives, "Girls, you care more about these things than I do, take your choice and I will be satisfied with what is left."

But something in her tone, an intimation that she was yielding to their covetousness, aroused their anger and they all refused to choose. And there stood poor Franklin Richards, who had done his very best to please his six wives, encountering a general boycott of his gifts. Jane Richards went into her room and cried. Her husband followed, complaining that she never cared for his presents. She begged him in the future to make the distribution to each wife himself. Then she went back to the commons room and announced, "Now, girls, I hope you will approve, he will distribute them according to his own discretion."

It took an enormous amount of good will on the part of everyone concerned to keep a polygamous marriage on track. For divorce under Utah territorial law could be easily obtained in cases when marriage became intolerable. Brigham Young had fifty-five wives, several of whom divorced him.

As for Jane Snyder Richards, she told of instances in which the wives quarreled, where the one who was washing said she would not wash for the other, and the one who was cooking said she would not cook for the other. And then the one who was washing threw some wrung-out clothes in the face of her rival.

Jane never got completely used to the arrangement. Mrs. John Taylor, the wife of the next Mormon president after Brigham Young's death in 1877, visited one day and asked her how she was getting along in plurality.

"Not very well, I guess," Jane replied.

"I think you have too much pride and grit to let your domestic troubles be known to the world," Mrs. Taylor declared. She stayed for dinner, and when someone began speaking about trials, Mrs. Taylor said, "Mrs. Richards thinks everything has its trials, even polygamy." It annoyed Jane Richards that Mrs. Taylor was joking about something she had been told in confidence. Gossip between wives, she reflected, was one of polygamy's worst features. To a neighbor who asked Jane's advice about her husband taking another wife, she said: "There isn't as much trouble in reality as there is in sweating about it beforehand."

Jane felt an interest in the children of other wives, but not the same as she did for her own. If Franklin's children were all drowning and only one could be saved, she would save hers, while Franklin would snatch up the first child he could get hold of.

In plural marriages, women unfailingly transferred their emotions from their husband to their children. But the paradox of polygamy was that instead of subjugating women, it carried the seeds of feminist independence. Mormon wives formed ties of sisterhood and learned to restructure their lives so that they had considerably more freedom than a monogamous wife.

Plural marriages brought unintended consequences, pushing women into new roles and breaking down sexual stereotypes. Since many-wived elders were often away on church matters, their spouses ran the farms and the businesses. Grouping together and dividing the labor, these women directed their energies to outside occupations.

Some of the women felt as grateful for the sharing of the marriage bed as for the sharing of any household chore. Martha Hughes Cannon, the country's first woman state senator, and the fourth wife of a polygamist, said, "If her husband has four wives, she has three weeks of freedom every single month."

Although excoriated as an enslaver of women, Mormon Utah pioneered women's rights. It was the first state in which women came to dominate the medical profession. And it was one of the first territories to have a newspaper for women. The *Woman's Exponent* became the voice for women's concerns between 1872 and 1914, expressing a feminist point of view that focused on the inequities between the sexes.

Aside from polygamy, another Mormon heresy was condemned as un-American—collectivist experimentation. In 1831, Joseph Smith had a revelation concerning a communistic society that had flourished among the ancient Americans, but then disintegrated as a result of individual selfishness. The revelation came at a time when the idea of collective living was in the air. A flurry of collectives were formed, among them New Harmony in Indiana, the Rappists in Pennsylvania, and Brook Farm in Massachusetts.

Within the Mormon movement, Smith founded the United Order of Enoch, whose members agreed to give all their property to the church. In 1874, Brigham Young launched a Second United Order and set up a village form of communism in Utah. Although pragmatically aimed at economic self-sufficiency in an alien world, the collectives were also a kind of social engineering, an attempt to create economic equality and a more altruistic human species.

In 1871, about two hundred Mormons who had tried to settle a place called Muddy Mission in the territory's southwestern corner moved out— the water was bad, the soil turned to alkali dust, and they were attacked by Indians. They went east to Long Valley and stopped at the headwaters of the Virgin River, right next to a small settlement by the name of Mount Carmel.

But when the Muddy Mission people started clearing tillable land and planting wheat and corn, the Mount Carmel settlers protested. The newcomers, they said, have moved in on their claims. In the Mormon manner, a meeting was held to address the dispute. A Muddy Mission elder named Orville Cox, speaking to the Lord as to an old friend, said: "We need thy help, O father, in reaching an amicable solution."

But Henry Clark interjected: "You folks just come pushing in, jumping claims right and left."

Tempers were high, so Israel Hoyt said: "We will dismiss this meeting with prayer, and then we each will go directly to our homes."

"I ain't got no home," an early settler said. "One of your holy Muddyites is living on my place."

Over time, the two communities worked out their differences. Some stayed put, and some moved. A Muddy Mission farmer who was squatting in an abandoned cabin said: "Pay for that mouse nest? There was a dead rattler in the fireplace. We'll build a decent new place."

In 1874, the Mount Carmel settlers heard that Brigham Young was organizing the villages of Dixie, as southern Utah was known, into a New Order of collectives. They held a meeting to discuss joining Young's order, and some people voiced opposition to the idea. "Count me out," one man said. "I'm not signing over all I've got to keep somebody else."

On March 20, Brigham's nephew, John R. Young, came to Mount Carmel to do a little missionary work. He explained that under the New Order, they would have to turn over all their land and property to the collective. They would be given work assignments, and all work would earn the same pay. Labor was not a duty, Young said, but a privilege. In the New Order, there would be no rich and no poor, and no more "This is mine." It would be, as revealed to Joseph Smith and Brigham Young, "This is ours."

Young called for a show of hands, and a large majority voted yes. Officers were then elected to a nine-member board. Those who had not raised their hands, however, expressed their discontent: "It's not right, a man ought to have control of his own work and his own property."

A division arose between those who wanted the New Order and those who did not. Someone proposed that those in favor of the collective move to a new location just north of Mount Carmel and build a town there. So in February 1875, 94 adults and 96 children moved to the new site, which they called Orderville. They gave their land to the order and received work assignments to build the town. The houses were joined in rows like motel cabins. In the center rose a communal dining hall, twenty-two by forty feet, with an adobe chimney and an adjacent kitchen that contained three huge vats.

Some grumbling over work assignments led to rotations. There was also grumbling about the alleged high-handedness of the treasurer, H. J. Jolley. "Some claim that the Jolleys think they're better than other people," it was said. In Orderville's egalitarian society, it didn't pay to be stuck-up. People drafted a petition, and the Jolley family was expelled.

Others left because they just didn't like the New Order. As Kendell Fletcher explained to Israel Hoyt: "It's the wife, you know. I talk till I'm purple, but she can't do it." "Brother Fletcher, we're sorry to lose you," Hoyt said.

On balance, however, the population increased, for more people arrived than departed. Orderville rapidly became a success, so much so that Brigham Young came to visit in 1876, and kept saying "Fine, fine" at everything he saw. The community was known as the most self-contained town in Utah. Ordervillians grew their own food and raised their own wool, which they scoured, carded, spun, and wove. They cultivated their own cotton and sugarcane and became famous for their molasses. In the fall, they picked potatoes and topped beets and carrots. A military discipline regulated daily life, complete with reveille and mess calls and a 9 P.M. curfew. Orderville was part kibbutz, part harem, and part garrison.

The brave new settlement's first commandment was "Thou shalt not be idle." Loafers were brought before the board and sometimes expelled. The cooper busily turned out barrels, buckets, tubs, and churns. The carpenters made tables, chairs, cupboards, picture frames, chests, and bed-steads. A pleasant smell wafted up from the clean white shavings curled and spread like a carpet over the floor, which crunched under visitors' feet. At Christmastime, the carpenters made presents for the girls—small brooms like their mothers' and miniature washboards and churns that really worked.

Outsiders from within the faith made jokes about the Ordervillians' clodhopper shoes, floppy straw hats, and clannishness. But nothing excited more ridicule than communal eating, men at one sitting, women and children at the next. A brother in Cedar City said, "They are just as happy as if they had good sense." Six cooks rotated each week around the huge vats in the kitchen. Three rows of tables extended the length of the hall, and six waiters attended at each meal. The floors were scrubbed twice a week with sand from the foothills, since soap was scarce.

The town had little trouble with the Indians, for the people of Orderville followed Brigham Young's precept: "It is easier to feed them than to fight them." A Paiute spoke at one of their testimony meetings and said: "Mormon good. Mormon friend. Makem water ditch. Plantem grain. White man son of a bitch."

In Orderville, full employment was the rule, and everyone was supposed to love his work—though there were complaints that labor skilled and unskilled was given equal credit. In Sunday school, Brother Harmon, who had a tuning fork, led the singing:

> The world has need of willing men,
> Who wear the worker's seal;
> We all have work, let no one shirk,
> Put your shoulder to the wheel.

In 1877, Orderville had a population of 450. That year Thomas Chamberlain, a member of the board, was named bishop at the age of twenty-three. It was also the year that Brigham Young died after thirty-three years as the Mormons' leader—his grieving flock mourned him as a giant among men. Brigham's death gave Chamberlain an even greater resolve to fulfill the promise of the New Order.

Yet even in Orderville, there was no denying human nature. Bateman Williams, the first counselor, refused to give up the use of tobacco. In addition, he was contentious, and jealous of other leaders, and the community forced his resignation.

Harry Esplin and his wife were sent to Leeds, thirty miles west of Orderville, to run the Order's fruit farm there. Miners at nearby Silver Reef asked Philena Esplin to do their washing and ironing. The money she made was spent on her children. When she returned to Orderville, other women complained: "She spent money that should have been turned in to the treasury. *Our* children don't get extras, however hard we work."

But even in the midst of collectivism, the Mormons could not help admiring examples of enterprise. One of the young men, John Carling, needed a new pair of pants. He had grown so much in a year that his long pants were now short pants. But under the New Order rationing, he would have to wait his turn for another pair of homespun trousers.

In the spring of 1878, Carling was assigned to a shearing team. The workers usually threw the lambs' tails away, but when the tails were "docked" (cut) that spring, Carling gathered them and sheared the little bit of wool left on each one, on his own time. Assigned to haul a load of wool to Nephi, 180 miles to the north, he secretly took along his sack of tail wool and exchanged it for a pair of store pants.

When he walked into the weekly dance held at the dining hall, his new pants created a sensation. The board asked for an explanation. When he told them what he had done, they commended him for his venture. The board then decreed that all pants should be designed like Carling's. The young man was directed to donate his pair, which were unseamed and used as a pattern for all future pants. When the news got out, all of Carling's peers wore down their old pants on the grindstone so they could qualify for new ones.

In 1881, floods hit Orderville, doing extensive damage to the town and to the crops. The dining hall was ruined, and for the first time people ate at home. The Ordervillians later saw the flood as a portent, for despite their isolation in Dixie, the might of the federal government was bearing down on them.

In the 1870s, the moral outcry against polygamy snowballed. The eastern press urged non-Mormon settlers to move to Utah and take preemption claims. Protestant ministers demanded military intervention. As the Reverend J. H. Peters said in Dayton: "I would that the guns at Fort Dayton were turned upon them and they were made loyal by this means if by no other."

In 1878, the Supreme Court ruled that polygamy was not protected under the freedom-of-religion clause in the Bill of Rights, which applied to freedom in doctrine and thought, but not to overt acts contrary to good order and morality.

This decision opened the door to legislative action. In 1882, George F. Edmunds of Vermont, known as "the Iceberg of the Senate," introduced an act that would make anyone found guilty of polygamy liable to five years in jail and a $500 fine. When the Edmunds Act became law, Mormon polygamists went underground. The government sent a five-man commission to Utah to supervise elections there and make sure professed polygamists were not allowed to vote.

The reaction in Orderville to the Edmunds Act was: "The whole thing is aimed at Mormons and only Mormons." Thomas Chamberlain wondered: "How soon before me and my brothers are forced into hiding?"

But being so far south, Orderville escaped the harassment that was taking place around Salt Lake City.

In May 1882, a correspondent for the *New York World*, Phil Robinson, toured Orderville and wrote that "the Communists bid fair to prove to the world that pious enthusiasm, if loyally tempered by business judgment, can make a success of the experiment." But he also noted that "the young men are complaining of a system which does not let them see the fruit of their work . . . they know that beyond Orderville . . . there are more brilliant opportunities for both the hand and the head."

In some ways, 1882 was a banner year. The lamb "crop" was the best ever, for they now had 5,000 sheep. The town was thriving, and the population had grown to more than 600. But Chamberlain had to agree with Phil Robinson: dissatisfaction was growing among the young men. The Silver Reef mines were creating wealth overnight in the area. Young Orderville men in their homespun clothes, clodhopper shoes, and floppy straw hats saw young men from other towns wearing high-heeled cowboy boots, Stetson hats, and bright silk neckerchiefs. They felt like dim-witted hayseeds. And in the pockets of the other young men's store-bought pants, coins jingled.

Some families packed up to leave. Chamberlain listened to their reasons: "Orderville is all work and no play." "We live too much in each other's hip pockets." "What will our children have when we are gone?" "It's not fair to give equal credit for unequal labor." Realizing that the system needed an overhaul, Chamberlain drew up pay scales according to skills.

In 1883, the young bishop told the Mormon president, John Taylor: "Dissension could well tear us apart." His warning fell on deaf ears. On June 2, 1884, Chamberlain received a letter from Taylor's number-two man, George Q. Cannon, chiding him for setting up different wage scales. The change in the system of credit, Cannon said, "opened the door to selfishness." They should return to the old system, and maintain the collectivist purity of the New Order.

For Thomas Chamberlain, the Mormon leader's stand-pattism signaled Orderville's failure. The system had broken down over the issue of fair pay. Chamberlain did not consider wages that matched the nature of the work as the introduction of selfishness but as a normal reward of industry and ability. Why should anyone take pride in skilled work if they had no incentive?

And people kept trickling out of Orderville. They came to Chamberlain and said, "Bishop, my wife is telling me that I can do better on the outside," or "Bishop, my boys have set their hearts on moving on." All Chamberlain could say was, "Be sure to write. Let us know where you are." Because in Orderville there was no coercion.

A solid core remained. But in the fall of 1884, an emissary from President Taylor arrived at Orderville with termination papers. His name was Heber Grant and he brought the word: "President Taylor sees breakers ahead for your group. Conditions change."

Sister Crofts, with disbelief on her face, asked: "Just give it up?"

"All aspects of the situation have been prayerfully considered," Heber Grant said.

The decision had less to do with Orderville, still functioning successfully as a collective, than with federal harassment of the Mormons in the north. The Mormon leadership had reason to believe that the government was about to pass laws calling for the seizure of property belonging to polygamists. Since the New Order legally owned Orderville, the town and all its assets were ripe for confiscation.

So the Orderville United Order was disbanded and property returned to private ownership. Family by family, folks moved to individual lots and built individual houses. By the spring of 1885, Orderville had been transformed from a communist enclave into a community of small farms. The experiment was over. Even if social engineering could have changed human nature, the long arm of the federal government was reaching out to strangle the collective.

In northern Utah, federal marshals disguised as peddlers tracked down polygamists. The government offered rewards for the arrest of prominent Mormons. Lawmen imprisoned a total of 1,035 "co-habs" under the Edmunds Act, swelling the population of the territorial jail at Sugar Rock. Among those jailed were President Taylor and Lorenzo Snow, one of the Twelve Apostles.

Just as the Mormon leaders had foreseen, when the Edmunds Act failed to do away with polygamy, Congress enacted an even more punitive law in 1887. The Edmunds-Tucker Act dissolved the church as a legal corporation nd required it to forfeit all property in excess of $50,000,. No Mormon could vote, serve on a jury, or hold public office unless he signed an oath swearing to support antipolygamy laws.

Under the Edmunds-Tucker Act, Orderville would have been confiscated. As it was, the act forced the men of Orderville with plural wives into hiding. Some of them fled to Moccasin Springs, across the Arizona line. Others were not so lucky. In 1888, Thomas Chamberlain was arrested as a "co-hab" and served six months in jail.

The Edmunds-Tucker Act sounded the death knell of a polygamous Mormon church, and when the Supreme Court upheld it in May 1890, the Mormon hierarchy jettisoned polygamy to save the faith. Four days after the high court decision, Wilford Woodruff, the Mormon president, agreed to end open polygamy and obey the laws of the United States.

In response, President Harrison and then President Cleveland extended amnesties to reformed polygamists, and Congress passed an enabling act for statehood. The Utah constitution, which outlawed polygamy and provided for the separation of church and state, was ratified in November 1895 and submitted to Congress.

Utah's long exclusion from the United States ended when Grover

Cleveland admitted it as the forty-fifth state on January 4, 1896. The population by then had reached 247,324, nine out of ten of them Mormons, plus 3,000 Indians, living mainly on reservations.

In 1896, Cuba was in revolt against Spain. In South Africa, the Boers had won a victory. In the Near East, Turks were massacring Armenians. In Vienna, Freud was treating hysteria with hypnotism. In France, André Michelin had put pneumatic tires on motorcars. In Cleveland, the Sherwin-Williams paint company adopted the trademark "It Covers the Earth." At the Colorado state line, eleven tons of illegally slaughtered Utah venison was impounded.

And in Salt Lake City at 9:13 A.M. on January 4, Superintendent Brown of the Western Union Telegraph Company was observed running out of his office into East Temple Street firing both barrels of a shotgun. The Mormons had finally reconciled themselves to the norms of Victorian America.

CHAPTER TWENTY-FOUR

THE LAST INDIAN FRONTIER, THE FIRST TWENTIETH-CENTURY STATE

I have no more land.
I am taken away from my home
Driven up the red waters.
Let us all go
Let us all die together.

A CREEK WOMAN

The National Archives
The last land opening in Oklahoma's Indian Territory took place on August 6, 1901, in El Reno. Thousands of would-be homesteaders arrived by train and horse-drawn bus to take part in the lottery, and some of them used the tops of freight cars for bleachers.

I am looking rather seedy now
While holding down my claim,
And my victuals are not always of the best.
And the mice play shyly round me as I settle
  down to rest,
In my little old sod shanty on the claim.

AN OKLAHOMA BOOMER

In 1951, Elizabeth Jacobs Quinton was interviewed in her kitchen in the town of Bokoshe, Oklahoma, not far from the Arkansas line. She was 112 years old, a tiny woman in a checked gingham apron who smoked a pipe and said, "I wake up in the night and have to have a draw or two."

Elizabeth was born in 1838 in Mississippi, and her family settled in Fort Smith, Arkansas, where she went to school with Choctaw children. "If they talked Choctaw," she recalled, "they gave them a teaspoonful of red pepper for each word." After the Civil War, her family moved to Oklahoma, where Elizabeth married and raised a family.

She lived through Oklahoma's passage from Indian Territory to territorial status to statehood, a period when the first lesson of life was self-reliance. "I've wove many a web of cloth in my time," she said. "Now people just live out of paper sacks. They made us learn how to do things right. That's the reason I can sew now, blind as I am."

When asked how she dyed her yarn, Elizabeth replied: "What do you want to know all that for? You don't want to make no cloth." Her comment on modern times was: "It's a sorry thing to see girls smoking cigarettes, but the worst thing is to see 'em wearin' britches and ridin' bicycles."

That hoary institution, the interview with the centenarian, closes the gap between two centuries and becomes a reminder of how recent American history is. One life takes us back to an antebellum time of the last Indian nations, and to the erosion and collapse of those nations in an America where most of the arable land had been homesteaded.

In Oklahoma, there was an acceleration of the process of Indian removal that had been going on since 1607, when the English landed at Jamestown. Going from east to west, the relocation of the tribes took exactly three hundred years from the settling of Jamestown to Oklahoma statehood. But in Oklahoma itself, the entire transformation, so long-drawn-out nationally, took only forty years—from Indian country to an industrial state rich in coal and oil.

In Oklahoma, settlement occurred in the twilight of the westward movement, as the country graduated from the nineteenth to the twentieth century. The United States changed as it did so, from a land of territorial expansion and pioneering, to one of trusts, conglomerates, and corpora-

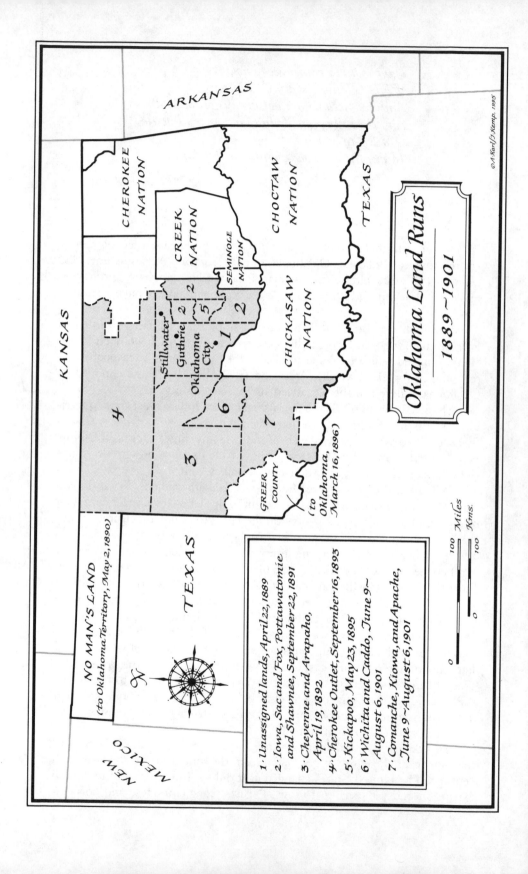

Oklahoma Land Runs
1889~1901

© A.Karl / J. Kemp. 1995

ARKANSAS

KANSAS

CHEROKEE NATION

CREEK NATION

SEMINOLE NATION

CHOCTAW NATION

TEXAS

Stillwater

Guthrie

Oklahoma City

CHICKASAW NATION

GREER COUNTY

(to Oklahoma, March 16, 1896)

NO MAN'S LAND
(to Oklahoma Territory, May 2, 1890)

TEXAS

NEW MEXICO

N

1 · Unassigned lands, April 22, 1889
2 · Iowa, Sac and Fox, Pottawatomie
   and Shawnee, September 22, 1891
3 · Cheyenne and Arapaho,
   April 19, 1892
4 · Cherokee Outlet, September 16, 1893
5 · Kickapoo, May 23, 1895
6 · Wichita and Caddo, June 9 ~
   August 6, 1901
7 · Comanche, Kiowa, and Apache,
   June 9 ~ August 6, 1901

100 Miles

100 Kms.

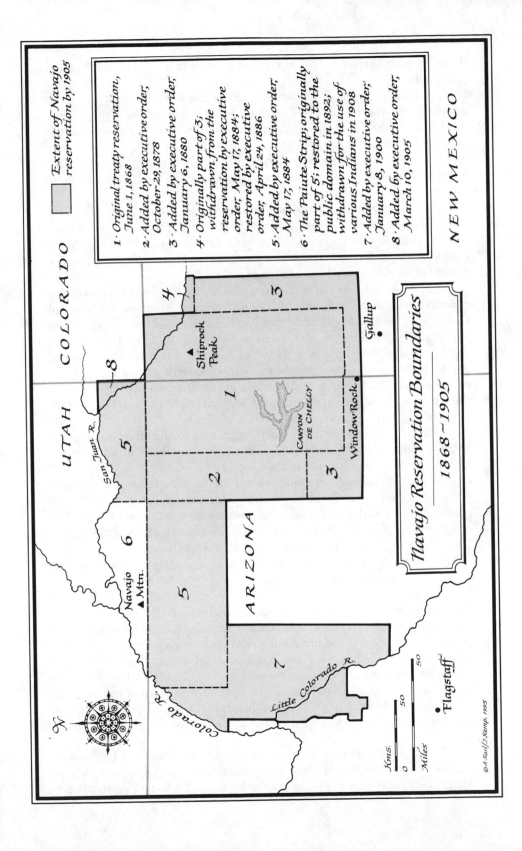

UTAH   COLORADO

NEW MEXICO

ARIZONA

Extent of Navajo
reservation by 1905

1 · Original treaty reservation,
June 1, 1868
2 · Added by executive order,
October 29, 1878
3 · Added by executive order,
January 6, 1880
4 · Originally part of 3;
withdrawn from the
reservation by executive
order, May 17, 1884;
restored by executive
order, April 24, 1886
5 · Added by executive order,
May 17, 1884
6 · The Paiute Strip; originally
part of 5; restored to the
public domain in 1892;
withdrawn for the use of
various Indians in 1908
7 · Added by executive order,
January 8, 1900
8 · Added by executive order,
March 10, 1905

Navajo Reservation Boundaries
1868–1905

Shiprock Peak ▲

CANYON DE CHELLY

Window Rock ●

Gallup ●

San Juan R.

Navajo Mtn. ▲

Colorado R.

Little Colorado R.

Flagstaff ●

Kms.
0   50
Miles
0   50

© A. Karl / J. Kemp, 1995

tions, its great surface easily encompassed by railroads, automobiles, and telephones.

Oklahoma's frantic land runs expressed the last hurrah of the spirit that believed "there's always something better beyond." As a slogan on a wagon in the 1889 rush put it, CHINCH-BUGGED IN ILLINOIS, BALD-KNOBBED IN MIZZOURI, PROHIBITED IN KANSAS, OKLIHOMMY OR BUST! Of course, there had always been the promise of a new dispensation, but that promise had just about vanished, for by then settlers had reached the Pacific and there was no beyond.

Now the machine age crashed into history, a blitzkrieg on nature, as the locomotive enveloped the landscape with its iron bands. No one missed the bad roads or the stagecoaches, already in museums. The U.S. Army Corps of Engineers was taming rivers and building dams. The quick growth of crops mirrored the growth of cities.

And in Oklahoma came the invasion of the last Indian enclave, an enormous territory surrounded by Texas, Arkansas, Missouri, Kansas, and Colorado. The Five Civilized Tribes had been relocated there in the 1830s and 1840s. Occupying 70,000 square miles in the middle of the United States, the Indians lived as if they had been forgotten by history—one nation isolated within another, the two nations dwelling in different centuries. As a local historian wrote, "Oklahoma represented the leftover after the garment of the public domain had been cut to fit the pattern of other states by the congressional tailors."

In their spacious enclave, which comprised the future state of Oklahoma without the panhandle (a no-man's-land unassigned to any state or territory), the 50,000 Indians of the Five Tribes—Choctaws, Chickasaws, Cherokees, Creeks, and Seminoles—lived undisturbed because white men were proscribed. They lived in a sort of golden penumbra with their own constitutions, tribal governments, court systems, and schools. Whiskey peddlers who visited the tribes were sent to Fort Smith chained to wagons. The Five Tribes were slave owners and kept a total of about 7,500 black slaves, emulating the plantation system, and decorating their towns with magnolia and pecan trees.

History caught up with the Five Tribes in 1861. Their enclave was squeezed between two secessionist states, Arkansas and Texas, with whom the Indians had in common "the peculiar institution." As soon as federal troops withdrew from the three military posts in Indian Territory in May 1861, the Five Tribes were subjected to rebel influences. Confederate agents swooped in, chief among them Brigadier General Albert Pike (author of the lyrics for "Dixie"), who in five months negotiated treaties with all five tribes, reversing their policy of neutrality. Indian Territory became an annex of the Confederacy, useful as a place to raise troops and obtain cattle.

The rebels formed regiments of mounted rifles among the tribes. The treaties banned the use of these troops outside Indian Territory, but in March 1862 some of them fought in the battle of Pea Ridge, in northwest-

The National Archives
Slaves held by tribes that occupied Oklahoma's Indian Territory were freed after the Civil War, and many of them became homesteaders.

ern Arkansas near the Missouri line. In the course of the battle, the Indians reverted to their habit of scalping, giving the rebels a bad press.

When Lee surrendered in 1865, the Five Tribes found themselves on the losing side, just as they had been in the War of Independence. "It was the white man's quarrel and the red man's woe," a local historian said. The war was disastrous for the Five Tribes, who were charged with treason for aiding and abetting the southern cause.

At a council in Fort Smith, the victors told the Indians that their lands would be confiscated. Following negotiations in Washington in 1866, the tribes lost the western half of Oklahoma and were forced to free their slaves and give them land. Many of the freed blacks remained in the truncated Indian Territory, running farms, or working as laborers for the Indians. Albert Richardson, the *New York Tribune* correspondent, was told at Fort Smith that "in fact the niggers are masters and do about as they please."

Even after the amputation, however, the Five Tribes kept 20 million acres, though many Indians had to go through the ordeal of relocation. The western half of Oklahoma that the Five Tribes had been pushed out of was used as a dumping ground for twenty or so unwanted Plains tribes standing in the way of settlement, while two million acres near the center remained "Unassigned Lands."

In October 1867, commissioners met on Medicine Lodge Creek, in Kansas, with the Comanches, the Kiowas, the Cheyennes, and the Arapahos. Under duress, the Indians agreed to relocate to Oklahoma. The Comanches and Kiowas moved to a reservation between the Red and the Washita rivers, while the Cheyennes and Arapahos settled in the area west of the Unassigned Lands.

The western half also received small tribes such as the Osages, the Pawnees, and the Kickapoos, who put up their tents along the streams. By 1883, only 15,000 Indians lived in the post–Civil War reservations, an area about the size of Ohio. But with the Plains Indians in its western half and the Five Civilized Tribes in its eastern half, Oklahoma became home to one-third of all the Indians in the United States.

That did not stop an expanding white presence in Indian Territory in the post–Civil War years. Each tribe had its agency, and in keeping with President Grant's peace policy, the agencies were staffed by Quakers. In July 1869, four months after Grant's inauguration, Quaker Lawrie Tatum arrived at Fort Sill in southwestern Oklahoma as the agent for the Kiowas and Comanches.

The Quakers wanted to elevate the Indians through kind and just treatment. But Lawrie Tatum soon discovered that the Kiowas did not want to be elevated—they wanted to go on hunting as they had always done. The Indians took little interest in the fifty-five acres of corn and vegetables the agency had planted for them. Returning from the hunt, they ate unripe corn and let their ponies loose to trample the fields. Though it was discouraging work, Lawrie Tatum nevertheless prepared more acreage for planting.

Rations were issued every two weeks, as a way of keeping the tribes on the reservation. If the Indians went on raids, their rations were reduced. When that happened, however, the tribe had various ways of displaying its displeasure in council. One brave would remove cartridges from his breech-loading rifle and put them back again. Another would twang his bow or snap it. One would vigorously apply his butcher knife to a whetstone. Still another would slip his hand under Tatum's vest and ask him if his heart was beating fast.

In September 1870, when beef rations were issued, Tatum warned the Kiowa chiefs to restrain their young men from running wild in the beef pens. As always, though, they killed more beeves than they were entitled to, so he held back half the Kiowa's supplies. The Kiowa chief Lone Wolf told Tatum: "You are foolish to get mad just as we have got entirely over our mad."

Tatum had to ask for an armed guard while doling out rations, which was anathema to the pacifist Quaker spirit. But nothing could be done to curb the Kiowas' marauding habits, and Tatum lost his Quaker idealism. In March 1873, his displeased superiors forced him to resign.

At the Osage Agency, northeast of the Kiowa-Comanche Reservation, James Edward Finney worked as a trader for the firm of Dunlap & Florer. In the early 1870s, when the buffalo still roamed, Finney traded hides for goods. He accompanied the Osages on their annual buffalo hunts, and in 1873 he went out with John Florer to scout locations for hunting camps.

Riding in their wagon to Pond Creek, near the Salt Fork of the Arkansas, the two men suddenly saw sunlight glittering and flashing off the long-bladed heads of Indian spears. Mounted warriors were riding toward them. "A war party, sure as fate," Florer said, "but they're not Osage." They counted eighteen Indians coming at full speed, all painted and naked but for loincloths, galloping through the tall blue-stem grass and shaking their spears.

Across the Salt Fork rose a steep bank. As the traders tried to climb it, the war party came so close behind them that Indian ponies splashed mud onto the backs of their wagons. Then they were encircled and a painted warrior seized one of their horses by the bit.

Recognizing some of the Indians behind the paint, Florer said, "I'll be damned if they're not Osage." In fact, they belonged to the Beaver band, led by George Beaver, who dismounted, looking vexed that he'd been recognized. When Beaver came up with outstretched hand, Finney whispered, "Act as if you do not know him."

Addressing Beaver in his own language, Finney said, "No, I will not shake the hands of men in a war party." Folding his arms across his chest, Beaver asked in a haughty tone, "What is your business in this country?"

"More business than you have," Finney replied. "You have no right to be here—no permit to be off your reservation. Do you know what we could do with you and all your men? Before another moon, we could have you in prison at Fort Smith with your hands this way"—and he crossed his wrists to suggest handcuffs.

"What!" George Beaver exclaimed. "Brother, you would not do that?"

"I am thinking about it," Finney said. "We have always been your friends and now you chase us over the prairie like coyotes."

"You know how many ponies I have and where they are," said George Beaver. "Drive on home and go down to my herd and pick out five of the best. That's to keep your mouth shut and say nothing about this."

"We have more ponies than we want," Finney answered. "How many years have you been carrying your buffalo robes to old Nahhutsak-hi-kah [Hiatt, a rival trader]? You never trade with us. Our mouths will not be shut unless you throw the trade of your band to our store."

Beaver held out his hand and said, "That is a promise. We will keep it." He was true to his word, and thereafter the Beaver band traded only with Dunlap & Florer. Old Hiatt could never figure out why.

• •

When the buffalo herds disappeared in the late 1870s, the Indians lost their one source of revenue. They soon found another one. With the establishment of cow towns like Dodge City in western Kansas, the Texas traildrivers started taking their herds further west, right through Indian Territory, over four major routes connecting Texas and Kansas. It was not long before hungry Indians began to station themselves on the trails, demanding a toll from passing herds.

Attracted to the rich grasslands of Indian Territory, the trail bosses contracted with the tribes to graze their herds for a few weeks to fatten them up. With the depletion of grasslands in Texas, the next step for the cattlemen was to pasture their herds permanently on the Indian reservations.

In 1882, the Dickey brothers made a deal with a band of Cheyenne to put 22,000 cattle on land that partly belonged to the reservation. In a short time, a tangled patchwork of illegal leases took shape. As a cattleman put it: "The big thing about the plains is that you don't have to feed stock. It can rustle for itself and the dollars just crawl into your jeans."

On the Kiowa-Comanche Reservation in 1882, the Indian agent P. B. Hunt had 4,179 Indians to feed. Abruptly, beef rations were cut by a third because Congress had failed to appropriate enough money to issue full rations. The solution, Hunt realized, was to let cattlemen graze on land that was going to waste, and take cattle as payment. Tens of thousands of unused acres could be converted into beef for the Indians, making up the shortfall in government beef.

As Hunt went ahead with his plan, to the north, on the Cheyenne-Arapaho Reservation, Agent John D. Miles struggled with the same situation. He was getting 80,000 pounds of beef per week for his Indians, who needed 125,000 pounds. He warned the Bureau of Indian Affairs that if he did not receive full rations there would be serious disturbances, but nothing was done.

Miles then asked the Department of the Interior if beef contractors might be allowed to pasture their cattle on the reservation to make up for the beef deficit. Interior refused, but Miles went ahead anyway and signed leases with seven cattlemen. They could graze on 3 million acres for ten years, at a cost of 2 cents an acre per year, or $60,000 annually.

Interior took a noncommittal attitude, neither sanctioning nor banning the move. So the seven cattlemen fenced and stocked their ranges, building bunkhouses for cowboys and corrals for branding. Instead of resisting the invasion, the tribes abetted it. They knew that fencing, for example, would facilitate the collection of grazing fees. Some cattlemen tried to win favors from John Miles with bribes, but he turned them down and told the Indians to hold out for the best prices.

John Miles resigned in 1884, having presided over the transition from buffalo to beef. His action had brought the grazing issue to a head. Interior tolerated grazing but stayed aloof, not wanting to get involved in the leasing. As a result, disputes arose, and in 1885, President Cleveland declared all the leases null and void and ordered the cattle removed from the reservations. But it was easier to remove the cattle than the hundreds of whites whom grazing policies had brought into Indian territory.

As the cattle herds crossed Indian Territory from the south, the railroads were poised to jump in from the north. For in their post–Civil War treaties, the Five Tribes had consented to allow railroad lines to cross their reservations. Congress granted a right of way to the Missouri, Kansas & Texas railroad across eastern Oklahoma, from Kansas to Texas.

In June 1870, the push started south from Kansas through Indian lands, creating the rail centers of Vinita and Muskogee. In 1872, the Atlantic & Pacific built a line from Missouri that connected with the line at Vinita. Some of these were Choctaw lands, and a Choctaw scholar went to Washington to testify before Congress on the need for regulation.

C. J. Hillyer, the attorney for the Atlantic & Pacific, described the testimony of the Choctaw scholar this way: "A sleepy-eyed, stupid-looking Indian pulled a few scraps of paper from his pocket, which were the tribe's constitution."

J. J. McAlester, a section foreman for the Missouri, Kansas & Texas, was laying track south of Muskogee when some Indians told him about "the rock that burned." He did a little digging and struck a coal vein. He took a load across the Kansas line to Parsons, where it was pronounced "the best steam coal west of Pennsylvania."

McAlester married a Choctaw woman, which gave him tribal citizenship, and leased mining rights, paying the Choctaws a royalty. He established the Osage Coal & Mining Company, along with a town named after him, seventy-five miles south of Muskogee. The Missouri, Kansas & Texas reached McAlester in 1872. The former railroad man opened a mine in nearby Krebs, hauling the coal in wagons to the railhead.

The coal industry changed the nature of some tribal governments, since the Indians became dependent on the mines for increased revenue. Tribal chiefs assumed roles as partners with the coal companies and the railroads, softening the white-Indian adversarial relationship. Twenty-three of the thirty-six members of the Choctaw Council were bribed to approve the sale of rich coal leases at $1.50 an acre. During miners' strikes, the chiefs aligned themselves with company management.

Thus, despite the fact that Indian Territory was in principle closed to white settlers, the area reserved for perpetual domain became a hive of commercial activity. The tribes, while benefiting from leasing their pastures and mineral rights, lost the management of their own affairs. Tribal rules that had been created to block the advance of white civilization were ignored, and the whites streamed in.

In 1888, sixteen-year-old Arthur Dunham, an agent for the Atchison, Topeka & Santa Fe, was sent to Oklahoma Station in the heart of Indian

Territory. Starting on the Kansas line at Arkansas City, among tidy fields and log farmhouses, Arthur's train passed through unbroken prairie and traversed the teepee-dotted Ponca Reservation in the Cherokee Strip, where Indians flashing agency passes paid a reduced fare.

Then came a bridge over the Salt Fork, and then the breaks of the Cimarron and a long trestled bridge at the junction of Cottonwood Creek and the small depot at Guthrie Station: two section houses and a water tank, all painted in the deep Santa Fe red. Fifteen miles south of Guthrie, Edmond Station consisted of a telegraph office, a two-story coal barn, and a cattle-loading chute. Then came Oklahoma Station, 120 miles from Arkansas City, and 30 miles from the next station south, Purcell.

Arthur Dunham arrived at Oklahoma station, a scruffy collection of tents, log cabins, and cattle pens, on February 20, 1888, disembarking with the traveling auditor for Wells Fargo. A shack across from the depot offered bed and board. On the ground floor, Indians were rolled up in blankets. For breakfast, there was sowbelly, soggy biscuits, and coffee.

Arthur was railroad agent, express agent, state agent, and Western Union manager. He bunked in the depot because he had to get up at four-thirty in the morning to let the stage out and look after passengers and baggage. Oklahoma served as a distribution station to supply the Indian agencies and Fort Reno, twenty miles to the west by Concord coach. Indian freight alone amounted to a million pounds a month. Arthur shipped out mostly cattle, and sometimes buffalo horns and bones gathered by enterprising nesters.

Whites came through all the time, illegal "boomers" trying to squat in Indian territory. The incursion had been going on for years, ever since David L. Payne, "prince of the Boomers," had set up squatter camps in border towns like Caldwell. Payne had led raids into Indian territory, and in 1880 he had started a settlement right where Arthur Dunham was now, at Oklahoma station. But the cavalry burned the town, arrested Payne, and whisked him off to Fort Smith for trial.

Payne had died in 1884, but the boomers were still at it, and cavalry detachments form Fort Reno still came after them. The boys in blue caught the squatters and sent them back to the Kansas line. Arthur could always tell when the boomers were being chased because of the way they scrambled to get to the depot. In a few hours, he'd sell 100 tickets to Purcell, the closest station out of the forbidden districts. When the raid was over, the boomers crept back, for the soldiers had too much territory to cover.

By 1888, so many squatters were living in the western half of Indian Territory that a bill was introduced in January for the organization of an Oklahoma Territory. Opponents said the proposed legislation violated treaty stipulations. But those in favor argued that the land was needed for homesteaders, since almost all the arable land in the rest of the country had been taken.

Having leased 6 million acres of reservation grasslands, the cattle lobby fought the bill tooth and nail. When the Oklahoma bill passed the House by 147 to 102 on February 1, 1889, cattlemen's lawyers laid siege to the Senate Public Lands Committee to have it defeated, or at least delayed until the Senate adjourned

But on March 3, Congress adopted the Springer Amendment (after William Springer of Illinois) to the Indian Appropriation Act. The amendment provided that 2 million acres of land ceded long before by the relocated Seminoles and Creeks, and still unassigned, should be opened to settlement under the Homestead Act.

Also on March 3, 1889, President Benjamin Harrison announced that these unoccupied acres would be opened to all comers for settlement on April 22 at noon. Anyone was free to join the race, but not to jump the gun. By April 22, the land would have been surveyed and laid out in 320-acre townsites and 160-acre homesteads.

Whoever wanted to join in had seven weeks to get ready, seven weeks to scout locations, organize land companies, buy equipment, and hatch schemes. The irregular rectangle of land being made available could be approached from any of its four sides, right up to where troops patrolled its 200-mile perimeter.

Since the Atchison, Topeka & Santa Fe ran across the entire strip, many chose to take trains, which left the various stations in time to reach the line at noon. Two Kansas towns on the Oklahoma border, Arkansas City and Caldwell, became the main staging points. From Arkansas City, you could drop through the Cherokee Strip down to Guthrie, one of the two land offices inside the tract.

Starting from Caldwell, Boomers could head south across the Cherokee Strip to Kingfisher, site of the other land office inside the zone, just south of the Cimarron. These two land office towns, Guthrie and Kingfisher, where every successful boomer would have to file his claim, were seen as having bright prospects.

Those coming north from Texas took the train to the Purcell station on the Canadian River, the zone's southern boundary. To the east, the line followed the Pottawatomie reservation, or "Pott line," fifteen miles from the Oklahoma station. This long border, crossed by gullies and thickets and hard to guard, was wide open for premature entries. To the west, the line ran from Kingfisher to Fort Reno, where the troops were garrisoned. As the day approached, sprawling Boomer camps formed around the perimeter, clustered in places like Fort Reno and Purcell.

This was the first time land in Indian territory was opened to settlers, 2 million acres in the "Oklahoma country." The much-publicized method of allocation astonished the world. On the appointed day, the correspondent for the Paris daily Le Figaro wrote, "Today, Monday, April 22, at exactly mid-day, there will take place in the United States an event which could not possibly be imitated in old Europe."

The "Harrison Horse Race" compressed and surpassed, in a few hours both glorious and wretched, all the features of the frontier, its energy,

combativeness, and unscrupulousness. It was simultaneously the triumph
of the pioneer spirit and a victory for greed and chicanery. In this chaotic
race, this frantic swoop, this inspired dash, this board-game played on real
land, this take-on-all-comers, win-at-all-costs aptitude test, was embodied
the formative event buried at the heart of the American experience—the
abundance and availability of land for private ownership, free for the taking, if you could beat out your rivals.

An estimated 50,000 hopefuls stood ready on the appointed day, the
Boomers' tents looking like flocks of migratory white cranes. On all four
sides teemed camps of devout believers in almost free land ($1.25 an acre).
The spectacle revealed an improvised parade of American types: West
Virginia lumber raftsmen, Tennessee mountaineers, Ohio bricklayers,
Pennsylvania miners, and Fort Leavenworth deserters. There were also
many non-Americans, mainly German and Irish, and including a doctor
who had studied at Heidelberg, a former officer in the Austrian army, and
a one-time exile in Siberia.

And then from the palisades of Fort Reno at ten to twelve, soldiers
yelled, "Everyone in line." When the hands on the clocks overlapped, the
Fort Reno howitzers boomed, and the blue-uniformed cavalrymen gave the
signal. Bugles sounded, whips cracked, teams tugged at harnesses, and
thousands were off and running, in wagons, on horseback, and on foot.

Hamilton Wicks was in New York in April when he heard President
Harrison was opening up 1,887,750 acres. Seized with Oklahoma fever, he
packed a valise and some maps and stepped aboard the Penn Limited to
Chicago, switching to the Rock Island to Kansas City, and then the Santa
Fe to Arkansas City. Canvas homes had been pitched in all the open spaces,
and Wicks managed to find an unoccupied tent corner.

On the morning of the twenty-second, five trains were made up ready
to start, but the excited mass of passengers wondered which one would
leave first. Wicks could not even find standing room until he offered a few
coins to a brakeman, who opened a caboose. Then the conductor called,
"Board for Oklahoma!" and as the train picked up speed through the Cherokee Strip, Wicks could see an army of Boomers moving across the plains
on the wagon road that ran parallel to the track.

Here was a prairie schooner, drawn by four scrawny horses; there a
couple of real estate men from Wichita lashing a spanking set of bays.
Six-mule teams and four-in-hands competed with hardy pedestrians. The
possibility of disappointment did not enter their minds. "April hopes, the
fools of chance," thought Wicks.

At the blast of bugles, all the curious equipages joined in a singular
race. This would occur but once for all time, thought Wicks, thorough-
breds, pintos, mustangs, thundering across the prairie, through pools,
down ravines, and into ditches, fanning out until lost to the viewer's sight.
The train crossed the trestle bridge spanning the Cimarron, then swung

around the hills between the river and the Guthrie town site, reaching Guthrie at 1:30 P.M.

Wicks saw a water tank, a station house, a Wells Fargo shanty, and a land office. He threw his valise out the window of his car and joined the scramble for a town lot. People wandered about like stray sheep, not knowing which way to turn, but Wicks fixed on a corner lot near the depot, where a street was planned. Jamming his location stick in the ground, he pounded the marker down with his heel. Then he unstrapped a small folding cot and threw a couple of blankets over it, figuring that he had now made enough improvements to make his claim unjumpable.

Wicks hired a man for a dollar a day to plow around his lot: 25 feet in front and 40 feet in depth. By dusk, he had put up a large wall tent. He saw tents everywhere and reflected to himself: "A city laid out and populated in half a day." Thousands of campfires flickered as far as the eye could see, and you could hear the hum of an indistinct multitude. That evening a roll call of states found settlers from every state and territory in the Union.

When Harrison announced the land opening in March, the railroad told Arthur Dunham to prepare for abnormal conditions at Oklahoma Station. "Everyone was on his toes for the Grand Rush," Arthur recalled. Drillers put down a well next to the station to supply water. News writers came in, and Arthur had to send out their copy, telling the night operator, "Here, clear this trash."

At noon on April 22, Arthur was standing on a boxcar alongside the depot and saw people spring up as if by magic, some with spades, some with stakes, some with pots and pans. The first train—from the south—steamed in about two-ten, so crowded that passengers swarmed over the tops of the cars. There were 2,000 people on that train, and Oklahoma City rose from the ground in days.

The trains from the north were behind schedule because eager Boomers kept jumping off and the conductors had to slow down to prevent injuries. Arthur would see a train approach and a homeseeker throw his baggage off, and then from a small cloud of dust a man would emerge, running his damndest.

Then came the "Sure Thing" men, and the "Knights of the Green Cloth," and the vendors of White Mule and Choctaw Beer. The demand for freight was so great there wasn't enough track room to hold the cars. Lumber came in and was retailed by the stick or the armload as the city went up.

In this formative period, there were so many trying incidents that Pimm & Banks, the furniture store, took up undertaking as a sideline. They came to Arthur with a body they wanted shipped to Council Grove, Kansas, and asked his permission to keep the deceased in the station overnight. A fellow came in that evening and used the coffin for a bed.

•   •

Cases involving Sooners—people who had come in illegally prior to the date and time set—were in the courts for years. In 1898, the Supreme Court ruled: "Manifestly, Congress did not intend that one authorized to enter the Territory in advance of the general public, solely to perform services therein as an employee of the government, should be at liberty, immediately on the arrival of the hour for opening the territory to settlement, to assume the status of a private individual and actual settler and make selection of a homestead, thus clearly securing an advantage in selection over those who, obedient to the command of the President, remained without the boundaries until the time had arrived when they might lawfully enter."

Sooner schemes abounded, and not just cases involving deputy marshals and other government employees. A typical example was that of Veeder Paine, who had once been an inspector of timber and logs in Michigan. In 1885, he published an article in *Harper's New Monthly* on how syndicates, by shrewd manipulation, acquired large parts of the public domain.

In 1889, Paine was working for the Saginaw Cattle Company, a firm that leased grassland on the Sac and Fox Reservation, to the east of the land that would open up on April 22. With two friends, Paine devised a plan to obtain a Guthrie homestead, which they could sell at a good profit to a townsite company.

At noon on April 22, Paine waited on the line north of Guthrie on a fast saddle horse. The night before, one of his cronies had sneaked inside the tract to the Guthrie site in a buckboard loaded with a tent, axes, and wood for stakes. The other friend was posted on the route to Guthrie with a relay horse.

On hearing the signal, Paine bolted into the lead and soon galloped out of sight, unencumbered by the provisions and equipment that were being carried for him in the buckboard. Passing many fine tracts, he headed for the Guthrie townsite. When his horse tired, his friend was conveniently waiting with the relay horse, and he reached his quarter section at 12:40 P.M. He and his two friends were the only ones there. Planting stakes and blazing trees on all four sides of the 160 acres, they marked their ownership.

Now it happened that a townsite company organized in Winfield, Kansas (just north of Arkansas City), had its eye on the land Paine claimed —Section Nine. On April 10, the company had sent a surveyor to plat the section's western half (320 acres). But when he got to Guthrie, the military would not let him proceed to the tract, which he was obliged to survey from the train window.

The surveyor returned to Winfield and made his plats. Having paid $10 to cover expenses, each member of the townsite company picked a lot. On April 22, the two hundred members arrived in Guthrie and headed straight for the western half of Section Nine. There they met Paine, who informed them that he occupied half their division, or 160 acres.

On April 25, Paine started building his house and fencing and sowing eleven acres of land. At the same time, the townsite people set up a city government and elected a mayor. Next they turned to harassing Paine and tore down his fences and destroyed his crops. By force of numbers they drove him off, and he sought redress in the courts.

At a hearing in the Guthrie Land Office on November 26, 1889, the register awarded the western half of Section Nine to the townsite claimants. But Paine persisted, and in 1891, Land Commissioner W. M. Stone decided in his favor. A final appeal came before Secretary of the Interior John Noble, who ruled against Paine on June 22, 1891, declaring him a Sooner.

Paine, Noble asserted, had arranged for his friends to enter the tract before the appointed hour, giving the three an unfair advantage on a claim they had taken for speculative purposes. Paine argued that his horse had stumbled and fallen on stony ground, bursting the forward girth of his saddle, and so he had to borrow his friend's horse and finish the journey. But if that was the case, Noble countered, why had he not exchanged saddles instead of horses? When the decision went against him, Paine wrote the Secretary to ask for a job as allotting agent in the Cheyenne and Arapaho country.

As one of the Boomers later put it, the Sooners had added to the old saying:

> *Aristocracy, to every man according to his breed;*
> *Plutocracy, to every man according to his greed;*
> *Democracy, to every man according to his deed;*
> *Mobocracy, to every man according to his need;*
> *Soonerocracy, to every man according to his speed.*

For more than a year, the Boomers who settled in the Unassigned Lands had no government, and each town improvised its own. But all that changed on May 2, 1890, when the Oklahoma Organic Act made the western half of the future state a territory. This included the Boomer settlements and the Indian reservations, as well as No Man's Land, that unwanted panhandle between Texas and Kansas.

Legislation gave rise to more legislation, and the Dawes Act ruled that the reservations should be parceled out to individual Indians. Commissioners then arrived in Oklahoma to make the allotments; the surplus was opened up to settlement. Thus, between 1891 and 1901, there were four more runs on surplus lands in Oklahoma Territory.

The first of these four runs took place on September 22, 1891. Twenty thousand persons scrambled for lots on what had been the Sac, Fox, Iowa, Shawnee, and Pottawatomie reservations, all land that lay to the east of the famous land run in 1889. In April 1892 came the run on Cheyenne and Arapaho lands between the Cimarron and North Canadian rivers. The following year the 8-million-acre Cherokee Strip, a large rectangle of land running across most of the northern third of Oklahoma, went up for grabs —the government had bought it under the allotment act for $8,595,736.12.

To prevent fraud, the Cherokee Strip run was more strictly regulated. Officials constructed nine registration booths along the line. Every Boomer was required to register prior to the run and had to present his registration certificate in exchange for the right to file. The booths opened on September 11, and the run took place on September 16. At towns with registration booths, such as Arkansas City, long lines began to form in the race for "life, liberty, and 160 acres." In stifling heat, thousands waited, as everyone from clergymen to stablehands prepared to cross the strip.

A. M. Thomas came by train to Arkansas City on Monday, September 10. He pushed his way into the crowd waiting to register and dared not leave his place in line. The next day when the booth opened, those waiting organized the line into squads of ten. Every tenth man was designated captain. It was his job to see to it that no one "Soonered" his squad, for speculators were trying to sell their place in line.

Having been picked as a captain, Thomas slept in line in a blanket. On Friday, he reached the booth and got his certificate, which entitled him to beat all rivals to a claim. In the time remaining until the run at noon on Sunday, horses were lightly fed, the wheels of vehicles were lubricated, and canteens were lashed to saddles.

That Sunday, vehicles of every description jammed into line. Wagons touched wheels and horsemen lined up like cavalry at inspection. At noon, an estimated 100,000 Boomers dashed forward from the starting points of Arkansas City, Caldwell, Kiowa, and Hunnewell (all on the Kansas side of the line), and from Orlando, Hennessey, and Stillwater on the southern boundary of the Strip.

A. M. Thomas rode off from Arkansas City south by southwest about fifteen miles to Blackwell, where he took some town lots. The next day Blackwell was a tent city. Thomas had some carpenters' tools and got a job building a restaurant, but the dust was so thick that when he drove a nail he couldn't see it.

On September 16, Jesse Dunn rode into Alva on the train from Kiowa. When the train stopped, everyone ran for town lots. Dunn's friend, A. H. Burtis, ran neck and neck with a tall woman and a one-legged shoemaker from Kiowa. The woman had her skirts up around her knees and the shoemaker was lunging and plunging on his wooden leg. Dunn laughed so hard he failed to get a lot. He felt like the Austrians defeated by Napoleon in Italy because "they did not know the value of five minutes."

The next day he found some land near the depot that no one wanted and planted his stake. He put up a tent, opened a law office, and set to work making out papers for other claimants. Dunn made $15 a day, more money than he'd ever seen. In the meantime, the offers kept going up for his lot, from $50 to $500.

Without planning or preparation, Alva grew into a city. The citizens got out of tents and into houses. A waterworks meeting was called to solve the water problem. It was wonderful to see all the saloon souses proclaiming the urgency of water. Finally, the abstemious F. W. Cowgill rose to his feet and said, "I would like to hear someone talk on this water question who uses water."

After 1895, the one major unsettled reservation left in Oklahoma Territory was the Kiowa-Comanche land in the southwest quadrant. It had in fact been ceded to the government by the Indians in 1892, but so much of it was already leased to cattlemen with friends in Congress that the actual opening for settlement was delayed until 1901.

Two million acres were ready to be opened in July 1901, with 450,000 acres, known as the "Big Pasture," reserved as grazing land for the Indians —that is, for the cattlemen. The military reservation of Fort Sill was enlarged to 56,000 acres and also kept from settlement, along with a forest preserve in the adjacent Wichita Mountains.

But this time, to avoid the chaos and crooked schemes of the runs, homesteads were doled out by lottery. In July, two offices opened, in El Reno and at Fort Sill, where homesteaders could register for the drawing, scheduled to take place on August 6.

The lottery had about 13,000 homesteads to distribute. More than 150,000 aspirants registered: 120,636 in El Reno, a town of 4,000 on a railroad line; and 29,888 at the more remote Fort Sill. The odds on getting land were less than ten to one.

People mistakenly thought that registering early would improve their chances, so they formed long lines in front of the six registration booths in El Reno, one of which was a booth for women so they would not get trampled.

Four thousand registered the first day and 6,000 the next. Booths and stands lined the streets of El Reno from end to end. Vacant lots were covered with cots for rent at a quarter each. Housewives checked grips and bundles. Children sold lemonless lemonade. Saloons extended their bars onto the sidewalks.

In Fort Sill, the lines stretched out into the vacant prairie, and a man was killed for trying to break in. An agent sent by the State of Texas opened a booth and hung out a sign: IF YOU LOSE IN THE GOVERNMENT LOTTERY, COME TO TEXAS. But enough frontier optimism still filled the air so that no one thought they would lose.

On August 6, there was a county fair atmosphere in El Reno as 50,000 hopefuls gathered to witness the drawing on the Irving schoolground. On a raised platform, batches of envelopes were stuffed into an octagonal pasteboard box, which was shaken briskly each time a blindfold boy drew one. They were opened by land-office officials, who called out the names of the winners to shouts and applause. This went on for several days at El Reno and also at Fort Sill, where the edge of the military reservation became an instant town, called Lawton. The winners set up tent encampments called "dog towns," while the losers went back to Kansas or Texas or wherever they had come from. The Oklahoma land openings were over.

The twentieth century had arrived, but you would not have known it from observing Oklahoma settlers, who lived much like those of the century before. In 1899, Roscoe Harper's father filed a claim four miles from the town of Buffalo, just south of the Kansas line in northwestern Oklahoma. The nearest post office was in Ashland, Kansas, thirty-five miles to the north. The county seat was Woodward, thirty-five miles to the south. You had to make a two-day round trip to Ashland or to Woodward, and so few houses appeared along the way that you took food and water.

This northwest corner of Oklahoma was perhaps the last place in America where buffalo still grazed in 1900. Practically none of the land had been plowed, and dust storms had already occurred. People still used cow chips for fuel. Roscoe saw his grandma reach over and pick up a handful, throw them into the stove, and put her hands back in the dough without washing them—and they sure were good biscuits.

The only community activity was debating. Was England right in the Boer War? Was a sheep more useful than a billy goat, or a dishrag than a broom? They had no telephone or telegraph, no store, no doctor. "Life was lonesome," Roscoe recalled. "Once I spent two weeks at a ranch without seeing anyone."

On the Washita River near Durham in western Oklahoma, Augusta Metcalf remembered her mother calling out, in the spring of 1900: "Water in the house!" It was sixteen inches and rising, and Pa said they better get to high ground. He snatched up a big quilt, an ax, some kindling, and little George.

When her parents died, Augusta farmed twenty-five acres of row crops and mowed thirty acres of bottomland, raking and bunching the hay to feed her cattle. In her eighties, she said, "I'm just as ready as ever to investigate who's shooting and where he's at."

Homesteading outside the town of Fletcher in 1901, Iva Allen and her husband were in their tent one evening when they heard thumps on the roof, and Charlie said, "Hail, oh our wheat crop." The noise sounded like a thousand machine guns going off at once, and the tent began to collapse from hailstones as big as eggs. Charlie grabbed a mattress and placed it on the table and Iva sat underneath, holding her two babies in her arms. Charlie kept saying, "This is ruining my wheat and thrashing down my half-ripened oats."

The storm ended almost as quickly as it had begun. They stood there staring at what only that morning had been a golden crop, seeing it all wiped out, nothing but shredded ruin. That afternoon Iva burned twelve chickens that had been battered to death by the hail. To keep her family alive, she gathered wild greens—dandelions, lamb's-quarters, pokeweed, sour dock, and wild lettuce.

•   •

When thirty-one-year-old C. F. Holmes arrived in Mangum, Greer County, in the spring of 1900, the southwestern Oklahoma town had a population of 700. Some residents lived in tents and others in dugouts. Holmes knew that people were fed up with circuit-riding dentists, who departed leaving boardinghouse bills unpaid and teeth unfilled, so when they asked him how long he intended to stay, he replied, "I expect to remain for 75 years."

Greer County was a million-and-a-half-acre triangle situated between the north and south forks of the Red River, claimed by both Texas and Oklahoma, and granted to Oklahoma in an 1896 Supreme Court decision. The only other dentist in this huge area was Dr. Laird, who wore a ten-gallon hat and had long hair dangling over his shoulders. He extracted teeth with his fingers, in the street before a crowd. He used no anesthetic, but had a couple of fellows in blackface keeping up a running patter of jokes to distract the patient. Meanwhile, his pretty wife in a fancy costume urged the victim to keep smiling.

That was the medicine-show school of dentistry. Dr. Holmes, however, thought of himself as a twentieth-century, state-of-the-art dentist. He administered cocaine as an anesthetic, once finding himself with three particularly susceptible patients stretched out on his office floor recovering from their doses.

Greer County was still pretty wild, and you never knew what to expect. It was not uncommon for a cowboy to ride in from the Texas panhandle, as far as a hundred miles away, to have a tooth pulled. One of them showed up one day and said he hadn't brushed his teeth for a year, and proceeded to do so with Dr. Holmes's toothbrush, which the doctor afterward prudently threw away.

A son brought in his mother, who needed dentures, but she said she did not want to lose her "tobacker" tooth, the one she used to bite off a piece of plug tobacco. Her son said: "I don't want maw's teeth to project out so much that she can bite a pumpkin through a crack in a brush fence."

Dr. Holmes thought to himself that here was a fellow with a keen sense of aesthetic values.

"And I don't want them set so far apart that she can't bite the cork out of a bottle," the son added.

"By avoiding either extreme," Dr. Holmes recalled, "I was able to make her presentable." His motto was: "A denture that is not paid for never fits."

The young trader James Edward Finney represented Dunlap & Florer at the Osage Agency throughout the 1870s. John Florer told Finney he was convinced the reservation was "underlaid with oil." Finney remembered Florer's words when an Indian took him to a spot on the banks of Sand Creek and pointed to a filmy rainbow on the water's surface. Finney soaked up the patch with a blanket and squeezed out enough crude oil to provide a sample.

In 1895, Florer asked the Osages for an oil and gas lease. The Indians hesitated at first, but relented in 1896 in exchange for 10 percent of earnings. The Phoenix Oil Company was formed and dug a couple of wells, but they didn't pay.

Then Michael Cudahy, a meatpacker from Omaha, took charge. In April 1897, at Bartlesville, forty miles north of Tulsa, Cudahy struck oil. A column of black gold spouted from the derrick, and the well was christened the Nellie W. Johnstone No. 1, after an Osage chief's daughter who owned the tract as her allotment.

But the company had no way to bring the oil to market until the Atchison, Topeka & Santa Fe extended rail service to Bartlesville in 1899. A two-inch pipeline was laid from the Phoenix wells to the depot, and a loading rack was built. The Standard Oil refinery in nearby Neodesha, Kansas, furnished tank cars and the first shipment of 6,216 barrels went out in May 1900, followed by 10,536 the next year.

Oil in the United States had first been found near Titusville, Pennsylvania, in 1859. At that time, it was used for lamps. Standard Oil was incorporated in 1870, and by 1900 it controlled 80 percent of the nation's oil production with its giant network of refineries, pipelines, and storage tanks.

In 1903, Prairie Oil & Gas, Standard Oil's pipeline subsidiary, constructed a 35,000-gallon storage tank at Bartlesville and connected the Osage wells to it with a pipeline. Standard Oil also built its Sugar Creek refinery near Kansas City, linking it up with Neodesha.

But the Oklahoma oil fields remained too unregulated for Standard Oil to take them over. Too many wells were opening up and too many independents were coming in. On the Osage Reservation, tracts were subleased to wildcatters, who became the key figures in Oklahoma oil development. A product of the late frontier, the wildcatter resembled the gold rusher from half a century before.

Oil was not an industry, but a gamble. The wildcatters had no geologists to guide them in leasing and drilling. They operated on hunches, or "witches" with "doodle bugs" (dowsers with wands). Of Tom Slick, "Prince of the Wildcatters," they said, "He may not be the country's greatest geologist, but he sure is the country's greatest poker-playing geologist."

Up to January 1903, 30 wells had been drilled on the Osage Reservation, 17 for oil, 2 for gas, and 10 dry holes. In 1904, an Oklahoma oil rush resulted in 361 wells on the reservation by the end of the year: 243 oil, 21 gas, and 97 dry holes. Gas flares at the wells and the dull clank of sledges pounding bits gave away the oil town.

With increased production, the Oklahoma parent company, Indian Territory Illuminating Oil (which had absorbed Phoenix Oil), dropped its price from $1.36 a barrel in January 1904 to 70 cents in January 1905 for light oil. With the Osage Reservation broken up into tracts, the government reserved oil and gas royalties for the tribe, which divided the money equally among its members. This made the 2,229 enrolled members of the

Osage tribe the richest community in the world on a per capita basis. Revenue in 1906 reached $228,267.34, and in 1923 climbed to $27,639,600. John Florer, one of the prophets of Oklahoma's oil wealth, died in 1907. In 1941 Indian Territory Illuminated Oil was merged with Cities Service.

The allotment system inspired by Dawes did not apply to the Five Civilized Tribes that had been relocated to a supposedly business-free sanctuary in the eastern half of Oklahoma. In 1893, however, Grover Cleveland appointed a commission to negotiate with the Five Tribes and convince them to hold their lands as individuals rather than as a nation. He also wished them to abolish tribal governments and come under state and federal laws.

According to the 1890 census, 51,000 Indians and 109,393 whites dwelled in Indian Territory—the latter a motley crew of coal miners, oil workers, Indian agency employees, and squatters. In principle, these white residents were noncitizens allowed on tribal land on a permit basis. Nonetheless, they lobbied Congress for the benefits of citizenship—namely land ownership and schools.

Congress responded by phasing out tribal government. Laws like the Curtis Act in 1898 invalidated tribal courts, making Indians subject to federal laws. Simultaneously, President Cleveland's commissioners secured agreements from the Five Tribes, drew up the tribal rolls, and started surveying Indian Territory and making allotments. In 1897, the Choctaws and Chickasaws were the first to sign, and by 1902 all five tribes had given their consent.

In April 1903, land offices opened at Atoka, on Muddy Boggy Creek, and Tishomingo, near the Blue River, in southeastern Oklahoma, so that the Choctaws and Chickasaws could select their homesteads.

A year and a half later, in October 1904, several thousand allottees had not yet appeared. A field party was sent out to find them, led by L. P. Bobo, a young surveyor. Bobo went to see one of the commissioners, Colonel Needles, at the Katy Hotel in Muskogee, for instructions.

Colonel Needles happened to be in the middle of his afternoon nap. Awakened, he told Bobo, "We want you to go out and do the job and not worry us. Put your own construction on the law." Bobo asked no more questions, and in November rode a hundred miles south to Farris, on Muddy Boggy Creek, with another surveyor, two interpreters, three good sixteen-hand horses, and a mule team.

Among the Five Tribes were a number of prominent recalcitrants referred to by white officials as "Snakes," such as the Cherokee Daniel Redbird and the Creek Chitto Harjo. These men wanted to keep the country as it was. They had no use, they said, for 320-acre allotments, when under the old system they owned thousands of acres. Some Choctaws were called "wigwam lawyers" for citing the Dancing Rabbit Treaty of 1830, which had granted them land "as long as the grass grows and water runs."

L. P. Bobo's field party had a complete roll of Choctaws and Chickasaws. They also had to find out which allottees had died, so that the land could be transferred to their heirs. To accomplish this, the party rode into Antlers, 10 miles east of Farris, and found Colonel Victor Locke at the Harvey Hotel. A Tennessean who had married a squaw, the colonel was in the business of furnishing coffins to the Indians, often on credit, so he kept a list of the deceased. The Harvey Hotel, Bobo reflected, was a nice change from sleeping on the ground in a blanket.

Bobo rode out to some improved acreage nearby and found a belligerent Snake in front of his cabin. "Why did you not go to the land office?" Bobo asked. "I don't want any land between the rocks" (that is, between subdivision corners marked by stones), the Indian replied. Picking up his shotgun, he ordered the whites off his premises. He had not seen a deer in two years, he cried after them; previously, the woods had been full of them. He called one of the interpreters a traitor to his tribe. The interpreter was so stung by this rebuke that upon returning to Antlers he quit.

Still looking for deceased allottees, the little expedition proceeded to Smithville, sixty miles to the east and not far from the Arkansas line. There they found Mary McClure, who taught in a Choctaw school. She said the water on her allotment was so impregnated with crude petroleum as to be unfit for human or animal consumption.

In Smithville, they uncovered a scheme of feigned recalcitrance— Indians who went to the land office and filed allotment claims where their Snake neighbors were located. They then preached the Snake doctrine— "Have nothing to do with the Dawes Commission"—so that their acquiescence to private ownership would not be found out by other members of the tribe. As a result, there were numerous disputes over allotments, and one of Bobo's tasks was to find suitable land where the genuine recalcitrants could go.

In the final rolls of the Dawes Commission, 23,405 freedmen in Indian territory were listed as obtaining allotments. These one-time slaves of the Five Tribes, more than any other group of blacks, realized the old Reconstruction dream of land for the landless. But like the Indians, they were often accused of sitting on the land instead of improving it. John R. Thomas, a federal judge assigned to Indian Territory, complained that "these negros won't work if they can avoid it and as long as they have 160 acres of land, they won't."

As the freedman J. Coody Johnson told Congress in 1906, the sales of their allotments for modest sums "made idlers of people who, before these restrictions were removed, were content to attend to their labors and were industrious people." Many freedmen, however, kept their lands and became small farmers, owning their farms, opening bank accounts, and keeping their heads above water.

In 1900, an Oklahoma statehood movement started gathering strength. The big question was whether there would be one state or two. The Republicans desired a single state that combined Oklahoma and Indian territories, for they feared that Indian Territory, with its southern inclinations, would go Democratic. The Five Tribes wanted a separate state, invoking a provision to that effect in the treaty signed by the Choctaws and Chickasaws in 1897.

The background to Oklahoma's struggle for statehood was a powerful reform movement sweeping the west. It also took root in Oklahoma, among workers and farmers who were wrestling with the demands and inequities of the turn-of-the-century market economy. These laborers had begun to question the assumptions of the Boomer philosophy. The unrestrained competition of 1889, the every-man-for-himself individualism of the frontier, no longer worked against the overpowering forces of eastern capitalism: the trusts, the railroads, the corporations.

This was the true finale of the frontier—not a geographic limitation as defined by the Census Bureau, but the demise of the frontier spirit, which became obsolete amid the complexities of twentieth-century industrial America. The impersonal market economy was disastrous for the little man, whose only means of fighting back was by forming associative movements.

Thus the rise of the Farmers' Alliance. Created in the 1880s, the Alliance aimed to curb the power of the railroads and the trusts and to lower interest rates. A companion group, the Farmers' Union, had organized 40,000 Texas farmers by 1903, and by 1904 had 150,000 members, 30,000 of them in Oklahoma.

In 1898, the United Mine Workers went into the coal fields of Indian Territory and chartered District 21. Unorganized, the miners lived in hovels; the company deducted their rent from their wages. The pay, dispensed in scrip, was redeemable only at company stores with high markups.

In addition, Indian Territory had the world's most dangerous coal mines, and ninety-six men lost their lives in an explosion at a Krebs mine on January 7, 1892. The "shot firers" who set off dynamite charges in the dust-filled tunnels didn't last long either. Though Washington provided for a territorial mine inspector, none had arrived by the time of the Krebs explosion. The job was finally filled by a company man, who concluded that accidents resulted from the miners' ignorance and carelessness.

When the UMW called strikes in Indian Territory, the mine operators brought in black strikebreakers. Edwin Ludlow, the mine superintendent for the Atoka Company, vowed to break the miners and their families, and "to make a dollar look as big as a wagon-wheel."

But the District 21 president, Peter Hanraty, coordinated strikes with two other UMW districts, 25 and 14. He forced the Southwestern Coal Operators' Association, which represented every mining concern in Kansas, Arkansas, Texas, and Indian Territory, to the bargaining table. In a landmark contract signed in August 1903 at Pittsburg, Kansas, the UMW won recognition of the eight-hour day, biweekly pay, the deduction of union dues from paychecks, the abolition of involuntary deductions, the creation of a pit committee to settle disputes, and wage increases to $2.56 a day.

Hanraty later wrote of the 1903 agreement that "since that time, the coal operators and the miners have been on very friendly terms." Labor and management had grasped the mutual advantage in giving up destructive rivalry and working together to standardize wages and maintain production levels.

No longer would the working man and the farmer remain frustrated spectators in an unregulated market economy. Oklahoma rode high on the wave of reform. The new synonym for "evil" was "trust." The people banded together against the monopolizers like U.S. Steel, International Harvester, Standard Oil, and the American Tobacco Company. These giants cared only for profits, price increases, and destroying the competition. No sooner did a Southwestern Lumber Manufacturing Association form than the price of lumber in Oklahoma rose by a third.

And while the railroads cut rates for powerful shippers like Standard Oil, they overcharged the farmers. The Interstate Commerce Act of 1887, meant to counter the railroad's pricing tactics, was ineffective. Theodore Roosevelt, in the White House from 1901 to 1909, got a rate bill called the Hepburn Act passed in 1906, but that didn't do much good either. In the west, people viewed politicians as being in a corrupt alliance with big business.

Oklahoma politicians routinely held the eastern plutocrats in derision as a vote-getting tactic. They seized on Mrs. Howard Gould, for example, who in her divorce suit said she needed $240,000 to make ends meet. Charles Haskell, the state's first governor, referred in a speech in Sulphur, Oklahoma, to Mrs. Gould's $500 gowns, saying, "I don't know how it is with the rest of you folks, but my wife goes to bed sometimes just to get her dress washed."

In this euphoria of populism and reform one segment of the population was left out. The progressive agenda did not extend to blacks; quite the contrary. At the same time that Oklahoma sought to check corporate power, equalize the tax burden, and get rid of certain kinds of social injustice, a Jim Crow backlash was directed at the black population.

The many southern white residents were accustomed to seeing black slaves grovel before the massa. But in Oklahoma, land-owning blacks lived free. They voted and held office in the territorial government, and kowtowed to no one. By 1900, there were twenty-eight all-black communities in the two territories, publishing their own newspapers and electing their own officials.

Many white Boomers looked askance at this black success story. They resented having to compete with blacks for jobs, land, and economic opportunities. In the selective process of migration, the blacks who left the south and came to Oklahoma tended to be more ambitious and assertive than the blacks who stayed behind.

The Jim Crow backlash expressed itself in growing segregation. Waurika, not far from the Texas line, warned blacks: "Don't let the sun set on you in this town." Legislation in 1897 segregated the territorial school system, stipulating, "It shall hereafter be unlawful for any white child to attend a colored school, or for any colored child to attend a white school." In progressive Oklahoma, racial segregation was enforced right down to the telephone booths and cemeteries.

Just as the politicians bashed the eastern rich to win votes, they used Negro-bashing to equally good effect. C. M. Cade, who was running for territorial delegate to Congress in 1902, said in a speech at Cushing (midway between Tulsa and Oklahoma city) on August 26: "I am glad that you ain't got no niggers in Cushing. There wasn't a nigger in the Democratic convention that nominated me for Congress, and thank God, there wasn't any nigger smell." Race-baiting was a surefire political tactic. The same men who shouted about the evils of eastern capitalism and the need for reform shouted just as loudly against equality for blacks.

In April 1905, Theodore Roosevelt, who had been inaugurated a month before for a second term, came by train to Indian Territory on a hunting trip, speaking at station stops in Vinita, Wagoner, Muskogee, and McAlester. In Muskogee, he declared: "Your territory, remember, in conjunction with Oklahoma, will soon be one of the greatest states in the Union."

Taking time out from hunting coyotes in western Oklahoma, Roosevelt said in Frederick on April 8: "The next time I come to Oklahoma I trust I will come to a state and it won't be my fault if this is not so."

Obviously, the president was pushing for a single state, to which the Five Tribes had long expressed their opposition. But the end was approaching for the Five Tribes, for an act of Congress set March 4, 1906, as the date on which tribal government would be terminated.

In a final attempt to make a separate state out of Indian Territory, the Five Tribes held a conference at Muskogee on July 14, 1905, where they expressed all-out opposition to single statehood. On August 7, they convened a mass meeting to choose delegates for a constitutional convention.

Held on August 21, the convention consisted of 182 Indian and white delegates. Among them was that picturesque figure William H. "Alfalfa Bill" Murray, a Texas dirt farmer who had come to Tishomingo in 1898 with his carpetbag and his derby, taken a Chickasaw wife, and become a legal member of the tribe.

The delegates drafted a constitution for a separate state to be named Sequoyah. It was ratified by the people and submitted to Congress. But the lawmakers in Washington refused to consider Sequoyah's admission to the Union.

Unintentionally, the Muskogee convention ended the two-state movement and stimulated the federal government to act on single statehood. In June 1906, Congress passed an enabling act and invited both territories to send delegates to a constitutional convention. The delegates, fifty-five from each territory plus two from the Osage Nation, assembled at the Oklahoma territorial capital of Guthrie on November 20, 1906. Ninety-nine Democrats and thirteen Republicans arrived in a city of 12,000, crosshatched by nine railroads and visited by forty-two passenger trains a day.

Imbued with the reformist spirit of the moment, the convention also embodied the prevailing racism. Alfalfa Bill Murray served as the convention president, with Pete Hanraty as his vice president. In a spirit of reconciliation, Murray asked the delegates to appoint one Union and one Confederate veteran as sergeants-at-arms. In a spirit of subjugation, he requested the designation of a black man as convention janitor.

"It is an entirely false notion," he said, "that the negro can rise to the equal of a white man. . . . the more they are taught in the line of industry the less will be the number of dope fiends, crap shooters, and irresponsible hordes of worthless negros around our cities and towns."

It took the delegates nearly four months, from November 20, 1906, to March 15, 1907, to draft what became the longest constitution in the nation's history—45,000 words combining reformist and racist measures, including the segregation of public schools. Other Jim Crow measures were deleted when President Roosevelt, who had been sent a draft of the constitution, threatened to reject it.

In many ways, the Oklahoma constitution expressed the territory's distrust of machine politics and eastern capitalism. Railroads were the delegates' prime target: the rail companies had to divest themselves of their mining operations and reduce their freight rate to 2 cents a mile; they also had to pay taxes on rolling stock as "movable property." State officials were required to swear that they "will not receive, use, or travel upon any free pass or free transportation during [their] term of office."

The constitution took aim at giant trusts, public health and safety, political machines, and farmer's welfare. It stipulated that all corporate records be open to public inspection and declared monopolies illegal; formulated a pure food and drug act; created insurance commissioners, mine inspectors, and a department of charities and corrections; proclaimed the eight-hour day and banned child labor. It set gubernatorial elections in a different year from presidential elections so that no candidate for state office could ride on the president's coat-tails. It required that agriculture be taught as a vocation in public schools.

Samuel Gompers, president of the American Federation of Labor, called Oklahoma's blueprint for statehood the most progressive constitution in existence. Frederick Upshaw Adams of the *Saturday Evening Post* wrote, "It was not merely the birth of a new state; it was the birth of a new kind of state." Except when it came to blacks and women.

Not everyone was gasping with admiration. President Roosevelt, though not wanting to interfere personally, dispatched his secretary of war, William Howard Taft, to Oklahoma to oppose the radicalism of what Taft called "a zoological garden of cranks." In a speech before a Republican audience in August 1907 at Oklahoma City, Taft said that this was not a constitution at all but a code of laws, a spurious combination of "Bour-bonism and despotism, flavored with Socialism"—referring to the state's strong Socialist Party. He urged Oklahoma Republicans to vote against it.

On September 17, 1907, however, the constitution was ratified by a vote in both territories of 180,333 to 73,059. On November 16, 1907, Theodore Roosevelt had no choice but to sign it into existence, and brought into being the forty-sixth state, which had the largest population of any new state, 681,115 in Oklahoma Territory and 733,062 in Indian Territory.

CHAPTER TWENTY-FIVE
THE LAST
HISPANIC FRONTIER

In my native tongue, the word relocation does not exist.

Message on a T-shirt,
Santa Fe, August 1988

The territory we have selected for our home is unlike any
other portion of the United States.

ED CROSS of Tubac, Arizona

The National Archives
A Navajo family near Fort Defiance, New Mexico, in 1873.

For over two centuries, New Mexico stagnated under Spanish rule. This somnolent rim of the old Viceroyalty of New Spain contentedly devoted itself to subsistence farming, to herding, and to the conversion of the sedentary Pueblo Indians.

In the summer of 1821, however, Mexico declared its independence from Spain. The new nation welcomed American traders into New Mexico to stimulate the economy. The response was almost instantaneous, for on September 1, 1821, William Becknell the Indian fighter left Arrow Rock, Missouri, with twenty-odd men and a packtrain of goods, getting to Santa Fe by mid-September.

Reversal of the Spanish prohibition brought an influx of American traders, trappers, and mountain men into New Mexico. In 1824, Senator Thomas Hart Benton asked Congress to appropriate funds for the blazing of the Santa Fe Trail and the protection of caravans. By 1825, an American consular office had opened in Santa Fe.

"The commerce of the prairies," as Josiah Gregg called it in his classic account, developed its own style and procedures. On the eight-hundred-mile route from Independence, Missouri, to Santa Fe, pioneers encountered much prairie, some sandy desert, little water, and many Indians. The traders banded together in caravans for convenience and self-defense.

Approaching the Mexican settlements, the Americans might see a lone buffalo hunter. Outside Santa Fe, the wagons stopped for customs inspection and paid the *derechos de arancel*—the impost duties. The *mordida*, or bribe, became so customary that in 1839 Governor Manuel Armijo decided on a flat rate: $500 per wagon regardless of the contents. Of course, traders started using larger wagons, loaded with more costly goods, and the measure was repealed.

They came into Santa Fe like ships into harbor, the crewmen impatient for leave. In this town of 3,000, people lived in one-story adobe houses flush with the street. There was a plaza with a governor's palace, the sunny side of which was crowded with beggars, and a couple of churches.

The traders livened up the sleepy town, which did its best to supply the usual trappings of a cosmopolitan commercial center: saloons, gambling houses, and women with rouged cheeks who danced the fandango and smoked cornhusk cigarettes in public. While enjoying the amenities, the hard-driving Protestant traders developed their stereotype of Mexicans as "a lazy gossiping people always lounging on their blankets and smoking cigarillos." Josiah Gregg said they lived "in darkness and ignorance . . . having inherited much of the cruelty and intolerance of their ancestors, and no small portion of their bigotry and fanaticism."

For too long, in the American view, these people had been the pupils of Spain and popery. And that was about to end. For in 1846, the United States and Mexico were involved in a border dispute; in April, Mexican troops crossed the Rio Grande, and in May, President Polk declared war. In September 1847, General Winfield Scott took Mexico City and the war in effect ended, though the treaty was not signed until February 1848.

On August 18, 1846, American troops under the command of Stephen Watts Kearny entered Santa Fe. In a flutter of changing flags on the plaza, the old regime disappeared. Kearny remained as military governor for four years.

Eighteen-year-old Louis Garrard, who was traveling with some mountain men, visited the Taos jail on April 9, 1847, the day of the first hanging under American rule. Garrard came upon a long-haired, dirty Missouri volunteer leaning against the doorframe, who asked: "Well, stranger, how are ye?"

"Quite well, thank you," Garrard said.

"Them's great britches of yourn'," said the volunteer, eyeing one of the mountain men's fringed buckskin pants. "Whar'd they 'riginate—Santa Fee? Beat linsey-woolsey all holler."

"Santa Fay," Garrard said. "Why, hoss, them's Californy."

"Californy! My-oh, way over yonder! Now you don't mean to say you was in them britches when they was *in* Californy?"

"That boy's been everywhar," another of Garrard's companions said. "He's stole more mule flesh from the Spaniards and raised more Injun hair than you could tuck in your belt in a week."

"Raise Injun hair?" asked the volunteer. "Like we raise corn 'n' hemp?"

"No, you darned fool—when an Injun's a gone beaver we take a knife and catch hold of the topknot and rip skin an' all right off."

The Taos court was in session for fifteen days, and during that time it charged seventeen men with murder and hanged fifteen of them before the ink on the court transcript had dried.

New Mexico was an unstable mix of very different people. There were 50,000 Hispanics, almost all Catholic, and almost none English-speaking. Most of them could not read or write. Overnight they became United States citizens, although in the rest of the country they were considered ill suited to take part in the blessings of democracy. About 10,000 Pueblo Indians, semi-Hispanicized and semiconverted, also occupied the territory, along with about 30,000 nomadic, marauding Indians, mainly Navajos, Cheyennes, and Apaches. Finally, there were several thousand traders and Missouri volunteers.

Hoping to create a fan of defense, the army built a string of forts in the heart of Indian country: Fort Yuma, where the Gila River runs into the Colorado in southwestern Arizona; Fort Union, a hundred miles northeast of Santa Fe; Fort Fillmore, forty miles north of El Paso on the Rio Grande; and Fort Defiance, in the middle of Navajo country, on the Arizona—New Mexico line.

Born in Pataborn, Westphalia, in 1827, William Kronig was twenty when he arrived in New York. He worked in an "underground grocery," but got fired because he would not pass counterfeit money. In 1849, he headed west, bound for the California gold mines. The wagon train passed through Las Vegas, New Mexico, a town of adobe huts that had strings of red and green chili peppers hanging from the rafters.

Then they came to Santa Fe, the wagons rumbling into the square. Business was flourishing, and women could be had for hire at most of the gambling places. William was embarrassed when a painted female standing at a window invited him in. He was also stone broke. He had arranged to cash a check for a hundred dollars in Santa Fe, but Mr. Cartwright, the owner of the brokerage house in Independence, Missouri, had in the meantime died of cholera, and the check was stopped while his estate was settled.

The day came when Kronig could not pay his hotel bill and had to sell his horse for $13. After that, he bunked with two fellow Germans, Schlesinger, a small, toadlike sycophantic fellow, and Viereck, the brother of an actress, a happy-go-lucky sort who never had a dollar to his name but was always in high spirits. Viereck opened a barbershop, but the three-card monte men got every dollar he earned, and the rest of Kronig's money as well.

Every morning people formed a line in front of Viereck's barbershop before it opened—not customers but bill collectors. There was the man who had built the barber's chair, the Mexican landlady, and the German doctor who had treated Viereck for the clap. Since neither Kronig nor the layabout Schlesinger could find a job, all three men responded to a call for volunteers in Taos, leaving behind their creditors.

At Taos, they enlisted for two months. Being the only one in his company who could read and write, Kronig was made orderly sergeant. When he drew rations for the company, the captains and lieutenants asked him to give them three rations each. But Kronig was that rare species, an honest man, and he refused, incurring their animosity.

The company was sent eastward to protect the settlements from the Utes. Kronig gave out rations every five days, exchanging the company's provision of candles for vegetables from the local farmers. When he discovered a mysterious shortage in the meat ration, the conscientious Kronig went to find the beef contractor, but the captain warned him that if he pressed the matter he would find himself in the guardhouse. He confronted the contractor anyway, who offered Kronig a percentage of the money he had cheated the army out of. Kronig told him that the men were entitled to their full ration.

When his two months were up, Kronig was mustered out. He happened to run into his regimental commander, Colonel Beall, who offered him $5 a day to recover a baby who had been captured by the Utes. Game for any opportunity, Kronig left in knee-deep snow with ten days' provisions. By the time he found the Indian camp, he was out of food and starving. The Ute chief, Belasquez, gave him buffalo meat with the hair still sticking to it, which Kronig gratefully devoured.

Kronig and the Indians held a council and smoked a pipe. The Ute chief said, "Tell your chief that we will come to Taos as soon as the grass is long enough so that it will keep the horses strong." Then he added that the baby was dead.

Before he left, the Indians asked Kronig for ammunition. He said no, explaining that he had to render a statement for everything he had taken along. As he was about to leave, Kronig asked about the curious ornaments on the chief's leggings. The chief pointed to one cluster and said, "These are Mexican fingernails," and then to two others, "American fingernails" and "negro fingernails."

Back in Taos, Kronig gave Colonel Beall his report and was paid in full. He felt like a rich man. He was a lucky man, too, for at the quartermaster's office, he ran into Quinn, the beef contractor who had tried to bribe him. Kronig was about to pretend not to know him when Quinn stopped him and asked if he wanted to open a business in Taos. Quinn said he needed a man he could trust; he himself would supply the capital. Kronig accepted, and for some years operated a highly successful general store.

As a result of the Compromise of 1850 negotiated between the northern and southern factions of Congress, New Mexico became a territory. On September 9 of that year, California was admitted as a free state and, as a counterweight, Utah and New Mexico (including Arizona) were admitted as territories under the doctrine of squatter sovereignty with no provision concerning slavery.

Thus began the longest territorial period that any state underwent— sixty-two years. The lengthy hiatus was due mainly to the large Hispanic population, which made New Mexico seem like a foreign country. Here were two distinct political and religious traditions, as compatible as water and oil. Two sets of habits and institutions had to be reconciled. For the Spanish way of doing things was to go to the palace and petition the governor, who listened all day to endless stories about a horse and a mule, or to a water-rights dispute.

Corruption in local office was the rule. An advertisement in the *Santa Fe Weekly Gazette* on August 20, 1853, offered a

HANDSOME REWARD

One blanket, two strings of peppers, one *almo* of beans, one pint of whiskey, and one roll of tobacco—this will be given to any person that will present a more partial *alcalde* [mayor] than we have in Las Vegas, or in other words a bigger fool.

On December 4, 1852, the secretary of war, Charles M. Conrad, presented to Congress a plan to administer the newly minted territory. The region, he said, was "so remote and inaccessible, and holds out so little inducement to emigration, that the struggle between the two races is destined in all probability to continue there long after it shall have ceased in every other portion of the continent."

Conrad was so pessimistic about New Mexico that he proposed the United States give it up. He pointed out that to protect a mainly Hispanic white population of 60,000 the government had to maintain a large military force at a cost of a million dollars a year. "Would it not be better," Conrad asked, "to induce the inhabitants to abandon a country which seems hardly fit for the habitation of civilized man by remunerating them for their property?" But Congress ignored him and built more forts, though Indian marauding remained the order of the day.

One of those remote military posts, Fort Massachusetts, rested along the base of Blanca Peak in today's southern Colorado, at 8,000 feet. In 1855, De Witt Clinton Peters, a twenty-six-year-old New Yorker, served as the post surgeon, one of eighty men in a wilderness garrison surrounded by hostile Indians. In a letter home, he wrote, "I wish some of our Washington gentlemen could see the true state of affairs in this country."

Indians were fighting each other over hunting grounds, but they left the post alone, seeing that the men were well armed. One Indian came peacefully into the camp holding a pole with eight scalps dangling from it. He sold De Witt a buffalo tongue for 10 cents.

In 1855, the Utes declared war, putting the fort under a state of siege. The soldiers had to send the mail out at night, south to Taos, a hundred miles away. The nearest fort to the north was Laramie, eight hundred miles away. "We are quite isolated in this vast territory where 10,000 Indians roam," wrote De Witt. "Most of the bands are at war with each other, very happily for us."

De Witt rode to Taos with the mail express man to get bandages and medicine. Outside Costilla, fifteen armed warriors began to chase them. They outran the Indians, though they could hear the yells the fellows kept up. In Taos, Kit Carson, the legendary scout, now an Indian agent in his mid-forties, complimented De Witt on his coolness.

De Witt and Carson went to a Mexican feast where they saw dances "which if performed in the states would be considered immoral and send them all to the penitentiary." Nevertheless, De Witt danced the fandango with pretty women wearing shawls. When he asked Carson when the festivities would end, Kit said, "Whenever beans make their appearance it is time to leave."

De Witt spent Christmas in Santa Fe. Though the Stars and Stripes flew from the palace, the territory was American in name only. The Indians roamed at will, and the Hispanic-controlled legislature then sitting in the palace was a disgrace and a farce.

In the Gadsden Purchase of 1853, the United States paid ten million dollars for southern New Mexico and southern Arizona, adding 45,535 square miles and 5,000 Indians to the part of New Mexico it already owned.

In 1854, surveyor William Pelham arrived in Santa Fe, entrusted with a formidable task. For much of the land in New Mexico was claimed under Spanish or Mexican grants with titles more or less valid. Shrewd Americans were buying some of the land grants that had been claimed under Spain or Mexico at nominal prices. They then enlarged them by fraud, so that the plots of land took on remarkable India rubber qualities.

A thousand claims awaited settlement, making New Mexico a paradise for lawyers—"men of low cunning and astuteness," as the reform governor E. G. Ross later described them. The fabrication of land titles was reported as early as 1849. Stamped Mexican blank paper could be bought and filled out by an "expert in penmanship." The transfer and enlargement of titles became commonplace.

Thus, in the 1850s, New Mexico remained a territory of remote military outposts and continuous Indian depredations. The insecurity and lack of public land for homesteads kept new inhabitants away. They had to wait until the Spanish and Mexican claims were settled and the land surveyed.

During the interim of the Civil War, Arizona fell briefly into Confederate hands, prompting Congress to separate it from New Mexico as an independent territory in 1863. But even after being divided in half, much of post–Civil War New Mexico remained a wasteland. The only Americans were the soldiers in the forts. Garrison life on the frontier meant days of boredom and moments of panic. To relieve the boredom, officers were allowed to bring their wives.

Josephine Clifford arrived in New Mexico in 1866 with her husband James, a captain in the 3rd Cavalry. Born Josephine Woempner in Prussia, she had emigrated to the United States with her parents in 1846 and had grown up in St. Louis, where she went to convent schools.

It was in St. Louis that she met Lieutenant James Clifford, a charming blue-eyed Irishman who had been promoted through the ranks. In 1863, they were married. What Josephine did not know at the time was that Clifford was already married to Margaret Dillon of New Orleans under his real name, James Ingram, and that he had four children.

In her wagon on the way to Fort Union, ten miles from Las Vegas, Josephine watched the infantrymen marching in front of her like a moving forest of bayonets. She admired the red-rock and desert landscape, the sculpted bluffs, the high cactus, and looked forward to discovering the southwest. But the isolated fort life brought out her husband's worst tendencies. He was never far from the whiskey bottle and usually in some kind of trouble. Once he was charged with stealing a hat from the quartermaster's store.

Soon the company moved to Fort Bayard, near Silver City, in southwestern New Mexico. There Josephine was the only wife. She rode sidesaddle on her horse Toby, exploring the mines and the town of Pinos Altos. But her husband's behavior did not improve. Once, in his cups, he told her he had killed a man in Texas a few years before. But having told her, he began to imagine that she was going to inform on him.

For six months, Clifford kept his wife a prisoner, refusing to let her leave the garrison. Whenever he got drunk, he threatened to kill her, and once he nearly strangled her. Pride kept Josephine from going to the post surgeon and showing her bruises. To hide them, she tied a strip of flannel around her neck and said she had a cold.

On occasion, Clifford played Russian roulette, aiming the pistol at Josephine's head, close to her temple, and letting the click of the hammer sound in her ears. At first, Josephine suffered her husband's abuse dazed and unresisting, like someone paralyzed. A natural reticence made her unable to seek help from the men in the garrison.

In January 1867, Clifford asked for a pass to Santa Fe, where he planned to lodge various charges against the colonel commanding the Fort Bayard post, who had cited him for insubordination. When his request was denied, he sent Josephine to seek redress for him. The post commander agreed to let her make the trip, for her efforts at concealment had not fooled anyone. In fact, a quiet conspiracy had taken shape to help her out of her predicament.

The night before Josephine left, Clifford begged for forgiveness. Declaring his love, he promised to reform. Though by now familiar with the cycle of abuse and repentance, Josephine was touched. When she set out the next day, she had every intention of coming back.

But once she was gone, Clifford's mind snapped and he jumped on a horse to pursue her. In San Antonio, south of Socorro, Josephine was preparing to leave for Albuquerque when her orderly noticed a rider approaching. When she saw who it was, "It turned my heart to stone, and paralyzed every nerve of my body."

Clifford had deserted from Fort Bayard and covered 150 miles in twenty-four hours, without food or rest. Worse, he was riding Josephine's beloved Toby, who was "trembling in every limb." "When Toby spied me," she recalled, "a low whinny reached my ear, and he moved forward a step to reach my side. But before I could reach him, he had tottered and fallen at my feet, with a deep, almost human groan." Moments later, the horse died.

Clifford told the terrified woman that when they got to Santa Fe, she must corroborate his version of persecution at the hands of his commanding officer. As soon as they reached the territorial capital, he locked her in their room at the inn. Afterward, he reported to General James H. Carleton, commander of the Ninth Military Department since 1862.

Carleton told Clifford that he would consider the accusations against the colonel at Fort Bayard. Then he ordered Clifford to return to the fort and place himself under arrest. To the other charges already pending against Clifford, the general added desertion. Carleton realized the nature of Josephine's situation, for he added in his report, "His wife is to be pitied." But since she had made no request for protection, the general's hands were tied.

Once again, something stopped Josephine from making good her escape. In early February 1867, she accompanied her husband back to Fort

Bayard, "leaving all hope behind." In Santa Fe, her orderly had given her a puppy. One evening when they were camped by the side of the trail, Clifford grabbed the puppy and beat its brains out with his pistol butt. Then he rubbed his hands clean in the sand of the trail. "I would not hesitate to dispatch you in a similar manner," he told Josephine.

At Fort Bayard, the colonel ordered Clifford to turn in his sidearms and placed a guard in front of his rooms. In response, Josephine fell into a state of depression. Around mid-April 1867, a court-martial convened at Fort Bayard to hear Clifford's case, among others.

Traumatized and numb, Josephine stayed in their quarters with her husband. One evening, Clifford threatened her with a hatchet and ordered her to kneel down, swearing that he was going to chop open her skull. When she calmly complied, he flew into a rage and threw some of her clothes into the fire. By this time, he was so drunk he passed out, and after a while Josephine fell asleep. She awoke to find him brandishing the hatchet a few inches from her face.

Finally, Josephine came to her senses. In the morning, with the help of the garrison command, she made plans to leave. The colonel gave her a letter to show at the posts she would pass: "Treatment [of Mrs. Clifford] is reported *Brutal* and anything you can do to assist her in leaving the country will be endorsed as a just cause."

Josephine reached Fort Union and joined a military train heading west. She made her way to California, where she got a divorce in 1869. At Fort Bayard, Clifford was cashiered, but he managed to get a medical leave, and went to Albuquerque. There he drew his gun on a superior, Lieutenant Colonel Duncan, accusing the officer of having helped his wife. Assault was added to the other charges, and Clifford was drummed out of the army. Josephine was also rid of him, ending this case of wife abuse in the frontier army of New Mexico.

The Indian problem in New Mexico had been inherited from the Spaniards, who made half-hearted attempts to keep the tribes at bay. There were two sets of tribes: The peaceful and sedentary Zunis and Tanos and Hopis had yielded to missionary influences. Becoming nominal Christians, they had kept their own rites, and farmed lands that the Spanish had given them. The marauding tribes, mainly Apaches and Navajos, earned their livelihood by stealing livestock and horses, threatening both the peaceful tribes and the Hispanic settlers.

These professional thieves did not change their way of life with the arrival of the Americans in 1847. They continued to live from plunder. The Navajos in particular proved to be such a menace that in 1855, David Meriwether, governor of New Mexico Territory, summoned a number of headmen to a conference and offered them a treaty confining their lands west of a boundary near today's Arizona–New Mexico border. "If we have a dividing line," he said, "so that we know what each other's country is, it will keep us at peace."

With the coming of the Civil War, the marauding tribes saw the whites fighting each other, and sensed a golden opportunity. In April 1860, the Navajos attacked the garrisoned post of Fort Defiance, fifteen miles northwest of today's Gallup, New Mexico. To retaliate, the army ordered a six-week campaign in October and November in the heart of Navajo country, whose target was "those audacious predatory hordes." But the campaign, led by Lieutenant Colonel Edward Canby, failed so miserably that a newspaper observed, "As well might we send boys into a cornfield to catch marauding crows."

It was not until September 1862 that the Indian menace was crushed, when General James Henry Carleton arrived in Santa Fe to replace Colonel Canby as commander of the Military Department of New Mexico (the Ninth). A native of Maine, Carleton had joined the cavalry in 1838 and been decorated in the Mexican War. He was one of those worrisome officers who aspires to perfection through attention to detail.

Carleton set about attacking each marauding tribe, one at a time. He chose Kit Carson to go into Navajo country in August 1863 with a force of about 800 volunteers. Carson's orders were to kill the Navajos' sheep, destroy their crops, cut down their orchards, and starve them out of their canyons. Believing ruthlessness to be the key to a short campaign, Carleton added, "The men are to be slain whenever and wherever they can be found."

Carson sent detachments on long rides through the wind-pocked land, burning cornfields and rounding up livestock. In December, in the snow and cold, worn out from a swelling aortal aneurysm that would kill him in 1868, Carson asked for leave over Christmas. Carleton replied: "*Now* while the snow is deep is the time to make an impression on the tribe."

Carson made a lasting impression by invading the last two Navajo strongholds, Canyon de Chelly and Canyon del Muerto, which were guarded by sandstone cliffs that stood 1,000 feet above the canyon floor. Most of his horses were out of commission; the mules stepped through the ice in shallow streams and stumbled under their loads.

Hiding on the mesas, the Navajos tried to survive on cedar berries and yucca fruit. In January 1864, ragged and hungry, they began to turn themselves in at Fort Defiance. As always, General Carleton had a plan: in eastern New Mexico, on the Pecos River, there was a well-watered million-acre reserve with some grassland and irrigable land. It was named Bosque Redondo, or Round Grove, for the patch of cottonwoods at its center.

Carleton believed that relocating the tribe was the only way to change its behavior. "The old Indians," he wrote, "will die off and carry with them all the latent longing for murdering and robbing; the young ones will take their places without these longings; and thus, little by little, they will become a happy and contented people."

The Navajos kept straggling into Fort Defiance. In March and April 1864, a total of 8,000 made the three-hundred-mile trek to Bosque Redondo. It was the exodus of an entire people out of the land of their fathers, except for about 400 die-hards who were never captured. Refusing to surrender, they fled northward into Colorado and Utah.

Bosque Redondo developed into a community of 10,000 (including soldiers and civilian workers). But the hope that the Navajos could become self-sustaining farmers there proved to be illusory. The waters of the Pecos were alkaline and made the Indians sick. The crops they planted were destroyed by a caterpillar called "the army worm." Once they had chopped down all the cottonwoods, they had to go fifteen and twenty miles for wood, digging mesquite roots out of a hard soil and packing them on their backs. The New Mexico papers called the place "Sweet Carletonia."

Unable to feed themselves, the Navajos relied on army rations that the military distributed every other day. "They cluster around the commissariat like steel filings around a lodestone," wrote General Carleton. When they were issued ration cards, they became adept at forging them, presenting the fake cards on behalf of "sick relatives." At one time, there were 7,000 Navajos and 10,000 cards. The cards had to be replaced by unduplicatable metal disks, made in Washington with an intricate design.

Proposals to move the sick and impoverished Navajos back to their homes in northern New Mexico began to reach Washington in 1866. But General William Tecumseh Sherman, who commanded the Division of the Mississippi, worried about the expense and wrote: "I think we could better afford to send them to the 5th Avenue hotel to board, at the cost of the U.S."

Still, in 1867 the movement for return found some followers in Congress, who argued that maintaining the Navajos in Bosque Redondo was costing the government an exorbitant $750,000 a year. It would be better and cheaper to send them back to their former home, these lawmakers maintained, on land that in any case was considered unfit for white habitation.

On May 28, 1868, General Sherman, the conqueror of Atlanta, and now the head of an Indian Peace Commission, arrived at Bosque Redondo. His mission was to negotiate a treaty with the Navajos, and he met with seven of their principal chiefs. They told Sherman that the reservation was inadequate to their needs and that the Diné (people) were being decimated. They wanted to return to their ancestral lands in the north.

"We have not planted this year," Chief Barboncito told Sherman. "It is true we put seed in the ground but it would not grow two feet high. . . . I think that this ground was not intended for us." The Navajos believed some lands to be bad luck, and Sweet Carletonia was one of them. "It seems that whatever we do here causes death," Barboncito went on. "A rattlesnake bite here kills us. . . . In our own country, a rattlesnake gives warning. . . . I am speaking to you as I would to a spirit or a god, and I wish you to tell me when you are going to take us to our own country."

On June 1, 1868, Sherman signed a treaty with the Navajos, who agreed to give up banditry. In exchange, Sherman would bring them back to their lands in the high plateaus, though restricting them to a 3,328,000-

acre reservation, a long, narrow rectangle straddling the Arizona-New Mexico line. The tribe would receive rations and clothing for ten years, as well as sheep and goats to build up their herds. They would have the right to hunt off the reservation.

Even though they were returning to an area that amounted to no more than one-fourth the land they had before, the Navajos were glad. For the reservation was not in a new and undesirable location. It lay on the lands they knew well, where mesquite and juniper grew, where mustard flowers dotted the plains and the clouds rolled in like galleons, where above 5,000 feet creosote, sage, and pine scented the air.

This was the Navajo's providential homeland, a country of umber cliffs, sandstone spires, and rock formations called skysupporters. Through the land's twisted trees and blowing sand flowed a tributary of the Colorado called the San Juan, carving its bed like the coils of a huge serpent wriggling through the desert. For the Navajos, each landscape feature held a particular significance, like the totem-pole rocks they used for rainmaking ceremonies, or the two ridges in southeastern Utah they called Bear's Ears, a nursery of medicinal plants.

The return of the 7,000 Navajos to their homeland in June 1868 was no trail of tears. The cost to the government, $56,000, was a bargain, since they were a changed people. Once martial, they were now domesticated and pastoral. Their four years of exile had taught them the futility of opposing a national army that could fight in all seasons. Armed resistance and violent raids only brought down the wrath of the military.

The Navajos returned chastened, but with a strong sense of tribal unity and a determination to survive in an Anglo world not of their making. They would now rely on more subtle strategies. In the twenty years to come, they offered a unique example of Indian success. Where other tribes saw their land holdings dwindle and their population decline, the size of the Navajo reservation and the Navajo population tripled. How this was accomplished, with the assistance of Indian agents and the federal government, runs quite contrary to the now familiar story of Indian heartbreak and despair.

The Navajos' good fortune had much to do with geography. Their reservation—a rectangle eighty miles north to south and sixty miles east to west—was in a picturesque but infertile area called the Four Corners, at the juncture of Arizona, New Mexico, Utah, and Colorado.

When the Navajos moved back there in 1868, no settlers were streaming in to encroach on the untillable reservation land. On the contrary, the Navajos started taking their herds off the reservation and grazing them on public lands.

The Four Corners soon became a crossroads for all sorts of people besides Indians. Mormons, Gentiles, cattlemen, miners, and traders competed with each other for public grazing land and water rights. The group with the most successful strategy would triumph, and the Navajo strategy was to avoid bloodshed, maintain peace with other tribes, curtail white settlement, and expand their land base. This last they did by ignoring reservation boundaries and grazing their sheep and planting their crops on public lands—that is by squatting, just as the whites had done for centuries.

The shifting migratory groups made for strange bedfellows. The Mormons, who had been in Utah since 1847, were moving south from Salt Lake City. By the early 1870s, they had reached the San Juan in the southeast corner of Utah Territory, only miles from the Navajo Reservation, where they founded the settlements of Bluff and Aneth. Other Mormon settlements started up in northern Arizona, at Tuba City and Moenkopi, again right next to the Navajos. Before long, the Mormons set about converting their neighbors.

The Navajos were receptive to the Mormon teaching, perhaps because of similarities to their own. The two groups saw themselves as a "chosen people"—the Navajos considered themselves different from other "earth surface" people, while the Mormons had moved west to get away from debased Gentiles. Both Mormons and Navajos looked to revelation to inform them about the future. Both regarded good and evil as products of the gods; and both practiced polygamy.

Thus, the Mormons and the Navajos were quite compatible, maintaining cordial relations with mutual gestures of goodwill. Navajos returned stolen Mormon horses, and Mormons helped Navajos with their irrigation and planting. The Mormons built a wool mill at Moenkopi, where Navajos could take their wool to market, and they also provided a trading post where the Indians could spend the proceeds.

Trouble in the Four Corners came mainly from non-Mormon settlers, who committed anti-Indian acts and tried to blame them on Mormons. In December 1873, four Navajos left the reservation without a pass to go on a trading expedition and got stranded in a snowstorm in southern Utah, on the Sevier River. Having bartered for a cow with some Utes and slaughtered it, they took shelter in a cabin and dried some of the meat.

A non-Mormon settler named McCarty had spotted the Indians with the cow, which he figured was stolen. He rounded up some men, and they attacked the cabin and killed three of the four Indians. The fourth escaped to Arizona. The Mormons were blamed for the killing but protested they had nothing to do with it.

Relatives of the dead Navajos asked the Indian agent, W. F. N. Arny, for compensation. Arny told them his hands were tied because the men had been killed while off the reservation without permission. Refusing to relent, the Navajos demanded 400 cows by May 1874. As the deadline approached, Arny worried that the tribe would go on the warpath, so he arranged for ten of the dead men's relatives to be invited to Washington. He personally accompanied this delegation of the bereaved to the nation's capital, and in addition issued extra rations in the amount of $17,364.71.

The Indian agent played the key role in the diplomatic history of the Four Corners. He had to investigate suspicious incidents, placate the

Navajos, and arbitrate disputes among Navajos, Mormons, and Gentiles. None of the agents could speak the Navajo tongue, and some made themselves unpopular with their wards. As a result, there was quite a turnover —fifteen agents between 1869 and 1900.

Arny himself quarreled with the chiefs over the distribution of annuities. About his replacement, Major Alexander G. Irvine, the *Weekly New Mexican* said in October 1875: "How he will succeed among a nation of breech-clouted brutes . . . is quite problematic." It was Irvine who first raised the possibility of enlarging the reservation with the Bureau of Indian Affairs. Irvine admired the Navajos, writing his superiors in March 1876 that Spanish-Americans were "inferior in both intelligence and industry."

By then, there were 10,000 Navajos, and Agent Irvine reported that "the tribe is increasing in numbers, their children are growing up, their flocks of sheep are increasing, and more land is needed than was given them eight years ago."

In 1878, John E. Pyle took over from Irvine and was instrumental in implementing a program to give the Navajos part of their annuity in sheep and goats, in order to increase their herds. In his dispatches, he described the Navajos, once the scourge of the plains, as having been transformed into peaceful herdsmen. "They have too much at stake in their immense herds of sheep, goats, horses, and cattle, their hundreds of thousands of pounds of grain in the field and the cache," he wrote in 1878, "to hazard it in a war."

In 1878, President Rutherford B. Hayes ordered a first land extension, and moved the reservation's western border twenty miles to the west, further into Arizona. Ten years after returning to their homeland, the Navajos obtained a boundary increase, whereas the usual practice on reservations was appropriation. Then in 1879, the new agent, Galen Eastman, forwarded a request for another extension on land that was absent of settlers. Hayes signed a second order, on January 6, 1880, granting a fifteen-mile extension to the east and south.

The western extension had given the Navajos improved access to the San Juan, which was practically the only reliable water source on the reservation. Settlers protested. One, William White, wrote Senator Henry M. Teller of Colorado in February 1881: "I hope our next Secretary of Interior may be a Coloradoan or other western man and not of the Dutch persuasion." (The secretary, Carl Schurz, was in fact German). "We may then stand an equal chance with an Indian." But the Navajos kept their extension.

Galen Eastman didn't last long. A reformer, he tried to ban liquor and squaw men. The Navajos called him "the tarantula" and accused him of giving them inferior goods and being niggardly with tobacco. But the real basis of their displeasure was that in remote villages the Navajos still kept slaves from other tribes, and Eastman was going into those villages and ordering them released.

In the Canyon de Chelly, Eastman reported, "One ol' villain wanted to know who was to take care of him if his slaves were taken away. I shut him up by telling him I would take care of him and the whole band if they were not set free."

By 1879, when Eastman arrived, non-Mormon settlers were trickling into the reservation's fringes on the San Juan, which curved down from southern Utah into northern New Mexico. One of them, a contentious fellow who fired off letters to every government department, was Henry L. Mitchell, a Missouri man who had settled near Aneth in 1878. He had a ranch at the mouth of McElmo Canyon. In one year, eighteen other families joined him, totaling about seventy persons. The Mormons lived in Aneth, but Mitchell said he would "soon give the damn Mormon outfit the same medicine that I gave them back in Missouri."

Mitchell's ranch had the Navajos to the south and the Utes to the east, and in 1879 he began reporting Indian acts of agression. In December, he said, the Navajos had herded 20,000 sheep around his ranch, which "cleared away all grass several miles back from the river."

Then in 1880, Henry Mitchell wrote Galen Eastman to inform him that his son Ernest and Ernest's friend James Merritt were missing. They had left a month before, Mitchell said, to look for a silver mine. Shortly afterward, the two young men turned up dead and scalped in Monument Valley, Utah. Henry Mitchell went to get the bodies, and blamed the Navajos for the murder. The Navajos blamed the Utes, while it later came out that it had been the Paiutes.

In any case, Mitchell felt that Galen Eastman was dragging his feet. He wrote the Ute agent Hiram Page on July 13, 1880: "I have been drove from my home on the san wan by the Indians, it being no longer safe for me to live there without protection . . . the mormans got the indians to do it. This is a horrible state of things . . . i am getting old and wore out and then to be robd and drove from my hom i think it is hard."

Mitchell kept up a barrage of complaints against his Navajo neighbors. On January 15, 1883, he sent a letter to the secretary of the interior, saying that the Navajos were again wandering off their lands, "robbing white men, claiming they own the land, threatening to kill all whites. . . . I know they intend to make trouble this spring."

Galen Eastman's replacement at the Fort Defiance Agency, Denis Riordan, looked into Mitchell's warning. Finding no sign of trouble, he figured that Mitchell was paving the way for a future claim of loss of property. Riordan had Mitchell pegged as an opportunist, playing all the angles, and suspected him of selling the Indians liquor and ammunition. He also discovered that Mitchell was issuing passes to the Navajos, allowing them to cross to the north side of the San Juan to graze their flocks on the public land used by the Mormons.

Some time after reporting in 1884 that "the Navajos are the best-behaved Indians in America," Riordan resigned, saying that the leaky houses at Fort Defiance had made his family ill. The new man, John

Bowman, lasted only a year as the result of a sex scandal with a Navajo squaw.

In the meantime, the reservation extensions continued, on the assumption that giving the Navajos more land would make them self-sufficient. William Parsons, a special agent from the Department of the Interior, proposed that the northern boundary be extended to the San Juan, increasing the reservation's river frontage. "It is in fact," he said, "all desert and mountain with the exception of 2000 acres of bottom land. . . . This land the Navajos must have in order to get water with their herds and flocks."

In 1882, President Chester A. Arthur created a Hopi reservation of 2,500,000 acres in Arizona, and later gave part of the land to the ever-expanding Navajos. In another executive order on May 17, 1884, Arthur extended the reservation northward into Utah, adding a strip between the San Juan and the Arizona border. This long east-west ribbon of land was the last Navajo extension of the nineteenth century.

The rationale for the extensions was that the donated land was not suitable for settlement. One report described the area as "merely a space on the map of so many degrees and parallels. Three fourths of it is about as valuable for stock grazing as that many acres of clear sky . . . no soil worthy of the name." The refrain was always: "Why not give them a few more square miles of barren sand?"

The next agent after Bowman, S. S. Patterson of Iowa, turned out to be a crook. In 1886, Congress appropriated $7,500 for irrigation on the reservation. Patterson hired Indian labor at a dollar a day to dig the irrigation ditches, then charged his workers 50 cents a day for board. The Indians called him "the old woman" and "the man who smells his mustache." He was charged with payroll padding, false expense accounts, and running a private boardinghouse for workers. Out of the $7,500 earmarked for irrigation, Patterson had pocketed $5,000. The irrigation project stalled, and the little work that got done was useless.

In 1887, in a reversal of the usual removal of Indians, settlers were forcibly removed from the banks of the San Juan in Utah, where the reservation had been extended. In April Patterson reported that about a dozen settlers "manifested a dogged determination to stay until paid for improvement." By July, only three families held out—the Carmans, the Whytes, and the Hendricksons. Mrs. Hendrickson made herself the spokeswoman for these die-hards, writing the Secretary of the Interior: "We came here to stay and we mean to if we can."

Orders came down for troops to move the settlers out. On August 25, two weeks past the August 10 deadline, the soldiers marched in, loaded Mrs. Hendrickson and her three children and their possessions into a wagon, and escorted them off the land. Mrs. Hendrickson appealed to the president, Grover Cleveland: "Why rob us of our homes when we toil so hard to build up, to enrich, and to beautify the valley of our wilderness?"

The Bureau of Indian Affairs replied on October 29 that the removal "was deemed necessary to permanently maintain peace between the Indians and settlers." On December 23, 1887, Mrs. Hendrickson shot off the last word: "Oh shame on a government that will willingly rob its citizens."

The year 1889 saw the Navajo population increase to 21,000, three times its size since the tribe's return from Bosque Redondo in 1868. The reservation acreage had also tripled, from 3,328,000 to 9,503,763. Agent Parsons observed that the Navajos' success made them less amenable to changing their ways. They clung to their long hair, red bandanas, and Indian dress. The agency had no leverage to Anglicize them because they were self-sufficient.

In 1892, Agent David Shipley reported that after the oil-rich Osages, the Navajos had become the wealthiest tribe in the United States. Their luck changed in 1893, when drought caused an economic collapse. Thousands of Navajos sank into destitution, and in 1895 they were killing horses for food.

Still, the resilient population grew and grew, needing more land. On January 8, 1900, President William McKinley signed yet another executive order that added 1,575,369 acres, extending the reservation westward as far as the Little Colorado. The new acreage swallowed up Tuba City and Moenkopi, and the government had to remove the Mormons from their two towns. Again, white settlers were evicted to make room for Indians, which did not happen every day. But for the Navajos it was normal. They were the elect. It was foreseen in their code of conduct, the "Blessing Way."

In 1903, the subagency of Shiprock was created, on the San Juan west of Farmington. William Shelton, the agent, protected Navajo interests—although in 1907 he had to send the cavalry against a rebellious medicine man who refused to have his sheep "dipped" (disinfected) against scabies, a contagious skin disease. When local whites complained that the Navajos were grazing their sheep off the reservation, Shelton told them that they "misunderstood the purpose of a reservation. Reservations are to keep white men off, not Indians on."

By 1909, the Navajo Reservation was the largest in the United States, consisting of more than 10 million acres, most of it at an elevation of between 4,000 and 10,000 feet, up there with the creosote and the grama grass. White settlers kept waiting for the land to be reduced by allotment, but only after statehood in 1912 was that process begun.

In 1868, when the telegraph reached Santa Fe, the territory of New Mexico had a population of 12,000 Anglos, who spark-plugged an economic boom. Two of the boom's by-products were lawlessness and political corruption. In Lincoln County, at 27,000 square miles the biggest county in the United States, the courts operated in such disarray that murderers did not stand trial, and in 1878, President Rutherford B. Hayes declared the county to be in a state of insurrection.

In Santa Fe, a corrupt machine of politicians, lawyers, and businessmen ran things. The Santa Fe ring was a bipartisan sub rosa government with friends in Congress, including among its members territorial governors, judges, and newspaper owners. It dealt in fraudulent land grants, cattle rings, and mining rings, until President Grover Cleveland finally cleaned the situation up.

In the climate of the times, men got shot over very little, often in saloons. Killings were the order of the day, for everyone was armed and fractious. Jimmy Morehead, an agent for a wholesale house in St. Louis, was staying at the St. Nicholas Hotel in Las Vegas. He told his friend Manuel Otero that a waiter had refused to bring him eggs for breakfast because he had arrived in the dining room a few minutes late.

"The same thing is liable to happen in the morning," Jimmy said, "for I am getting to bed late tonight and I don't intend to regulate my hours of sleep and my habits to suit the waiter of a hotel where I am paying a good price for the poor service."

The next day Morehead came down to breakfast at nine sharp, but the waiter said, "You are too late to get eggs; you will have to take what you can get."

"Look here, young man," Morehead said, "I want no more of your impudence."

"I'm just as good as you are in any way you want to take it," the waiter said.

"You damn scrub," Morehead responded.

"You're a damn sight more of a scrub than I am," the waiter said.

Morehead picked up a chair, saying, "You damn son of a bitch, don't open your mouth to me again."

The waiter ran into the kitchen and got his gun. He came out and said, "You infernal son of a bitch, get down on your knees and beg my pardon, or I'll kill you."

Morehead jumped at the waiter, who fired, shooting the wholesaler in the gut. They carried Morehead up to his room, and when the doctor came, he couldn't find the bullet's point of exit. Lifting Morehead's shirt, he saw a small blue spot on his back and made an incision. Then he pressed on both sides and the bullet popped out. That afternoon Morehead died.

In April 1880, twelve-year-old Jim Hastings accompanied his father to Silver City in southwestern New Mexico. "New Mexico has 121,666 square miles," his father said, "and probably one person per square mile." Mr. Hastings was the superintendent of a quartz mill that crushed the silver ore from two mines.

Mule teams hauled ore down from the mines in giant wagons that had boiler-plated beds. The mill ran twenty-four hours a day, seven days a week, ten months a year. In the heat of summer, they laid off for repairs. The ore was crushed to a fine dust by stamps that rose and fell with a deafening noise, and the dust was washed into massive pans and ground still finer under monster shoes that worked like millstones.

In the last set of pans, workers added quicksilver to the silver dust to form an amalgam. Then they poured the amalgam into strong canvas bags and drained off most of the quicksilver, much as a farmer's wife made cottage cheese by twisting the sack and squeezing the whey out. The result was called a "goose egg." These were heated in a retort until the silver was pure, when it was cast into three-hundred-pound bricks.

The Adams and Wells Fargo express companies took the bricks in coaches to the railhead at Deming, fifty miles to the southwest. One time a brick broke through the coach floor in the desert. All the driver could do was leave it there, which was safe enough, for no pack mule could carry it, and any wagon that did could be tracked. In any case, the abandoning of a $5,000 silver brick did not bother Mr. Hastings. Once the Wells Fargo driver had signed for the load, it was his responsibility.

All the food in Silver City came via the railroad. But when the Mescalero Apaches were in the vicinity, the Mexican conductors refused to make the food run to the mines, and Silver City's inhabitants had to go on a cornbread diet. Jim Hastings remembered his three-year-old sister going to the birdcage and plucking a lump of sugar out between the wires and scraping her teeth across it. But with a shake of her curls, she returned the lump to the cage.

One Sunday morning Jim saw two soldiers come down the street driving two horses hitched to a coach that was punctured by bullet holes and covered with blood. Hiding behind yucca stumps, the Apaches had jumped the coach around sunrise near Fort Cummings, a six-company post. They killed every mortal inside. The mail from the recovered sacks was splattered with blood.

The Indians, Jim believed, were made to hate the white man by a minority of scoundrels. Jim's father told him that once he had gone to Fort Cummings and seen a log-cabin guardhouse where an Apache had been confined for some misdemeanor. Soldiers made a campfire near the cabin, and one of them heated a steel rifle-cleaning rod in the fire, stuck it between the guardhouse logs, and burned the sleeping Apache. In his pain and fright, the Indian broke out of the cabin. The guard, who thought he was trying to escape, shot him dead.

Jim had no school to go to. Sometimes a traveling schoolmaster came through, staying long enough to earn sufficient money to move on, but most of the time Jim did odd jobs at the mines, working alongside ex-slaves, Mexicans, and Canton Chinese. Sometimes he flagged in the mine shafts for the surveyor, using a candle for a flag. Accustomed to the routine of the mine, he listened for the black cook to blow the whistle on the hoist and call, "Come and get it." When one day Jim asked the cook to come down in the mine shaft with him, the man said, "No sah, mister Jimmie, I can go out the doah and dig a hole six inches deep and get into that and it is deep enough for me."

Their camp wasn't far from the border, and Mexican horsemen came through with skinny fowls hanging from their saddles, asking for two *reals* each, or 25 cents. You could always tell the smugglers' carts, because only the thieves greased the spindles on the wooden wheels, which otherwise made a wail that could be heard for miles around.

Jim's usual task was to keep the water pails brimming. He went to the St. Vincent spring where the Mexican women were gossiping and where, if you had taken the trouble to learn border Spanish, you could get an earful. When he had free time in the morning, Jim would watch the Concord coaches leave town for the railhead. The Adams express would race the Wells Fargo coach, which had four small mules. Bill Green, the Adams driver, once ran over a rattlesnake but turned his four horses out to avoid crushing a terrapin in a wheel rut.

The Mexicans brought in stove-length wood on burros. When he sold his load, the muleteer pulled one thong from the rawhide rope holding it on and the bundle of merchandise all fell to the ground. The burros had to pick their way out of the pile. When Jim had neatly ricked that wood near the kitchen door, he was free to go afield.

Some things the young boy would never forget as long as he lived: riding all afternoon on top of a swaying Concord coach between two infantrymen dressed in blue holding their Long Tom rifles, while to the north signal fires blinked from the summit of a flat-topped mountain.

Or, when as a thirteen-year-old flagman standing on a mountaintop, he saw the valley of the Rio Grande in the distance, the river winding across it like a white thread on the desert floor, and through the clean air the smoke of the construction trains, building the lines that would span the continent.

In March 1881, the Atchison, Topeka & Santa Fe reached Deming and connected with the Southern Pacific. The arrival of the railroad brought new towns and a jump in property values. It meant the replacement of mercantile capitalism by industrial capitalism.

In April 1884, Mary Bloom rode on the Santa Fe main line out of Albuquerque, going south to Las Cruces with her four-year-old daughter Maude and her seven-year-old son Ralph. They had come from Springfield, Illinois, to join Mr. Bloom, who had been appointed legal counselor to the new United States Land Office at Mesilla on the Rio Grande, 223 miles south of Albuquerque.

The train was going through a flooded area, and twenty-four-year-old Mary Bloom, the youngest of seven sisters, began to regret her husband's decision. Why had he given up the speakership of the Illinois House of Representatives to come to this godforsaken place where the river had washed away the county seat at Mesilla, so that the land-office papers had to be moved by boat to Las Cruces, getting soaked in the process.

"Oh, I simply can't stand this horrible rolling brown water," Mary Bloom said. She longed for the oaks and never-ending lawns of her home in St. Louis, where she lived before moving to Springfield. Oh, for the pride-of-the-prairie roses and the second-story veranda overlooking the placid stream of clear clean water. "I am not a hen to moult all my nice past life," she said. "Like Papa!"

"Papa couldn't be a hen anyway," Ralph observed. "He'd be a rooster." At which Mama slapped him.

At Rincon Junction, they had to switch trains and take a branch line to Las Cruces. The big train was going west to California over a steel bridge that lay half under water—still passable, the conductor said, although some of the men were shaking their heads.

The branch line, one yellow car with a funny little engine, arrived in front of the station. The passengers felt the train sink into the raging flood water of two big arroyos pouring down from the Rincon Mountains to the east. Two trainmen on the rear platform kept signaling with their lanterns to the handcar that followed.

Mary Bloom was frantic, and said, "This engine is going to fall into the river." The conductor came by to calm her down, assuring her that the roadbed wound above the water on rocky hillsides through the narrows between Rincon and the Robledo Pass. He handed the children free tickets to the circus in El Paso (forty miles from Las Cruces). But Mary Bloom worked herself up into a fit and started screaming that they had to go back to Rincon or they would all drown. The conductor gave her a shot of whiskey to quiet her nerves.

They reached Las Cruces without incident. Maude saw her father standing beside the tall uniformed army doctor, and when she hopped off, her dad picked her up and gave her a big hug. After the Las Cruces stop, the train went on for a few miles and toppled into the torrent. Mary Bloom, who would be teaching Sunday school, asked if she could have the bell for her little adobe chapel, which was in the aptly named hamlet of Cantarecio, meaning "the place where the water sings loudly." It was the first Protestant church with a bell in the Mesilla valley.

In 1889, Sam and Carrie Sutherland moved to La Luz in southern New Mexico, eighty miles north of El Paso. Sam became a cattleman, exploiting the steady market of thousands of reservation Indians who received beef rations from the government. But thieving Indians and rustling Anglos cut into profits, and range wars pitted the nesters and small cattlemen against the big outfits.

When Sam complained to the sheriff about loss of cattle, he made the rustlers sore, and they decided to make an example of him. They arrived on his range in broad daylight and proceeded to lasso his herd. One big rustler reached over to shake Sam's hand in a friendly gesture, grasped it, and pulled him out of the saddle to the ground.

Sam's six-shooter fell out of its holster, and as he lay sprawled, he reached for it, but the rustler kicked it out of reach, saying, "Oh no you don't, you son of a bitch." Then he planted his bootheel in Sam's face and ground it in. The imprint remained in Sam's jaw until he died in 1928.

There was no doctor in La Luz, and Carrie Sutherland nursed the sick in her home, setting bones and arranging for the isolation of smallpox and diphtheria victims. She helped lay out the dead and preached a bit at their burials. "I just do what has to be done," she said.

One Fourth of July at the turn of the century, some drunken Apaches rode into Alamogordo, where the parade was. They started fighting, and an old chief had his right forearm mangled by a shotgun blast. By this time, a doctor had come to Alamogordo; he had his office over Frank Rolland's drugstore. The doctor, who was new in town, asked Carrie to help.

They gave the old chief enough chloroform to knock out a horse. "He looks like a tough old hombre," the doctor said. "I'll bet he's killed a lot of people in his time."

"*Oh sí, señor,*" said the Indian, still wide awake.

The doctor cut off his arm below the elbow, folding the flesh back over the ulna and radius bones, stitching the wound, and bandaging the stump. Carrie made a sling from a towel. The old Apache, though conscious during the entire operation, did not flinch or even grunt. Once bandaged, he got off the table, put on his big felt hat over two long braids of black hair, and walked out. At the stairs, he went down backward as though descending a ladder, for he had never before been in a house with stairs.

Later in the day, Carrie Sutherland saw the old man lying in the shade of an old cottonwood, while a squaw fanned flies from his face with a horsehair switch. His stump was wrapped in a red bandanna. A little way off, a horse was being saddled for his return trip to the reservation.

To the west of New Mexico, Arizona was developing by fits and starts. At the end of the Mexican War in 1848, all there was to Arizona besides Apaches was two mud-ball presidios at Tubac and Tucson manned by a few ragged troops. The non-Indian population numbered 600.

The Arizona predicament was described on March 3, 1859, by Edward E. Cross in the first issue of the *Tubac Weekly Arizonian*, which was published on a handpress brought from Cincinnati: "The territory we have selected for our home is unlike any other portion of the United States. . . . Attached as we now are nominally to the territory of New Mexico and situated many hundreds of miles from its seat of government, the western portion of Arizona is a region without the shadow of anything that claims to be law. . . . So far as we know, no judge or justice, either federal or territorial, has ever visited this portion of the country."

At the outset of the Civil War, Arizona was occupied by rebels but soon slipped from the Confederate grasp. When Congress debated a separate Arizona Territory in 1863, the lawmakers' initial response was not enthusiastic. The principal Arizona lobbyist, Charles Debrille Poston, went to see Senator "Bluff Ben" Wade of Ohio, who said: "Oh yes, I have heard of that country—it is just like hell—all it lacks is water and good society."

But John S. Watts, the Arizona delegate, addressed Congress holding a specimen of silver ore in his hand, a little nugget that was worth $5,000 a ton. It quickly became apparent that Arizona would help fill the Union war chest. The bill passed, and President Lincoln signed it on February 24, 1863.

Arizona's principal difference from New Mexico was that it did not have a large Hispanic population. From the first, the territory was Anglo in character, naming its capital Prescott, after William H. Prescott, the historian of the conquistadors. In Prescott, the houses were not adobe but made of wood and painted white. The first settlers were soldiers, surveyors, and miners. Arizona was a territory founded on venture capitalism in its three prevailing western forms: mining, railroads, and livestock.

For business to be successfully conducted, a minimal amount of law and order was required. When Milton B. Duffield arrived in Tucson as the first U.S. marshal in 1863, the town lay half in ruins, with dirt and manure piled up at the corners of ungraded streets. There was no hotel, boardinghouse, or restaurant, but plenty of mescal shops, monte tables, and whorehouses. The population consisted of 1,200 Mexicans, 100 Anglos, and 150 soldiers. The troops lived in debauchery and drunkenness, stealing chickens, pigs, and garden vegetables from the people they were supposed to protect.

Duffield spent much of his time writing poison pen letters concerning his fellow territorial officers. The governor, John N. Goodwin, Duffield wrote in 1865, was selling arms to the Mexicans, trafficking in provisions, and "affiliating himself with men who rejoiced at the assassination of president Lincoln." Charles Poston, the Superintendent of Indian Affairs, neglected his duties to go prospecting, Duffield said, and the superintendent's brother, Sanford Poston, had received $8,000 for "pretending to carry mail from Albuquerque to San Bernardino." "Some of these speculative and tricky officials," reported Duffield, "ought to be in Andersonville prison."

Duffield called Arizona "a rogue's paradise." He offended so many people that he was soon replaced as marshal. The editor of the *Weekly Arizonian* called him "a wanton disturber of the peace and a barterer of confidence."

Duffield became known in Tucson as a quarrelsome drunk, though people still feared him as a gunman. When "Waco Bill" came to town, "saturated with the vilest coffin varnish around," in the words of a contemporary account, the gunslinger went asking, "Whar's Duffield? He's my meat . . ." Waco Bill found Duffield and drew, but Duffield beat him to it. Into Waco Bill's groin "went the sure bullet of the man who wore crepe on his hat in memory of his [Duffield's] departed virtues."

On August 8, 1873, Tucson was the scene of a bilingual public lynching. For three Mexicans who had murdered a pawnbroker and his pregnant wife, a four-rope gallows was improvised on the plaza. The fourth was for John Willis, who had been sentenced to death for murder, and whom the lynchers thought convenient to expedite with the others.

Since the mob, as well as the lynchees, were both Hispanic and Anglo, a public-spirited citizen jumped on the platform to address those gathered in both languages.

"What punishment do the prisoners deserve?" he asked. "*¿Qué castigo merecen los prisioneros?*"

The crowd responded with "Death!" and "*¡Que mueran!*"

Duffield, who had been drinking, spoke up: "You can hang a Mexican, and you can hang a Jew, and you can hang a nigger, but you can't hang an American citizen."

From the crowd came shouts of "Jug him!"

So Duffield was tied up and guarded while the four prisoners were hoisted on top of horse-drawn wagons with halters around their necks. The horses trotted off followed by the wagons, leaving the men dangling. Later that year one of Duffield's numerous enemies shot and killed him. The obituaries called him "a miserable, blatant driveler," and "a pompous vilifier." Such was Arizona in its early youth: a refuge for gunslingers and mudslingers, and an arena for eccentrics. Robert Forbes, the pioneer agronomist, condemned the "shiftless, live-for-today, Texas spirit."

The Americans inherited the Apache problem from the Mexicans, who offered bounties for Apache scalps, a provocation that incited the Indians to increase the raids upon which their economy depended. War broke out between Apaches and Americans when gold was found on Apache lands near Prescott in 1863. Atrocities were committed on both sides, and General George Crook went into the southwest at the head of 3,000 men to round up the tribe. He did so with such efficiency that by 1873, 5,000 Apaches were living on five reservations: Fort Apache, north of the Salt River; Camp Verde, beside the Verde River; San Carlos, between the Salt and the Gila; Chiricahua, in the territory's southeast corner; and Warm Springs, in western New Mexico.

In 1874, a brash twenty-three-year-old named John P. Clum was placed in charge of the San Carlos Reservation. The son of a farmer in Claverack, New York, Clum graduated from Rutgers and in 1871 joined the U.S. Army Signal Corps and was sent to Santa Fe. Three years later he was on his way to Tucson to take up the post of Indian agent.

Clum's policy at San Carlos was to run things without the army. He got rid of the cavalry detachment, formed an Apache police, and set up a court system. Confrontational by nature, he feuded with the military, and as a result, the army issued orders to ignore Clum's requests for assistance in case hostilities broke out at the reservation. But Clum counted on maintaining order with his Apache police, whom he armed with Springfields.

Police loyalty was tested in December 1875, when Chief Disalin ran amok. Disalin had two wives. He was jealous of the prettier of the two, who went to Clum to complain that the chief beat her regularly, sometimes tying her to a tree and throwing a hunting knife at her, for practice. Clum called the chief in and told him that all Indians at San Carlos were entitled to protection from bodily harm.

The next day the brooding Disalin, resenting this interference in his domestic affairs, slipped into the agency building with a gun concealed under a blanket and started shooting. The Apache police sergeant, Tauelclyee, shot him dead, then said to Clum: "*Enjuh*—it is well. I have killed my own brother. But he was trying to kill you, and I am a policeman. It was my duty."

Clum ran the agency with only two other white men—a clerk and a doctor. He kept the Indians busy planting two hundred acres of crops and also gave them shovels and picks to dig two miles of seven-foot-deep irrigation ditches. Instead of using outside contractors for construction, he hired Apaches to build a guardhouse and a hospital, paying them wages. He had the Indians vaccinated, issued them soap, and raided the brewers of Tulepai, a fermented grain beverage, to keep his wards sober.

Clum's agency was such a success that it became a dumping ground for Apaches from other parts of Arizona. By 1877, there were 4,200 of these newcomers. That February, renegade Apache chiefs had resumed raiding, notably Geronimo. He was reported to be in southwestern New Mexico—near the Warm Springs agency, between the headwaters of the Gila and the Rio Grande—where he was stirring up the tribes. The cavalry had been unable to catch him, so on March 20, Clum was ordered to go there and move Geronimo's Mimbreño Apaches to San Carlos. He left on foot on April 8 with 40 Apache policemen, traveling south to Fort Bowie and then east to Silver City.

On April 20, after a forced march, Clum arrived at the Warm Springs Agency east of Silver City. His 40 men were joined by 80 army reserves, whom he concealed in a commissary building, Trojan Horse–style. Geronimo, he learned, was camped three miles away, with other prominent renegade chiefs.

Unaware that Clum had 120 men, Geronimo accepted an invitation to parley. He came to the camp with six other chiefs, including Gordo, Ponce, and Francisco, their faces smeared with paint. Clum told Geronimo that he was taking them to San Carlos. Geronimo replied that if Clum tried anything like that, "your bodies will stay here at Ojo Calientes to make food for coyotes."

At that point, Clum touched the brim of his sombrero and the reserves swarmed out of the commissary, their guns trained on the renegade Indians. When Clum saw Geronimo's thumb creeping toward the hammer of his Springfield, he gave another signal, and his men surrounded the renowned chief with cocked rifles. Clum personally disarmed him. Later he recalled that "I have seen many looks of hate in my life, but never one so vengeful." He kept Geronimo's rifle as a souvenir.

Clum placed Geronimo and the others in ankle irons, fashioned on the spot by a blacksmith from strips of iron wagon tires. He went back to San

Carlos on foot leading 450 Mimbreños, having provided wagons for the seven shackled chiefs. Upon his return, he was told to his dismay that troops would have to be brought in to guard the renegade Apaches. In June, he wrote the commissioner of Indian Affairs: "If your department will increase my salary sufficiently and equip two more companies of Indian police, I will volunteer to take care of all Apaches—and the troops can be removed."

When Clum's offer was refused, he resigned. The real reason for insisting on troops, he believed, had been given by a Tucson merchant, who told Clum: "What are you trying to do, ruin my business? Most of our profit comes from feeding soldiers and army mules."

After Clum's departure in July 1877, conditions on the San Carlos Reservation deteriorated. Contractors who wanted to keep the Apaches on rations hired men to destroy the crops that Clum had made the Indians plant. Pieces of the reservation were lopped off and opened to miners and settlers.

Despite the presence of troops, Geronimo and other Apache leaders escaped San Carlos and resumed their raids. They killed so many settlers that in the early 1880s, 5,000 soldiers—one-fourth of the United States Army—were stationed in southern Arizona and New Mexico for the purpose of chasing Apaches. Finally, they received permission for "hot pursuit" into Mexico. Thus, in the spring of 1886, troops cornered and took prisoner Geronimo and two dozen of his people in their Mexican stronghold of Sonora. The Indians were sent to Florida, then to Alabama, and in 1894 they were moved to Fort Sill, Oklahoma.

On March 5, 1905, John Clum, now a newspaper correspondent, was in Washington covering Theodore Roosevelt's inauguration. He watched the parade proceed down Pennsylvania Avenue, in a blur of waving flags, led by the beaming and mustached president, who doffed his silk top hat to half a million cheering citizens.

Then Clum began to hear cries of "Hey, it's Geronimo! Hooray for Geronimo!" Astride a calico pony, clad in buckskins and beads, his wrinkled brown face daubed with paint and a feather stuck in his graying hair, sat the Apache leader. Now seventy-six years old, he had been brought from Oklahoma to take part in the inaugural parade.

The way in which his old enemy had been turned into a living museum exhibit, cheered by the crowd, made Clum's blood boil. This was the man he had covered 800 desert miles to capture, the man responsible for the deaths of more than 100 Americans. They had made, so Clum thought, the greatest villain in the Apache nation into a hero.

Clum was sitting in the reviewing stand in front of the White House, quite close to the president, so close that he could not resist asking: "Why did you select Geronimo to march in your parade, Mr. President? He is the greatest single-handed murderer in American history."

Barely listening, waving and smiling and intent on the proceedings, Roosevelt replied, "I wanted to give the people a good show."

Geronimo died in 1908 at Fort Sill. John Clum lived on until 1923, a short, slight man whose baldness at twenty-one had earned him the Apache nickname "Boss with the High Forehead."

Of the 35 million immigrants who came to the United States between 1865 and 1915, 2 million were Jewish, representing 15 percent of all the Jews in Europe. Among those fleeing czarist persecution and the pogroms of Russia and eastern Europe were a large number of peddlers and tailors, at the bottom of the social ladder.

Accustomed to travel, and adaptable to new environments, many of these peddlers headed west. In Arizona, every ranch had its Jewish drummer, every garrison its Jewish sutler, every settlement its Jewish storekeepers. Fleeing from a static feudal society that beat them down, they joined a society in the making, unregulated and open to enterprise, in which they flourished.

In Arizona these Jewish traders, in daily contact with the population, linked the outland with the cities and promoted a live-and-let-live attitude. Because they were scattered over a large area and provided a useful service, they escaped ethnic animosity. Carrying not one ounce of the macho bravado that characterized western men, they got along with everyone and became smoothly working cogs in the territorial machinery.

Isaac Solomon arrived in the territory in 1876 to work for the Liszynsky brothers at their copper-smelting operation in Clifton, in southeast Arizona on the San Francisco River. The company sent him to the Gila Valley with a contract to burn mesquite timber into charcoal for use in the smelter. In the valley, he opened a general store, which grew into a crossroads village called Solomonville.

Isaac Solomon became a contractor for the army, supplying hay and grain to the forts. In 1880, he went to Prescott to collect a payment that was owed him by the army quartermaster, who gave him one check for $1,000 and another for $960. Having no cash for small expenses on the return trip to Phoenix, Solomon went to Colonel Head's store and cashed a personal check for $25.

On the stagecoach back, the other passengers were a doctor and an army captain stationed at Fort Grant. They left Prescott at 2 P.M. As soon as night fell, the coach was stopped by two masked men, who instructed the passengers to throw up their hands.

Solomon was wearing a gold watch attached to a silk cord. One outlaw cut the cord and took the watch along with the storekeeper's $25. Next, they demanded that the Wells Fargo box be handed down from the driver's seat. Deciding to make the best of a bad situation, Solomon set about ingratiating himself with the robbers. In his rather stilted, formal way, he praised them for obtaining a substantial amount of cash without doing bodily harm to anyone.

As Solomon was expressing these sentiments, they heard the stage from Phoenix to Prescott rumbling toward them. The gunmen stopped it and ordered the occupants out, one of whom was a well-known lawman, Dick Nagle. When the Prescott-bound passengers had been divested of their valuables, Solomon again complimented the bandits and thanked them for doing a difficult job with considerable courtesy.

Solomon then asked if he could have his watch back, saying he regarded it as an heirloom. It had little monetary value, he said, but had been given to him by a beloved relative. He knew the thieves were gentlemen and would not mind returning it. Unaccustomed to flattery, the robbers produced about ten watches and asked Solomon which was his. The one on the silk cord, he said, retrieving it.

Inspired by Solomon, Dick Nagle said: "Gentlemen, I hope you will also return my watch. I prize it very highly because it was given me by prominent citizens of Tombstone after I had served that city as chief of police. The names of my Tombstone friends are engraved on the watch, as well as my own. If you will return it to me, I will give or send $100 to any place in Arizona you care to name."

The robbers hesitated, for police chiefs were not among their favorite kinds of people. But since they had grown comfortable with their new roles as gentlemen, they said, "Here, take your confounded watch."

Then Solomon asked them if they wouldn't mind returning enough money so that he could invite the other passengers to breakfast in Phoenix and buy drinks all around. One of the outlaws held out a hand filled with silver and told Solomon to take what he needed.

"Boys," Solomon said as the robbers mounted their horses, "you sure are regular fellows."

As early as 1864, the daily prayer of the *Arizona Miner* was "O Congress, give us a railroad." In 1880, the prayer was answered and the Deming connection in western New Mexico put Arizona on the east-west line. Most of the traffic was just passing through to California, causing the population of Los Angeles to jump from 11,000 in 1880 to 100,000 in 1890. San Francisco in 1900 had more people (343,000) than Arizona and New Mexico combined (315,000).

Still, the railroads ended "the tyranny of distance," and the world was at Arizona's doorstep. Washington was now less than a week by train from Phoenix, which became the territorial capital in 1889. Small, independent lines started crisscrossing Arizona, such as the Globe & Northern in the Gila Valley, built by William Garland. Work began at Bowie in the southeast corner of the territory in 1894, and by 1895 track had been laid to Pima, forty miles north on the Gila River.

But right-of-way problems frustrated these trunk lines in settled areas. The Bowie–Pima line went through land owned by an obstreperous settler, Patrick Sullivan. On February 1, 1895, the first train from Bowie to Pima started out, with William Garland aboard.

When they arrived on Sullivan's land, an obstruction appeared ahead. Coming closer, they saw that Sullivan had built a shanty with a wire fence around it right on top of the track. He and his wife were occupying this improvised dwelling, as if daring the iron horse to run them down.

The train came to a halt a few feet from the fence, which the furious Garland began to knock down. Sullivan pointed his double-barreled shotgun at Garland and said, "Keep your hands off my property."

Garland went back to Solomonville and swore out a warrant for Sullivan, who was arrested by the sheriff and later released on bond. Before they set him free, Garland's crew razed "Fort Sullivan," clearing the track so the train could proceed to Pima. But the next day, when another train arrived from Bowie, Sullivan's rebuilt shack was again astride the track.

Again warrants were issued, this time for both Sullivan and his wife. The sheriff went out to the shack to read the warrant. Sullivan said he would not leave unless he was carried off. But when the sheriff threatened to jail him for resisting an officer, he allowed himself to be led away.

The shack was torn down a second time and the train continued on to Pima. A court order restrained Sullivan from further interference. When his case came to trial, a judge awarded him payment for right of way, and the track remained clear.

When the Globe & Northern line advanced north of Pima, on its way to Globe, another right-of-way obstacle presented itself. For the route went across the San Carlos Reservation. In 1895, Mark Smith, the Arizona delegate to Congress, lobbied for a bill granting the right-of-way, which was passed by both houses of Congress. But President Cleveland vetoed it, saying that the Apache Indians who lived on the reservation had to give their consent. Globe & Northern completed the track just up to the reservation line, halting construction while Garland waited for a more favorable political climate.

When William McKinley was inaugurated in 1897, his administration ruled that the right-of-way required the consent not of all the Indians but only of a majority. The matter would be put to a vote. With the help of the Indian agent, Lieutenant Sedgwick Rice, Garland lobbied the San Carlos Apaches for approval.

The day of the vote was February 9, 1898, at the Indian agency. Indians began to arrive from every direction several days before. The mesa was covered with campfires, which the Indians sat around, while their squaws cooked the food that Garland had provided. They danced all night, with some of the squaws choosing white visitors as partners.

At noon on February 9, just before the vote, Garland handed out more rations. Then Lieutenant Rice explained the right-of-way proposition and several chiefs spoke in its favor. Chief Bailish said he had been to Washington, where he had seen a great mill grinding out money by the bushel, so he knew from experience that money was not scarce.

The casting of ballots lasted two hours and in the end there was only one negative vote. The next stage was to negotiate the amount of compensation. Garland offered $6,000, the chiefs demanded $10,000, and they settled on $8,000—including an added benefit of free rail transport for thirty years. Less than twelve months later, the Globe & Northern was running trains from Bowie to Pima to Globe (fifty miles northwest of Pima), with the track running across the San Carlos Reservation from east to west.

The territories of New Mexico and Arizona experienced the longest admission struggles for statehood in the nation's history—sixty-two years for New Mexico and forty-nine for Arizona. People in both territories were desperate to determine their political destinies and elect their own officials. As Governor Conrad Zulick of Arizona put it, the situation was "repugnant to the enlightened sense of the American people."

But the question remained: Were New Mexico and Arizona ready for statehood? According to the 1890 census, more than a third of New Mexico's 154,000 residents were illiterate, and only a quarter of the 44,000 school-age children were in school. In 1890, not a single public school or college existed in either territory.

Another stain on New Mexico's blotter was the corruption of the Santa Fe ring and the attendant land fraud. President Cleveland cleaned up the ring when he appointed two reform-minded abolitionists as governor and surveyor general: Edmund G. Ross of Kansas and George Washington Julian of Indiana.

Ross came to think that the only way to reform New Mexico was to make it a state, but both he and Julian made so many enemies that they were replaced, and the remnants of the Santa Fe ring breathed a sigh of relief.

When Miguel Otero, member of a respected family of merchants, was appointed governor of New Mexico Territory in 1897 by President McKinley, he became a leader of the statehood movement. Those who argued that statehood would add to their taxes, he said, were "unworthy of American manhood."

Otero realized that stumbling blocks to statehood existed not only in New Mexico but in the east, due to "persistent misunderstandings" of conditions in the territory. Tourists came with their Brownies and "pressed the button on every burro they met." Eager to "catch the features of a worthless old Indian," they spread the impression that New Mexico was backward and unprepared for statehood.

Theodore Roosevelt, inaugurated in 1901, was sympathetic to New Mexico and Arizona statehood because so many young men from those parts had volunteered for his regiment in the Spanish-American War, the Rough Riders.

But in Congress, lawmakers viewed with misgivings the prospect of four new senators representing 195,000 persons in New Mexico and 123,000 in Arizona. Leading the opposition in the Senate was Albert J. Beveridge of Indiana, who had two reasons to be against New Mexico statehood. The first was that as a Progressive, he suspected (and rightly so) that special interests such as the railroads and the mines were pouring money into the statehood drives so they could manipulate the state governments. His second objection was based on a strong anti-Hispanic prejudice. Beveridge saw Hispanics as second-class citizens, passive and pliant. He viewed their refusal to learn English as tantamount to treason. In 1902, Beveridge traveled to the southwest to confirm his views. He found enough illiterate Hispanics in New Mexico to satisfy him, and described Arizona as still "a mining camp."

In 1904, a bill that called for New Mexico and Arizona to form one state, perhaps to be called Montezuma, passed the House but not the Senate. One advantage of "jointure" was that it would maintain the balance of power in Congress. But in Santa Fe, Governor Otero fought jointure as unfair and unwise—the population was too scattered to be governed by one capital.

In Congress, the movement for jointure gathered steam despite the Senate defeat. Senator Beveridge was for it, prompting the Arizona delegate Mark Smith to comment that Beveridge "proceeds from his own argument that one rotten egg is bad, but two rotten eggs would make a fine omelet." An enabling act for the union of both territories passed, but Smith got an amendment added that jointure be put to a vote. If either territory refused, it was void. In November 1906, New Mexico voted for a single state, but Arizona voted against, not wanting to be outnumbered by "greasers."

Both territories had to start over. William Howard Taft occupied the White House after Theodore Roosevelt had served out his two terms. Taft had no strong inclinations to grant statehood, though he resolved to do nothing to keep the territories out. In January 1910, Edward L. Hamilton of the House Committee on Territories introduced enabling acts to admit New Mexico and Arizona as two separate states, which passed both houses of Congress.

Separate constitutional conventions assembled in the fall of 1910. In Santa Fe, a hundred delegates met from October 2 to November 21 in smoke-filled rooms at the Palace Hotel, swigging Old Taylor whiskey and making the brass spitoons ring. They drew up a conservative document that denied women the vote and rejected most Progressive ideas. It was called "a perfect 1810 constitution."

President Taft signed a statehood bill on January 6, 1912, telling the prominent New Mexicans who attended the ceremony: "Well, it is all over, I am glad to give you life. . . . I hope you will be healthy."

In Arizona, on the other hand, the Progressives captured the convention in Phoenix and passed a number of reform-minded articles, including provisions for women's suffrage and limitations on the power of trusts. "The crimping of corporations is proceeding merrily," the *Daily Globe* reported. They passed water-rights clauses to fit the needs of a state that depended on irrigation. They passed antilobbying clauses and railroad rate clauses.

President Taft became so concerned that he traveled to Arizona to denounce the "crank constitution." When it landed on his desk with a provision to recall sitting judges for malfeasance, he vetoed it, contingent on the removal of the objectionable features. The sanitized constitution was returned to him on February 14, 1912, and Arizona became the forty-eighth state.

New Mexico and Arizona were the last two territories in the continental United States to become states. The work of Manifest Destiny was done. The great land mass "from sea to shining sea," won by treaty, conquest, and the blood of settlers and Indians, had been divided into forty-eight states over a period of 120 years—years of struggle on the part of men and women who were usually ahead of a government that followed as best it could, assisting the people's endeavors with military protection and cheap public land. With the end of the territories came the end of the frontier and its promise of the unattained.

What would replace in the American psyche the sense of possibility and aspiration that the frontier represented? In 1890, the United States Census of Manufactures included for the first time separate figures for the automobile industry; for in that year, thirty American carmakers produced 2,500 cars.

It was as if the era of the automobile had come along just in time to provide a continuation of the frontier momentum. Like the westward movement, the car culture made the country available to the masses. Americans had a continent to cross, at first over bad roads, but the first transcontinental automobile crossings in 1903 showed that the average driver could do it.

The rise of the car culture became an appendix to the history of the frontier. Thanks to the car, Americans could cling to the idea that "it's better beyond," to all the mythic associations that the frontier held of a destiny still to be accomplished. The automobile excited the American people because speed, mobility, and distance had become part of their character through the frontier experience.

The automobile revitalized the frontier myth with the promise of untrammeled and unregulated personal mobility. For at first, no laws or regulations governed driving, and there were no speed limits or drivers' licenses. Here again, the government lagged behind the individual and had to catch up.

The automobile provided the answer to the eastern urban anthill, to the octopus of trusts crushing the little man, to the ponderous federal bureaucracies mushrooming in the west. Because like any restless pioneer, a person could just get into a car and hit the road.

The rise of the car culture was swift. In 1906, a Stanley Steamer was clocked at 126 miles per hour at Daytona Beach. In 1908, Henry Ford introduced the Model T; affordable and adapted to unpaved rural roads, it captured 50 percent of the market. By 1910, 458,000 automobiles were registered in the United States. Automobile manufacturing went from 150th to 12th in value of product among American industries.

In Arizona, Tucson required that cars be licensed as early as 1905. By 1911, Phoenix had a Ford dealership that sold roadsters for $690. In 1912, the year of statehood, 1,800 owners had registered their cars in Arizona.

The age of touring created a benign frontier of blanket Indians and defanged wolves, where nature was an attraction, native artifacts were on sale at roadside shops, and the desert was user-friendly. But for the aspiring motorist, his new contraption posed its own hazards. He needed a strong arm for cranking and pushing, and plenty of patience between garages, which were usually converted livery stables. Drugstores sold gas and motor oil, blacksmiths repaired broken parts, stationers offered road maps, and clothing stores provided dusters and goggles. Teddy Roosevelt had worn his linen duster when in 1911 he went by car to inaugurate the dam in Arizona named after him.

One of those 1,800 cars registered in Arizona, a four-cylinder Studebaker, belonged to Sam and Edith Kitt of Tucson, who decided in May 1914 to drive to the Grand Canyon. They left on May 28, with a box on the running board filled with provisions.

Their route was circular, beginning and ending in Tucson, which evokes the circling of wagons, or a desirable insularity impossible to maintain as the era when America could mind its own business came to an end.

Seventy miles northwest of Tucson they reached Florence, having driven through a landscape of palo verde and ironwood. "The people of Florence sit tilted back in their chairs on the hotel porch waiting for a boom," Edith Kitt noted. "They were doing that when I was a girl." In Mesa, outside Phoenix, the Kitts looked down on the Salt River Valley, and in the early evening, a light purple mist rose from the irrigated land.

In nearby Tempe, they passed the State Normal Insane Asylum and the Pacific Creamery. A big truck traveled up and down the valley daily, collecting milk from farmers. As for Phoenix, with its paved streets and four-story buildings, it was some town, though Edith hated to admit it, being from Tucson.

Grades gave them trouble because the gasoline would not travel uphill into the carburetor on an incline. They moved slowly into the high plateau of the Kendrick Mountains with the hood up, while Edith sat on the fender squirting gas from a can into the carburetor.

From Wickenburg, the Kitts drove eighty-one miles to Prescott, a mile-high town situated on either side of a small creek, its courthouse facing a Rough Rider monument. At Prescott, they went to a garage to have the carburetor fixed so the gas would flow uphill.

Out of Prescott, they drove up the Big Chino Valley on a road straight as a rail, over some low juniper-colored hills to Ash Fork, where the Phoenix branch met the main line of the Santa Fe. They found a pretty railroad hotel next to the station, and Edith asked the man at the desk how the road to Williams was. "Steep and bad," he said, "rises 2,000 feet in 20 miles." But then a man who had just come in from Williams in a big auto said, "Fine as silk, fine as silk."

Williams itself was in a pine forest. There the couple met a dairy farmer, Mr. Owens, who had thirty Jersey cows, a number of which had taken prizes at the Phoenix fair. The road north was good, except for prairie-dog holes, and they rumbled over the sixty-five miles to the Grand Canyon, which they reached on June 8.

The Kitts spent three days viewing the canyon from different points, because it took them a while to grasp the bigness of it all. The river glinted a mile down, and the opposite wall loomed thirteen miles away. They watched the light and shadows strike each stone dome and turret, and saw the colors change. Following the trail down to the black granite canyon through which the Colorado rushed, they ate lunch with the smell of muddy water in their nostrils. On mules, the journey down and back took seven hours and the only store was a dilapidated shack that sold canned food to the Indians.

Leaving the Grand Canyon, the Kitts headed south to Flagstaff, passing through Schultz Pass, lying at the base of the San Francisco peaks. This was sheep country, and logging country, and they saw timber being hauled to the railroad track, the big crane swinging out and grabbing a log, which a man with a log pole maneuvered into a pile. Flagstaff had three sawmills and a rock quarry of solid red sandstone, which Edith Kitt noted was used for the best buildings in Los Angeles, including the post office.

From Flagstaff, they drove due east to Leupp. The stubble growing out of the road was so thick it lifted up one wheel after the other, but Edith decided that stubble beat sand. They crossed a six-mile dry lake smooth as glass before entering Winslow, nestled in low juniper hills, pink volcanic peaks rising on each side. Winslow was a railroad town where the Babbitts had a store. From there, the Studebaker pushed on thirty-eight miles east to Holbrook, a small town in the bed of the Little Colorado, where the streets were sand.

While Mr. Kitt was buying provisions, Edith sat in the car near the town pump, watching the line of people getting water. Groups of cowboys in boots and chaps watered their horses and chatted around the pump, joined by young ranchers in khaki breeches along with road-soiled tourists. Holbrook, it turned out, was on the new ocean-to-ocean highway.

The travelers followed the Little Colorado down to Springerville, crossing two bad washes. At 7,000 feet, and surrounded by the White Mountains, Springerville sat twelve miles from the New Mexico line. Julius Becker, who practically owned the town, kept a register of tourists, which he showed the Kitts—109 autos carrying 328 persons had come through since the start of the year, and it was only June 24.

Then it was into the White Mountains to Cooley's Ranch, where they learned that a man had been ordered off the forest reserve with his 8,000 sheep. Things sure had changed since the days of public grazing, thought Edith. Their tires were chewed to a frazzle, and two of them blew within half an hour of each other. Each time some good Samaritan pushed them up a hill Edith asked, "Do you get many stuck here?" and the reply was always "Oh yes, lots."

Twenty miles west of Cooley's and out of the pines, they came to Fort Apache. The vegetation was Spanish bayonet and now and then a juniper tree. Apache huts were scattered everywhere. The women were dirty and degenerate looking, Edith thought. Many Indians were mounted, and men and women rode at a gallop. The men were big, strapping, good-looking fellows, completely different from the small Oriental-looking Hopis Edith had seen at the reservation near Leupp. They wore their hair long, and it floated in the wind as they rode. At the government sawmill nearby, they made shingles, to give the Apaches work.

At Rice, west of Fort Apache, the Kitts found a big Indian school, where they bought a dandy Apache basket from Mr. Tiffany, the railroad agent. At Tuttle's Ranch they bought gas at 55 cents a gallon. From Rice to Globe they covered twenty miles, then thirty more to the Salt River and the Roosevelt Dam, a huge masonry structure rising 284 feet between two steep canyon walls. One hundred and eighty-four feet thick at the base, the dam harnessed the floodwaters and stored up to 1.4 million acre-feet of water.

From Roosevelt Dam to Mesa it was sixty miles—at Mesa, the Kitts closed the 1,300-mile circle of their journey. Then they drove home to Tucson, where on the last leg of their tour the transmission broke and they had to hitch a ride on the prison truck. It was an inglorious ending, but as Mr. Kitt said of their trip, "I wish I were starting out tomorrow to take it all over again."

PART SEVEN
THE FAR-FLUNG STATES

CHAPTER TWENTY-SIX

THE HAWAIIAN FRONTIER

If a big wave comes in, large fishes will come from the dark ocean which you never saw before, and when they see the small fishes they will eat them up. The ships of the white man have come, and smart people have arrived from the great countries which you have never seen before. They know our people are few in number and living in a small country. They will eat us up.

DAVID MALO

The National Archives
Pineapple fields in 1927 using mainly Filipino and Japanese labor.

*If you go back several thousand years, the Western world
revolved around the Mediterranean, then you go back
three or four hundred years, it's been the Atlantic. Now
it's the Pacific. It's where the population of the world is.*

THOMAS HITCH

For twelve centuries, the Polynesians lived unbothered with their gods and their volcanoes. Then came the white man, in the form of James Cook, who in his three circumnavigations between 1768 and 1779 literally put the Pacific Ocean on the map.

In 1778, Cook came upon the Hawaiian chain. The only land mass of any size in the north-central Pacific, the Hawaiian islands were the last to be discovered because of their isolation. Ten months later, in February 1779, Cook returned to Hawaii's west coast, playing the role of point man for the industrial revolution. This time there was trouble. When the Hawaiians stole one of his longboats, Cook went ashore to take the chief hostage. A warrior protecting the chief struck him, and in the ensuing fracas the explorer was killed. He left behind his journals, the base line for all studies of the Hawaiian people.

After Captain Cook's death, a local chief, Kamehameha, extended his control over the other islands in wars of conquest and established a dynasty that ruled Hawaii for a hundred years. Under Kamehameha's reign, the islands became a resource base for New England merchants. Soon the ships began taking on cargoes of sandalwood to exchange for tea and silk in Canton.

By the time the sandalwood trade had collapsed because of overcutting, the deepwater port of Honolulu had emerged as the rendezvous for the whaling fleets of the Pacific. There were times when four hundred ships could be counted in the ports of Honolulu and Lahaina, and 80 percent of them were American.

In 1820, the missionaries arrived, bringing to the Pacific the doctrines of original sin, the sufficiency of the Scriptures, and the godliness of private property. The reverends became advisors to the native rulers, in an increasingly mixed Hawaiian society where Polynesian traditions clashed with the boisterous go-getter mentality of the traders and sea captains. The missionaries were a dynamic group, the Lord's entrepreneurs; they opened schools, created a Hawaiian alphabet, and printed a speller and a reader. But behind all their reforms lurked a sense of superiority, and a fear of contamination by the native culture.

In the meantime, Uncle Sam was gradually placing a friendly arm around Hawaii, an unlikely frontier for religious and commercial expansion, 2,000 miles from the mainland. Under the American influence, a shift occurred from feudalism to democracy. In 1840, the Hawaiian monarchy drafted a constitution, based on those of New York and Massachusetts. This was followed by diplomatic relations with the United States in 1843 and a commercial treaty in 1849.

In 1850, Honolulu had become the capital of a young Pacific kingdom, a town of 15,000 where English was spoken and trade was brisk. Hawaii still depended on whaling, though the sugarcane industry had begun to stir. When whales grew scarce after 1860, Hawaii evolved into the Sugar Islands. After sandalwood and whales, the Hawaiian economy was transformed by outsiders for the third time.

The missionaries were still active, trying to stop prostitution, drinking, and social dancing. A popular saying at the time expressed the native's demoralization at having it drummed into them that their past and their culture were shameful: "The people freely dismissed their souls and died."

This was literally true in terms of the declining population. Captain Cook in 1778 had estimated the population of the islands at 300,000. But by 1850, the diseases the white men had brought, smallpox and measles, had reduced the number of islanders to 84,000. The death rate soared so high that the islands seemed to be heading toward extinction. As a result, sugar plantations were shorthanded, though in any case plantation managers complained that native workers were worthless.

In 1850, the monarchy passed a law to allow imported labor, for sugar exports had increased from 8,000 pounds in 1836 to 750,238 pounds in 1850. The need for labor was urgent. Judge William L. Lee, president of the Royal Hawaiian Agricultural Society, said in a report on August 11, 1851: "More labor we must have; and it is clear we cannot depend on the islands for an increase. It only remains, then, for us to look abroad."

China was chosen because it was close and coolies came cheap. Captain John Cass was engaged to sail there on his ship the *Thetis* and round up a shipload of "pigtails"; he would be paid $50 for each one delivered in good physical condition. In Honolulu, Cass signed on a Chinese ship's carpenter named Alook, to help in recruiting.

Cass sailed on August 12 and headed straight for the coastal city of Amoy in the southeastern province of Fukien, establishing a pattern of emigration that continues to this day. In Amoy, he rounded up 199 coolies, who signed five-year contracts at $36 per annum.

Captain Cass landed his cargo in Honolulu on January 3, 1852. Later that year he went to Amoy once more, and this time brought back 98 coolies. They proved to be good workers, diligent though not quick; obedient but requiring looking after. The king's foreign minister, R. C. Wyllie, said that "both in industry and morals, they are vastly superior to our Hawaiian Christians."

The Civil War provided Hawaii with a bonanza, for the removal of southern sugar from northern tables left a demand waiting to be filled. But when the war ended, demand dropped off and the bottom fell out of the Hawaiian sugar economy. To make matters worse, tariff policies restricted access to American markets. The planter oligarchy campaigned for low tariffs or annexation.

With 90 percent of Hawaiian exports going to the United States, annexation was in the air. But in post–Civil War Washington, there was little interest in Hawaii, and when annexation did not come, the planters lobbied for a reciprocity treaty that would remove trade barriers. Congress passed that legislation in 1876. An automatic windfall resulted from not paying duty, and sugar production doubled.

Sugar depended on cheap land, cheap money, and cheap labor. The first two the planters had, but the last remained uncertain. Not wanting to rely only on the Chinese, they started bringing in Japanese. Recruiters scoured Hiroshima and Yamaguchi prefectures for sturdy peasants, displaced samurais, palanquin-bearers, and the like.

Portuguese peasants from the Atlantic islands of Madeira and the Azores, where land was scarce, also started arriving. If Hawaii could be called a frontier, it was a frontier settled by contract laborers, not unlike the indentured servants who had come to Maryland under the Calverts, except that this was an Asian migration: mainly Chinese, Japanese, and Filipino. Soon the immigrants outnumbered the natives. The social history of Hawaii can be largely told as a process of accommodation among the various races and nationalities brought in as a workforce for the sugar plantations.

Juan Soares was born in 1874 on San Miguel, the largest of nine islands in the Azores chain, at Punta Dagalda, a tidy village that went back to the seventeenth century and whose streets were lined with orange and lemon trees. The climate was mild, and every day the sun came up from the sea and returned to the sea. Juan's father, a tenant farmer, finally realized at the age of forty-one that he would never have land of his own.

He came home one day and told Juan's mother, "It's no use to work and work." She said they should go to Brazil. His father said Brazil was no good because the yellow fever killed everybody. Some friends Señor Soares went to for advice told him: "Terra Nova, go to Terra Nova" (Hawaii). But his brother said, "Jose, you crazy go to Terra Nova. The people just like wild animals. They gonna eat you up."

The elder Soares decided to take a chance on Hawaii anyway. In Punta Dagalda, the family caught the German steamer *Albergeldie*. On the boat, Pedro's mother could not stop crying. But she sighed and said, "Maybe we going to be more happy in Terra Nova." They reached Honolulu on May 10, 1883—264 men, 195 women, and 453 children, one of them nine-year-old Juan Soares. His mother said, "Just like San Miguel, no?"

A man came around and Juan's father signed two papers. Then they went aboard a smaller steamer, which rocked like anything. It *was* just like the Azores, Juan thought, because there were islands all around. The boat docked at Hilo, on the big island, and the very next day, Juan's father went to work in the fields as a *hoe-hana* man, a cane-cutter.

The Soares family lived in a long house in Camp 4, with five other families. One of them was Portuguese, and Juan recalled that "we come good friends. We never pay attention to the other families. My father cut a door in the wall and the children can go between the two apartments. The kitchen was outside and the floor was dirt. When it rain, we were like ducks in the mud. . . . My father got $9 the first month and then later he got $18. My mother washed and sewed for the single men folks. She got about $10 in one month and buy our clothes."

"Little by little the Japanese come," Juan went on. "Every time a green bunch come, the Portuguese go help them fix the house. The Portuguese smart. They know the Japanese got good sake and if they help they all get good drink. Our camp, the Portuguese and Japanese all good friends. No fights anytime. On way to work we hear them say to my father, 'Jo-san, o-hay-o' [Joe, good morning]."

In 1884, when Juan was ten, he went to the fields as a hoe-hana, at $8 a month. He hated the job, which was hot, dirty, and uncomfortable, and managed to get reassigned as a waterboy. He would sit down and chat with each group of workers he brought water to, until the *luna* (foreman) told him; "John, you a loafer, shake a leg."

"One day," Juan recalled, "I get tired with water-boy job. I see manager and say I like drive mules. All right, he say, you got the job. I get up early and get mules from stable boss. My father say, 'Who did the plowing, you or the mules?' My mother say that in my sleep I yell 'Gi-dap.' "

"By the time I was 17, I get the biggest plow on the plantation. I get $10 a month. When payday come, my mother go down to the market and buy one big fish. Weekdays we work till four, Saturdays till half past two. The boss give us time off early because we have to go for firewood."

The workers' lives revolved around the plantation. In 1896, at the age of twenty-two, Juan met the sixteen-year-old daughter of another Portuguese family and married her in the Catholic church at Hilo. He went to night school and learned to read and write English.

The day came when the boss said, "John, I give you one acre and half cane you cultivate that and see what you can do." "I was glad," Juan recalled, "because that cane was Lahaina cane, the best in the world. That cane is soft, juicy, and plenty of sugar. My wife and I work together and that cane grew like anything. When harvest time come, we find the rats ate everything. The rats sure knew I had good cane and I learned a good lesson."

Having arrived at the plantation at the age of nine, Juan Soares spent the rest of his life there. He had no complaints. He had worked hard, and management had taken care of him and his family. In Hawaii, there was social mobility, and his children would have education and job opportunities. "I know that my children not going to be plantation workers," Juan said. "That is one thing I am glad I come here. If we stay in Azores we no get this kind life."

As contract labor replenished the population, making native Hawaiians a minority in their own land, the opéra bouffe monarchy that had ruled for nearly a century began to totter. The weakness of the regime was one fact that cheered advocates of annexation. Another was that by 1886, when the reciprocity treaty was renewed, Hawaii had become an economic satellite of the United States. In Washington, a new generation of politicians was oriented toward empire building. The movement for annexation picked up speed when James Blaine, Benjamin Harrison's secretary of state, called Hawaii "the outlying district of California."

By then, the haoles (whites) owned four-fifths of the land. But in 1891, the sugar planters got hit with the McKinley Tariff, which allowed all imported sugar into the United States duty-free, while authorizing a subsidy of 2 cents a pound to the makers of domestic sugar. Hawaii lost its most-favored-island status, and had to compete with Cuba and Jamaica. Sugar prices plummeted. For Hawaiian planters, annexation became all the more urgent.

On January 14, 1893, the independent-minded Queen Liliuokalani announced a new constitution, under which all cabinet ministers served at her pleasure, allowing her to get rid of her white advisors. This led to a plot to topple the monarchy. The Marines landed, the white leaders of the coup seized the government buildings, and the monarchy was dissolved.

But congressional halls echoed with considerable antiannexation grumbling. It was an ugly business, this tiny cabal of Americans overthrowing the popular monarch of a nation whose people wanted to maintain their sovereignty. What did the United States want with colonies in the middle of the Pacific? And what was this coup in Hawaii but a sugar planter's scheme to share in the bounty paid on domestic sugar?

Inaugurated (for the second time) in March 1893, Grover Cleveland opposed annexation. The issue was shelved during his term in office. For the next five years, Hawaii was a republic, governed by the clique that had ousted the queen.

During those years, however, support for annexation grew. In November 1896, the election of William McKinley revived expansionist hopes. When the annexation debate revived in 1897, the nativist viewpoint was best expressed by Representative Champ Clark of Missouri, who envisaged the day when Hawaii would be a state. "How could we endure our shame," he asked, "when a Chinese senator from Hawaii with his pigtail hanging down his back, his pagan joss stick in hand, shall rise from his curule chair and in pidgin English proceed to chop logic with George Frisbie Hoar or Henry Cabot Lodge [the two senators from Massachusetts]? A Chinaman can never be fit for American citizenship."

Along with the domestic sugar interests and the nativists, organized labor also opposed annexation, fearing that it would bring contract labor to the United States and undermine the Chinese Exclusion Act. Labor newspapers called Hawaii "a slave state," while Samuel Gompers of the AFL said it would threaten American labor with coolie contracts.

On the other side stood the principal supporter of annexation: the navy. There was at the time a clamor for a powerful navy, second to none, equipped with overseas bases for logistical support. With its mid-Pacific location, Hawaii made an ideal base, and Admiral George Belknap told Congress that the islands were necessary for national security. With his usual bluntness the assistant secretary of the navy, Theodore Roosevelt, said, "If I had my way, I would annex those islands tomorrow."

But the "jingo bacillus" had infected Congress, and an attempt to ratify an annexation treaty in 1897 ended in defeat. Congress was about to have a change of heart, however. For on February 15, 1898, two explosions destroyed the battleship *Maine* in Havana harbor, killing 260 men, and providing a *casus belli* for war with Spain.

In April, Congress declared war on a country which, besides Cuba, owned Puerto Rico in the Caribbean and Guam and the Philippines in the Pacific. The whole business took about ninety days, and when the smoke of battle lifted, the map of the United States looked quite different.

While the war was being fought, the navy used Oahu as a coaling station as well as a stopover for troops en route to the Philippines. Opposition to annexation now seemed unpatriotic. Thus, annexation was passed in a joint resolution of both houses of Congress on July 7, 1898.

The headline in the *Honolulu Advertiser* said HAWAII BECOMES THE FIRST OUTPOST OF A GREATER AMERICA. Other outposts were soon to come. The treaty signed with Spain in Paris on December 10, 1898, established Cuba as an independent state, but ceded Puerto Rico, the Philippines, and Guam to the United States. Overnight, America acquired both an overseas empire and the image of a colonial power in the eyes of Europe. The Pacific north of the Equator became an American lake.

To American anti-imperialists, the drift into colonialism brought a loss of innocence. It meant the end of America as a virtuous republic, a City upon a Hill. How could the nation remain true to its principles when it became the overseer of backward natives in Hawaii, the Philippines, and Puerto Rico? America was now extended far beyond its borders, on an enlarged domain that required a greater degree of military preparedness— perhaps turning Athens into Sparta.

As for Hawaii, under the Organic Act of 1900, it became a territory. But its new status placed Hawaii under the jurisdiction of the Exclusion Act of 1882, which not only put a stop to any further importation of Chinese laborers, but denied citizenship to residents of Asian birth already in Hawaii: 26,000 Chinese and 61,000 Japanese out of a total population of 154,000.

To make up for the shortfall in Chinese and Japanese labor, the planters began bringing thousands of Filipinos to Hawaii in 1906. One of them was Mariano Quinto, who came from the village of Bulac on the skinny little island of Cebu. One day in 1906, two fast-talking recruiters came to his village looking for workers. They talked Hawaii up as a wonderful place where you could get water by turning a little handle instead of going to a spring, and where, after working for a few months, you could buy your own car.

Mariano wanted to take along his wife and three children, but the recruiters were asking for $5 per person for the trip to Manila. Mariano raised the $25 for them all by selling some of his wife's jewelry, and they sailed for Manila with thirty other Cebuans. But once in Manila, the two snakeheads who had taken their money left them stranded.

Mariano was wondering what to do next when someone at the hotel told him that if he went to the immigration office he could find passage to Hawaii. He stood in a long line waiting to be examined. Then he was given some clothing and bedding and hustled with two hundred others into the ship's hold, where they slept on mats on the floor.

It was a difficult two-month crossing, fatal to many of the passengers. No one was allowed to go on deck for fresh air, and the stink of oil, food, and machinery made the immigrants sick. The food arrived in large buckets, and tasted so awful that many of them threw it up. One day Mariano saw a Chinese steward serving soup from a bucket that some other people had vomited into not long before.

Then the fever struck. Each day the Chinese stewards removed the dead, stacked them two or three to a coffin, and dropped them overboard. Attrition made for more room in the hold, but everyone wondered who would be next. Mariano's wife and two youngest children caught the fever, and the children died. His wife had dwindled to a sack of bones, but she survived, as did his oldest child. Two Japanese doctors came each day to examine them, but all these physicians did was stare. They obviously had no inkling of what the fever was.

As the boat neared Hawaii, the warm climate helped the sick to recover, but only a handful of the original two hundred passengers were still alive. When they landed at Honolulu, everyone received a supply of new clothing. Mariano and his shattered family were taken to the Ewa Plantation, twenty miles from Honolulu, where the workforce was Portuguese, Chinese, and Japanese. No group mingled with any other. The whole place was covered with algaroba trees, which Filipinos believed contained little people.

Mariano was put to work clearing ground for new cane fields. Later he was promoted to planting. The hardest job of all was *hapaiko*, hauling the cane on one's back in the blazing sun. Mariano worked overtime to increase his wages, so that each month he brought home $80 or $90. Soon there were enough Filipinos so that they had their own camp. Mariano's wife began to cook for the bachelors and soon began making as much as her husband did. She charged $15 a month for three meals a day.

Their fellow workers began to think that they were well-to-do and borrowed money from them, using jewelry as collateral. Before long, the Quintos were running a pawnshop. From contract worker, Mariano Quinto had become a small-time entrepreneur, with his wife's help. "My wife and I took great delight in counting our money every payday," he said. Mariano worked at Ewa for twenty-five years, rising to the rank of *luna*, and saved enough money to buy a house and retire.

In the early days, the top management of the plantations was lily-white. It helped to have a connection to the old haole families, though a newcomer with a good idea could also prosper. One example of overnight success was James Drummond Dole. The Boston-born son of a Unitarian clergyman, James was related to Sanford B. Dole (himself a missionary), president of the five-year Hawaiian Republic and first governor of the territory.

Jim Dole went to Harvard, but did not shine as a scholar. He seemed to be the classic underachiever, aimless and lackadaisical, showing no interest in embarking upon a career. In 1899, at the age of twenty-two, he left for Hawaii with a graduation present of $1,200 in his pocket, saying he wanted to grow something and be his own boss. His ambition, he declared, was to "spend the rest of my life in a hammock smoking cigars rolled from tobacco grown on my own place."

Dole went to Wahiawa, twenty miles north of Pearl Harbor, and bought sixty acres of homestead land on this fertile plain cut by deep gulches. The soil was not right for tobacco, but Dole became intrigued with the *ananas comosus*, or pineapple, with its armadillolike carapace, bayonetlike fronds, and fleshy golden fruit. One pineapple could weigh as much as four pounds, and you could grow 20,000 of them per acre.

Knowledgeable Hawaiians scoffed when the twenty-four-year-old Jim Dole announced in 1901 that he was launching the Hawaiian Pineapple Company, and that it was his intention to "extend the market for Hawaiian pineapples into every grocery store in the United States."

Undiscouraged, Dole converted an old barn into a small cannery using hand-operated equipment and handmade cans. Workers stuffed broken pieces of pineapple into a small hole in the top of the can, and then soldered it shut. In his first year of canning, Dole had twenty employees and an annual payroll of $4,720. That year, he packed 189 cases of 24 cans each.

From the first tentative years, the business grew exponentially—8,810 cases in 1904, 25,000 cases in 1905, and so on. In 1906, the Hawaiian Pineapple Company made a profit of $30,489.

The true proof of success was competition, and by 1907 there were seven other pineapple canneries in Hawaii, including the giant outfit of Libby, McNeil & Libby. But that year a financial panic struck the mainland, resulting in a stock-market free fall, bank closings, and magnates throwing themselves out of windows.

Concerned that pineapple was an easy product not to buy in hard times, Dole assembled the other packers. He won their agreement to cut prices and launch an advertising campaign to sell their annual production of 400,000 cases. A million leaflets were printed saying, "Don't ask for pineapple alone—insist on Hawaiian pineapple." "The objective," Dole explained, "is to make Hawaiian mean to pineapple what Havana means to tobacco." Orders poured in despite the panic, and the consumption of Hawaiian pineapple quadrupled.

In 1913, Dole was packing 10,000 tons of pineapple a year, raised from the rich soil of Oahu—either grown in his own fields or bought from other growers. But there was a bottleneck in canning, because the hand-operated equipment could only process two or three pineapples per minute. Dole hired a mechanical draftsman, Henry Ginaca, to design a high-speed peeling and cutting machine.

Ginaca came up with a Rube Goldberg contraption that could size, peel, core, and cut the ends off pineapples, delivering golden cylinders to the packing tables, and enabling the cannery to process a hundred fruits per minute. Production jumped to a million cases in 1918. By that time, the company had gone international, buying pineapples in Mexico, Fiji, the Philippines, Malaya, and Australia.

His next move was to pioneer brand identity. Originally, he had marketed his fruit under such brands as Diamond Head and Outrigger. In 1927, he created a campaign to make Dole a household word. His name appeared on the can, and a radio slogan said, "You can thank Jim Dole for canned pineapple."

Dole had long ignored the rules of Hawaii's "Big Five" economy, according to which five firms ran things by keeping out competition from the mainland, and by blackballing cutthroat and un-American Oriental firms.

The way it worked, said a 1923 magazine article, was that "you can start a department store in Honolulu if you want to, but as soon as its business begins to approach that of the Big Five's Liberty House, for God's sakes look out; the Matson Navigation Company will leave your freight on the wharf at San Francisco 'by mistake.' "

During the Great Depression, the Hawaiian Pineapple Company almost went under. Sales slowed to a trickle, while inventories mounted. Thousands of tons of pineapple were left in the fields to rot. Ever the individualist, Dole had gone outside the Big Five and bought cement from a mainland firm to save money. Now, in 1931, in the midst of the Depression, he transferred his shipping from the Big Five's Matson Navigation to the Isthmian Steamship Line on the mainland.

That proved to be his undoing. He soon found that Hawaiian banks would not renew his loans. The directors of his board, the same men who sat on all the other boards in Honolulu, ousted him as general manager in October 1932, though he stayed on with the honorific title of president.

Dole retired in 1944 at the age of sixty-seven. He was one of those legendary entrepreneurs, like Uncle Ben in Arthur Miller's *Death of a Sales-*

man, who says: "When I was seventeen, I walked into the jungle, and when I was twenty-one, I walked out, and by God I was rich."

It was said that Jim Dole had such an amazing memory that even when the payroll numbered in the thousands, he knew every employee by name. But that kind of paternalism was reversible, and Dole did not hesitate to take advantage of labor trouble to hire seasonal workers. During the 1909 sugar strike, for example, he placed ads in the Japanese-language newspapers in order to recruit sugar workers as pineapple pickers. Like sugar, pineapple needed cheap labor.

With time, most of the pineapple workers became members of the International Longshoremen's and Warehousemen's Union, the ILWU. Under union rules, they worked five 8-hour days with a half-hour lunch break—from 6:30 A.M. to 3 P.M. Management still had problems with absenteeism, with people going "Hawaii sick," but Stone Age policies like piecework and *hanapau* (work allotments) had been replaced by incentive programs.

The union broke down paternalism. Gone were benefits such as free rent, free utilities, and free medical care, along with perks such as the May Day picnic, the Fourth of July and harvest festivities, and the Christmas packages with toys for the kids. Under paternalism, the company cast its shadow everywhere, governing not only work schedules, but social relations and private behavior.

Workers under the old system had to maintain a falsely cordial, hat-in-hand attitude to get on the good side of the *luna*. Housing and work assignments often depended on favoritism, which bred the conviction that management was unfair. But with union negotiations replacing the *luna*'s arbitrary power, a number of unpleasant worker types became extinct: the brownnosers, the tattlers, the gift givers.

As a Filipino worker put it: "Before, jackass better than worker. When jackass sick, plantation call doctor from downtown. When we sick, we *make* [die]. Doctor no come to us. Now we get union, at least worker as good as jackass."

The union also promoted interethnic harmony in pursuit of common goals. As one worker put it: "It used to be We Japanese and We Filipinos must stick together. Now it's We Workers in the common fight." The unions pushed for changes in management, urging that promotions be based on language and job skills rather than race. As the workers learned English and became Americanized, middle management became interracial. Differences which under paternalism had pitted the haoles against all the other races, were now simply labor-management disputes.

Besides the union, the other major agent of change on the plantation was generational. Children born in Hawaii did not want to follow in their parents' footsteps, either in maintaining traditional ethnic attitudes or in staying on the plantation. Here is a conversation between a Filipino father and son in preunion days:

FATHER: Why not work on plantation? At least you got security. Free house, store can charge. Plantation not so bad if you get used to it. Not much pay but at least you can get married and live.

SON: Heck, what you think? You think I only like free house, free this, free that? I like one good job. Look how cheap the pay. Downtown get better jobs. What kind chance I got? You gotta suck around, no can squawk back, any time you get cocky luna can tell you go home, aw waste time.

The second generation had to find a way between the pull of the old country and the adjustment to American Hawaii. In public school, they were taught to express themselves, but to their parents they seemed ill-mannered and obstinate.

A young Japanese man said he'd seen his parents wither away from the daily work routine. Their lives were drab and empty, and they were prematurely aged. He wanted something better. "But I'm the first-born and I have to obey my parents. Everything is *oyakoko* [filial piety]. When I went to school, I wanted to be like other kids, but my mother gave me Japanese food for lunch, rice, the cheapest canned tempura, and *umeboshi* [pickled small plums].

"When I was in the fifth grade my eyes were bothering me, but my father wouldn't give me glasses because he thought I was being *hokano* [show-off]. The teacher had to tell him to do it. Then in high school I wanted a suit to go to the dance, and my mother asked him and he said, 'What's the matter with you, do you want him useless and good-for-nothing? A new suit for his graduating is good enough.'"

His parents had found a wife for him, very Japanified, but here he drew the line—he would find his own wife. "When I get married," he said, "I don't want this Japanese clothes, and the *yuino* [bridal gift of money], and all the rest, I'm saying nuts to that and getting a Protestant wedding."

The second generation felt a certain amount of ethnic confusion. "We are not good Japanese in the eyes of our parents," one Japanese youth said, adding that "the Americans do not believe we are really Americans. Just what are we?"

Even more than the influence of unions and the change in the younger generations, the Japanese attack on Pearl Harbor on December 7, 1941, accelerated the Americanization process among the tradition-minded Chinese and Japanese.

Chinese weddings, which normally went on for several days, now had to end before the curfew imposed by blackout regulations and gasoline rationing. The same was true of the Chinese funerals that had gone on all night, with wailing and marching around the coffin. The months of mourning in seclusion were dispensed with by those whose attendance was required at war plants.

The Chinese New Year lost some of its clamor now that the strings of fireworks were banned. And along with other foreign-language radio programs, the authorities canceled the Sunday afternoon Chinese hour, the only respite of China-born elders from American jabbering and nerve-racking jazz. Chinese-language schools, where children learned to write their mother tongue, were closed as well. Thus, a sort of Americanization by deprivation occurred, since the Chinese could no longer practice their customs.

In the case of the Japanese, Americanization was an urgent matter of proving their loyalty. Overnight, the war undermined the traditional society they had sought to preserve, and their status as a group declined to the point where they were treated as suspects or enemy aliens.

Following the Pearl Harbor attack, Hawaii became the first territory in American history to be governed under martial law. But attempts to intern the Japanese were fought by the general in command, Delos Emmons. He opposed locking up one-third of the population, which would require building materials to house them and troops to guard them. Most of the skilled labor on the island of Oahu, including 90 percent of the carpenters, were Japanese. The military needed them to rebuild the defenses destroyed by the Pearl Harbor debacle. As a result, only 1,875 of the 158,000 Japanese in Hawaii were removed for internment on the mainland.

Even though relatively little Japan-bashing took place in tolerant Hawaii, the Japanese community was demoralized and cast down. "What is going to become of us?" they asked. They had deliberately segregated themselves, making little effort to adopt American ways. Now they had to rapidly acquire Americans standards of behavior to avoid being stigmatized. In 1942, 2,400 Japanese filed petitions to Anglicize their names. To display their patriotism, large numbers of Japanese bought war bonds, donated blood, and volunteered for civic service groups.

The war situation also reversed the parent-child roles. Japanese-born parents had been blindly obeyed, but now that they risked classification as enemy aliens, they lost their authority. They had to depend on the judgment of their American-born children, who taught them the do's and don't's: "Don't talk in Japanese." "Don't wear a kimono." "Don't bow like a Japanese." Any parental disapproval could now be met with an appeal to "American custom." For the duration of the war, Japanese parents were subjected to the tyranny of their children. Nor were Japanese husbands able to maintain their traditional ascendancy over their wives, who joined the Red Cross, the YWCA, and the USO to affirm their American credentials.

The proudest Japanese families were those with sons in the service. Families with only daughters were even more apologetic than traditionally had been the case. A Japanese woman working at the YMCA in 1943 said: "My son is in Europe fighting the enemy. I feel that I am fighting too. I make Red Cross slippers for the soldiers with my body, mind, and soul."

Kimonos were packed away in mothballs, and in a Main Street store this comment was heard about die-hard traditionalists who still wore them: "It's hard enough for us already without having them strut about."

Fear of mass internment lingered even though it did not occur. Every Japanese family expected the knock on the door. "Don't speak Japanese on the bus," people said, "because there are FBI agents all over the place, and they can pick you up at any time." Stories abounded about FBI men visiting Japanese homes: "Why they even tried to take away the little boy's toy, which happened to be a miniature Japanese destroyer sent to him by his grandpa. But he cried so hard they gave it back to him."

The war years of accelerated assimilation had a lasting effect. But the notion that Americanization would lead to a racial paradise honoring ethnic pluralism was a pipe dream. Instead, a curious form of reverse racism sprang up.

Ethnicity had been a form of alienation that fostered a ghetto mentality. As long as the Japanese and the other groups refused to speak English and clung to the old ways, the haoles were able to maintain their power. But once Americanized, these Asian groups, who made up a majority, gave as good as they got. The haole became the god-damned haole, the stupid haole, the fuckin' lazy haole. The haoles, who had been dishing it out for more than a century, did not like being on the receiving end. Or being served last at a Japanese lunch counter as they sat among Japanese customers. Or being turned down for an apartment because landlords thought haoles were messy.

Haoles now griped about under-representation in education and the professions. The "orientals," they said, ran everything: the government, medicine, dentistry, the law. The Chinese seemed to own all of downtown Honolulu. Haoles sometimes felt they were being scapegoated for the sins of Captain Cook, the puritanical missionaries, and the cabal that overthrew the monarchy. One white migrant from Alabama to Hawaii complained: "It's like the south where I come from. Nigger, do you want to live here? You keep your mouth shut."

In 1952, when Robert Bean was between junior college and college, he found a job in a tire-recapping plant. His haole boss told his new white employee that the big problem would be getting along with the other workers, who were Japanese. The boss had tried Hawaiian, Portuguese, and haole boys before, but they never lasted very long. In fact, all the tire-recapping shops in Honolulu had close-knit Japanese employees.

The boss took Bob to meet his Japanese supervisor and said: "He's all yours—work hell out of him." All day long, Bob painted rubber cement on tires. The other workers ignored him and spoke in Japanese. They thought he was some kind of stooge for the bosses, who were all haoles, from the president of the company down to the general manager.

Bob's pidgin English got him over the first hump, and then came the big party at a Japanese teahouse, held to celebrate the company's fifteenth anniversary. Bob sat with his coworkers and showed them that he could use chopsticks as well as they could, and eat every Japanese dish they ate. This established the fact that he was a local boy and not a stuck-up coast haole.

After dinner, they all got drunk, which was a great equalizer. One Japanese fellow whom Bob didn't know sat down next to him and said, "I don't like you goddamned haoles and I never will; you think you're too damned good and are always shoving us around."

"I'm sorry you feel that way," Bob said, "but it's okay with me. Let's try to stay out of each other's way. I think there's enough room for both of us here in this company." They shook hands and the drunken coworker staggered off. Bob later learned that he had wanted to transfer from another department to the recapping shop and felt that the white management had given Bob the job that he deserved.

When the other workers had satisfied themselves that Bob had no great ambitions in the recapping trade, they were more at ease. Then a Filipino was hired. He knew his job and worked hard, but the Japanese workers told Bob, "Filipinos can't be trusted, be careful where you leave your things, you better start locking your locker."

One day Bob overheard a conversation between the Filipino and one of the Japanese workers and realized they were talking about him.

"He's a pretty good haole, no?" the Filipino asked.

"The only good haole is a dead haole," the Japanese replied.

Bob interrupted them, saying. "I thought that phrase applied to Indians."

"I meant Portagees, not regular haoles," said the Japanese.

Bob tried hard to fit in. When he had a problem, he did not go over the Japanese supervisor's head to the big boss, haole-to-haole, but took it to the supervisor. In the spring, he signed up for the softball team, but the other workers told him they preferred to keep the team all-Japanese. Bob went to the games and rooted, hoping they would change their minds, but they never did.

And right up to his last day at work, Bob was never called "haole" but "damned haole." It reminded him of the junior college he'd attended on the mainland, where the whites had mocked a student of Japanese ancestry as a "damned Buddhahead."

In June 1957, Janet O'Brien stepped out of a navy boat at Keehi Lagoon and went on shore with her two daughters, two and four, to join her husband, an enlisted man. There was a waiting list for navy housing, so her husband had found a small four-room apartment near Punchbowl, on the Ewa side of Pearl Harbor.

The place was $100 a month, furnished. Six months pregnant, Janet felt exhausted from the trip, and her first glimpse of the apartment did not make her feel any better. The bathtub was ancient and streaked with dirt, the mattress was stained, and termite holes riddled the furniture. When the Filipino landlady showed up, she shrieked: "I didn't know the children were so small. Everyone knows you people let children do anything they want."

Janet was too tired to argue, but the landlady went on: "I knew I should have rented to Japanese—they're clean and they don't scratch up the floor with shoes. You'll have to pay another $50 deposit." That was a big bite on an enlisted man's pay, but her husband had no choice.

That afternoon Janet made her way downtown to buy some sheets before the stores closed. On the bus, she wondered, "Good heavens, where are the Hawaiians? Where is the spirit of aloha I heard so much about? Is this China or Japan? What are all these Orientals doing here?"

The next day her husband put out to sea and Janet went into the courtyard to hang up her wash and met an Oriental woman hanging hers. "Good morning," Janet said, "we just moved in." Without uttering a word, the other woman turned and walked back into her house.

Janet had the feeling that in Hawaii every ethnic group disliked every other group, although they were always talking about how well everyone got along. Navy personnel were generally thought of as a necessary evil, even by the other whites—for haoles, missionary ancestry was the thing; it was like having come over on the *Mayflower*. At first, interracial marriage seemed wrong to Janet, but despite the ethnic tensions, miscegenation was so common in Hawaii that soon she wondered what all the fuss was about. In spite of all the rude behavior she encountered, and the ethnic confusion, she concluded that "it all comes down to this: this is certainly America and anyone who can't see it just isn't looking."

That Hawaii was certainly America was not immediately apparent to many persons on the mainland, particularly congressmen. Hawaii's struggle for statehood was so protracted that it began to seem like one of those never-ending stalemates of history, such as the Hundred Years' War.

In the case of Hawaii, the pre–Civil War battle over free states and slave states repeated itself. For the issue of Hawaiian statehood became part of the struggle in Congress over civil rights legislation. Southern congressmen opposed to civil rights feared that the tolerant multiracial Hawaiian islands, if admitted to statehood, would undermine their stand.

There were in any case compelling reasons against statehood. Hawaii was noncontiguous with the rest of the United States, an island chain in the mid-Pacific, 2,000 miles from the West Coast. The admission of an insular territory as a state, extending the boundaries of the United States far beyond its continental limits, had no precedent. Hawaii was also a territory with an Asian majority, and grave doubts were expressed in Congress as to whether Asians would make good citizens.

But by 1934, big business in Hawaii had put its considerable weight behind statehood as the result of two pieces of New Deal legislation. The first was a 1933 bill allowing President Roosevelt to appoint a nonresident as governor, which might have curbed the powers of the Big Five—the companies that ran the banks, the utilities, transportation, and the sugar industry. A heartfelt protest arose from Hawaii's establishment that imposing an outside governor was unfair and undemocratic.

When the Colorado judge Ben Lindsey was proposed, the *Honolulu Advertiser* wrote, "Give us Ely Culbertson [the bridge champion] or Al Jolson, but not Ben Lindsey." The appointment finally went to the Oregon judge Joseph Boyd Poindexter. But Hawaiians felt more than ever that they had no say in their own affairs.

Another blow to Hawaiian interests came with the 1934 Agricultural Adjustment Administration hearings on the sugar quotas. The upshot of those deliberations relegated Hawaii to the category of a foreign producer of sugar. This made the Hawaiian sugar interests understand the value of a voice in Congress, and they became energetic statehood boosters.

In 1940, Hawaii organized a plebiscite on statehood. Lectures, films, and leaflets made the point that Hawaii was ready—it was bigger than Connecticut, had more people than Wyoming, and in 1939 the island territory paid more federal taxes than fourteen of the mainland states. On November 5, 1940, the voters were asked, "Do you favor statehood for Hawaii?" While 20 percent of the registered voters cast no ballot, 46,124 said yes, and 22,428 said no.

But just when the statehood engine began to hum, Pearl Harbor caused another four-year delay. Afterward, however, Hawaiians felt that the war had wiped out all objections to statehood. Had they not taken the first blow? Had not 30,000 Hawaiians served in the armed forces? Yet Hawaii had a mixed population of 500,000 that was 34 percent white and 32 percent Japanese; the remaining 34 percent was mainly Filipino, Chinese, and native Hawaiian. And this was the factor that now made Hawaii a pawn in the civil rights debate that lasted from 1947 to 1959.

President Truman had taken office after Roosevelt's death in April 1945. The following year, he appointed a Civil Rights Commission, which recommended that Congress enact civil rights legislation. In its landmark report in 1947, the commission called the 1896 separate-but-equal doctrine justifying segregation "one of the outstanding myths of American history, for it is almost always true that while indeed separate . . . facilities are far from equal."

The lines in Congress were drawn for a major fight over civil rights. Truman's program included antilynching and antipoll-tax legislation, and an end to segregation in the armed forces. Stuck into this package was the president's recommendation of statehood for Hawaii and Alaska, which led to the drafting of another statehood bill.

The House voted on the bill on June 30, 1947; it passed by 196 to 133. The opposition consisted mainly of Democrats from southern and border states who feared that traditionally Republican Hawaii would swell the Republican majority in the Senate. Some Democrats wanted to pair Hawaii with Democratic Alaska as a way to preserve the status quo in Congress.

Of course, these southern congressmen also worried that multiracial Hawaii's senators and representatives would promote civil rights legislation in Congress. They foresaw that Hawaii's admission would reduce the ability of the southern states to determine their own racial politics, adding to the growing antisegregation block in the Senate. It would dilute southern strength in their life-and-death struggle to preserve states' rights and a segregated way of life.

In the ensuing 1947 House debate, Prince Preston of Georgia coached these fears in anti-Japanese rhetoric, still effective only two years after the war. "What does the Hawaii bill do?" he asked. "It makes citizens with equal rights with you and me of 180,000 Japanese. . . . When you give these people the same rights we have today you will have two senators speaking for those 180,000 Japanese."

The southern senators also had Republican allies, conservatives such as Senator Hugh Butler of Nebraska, who consistently voted against Hawaiian statehood from 1941 to 1952. In 1946, when Butler became chairman of the Committee on Public Lands, he wrote his constituents: "A lot of people have asked me if I want to see two Japs in the United States Senate. No, I don't." By exerting pressure through his presence on key committees—Public Lands, Interior, and Insular Affairs—Butler became the chief wrecker of Hawaii's statehood hopes.

In the House after 1947, however, the anti–civil rights faction did not have the numbers to block statehood legislation. Still, the House Rules Committee, under the sway of southern Democrats, was able to bottle up Hawaii bills by combining them with Alaska bills that most Republicans found unacceptable.

In 1952, Hawaii's political prospects dramatically improved when Eisenhower was elected and the Republicans gained a majority in the House and a one-seat majority in the Senate. Ike promoted Hawaiian statehood while rejecting Democratic Alaska, which caused bitter party divisions. But some Republican opponents of Hawaii, like Hugh Butler, now hewed the party line. Butler notified his constituents that he had changed his mind on Hawaiian statehood (which he did not live to see, for he died in 1954).

On March 10, 1953, the Hawaii bill made it through the House for the third time. When the Senate took it up in March 1954, Minority Leader Lyndon B. Johnson said the Democrats would oppose it because Ike had made statehood a partisan issue by refusing to promote Alaska. Even if separate bills were passed, Johnson said, Ike would veto Alaska to maintain Republican strength in Congress.

At the same time, Democratic Senator James O. Eastland of Mississippi indicated that any Hawaii statehood bill would be filibustered. Hawaii, he declared, was "tinctured with Communism," and statehood would mean "two votes for socialized medicine . . . two votes for government ownership of industry . . . two votes against all racial segregation, and two votes against the south on all social matters."

After much haggling, the Senate proposed a combined Hawaii-Alaska bill. This legislation passed on April 1, but only because of assurances that the House would reject it. In July, the Rules Committee refused to forward the bill to the floor of the House. Tying Hawaii to Alaska doubled the difficulty of passage, for objections to one would sink the chances for both. Each party wanted a different state, but neither party wanted the two states together. Meanwhile, the opposition was becoming farcical. Democratic Senator Tom Connally of Texas announced that he was a better citizen than anyone living in Hawaii. Democratic Senator J. Strom Thurmond of South Carolina quoted Kipling: "East is East and West is West and never the twain shall meet."

Citizens of Hawaii watched with dismay as one statehood bill after the other was buried. In 1954, they responded to farce with farce. Dorothy Lamour, on the basis of her expertise with sarongs, declared her ardent support for statehood. In Honolulu's Bishop Street, a roll of newsprint weighing half a ton appeared alongside beauty queens who urged passersby to sign. People waited in a block-long line to put their names to the massive petition, which was sent with 110,000 signatures to Vice President Nixon.

Despite all these efforts, Hawaiian statehood made no progress in 1954, though the year was a turning point in civil rights. On May 17, the unanimous Supreme Court decision of *Brown* v. *Topeka Board of Education* prohibited segregation in public schools. A year later the court ordered the desegregation to be carried out "with all deliberate speed." With this landmark bill, the southern block lost its momentum, since the constitutional underpinnings to segregation had crumbled.

As if mainland America were mimicking Hawaii's ancient volcanoes, the country erupted. In short order came the Montgomery bus boycott, Martin Luther King's nonviolent disobedience, and the start of the black civil rights movement. The battleground was no longer Congress but the schools, and in 1957 Eisenhower had to use federal marshals and troops to enforce the right of black children to attend the previously all-white Central High School in Little Rock, Arkansas.

In all this tumult, opposition to Hawaiian statehood began to seem irrelevant. It was plain to see that the fate of civil rights was being determined in the courts, not in Congress. Between 1957 and 1959, the sectional opposition to Hawaii's aspirations gradually broke down. A majority coalition of moderate Republicans and northern Democrats emerged in the Senate and passed important civil rights legislation—most notably the 1957 civil rights bill protecting the Negro's right to vote.

Realizing that they could no longer block such legislation, conservatives tried to amend it. This strategy of compromise had significant implications for Hawaiian statehood. For the addition of four senators from Alaska and Hawaii would hardly matter in the present climate of civil rights reform. After 1957, civil rights opponents became more amenable to compromise on statehood. Having lost control of Congress, the best the southern segregationists could do was try to maintain some influence.

By 1958, both houses of Congress favored statehood for Alaska but not for Hawaii. Lyndon Johnson and Sam Rayburn, the speaker of the House, convinced John A. Burns, the Hawaiian delegate to Congress, to agree to an "Alaska first" strategy. Alaska would be admitted and hold the door for Hawaii. Though he was criticized back home for further delaying statehood, Burns saw the wisdom of the strategy and went along with it.

In May and June 1958, a separate Alaska bill passed the House and Senate. The same coalition of liberal Democrats and moderate Republicans who had gained the passage of the 1957 Civil Rights Bill voted for Alaska statehood. For the first time, a separate statehood bill for Alaska or Hawaii was not scuttled by delaying tactics. On January 3, 1959, Alaska became the forty-ninth state.

The open-door strategy worked. In March 1959, Hawaii's statehood bill sailed through both houses practically without debate. In one of the speediest congressional actions on record, the House approved the measure on March 11 and the Senate on March 12. As Daniel K. Inouye, the present senator from Hawaii, recalled: "The argument against the statehood bill . . . was that if Hawaii became a state you would have representation by a strange-looking people. As one senator said, 'How would you like to be sitting next to a fellow by the name of Yamamoto?' . . . Johnson . . . was able to convince those opposed . . . to weaken their resistance and it went through."

In June, the Hawaiians ratified the statehood bill. Of 240 precincts, only the tiny island of Niihau, whose 107 registered voters were native Hawaiians, rejected it. President Eisenhower signed the legislation on August 21, 1959, making Hawaii the fiftieth state. On that very day, a local boy in a Honolulu bar, whose patrons were the usual mix of racial strains, looked at himself in the wall mirror, raised his glass, and proposed this toast: "Now we are all haoles."

CHAPTER TWENTY-SEVEN
THE LAST FRONTIER

*In a land whose very features were unfamiliar, where even
the rules of life were strangers, where the past had been
abolished so that everyone could feel they were starting life
as equals from a line of opportunity which was the same
for all; in such a land, with such a task, you had to learn
to depend on yourself, to make a religion, as Emerson did,
of "self-reliance," and become a handyman, a "jack-of-
all-trades," as it was put; but it was also true that when*

In 1900, native Alaskans in their riverside hamlets still placed totem
poles in front of their homes bearing the likenesses of their human
and animal ancestors.

*you did need others you desperately needed them — to form
a posse, raise a roof, to bridge a stream — nor did you
have the time or training, in order to discover whether another person was a friend or an enemy, a worker or a wast-
rel, dependable or weak, an honest man or a rustler; so
you wanted to know immediately "how the land lay," and
the frank and open countenance was consequently prized.*

WILLIAM GASS

*This is the law of the Yukon, and ever she makes it
   plain:
Send not your foolish and feeble; send me your strong and
   your sane.*

ROBERT SERVICE

In 1980, the Census Bureau in Alaska decided to make a determined effort to count the hundreds of residents classified as "subsistence homesteaders" who lived in the wilderness, far from inhabited areas. The bureau sent out census takers in pontoon planes that could land on water, since most homesteaders dwelled on rivers and lakes. They flew around at treetop level, landing wherever they saw a cabin. Never had the Census Bureau spent so much money to add so few people to the rolls, but it had to be done.

One day that spring, Miles Martin, who had been living in Alaska for eight years as a homesteader and trapper, looked out the window of his cabin on the Bearpaw River and saw a chartered plane overhead. The Bearpaw is about 120 miles from the town of Nenana, where Miles (known as "Sunshine") keeps a post-office box. The Bearpaw runs into the Kantishna, which runs into the Tanana, which runs into the Yukon. Miles's twenty-nine-acre homestead is in a forest, far from any trail or road, and he has no neighbors. His mode of travel when the rivers are running is by an outboard-motor-driven fiberglass boat. In the winter, he gets around by dogsled.

Miles watched the plane land on the Bearpaw outside his cabin. Two census takers, a man and a woman, paddled a rubber dinghy to shore and warily approached. He went out to greet them, and the woman said: "You never know how homesteaders will react. One of them took a shot at us."

Miles invited them in, and showed them the wall of his cabin that is covered with approximately two hundred skulls of the animals he's killed, from a porcupine to a grizzly.

"How do you get the skulls so clean and white?" the woman asked.

The National Archives
Miles Martin, one of the last Alaskan bush rats, with some of the
furs he trapped in 1993.

"I cut off the heads and bury them for six months," Miles said, "and
the maggots and the worms do the rest."

The census takers found Miles so talkative and friendly that they
decided to give him the long form, and started asking questions.

"Any running water?" one asked.

"Sure," Miles said.

"Where?"

"Right outside," Miles said, pointing to the Bearpaw.

"Any plumbing?" the other asked.

"Yes," Miles said.

"Where?"

"I dump the slop bucket on the ice and it flushes when the ice breaks."

One of the census takers said, "I think we'd better give him the short
form."

Alaska is the only state in the Union where the federal government
arrived ahead of the settlers. When the United States bought the area from
Russia in 1867, there were no American squatters claiming land. Located
in the distant north, Alaska was not the place for pioneer wagons and small
farms, and Americans did not come there in large numbers until the Yukon
gold strike of the 1890s.

The purchase of Alaska was the achievement of a single man, Lincoln's secretary of state, William Henry Seward. This lumpy-nosed New Yorker believed that the United States needed naval outposts outside its borders. In the last months of the Civil War, when the Confederate raider *Shenandoah* was attacking American whalers in the Bering Sea, Seward had occasion to reflect on the advantages of an American naval presence in the area.

Fur had brought the Russians to the North American continent in the mid eighteenth century. The *promyshlenniki* (trader-explorers) leapfrogged across the Aleutians, chasing seal and otter, which they practically exterminated. They ruled with the sword and the knout, enslaving the Aleuts. "God is on high and the czar far away" was their motto. By the middle of the nineteenth century, the fur trade was in decline, and the czar started wondering, "What do I want with this huge frozen area?" At a time when he couldn't even defend Crimea against the British, the cost of keeping Alaska didn't seem worth it.

Alaska was a buyer's market, for the czar eagerly wanted to sell. But in Washington, no one besides Seward had much interest. The secretary's only ally was the urbane and mutton-chop-whiskered Russian ambassador, Baron Édouard de Stoeckl, who had married an American. Stoeckl bragged to Alexander II that his wife, who hailed from Springfield, Illinois, was "stately as a queen."

Stoeckl saw Russian America as a liability. He told his foreign minister, Prince Gorchakov, that if they didn't sell it to the Americans, the British would grab it. The prince took heed. In 1867, when Andrew Johnson was president, Gorchakov instructed the baron to put Alaska on the market at no less than $5 million. A period of haggling ensued, and Seward bid $7 million plus $200,000 to cover any claims on the part of the Russian fur company that had installations there.

On Friday, March 29, 1867, the baron called on Seward at home and found him playing whist. Stoeckl had good news. St. Petersburg had approved the terms, and he was ready to sign the treaty. Thus, Seward concluded the greatest real estate deal since the Louisiana Purchase, buying a piece of ground twice the size of Texas, with 31,000 miles of shoreline, for less than 2 cents an acre.

But would the Senate approve such a monumental land transfer in an area that was not contiguous with the United States? Much depended on the Massachusetts senator Charles Sumner, chairman of the Foreign Relations Committee. The press, meanwhile, called Alaska "Icebergia," "Walrussia," and "Seward's Folly." *Harper's Weekly* wrote that the ice crop was promising and the cows gave ice cream instead of milk. On April 8, however, the Senate Foreign Relations Committee voted in favor, and Sumner proposed the name Alaska—Aleut for "mainland." On April 9, Sumner delivered a three-hour oration that exhausted, it was said, both his subject and his audience. Afterward, the full Senate approved the purchase by a vote of 37 to 2.

On October 18, 1867, at the Russian capital of Sitka, the United States took possession of Alaska. The outgoing Russian garrison faced a company of U.S. Army troops that stood at attention as the czarist double eagle floated down and the Stars and Stripes ascended over the abandoned barracks. Batteries fired a salute, and Alaska became American property.

There remained, however, the problem of payment, which had to be appropriated by the House. The Alaska purchase became entangled in the House feud with President Johnson, for on November 25, the House Judiciary Committee voted for impeachment. A short time later, the full House voted 93 to 43 to approve no more funds for Alaska.

In March 1868, the House postponed consideration of the Alaska appropriation for two months. This was a violation of a clause in the treaty that said Russia had to be paid in full within ten months of Senate ratification.

Seward lobbied House leaders, arguing that the Alaska purchase should be disassociated from the anti-Johnson feeling, and pointing out the value of Alaska's resources. On May 16, 1868, the vote in the Senate to impeach the president was 35 to 19, one vote short of the two-thirds required. On July 14, the House finally relented and passed the Alaska purchase appropriation by a vote of 113 to 43. In August, the U.S. Treasury paid Baron Stoeckl in full.

In Alaska, where almost free land is still available to those willing to build a cabin and settle on it, the homesteaders are known as "bushrats." Miles Martin is not a bushrat from central casting. He is more Wally Cox than John Wayne, short and mild-mannered, with expressive brown eyes, seemingly untouched by the hardness of the country, and thinning brown hair. He does not smoke or drink, and cusses rarely. In his twenty-two years as a homesteader and trapper, he's lost some of his teeth and hair to scurvy, the disease that killed off Jacques Cartier's men in Canada in the sixteenth century.

Born in 1952, Miles moved as a boy from Ohio to Michigan, where his father was a college professor and dean. Rebelling against parental authority, Miles enlisted in the navy at the age of seventeen instead of going to college, and spent four years aboard the *Wasp*, an aircraft carrier in the North Atlantic.

When Miles got out of the navy in 1972, Alaska beckoned. After being cooped up on an aircraft carrier with 5,000 men below decks, he wanted spaciousness and isolation. He had been reading Thoreau, who said that a forced self-reliance and a life free from encumbrance could be found on the frontier. "Our lives . . . need the relief of the wilderness," Thoreau wrote, "where the pine flourishes and the jay still screams."

"I felt like an Alaskan before I came to Alaska," Miles said, meaning that what he imagined Alaska to be like was compatible with his needs. It was the last frontier, after all, with plenty of virgin land that was being given away.

Unlike most of us, Miles acted on his impulse. One bright August day he walked into bush pilot Al Wright's office in Fairbanks and said, "Fly me into the bush—I don't care where."

"When do you want to be picked up?" Wright asked.

"I don't," Miles said.

It turned out that with the cost of supplies and the air charter, Miles was $300 short. So he negotiated a deal that he would work at Al Wright's fishing camp on the Yukon for the rest of the year. The job involved catching salmon, cutting it in strips, and smoking it, and he could keep half the fish he smoked.

Miles was a happy man. He had turned his back on civilization and labored alone at the camp, dipping the pieces of salmon in a mixture of brown sugar and brine and then letting them hang over the curling smoke. The river Indians called it "squaw candy."

Miles's job at the fishing camp ended in 1973, but he decided to stay on the Yukon on his own. He bought supplies and a boat, then built a cabin and a boat landing. The winter of 1973 found him in his cabin trapping. One bad mistake he made was not observing the proper etiquette with the Yukon River Indians, the only other inhabitants near the fishing camp.

"I didn't even ask, may I build a cabin," he recalled. "I didn't pay a call. I didn't put them at ease." Miles had stored his supplies on the boat, and one day he saw another boat come by carrying a squaw and two children. "I went down to the landing and she smiled and said, 'Have a nice winter.' Then I saw my stuff was missing, but with my little eighteen-horse there was no way I could catch her. They'd taken my beans and rice, my smoked fish, my lantern and kerosene, and my ax. You don't take someone's ax, that's like committing murder."

Miles found himself three hundred miles from Fairbanks at the start of winter with no supplies, but he stayed on because he was overconfident. "I made it last year," he told himself, "I'll make it this year." He had some flour, rice, and sugar, and a jar of peanut butter, and he figured he'd eat the meat from his traps. "Lynx meat was pretty good," he recalled, "close to chicken."

He had no clock and no calendar, and didn't know what day or month it was. In spite of rationing, his food was running out, and the game became scarce. Miles realized he had to get out or die. He knew he was thirty miles from the pipeline haul road. He could hear them dynamiting. In what he thought was March or April 1974, he started out on snowshoes with the last of his supplies, but they were the wrong snowshoes, made for trails, not for breaking new trails. He also had the wrong boots. The snowshoe harness straps rubbed through the nylon, letting in the snow, which froze over his feet.

Miles covered ten miles the first day, following the river. But the second day it was 50 below through heavy snowdrifts and he only made three miles. His army duck-feather sleeping bag got wet; the mistakes seemed to be piling up. He ate most of his food to keep his strength up, reserving some taffy he'd made from mashed berries and sugar for the next day. That night, after he had lit his fire and fallen asleep, Miles rolled into the flame and burned holes the size of footballs in his sleeping bag.

On the third day, Miles had no food and no sleeping bag. The snow was so deep that first he broke trail, and then he went back for his backpack, an army duffel with a strap and no armature. He said to himself: "There's only so much a person can endure." His toes and fingertips were freezing, and his strength was failing. He got to the point where he would take ten steps and then rest for half an hour, and eat a little taffy. After that, he'd be good for ten more steps.

As the sun was setting and Miles stopped to make camp, he saw that a pack of wolves had gathered across the river, sitting and watching. He wasn't afraid, because he knew they'd wait until he was dead. He considered playing dead and killing the first wolf who approached him with his knife, for food. But then he thought, "I might not be pretending."

On the fourth day, he set out again. By midafternoon, when he was ready to make camp, he turned around and saw his last camp a mile away. He had gone one mile in one day. If he was going to die and his body was found, he wanted his track to be straight. No eccentric behavior. The best thing to do was stay in one place and make it a rescue operation.

So with his last remaining energy, when dawn broke on the fifth day, Miles stomped out a big triangle in the snow, placing a piece of dark blanket at each of the three corners, walking back and forth to beat out the triangle, three hundred feet to a side.

On the next and sixth day, Miles sat inside the triangle and ate the last of his food, a teaspoon of peanut butter. He didn't think he was going to make it. At sunset, he saw the trail of a 707 Wein Airline jet going from Fairbanks to Prudhoe Bay. He jumped up and waved, afraid that the jet was too high to see him. Luckily, a passenger who was looking at the river spotted the triangle and alerted the stewardess, who told the pilot.

Miles watched the jet turn around and fly over the treetops, as if in slow motion, its windows lit up and the passengers' faces framed against the glass. A jet can't tip its wings, but Miles knew the pilot had seen him. Inside his distress signal, he waited by the fire.

The pilot called the Eielson air base for a rescue helicopter. An hour later, Miles saw a light on the river, which came from the spotlight of the Chinook. He heard the rotor, and snow blew all around him as the chopper landed with its blade windmilling. Guys with headsets on pulled him in, and the first words he heard were "My God, you smell like a forest fire."

The lesson Miles had learned was that "an adventure is a mistake. The fewer mistakes you make, the less adventures you'll have." Miles now wanted to save enough money to go back into the interior. He remembered all the people who had told him he'd never make it in the bush, and he wanted to prove them wrong.

•   •

After the purchase of Alaska, Congress established a small military force and a customs district there. During the seventeen years of military rule, twenty-five bills providing for civilian government were buried in committee, for Congress had a presumption of worthlessness about the "frozen wastes."

The American presence was thin—troops in Sitka, and revenue cutters patrolling the coast. As Kipling wrote, "There's never law of God or man runs north of 53" (latitude). This neglect had a prohibitive effect. Since all the land belonged to the government, and since it had not been surveyed, no settler could obtain title to property, and no prospector could stake a mining claim. No courts and no justices of the peace meant no crimes punished and no marriages celebrated. A man could not even make out a legal will. If he cut wood for his fire, he was defying a congressional restriction.

In 1884, Congress finally passed an organic act giving Alaska a civilian government. But unlike other territories, Alaska was denied a legislature and a delegate to Congress, although it now had a governor and judges. There were still no land laws and thus no private ownership. On the bright side, there were no taxes.

Alaska remained in its preliminary phase, unsettled, unmapped, unsurveyed, and largely unexplored. In the case of a few men, the region had become a fixation. The Kentucky-born West Point graduate Henry T. Allen wrote his fiancée in 1883: "I am willing to forego almost any benefit that I might receive for an attempt at exploration in Alaska."

A year later Allen was in Sitka, proposing to lead a three-man mission to the Copper River delta up the coast, about fifty miles west of the Yukon border. In March 1885, he started out, accompanied by Sergeant Cady Robertson and Private Fred Fickett of the Signal Corps. Their equipment consisted mainly of a sextant for mapmaking, a camera with plates and chemicals, and sleeping bags made of linen sailcloth waterproofed with beeswax and linseed oil.

The expedition set out up the coast in the *Pinta*, a fourth-rate man-of-war with small armament. Reaching the delta, they looked for Indian packers and guides, but found them reluctant to go, until Lieutenant Allen tried the old Tom Sawyer ploy. "These Indians promised one hour to go and the next refused all connection," he noted in his journal. "In order to persuade them that it was a great privilege I was extending, I decided to take only five and had them draw lots to determine the one to remain. This had the desired effect."

On March 29, 1884, they began to ascend the Copper in five canoes. Rain, soft snow, shallow channels, and floating ice forced the party to crisscross the river with both canoes and sleds. On March 30, they abandoned half their ammunition, clothing and food, so that each man would have no more than he could carry in a fifty-pound pack. On April 4, they saw the sun for the first time.

Lieutenant Allen made a side trip in the snow to Taral (today's Chitina). There he found John Bremner, a copper prospector, trapped by the weather. Bremner, wrote Allen, was "certainly the most uncouth specimen of manhood that I had, up to that time, ever seen. He was a picture of wretchedness, destitution, and despair, suddenly rendered happy. John was reduced to a single round of powder, which he fired in answer to us. . . . In the meantime he had been living on rabbits which he snared, with occasionally a piece of dried salmon as a luxury. He was shortening his belt one hole every other day."

At Taral, after picking up a second prospector, Lieutenant Allen explored the Chitina River, a tributary of the Copper. He took along four other men and four days' rations. "We began to realize the true meaning of the much-used expression 'living upon the country.' . . . Our main dependence was on rabbits, the broth of which was thickened with a handful of flour." On April 13, an Indian brought scraps of a moose killed by wolves. Lieutenant Allen celebrated his twenty-sixth birthday with rotten moose meat.

Food shortages remained a problem. Allen decided to portage north of the Chitina to a community of Copper-Chitina Indians headed by a chief of some repute called Nikolai. At the village, the famished five gorged on moose, beaver, lynx, and rabbit, cooked native-style, entrails and all.

Nikolai asked Lieutenant Allen why, if he was a genuine chief, he carried his own pack and pulled with the others. Allen realized that the natives had a stricter sense of rank than existed in the army. "None of the natives would sell us any food without consulting [Nikolai]," he noted, "and he advised prices that would make a commissary shudder. They realize full well our dependence."

Arriving at the mouth of the Tazlina River on May 15, Lieutenant Allen now crossed country never before seen by white men. Even the natives knew little about this land. The party pulled on up the river, slowly cordelling. On May 27, a crippled and hungry Indian came into their camp along the water to offer his services, which they refused, as they did not have enough food. But he followed them like a stray dog, always appearing at mealtime. They finally adopted him, and he earned his keep with his root-digging abilities.

On May 30, Private Fickett noted: "Arrived at Indian house at 11 A.M. Hungry. Decided to abandon boat. Indian gave us dinner of boiled meat from which he scraped the maggots by handfulls before cutting it up. It tasted good, maggots and all."

Continuing northward on foot, the men reached the mouth of the Siana River and cut north through the Siana Valley to a mountain pass. At Lake Suslota, they found salmon. Then they went up a divide, with barren bluffs on each side, to 4,500 feet. The sun was rising, but not in the east, for they had reached the land of the midnight sun, which rose in the north. At the top of the pass, yellow and white buttercups poked out of the remaining patches of snow. Allen forgot his fatigue and hunger and was overcome with joy at seeing a landscape known until then only to Tanana Indians.

Then it was down the muddy Tanana, and on June 25 they reached the 2,000-mile-long Yukon River, Alaska's Mississippi, and followed this main waterway to its juncture with the Koyukuk. The Koyukons had the worst reputation of all the river Indians, but Lieutenant Allen found them hospitable. The tribe invited him and his men to dine on fish fried in machine oil.

After resting on the Yukon, Lieutenant Allen and his men headed for home in August. They canoed down the big river as far as today's Kaltag. There they portaged to the Unalakleet, which took them into Norton Sound. From St. Michael, on the sound, they embarked on a ship to the United States.

Lieutenant Allen had completed an original exploration of 1,500 miles of virgin wilderness, crossing the Alaska Range and going from the 61st parallel to the Arctic Circle. Three major river systems—the Copper, the Tanana, and the Koyukuk—were charted for the first time. But because Allen did not leap into print, his exploits went unheralded. Only specialists knew what he had accomplished. Walter C. Mendenhall, the chief of the U.S. Geological Survey, observed that "no geographer in recent years has made greater contributions to our knowledge of the territory in so limited a time in the face of such obstacles." General Nelson A. Miles, Allen's commanding officer, said that the lieutenant's expedition was the first major exploration of the continent since Lewis and Clark.

Allen performed his greatest feat while still in his twenties. He went on to a distinguished military career, serving as military attaché in St. Petersburg and Berlin. He commanded the 90th Division in World War I, and after 1918 served as commander of the United States occupation forces in Germany. But all his life he remembered with a special fondness the difficult days in the Alaskan wilderness.

After his dramatic rescue on the Yukon in 1974, Miles Martin worked on an army base for two years. When he had saved enough money, he ordered a houseboat from Larrabee's Marine in Delta Junction, on the Tanana 75 miles southeast of Fairbanks. In the spring of 1976, he quit his job and took his new houseboat down the Tanana, and then west on the Yukon about 450 river miles to Galena.

But Galena was close to an air force base, which for Miles spoiled the wilderness. So he took his houseboat back up the Yukon, up the Tanana, and up the Kantishna, to a remote area around Lake Minchumina. But that didn't work out either. Miles wanted to trap. As a boy growing up in Cleveland, he'd caught rats for bounty. Neighbors paid him 50 cents a rat, and he was good at it. Yet even in the wilderness, even here at the end of nowhere on Lake Minchumina, someone was always ahead of you. The five trappers on the lake had already laid claim to two hundred square miles. If he started trapping in their purview, Miles knew, he would have to go to war. The first time, they'd pull a gun and say, "Don't come around here again." The second time—well, the second time would be the last time.

Then Miles met an old-timer who told him about a trapline he'd stopped using, a hundred miles down the Kantishna. "Use my trapline," he said. This was on Hansen Lake, where the old-timer also had a cabin, long deserted. Miles went there and found a note under the coffee cup that said: "Stopped by to see you. Sorry I missed you. June 1952." That was the year of Miles's birth.

Miles squatted for three years on Hansen Lake, but felt the age-old squatter's insecurity. He didn't dare put in a vegetable garden or make improvements, since the land wasn't his, and the state could take it away. So when homesteads opened up a hundred miles downstream from the lake under a lottery system, Miles jumped at the chance. He was one of eighty winners.

The next step was to stake and blaze his five-acre homesite. Paying $5 for his staking packet, he paddled up a creek, portaged over a beaver dam, and staked out his acres deep in the forest, driving in corner posts painted red on top. Between the posts, he flagged tree branches with orange surveyor tape. Of the eighty winners, only four stayed. Most of them couldn't come up with the $250 survey deposit. The survivors had to contend with all the old frontier problems, from homesteaders moving each other's corners to Indians ripping up the posts.

Now Miles had five acres and a houseboat, and he built a cabin to "prove up" his claim. Some of the homesteaders didn't even bother to do that—they just walked into the land office with a snapshot of someone else's cabin.

Miles started trapping marten, an animal the size of a house cat with soft, dark, lustrous fur, which he then sold for about $50 a pelt. No one had found a way to raise them in the United States in captivity, though the Russians had done it.

The first winter, in 1976, Miles went out on snowshoes and set his traps haphazardly. He had open-jaw traps for foxes and wolves, whose fur he sold for parkas. For marten, his bread and butter, he put down pole traps. The pole trap was made with a notched pole stuck upright in the ground. You fitted the limb of a tree into the notch so that it leaned from the ground to about five feet in the air. At the base of the upright pole Miles rubbed some of his secret bait (a mix of boysenberry extract, marten bladder, moose brain, and baby oil). At the upper end of the limb, he nailed some fishbait, tucked on the underside so the birds couldn't see it. Lured to the trap, the marten climbed up the tree limb but, while heading for the fish, tripped the trap's steel jaw.

Miles found that on foot he could cover no more than twenty miles a day. He hoofed it for two winters, but in 1978 decided to get dogs. That changed his style of trapping, for with dogs you had to go on designated trails, and those trails had to be cut. Over the years, he extended his traplines to two hundred miles. When he bought the houseboat, he had wanted to remain nomadic, traveling the rivers where it pleased him, but now he had a commitment to the land. He registered the traplines and became a professional trapper.

When Miles bought his first six-dog team in 1978, he knew nothing about dogs. As a result, he acquired a collection of every type of undesirable canine—the "give-away" (worthless), the "shooter" (only worth shooting), the "biter" (that starts fights), and the "chewer" (that chews its harness). The only good dog was Thunder, sixteen years old, by which age most dogs have retired. Miles didn't know how to put harnesses on and was too embarrassed to ask. Thunder knocked the harness out of his hands to tell him he was putting it on wrong.

It took Miles years to get really good dogs, dogs that didn't fight or chew, with good feet, good lung capacity, long hair, and long legs. They had to weigh from forty to sixty pounds, and be capable of pulling twice their weight. Always on the lookout for the right kind of dog, Miles heard of a woman homesteader living alone who bred dogs and had one for sale. He went to see her and said, "I want a male, I've got an all-male team."

"That's interesting," she said, "I've got an all-female team."

"Why don't you want males?"

"Oh, they're always stopping to piss against trees. I can't make them go."

"Well, I can deal with that," said Miles. "It's only a male being a male. It's not that they need to piss—it's territorial. They want to leave their mark. Sometimes I stop and piss on the tree myself and that satisfies them."

"Why don't you want females?" the lady breeder asked.

"If one does something wrong," Miles replied, "and I want to smack her, she smiles and rolls over and looks cute. How can you hammer on a cute dog? Then she jumps up and does the same thing all over again!"

"Well," said the lady breeder, "it's just a female being a female. I can live with that."

When Thunder was seventeen, he didn't want to work anymore. He lay down and refused to get up, which communicated itself to the other dogs, so that the entire team went on a sit-down strike. There was only one thing Miles could do. He picked up his rifle and unhooked Thunder, who knew it was time and was not afraid. Loping out on the frozen lake toward a piece of driftwood, the dog stopped there and waited. He didn't try to run away. As Miles approached, Thunder looked all around the lake and then he looked at Miles. His eyes said, "This is as good a spot as any." And Miles said, "So this is the spot, is it?" and shot his old friend between the eyes.

Miles thought of dog handling as something like coaching a football team. He had to trade the players that didn't fit in, because his life depended on those dogs. One member of the team he had trouble with was Scorpion, a wolfhound and a fighter. Scorpion wanted to be the lead dog, and resented being the wheel dog next to the sled, that being the worst position.

So Scorpion tried to prove his leadership qualities by fighting with the leader, but Miles needed every dog and couldn't allow fights. Then on a trip to Lake Minchumina, Scorpion sat down, and the other dogs couldn't go on without him. It was a dangerous situation. Miles picked up a stick to whip him and Scorpion gave him a look that said, "Without that stick you're just shit."

Miles dropped the stick. The other dogs formed a circle around them. It was like the fight for leadership of a wolf pack. Scorpion jumped for his throat. Miles reached out his arms while the dog was in the air, and with the strength of anger held the dog by the throat with his thumbs on the animal's windpipe for a full five minutes, until he saw that Scorpion was weakening. Then he threw the renegade dog on the ground and strangled him until he was dead. "No dog is going to go for my throat and live," Miles shouted at the other dogs.

Dogs were a full-time job. You had to feed them, give them their shots, and break up fights. In the winter, it took Miles a week to run a hundred miles of traplines. It was 60 below, and the sun rose at 11:30 A.M. and set at 1:30 P.M. Miles didn't mind it because he liked extremes, all dark and then all light. That's what got the blood going. That was the way the world was meant to be.

In a good week, he'd collect a hundred pelts. In a bad week, entire sections were lost to snowdrifts; he couldn't get to the traps, and the animals rotted. He was also having problems with nesters who didn't understand the amount of land a trapper needs, and with other trappers horning in.

One young fellow came around who was catching mink for bikinis. "With one mink you can make five bikinis," he said. Whenever Miles found an unknown trapper on his trails, he'd ask him, "Are you lost?" And if he saw him a second time, he'd set a big-jawed trap for the poacher, or stretch a wire across the trail to snare the intruder's dog team. Those were warnings. At a last resort, he said, "Poachers just get buried out here. But that brings in the authorities."

Sometimes Miles got letters from people in the Lower Forty-eight, referred by the Department of Natural Resources, wanting homesteading advice. One fellow from California asked, "Can you tell me what church I'd be going to, and where the hospital is, and how much free land you can get?"

Miles replied: "If you want churches and hospitals, stay where you are. As for free land, the land is not free, you pay for it with your blood."

On August 16, 1896, gold was found in the Klondike River, a tributary of the Yukon, fifty miles east of the Alaskan border. Miners swarmed there to stake claims, and Dawson City popped up at the confluence of the two rivers. In the ensuing gold rush, during the last three years of the nineteenth century, 100,000 people left for Alaska. Those who couldn't get claims in the Klondike spread to other areas.

In December 1897, the prospector H. L. Blake came through Cheenik on his way to Nome, on the southern shore of the Seward Peninsula. Nels O. Hultberg, a missionary for the Swedish Mission of America, suggested that Blake take some of Hultberg's reindeer and proceed to Nome by sled. In 1891, the federal government had brought reindeer from Siberia to Alaska to provide meat for the natives, and the missions sometimes managed the herds. Hultberg joined Blake and the two men found samples of good ore.

In August 1898, they returned in a whaleboat and two canoes to Nome with four others. They arrived off Cape Nome on August 4 in the middle of a storm, and breakers threw the whaleboat onto a gravel bar in the middle of the Snake River. Soaked through, the six men crossed the tundra on foot and reached Anvil Creek. Blake washed out sand gravel and found color.

Hultberg said, "Let me try my luck." Grabbing a pan and a shovel, he went upstream and was gone for two hours. When he came back, Blake asked "Well, what luck?" "Dey is not any gold up dere," replied Hultberg. The two men then separated. A furious Blake later wrote that "this sly, crafty, avaricious, God-fearing, Eskimo-loving missionary fooled me. He got a boat at the mouth of the Snake, slipped off in the night, went directly to Golovin Bay [50 miles east of Nome], and located [filed claims on] the whole country."

Hultberg and his Swedish friends located ninety of the two thousand claims that were recorded by June 1899. As Hultberg had realized, Anvil Creek overflowed with gold, and a mining district was organized in Nome in October 1898. But after the miners had staked their claims, they realized that they could not prospect after the end of October, when the creeks froze.

Soon the word spread about a strike "richer than the Klondike." Before long, "stampeders" claimed the entire Nome Mining District. "From sea-beach to skyline the landscape was staked," wrote one observer. People kept coming, and just when all the claims had been filled they discovered gold on the beach. You could wash it out of the sand between high tide and low tide. There it was, not hidden in some mountain crevice, but glittering in plain sight for anyone who owned a bucket. And since no claim could be legally staked on land that the sea submerged at high tide, the right to pan on the beach was as free as the right to fish.

Ads for the shipping companies that transported suckers to Nome advertised that "gold clung to the ships' anchors when they were drawn up." The gold seekers arrived a thousand a day and lived in tents on the beach. Soon there was not even tent room, and the crowded stampeders contaminated the drinking wells. Instead of gold, they collected smallpox and typhoid. The pesthouses filled up, and the diseases spread to the Eskimo villages, wiping them out.

At one point, 30,000 hopefuls thronged the beach at Nome, most of them stranded and penniless. Revenue cutters took some of the worst cases back to the States. But many stayed, spreading to other parts of Alaska and finding other occupations. Thus, the gold rush was the main event in the settlement of the territory. By 1900, Alaska had a population of 63,592, double the 1890 count, and more than half of these inhabitants were settlers.

The population boost gave a stimulus to home rule. In 1904, private surveys were permitted and people could buy homesteads for $2 an acre— up to 160 acres for an individual. Two years later, Alaska elected a delegate to Congress. In 1908, the big money moved in, when J. P. Morgan and the Guggenheims formed what was called the Alaska Syndicate. This was the equivalent of Hawaii's Big Five, a cabal that stifled every enterprise it could not control. It bought gold and copper mines and built railroads from the mines to the harbors. There the cargo was loaded onto vessels of their steamship company. The syndicate moved into the salmon industry, and operated canneries on the river without any sort of regulation or taxation. As a result, the salmon population declined.

Alaskans wanted a territorial legislature, but the syndicate opposed it, fearing that such a body would levy taxes on their operations. The governor, Wilford B. Hoggatt (1906–10), a stooge for the syndicate, wrote Theodore Roosevelt in 1908 that "the conservative businessmen of Alaska, those men who are doing the most for the development of the country," feel "that the time is inopportune for this form of government," which was favored "by the saloon element."

In 1909, after succeeding Roosevelt, William Howard Taft visited the Alaska Exposition in Seattle, finding the display "most attractive." But Alaskans were stunned when Taft proposed that the territory be placed under the War Department's Bureau of Insular Affairs, which governed the Philippine Islands (where Taft had served as commissioner). So now, said the Alaskans, they were to be lumped with the Filipinos, and governed like an Asian protectorate.

In 1912, however, thanks largely to the efforts of the Alaska delegate to Congress, James Wickersham, Congress passed a second organic act, which finally gave Alaska a legislature. Eight senators and sixteen representatives, coming from a total of four electoral districts, sat on the smallest territorial legislature in the nation's history.

Though small, the legislature was feisty. In their first session in 1913, the lawmakers enfranchised women (a gesture that some regarded as an attempt to lure the fair sex to the frozen wastes). In its second session in 1915, the legislature enacted an old-age pension plan that predated the New Deal's Social Security by twenty years. It also entitled Alaskan indigents to a monthly pension of $12.50. Alaska was now a full-fledged territory, but still nearly half a century away from statehood.

•   •

By 1981, Miles Martin had lived in the Alaska backcountry for ten years. He had three homesteads on the Kantishna, in places where the landscape features hadn't even been named yet. The closest was fifty miles from the town of Nenana, where Miles went periodically to pick up his mail and supplies.

Homesteading was not fun, it was backbreaking labor, with a work day that started at six in the morning and ended at nine-thirty at night. Just to feed his dog team through the winter, Miles had to catch two thousand pounds of salmon, fishing for days and weeks before the freeze-up. Miles had seen the wannabes come and go, the ones who lasted a few days or a month. The one who brought his guitar, but no gun and no food. The one who couldn't tell a caribou from a moose. The one who flew in all his supplies, including cement for a fireplace, and lasted four days.

Sometimes, Miles asked himself, "What am I trying to prove?" And then he'd see the cotton grass by the pond, and the light catching the birch trees, and a bald eagle sitting on a driftwood pile under a double rainbow. But scenery wasn't enough. He liked having acquired wilderness skills, and seeing the results of his efforts, as in skinning and gutting his kill, or cutting a cord of wood. He liked living off the land, catching salmon in the summer, and hunting moose, caribou, and Dall sheep in the winter. He paid a price, in terms of discomfort and cabin fever, but he knew that if he lived in the city he'd end up committed, because he couldn't stand the overregulation: "Do you have a license?" "Oh, that won't meet the fire code." My God, they were drowning in red tape.

What Miles missed most was female companionship—but was there a woman who could stand the life? In Nenana, he met Jane Campbell, who asked to go on a dog-mushing trip. Jane, who with her high cheekbones and raven hair looked part Indian, was divorced from a biologist at the University of Fairbanks, and had two daughters. Their trip turned out to be a success—this was romance bushrat-style, where you had to prove your wilderness skills to win a woman's heart. Miles and Jane decided to live together in the backcountry with her kids.

Miles took another homestead on the Kantishna and built a cabin big enough for four, which he called "the estate." The nearest school was in Nenana, 120 miles away, but Alaska had a good home studies program. Once a month the teacher flew in to give the girls tests and teaching aids. Whatever they asked for, they got—globes, microscopes, battery-operated VCRs, cross-country skis. The girls were happy and didn't want to go back to town. They learned to run traplines and took up dogsledding.

But then their father asked for custody. He made the argument that living in the wilderness was a substandard existence that deprived his daughters of access to children their own age. The court appointed an arbitrator. Flying in to inspect their cabin, he asked what Miles thought of as "the usual stupid questions."

"Do you have running water?"

"Do the children have separate rooms?"

"Are any religious services available?"

The court decided on joint custody, a settlement Miles couldn't fault, because the girls did need to be with other kids.

The arrangement with Jane lasted four years. Oddly enough, when they split, it wasn't because Jane wanted more comfort and conveniences. On the contrary, she proved to be too much of an outdoors purist. Since Miles had a lot of wood to cut for the stove, he used a chain saw, but Jane insisted he cut the wood by hand. She wanted to live exactly as pioneers had lived in the eighteenth century, without electricity or appliances. She didn't even want a radio around. She protested against the use of money, and said they should strive for complete self-sufficiency.

Miles began to think, "Is this the way I want to live?" Arguments erupted over the children. One of the girls was having trouble with long division, and Miles said, "Forget it, you can live without it." But Jane upbraided him for his negative attitude and insisted that her daughter had to learn it. Miles felt she was too bossy. She was even telling him what harnesses to put on the dogs. Then one day she said they should tear down the cabin because it depreciated the value of the property and Miles wondered whether she expected them to live outdoors when it was 50 below. Enough was enough.

After they split, Miles put an ad in *Mother Earth:* "Homesteader-Trapper, has Houseboat, Seeks Female Partner." He got shopping bags full of mail and was spending so much money on stamps that he got picky—if he didn't like the perfume on the letter, he threw it out. But most of the women who said they were coming were no-shows. One who did turn up had lied about her age: she was a sixteen-year-old runaway from Georgia. "She lasted exactly three days," Miles recalled. "I gave her some money and said, 'Ellen, do what you want.' She went to Manley Hot Springs and married one of these hippie losers you get around here, the kind with tattoos and hair down to their shoulders."

When Seward bought Alaska in 1867, he envisioned a gradual and orderly advance to statehood. Instead, the government treated Alaska like a distant, slightly retarded relative, incapable of improvement and therefore unworthy of receiving federal benefits. When Congress passed the first Federal Highway Act, for example, Alaska was left out. James Wickersham, the delegate to Congress, concluded that only with statehood would Alaska obtain its rightful slice of the federal pie. In 1916, he introduced the first legislation to make Alaska a state, but it got nowhere.

In 1923, Warren Harding was the first president to visit Alaska, when he drove the golden spike for the Anchorage–Fairbanks railroad at the Tanana Bridge. After his visit, Harding announced a policy of conservation for the territory. We must "regard life in lovely, wonderful Alaska as an end and not a means," he said, and reject the policy of "looting Alaska and . . . turning Alaska over to the exploiters." He died a week later, but his words were prescient, for the Teapot Dome scandal broke out some time afterward. That affair involved the leasing, without competitive bidding, of government oil reserves in California and Wyoming to cronies of the secretary of the interior, Albert B. Fall. He was convicted of accepting bribes and served a year in prison.

Realizing that they could get no help from Washington, Alaskans sometimes took matters in their own hands. In 1938, when Japanese fishing vessels began to encroach on Alaskan waters, local fishermen went after them with rifles, thereby answering the question "Are Alaskan Salmon American Citizens?" in the affirmative.

In World War II, Alaska became a military base, which created a second population boost since some GIs decided to stay. Yet only in 1944 did the territorial legislature enact an income-tax bill, preparing the way to statehood. Indeed, in 1950 a statehood bill passed the House. But the Seattle-controlled salmon industry fought the bill, for the cannery operators feared the restrictions that a state government would impose, and it was defeated in the Senate.

One of the key opponents to Alaska statehood was Senator Hugh Butler of Nebraska, who had also stalled Hawaiian statehood. Butler derided statehood for a mere 108,000 Alaskans. In 1953, when the Nebraska senator held hearings on Alaska statehood, his committee heard 140 witnesses, of whom less than 20 were against it. But Butler still did not get the message and announced that "most of the clamor for statehood came from politicians who wanted to run for office."

Then came a defense construction boom when the air force spent $150 million to build the Distant Early Warning (DEW) radar system on the Arctic and Bering seacoasts. This infusion of cash into the Alaskan economy helped statehood advocates like Governor Ernest Gruening to press their case.

But President Eisenhower was against statehood. As a military man, he felt that in a defense emergency, Alaska could function more efficiently as a territory that could be placed under martial law, as Hawaii had been in 1941. As a Republican, he wanted to protect his narrow majority in the Senate from two Democratic senators from Alaska.

Once again, Alaskans seized the initiative and held a constitutional convention in 1955. The elected delegates met in Fairbanks in November and after seventy-five working days released a 14,400-word document. The convention also asked voters to approve the so-called Tennessee Plan. Tennessee had been granted statehood in 1796 after an elected delegation from that territory had gone to Washington to plead for admission.

Alaskan voters approved the constitution. They also endorsed the Tennessee Plan, presumptuously electing a congressional delegation of two senators (Governor Gruening and State Legislator William Egan) and one representative (State Legislator Ralph J. Rivers). But when the three men arrived in Washington in 1957, Congress refused to seat them. They were told that after statehood they would have to run again.

The turning point for Alaska came when Speaker of the House Sam Rayburn dropped his opposition. Everything fell into place after that. In June 1957, the House Interior and Insular Affairs Committee recommended admission. The statehood bill was passed by both the House and the Senate in 1958, and Ike signed it on January 3, 1959.

In the 1980s, Miles Martin began to feel the hot breath of government down his neck. In the spring of 1983 came the "Big Moose Bust." Miles was in his cabin fifty miles from the town of Nenana when a helicopter landed and three game wardens from the Alaska Department of Fish and Wildlife Protection jumped out. "It costs them seven hundred dollars an hour to operate the chopper," he recalled, "and when they come looking for you, you can bet they're not going to go home empty-handed."

They sniffed around and found some old moose bones, which they claimed as evidence. They confiscated Miles's diary, in which an entry for October said, "Got a moose."

Miles had in fact shot a moose out of season, and someone must have snitched on him for the reward, which could be as much as $1,000. As a subsistence person, he was entitled by law to kill a winter moose, but only in a "subsistence management area"—that is, government land, about a hundred river miles away, with no trail, which was not feasible.

Nor could he kill a moose during the legal season, twenty days in September, since the meat would spoil before winter. The rules seemed to be designed for affluent hunters with freezers, not for subsistence people who had to wait for winter. A single moose provided a thousand pounds of meat. Miles needed only one to see him through the winter, but he had to kill it late enough so that nature would freeze it.

The wardens gave Miles a citation to appear in court in Fairbanks in thirty days, which they knew he could not do, as the river was breaking up and he could not travel by boat and there was no road from his cabin. They told him that if he did not appear they would ask the judge for an arrest warrant. If he was found guilty, the fine would be $1,000, and he might lose his hunting and fishing privileges.

Fish and Wildlife was making this a test case. The agency's attitude was, "There's no such thing as subsistence, and we're going to prove it." They wanted to prove that people hunted and fished indiscriminately while claiming subsistence. But when his case came up, the judge dismissed it on a technicality.

Nonetheless, Miles felt like a misfit, as if he were living in the wrong century. He had come to Alaska to live an authentic frontier life, to be free of authority and rules, self-regulating and autonomous. All true frontiersmen, he believed, were antisocial types of some sort. "What they have in common is a desire to do for themselves and be left alone," he said. "They don't want either protection or interference from the government. 'I can take care of myself' is the watchword."

But Alaska was crippling the very lifestyle it promoted in brochures by harassing the subsistence people. Then Miles had to contend with the animal rights groups, who didn't want him to trap for fur, or to kill the wolves that destroyed the caribou he also counted on for food, or use dog teams to inspect his traplines. He was considered a villain because he used steel traps, which conjured up images of cruelty—animals with bloody paws struggling to free themselves from the metal teeth.

But to Miles, Fish and Wildlife were the villains. Miles needed two thousand pounds of salmon a year to feed his dogs. Fish and Wildlife tried to get a law passed that dogs could not be fed fresh salmon, which he felt was aimed at him personally. When that one didn't get by, they made rules that you could only catch certain types of salmon and had to throw the rest back. If he abided by that, he'd have to be inspecting his nets ten times a day.

So Fish and Wildlife went after him, seizing his nets and charging him with selling salmon roe. By now, Miles had five homesteads on the Kantishna and he moved from place to place during the fishing season, painting his fish floats black so they couldn't be seen from the air.

"I felt like a peasant during the Vietnam War," he said. "Why mess with someone like me, who's barely making ends meet? We have no clout, no money, no influence, and they are trying to shut us down. We're less well off than the Indians, who can work with ivory, but we can't." Miles by then had started making jewelry and carvings during the long winter months, using animal bones and teeth, gold and silver, and semiprecious stones. He sold his wares to gift stores and art galleries in Fairbanks.

Some of his homesteader friends, also harassed by Fish and Wildlife, had given up, moved to Fairbanks, and gone on welfare. "Can you imagine that?" Miles asked. "To be a homesteader on welfare? That's a contradiction in terms."

In his cash-starved subsistence life, feeding the dogs was the main problem. If he didn't feed them salmon, it would cost him $2,000 a year in commercial dog food, plus hauling. The alternative was a snowmobile. "Dogs are slower but they always make it," Miles said. "The snowmobile breaks down, or sometimes the gas is doctored, but you can't beat a dog team."

In the summer of 1992, Miles celebrated his twentieth anniversary in the wilderness. He was still hanging on, raising barely enough cash with his furs and his jewelry. There were days when he thought he owned the blue sky, the warm day, the ducks and geese. There were other days when he cursed the invasion of his domain on the Kantishna by people building vacation homes. Most of them had private planes, and they had the right to hunt and fish from the air. It seemed to Miles that the vacation-home people could do pretty much as they pleased, while he was constantly tormented by Fish and Wildlife.

So much so that he now had a lawyer in Nenana, Marc Grober, a bushy-haired, potbellied, slightly hyper refugee from New York. Miles paid his attorney a visit that August. Grober agreed that the laws had become so intrusive that "they're turning homesteaders into criminals. If you scratch your ass while you're cutting strips, you're breaking the law. They tell you the mesh size of your net, they tell you that your cutting table must be made of stainless steel, they tell you to cut the dorsal fin closest to the tail and send it in so they know how many fish you're catching —I don't know a single subsistence fisherman who obeys those laws." Grober advised Miles to put a float line across the river with no net. That way the wardens would spend money foolishly and perhaps give up further inspections.

Miles walked down Nenana's main street to the saloon, the Corner Bar, where he had a beer with Morris, an old-timer who had come to Nenana in 1916 as a boy. Morris recalled that in those days on the Tanana you'd see catches of fish lying along little wooden platforms perched on stilts, next to stacks of cordwood, rows of doghouses, and fishwheels revolving lazily with the current.

Then in 1916, Morris reminisced, Nenana became a base for railroad construction, the point where the trains connected with the Yukon steamers. "At that time," Morris said, "Nenana had a population of 18,000 and a whorehouse with seventy-five girls. I used to bring them baskets of berries and they'd say, 'Here comes that nice berries boy.' "

Morris was a homesteader, and rarely left the wilderness. Recently, though, he'd been to visit his brother in Seattle, and in the big city he'd gotten mugged. He woke up in the hospital with his ribs broken and a finger almost torn off where they'd tried to get his ring. "I sure was glad to get back here where it's safe," he said.

After the Corner Bar, Miles, who doesn't drive, hitched a ride to Fairbanks, where he had an appointment with Keith Schultz, an official from the state Department of Fish and Game in charge of commercial fishing in the interior. Miles wanted Schultz to clarify his position on the Kantishna.

"No more gill nets on the river," said Schultz, an amiable, light-haired outdoorsman of the "I'm-just-doing-my-job" variety. "Gill nets are banned on the entire river." A gill net is like a volleyball net, with a lead line to hold the bottom down and a float line to keep the top up—the fish are caught in large numbers because they can't get through the mesh.

"Yeah," Miles said, "but Fish and Game themselves use gill nets to catch and release fish . . ."

"They used to, but . . ."

"If I'm forced to use a fish wheel and I don't have a spot where the wheel can go . . ."

"You can go to the Tanana and fish."

"That's eighty miles away. That's like asking you to commute to work eighty miles every day. It costs me twenty-five dollars an hour to run my boat."

"Build a fish wheel."

"I'll need two hundred dollars to build a wheel when I'm already set up to fish with nets."

"There aren't that many fish anyway."

"There used to be so many fish I could walk across the river over them," Miles said. "That was only three years ago. I could take a gig in the dark and stick it in the river and come up with a fish."

"Well, the board decided to stop fishing on the Kantishna to protect the chum [a type of salmon]," Schultz said.

"When's it coming up again?" Miles asked.

"In 1996. You can attend the meeting."

"Sure. The last meeting was in Bethel, five hundred miles away. You think I'm going to fly down there in the middle of trapping season to talk to a board made up of commercial fishermen about the problem of a subsistence fisherman?"

"It won't be in Bethel."

"Their real interest is to protect fishing on the lower river, and shut down fishing in the interior. If that's your goal say so."

"Every five years the fish return," Schultz said.

"I can't feed my dogs every five years."

Miles was getting testy, and both men felt there was nothing more to be said. The bushrat walked out of Schultz's office shaking his head and asking himself, "How can I live the way I do and stay legal?"

In the summer of 1993, Miles's surveyor friend, Rick Gray, offered him a job at $130 a day, plus food and lodging (in a tent). The client, a professor at the University of Fairbanks, had a forty-acre homestead a few miles outside town. His ten-year proving-up time was almost up, and if the survey wasn't done within two months, the parcel would be returned to the state.

Miles and Rick were hoping to run a three-wheeler to the homestead to bring supplies in, but a creek had washed out the log bridge (due to record snows that winter), and trees were down all across the trail.

Instead, they hauled their gear and supplies in on foot, after putting in a full ten-hour day. As they trudged by with heavy packs, the client told them he had named his parcel Dreamland, to which they nodded and smiled. "This is a very pleasant stroll," the client said. "I wish there was more for me to carry so I could make another trip. I really love this land and its diverse vegetation."

Carrying his packload, Miles was completely worn out. All day long, it was up hills and down valleys and through swamps, cutting five miles of trail a day, running the chain saw for ten hours and cutting a straight line through the "diverse vegetation." Mosquitoes were chewing through the sweat that ran down his brow.

Miles was getting up at 6 A.M. and staggering back to camp at 9 P.M. When he told the client he'd never driven a car in his life and never owned a driver's license—that he only ran dogs or his boat or his snowmobile—

the client exclaimed: "I want to shake your hand. I truly admire you, you're truly close to the land." Miles thought he was going to be sick.

When they were done surveying, it was just another job. This one would be remembered as the "diverse vegetation" client. The one before had been the "our friends the squirrels" client. And the one before that was the "tree hugger."

Their job completed, Miles and Rick went into Fairbanks to socialize a bit. Just as people unused to the wilderness had to adjust to the claustrophobic feeling that comes with winter darkness, whenever Miles came to Fairbanks he had to adjust to the commercialization of the frontier. In Fairbanks, there was a Sourdough Fuel, a Glacier Cinema, and radio station K-WOLF. On the tube, a bearded prospector looked up from his panning and said, "Alaska has always appealed to independents, and Frontier Credit of Fairbanks wants to preserve that spirit." The frontier spirit had become a marketable commodity while the government was threatening the die-hards still trying to live the frontier life.

Having been a homesteader for twenty-one years, Miles had the old-timer's gripe that newcomers were coming in and spoiling things. Too many of them came from the Lower Forty-eight to pick up a fast buck. Miles now saw homesteaders who swapped wives and injected heroin. When they needed money, they turned in a neighbor for shooting moose out of season, even though they did it too. All too often, Miles heard, "I'll give it a couple of years and see how it works out."

In need of a new rifle, Miles stopped by Caribou Loans, the pawnshop where he buys his guns. He was chatting with the bearded owner and his rather massive wife when a raffish fellow sauntered in wearing a porkpie hat and a red T-shirt that said I'VE CALLED IN SICK SO OFTEN I'M GOING TO HAVE TO CALL IN DEAD.

The man went up to the counter and told the owner, "Times are gettin' tough and I have to ransom my baby again." He plunked a hunting rifle with a scope down on the counter.

"How much do you need?" asked the beady-eyed Madam Caribou.

"I need two thousand dollars," the man said, "but last time you gave me a hundred twenty-five."

"Will a hundred twenty-five do it for you?" Madam Caribou asked. "With the interest you'll owe a hundred eighty dollars."

"Okay," the man said, "and I hope this time it don't take so long."

Miles wondered how much longer he could last, how many years of hard outdoor work he had left in him. Maybe ten? At forty-two, his hair was turning gray, his teeth were falling out, his eyes were going, and he no longer felt the old excitement about being out in the weather. What, he wondered, would give out next—mind, heart, liver?

Fish and Wildlife was squeezing him, but what else could he do? He had no pension, no insurance, no health plan. To raise a little cash, he peddled his jewelry and carvings. From this seemingly innocuous sideline came the blow that almost sent Miles over the edge. In November 1993, while he was at one of his homesteads, frozen in for the winter and working on his traplines, he heard there was a warrant out for his arrest in Raleigh, North Carolina.

A couple of years before, he had met a woman at a fair in Fairbanks who bought some of his bear claws decorated with inlaid metal strips. She said she was going to travel through the Lower Forty-eight in her mobile home selling them, and wanted to become known as "the claw lady."

Miles kept supplying her by mail, but one day the woman wrote him that she had set up a table with his bear claws at a bazaar in Raleigh, and a Fish and Wildlife agent made a buy and busted her for the illegal sale of bear parts. She had to pay a $750 fine.

Soon after that, Miles received an inquiry from a gift company asking for "bear parts." When he saw that the return address was Raleigh, he thought, "Damn, that's where Joy's in trouble." He replied that he was phasing out bear parts, which came from bears he killed in self-defense.

Then came an order from the court in Raleigh to pay a $750 fine or show up to answer charges. By then, he was in his winter quarters, and by the time he saw the order the date to pay had long passed. The Raleigh court issued a warrant for his arrest and asked for his extradition.

Miles was broke, and his lawyer told him, "You're going up against the feds—you could get sent to North Carolina in handcuffs." He was appointed a public defender, Rich Curtner, who discovered that Miles was now charged with violating a federal law for "using the mail to transport an illegal substance." The offense carried a maximum sentence of ten years in jail and a $100,000 fine.

At a hearing in Fairbanks in December 1993, the judge ruled that North Carolina would not have issued a warrant without "probable cause," in effect granting extradition, and set January 28 as the day Miles had to appear in court in Raleigh. The court supplied him with a one-way ticket.

While the public defender tried to make a deal, Miles went back to his cabin, convinced that his case was being used to crack down on subsistence people. He was getting a little paranoid. He felt like "the mad trapper of Rat River waiting for the SWAT team." No way was he going to North Carolina, where, as he'd heard it, they put you on the chain-gang for jaywalking—he'd shoot it out first, or kill himself.

On January 21, a week from the due date, the deal came down, approved by the Fairbanks judge and the Raleigh court: a $500 fine, with six months to pay. Miles had to pledge to never again sell bear claws.

Though relieved, he asked himself: "So this is law and order, dragging me in and out of court? All I want is to be an old-time trapper, with a log cabin and a canoe, a hundred miles from the nearest road and my old snowshoes hanging on the wall, getting my mail once a month, but they won't let me. What am I supposed to do? Join organizations, go to meetings, write proposals, get a phone and a fax machine?"

"First came the frontiersman," he thought, "first on the land, breaking the way. Then came the settlers, with their wives-and children. Last came the government, the big, slow-moving beast. But once in motion, watch out; the big head slowly lifts its eyes and blinks, and the frontiersman goes 'Oh, damn,' while the settler goes, 'Well, maybe.' "

Finally, the land was organized and the cities were built and antagonism built up toward the original frontiersman—who dresses funny, smells funny, acts funny. There was no more pride in what the frontiersman had done. Now he was a nuisance, and soon he'd be a memory. My, but those times must have been something, huh?

APPENDIX:
THE STATE-MAKING PROCESS

The original thirteen states were colonies of Great Britain who, after winning their war of independence, entered the state-making process and became states upon ratifying the Constitution, drafted in 1787 and adopted in 1788 after ratification by nine of the thirteen. The ratification of all thirteen states took more than two years.

STATE	YEAR MADE A TERRITORY	DATE OF STATEHOOD	TIME AS TERRITORY	REMARKS
Delaware		Dec. 7, 1787		1st to ratify.
Pennsylvania		Dec. 12, 1787		2nd to ratify.
New Jersey		Dec. 18, 1787		3rd to ratify.
Georgia		Jan. 2, 1788		4th to ratify.
Connecticut		Jan. 9, 1788		5th to ratify.
Massachusetts		Feb. 6, 1788		6th to ratify.
Maryland		Apr. 28, 1788		7th to ratify.
South Carolina		May 23, 1788		8th to ratify.
New Hampshire		June 21, 1788		9th to ratify, putting over the Constitution.
Virginia		June 25, 1788		10th to ratify.
New York		July 26, 1788		11th to ratify.
North Carolina		Nov. 21, 1789		12th to ratify.
Rhode Island		May 29, 1790		13th and last to ratify.
Vermont		Mar. 4, 1791		Vermont was never a territory and was made the 14th state after having been a republic since 1781.
Kentucky		June 1, 1791		Kentucky, the 15th state and the first trans-Appalachian state, was detached from Virginia and was never a territory.

Tennessee	1789	June 1, 1796	7 years	Tennessee, the 16th state and the first territory to attain statehood, was ceded by North Carolina to the Union and organized as the "Territory South of the River Ohio," known as Southwest Territory.
Ohio	Ohio was a part of the Northwest Territory, established in 1787 under the Northwest Ordinance. In 1800, it was divided into Ohio and Indiana territories.	Mar. 1, 1803	15 years	Ohio was the 17th state, and the first to be carved out of the Northwest Territory, won by conquest from the British.
Louisiana	Became Orleans Territory in 1804.	Apr. 30, 1812	8 years	Louisiana was the first state to be formed from the Louisiana Purchase of 1803, and the 18th state.
Indiana	1800	Dec. 11, 1816	16 years	19th state.
Mississippi	1798	Dec. 10, 1817	19 years	20th state.
Illinois	Lopped off from Indiana Territory in 1809.	Dec. 3, 1818	9 years	21st state, with a population of 46,620. One of three states that did not meet the population requirement of 60,000.
Alabama	Removed from Mississippi Territory in 1817 when	Dec. 14, 1819	2 years	22nd state.

	Mississippi became a state.			
Maine	No territorial period, ceded by Massachusetts.	Mar. 15, 1820		23rd state.
Missouri	Formed from Louisiana Territory in 1812, when Orleans Territory became the state of Louisiana.	Aug. 10, 1821	9 years	Missouri became the 24th state as the result of the Missouri Compromise on slavery.
Arkansas	Formed from Missouri Territory in 1819.	June 15, 1836	17 years	25th state.
Michigan	Lopped off from Indiana Territory in 1805.	Jan. 26, 1837	32 years	Michigan was the 26th state, paired with Arkansas under the Missouri Compromise.
Florida	Ceded by Spain in 1821, Florida was under military rule until 1822, when it was made a territory.	March 3, 1845	24 years	Florida, the 27th state, was paired with Iowa under the Missouri Compromise.
Texas	An independent republic from 1836 to 1845, Texas was annexed as a state by joint resolution of Congress.	Dec. 29, 1845	Texas bypassed the territorial stage.	28th state.
Iowa	1838	Dec. 28, 1846	8 years	29th state.
Wisconsin	1836	May 29, 1848	12 years	30th state.

California	Ceded by Mexico in 1848, California became a state two years later without having been a territory.	Sept. 9, 1850		31st state, under military rule from 1848 to 1850.
Minnesota	1849	May 11, 1858	9 years	32nd state.
Oregon	1848	Feb. 14, 1859	11 years	33rd state, with a population of 48,460. The second state that did not meet the population requirement of 60,000.
Kansas	Kansas became a territory in 1854 under the Kansas-Nebraska Act.	Jan. 29, 1861	7 years	34th state.
West Virginia	West Virginia seceded from Virginia during the Civil War and went directly to statehood.	June 20, 1863		35th state.
Nevada	1861	Oct. 31, 1864	3 years	With a population of 21,140, Nevada was the third state under the 60,000 minimum. It was made the 36th state after only three years because the Union needed the revenues from its gold and silver mines.
Nebraska	1854	Mar. 1, 1867	13 years	37th state.
Colorado	1861	Aug. 1, 1876	15 years	Centennial state, 38th.

North Dakota	Spun off, with South Dakota, from Minnesota in 1858, when Minnesota became a state.	Nov. 2, 1889	31 years	39th state.
South Dakota	1858	Nov. 2, 1889	31 years	40th state.
Montana	1864	Nov. 8, 1889	25 years	41st state.
Washington	Spun off from Oregon Territory in 1853.	Nov. 11, 1889	36 years	42nd state. The Dakotas, Montana, and Washington were all four made states as part of the Omnibus Bill of 1889.
Idaho	Idaho Territory, created in 1863, at first included Montana and Wyoming, which were spun off.	July 3, 1890	27 years	43rd state.
Wyoming	Created in 1868, Wyoming Territory was taken from pieces of North Dakota, Idaho, and Utah.	July 10, 1890	22 years	44th state.
Utah	Utah Territory was created as part of the Compromise of 1850.	Jan. 4, 1896	46 years	Utah's long wait before it became the 45th state had to do with polygamy, which the Mormons had to forswear.
Oklahoma	In 1890, the western half of Oklahoma	Nov. 16, 1907	17 years	46th state.

	became a territory, while the eastern half remained Indian Territory.			
New Mexico	Ceded by Spain in 1848, New Mexico was under military rule until becoming a territory in 1850.	Jan. 6, 1912	62 years	47th state. New Mexico holds the record for time spent as a territory, due largely to objections over its Hispanic population.
Arizona	Arizona Territory was spun off from New Mexico in 1863.	Feb. 14, 1912	49 years	48th state.
Alaska	Alaska went through several territorial stages but did not achieve full territorial status until 1912.	Jan. 3, 1959	47 years	49th state.
Hawaii	1900	Aug. 21, 1959	59 years	50th state.

NOTES

INTRODUCTION

On the territorial system: Earl Pomeroy, *The Territories and the United States* (London, 1947); J. E. Eblen, *The First and Second United States Empires* (Pittsburgh, 1968).

ONE: THE MISSOURI FRONTIER

On Stoddard and Delassus: F. L. Billon, *Annals of St. Louis* (St. Louis, 1886).

"to demand and receive": Ibid.

averse to the cession: C. E. Carter, ed., *The Territorial Papers of the United States* (Washington, D.C., 1934), vol. 13 (hereafter, *TP*).

"thirst for money": Ibid.

"the Hudson, the Delaware": Ibid., vol. 9.

On the Louisiana Purchase: Dumas Malone, *Jefferson the President* (Boston, 1970): *TP*, vol. 9.

Livingston's negotiations: Livingston Papers, New-York Historical Society.

"We are to give money": Malone, *Jefferson.*

"for the purpose of": *TP*, vol. 9.

On Lewis and Clark: Malone, *Jefferson;* David Lavender, *The Way to the Western Sea* (New York, 1988).

On the expedition: Gary E. Moulton, ed., *The Journals of the Lewis and Clark Expedition*, 3 vols. (Lincoln, Nebr., 1987); Donald Jackson, *Among the Sleeping Giants* (Urbana, Ill., 1987).

Lewis and Clark and tribal politics: J. P. Ronda, *Lewis and Clark Among the Indians* (Lincoln, Nebr., 1984).

Osages to Washington: Ronda, *Lewis and Clark.*

Osages in Congress and performing dances: Charles William Janson, *The Stranger in America* (London, 1807).

Lewis and Clark among the Arikaras and Mandans: Ronda, *Lewis and Clark;* Moulton, *Journals.*

Eagle's Feather in Washington: Ronda, *Lewis and Clark.*

"Man must die": Ibid.

"what is more especially to be regretted": *TP*, vol. 5.

On Georges Drouillard: M. O. Skarsten, *Georges Drouillard* (Glendale, Calif., 1964).

On Manuel Lisa: R. E. Oglesby, *Manuel Lisa and the Opening of the Missouri Fur Trade* (Norman, Okla., 1963).

On Sergeant Nathaniel Pryor and Big White: Oglesby, *Manuel Lisa.*

Big White sent home: Thomas James, *Three Years Among the Indians and Mexicans* (Lincoln, Nebr., 1984).

On decline and suicide of Lewis: Donald Jackson, ed., *Lewis and Clark Papers* (Urbana, Illinois, 1978).

"while he lived with me": Malone, *Jefferson.*

On Wilson Price Hunt: Nancy M. Peterson, *People of the Troubled Water* (Frederick, Colo., 1988).

On John Bradbury: John Bradbury, *Travels in the Interior of America* (Lincoln,

Nebr., 1986); Susan Delano McKelvey, *Botanical Exploration of the Trans-Mississippi West, 1790–1850* (Cambridge, Mass., 1955). .

On Henry Brackenridge: R. G. Thwaites, ed., *Early Western Travels*, vol. 6 (New York, 1910).

"unruly hands to manage": Ibid.

"That species": Bradbury, *Travels*.

On the 1812 Lisa expedition: Stella M. Drum, ed., *Journal of John C. Luttig* (Missouri Historical Society, n.d.).

"I go a great distance": Oglesby, *Manuel Lisa*.

TWO: THE MISSISSIPPI FRONTIER

On Orleans Territory: *TP*, vol. 9.

On Claiborne: Ibid.; Malone, *Jefferson*.

"The government of a city": Gallatin Papers, New-York Historical Society.

"had scarcely a nerve": *TP*, vol. 9.

to be "disgraced": Ibid.

"uninformed, indolent": Ibid.

On the trouble with the French: Ibid.

"Favoritism is like fire": Ibid.

Claiborne's problems: Ibid.

"they begin to view": Ibid.

"Scarcely a week": Ibid.

"You Americans": Ibid.

"The time will come": Ibid.

On Andrew Ellicott: Catharine Mathews, *Andrew Ellicott, His Life and Letters* (New York, 1908); Andrew Ellicott, *Journal* (Philadelphia, 1814).

Ellicott down the Mississippi: Ellicott, *Journal*.

"the flag wore out": *TP*, vol. 5.

On Spanish arguments: Ibid.

"fix their attachment": Ibid.

"a federal governor": Ibid.

"We met and saluted": Mathews, *Ellicott*.

"Dey is jes as sly": *Mississippi Historical Publications*, vol. 8.

On Gideon Lincemum: Ibid.

When Mobile was Spanish: R. Reid Badger and L. A. Clayton, eds., *Alabama and the Borderlands* (Mobile, 1960).

On George Strother Gaines: Joel Campbell DuBose, *Sketches of Alabama History* (Philadelphia, 1901).

On Hughes and Mitchell: *TP*, vol. 18.

"I have the mortification": *TP*, vol. 18.

THREE: THE FLORIDA FRONTIER

"Florida, sir . . .": *TP*, vol. 23.

"I have full confidence": Ibid.

"the stranger was accosted": Ibid.

"some dissatisfaction": Ibid.

Treaty of Moultrie Creek: Ibid.

On fugitive slaves: Ibid., vol. 22.

On plantation life: *Florida Historical Quarterly*, October 1927.

"Nineteen-twentieths": *TP*, vol. 23.

On Abraham: *Florida Historical Quarterly*, July 1946.

"Let alone the mad water": *TP*, vol. 23.

"Here our navel strings": Ibid.
"these people have been": Ibid.
On Gad Humphreys: Ibid.
On Indian policy: F. P. Prucha, *The Indians in American Society* (Berkeley, 1985).
On Indian removal under Jackson: Grant Foreman, *Indian Removal* (Norman, Okla., 1932).
"shall receive two hundred dollars": *TP*, vol. 23.
On John Phagan: Ibid.
"You say our people": Ibid.
"We have a perfect": *Florida Historical Quarterly*, July 1946.
"of the vouchers": *TP*, vol. 23.
"If you asked for": Ibid.
On Seminole war: M. M. Cohen, *Notice of Florida* (Gainesville, 1964); A. E. Francke, Jr., *Fort Mellon* (Miami, 1977); *Army and Navy Chronicle* (Washington, D.C., 1836); John K. Mahon, *History of the Second Seminole War* (Gainesville, 1967).
On Thompson and Carter: *TP*, vol. 25.
On Tennessee volunteers: *Tennessee Historical Quarterly*, December 1942.
On White and Jackson: *TP*, vol. 25.
"At the Cypress": *Florida Historical Quarterly*, July 1946.
"Alligator is a most": *Army and Navy Chronicle*.
"Put us even down upon the capes": *Florida Historical Quarterly*, October 1927.
"I can have no agency": *TP*, vol. 25.
"I shall send out": Ibid.
On the bloodhounds: Ibid.
"Oh my dear wife": Ibid.
"be confined to tracking": Ibid.
"The emigrants went off": Ibid.
"a few Indians": Ibid.
On Hezekiah Thistle: Ibid., vol. 26.

FOUR: THE INDIANA–ILLINOIS FRONTIER

On the Knox County petition: *TP*, vol. 6.
On Fort Wayne: Charles Poinsatte, *Outpost in the Wilderness: Fort Wayne, 1706–1828* (Fort Wayne Historical Society, 1976).
On Oliver and Howard Johnson: *Indiana Historical Society Publications*, vol. 7.
On the couple near Lafayette: William M. Cockrum, *Pioneer History of Indiana* (Oakland City, Ind., 1907).
On Oliver Smith: O. H. Smith, *Early Indiana Trials and Sketches* (Cincinnati, 1858).
On courtroom behavior: Usher F. Linder, *Reminiscences of the Early Bar and Bench of Illinois* (Chicago, 1879).
On the mountaineer and his wife: A. C. Bogges, *The Settlement of Illinois* (Chicago, 1908).
"Such is the terror": *TP*, vol. 8.
"The tickets for the whole": Ibid.
On the military tract: T. L. Carlson, *The Illinois Military Tract* (Urbana, Ill., 1951).
On the Burlands: Rebecca Burland, *A True Picture of Emigration* (Chicago, 1936).
On Free Frank: Juliet E. K. Walker, *Free Frank* (Lexington, Ky., 1983).

FIVE: THE ARKANSAS FRONTIER

"Many of the southern": *Letters of William Plumer Jr.* (Missouri Historical Society, 1926).

On Missouri Compromise: Glover Moore, *The Missouri Controversy* (Lexington, Ky., 1953).

On John Benedict: *Arkansas Historical Quarterly*, Summer 1951.

"I am here among": *TP*, vol. 19.

"You are going contrary": Ibid.

Lovely's Purchase invaded: Grant Foreman, *Indians and Pioneers* (Norman, Okla., 1936).

"It should be remembered": *TP*, vol. 19.

On George Featherstonhaugh: George Featherstonhaugh, *Excursion Through the Slave States* (London, 1844).

On Choctaw removal: Foreman, *Indian Removal*.

"The rain came down": Grant Foreman, *Pioneer Days in the Early Southwest* (Cleveland, 1926).

"There on his own floor": Foreman, *Pioneer Days*.

Des Arc: *Arkansas Historical Quarterly*, Winter 1952.

SIX: THE MICHIGAN FRONTIER

"If the Indian": *TP*, vol. 10.

On Lewis Cass: Frank B. Woodford, *Lewis Cass* (New Brunswick, N.J., 1950).

"The British medals": *TP*, vol. 10.

"for a large portion": Ibid.

"It is with the utmost": Ibid.

On Puthuff: *Pioneer and Historical Collections*, vol. 16 (Lansing, Michigan, 1890).

"How Major Puthuff": *TP*, vol. 10.

"his plea": Ibid.

"foreigners who are odious": Ibid.

On Matthew White: *Pioneer Collections*, vol. 14.

On Dr. Madison: Ibid., vol. 1.

On George Moran: Ibid., vol. 5.

On the slave catcher: *TP*, vol. 11.

On Saginaw: *Pioneer Collections*, vol. 3.

On Jesse Turner: Ibid., vol. 6.

On Henry Raymond: Ibid., vol. 10.

On James Lawrence: *Pioneer Collections*, vol. 18.

On Michigan statehood: Henry M. Utley, *Michigan* (New York, 1906).

On Van Buren: *Pioneer Collections*, vol. 14.

On Oceana County: *Pioneer Collections*, vol. 10.

SEVEN: THE WISCONSIN FRONTIER

On Charles Réaume: *Wisconsin Historical Collections*, vol. 19.

"I'll make . . . de man": Ibid., vol. 2.

"But I don't understand": Ibid.

On Colonel Talbot Chambers: Ibid., vol. 19.

On Ebenezer Childs: Ibid., vol. 4.

On Fort Winnebago: Ibid., vol. 6.

On Alexis Clermont: Ibid., vol. 15.

On Major Green's talk: *TP*, vol. 27.

On Charles Cole: *Wisconsin Historical Collections*, vol. 6.

On Judge William C. Frazier: Ibid., vol. 7.

On Elijah Keyes: Ibid., vol. 11.

On lead mines: Joseph Schafer, *The Wisconsin Lead Region* (Madison, Wis., 1932).

"I verily believe": *TP*, vol. 7.

On Moses Meeker: *Wisconsin Historical Collections*, vol. 6.
On Theodore Rolfe: Schafer, *Wisconsin Lead Region*.
On statehood: *TP*, vol. 27.

EIGHT: THE IOWA FRONTIER

On the Burlington couple: *Annals of Iowa*, 1868.
On the Davenport treaty: Ibid., 1865.
On the Dubuque trial: Ibid., 1870.
On the frontier wedding: Ibid., 1872.
On the Iowa land rush: R. P. Swiereng, *Pioneers and Profits* (Ames, Iowa, 1968).
On Wapello County: Harrison L. Waterman, *History of Wapello County* (Chicago, 1914).
On R. B. Groff: *Annals of Iowa*, 1870.
On the Constitutional Convention: B. J. Shambaugh, *History of Iowa* (Iowa City, 1897).
On James Lyon: T. H. Macbride, *In Cabins and Sod-Houses* (Iowa City, 1928).

NINE: THE OREGON FRONTIER

On the Oregon question: *Oregon Pioneer Transactions*, vol. 1.
On John McLoughlin: Charles Henry Carey, *Oregon* (Chicago, 1922).
On William H. Ashley: LeRoy R. Hafen, editor, *Mountain Men and Fur Traders of the Far West* (Lincoln, Nebr., 1982).
On Jedediah Smith: Hafen, *Mountain Men*.
On James Clyman: Charles L. Camp, "James Clyman, American Frontiersman," *California Historical Society Quarterly*, *1925–1927*.
"To rendezvous for all our parties": Dale L. Morgan, ed., *The West of William H. Ashley* (Denver, 1964).
On the rendezvous: Fred R. Gowans, *Rocky Mountain Rendezvous* (Layton, Utah, 1985).
"sky a copper": Gowans, *Rendezvous*.
On Joe Meek: Harvey E. Tobie, *No Man Like Joe* (Portland, Oreg., 1949).
On Jim Bridger: Hafen, *Mountain Men*.
On Dr. Marcus Whitman: C. M. Drury, *Marcus Whitman* (Caldwell, Idaho, 1937).
"Come, we are done": Tobie, *No Man*.
On Peter Skene Ogden: *Peter Skene Ogden's Snake Country Journals* (London, 1971).
"Shoot her, Shoot her!": Ibid.
On the move to Oregon: Dale Morgan, ed., *Overland in 1846* (Georgetown, Calif., 1963).
On Elijah White: Carey, *Oregon*; *Oregon Pioneer Association Transactions*, vol. 1.
On Peter Burnett: *Oregon Historical Quarterly*, vols. 5, 6.
On John Minto: Ibid., vols. 1, 2, 5, 6.
On Manifest Destiny: Frederick Merk, *Manifest Destiny and Mission in American History* (New York, 1963).
On Francis Parkman: Francis Parkman, *The Oregon Trail* (Madison, Wis., 1969); Wilbur R. Jacobs, ed., *Letters of Francis Parkman* (Norman, Okla., 1960).
On Heinrich Lienhard: Heinrich Lienhard, *From St. Louis to Fort Sutter* (Norman, Okla., 1961).
On Benton and Oregon Territory: W. M. Meigs, *Thomas Hart Benton* (Philadelphia, 1904).
On Benton and Butler: Ibid.
On Oregon and gold: *Oregon Historical Quarterly*, vols. 5, 6.

"Come out and see": Morgan, *Overland*.
On Oregon statehood: Carey, *Oregon*.

TEN: THE CALIFORNIA FRONTIER

On the Spanish occupation and the friars: Ramón A. Gutiérrez, *When Jesus Came, the Corn Mothers Went Away* (Stanford, Calif., 1991).
The missions: Richard Henry Dana, *Two Years Before the Mast* (New York, 1840).
"The Californians": Dana, *Two Years*.
On John Augustus Sutter: H. H. Bancroft interview, Bancroft Library, Berkeley, Calif.; Henrich Lienhard, *A Pioneer at Sutter's Fort 1846–1850* (Berkeley, 1941).
"I noticed": Bancroft interview.
"I was everything": Ibid.
"My God, how can you manage?": Ibid.
On Captain John C. Frémont: Allan Nevins, *Frémont* (New York, 1955).
"I have heard of you": Bancroft interview.
"No one else": Ibid.
"Revolutions are matters": Dana, *Two Years*.
"What will the settlers": Bancroft interview.
On war in California: George Sanderlin, *The Settlement of California* (New York, 1972).
"You do not know": Ibid.
On Sutter and Lienhard: Lienhard, *A Pioneer*.
"I want two bowls": Bancroft interview.
"We have some gold": Ibid.
On Sutter and the discovery of gold: J. P. Zollinger, *Sutter* (New York, 1939).
On Sutter and stealing: Bancroft interview.
On William Grimshaw: Ibid.
On Joseph Wadleigh: Ibid.
On the end of Sutter: Zollinger, *Sutter*.
On the gold rush: Sanderlin, *Settlement*.
On Alfred Green: Bancroft interview.
On J. P. C. Allsopp: Ibid.
On John Currey: Ibid.
On Alex Todd: Ibid.
On Chinese miners: Stephen Williams Stanford, *The Chinese in the California Gold Mines* (Stanford, 1930).
On California statehood: Sanderlin, *Settlement*.
On Douglas and the Compromise of 1850: Robert W. Johannsen, *Stephen A. Douglas* (New York, 1973).
On mining: Ernest A. Wiltsee, *The Pioneer Mind* (San Francisco, 1931); E. G. Buffum, *Six Months in the Gold Mines* (New York, 1966); James H. Carson, *Recollections of the California Gold Mines* (Oakland, 1950); Henry Vizetelly, *Four Months Among the Gold-Finders in Alta California* (London, 1849).
"Have you seen the elephant?": *The Shirley Letters* (New York, 1949).
On Ed Morse: *California Historical Quarterly*, vol. 6.
On Lemuel McKeeby: Ibid.
On J. D. Borthwick: J. D. Borthwick, *Three Years in California* (London, 1857).
On David Anderson: Bancroft interview.
On Louise Clapp: *Shirley Letters*.
On Alfred Green: Bancroft interview.
On Dr. Beverly Cole: Ibid.
On John Manrow: Ibid.

ELEVEN: THE MINNESOTA FRONTIER

"With judicious conduct": *TP*, vol. 6.
On Lieutenant Colonel Henry Leavenworth: *Minnesota Historical Collections*, vol. 1.
On Snelling: Ibid., vol. 2.
On Fort Snelling: Steve Hall, *Fort Snelling* (St. Paul, 1987).
On the regular army: Hall, *Fort Snelling*.
On Martin Scott: *Minnesota Historical Collections*, vol. 3.
On Lawrence Taliaferro: Ibid., vol. 6.
"I have had more than 1,400": Ibid., vol. 2.
On Dr. Nathan S. Jarvis: Jarvis Letters (unpublished), New York Academy of Medicine.
"I cannot preach": Samuel W. Pond, *The Dakota Sioux* (St. Paul, 1986).
On Dred Scott: Frank B. Latham, *The Dred Scott Decision* (New York, 1968).
On Taliaferro and the Sioux: *Minnesota Historical Collections*, vol. 6.
On Franklin Steele: Ibid., vol. 8.
On James Goodhue and Richard Johnson: Ibid.
On Minnesota Territory: Ibid., vols. 1, 7.
"The gentleman may be": Ibid., vol. 8.
On Charles Flandreau: Ibid.
On Daniel Johnston: Ibid., vol. 15.
On Minnesota statehood: Ibid., vol. 8.
On the Kansas-Nebraska Act: James C. Malin, *The Nebraska Question* (Lawrence, Kans., 1953).

TWELVE: BLEEDING KANSAS

On the Kansas-Nebraska Act: Alice Nichols, *Bleeding Kansas* (New York, 1954).
On the Emigrant Aid movement: *American Historical Review*, vol. 41.
On the founding of Lawrence: *Kansas Historical Collections*, vol. 3.
"I would be ashamed": Ibid., vol. 2.
"Sound on the Goose": Ibid., vol. 7.
On Andrew H. Reeder: Ibid., vol. 3.
"Free ferry": Ibid., vol. 7.
"They been a jawin' me": Ibid., vol. 8.
On James McClure: Ibid.
On Dewitt Goodrich: Ibid., vol. 12.
On the March 1855 election: Ibid., vol. 8.
Robinson asks for rifles: F. W. Blackmar, *Charles Robinson* (Topeka, 1902).
"Kansas has been invaded": *Kansas Historical Collections*, vol. 1.
Reeder and the Pawnee lands: L. W. Spring, *Kansas* (Boston, 1973).
On Lemuel Knapp: *Kansas Historical Collections*, vol. 12.
On James Lane: Ibid., vol. 3.
On Albert Morrall: Ibid., vol. 14.
On the sack of Lawrence: Ibid., vols. 1, 2; Nichols, *Bleeding Kansas*; W. F. Zornow, *Kansas* (Norman, Okla., 1937).
"Gentlemen, I'll go": *Kansas Historical Collections*, vol. 1.
On Morrall in Lawrence: Ibid., vol. 14.
"You blame Pierce": Zornow, *Kansas*.
"Oh, don't shoot my husband": *Kansas Historical Collections*, vol. 1.
On Coffin, Hiatt, and Johnson: Ibid., vol. 6.
On the 1857 election: Nichols, *Bleeding Kansas*.

On the Lecompton constitution: Ibid.
"Kansas is at this moment": Zornow, *Kansas.*
On Captain James Montgomery: *Kansas Historical Collections*, vol. 3.
"Shut up and dismount": Ibid., vol. 14.
It's crimes like this": Ibid., vol. 3.
On Lincoln in Kansas: Ibid., vol. 3.
"If the people of Illinois": Ibid.
"Not only will I": Ibid.
On Kansas statehood: Zornow, *Kansas.*
On David Hougland: *Kansas Historical Collections*, vol. 9.

THIRTEEN: THE WEST VIRGINIA DILEMMA

On the dispute with Virginia: C. H. Ambler, *West Viginia, the Mountain State* (New
    York, 1940).
On Harper's Ferry: Ibid.
"I have hearn tell of you": *West Virginia Historical Magazine*, vol. 3.
"marked by a vulgarity": Ibid.
On the Virginia secession: Elizabeth Cometti and Festus P. Summers, eds., *The
    Thirty-Fifth State* (Morgantown, W. Va., 1966).
On the West Virginia quandary: *West Virginia Historical Magazine*, vol. 1.
On West Virginia battles: Ambler, *Mountain State.*
"In our scouting expeditions": General Jacob D. Cox, *Military Reminiscences of the
    Civil War* (New York, 1900).
On West Virginia statehood: *West Virginia Historical Magazine*, vols. 1, 2.
"We already have": Cometti, *Thirty-Fifth State.*
"The Baltimore & Ohio": *West Virginia Historical Magazine*, vol. 1.
"was nothing less": Ibid.
". . . I do not believe": Ibid.
Lincoln troubled: Ibid., vol. 2.
"I wish I had more": Ibid., vol. 1.
"This is by far": Ibid.
"Do you see that signature?": Ibid.
On Lincoln's reasoning: Ibid., vol. 2.

FOURTEEN: THE NEVADA FRONTIER

On Thomas Knott: Bancroft interview, Bancroft Library, Berkeley, Calif.
On the Mormons in Nevada: E. M. Mack, *History of Nevada* (Glendale, Calif.,
    1936).
On Nevada mining: C. H. Shinn, *Mining Camps* (New York, 1948); C. C. Spence,
    Mining Engineers and the American West (New Haven, 1970).
Language of mining: Spence, *Mining Engineers.*
Ore samples and mining stocks: Ibid.
"I particularly recommend": Russell R. Elliott, *Nevada* (Lincoln, Nebr., 1987).
"I never knew": Spence, *Mining Engineers.*
On Alfred Doten: *The Journals of Alfred Doten* (Reno, Nev., 1973).
"damned son of a bitch": Ibid.
On near-lynching: Ibid.
On the affair with Mrs. Morton: Ibid.
On the Emancipation Proclamation: John Hope Franklin, *The Emancipation Procla-
    mation* (New York, 1963).
"I am very anxious": Charles A. Dana, *Recollections of the Civil War* (New York,
    1898).

Nevada statehood: Elliott, *Nevada*.
"DON'T WANT ANY CONSTITUTION": Ibid.
"I am glad to see you here": Mack, *History of Nevada*.
"I have sometimes heard": Dana, *Recollections*.
"The news cast": Doten, *Journals*.

FIFTEEN: THE NEBRASKA FRONTIER

On the "permanent Indian boundary": Francis P. Prucha, *The Great White Father* (Lincoln, Nebr., 1986); Francis P. Prucha, ed., *Documents of United States Indian Policy* (Lincoln, Nebr., 1990).
On the Pawnees: G. E. Hyde, *Pawnee Indians* (Denver, 1951).
On Dunbar and Allis: *Kansas Historical Collections*, vol. 14, "Letters Concerning the Presbyterian Mission to the Pawnee Country, 1831–1849."
"They are very accommodating": Ibid.
"abominably lazy": Ibid.
"Their minds are dark as": Ibid.
"he is like your president": Ibid.
"I wish the board": Ibid.
"red niggers": Ibid.
"a thorough-going man": Ibid.
"It is hard": Ibid.
"lie exposed": Ibid.
"My father, I am poor": Ibid.
On James Mathers: Ibid.
"Tell me just how you feel": Ibid.
"I wish my father": Ibid.
Major Miller replaced: Ibid.
"I consider you responsible": Ibid.
"If I had": Ibid.
Evacuation of the mission: Ibid.
On Indian agents: *Iowa Journal of History and Politics*, vol. 14.
On Douglas: Robert A. Johannsen, *Stephen A. Douglas* (New York, 1973).
"Douglas wanted": Ibid.
"It is utterly impossible": Ibid.
On George W. Manypenny: Hoopes, *Indian Affairs*.
"you cannot fix bounds": Johannsen, *Stephen A. Douglas*.
"I passed": Ibid.
"on the western boundary": Ibid.
Early days in Nebraska: J. C. Olson, *Nebraska* (Lincoln, Nebr., 1955).
"Oh, what was your name in the States": Everett Dick, *Law of the Land* (Lincoln, Nebr., 1970).
Nebraska homesteaders: Everett Dick, *The Sod-House Frontier* (New York, 1937).
On George Klein: Dick, *Law of the Land*.
On C. C. Akin: Ibid.
On Andrew Murphy: Western Heritage Museum exhibit, Omaha.
"That was my slogan": Dick, *Sod-House Frontier*.
On Peter Jansen: Ibid.
On Bierstadt: Nancy K. Anderson and Linda S. Ferber, *Albert Bierstadt, Art and Enterprise* (Brooklyn, 1990).
On Bierstadt's 1863 trip: Fitz Hugh Ludlow, *The Heart of the Continent* (New York, 1870).
"I cannot breathe free": Ibid.
"Cuss his tough hide": Ibid.

"Now boys": Ibid.
On Bierstadt and the buffalo: Ibid.
"his coat-tails stuck": *Nebraska Pioneer Reminiscences.*
On Nebraska statehood: Olson, *Nebraska.*
On trees and the prairie: Dick, *Sod-House Frontier.*
On Omaha: Western Heritage Museum exhibit.
On front porches: Ibid.

SIXTEEN: TEXAS AND THE CATTLE FRONTIER

On the Homestead Act: Roy M. Robbins, *Our Landed Heritage* (Princeton, 1942).
On railroads: Stewart H. Holbrook, *The Story of American Railroads* (New York, 1947).
On transcontinental railroad: J. P. Davis, *The Union Pacific Railway* (Chicago, 1894).
On the Texas cattle tradition: E. E. Dale, *The Range Cattle Industry* (Norman, Okla., 1960).
The post–Civil War market: E. S. Osgood, *The Day of the Cattleman* (Minneapolis, 1954).
On the Chicago stockyards: William Cronon, *Nature's Metropolis* (New York, 1991).
"I was coming": E. C. Abbott, *We Pointed Them North* (Norman, Okla., 1939).
On Jim Cook: James H. Cook, *Longhorn Cowboy* (Norman, Okla., 1960).
On Bill Jackman: J. Marvin Hunter, *Trail Drivers of Texas* (Nashville, 1925).
On James Cape: Jim Lanning and Judy Lanning, eds., *Texas Cowboys* (College Station, Tex., 1984).
On James Daugherty: Hunter, *Trail Drivers.*
On Joseph McCoy: Joseph G. McCoy, *Historic Sketches of the Cattle Trade* (Washington D.C., 1932).
"to establish a market": Ibid.
"It occurs to me": Ibid.
"A small dead place": Ibid.
"the butcher's nightmare": Cronon, *Nature's Metropolis.*
On William Slaughter: Hunter, *Trail Drivers.*
On George Sanders: Ibid.
"Want to go up the trail?" Abbott, *North.*
"I ain't kicking": Ibid.
On George Hindes: Hunter, *Trail Drivers.*
On buffalo hunters: Homer W. Wheeler, *Buffalo Days* (Lincoln, Nebr., 1990).
On Andy Adams: Andy Adams, *The Log of a Cowboy* (Boston, 1903).
"I'll not ship": Ibid.
"I was selling": Ibid.
On the decline of the buffalo: Walter P. Webb, *The Great Plains* (New York, 1931).
On Hammond and Swift and refrigeration: Cronon, *Nature's Metropolis.*
On the end of the trail drive: Dale, *Range Cattle.*
On public grazing: Webb, *Great Plains.*
On Glidden and barbed wire: Ibid.
"It jest won't do!": Ibid.
"Now there is so much land": Ibid.
On the end of the cowboy: Paul I. Wellman, *The Trampling Herd* (New York, 1974).
On illegal fencing: Webb, *Great Plains.*
On the cowboy: Philip Ashton Rollins, *The cowboy* (New York, 1922); Webb, *Great Plains;* A. J. Sowell, *Rangers and Pioneers of Texas* (New York, 1964).
"Why the bandana?": Lanning and Lanning, *Texas Cowboys.*
"That's Bill Adams": Webb, *Great Plains.*
"sold his saddle": Adams, *Log.*

"I wasn't bigger": Lanning and Lanning, *Texas Cowboys*.
"A man sure can": Adams, *Log*.

SEVENTEEN: THE COLORADO FRONTIER

On Mr. and Mrs. Henry Tabor: *Colorado Magazine*, vol. 3.
On Evelyn Silverthorn: Ibid., vol. 2.
On Emily and David Witter: Ibid., vol. 3.
Statehood defeated: Marshall Sprague, *Colorado* (New York, 1976).
On Dr. Henry Parry: Parry Letters, *Annals of Wyoming*, vol. 30.
On A. K. Clarke: *Colorado Magazine*, vol. 5.
On Charles Thomas: Ibid., vol. 1.
On Denver & Rio Grande: Ibid., vols. 22, 23.
On William Walk: Ibid., vol. 24.
On John Taylor: Ibid., vol. 18.
On Zimri Bowles: Ibid., vol. 14.
Colorado statehood: Sprague, *Colorado*.
On Fourth of July parade: *Colorado Magazine*, vol. 11.
On Fred Vaille: Ibid., vol. 5.
On La Junta: Ibid., vol. 9.
On Nathan S. Meeker: J. F. Willard, *The Union Colony* (Boulder, Colo., 1918).
"to prevent uncongenial": Ibid.
"an emancipation": Ibid.
Meeker among the Utes: Robert Emmitt, *The Last War Trail* (Norman, Okla., 1954).
"You are here to teach": Ibid.
"They would listen": Ibid.
"I HAVE BEEN ASSAULTED": Ibid.
"A good many times": Ibid.
"It was made known": Ibid.
"I want the privilege": Ibid.
"I don't think": Ibid.
On R. E. Arnett: *Colorado Magazine*, vol. 22.
On Bill Burt: Ibid., vol. 29.
On H. A. Sumner: Ibid., vol. 24.
"The altitude here": Ibid.
On E. A. Meredith: Ibid.

EIGHTEEN: THE DAKOTA FRONTIER

On John Blair Smith Todd: Dale Gibson, *Attorney for the Frontier* (Winnipeg, Man., 1983).
On the Upper Missouri Land Company: Gibson, *Attorney*.
Early Yankton: H. R. Lamar, *Dakota Territory* (New Haven, 1956).
On Pembina: Ibid.
On the Pony congress: Ibid.
On the territorial mentality: Ibid.
"ANOTHER SURVIVOR": *North Dakota Historical Quarterly*, vol. 7.
"Why, Dakota's no place": Ibid.
On Frank Trumbo: *South Dakota Historical Collections*, vol. 5.
On Horatio Larned and Captain Fisk: *North Dakota Collections of the State Historical Society*, vol. 7.
On Larned and Porcupine: Ibid.
"One of the men": Ibid.
"I did the best I could": Ibid.

"You saved my life once": Ibid.
On Dakota and the railroads: Ibid., vol. 1.
On the Northern Pacific: Henry Villard, *Memoirs* (New York, 1969).
On Croffords: *North Dakota Historical Quarterly*, vol. 7.
On Jay Cooke: *North Dakota Collections*, vol. 1.
On the Black Hills: Donald Jackson, *Custer's Gold* (New Haven, 1966).
On General Philip Sheridan: C. C. Rister, *Border Command* (Norman, Okla., 1944).
On Custer: Evan Connell, *Son of the Morning Star* (San Francisco, 1984); F. F. Van
    De Wate, *Glory-Hunter* (Lincoln, Nebr., 1934).
"more fresh laurels": Jackson, *Custer's Gold*.
"gold has been found": Ibid.
"He wanted to be first": Ibid.
"to use the forces": Rister, *Border Command*.
"At Yankton you can": *North Dakota Historical Quarterly*, vol. 6.
"Once in a while": Ibid.
On Phillip Wells: Ibid., vol. 8.
"I understand that the president": Rister, *Border Command*.
"for such action": Connell, *Morning Star*.
"We have two ways": A. B. Adams, *Sitting Bull* (New York, 1973).
On T. E. Cooper: *North Dakota Collections of the State Historical Society*, vol. 2.
On Linda Slaughter: Ibid., vol. 1.
On Thomas Riggs: *South Dakota Historical Collections*, vol. 2.
On the statehood movement: Lamar, *Dakota*.
On Livingston: Ibid.
On Villard: Robert S. MacFarlane, *Henry Villard and the Northern Pacific* (New York,
    1954).
"I hate you": Ibid.
On Ordway: Lamar, *Dakota*.
On the Dakota statehood movement: *South Dakota Historical Collections*, vol. 12.
"Why rush new states": Ibid.
On statehood: Ibid.
On Dolwig: *North Dakota Historical Quarterly*, vol. 3.

NINETEEN: THE MONTANA FRONTIER

On fur traders and Indians: Lewis O. Saum, *The Fur Trader and the Indian* (Seattle:
    1965).
On Denig: E. T. Denig, *Five Indian Tribes of the Upper Missouri* (Norman, Okla.,
    1961).
"Committed fortification": Saum, *Fur Trader*.
On Fort Sarpy: "Original Journal of James H. Chambers, Fort Sarpy," *Contributions
    to the Historical Society of Montana*, vol. X.
"prodigal liberality": Ibid.
"filling their gut": Ibid.
"Oh, Six": Ibid.
"a dirty little lousy slut": Ibid.
"the target was": Ibid.
"the bucks are raping": Ibid.
On the arrival of the miners: Michael P. Malone and Richard B. Roeder, *Montana,
    A History of Two Centuries* (Seattle, 1976).
On vigilantes: L. L. Callaway, *Montana's Righteous Hangmen* (Norman, Okla., 1982).
On Montana territory: Malone and Roeder, *Montana*.
On Lyman Munson: *Montana Magazine of History*, vol. 1.

On William T. Hamilton: E. L. Silliman, *We Seized Our Rifles* (Missoula, Mont., 1982).
On Langford: *Montana Magazine of History*, vol. 3.
"I owe no allegiance": Ibid.
"I was sent here": Ibid.
"Don't say another word": Ibid.
"I suppose": Ibid.
"Great Caesar!": Ibid.
On Langford and Yellowstone: *Minnesota Historical Society Collections*, vol. 15.
On Peter Koch: *Contributions to the Historical Society of Montana*, vol. 2.
"You miserable": Ibid.
On Langford: *Montana Magazine of History*, vol. 3.
"The ladies are very fond": Malone and Roeder, *Montana*.
On cattlemen and sheepmen: Bill O'Neal, *Cattlemen vs. Sheepherders* (Austin, Tex., 1989).
"They just drift around": Ibid.
"He feeds me": Ibid.
"This is no place for a dog": Brown and Felton, *Before Barbed Wire*.

TWENTY: THE WASHINGTON FRONTIER

On logging: R. E. Ficken, *The Forested Land* (Seattle, 1987).
On William Renton: D. J. Chasan, *The Water Link* (Seattle, 1981).
Petition to Congress: K. D. Richards, *Isaac L. Stevens* (Provo, Utah, 1979).
On Washington Territory and its governor: Ibid.
On Stevens and Indian treaties: Ibid.
"Goods and earth": Ibid.
"We trust they will": Ibid.
Stevens declares martial law: Ibid.
"a most despotic": Ibid.
On Charles Prosch: Charles Prosch, *Reminiscences of Washington Territory* (Fairfield, Wash., 1969).
"We are informed": Ibid.
"There is probably": Ibid.
On Asa Shinn Mercer: *Oregon Historical Society Quarterly*, vol. 5.
"I had been taught": Ibid.
"Sit down, Mercer": *Oregon Historical Society Quarterly*, vol. 5.
"There is no law": Ibid.
"I understand": Ibid.
"It may well be": Ibid.
Account of the trip: Roger Conant, *Mercer's Belles* (Seattle, 1960).
"Oh, Mr. Mercer": Ibid.
"I don't see": Ibid.
On hopeful bridegrooms: Ibid.
On John McGilvra: Ficken, *Forested Land*.
"It would be better": Ibid.
"the perpetration": Ibid.
On the Northern Pacific: Ibid.
On Stevens and Tuttle: Ibid.
"I am much pleased": Ibid.
"make an honest business": Ibid.
On T. H. Cavanagh: Ibid.
"the agent can be fixed": Chasan, *Water Link*.

"the timber contiguous": Ibid.
On Job Carr: Murray Morgan, *Puget Sound* (Seattle, 1979).
"I raised on my feet": Ibid.
On McCarver: Ibid.
"I can frequently": Ibid.
"unhesitatingly decide": Ibid.
"Seattle! Seattle!": Thomas Ripley, *Green Timber* (Palo Alto, Calif. 1968).
Washington statehood: D. O. Johansen, *Empire on the Columbia* (New York, 1957).
"What is the greatest?": Chasan, *Water Link*.

TWENTY-ONE: THE WYOMING FRONTIER

On the telegraph: Edwin Gabler, *The American Telegrapher* (New Brunswick, N.J., 1988).
On Oscar Collister: *Annals of Wyoming*, vol. 50.
"I don't want to kill": Ibid.
"What prompted them": Ibid.
"The Indians are almost": Ibid.
"When the grass": Ibid.
On the mail at Fort Reno: Ibid.
On the *Frontier Index:* File of extant copies, Bancroft Library, Berkeley, Calif.
On the Freeman brothers: Leigh R. Freeman, *History of the Frontier Index* (Evanston, Ill., 1943).
"The Pioneer paper": Index, Bancroft Library.
"The Index is . . .": Ibid.
"the smelliferous": Ibid.
"the town is only": Ibid.
"our office was burned": Freeman, *History*.
On Wyoming Territory: L. L. Gould, *Wyoming* (New Haven, 1968).
"We now expect": Ibid.
On women's suffrage: *Annals of Wyoming*, vol. 11.
On Eliza Stewart: Ibid., vol. 21.
"This woman suffrage business": Ibid., vol. 11.
On Jesse Knight: Ibid., vol. 50.
On T. S. Garrett: Ibid., vol. 1.
On Edward Day Woodruff: Ibid., vol. 7.
On the Chinese massacre: Ibid., vol. 11.
On David Thomas: Ibid., vol. 19.
"Why did you kill": Ibid.
On statehood: Gould, *Wyoming*.
On Hank Mason: *Annals of Wyoming*, vol. 1.

TWENTY-TWO: THE IDAHO FRONTIER

On Elias Davidson Pierce: Merrill D. Beal, *Idaho* (New York, 1959).
"Yes sirree . . .": Ibid.
"to attempt to restrain": Ibid.
On Mr. and Mrs. Schultz: Bancroft interview, Bancroft Library, Berkeley, Calif.
On Alonzo Brown: Alfreda Eisensohn, *Idaho County* (Caldwell, Idaho, 1947).
On Boise: Beal, *Idaho*.
"Ye pining . . .": F. R. Peterson, *Idaho* (New York, 1976).
On J. M. McConnell: Bancroft interview, Bancroft Library.
On Indian affairs: T. G. Alexander, *A Clash of Interests* (Provo, Utah, 1977).

On Chief Joseph and the Nez Percés: C. E. Trafzer, *The Nez Percés* (New York, 1992).
On Grant's Indian policy: Alexander, *Clash.*
On the Indian police: W. T. Hagan, *Indian Police and Judges* (New Haven, 1966).
On the McBeth sisters: Kate C. McBeth, *The Nez Percés Since Lewis and Clark* (New York, 1908).
On the Fourth of July incident: *Idaho Yesterdays,* vol. 13.
"The real aim": Trafzer, *Nez Percés.*
On Alice Fletcher: E. Jane Gay, *With the Nez Percés* (Lincoln, Nebr., 1981).
On the implementation of the allotment policy: Ibid.
"I was not aware": Ibid.
"Why in thunder": Ibid.
"You will have": Ibid.
"Oh no, I cannot": McBeth, *Nez Percés.*
On surplus lands: *Idaho Yesterdays,* vol. 13.
On Caleb Lyon: Peterson, *Idaho.*
On anti-Mormon feeling: Ibid.
On Fred Dubois: Rafe Gibbs, *Beckoning the Bold* (Moscow, Idaho, 1976).
"Mr. President": Ibid.
"Another mining camp": Ibid.
"New York be blowed": Ibid.

TWENTY-THREE: THE UTAH FRONTIER

On Louisa Barnes [Pratt]: "Journal of Louisa Barnes Pratt," in Kate B. Carter, *Heart Throbs of the West,* vol. 8 (Salt Lake City, 1947).
"She shall see:" Ibid.
On Brigham Young: N. G. Bringhurst, *Brigham Young* (Boston, 1986).
"The oxteam salvation": Pratt, "Journal."
"That cow is no Mormon": Ibid.
On the exodus to the Missouri: Richard E. Bennett, *Mormons at the Missouri* (Norman, Okla., 1987).
On Captain James Allen: Bennett, *Mormons.*
"You do not seem": Pratt, "Journal."
"If you stop": Dean L. May, *Utah: A People's History* (Salt Lake City, 1987).
"For heaven's sake": Ibid.
Early days in Salt Lake City: *Utah Historical Quarterly,* vol. 1.
On John Nebecker: Ibid., vol. 2.
"It is her greatest": Pratt, "Journal."
"My heart shrank": Ibid.
"I found my spirit": Ibid.
On Almon Babbitt: *Utah Historical Quarterly,* vol. 26.
On Topponce: May, *Utah.*
On Scandinavian Mormons: *Utah Historical Quarterly,* vol. 21.
On Christian Nielsen: Ibid.
On Priddy Meeks: *Utah Historical Quarterly,* vol. 12.
"They have the appetite": May, *Utah.*
On Susie: *Utah Historical Quarterly,* vol. 12.
"is going to pieces": Bringhurst, *Brigham Young.*
"There is a batch": May, *Utah.*
On polygamy: Lawrence Foster, *Religion and Sexuality* (Urbana, Ill., 1984); Klaus J. Hansen, *Mormonism and the American Experience* (Chicago, 1981).
"on patrol guard": Juanita Brooks, ed., *Hosea Stout Diary* (Salt Lake City, 1964).
"He has lain": Bennett, *Missouri.*

"no adultery": *Utah Historical Quarterly*, vol. 35.
On Eliza Snow: Bancroft interview, Bancroft Library.
On Jane Snyder Richards: Ibid.
"Girls, you care more": Bancroft interview.
"Not very well": Ibid.
"There isn't as much": Ibid.
On Martha Hughes Cannon: Foster, *Religion*.
On Mount Carmel: Lucy Parr, *Not of the World* (Bountiful, Utah, 1975).
"We will dismiss": Ibid.
"Count me out": Ibid.
On Orderville: *Utah Historical Quarterly*, vol. 6.
"The world has need": Ibid., vol. 7.
On Harry Esplin: Ibid.
On John Carling: Ibid.
"I would that the guns": May, *Utah*.
On the Edmunds Act: Ibid.
"How soon before": Parr, *World*.
"the Communists bid fair": Ibid.
"Orderville is all work": Ibid.
"Dissension could well": Ibid.
"President Taylor": Ibid.
On Lorenzo Snow: Unsigned pamphlet, *His Ten Wives* (Butte, Mont., 1887).
On the Edmunds-Tucker Act: May, *Utah*.
On Superintendent Brown: *Utah Historical Quarterly*, vol. 32.

TWENTY-FOUR: THE LAST INDIAN FRONTIER,
THE FIRST TWENTIETH-CENTURY STATE

On Elizabeth Quinton: *Chronicles of Oklahoma*, vol. 29.
"Chinch-bugged in Illinois": Stan Hoig, *The Oklahoma Land Rush of 1889* (Oklahoma
City, 1984).
"Oklahoma represented": *Chronicles of Oklahoma*, vol. 22.
On the Indian nations during the Civil War: Ibid., vol. 25.
"It was the white man's quarrel": Ibid., vol. 29.
"in fact the niggers are masters": Ibid., vol. 25.
On Albert Pike: Ibid., vol. 18.
On Lawrie Tatum: Ibid., vol. 17.
"You are foolish": Ibid.
On James Edward Finney: Ibid., vol. 33.
On P. B. Hunt: Ibid., vol. 10.
"The big thing about the plains": Ibid., vol. 21.
On John Miles: Ibid., vol. 6.
"A sleepy-eyed": John Thompson, *Closing the Frontier* (Norman, Okla., 1986).
On J. J. McAlester: A. M. Gibson, *Oklahoma* (Norman, Okla., 1984).
"the best steam coal": *Chronicles of Oklahoma*, vol. 12.
On Arthur Dunham: Ibid., vol. 14.
On the organization of Oklahoma Territory: Gibson, *Oklahoma*.
On the 1889 land rush: Hoig, *Oklahoma Land Rush*.
"Today, Monday": Ibid.
On Hamilton Wicks: *Chronicles of Oklahoma*, vol. 4.
On Arthur Dunham: Ibid., vol. 14.
"Manifestly, Congress": Ibid., vol. 33.
On Veeder Paine: Ibid.
On A. M. Thomas: Ibid., vol. 21.

On Jesse Dunn: Ibid., vol. 3.
On the lottery opening: Ibid., vol. 9.
On Augusta Metcalf: Ibid., vol. 33.
On Iva Allen: Ibid., vol. 18.
On C. F. Holmes: Ibid., vol. 35.
On James Edward Finney: Ibid., vol. 33.
On the Oklahoma oil fields: Ibid., vol. 30.
"He may not be": Ibid.
On the allotment system: Thompson, *Closing*.
On L. P. Bobo: *Chronicles of Oklahoma*, vol. 23.
"Why did you not?": Ibid.
"these negros won't work": Goble, *Progressive*.
"I know of a number": Ibid.
Progressive movement: Ibid.
United Mine Workers: Ibid.
"since that time": Ibid.
"I don't know how": Ibid.
On the Jim Crow backlash: Ibid.
"I am glad": Ibid.
On Theodore Roosevelt: Ibid.
On the Muskogee convention: *Chronicles of Oklahoma*, vol. 28.
On "Alfalfa Bill" Murray: Wayne Morgan, *Oklahoma* (New York, 1977).
"It is an entirely false notion": Goble, *Progressive*.
On the Oklahoma constitution: Ibid.
"It was not": Ibid.
"a zoological garden": Morgan, *Oklahoma*.

TWENTY-FIVE: THE LAST HISPANIC FRONTIER

On William Becknell: Marc Simmons, *New Mexico* (New York, 1977).
On traders in Santa Fe: David Lavender, *The Southwest* (Albuquerque, N.M., 1980).
On Louis Garrard: *New Mexico Historical Review*, vol. 24.
On William Kronig: Ibid.
Handsome Reward: Ibid.
"so remote and inaccessible": Ibid.
On De Witt Clinton Peters: Peters Papers, Bancroft Library, Berkeley, Calif.
On land titles and Civil War: Lamar, *Far Southwest*.
On Josephine Clifford: C. J. Foote, *Women of the New Mexico Frontier* (Niwot, Colo.,
     1990).
"If we have a dividing line": *New Mexico Historical Review*, vol. 28.
On the Canby campaign: Ruth M. Underhill, *The Navajos* (Norman, Okla., 1956).
On Carleton: Lavender, *Southwest*.
"The men are to be slain": *New Mexico Historical Review*, vol. 11.
"*Now* while the snow is deep": Ibid.
On Bosque Redondo: Underhill, *Navajos*.
"They cluster around": *New Mexico Historical Review*, vol. 13.
"I think we could": Ibid.
"We have not planted": Ibid.
On the Four Corners: Robert S. McPherson, *The Northern Navajo Frontier* (Albu-
     querque, N.M., 1988).
On W. F. N. Arny: *New Mexico Historical Review*, vol. 13.
"How he will succeed": Ibid.
"They have too much at stake": Ibid.
First reservation extension: McPherson, *Northern Navajo Frontier*.

On Galen Eastman: *New Mexico Historical Review*, vol. 18.
"I hope our next": Ibid., vol. 21.
"One ol' villain": Ibid., vol. 18.
"soon give the damn Mormon oufit": McPherson, *Northern Navajo Frontier*.
"I have bin drove": Ibid.
"It is in fact": Ibid.
"merely a space on the map": Ibid.
"Why roh us?": *New Mexico Historical Review*, vol. 21.
"Oh shame": Ibid.
McKinley extension: McPherson, *Frontier*.
"misunderstood the purpose": Ibid.
On the Santa Fe ring: Lamar, *Far Southwest*.
On Jimmy Morehead: Miguel Antonio Otero, *My Life on the Frontier* (Albuquerque, N.M., 1987).
On Jim Hastings: *New Mexico Historical Review*, vol. 26.
On Mary Bloom: Ibid., vol. 16.
On Sam and Carrie Sutherland: Ibid., vol. 26.
On early Arizona: Lamar, *Far Southwest*.
"The territory we have selected": Ibid.
"Oh yes, I have heard": Ibid.
On Prescott: M. F. Maxwell, *A Passion for Freedom* (Tucson, 1982).
On Milton B. Duffield: *Journal of Arizona History*, vol. 8.
On the Apaches: D. E. Worcester, *The Apaches* (Norman, Okla., 1979).
On John P. Clum: W. Clum, *Apache Agent* (Cambridge, Mass., 1936).
"your bodies will stay here": Ibid.
"I have seen": Ibid.
"If your department": Ibid.
"Why did you select?": Ibid.
On Isaac Solomon: *Arizona Historical Review*, vol. 1.
On the Globe & Northern: Ibid.
On the statehood movement: *New Mexico Historical Review*, vol. 16.
"repugnant to the enlightened sense": L. C. Powell, *Arizona* (New York, 1976).
"Hovered over the territory": Lamar, *Far Southwest*.
On Governor Otero: Otero, *My Life*.
"pressed the button": Ibid.
On Beveridge: Lamar, *Far Southwest*.
"proceeds from his own argument": Powell, *Arizona*.
On the constitutional convention in Santa Fe: *New Mexico Historical Review*, vol. 27.
On the conservative movement: Richard White, *A New History of the American West* (Norman, Okla., 1991).
"Well, it is all over": Simmons, *New Mexico*.
"The crimping of corporations": Lamar, *Far Southwest*.
"crank constitution": Lamar, *Far Southwest*.
On Sam and Edith Kitt: *Journal of Arizona History*, vol. 12.
"I wish I were starting out": Ibid.

TWENTY-SIX: THE HAWAIIAN FRONTIER

On Cook and the Polynesians: Harold Whitman Bradley, *The American Frontier in Hawaii* (Stanford, Calif., 1942).
On Kamehameha: Noel J. Kent, *Islands Under the Influence* (New York, 1983).
"The people freely dismissed": *Hawaii Journal of History*, vol. 3.
"More labor we must have": Ibid.
On Captain John Cass: Ibid.

"both in industry and morals": Ibid.
On Juan Soares: *Social Process in Hawaii*, vol. 1.
"the outlying district": Kent, *Islands*.
On the sugar tariff: T. J. Osborne, *Empire Can Wait* (Kent, Ohio, 1981).
On the plot to topple the monarchy: Kent, *Islands*.
"How could we endure": *Hawaii Journal of History*, vol. 9.
"If I had my way": Osborne, *Empire*.
Spanish-American War: *Dictionary of American History*, vol. 6.
On Mariano Quinto: *Social Process in Hawaii*, vol. 4.
On James Drummond Dole: Henry A. White, *James D. Dole* (Newcomen Society Pamphlet, New York, 1957).
"spend the rest": Ibid.
"Extend the market": Ibid.
"The objective": Ibid.
"You can thank": Ibid.
"you can start": Tabrah, *Hawaii*.
On the plantation unions: *Social Process in Hawaii*, vol. 15.
"Before, jackass better": Ibid.
"It used to be": Ibid., vol. 15.
"Why not work?": Ibid.
"When I get married": Ibid.
On World War II and assimilation: Ibid., vol. 8.
On martial law: *Personal Justice Denied*, Report of the Commission on Wartime Relocation and Internment of Civilians (Washington D.C., 1982).
"My son is in Europe": Ibid.
"It's hard enough": Ibid.
"Why they even tried": Ibid.
On reverse racism: Elvi Whittaker, *The Mainland Haole* (New York, 1986).
"It's like the south": Ibid.
On Robert Bean: *Social Process in Hawaii*, vol. 18.
On Janet O'Brien: Ibid., vol. 19.
"it all comes down": Ibid.
"Give us Ely": Alexander McDonald, *Revolt in Paradise* (New York, 1944).
another statehood bill: *Hawaii Journal of History*, vol. 6.
On Hugh Butler: Ibid., vol. 9.
"tinctured with Communism": Ibid., vol. 6.
On the Honolulu petition: Tabrah, *Hawaii*.
On statehood: *Hawaii Journal of History*, vol. 6.
The argument against": Robert Dallek, *Lone Star Rising* (New York, 1991).
"Now we are all haoles": Kent, *Islands*.

TWENTY-SEVEN: THE LAST FRONTIER

On Miles Martin: Interviews with author.
On Alaska purchase: John M. Taylor, *William Henry Seward* (New York, 1991).
"God is on high": Merle Colby, *A Guide to Alaska* (St. Clair Shores, Mich., 1976).
On early Alaska: W. R. Hunt, *Alaska* (New York, 1976).
"I am willing": Morgan B. Sherwood, *Exploration of Alaska* (New Haven, 1965).
"These Indians promised": Ibid.
"We began to realize": Ibid.
"Arrived at Indian": Ibid.
"no geographer": Ibid.
On Blake and Hultberg: M. B. Sherwood, ed., *Alaska and its History* (Seattle, 1967).
"gold clung to the ships' anchors": Ibid.

"the conservative businessmen": Hunt, *Alaska*.
"regard life in lovely": Colby, *A Guide to Alaska*.
"Are Alaskan Salmon": Ibid.
On statehood: Hunt, *Alaska*.
"most of the clamor": *Hawaii Journal of History*, vol. 9.

INDEX